THE OXFORD HA

ARABIC LINGUISTICS

THE OXFORD HANDBOOKS IN LINGUISTICS

THE OXFORD HANDBOOK OF COMPUTATIONAL LINGUISTICS
Edited by Ruslan Mitkov

THE OXFORD HANDBOOK OF COMPOSITIONALITY
Edited by Markus Werning, Edouard Machery, and Wolfram Hinzen

THE OXFORD HANDBOOK OF FIELD LINGUISTICS
Edited by Nicholas Thieberger

THE OXFORD HANDBOOK OF GRAMMATICALIZATION
Edited by Heiko Narrog and Bernd Heine

THE OXFORD HANDBOOK OF THE HISTORY OF LINGUISTICS
Edited by Keith Allan

THE OXFORD HANDBOOK OF JAPANESE LINGUISTICS
Edited by Shigeru Miyagawa and Mamoru Saito

THE OXFORD HANDBOOK OF LABORATORY PHONOLOGY
Edited by Abigail C. Cohn, Cécile Fougeron, and Marie Hoffman

THE OXFORD HANDBOOK OF LANGUAGE EVOLUTION
Edited by Maggie Tallerman and Kathleen Gibson

THE OXFORD HANDBOOK OF LANGUAGE AND LAW
Edited by Peter Tiersma and Lawrence M. Solan

THE OXFORD HANDBOOK OF LINGUISTIC ANALYSIS
Edited by Bernd Heine and Heiko Narrog

THE OXFORD HANDBOOK OF LINGUISTIC INTERFACES
Edited by Gillian Ramchand and Charles Reiss

THE OXFORD HANDBOOK OF LINGUISTIC MINIMALISM
Edited by Cedric Boeckx

THE OXFORD HANDBOOK OF LINGUISTIC TYPOLOGY
Edited by Jae Jung Song

THE OXFORD HANDBOOK OF TRANSLATION STUDIES
Edited by Kirsten Malmkjaer and Kevin Windle

THE OXFORD HANDBOOK OF SOCIOLINGUISTICS
Edited by Robert Bayley, Richard Cameron, and Ceil Lucas

THE OXFORD HANDBOOK OF ARABIC LINGUISTICS
Edited by Jonathan Owens

THE OXFORD HANDBOOK OF THE HISTORY OF ENGLISH
Edited by Terttu Nevalainen and Elizabeth Closs Traugott

THE OXFORD HANDBOOK OF LANGUAGE AND SOCIETY
Edited by Ofelia García, Nelson Flores, and Massimiliano Spotti

THE OXFORD HANDBOOK OF WORLD ENGLISHES
Edited by Markku Filppula, Juhani Klemola, and Devyani Sharma

THE OXFORD HANDBOOK OF LANGUAGE POLICY AND PLANNING
Edited by James W. Tollefson and Miguel Pérez-Milans

THE OXFORD HANDBOOK OF ENDANGERED LANGUAGES
Edited by Kenneth L. Rehg and Lyle Campbell

THE OXFORD HANDBOOK OF

ARABIC LINGUISTICS

JONATHAN OWENS

OXFORD
UNIVERSITY PRESS

Oxford University Press is a department of the University of Oxford. It furthers the University's objective of excellence in research, scholarship, and education by publishing worldwide. Oxford is a registered trade mark of Oxford University Press in the UK and certain other countries.

Published in the United States of America by Oxford University Press
198 Madison Avenue, New York, NY 10016, United States of America.

First issued as an Oxford University Press paperback, 2019

Library of Congress Cataloging-in-Publication Data
Owens, Jonathan.
Th e Oxford handbook of Arabic linguistics / Jonathan Owens.
p. cm.—(Oxford Handbooks)
Includes bibliographical references and index.
ISBN 978-0-19-976413-6 (hardcover : alk. paper)
ISBN 978-0-19-091280-2 (paperback : alk. paper)
1. Arabic language—Grammar. I. Title. II. Title: Handbook of Arabic linguistics.
PJ6106.O96 2013
492.7'5—dc23
2012027454

To the once and future study of the Arabic language

Contents

Contributors

Enam Al-Wer Essex University

Elabbas Benmamoun University of Illinois

Ramzi Baalbaki American University of Beirut

Peter Behnstedt PD Hamburg University

Abdelali Bentahila Abdelmalek Essaadi University, Tangier

Sami Boudelaa United Arab Emirates University

Tim Buckwalter University of Maryland

Lina Choueiri American University of Beirut

Peter T. Daniels Independent Scholar

Eirlys Davies Abdelmalek Essaadi University, Tangier

Everhard Ditters Nijmegen (Radboud) University

Lutz Edzard Oslo University

Mohamed Embarki University of Besançon

Sam Hellmuth University of York

Clive Holes Oxford University

Maarten Kossmann Leiden University

Pierre Larcher Université de Provence

Stefano Manfredi University of Naples "L'Orientale" and University of Turin

Daniel L. Newman University of Durham

Jonathan Owens Bayreuth University

Dilworth B. Parkinson Brigham Young University

Robert Ratcliffe Tokyo University of Foreign Studies

Jan Retsö University of Göteburg

Karin Christina Ryding Georgetown University

Solomon I. Sara Georgetown University

Yasir Suleiman Cambridge University

Mauro Tosco University of Turin

Manfred Woidich University of Amsterdam

Abbreviations[1]

AH/CE, e.g., Ibn Sīda (458/1066) = Islamic calendar = AH 458/Gregorian calendar = CE 1066,

(*X) token not correct with material in brackets

*(X) token not correct without material in brackets

< > encloses root consonants or specified phonological element

⟨ ⟩ orthographic unit

e.g. [Larcher, "ALT II"] Refer to the article "Arabic Linguistic Tradition II" written by Pierre Larcher in this volume.

1	first person
2	second person
3	third person
4M	4M model of codeswitching
ACC	accusative
ADV	adverb
AGT	Arabic grammatical tradition
ALT	Arabic linguistic tradition
ANT	anterior
AP	active participle
AP	adjective phrase
ATR	advanced tongue root
AUX	auxiliary
C	consonant
CA	Classical Arabic
CL	computer linguistics
CLLD	clitic-left dislocation
CMC	computer-mediated communication
CMPL	completive
CollA	colloquial Arabic
COMP	complementizer

[1] Because Chapter 9 on Arabic computational linguistics introduces a plethora of abbreviations, which are listed in a separate appendix in that chapter, only key abbreviations from that chapter are included in the current list. In a few cases abbreviations are ambiguous; for example, JA = both Jordanian Arabic and Juba Arabic. The context of the article always provides clear disambiguation in these cases.

CONJ	conjunction
COP	copula
CP	complementizer phrase
CS	codeswitching
CS	construct state
CV	consonant vowel
D	determiner
DEF	definite
DP	determiner phrase
DG	dependency grammar
e	in syntax, indicates structurally relevant gap
EEG	electroencephalography
EgA	Egyptian Arabic
EL	elative
EL	embedded language
EMA	electromagnetic midsagittal articulometry
ENS	educated native speaker
EXS	existential
F1 (etc.)	first formant
F	feminine
FP	functional projection
FT	future
fMRI	functional magnetic resonance imaging
Fr.	French
GEN	genitive
GPA	Gulf Pidgin Arabic
HAB	habitual
Hz.	Herz
IA	Iraqi Arabic
IC	immediate constituent
IDF	indefinite
IMPF	imperfect
INDC	indicative
IP	inflectional phrase
IPA	International Phonetic Alphabet
IRR	irrealis
JA	Jordanian Arabic
JSV	jussive
L1	native language
L2	second language
LA	Lebanese Arabic
LAD	language acquisition device
M	masculine

MA	Moroccan Arabic
MEG	magnetoencephalography
ML	matrix language
MLD	Moroccan-flavored Dutch
MLF	Matrix Language Frame model
ms.	milleseconds
N	noun
NA	Nigerian Arabic
NEG	negative
NegP	negation phrase
NLP	natural language processing
NOM	nominative
NP	noun phrase
Num	numeral
NumP	number phrase
OA	Old Arabic
OBJ	object
OT	optimality theory
P	phrase
PA	Palestinian Arabic
P/C	Pidgin/Creole
PET	positron emission tomography
PL	plural
P	preposition
PP	prepositional phrase
PRE	preformative vowel of imperfect
PRED	predicate
PRES	present
PROG	progressive
Pron	pronoun
PRT	participle
PSSD	possessed
PSSR	possessor
PST	past
PSV	passive
PT	processability theory
Q	quantifier
QP	quantifier phrase
R&P	root and pattern (theory)
REL	relative
RP	resumptive pronoun
SA	Standard Arabic (also known as Modern Standard Arabic)
SBJ	subjunctive

SG	singular
SILL	strategy inventory for language learning
SLA	second-language acquisition
Spec	specifier
SQUID	superconducting quantum inference device
SUBJ	subject
SVO	subject–verb–object
T	tense
TAD	traditional Arabic dialectology
TAFL	teaching of Arabic as a foreign language
TJA	Tripolitanian Jewish Arabic (Libya)
TL	target language
TMA	tense, mode aspect marker
TMS	transcranial magnetic stimulation
TP	tense phrase
UG	universal grammar
UPSID	University of California–Los Angeles Phonological Segment Inventory Database
V	verb
V	vowel
VOS	verb–object–subject
VOT	voice onset time
VS	verb–subject
WAD	*Wortatlas der arabischen Dialekte*
WFR	word formation rules
WSA	Western Sudanic Arabic

Journals, Book Series, and Organization Abbreviations

ACTFL	American Council for the Teaching of Foreign Languages
AIDA	Association Internationale de la dialectologie Arabe
AL	*Anthropological Linguistics*
BSOAS	*Bulletin of the School of Oriental and African Studies*
CERES	Centre d'Études et de Recherches Économiques et Sociales
EALL	*Encyclopedia of Arabic Language and Linguistics*
EI2	*Encyclopedia of Islam/Encyclopédie de l'Islam, nouvelle édition*
GLECS	Groupe Linguistique d'Études Chamito-Sémitique
GURT	Georgetown University Round Table on Languages and Linguistics
HSK	Handbücher zur Sprach- und Kommunikationswissenschaft/Handbooks of Linguistics and Communication Science
IFAO	Institut Français d'Archéologie orientale.
ILR	Interagency Language Roundtable

INALCO	Institut National des Langues et Civilisations Orientales
IULC	Indiana University Linguistics Club
JAOS	*Journal of the American Oriental Society*
MAS Gellas	Matériaux Arabes et Sudarabiques
PAL	Perspectives on Arabic Linguistics (book series, Benjamins)
ZAL	*Zeitschrift für arabische Linguistik*
ZDMG	*Zeitschrift der deutschen morgenländischen Gesellschaft*

THE OXFORD HANDBOOK OF

ARABIC LINGUISTICS

CHAPTER 1

A HOUSE OF SOUND STRUCTURE, OF MARVELOUS FORM AND PROPORTION

an introduction

JONATHAN OWENS*

1.1 The Interest of Arabic: Proposition 1

ARGUABLY, for the linguist, Arabic is the most interesting language in the world. I will term this "Proposition 1." This claim will certainly strike most as either arrogant or woefully wrong-headed, otiose, and lacking any measurable basis of substantiation. It furthermore runs afoul of deeply embedded beliefs in linguistics itself.

In particular is the assumption that all languages are, for purposes of linguistic analysis and insight they give into the universal properties of language, equal. Indeed, on this basis one can agree only that there is no a priori reason to think that the structure of Arabic will tell us more about language than will, say, the structure of Dγwed'e, a Central Chadic language spoken by perhaps 40,000 speakers. In terms of its grammatical properties alone, Arabic has no more claim to the attention of linguists than does any other language.

To hypothetically formulate a second objection, it might be argued in some circles that Arabic should have a special linguistic place due to being the language of Quranic

* I would like to thank Ms. Nadine Hamdan and Ms. Smaranda Grigore for their invaluable help in preparing the volume for publication. I would also like to thank Enam Al-Wer for her critical comments on a draft of the Introduction.

revelation. While this position may have its partisans among some, it in fact has no inherent connection to its status within linguistics, as indeed was recognized by many of the Classical Arabic grammarians themselves (e.g., Ibn al-Nadim, cited in [Owens, "History"]).

A third objection is simply that there is no basis for defining what "interesting" means. This brings us to the defense of the proposition.

1.1.1 The Geographical, Demographic, Chronological, Cultural Gestalt

First, and most basically, once one factors away the grammatical, semantic, pragmatic, and formal aspects of languages, it is clear that not all languages are equal.

This can be measured first of all with simple quantitative standards. There are large languages and small languages. Arabic is one of the world's largest, spoken natively by about 300 million speakers, and as a second language (L2) by perhaps another 60 million. It is by a large margin the largest language in Africa (nearly 200 million speakers) and one of the biggest in Asia (120 million). It has been estimated to be the fifth largest language in the world in terms of native speakers. Strength of numbers alone guarantees it communicative centrality in the world language system (de Swaan 1998, 2001).

Arabic is equally spoken over one of the largest land areas of any native language. It is spoken continuously in the east from Iraq and Khuzistan in southwest Iran, all the way to Morocco and to northeastern Nigeria in the west, an area covering nearly a seventh of the latitudinal distance of the globe. In addition, a number of Arabic-speaking Sprachinseln can be found outside of this area (see Map 1.4 in the Appendix at the end of this chapter).

Arabic is furthermore the language of the Quran, Islam being the only one of the large religions whose holy book is revealed in a specific language. Hence, it is learned to one degree or another for religious, ritual, cultural, and legal purposes by nearly all Muslims,[1] and equally important, is therefore revered as the purveyor of God's word. It is the language of the great texts of Arabic–Islamic culture. "Arabic" thus binds the

[1] For native speakers, Procházka's (2006) estimate of 280 million strikes us as reasonable, if perhaps slightly low. In addition, Arabic is spoken fluently as a second-language lingua franca in particular in Algeria, Morocco, Mauretania, Libya, Yemen, Chad, Tunisia, and the Sudan.

An estimate of 452 million "total" speakers, such as found at http://en.wikipedia.org/wiki/List_of_languages_by_number_of_native_speakers#30_to_50_million_native_speakers, should be treated with great caution. Estimating total number of speakers in a language like Arabic begs the question of what a language speaker is. In a survey carried out among Kanuri, one individual reported to me that she uses Arabic "often" (Owens 1995). When I thereupon addressed her in Arabic, she could not understand a word. She explained that she began many acts with *bi sm illaahi* ("in the name of God"). Defining "total" (of what?) is no less a slippery task than defining "often."

communicative, intellectual, and emotional in one linguistic gestalt, in a way perhaps no other language in the world today does.

The history, both written and orally reconstructible, of the Arabic-speaking peoples is, compared with most languages, well documented, even if from the specialist's perspective gaps in the history are perhaps more prominent than what is available. The first reference to Arabs, which may be inferred to be a reference to Arabic speakers, dates from 853 BCE, North-Arabic clan names are mentioned even earlier (Lipiński 2000: 101, 457), and Arabic begins spreading with great rapidity out of its core Middle East location in the Arabian peninsula, Iraq, and Syrian and Jordanian desert at the beginning of the Islamic era (nominally, 622 CE). By 92/711, relatively large and self-contained groups of Arabic speakers stretch from Uzbekistan in the east to Spain (Andalusia) in the west. A further significant expansion out of Upper Egypt into the Lake Chad area around 800/1400 extends this region. With the exception of Spain, and allowing for modern, "global" diasporas, this essentially defines the limits of the Arabic-speaking world until today (see Owens 2009, chapter 1, for broader summary).

The linguistic consequences and challenges of this geo-history are self-evident. While Arabic has even in pre-Islamic times always been dialectally diverse (Rabin 1951), this diversity has probably increased in the wake of the great Arab–Islamic expansion. If till today simple models for classifying Arabic dialects elude us [Behnstedt and Woidich, "Dialectology"], it is no doubt in large part because an originally diverse proto-situation has continued to diversify across the vast geographical region where Arabic is spoken. Hand in hand with cataloguing the dialectal diversity goes the challenge of developing an historical linguistic model that accounts for the present-day situation. If, as argued in this volume [Owens, "History"], traditional accounts of Arabic language history have generally failed to provide linguistically adequate models of historical development, work on a comprehensive account is largely in its incipient stages.

Not surprisingly, in its expansion across a seventh of the earth's latitudinal distance, speakers of Arabic have come into contact with a large number of languages. The degree to which spoken Arabic itself has been globally affected by this contact is a matter of ongoing debate, with some scholars, such as Versteegh (particularly 1984), arguing that the effects have been profound, whereas others, including Kossmann ["Borrowing"], see Arabic often as the dominant, hence imposing, language in contact situations. Certainly the latter perspective receives support from those well- or fairly well-documented extreme situations where unquestionably, or arguably, new varieties arise from the contact. One of these concerns the emergence of Pidgin and Creole varieties in the Sudanic region and East Africa, varieties that emerged from a common ancestor in the 19th century, today variously known as Turku, Juba Arabic, and Nubi or Kinubi. Since Versteegh's (1984) argument that the structure of Arabic dialects is to be accounted for by having passed through a stage of Pidginization, a counterconsensus ([Tosco and Manfredi, "Creoles"]) has developed that these Pidgin/Creole varieties are indeed entirely new languages, following the classical model of creolization, with little implication for understanding mainstream historical developments of contemporary Arabic dialects. Relatively underdebated are Uzbekistan and Afghanistan Arabic, spoken by very small populations. Whereas these varieties have classic features of Arabic verbal morphological structure, in other areas of grammar they display marked deviations from any other variety of Arabic, for instance, in having a fixed subject–object–verb (SOV) word order. All deviations are readily explicable as influence from the Dari, Tajik, and Uzbek adstrates, and therefore the question can be raised as to whether these varieties are typologically mixed languages ([Tosco and Manfredi, "Creoles"]).

Before adducing more evidence in favor of Proposition 1, it is relevant here to take stock of the argument to this point. Beginning from older, classical perspectives on language, issues in Arabic dialectology and language history are multifarious, the challenge of building a comprehensive descriptive database remains high, and questions of language contact all along the vast geographical expanse of Arabic are open. Each of these domains represents a significant linguistic challenge, certainly descriptively but also methodologically and theoretically: what is the role of contemporary dialects in reconstructing language history; what determines direction of influence (van Coetsam 2000); what domains of language are more liable to contact influence; why do ostensibly similar global social conditions among communities of Arabic speakers lead to radically different linguistic outcomes (Owens 2000: 23); indeed, does a definable construct "Arabic" exist [Retsö, "Arabic?"]. But matters become even more interesting linguistically when the two peripheral varieties, Juba Arabic/Nubi and Uzbekistan Arabic, are added. Arabic is the only language in the world from which have emerged both Creole varieties and, arguably, mixed-language varieties. Arabic thus provides a living model for linguistics as a whole to address classic questions of historical and contact linguistics: what happens structurally to a language in the case of normal transmission (in general, the end product of the contemporary dialects) versus, by way of comparison, extreme situations of sociopolitical upheaval or cases of intense contact in a minority situation (Thomason and Kaufman 1988). Interim positions along the continuum formed by these poles can be integrated into linguistic typologies (e.g., Maltese, Kormakiti Arabic in Cyprus, Anatolian Arabic). Certainly, in the domains of phonology and morphology and also to some degree syntax, rigorous measures of core (necessary, not sufficient) Arabic could be constructed. Lurking in the background is the question of how inferences can be drawn from today's situations to interpret issues of Arabic historical linguistics and how, proceeding from contemporary sociolinguistics methodologies, determining factors in such developments can be extrapolated.

1.1.2 The Classical Language, the Linguistic Tradition

The factors summarized in the previous section alone are of enticing interest to linguistics, without mention even having been made of what is unquestionably the most central icon of Arabic: the classical language. It is remarkable that what today is for some *the* form of Arabic—the ʕArabiyya, or the Fuṣħaa, popularly known as Standard or Modern Standard Arabic—is by and large identical to the form of Arabic broadly described by the late 2nd-/8th-century grammarian Sibawaih.

The functions of the ʕArabiyya are legion. Most centrally, it is, roughly, the variety of Quranic revelation. It is the variety that came to symbolize the remarkable intellectual and cultural flowering in the Islamic era and the variety around which the Arabic script developed [Daniels, "Writing"]. It is the variety that became a central cultural and political pillar of the Arabic nahḍa "renaissance" movement of the 19th century ([Newman, "Nahḍa"]) and enjoys the status of official language in 23 nation states today (see Map 1.3 in the chapter Appendix) with its concomitant importance in modern educational systems, it is the variety typically taught in non-Arab universities [Ryding, "Acquisition"], and it continues to be an essential element in any debate on Arab identity [Suleiman, "Folk Linguistics"].

Each and every one of these associations implies linguistic issues of different types: descriptive, historical, political, second-language acquisition. What is most remarkable, however, is the Arabic linguistic tradition itself, which was built on the basis of one of the true classics of linguistics, the *Kitaab* of Sibawaih (Baalbaki 2008; ["ALT I"]). The very first book on Arabic grammar (so far as our documented record of transmission goes) is a comprehensive (nearly 1,000 pages) descriptive work built on a highly elaborated grammatical theory. While opinions differ as to the origin of the post-Sibawaih Arabic linguistic tradition, it is clear that a highly sophisticated and differentiated theoretical grammatical and pragmatic discourse continued to develop for at least the next 500 years [Larcher "ALT II"]. No less interesting and significant is the voluminous lexicographical tradition that developed in tandem with the grammatical [Sara, "Classical Lexicography"].

Students of Arabic therefore deal not only with the varieties of Arabic themselves but also with a metadiscourse, as it were, which was established within Arabic–Islamic culture. Arabic texts were passed down to us, along with a theoretical framework for analyzing them, constitutive of the Arabic–Islamic tradition, which continues to be of central importance in the contemporary teaching of Arabic and which challenges the interpretive acumen of linguists studying this tradition.

Thus, with respect to Proposition 1, it is not only that Arabic is one of the few languages of the world within which developed a linguistic tradition; also, it is a tradition that continues to exercise its influence on today's Arabs and Arabic society and beyond to Islamic society.

1.1.3 Arabic and Arab Identities

The two previous points set the stage for the inherent language tension that exists in contemporary Arabic societies. Arabic, the mother tongue of its approximately 300 million speakers, is not the same Arabic as the Arabic that is codified and has official political status and cultural centrality through its association with the Quran and with pan-Arab identity.

On one hand, these two broadly defined varieties can be represented as mutually opposed: official versus unofficial, written versus spoken, formal versus informal, pan- versus local, learned formally versus acquired as a first language (L1). The functional contrasts were made famous by Ferguson (1959). Equally, one can emphasize the complementarity of the codes. The native colloquial is the language not only of home and friends but also of all that is informal, unofficial, spontaneous, and intimate. The growing entertainment industry in its diverse media manifestations is thus wholly dominated by the colloquials, as is the informal world of texting and twittering [Holes, "Orality"]. Blogging, a domain awaiting comprehensive linguistic research, appears to cover a spectrum of styles.

The difference between the two is also one of ideology versus practice, of ideal versus real. The fuṣħaa, even if in its perceptions and usage it is a variety of fuzzy contours (Kaye 1972; Parkinson 1991) and is rarely[2] used in the real world in its prescribed form, is the variety of preeminent cultural importance [Suleiman, "Folk Linguistics"].

Sociolinguistics, a subdiscipline of linguistics of relatively recent provenance closely related to the older dialectology, shows the degree to which ideal and real can differ in the realm of spoken Arabic. The careful microdocumentation of speech communities consistently has shown (studies from the Arabian–Persian Gulf, Saudi Arabia, Jordan, Damascus, Bethlehem, Cairo, Casablanca, and northeast Nigeria) that features of spoken colloquial varieties are what drive language change [Al-Wer, "Sociolinguistics"]. Moreover, when Arabic meets other languages bilingually, it is again the colloquial that always forms the basic matrix of contact [Davies et al., "Codeswitching"]. Even in mixed colloquial–fuṣħaa exchanges such as on media talk shows, the colloquial can have a dominant role.

The vibrant co-existence of quite differentiated varieties, a situation hardly unique to Arabic, nonetheless takes on a special, perhaps unique status in the world's languages, precisely because each variety, beyond its linguistic profile, embodies a different history, a different symbolism, a different legitimization. While these differences are of central interest to students of linguistics, they extend beyond the academic lecture hall to the real world of language teaching and language policy. To which variety, for instance, should a program of second-language teaching be tailored, or, if the varieties have different cognitive profiles, what are the implications for L1 teaching? These are questions best not answered by policy fiat. Indeed, the experience of Arabic in post-9/11 America represents probably the sorriest example ever of huge resources expended for developing language teaching programs, largely divorced from the fundamental research on

[2] The crucial adverb *rarely* should be understood as follows. Arabic is spoken by, conservatively, 300 million individuals. Each individual, probably conservatively, speaks for two hours per day, at 10,000 words per hour (slightly low probably), giving 6 trillion words of Arabic per day. The only forums where a normative, spoken Standard Arabic is used are certain media broadcasts (e.g., the excellent news channels al-ʕArabiyya or al-Jaziyra, national and commercial channels mainly for information-orientated topics such as news and documentaries) and in various official meetings, including some but hardly all educational formats (see Mejdell 2006; also [Holes, "Orality"]). Of the 300 million speakers, only a tiny minority of them are engaged at any one time in a function prescribing the use of Standard Arabic. Otherwise, for most individuals nearly always, and for all at some time, the basis of everyday speech is a colloquial variant.

the language being taught that would make for a more rational and efficient teaching program [Ryding, "Acquisition"]. Research from across the spectrum of linguistics is implicated in any academicization of Arabic teaching, whether as an L1 or L2.

1.1.4 Grammar

Arabic is thus a language of rare breadth and extension in the world, a language like perhaps no other in the degree to which it embodies the culture and politics of its speakers. It is, however, a language, and it has been studied from a number of classical grammatical perspectives. Even here Arabic has structural features that set it apart from many, sometimes most, of the world's languages.

The phenomenon of emphasis (pharyngealization) of consonants is a hallmark of the language and has engendered numerous studies both in phonetics [Embarki, "Phonetics"] and in phonology [Hellmuth, "Phonology"]. What is emblematic of Arabic, however, hardly exhausts the interest of Arabic for linguistics. As Hellmuth points out, for instance, stress in Arabic has been of central interest in phonological theory.

In morphology, an ongoing debate surrounding Arabic and many other Semitic languages is the status of the consonantal root as a morphemic element. As Ratcliffe ["Morphology"] points out, the Arabic grammatical tradition itself viewed the stem, not the root, as the basis of morphology, and arguments from within contemporary morphological theory have been developed for this as well. But equally, psycholinguistic studies on the basis of carefully constructed experiments have interpreted the consonantal root as having a crucial role in morphological processing [Boudelaa, "Psycholinguistics"].

Besides the Arabic grammatical tradition itself (1.1.2), there are two further prominent approaches to Arabic grammar. The older one is the philological tradition [Edzard, "Philology"], with which the study of Arabic grammar in the West began. Besides its general interest in Arabic grammar, this tradition incorporates cultural issues and has been present at the interface of Arabic texts of all genres and language. The other is more recent and is based on the precepts of theoretical grammar, particularly syntactic theory in the generative tradition, which endeavors to locate what is specifically Arabic within a broader program of universal grammar [Benmamoun and Choueri, "Syntax"].[3] All of the formal grammatical domains feed into the growing domain of computational linguistics and into the broader field of natural language processing [Ditters, "Computational"].

Finally, the classical lexicographical tradition has its counterpart in contemporary lexicography, a field increasingly drawing the vast online publishing industry in Arabic

[3] Chapter 6 is a double chapter; the original intent was to have two separate chapters, one on the standard language and the other on dialects. Individual circumstances required conflating the two into one.

for its sources [Buckwalter and Parkinson, "Modern Lexicography"]. Here again one experiences the special challenges confronting the Arabic lexicographer, for instance, whether to lemmatize according to root or stem, how to sublemmatize parts of speech, and whether to lump polysemously or to differentiate identical forms.

The articles in this handbook describe a language that, when looked at in its totality, is of rare thematic linguistic differentiation.

1.2 Scope and Choice of Chapter Topics

Proposition 1 encapsulates an ideal. The handbook is intended to reflect the full breadth of research on Arabic linguistics in the West. Realistically, this implies that it includes only chapters on topics judged to have a critical mass of background research. The reader will therefore miss domains that might be expected in a linguistics handbook. Asymmetries will be noticeable. There is a chapter on L2 acquisition but none on L1 acquisition, a chapter on sociolinguistics, but none on oral discourse, a number of chapters on grammar but none on semantics. The gaps are regrettable but unavoidable so long as the focus of the chapters is on the domains of Arabic linguistics that do indeed enjoy a fairly broad and deep coverage rather than on Arabic-flavored general linguistics, as it were.[4]

The chapters themselves reflect domains of research with great disparities of detail. In some cases the chapter is able to cover nearly all of the published research on a given domain, for instance, the chapter on Pidgins and Creoles and even, surprisingly (see remark at end of 1.1.3), work on L2 Arabic language acquisition. In others the breadth of available material has meant that authors could summarize only broad lines of research, illustrating the topic in greater detail with selected examples. Arabic language contact, particularly as reflected in loanwords, for instance, has a very large literature; the research on Arabic dialects is immense, and the research on the Arabic grammatical tradition is large. As far as Western research goes, these disparities to some degree reflect the relative age of the subdomain. In general, codeswitching, psycholinguistics, sociolinguistics, and pidgin and creole linguistics, for instance, are barely 30 or 40 years old as independent specializations of linguistics. Research on Arabic dialects, on the other hand, was already well established in the 19th century. This does not, however, imply

[4] For instance, the justifiably well-regarded *Encyclopedia of Arabic Language and Linguistics* has a chapter on "Cohesion" (Khalil 2006) with nine non-Arabic items in the bibliography and ten on Arabic. Unfortunately, this breakdown realistically reflects the dearth of material on spoken Arabic discourse, for instance, only one book-length work, an edited volume (Owens and Elgibali 2010), which is too little in the editor's view to merit a separate chapter here. The article preceding Khalil's on "Coherence," a central topic equally in literary and spoken texts, treats the subject only as it is reflected in the Classical literary tradition (Faiq 2006). The limitation is regrettable but does reflect the unbalanced state of the art in this domain.

that any domain of Arabic linguistics has been exhaustively treated. As Behnstedt and Woidich point out ["Dialectology"], many dialects, for instance, are poorly described, and the integration of dialectology and sociolinguistics, an essential element of sociolinguistics in the West, has seen only modest progress in the case of Arabic, while historical dialectology, a part of the general field of Arabic historical linguistics, is meager at best.

Gaps should certainly be seen as a challenge to open up wider avenues of research.

1.3 The Real World of Research on Arabic: A Critical Look

Given the current state of research on Arabicist it may be asked: if Proposition 1 is correct, does the linguistic research match the inherent interest of the language?

Here I would answer with only a very conditional "yes." On one hand, as noted in the previous section, there are areas of research with a large literature and well-established research tradition. On the other hand, there are topics central to the study of any language with only modest research traditions in Arabic. Studies on spoken Arabic discourse are rare (see note 4), while more recent domains of linguistics such as psycholinguistics, sociolinguistics, or the study of spoken Arabic pragmatics, though growing, are still in their incipient stages.

Ultimately, however, the study of a language must be more than the sum of its parts. It will be suggested here that, as far as Arabic goes, a holistic linguistic tradition remains an as yet unrealized desideratum. In the past and currently, a number of factors militate against this development. Four factors can be identified.

1.3.1 Arabic Is Large

The first is simply the immensity of the field itself. Arabic presents prima facie anything but a unified domain of inquiry. Consider, for instance, the two basic media that Arabic linguistics works with: the written and the spoken word, the former of which is associated with the Classical and Standard language and the latter with the dialects. These two media are in important respects of a different nature. The written domain is a learned domain, one that itself continues a heritage dating back to the 2nd/8th century, whose standard and norms have been long established. While one might be able to change certain aspects of the Standard language, such as the idiomatic domain ([Newman, Kossmann]), one cannot change its morphology or syntax. The spoken domain, on the other hand, is beholden to contemporary methods of descriptive and field linguistics, associated with, inter alia, corpus collection and language documentation, work with expert consultants, and instrumental phonetics of the spoken language. Norms, such as there are in this domain, emerge from the individual research studies undertaken in it.

Experience, moreover, has shown that in the Western tradition these two domains exist largely in parallel universes, with scholars linked to one or the other but not both. Those concerned with the written language, for instance, to the extent that they move outside the field of the linguistics of the written varieties, gravitate toward the other literary domains of Arabic such as Arabic literature, law, and medical texts. Many such individual cases could be cited, but quite typical in this respect is Carl Brockelmann, whose *Grundriss der semitischen Sprachen* (1908, 1913) remains a standard reference work. After publishing this work, he went on to write another well-regarded book, *Geschichte der islamischen Völker* (1943) (*History of Islamic Peoples*). Brockelmann never studied a spoken variety of Arabic, and his *Grundriss*, while a work of compendious scholarship, is marked by a decided antipathy toward theoretical issues in historical and contact linguistics (Owens 2009: 43), precisely two areas where Arabic is particularly implicated, as discussed already.[5]

Those working in the realm of the spoken language, on the other hand, are faced initially with a plethora of challenges, for instance, which aspect of language to concentrate on or which varieties of Arabic to try to delineate. Finding a format to integrate these in turn with the Classical or Standard varieties may imply defining variables that are central to neither tradition.

Edzard ["Philology"] correctly notes that there is in principle no contradiction between a philological (written) orientation and a "theoretical" linguistic one; experience has nonetheless shown that relatively few scholars not only work in both domains but also, more importantly, attempt a synthesis of the two.

1.3.2 Stovepiping

The problem is at once abetted and exacerbated by the stovepiping characteristic of contemporary academia. Whereas 30 years ago one could claim to be a linguist, today it is more likely that one will be a sociolinguist, psycholinguist, or general or specialized syntactician. Certainly these developments follow their own internal logic, as methods and theoretical perspectives have become more specialized during this period. At the same time, in this there is the danger that the academic apparatus defines the language rather than the language being served by the apparatus.

To take an example from sociolinguistics, one can ask how many studies are needed to define the social status of the "qaf" variable. On one hand, the fact that there have been fruitful studies on this variable means that it provides a necessary and interesting comparative breadth; on the other hand, certainly many other variables, some of broad

[5] Indeed, it is striking that while comparative Semitic and comparative Indo-European literature both came of age in the same era, the 19th century, and to a large degree in the same region—Central Europe—the theoretical contribution of the former to the development of general principles of historical linguistics was negligible whereas that of the latter was essential.

comparative potential and others of particular local interest, await treatment. Added to this, embedding the findings on a comparative basis in the vast Arabic world is a challenge that has received relatively little attention from Arabic sociolinguists.[6] Beyond this is the ever-present danger of calling the game over as soon as a sociolinguistic phenomenon has been studied from within a particular theoretical perspective, as often as not one initially defined from outside of the Arabic-speaking world. Al-Wer's perspective in ["Sociolinguistics"] is better; she shows that ultimately constructs need to be interpreted within a context that does justice to the particularities of a given part of the Arabic world, illustrating her point with the interpretation of the ostensibly universal or at least very general "education" variable as a proxy for other, community-immanent variables.

1.3.3 Clash of Traditions

Complementing the two previously defined issues is that academic and cultural traditions provide ready barriers against synthetic perspectives. Within the West, for instance, Carter (1988: 207) proposed a distinction between Arabic linguistics and Arab linguistics. "... 'Arabic linguistics'.... detaches the language entirely from its environment so that it becomes a pure abstraction." On the other hand, Arab linguistics, the legitimate study of the Arabic language, is "... the vast and continuing output of traditional works, both editions of texts and secondary sources, which remain wholly within the historical norms of Islamic scholarship" (ibid.). However valid this perspective may have been thirty years ago, the prerequisites for an integrative Arabic linguistics are certainly in place today.

To be fair, one of Carter's objections to an Arabic linguistics deserves attention. "Solving" a problem in Arabic within a general linguistic theory runs the danger of importing an issue, a technique of inquiry, a focus on a grammatical construction whose ultimate interest is dictated from outside of Arabic and whose "solution" offers little to those interested in the complex structure of Arabic. At the same time, however, as noted already, trivial an observation though it is, Arabic is simply a language, so linguistic approaches will want to understand it within general theories of language. Moreover, as argued in Sections 1.1.1 and 1.1.2, Arabic itself has unique geographical, social, historical, and cultural properties that have, as it were, pushed the language in directions hardly encountered elsewhere. Linguistic theory can hardly avoid it, even if, in practice, non-Arabicist linguists often do so (see, e.g., criticisms in [Tosco and Manfredi, "Creoles"] or Ryding ["Acquisition"] on the barriers confronting researchers

[6] For instance, despite relatively well-documented accounts of "qaf" variation covering thirty years of research in the Arabic world from the Gulf to Morocco (e.g., Sallam 1980; Holes 1987; Haeri 1996; Amara 2005; Hachimi 2007), no studies have synthesized these accounts with a view toward defining the extent to which a common social dynamic lies behind "qaf" usage. It is, for instance, no sociolinguistic accident that the "qaf" variable is of such marginal interest in Nigerian Arabic, a distinctly minority language in northeast Nigeria, that it was not included as a variable in Owens (1998).

of second-language acquisition due simply to lack of language knowledge). It is easy to formulate a solution to this problem: practitioners need to be as well versed in Arabic in all its linguistic ramifications as they are in the methodologies and theories of linguistics. Nonetheless, its implementation implies a commitment of both individual and institutional time and intellectual resources, which are not necessarily easy to come by.

Perhaps more pernicious than the delegitimization of a linguistic approach to Arabic is Mahdi's (1984: 37) admonition to study dialects to be rid of its debilitating influence on the Standard (fuṣħaa).[7] This perhaps well-intentioned perspective derives most directly from a normative 19th-century tradition (see [Newman, "Nahḍa"], which attempts to lay the blame for the ill learning of the Standard language on the use of dialects and can justify the study of dialects only against a possible benefit for the Standard. Such a perspective is not uncommon in the Arabic world.[8] Leaving aside the cultural and political issues inherent in this position [Suleiman, "Folk Linguistics"], adopting this perspective would necessarily mean excluding Chapters 10, 12, 13, 14, 15, and 22 from this volume while requiring severe reductions in most others, since the dialect is nothing less than the mother tongue. It is not so much an approach foreign to general linguistic inquiry as it is a rejection of the scientific and empirical study of the world, defining in narrow political-cultural terms the goals of research on one of the most ineffable and undefined domains of human experience: language.

1.4 Attitudes

The reader may be confused at this point. On one hand, Proposition 1 claims that Arabic is, for the linguist, an intellectual challenge like no other. On the other, this challenge is often met by traditions, theories, academic structures, and attitudes that at best ensure a fragmented understanding of the language and at worst succeed in a holistic characterization of "Arabic" only at the expense of defining whole domains of language experience into nonexistence.

It can be suggested, without exaggerating the professional and even ideological differences that accrue in the study of Arabic, that the only approach that does justice to Proposition 1 is one grounded on radically open-minded empiricism.

[7] Mahdi speaks of the sicknesses of the dialects, which require treatment (الامراض التي يجب علاجها). The passage in fact comes in the Introduction to a well-edited edition of *1001 Nights*, which left the original "Middle Arabic" style intact rather than classicizing out its authenticity, as is the current custom (e.g., the version on arabicorpus).

Another popular approach is the regulation of language use by legal fiat. Munṣif al-Marzuqi, who writes an occasional column for Jezira Net, for instance, would (article of Nov. 6, 2011) criminalize the use of what he terms "Creole" Arabic, by which he intends, in the parlance of contemporary linguistics, a codeswitched variety of Arabic (*tajriym istiʕmaal luɣat al-kriyuwl*).

[8] For instance, generally speaking, "Arabic" in Arabic departments in the Arabic world stop with the classical language.

MAP 1.1 Countries with Arabic as a majority language.

MAP 1.2 The Arab league.

MAP 1.3 Arabic as official language.

MAP 1.4 Arabic as minority language.

the 13th century, they supposedly produced the first representation of the vocal tract with the main consonantal articulations (ibid.). This representation is distinguished by its modernity because it shows precisely both place of consonantal articulation and the articulators. Figure 2.1 provides a diagram of the vocal tract borrowed from Bakalla (1982) and quoted by Heselwood and Hassan.

Although phonetics was not yet a structured discipline and tools for observation did not exist, the early Arab grammarians still gave us ample, precise indications about the articulatory characteristics of consonants as well as on their acoustic and perceptive properties (Bonnot 1976; Heselwood and Hassan 2011). Thanks to the most modern equipment, researchers today can compare their own observations with those of the early Arab grammarians.

This, however, is not without disagreement: for example, Sībawayhi distinguished between the opposing *mažhu:ra* lit. "made loud" and *mahmu:sa* "whispered," which many modern phoneticians and phonologists translate with voiced versus voiceless, with the exception of Jakobson (1957), who uses *lenis* versus *fortis* to describe this contrast. Instead of doing a chronological presentation of the main research in Arabic experimental phonetics, I have chosen to present the most important conclusions of the works, which pertain to (1) pharyngeal consonants, (2) pharyngealized consonants, (3) length, and (4) consonantal and vocalic variation.

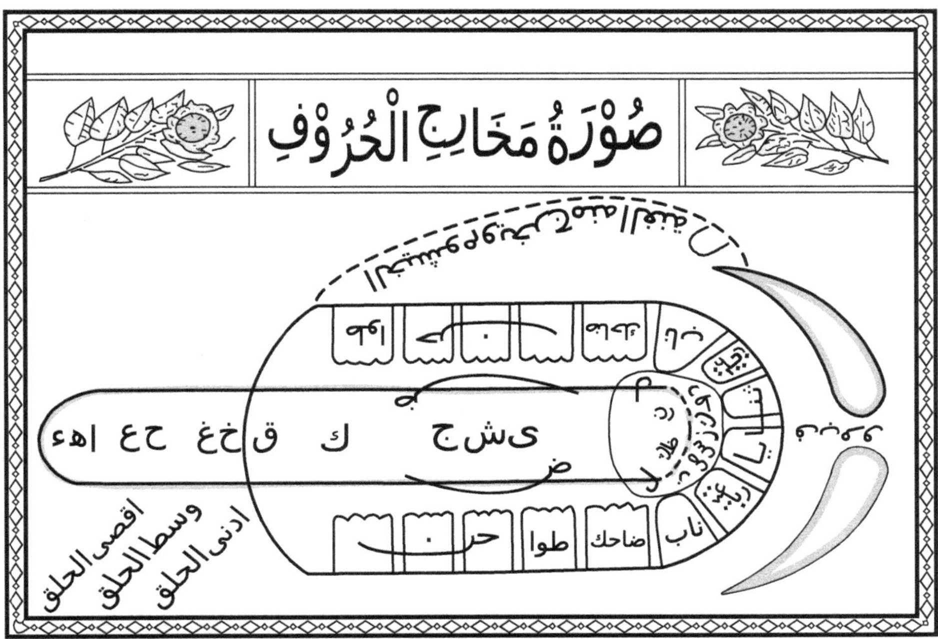

FIGURE 2.1 Vocal tract diagram titled *Ṣūrat makhārij al-ḥurūf* (Picture of the points of articulation of the letters) from *Miftāḥ al-ʿUlūm* (The key to the sciences) by Al-Sakkāki. Dotted line indicates the nasal passage with a nostril above the lip (from Bakalla 1982: 87, quoted by Heselwood and Hassan 2011: 7).

2.3.1 Pharyngeal Consonants

Modern phoneticians qualify the two guttural consonants (حلقية) "'ayn" (ع) /ʕ/ and "hā'" (ح) /ħ/ in Al-Khalīl as pharyngeal. However, not all researchers agree that they belong phonologically to a so-called natural class (see Zawaydeh 2003 for an extensive review of that point). Yet Sībawayhi does not use the same terms to describe these two consonants. The sound /ħ/ is described as fricative (raxw), while the sound /ʕ/, which is situated between the stop (ʃadi:d) and fricative, is produced with [tardi:d], according to Sībawayhi's terminology. Ghali (1983) and, following him, Hassan (2011) use the quality (taraddudijja) "frequentative" to designate the consonant /ʕ/.

Al-Ani (1970) is considered the first experimental work in Arabic phonetics. His research is based on cineradiographic data (x-ray), which give accurate images of the surface of the vocal tract, lips, tongue, uvula, and pharyngeal movements combined with acoustic data to describe the consonants and vowels of Modern Arabic. Relying on the productions of four Iraqi native speakers, Al-Ani (ibid., 59–60) confirms Sībawayhi's description of /ħ/ as a fricative voiceless consonant. If he accepts the pharyngeal place of the consonant /ʕ/, he describes it, however, as a voiceless stop in all positions (initial, medial, final) whether singleton or geminated (ibid., 62–63).

If we carefully examine the mid-sagittal sections from the cineradiographic films (Al-Ani 1970 72–74) and the spectrograms (ibid., 65–71), we can observe that /ʕ/ presents a constriction lower in the pharynx with the body of the tongue in more retracted position compared with /ħ/ (see Figure 2.2). On the acoustic level, /ʕ/ does not have the profile of a stop or even that of a fricative as is /ħ/; one can, however, see that it is clearly voiced.

The stop articulatory manner of /ʕ/ described by Al-Ani was not often followed by other phoneticians. Using the same techniques (x-ray and acoustic measurements), Ghali (1983: 440) chooses the feature frequentative for /ʕ/, which Sībawayhi also uses, and assigns it the "trill" articulatory manner. Besides / ʕ /, Ghali (ibid., 441) classifies four further consonants in the trill category: the alveolar /r/; the two uvulars /x/; the /ɣ/; and the glottal /ʔ/.

In the last two decades, more sophisticated technologies such as ultra-fast imaging have been used. Some researchers successfully applied these techniques to perfect our knowledge of Arabic consonants. Zawaydeh (2003) uses the endoscopic technique to visualize articulatory adjustments during the production of these two consonants in Jordanian Arabic.

The results indicate that, during the production of /ħ/ and /ʕ/ as well as during the production of pharyngealized consonants, the distance between the epiglottis and the pharyngeal wall is reduced (Zawaydeh 2003: 287). These results are similar to those obtained by Ghazeli (1977), who uses cineradiography to study pharyngealized consonants. In a recent study of Iraqi Arabic, Hassan et al. (2011) employs ultra-fast laryngoscopy (an imaging technique using endoscopy), combined with electroglottography (EGG). This technique captures vocal fold vibrations by positioning two electrodes on the neck on both sides of the thyroid cartilage.

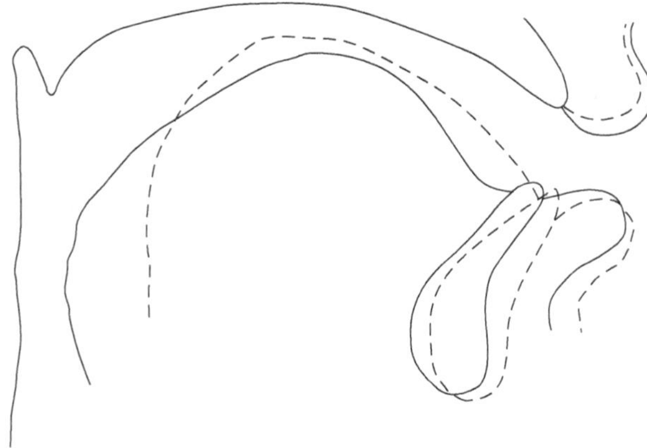

FIGURE 2.2 X-ray tracing of the articulation of /ħ/ (dotted line) and /ʕ/ (plain) in the context of /Ci/ (from Al-Ani 1970: 72).

These physiological data were combined with acoustic data to complete our knowledge of the features of /ħ/ and /ʕ/. While confirming their pharyngeal place of articulation, Hassan et al. (2011: 834) confirm that these two consonants are pronounced by Iraqi speakers as aryepiglotto-epiglottal fricatives, transcribed as voiceless /ʜ/ and voiced /ʢ/, and are considered as variants of /ħ/ and /ʕ/, respectively. Heselwood (2007: 5), relying on Laufer (1996: 114), indicates that /ʕ/ in the production of 21 speakers from 11 different Arab countries is never pronounced as a fricative consonant; it does not inherit this characteristic except through the fact that it is phonologically paired with /ħ/, which is a real fricative.

On the basis of articulatory and acoustic data, Heselwood (2007: 9–28) describes /ʕ/ as a "tight approximant," which he proposes to represent using the following symbol /ʕ̝/. On the basis of acoustic and articulatory data from Moroccan speakers, Yeou and Maeda (2011: 155) conclude that /ħ/ and /ʕ/ are real approximants, since, unlike certain fricatives such as /s/, the two pharyngeals have a larger articulatory constriction and the turbulence is present only for the voiceless consonant.

2.3.2 The Pharyngealized Consonants

Arabic has a specific phonological contrast that opposes plain dental or dento-alveolar consonants to their pharyngealized cognates. Modern Arabic has four pharyngealized consonants /tˤ dˤ đˤ sˤ/; some modern Arabic dialects have slightly more, while others have less.

Ferguson (1956) shows that allophonic phraryngealized variations exist in Modern Arabic for the /l/. I exclude the consonant /q/ from this correlation and adopt Bonnot's (1976) point of view, who dedicates a long chapter to the relation between the two stops /k/ and /q/ and concluded, based on articulatory and acoustic data, the absence of the pharyngealized feature during the production of the consonant /q/.

The pharyngealized consonants /tˤ dˤ đˤ sˤ/ existed in Classical Arabic with presumably a slightly more backed place of articulation and a different articulation manner for some of them (see Al-Wer 2003: 28–29 for the evolution of /dˤ/; see Roman 1981 for the evolution of the emphatic among the guttural consonants). These consonants were often designated by a plurality of Arab terms such as "istiʕla:ʔ," "tafxi:m," ""itˤba:q," or ""iħsˤa:r," which modern linguists translated by "emphatic" (see Bonnot 1976, esp. chapter dedicated to emphasis, 84–118).

The main dental or dento-alveolar articulation of these consonants is not a major point of disagreement among researchers, but the same cannot be said of their pharyngealized secondary articulation. According to Ladefoged and Maddieson (1996: 365–366), the place of constriction of the secondary pharyngeal articulation is formed midway between the uvula and the epiglottis. The sagittal sections presented by Al-Ani (1970: 57–58; see Figure 2.3) show that the back of the tongue has a rather flat position and that its root has a more backed position for the pharyngealized consonant compared with its non-pharyngealized counterpart.

The narrowing at the origin of the constriction seems to be produced in the median region of the oropharynx. The acoustic data deal more with the effects of the adjacent vowel showing that the secondary pharyngealized articulation leads to a rise of the frequency of the first formant, F1, and a lowering of the frequency of the second formant, F2 (Al-Ani 1979: 44–56).

Shahin (1997) interprets this acoustic pattern in phonological terms. The observed rise of F1 associated with pharyngealized consonants is shared by other guttural consonants (the glottals, pharyngeal, and uvulars); the author regroups them in a class called *pharyngealization harmony*. The lowering of F2, however, concerns only pharyngealized consonants, and Shahin proposes regrouping them in a different class called *uvularization harmony*.

Ghazeli's (1977) study using the same instrumentation as Al-Ani (1970) shows that the main characteristic of Arabic pharyngealized consonants on the articulatory level is a retraction of the root of the tongue and a flattening of its posterior part in the shape of a plateau, a tightening of the pharyngeal cavity above the epiglottis, and a slight labial protrusion. Based on the cineradiographic data of a Saudi speaker, Bonnot (1976: 369) determines that the constriction of a pharyngealized consonant goes from the uvula region up to the deepest level of the pharynx. Compared with its non-pharyngealized counterpart, a pharyngealized consonant is distinguished by a more backed place of articulation and a superior articulation strength as well as by a slight increase in its length and a shortening of the adjacent vowel (ibid., 472–473). These data are confirmed in Elgendy's (2001) study on pharyngealization.

Several chapters of Hassan and Heselwood (2011) examine the articulatory and acoustic properties of pharyngealized consonants using modern techniques such as nasoendoscopy, videofluoroscopy, electromagnetic midsagittal articulometry (EMA), and ultrasound. In addition to the retraction of the tongue body and the flattening of its posterior part, these data show that pharyngealized consonants are different from their non-pharyngealized counterparts in the volume of buccal and pharyngeal resonance

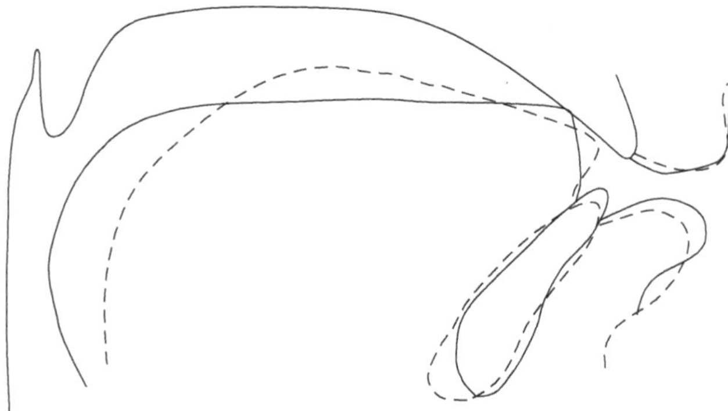

FIGURE 2.3 X-ray tracing of the articulation of /t/ (dotted line) and /tˤ/ (plain) in the context of /Ci/ (from Al-Ani 1970: 57).

cavities; the adjustments of the body of the tongue and its root; the height of the lower jaw; and the different positions of the hyoid bone, the epiglottis, the aryepiglottic cords, and the larynx.

According to Al-Ani (1970), acoustic data focus the effects of pharyngealized consonants on their phonetic environment. These effects manifest themselves through an important modification of the first two formants of the vowels, shown by a significant increase of F1 and a substantial decrease of F2. Jongman et al. (2011: 89) report significant effects on the third formant, F3, in the production of 12 Jordanian speakers. The frequency of F3 increases significantly when the vowel is placed next to a pharyngealized consonant.

Bonnot (1976: 451) shows that F1 and F2 are very close in a pharyngealized consonantal environment compared with a non-pharyngealized environment. Embarki et al. (2011b) analyzes the influence of pharyngealization on Jordanian, Kuwaiti, Moroccan, and Yemeni speakers by comparing $V_1C^{ʕ}V_2$ sequences, where C is /tˤ dˤ đˤ sˤ/, with similar V_1CV_2 sequences containing the non-pharyngealized cognates /t d đ s/. The frequency measures of the first two formants F1 and F2 as well as the distance F2 – F1 (Fv) taken at three different landmarks of the vowel (*onset*, *midset*, and *offset*) confirm the frequency differences indicated in the literature, that is, the increase of F1, lowering of F2, and closeness of the two formants (ibid., 146).

The study also shows that the values of Fv in the environment of a non-pharyngealized consonant are on average greater by 348 Hz than the corresponding pharyngealized one. Also, the differences of Fv between the two contexts (non-pharyngealized–pharyngealized) are stronger at the onset of V2 than at the offset of V1 (Embarki et al. 2011b: 147). Embarki et al. conclude that the influence exercised by a pharyngealized consonant on the vocal environment is stronger than its non-pharyngealized cognate. Jongman et al. (2011: 88–89) show that the effects of the pharyngealized consonant in initial or final position of a word significantly impact the three first formants of the adjacent vowel, influencing the vowel in a constant way from the onset to the offset via the midset. While confirming the effects of pharyngealization on the two first formants of the adjacent vowels, Ghazeli (1981: 275) shows that the direction of the pharyngeal coarticulation has a more regressive or persistent (carry-over) (left–right) nature than a progressive or anticipatory (right–left) one.

Ali and Daniloff (1972) use cinefluographic data in Iraqi Arabic to highlight this characteristic: a left–right effect being more important than a right–left effect both in the magnitude of the retraction gesture of the tongue and in the number of segments affected by the spread of pharyngealization. However, in a study based on articulatory data (EMA) of a Tunisian speaker, Embarki et al. (2011a: 210) indicate that the effect of a pharyngealized consonant in C_2 position (medial position) starts with the first vowel of the word (V1) and continues above the stationary part of the vowel of the second syllable (V2), indicating that the pharyngealization has carryover as well as anticipatory effects. The acoustic data of the study of Jongman et al. (2011: 91) show that the pharyngealized consonant placed in the final position of a word has significant effects on the non-pharyngealized consonant placed at initial position. On the other hand, the same pharyngealized consonant placed in initial position of a word has no significant effect on the final consonant. This shows that the anticipatory effects (right–left) of pharyngealization are more important than the carryover effects (left–right).

Another interesting piece of data in Ghazeli's (1981) work is the spread of pharyngealization in relation to morphemic boundaries. Ghazeli confirms that the spread of phrayngealization effects stops at the boundaries of the word (ibid., 275). These effects do not seem to cross from one word to the other.

The coarticulatory effects of the pharyngealized consonant on adjacent vowels were measured, among other ways, by a linear regression (i.e., the locus equation; see Lindblom 1963) quantifying the coarticulation degree between the consonant and the vowel between extremes: 0 for a null coarticulation; 1 for a maximal coarticulation. Yeou (1997) shows that the value of the slope of a pharyngealized consonant in Modern Arabic produced by Moroccan speakers is weaker than the value of the slope of its non-pharyngealized counterpart. This same pattern is confirmed in Embarki's et al. (2011a) study of the production of pharyngealized consonants in Modern Arabic and Arabic dialect of 16 native speakers from four different countries, Jordan, Kuwait, Morocco, and Yemen.

2.3.3 Duration

Duration is a phonetic parameter that is specific to all linguistic units, consonants, vowels, syllables, words, and sentences. As Coates (1980: 4) says, "Time is vital in the understanding of phonological processes and processing. *A fortiori*, it is vital in phonological representation too."

Traditionally, the rubric *duration* deals with contrastive length that pertains not only to vowels in a large number of natural languages (Ladefoged and Maddieson 1996: 320) but also to consonants, although to a lesser degree. Arabic is among the languages that use quantity contrast both for consonants and vowels. In addition to these two categories, I will include voice onset time (VOT), which is also mainly a temporal phenomenon. However, I will not talk about the effects of consonantal voicing on the duration of both the consonant and the vowel. In this respect I refer the reader to the works of Port et al. (1980) and Mitleb (1984a).

2.3.3.1 *Vowel Length*

As for vowels, most languages using vowel quantity have a duration opposition between two vowel categories, the short and the long ones. Ladefoged and Maddieson (1996: 320–321) explain that quantity can oppose three or even four vowel categories in some languages. The ratio of duration between vowels (the duration of the long vowel divided by the duration of the short vowel) varies enormously among languages. Some languages use a low ratio, for example 1.3, while others use a significantly longer ratio, such as 3.2 (Lehiste 1970).

In Arabic, studies show that the quantity ratios between vowels vary a great deal. Al-Ani (1970: 75) shows that the relative duration of short isolated vowels is 100 to 150 ms, while with the long ones it is 225 to 350 ms, which makes the ratio long to short more than two to one. Port et al. (1980) present a ratio of 2.6 for Egyptian, Iraqi, and Kuwaiti speakers. Mitleb's (1984b: 231) study on Jordanian Arabic showed that the Arabic long vowel is 65% longer compared with its short counterpart, a 1.5 ratio. Belkaid (1984) presents a ratio slightly greater than 2 for speakers of Tunisian origin. Studying three speakers of different dialectal origin, Abou Haidar (1991) presents varying ratios, but an average of around 2.6. Alioua (1992) finds a mean ratio of 2 for three Moroccan speakers. Jomaa (1994) proposes an intermediate ratio of 2.4 for several dialects. These ratios are, nonetheless, less than those of Modern Arabic and are between 1.3 and 2, with higher relationships in eastern dialects and lower ones in dialects from the Maghreb (Jomaa 1994).

The contrastive vowel length is conveyed essentially through duration (Lehiste 1970). In Al-Ani's (1970: 22–25) study, it seems that quantity contrast is accompanied, in an insignificant way, by vowel quality (see Section 2.2.2.2). The length ratio between short and long vowels is affected by other linguistic parameters. For example, Mitleb (1984b) shows differences that are inherent to the nature of the adjacent consonant, whether it is singleton or geminated (see the previous discussion). De Jong and Zawaydeh (2002: 319) show that long, stressed vowels in Arabic were lengthened 120% by native Jordanian speakers in contrast with their short counterparts. Canepari (2005: 319) indicates that, in a unstressed position, long vowels in Arabic are realized like semi-long vowels.

However, the sensitivity is limited by the theory of acoustic invariance, which is based on the hypothesis that invariable acoustic properties correspond to a segment or to phonetic features, independently of context, speaker, and language (Lahiri et al. 1984; Pickett et al. 1999). Thus, according to Zawaydeh and de Jong (1999), contrastive vowel length is maintained in Arabic fast speech. Port et al. (1980) and Mitleb (1984b: 233) indicate that the length domain in Arabic is determined at the segmental level, while in other languages it is determined at the syllable level such as in Swedish or at the word level such as in English.

2.3.3.2 *Gemination*

Consonant length is treated in languages in terms of gemination. Duration and gemination refer to different aspects of articulation. Quantity is a matter of length, while gemination applies to the repetition of the same articulation. The question of whether Arabic consonants are really geminated or simply long has been discussed by researchers.

In his study of pharyngealization, Bonnot (1976: 225) uses cineradiographic data to prove that the closure release of the geminated /tˤ/ occurs only at the final occlusion, which leads him to conclude that gemination in Arabic is not present with stops in a two-phase articulation but rather in one single phase (ibid., 450). According to Bonnot, the most important criterion is an increase in duration, and the so-called geminated consonants are in reality long consonants.

Languages such as Arabic, which combine both vowel and consonant quantity, are less numerous. In Modern Arabic, the distribution of the 28 consonants is completely regular, with each consonant occupying three positions: initial, medial, and final. All consonants can be singleton or geminated (Kaye 2009: 563). Contrary to the majority of languages where stops are geminated preferably in the medial position of the word (Ladfoged and Maddieson 1996: 92–93), dentals and dento-alveolars in Arabic can be geminated in initial position as well, as with all so-called solar consonants.

Gemination is thus phonological in Arabic, and it is highly contrastive in distinctions of morphological nature (Watson 2002; see, under the morphology subsection of the chapter of Arabic, Kaye 2009: 572–574; [Ratcliffe, "Morphology"]). Al-Ani (1970: 75–77) shows that the duration of geminated consonants increases until it reaches twice the duration of its singleton counterpart. This ratio between a consonant and its geminated counterpart varies slightly in the literature to the point that sometimes overlaps are noticed between the lowest average durations for a geminated consonant and the highest durations for its singleton counterpart.

Bonnot (1976) indicates that the geminate pharyngealized stop /tˤtˤ/ is distinguished from its singleton counterpart /tˤ/ essentially through the duration of the complete closure, which is longer for the geminated one than for its singleton counterpart, with overlapping zones. Al-Ani (1970: 33) indicates that the duration of the geminated consonant is twice that of its singleton counterpart. In Arabic, the geminated consonant can be preceded by a short vowel (V) or a long vowel (V:); the temporal pattern can also be globally affected without reducing a long vowel to the point of confusing it with a phonologically distinct short vowel (Hassan 2003: 46). Khattab (2007: 156) shows that the geminate–singleton ratio in Lebanese is higher when the preceding vowel is short (2.5) compared with a long vowel context (2.09).

Hassan (2003) indicates that the temporal pattern is different when a long vowel is followed by a singleton consonant (V:C) compared with the short vowel context followed by a geminate (VC). Mitleb (1984b) finds the same distributional pattern.

Bonnot (1976: 235) uncovers a difference in the closure duration of the consonant when it is preceded by a short vowel or a long vowel. In the first case, the closure can have a longer duration of up to 50 ms compared with the second case.

Basing his findings on electromyography (EMG) data for Estonian and English, Lehiste et al. (1973: 146–147) indicate that singleton and geminated consonants are different through the duration of the closure and the amplitude of the peaks. Al-Tamimi and Khattab (2011: 214–215) show that the differences between singleton and geminated consonants of Lebanese speakers included, in addition to the duration, other acoustic parameters such as F0, intensity, and the degree of voicing of the consonant. Bonnot (1976) notices articulatory differences illustrated by the lowering of the lower maxillary. Indeed, the lower maxillary is lowered less during the production of the singleton consonant /t: tˤ:/ (ibid., 255, 346). Bonnot also indicates that the position of the tongue varies for a singleton pharyngealized consonant and its geminated counterpart. Unlike the front part of the tongue, which does not show differences, the geminated consonant causes a tightening of the posterior part of the back of the tongue (ibid., 371). Other results show that the geminated stop is distinguished from its singleton counterpart through the VOT duration.

2.3.3.3 *VOT*

VOT is defined as the temporal difference between the release of the complete closure and the onset of quasi-periodical vibrations of the vocal folds. This parameter applies only to stop consonants. It is described as positive when the first voiced periodical resonance starts immediately after the release of the consonant, as is the case of voiceless stops. It is described as negative when the vibrations of the vocal folds begin before the closure release, as is the case with voiced stops. Lisker and Abramson's (1964) classic study, based on the examination of stop consonants in 11 languages, showed that this temporal interval, which is the VOT, allowed for the distinction among three categories of stops in those languages: (1) voiceless unaspirated stops, with a positive VOT between 0 and 25 ms, or *short lag*; (2) voiceless aspirated stops with a positive VOT of 60 to 100 ms, or *long lag*; and (3) voiced stops, with vibrations beginning before the closure release. Some languages use the three patterns to oppose stops, while other languages use a binary opposition only between the two patterns.

Lisker and Abramson (1964) show that the VOT duration varied according to the place of articulation of the consonant: longer for the velars, shorter for the labials, and intermediate for dentals. Cho and Ladefoged (1999: 213) mention six criteria as the origin of the VOT variation, including the cavity volume in front of and behind the constriction, the movement of the articulators, and the contact zone between the articulators.

Al-Ani (1970: 76) indicates that Arabic has a negative VOT for voiced consonants; the duration of this prevoicing varies between 50 and 300 ms according to the position of the consonant (initial, medial, or final) and its nature (singleton or geminated). On the other hand, Arabic has a positive VOT for voiceless consonants that varies between 20 and 40 ms for unaspirated and 35 and 60 for aspirated variants.

In their study of Lebanese Arabic, Yeni Komshian et al. (1977: 38) indicate that stops are characterized by a binary VOT, a long prevoicing, or negative VOT for the voiced consonants /b d dˁ/ varying between 40 and 80 ms and a short interval or positive VOT for the voiceless consonants /t tˁ k q/ between 15 and 35 ms. This study did not examine the VOT of the glottal consonant /ʔ/. Al-Ani (1970: 60–62) describes the latter with a short VOT of 15 to 20 ms.

Al-Ani's (1970) study shows VOT differences according to pharyngealization contrast. The VOT of /t/ is longer than that of its pharyngealized /tˁ/ counterpart, by 40–45 ms for the first and only by 20–30 ms for the second (Al-Ani 1970: 44–45). Yeni-Komshian's et al. (1977: 42) results show differences between pharyngealized consonants /tˁ dˁ/ and corresponding non-pharyngealized /t d/ presented in the form of overlapping zones of 0 to 30 ms. The VOT of voiceless consonants /t tˁ/ appears to be different; it is clearly shorter for the pharyngealized consonant (ibid., 40). Ghazeli (1977) confirms this distribution: the VOT of /tˁ/ is positive although very short (15 ms) compared with the double (30 ms) for the non-pharyngealized consonant /t/. Zeroual et al. (2007: 400) also show that the voiceless pharyngealized stop /tˁ/ has a positive VOT, 14 ms shorter than its non-pharyngealized counterpart /t/ (48 ms).

In Arabic phonology, the question of whether there is a phraryngealized relation that links the consonants /k/ and /q/ is amply discussed (see Section 2.2.1). VOT seems to be one of the elements taken into consideration. Al-Ani (1970: 32) found the same pattern in Iraqi speakers: a longer VOT for /k/ between 35 and 44 ms; and a shorter VOT for /q/ varying between 20 and 26 ms. On the other hand, Yeni-Komshian et al. (1977: 42) presented averages of positive VOT that seem similar for the two consonants: 25 to 30 ms for /k/; and 25 to 35 ms for /q/. This is probably because Lebanese speakers utter a /k/ that is close to a uvular consonant.

The dominant VOT pattern for /k/ and /q/ could be explained by the idea according to which the relation linking these two consonants is of the same nature as the one linking /t/ and /tˁ/—that is, a pharyngealized relation that materializes, inter alia, through a long VOT for /t k/ opposed to a short VOT for /tˁ q/. Lisker and Abramson (1964) indicated that the duration of the VOT varies according to the place of articulation of the consonant: longer for velar consonants; shorter for labial consonants; medial for dentals. However, this is not the case here, and, despite a more backed place of constriction than that of /k/, /q/ inherits a shorter VOT. The explanation is given in part in Cho and Ladefoged (1999: 213), which explains the VOT variation in terms of the volume of the cavity in front and behind the constriction, the movements of the articulators, and the contact zone between the articulators. Basing his data on cineradiographic data, Bonnot (1976: 440) gives details on the articulation of the two consonants and on the contact zones between articulators; these details explain the long release of /k/ and nearly simultaneous release of /q/.

Besides the variation according to the place of articulation of the consonant, Yeni-Komshian et al. (1977: 43) show that the duration of the VOT with Lebanese speakers varies according to the adjacent vowel: the VOT is longer with front vowels.

2.3.4 Consonant and Vowel Variation

Variation concerns all segmental units of Arabic—consonants as well as vowels. The best-known phenomenon for consonants is that of assimilation. Kaye (2009: 564) indicates several consonant assimilation cases. The assimilation in Arabic concerns all consonants and can be partial or total. The hamza, the glottal stop /ʔ/, is considered by some as a consonant that gets completely assimilated by the solar adjacent consonant when it is at a word initial position (Canepari 2005: 325). The Arabic linguistic tradition, on the other hand, considers this purely graphic hamza as a latent consonant.

Assimilation as a phonetic phenomenon was well studied by early grammarians, who precisely described the assimilation of /n/ in [ŋ], [nˤ], or [m] before /q, k, ʃ, j, s, z, sˤ, d, t, tˤ, dˤ θ, đ, đˤ, f/. They underlined the dependency of the nasal expansion on the place of articulation, thus showing that the guttural (stops and pharyngeal fricatives /ħ/, /ʕ/, and glottals /ʔ/ /h/) blocked this assimilation (Bakalla 1983). Consonant assimilation was also explored in its phonological dimension (Abu Salim 1988).

As presented already, early Arab grammarians emphasized the allophonic variants of consonants (see Sībawayhi's description of secondary articulations, mustaḥsana and ġayr mustaḥsana). Embarki et al. (2011a) explain that the differences for locus equations of pharyngealized consonants between Modern Arabic and Dialectal Arabic and among the four countries used in the study (Jordan, Kuwait, Morocco, and Yemen) were due to a weakening of the pharyngealization gesture. Indeed, pharyngealized consonants tend to be articulated like their non-pharyngealized counterparts with very few retraction effects in the back of the tongue; this tendency is very clear in the realization of the consonant /sˤ/ (ibid., 204).

As explained in Section 2.2.2.2, the Arabic vowel system consists of three cardinal qualities that contrast in terms of length: /i u a/ versus /i: u: a:/. This configuration is absolute and does not consider the allophonic realization of phonemes, which is slightly richer. Early Arab grammarians such as Sībawayhi, described these variations, such as the precision of the imala phenomenon (cf. Sara 2007; [Sara, "Classical Lexicography"]). Kaye (2009: 565) explains that variation affects Arabic short vowels more than long ones. He lists a total of 16 different allophones for the six basic phonemes; Al-Ani (1970: 23–24) lists 17 allophonic realizations. Canepari (2005) illustrates on a diagram the principal allophonic realizations of six vowels in Modern Arabic (see Figure 2.4).

These allophonic realizations essentially depend on the phonetic context (the nature of the adjacent consonant) and the prosodic nature (stressed vs. unstressed syllable). The aforementioned studies, which are specific to pharyngealization, show without exception that in a pharyngealized context the frequency of F1 increases and the frequency of F2 decreases noticeably. The phonetic contiguity of certain consonants pushes the cardinal vowels toward less peripheral frequencies. Embarki et al. (2006) show that the formants of three short cardinal vowels of Modern Arabic presented

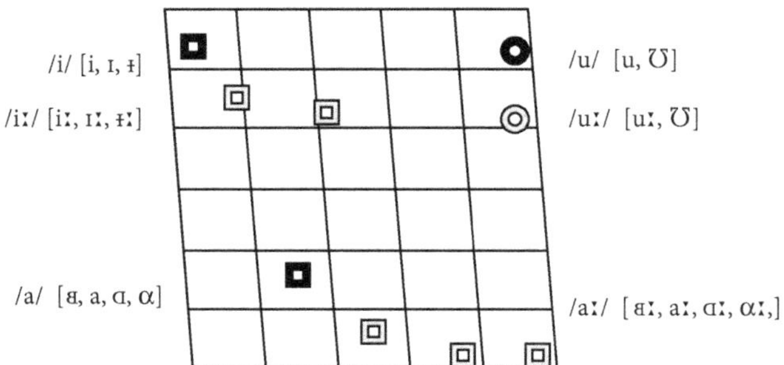

FIGURE 2.4 Articulatory space of vowels in modern Arabic and their allophones (from Canepari 2005: 317).

acoustic signs of nasalization when these vowels were used in the morphologic process of tanwin (_VN#).

In a literature review, Newman (2005) lists the different formant values (F1 and F2) in Modern Arabic in a non-pharyngealized context (see Table 2.4).

These values show a rather important dispersion that indicates a possible free variation around the six Arabic vowels. Can we really talk in such a case of free variation? The very different values listed in the literature can be explained by the nature of the corpus, the phonetic context and the geographical and dialectal differences of the speakers in the studies in question. The speakers are either from a unique dialectal origin, Iraqi (Al-Ani), Tunisian (Belkaïd), or Egyptian (Newman), or are from different countries (Abou Haidar; Ghazeli).

The question that poses itself is how the subjects perceive this variation. Jongman et al. (2011: 93) show that the vowels extracted from phonetic sequences that were affected by pharyngealization and used in perception tests obtain high identification rates. This demonstrates that the Arab subjects have internalized this vowel dispersion and that they use it optimally in lexical treatment tasks.

Table 2.4 Vowel dispersion according to the frequency of the first two formants F1/F2

	iː		i		uː		u		aː		a	
	F1	F2	F1	F2	F1	F2	F1	F2	F1	F2	F1	F2
Al-Ani	285	2200	290	2200	285	775	290	800	675	1200	600	1500
Ghazeli	310	2225	455	1780	330	900	450	1125				
Belkaïd	285	2195	355	1830	310	790	340	995	425	1720	400	1640
Abou Haidar	315	2230	485	1750	335	835	500	1120	690	1500	675	1585
Newman	390	1870	435	1790	465	1075	480	1170	620	1455	615	1460

Source: Newman (2005).

2.4 Conclusion

This chapter shows the range and uniqueness of experimental phonetic studies. The studies cited here indicate that the Arabic language is a distinct language with specific phonetic contrasts and that it shares universal phonetic features with other languages. If we can be reasonably satisfied with the degree of precision of the phonetic descriptions, exclusively sensorimotor here, much remains to be done in the field of speech perception in Arabic. Detailed studies on perception should be conducted to uncover not only robust contrasts but also subtle articulatory and acoustic features. An important part of this chapter was dedicated to the articulatory and acoustic features of pharyngeal and pharyngealized consonants, where the literature is extensive. Little data, however, have been published on the perception of these consonants or on their vowel environment. Our phonetic knowledge should be enhanced by techniques such as functional magnetic resonance imaging (fMRI), which have not been used here.

Research still needs to be conducted to complete our understanding of listeners' and speakers' use of contrasts specific to Arabic to work out, convey, and interpret the most diverse meanings as well as the mobilization of these contrasts in morphology and psychology.

References

Abou Haidar, Laura. 1991. *Variabilité et invariance du système vocalique de l'arabe standard*. PhD diss., Université de Franche-Comté, Besançon.

Abu Salim, I. M. 1988. Consonant assimilation in Arabic: An autosegmental perspective. *Lingua* 74: 45–66.

Al-Ani, Salman H. 1970. *Arabic phonology: An acoustical and physiological investigation*. The Hague: Mouton.

Al-Tamimi, Jalal and Ghada Khattab. 2011. Multiple cues for the singleton-geminate contrast in Lebanese Arabic: Acoustic investigation of stops and fricatives. *Proceedings of the 17th International Congress of Phonetic Sciences, Hong Kong*, 212–215. http://www.icphs2011.hk.

Al-Wer, Enam. 2003. Variability reproduced: A variationist view of the [dˤ]/[đˤ] opposition in modern Arabic dialects. In *Approaches to Arabic dialectology*, ed. Martine Haak, Rudolf de Jong, and Kees Versteegh, 21–31. Amsterdam: Brill.

Ali, Latif and Raymond Daniloff. 1972. A contrastive cinefluorographic investigation of the articulation of emphatic–non emphatic cognate consonants. *Studia Linguistica* 26: 81–105.

Alioua, Ahmed. 1992. De la corrélation entre la durée et l'aperture des voyelles brèves en arabe littéral. *Travaux de l'Institut de Phonétique de Strasbourg* 22: 1–8.

Bakalla, Muhammad H. 1982. *Ibn Jinnī: An early Arab Muslim phonetician*. Taipei: European Language Publications.

——. 1983. The treatment of nasal elements by early Arab and Muslim phoneticians. In *The history of linguistics in the Near East*, ed. C. H. M. Versteegh, Koerner Konrad, and Hans-Josef Niederehe, 49–71. Amsterdam: John Benjamins.

Beeston, Alfred. 1962. Arabian sibilants. *Journal of Semitic Studies* 7: 222–233.

Belkaïd, Y. 1984. Les voyelles de l'arabe littéraire moderne: analyse spectrographique. *Travaux de l'Institut de Phonétique de Strasbourg* 16: 217–240.

Bonnot, Jean-François. 1976. *Contribution à l'Etude des consonnes emphatiques de l'Arabe à partir de méthodes expérimentales*. PhD diss., Université des Sciences Humaines de Strasbourg.

Boudelaa, Sami and William Marslen-Wilson. 2001. Morphological units in the Arabic mental lexicon. *Cognition* 81: 65–92.

Bowern, Claire. 2008. *Linguistic fieldwork: A practical guide*. New York: Palgrave MacMillan.

Bybee, Joan. 2003. *Phonology and language use*. Cambridge, UK: Cambridge University Press.

Canepari, L. 2005. *A handbook of pronunciation*. München: Lincom Europa.

Cantineau, Jean. 1960. *Etudes de linguistique arabe*. Paris: Klincksieck.

Chelliah, Shobhana L. and Willem De Reuse. 2011. *Handbook of descriptive linguistic fieldwork*. New York: Springer.

Cho, Taehong and Peter Ladefoged. 1999. Variation and universals in VOT: Evidence from 18 languages. *Journal of Phonetics* 27: 207–229.

Coates, Richard. 1980. Time in phonological representations. *Phonetics* 8: 1–20.

de Jong, Kenneth J. and Bushra Zawaydeh. 2002. Comparing stress, lexical focus, and segmental focus: patterns of variation in Arabic vowel duration. *Journal of Phonetics* 30: 53–75.

Elgendy, Ahmad M. 2001. Aspects of pharyngeal coarticulation. In *Proceedings of the Institute of Phonetic Sciences, University of Amsterdam*, vol. 24, 197–199.

Embarki, Mohamed. 2014. Evolution et conservatisme phonétiques dans le domaine arabe. *Diachronica* 31(1).

Embarki, Mohamed and Christelle Dodane (eds.). 2011. *La Coarticulation des indices à la representation*. Paris: L'Harmattan.

Embarki, Mohamed, Christian Guilleminot, and Melissa Barkat-Defradas. 2006. Expansion nasale en arabe standard: Indices acoustiques d'une coarticulation anticipatoire. *Revue Parole* 39–40: 209–234.

Embarki, Mohamed, Christian Guilleminot, Mohamed Yeou, and Sallal Al Maqtari. 2011a. Agression coarticulatoire des consonnes pharyngalisées dans les séquences VCV en arabe moderne et dialectal. In *La Coarticulation des indices à la representation*. Ed. Mohamed Embarki, and Christelle Dodane, 143–54. Paris: L'Harmattan.

Embarki, Mohamed, Slim Ouni, Mohamed Yeou, Christian Guilleminot, and Sallal Al Maqtari. 2011b. Acoustic and electromagnetic articulographic study of pharyngealisation: Coarticulatory effects as an index of stylistic and regional variation in Arabic. In *Instrumental studies in Arabic phonetics*, ed. Zeki M. Hassan and Barry Heselwood, 193–215. Amsterdam: Benjamins.

Ferguson, Charles A. 1956. The emphatic *l* in Arabic. *Language* 32: 446–452.

Flemming, Edward S. 2001. Scalar and categorical phenomena in a unified model of phonetics and phonology. *Phonology* 18: 7–44.

Ghazeli, Salem. 1977. *Back consonants and backing coarticulation in Arabic*. PhD diss., University of Texas, Austin.

——. 1981. La coarticulation de l'emphase en arabe. *Arabica* 28: 251–277.

Ghali, M. M. 1983. Pharyngeal articulation. *Bulletin of the School of Oriental and African Studies* 46: 432–444.

Gordon, Matthew. 2007. Functionalism in phonology. In *The Cambridge handbook of phonology*, ed. Paul de Lacy, 61–77. Cambridge, UK: Cambridge University Press.

Hassan, Zeki M. 2003. Temporal compensation between vowel and consonant in Swedish and Arabic in sequences of CV:C and CVC: and the word overall duration. *PHONUM* 9: 45–48.

Hassan, Zeki M., John Esling, Scott Moisik, and Lise Crevier-Buchman. 2011. Aryepiglottic trilled variants of /ʕ, ħ/ in Iraqi Arabic. In *Proceedings of the 17th International Congress of Phonetic Sciences, Hong Kong*, 831–834. http://www.icphs2011.hk.

Hassan, Zeki M. and Barry Heselwood. 2011. *Instrumental studies in Arabic phonetics.* Amsterdam: John Benjamins.

Heselwood, Barry. 2007. The "tight approximant" variant of the Arabic "ayn." *Journal of the International Phonetic Association* 37: 1–32.

Heselwood, Barry and Zeki Hassan. 2011. Introduction. In *Instrumental studies in Arabic phonetics.*, ed. Zeki Hassan and Barry Heselwood, 1–25. Amsterdam: Benjamins.

Jakobson, Roman. 1957. Mufaxxama—the emphatic phonemes in Arabic. In *Studies presented to Joshua Whatmough*, ed. E. Pulgram, 105–115. The Hague: Mouton.

Jomaa, Mounir. 1994. L'opposition de durée vocalique en arabe: essai de typologie. *Actes des XXèmes Journées d'Etudes sur la Parole (JEP)* 20: 395–400.

Jongman, Allard, Wendy Herd, Mohammad Al-Masri, Joan Sereno, and Sonja Combest. 2011. Acoustics and perception of emphasis in Urban Jordanian Arabic. *Journal of Phonetics* 39: 85–95.

Kaye, Alan J. 2009. Arabic. In *The world's major languages*, ed. Bernard Comrie, 560–577. London: Routledge.

Khattab, Ghada. 2007. A phonetic study of gemination in Lebanese Arabic. In *Proceedings of 16th International Congress of Phonetic Sciences, Saarbrücken*, 153–158. http://www.icphs2007.deand

Kingston, John. 2007. The phonetics–phonology interface. In *The Cambridge handbook of phonology*, ed. Paul de Lacy, 401–434. Cambridge, UK: Cambridge University Press.

Ladefoged, Peter. 2003. *Phonetic data analysis: An introduction to fieldwork and instrumental techniques.* Malden, MA: Blackwell.

Ladefoged, Peter and Keith Johnson. [2001] 2010². *A course in phonetics.* Boston: Wadsworth.

Lahiri, A., L. Gewirth, and S. Blumstein. 1984. A reconsideration of acoustic invariance for place of articulation in diffuse stop consonants: Evidence from a cross-language study. *Journal of the Acoustical Society of America* 76: 391–404.

Laufer, Asher. 1996. The common [ʕ] is an approximant and not a fricative. *Journal of the International Phonetic Association* 26: 113–117.

Lehiste, Ilse. 1970. *Suprasegmentals.* Cambridge, MA: MIT Press.

Lehiste, Ilse, Katherine Morton, and Marcel Tatham. 1973. An instrumental study of consonant gemination. *Journal of Phonetics* 1: 131–148.

Lindblom, B. 1963. On vowel reduction. Report 29, Royal Institute of Technology, Stockholm, Speech Transmission Laboratory.

Lisker, Leigh and Arthur Abramson. 1964. Cross-language study of voicing in initial stops: Acoustical measurements. *Word* 20: 384–422.

Lodge, Ken. 2009. *A critical introduction to phonetics.* London: Continuum.

Maddieson, Ian. 1984. *Patterns of sounds.* Oxford: Oxford University Press.

Mitleb, Fares. 1984a. Voicing effects on vowel duration is not an absolute universal. *Journal of Phonetics* 12: 23–28.

——. 1984b. Vowel length contrast in Arabic and English: A spectrographic test. *Journal of Phonetics* 12: 229–235.

Murtonen, A. 1966. The Semitic sibilants. *Journal of Semitic Studies* 11: 135–150.

Newman, Daniel L. 2005. Contrastive analysis of the segments of French and Arabic. In *Investigating Arabic: Current parameters in analysis and learning*, ed. Alaa Elgibali, 185–220. Leiden: Brill.

Owens, Jonathan. 2001. Arabic sociolinguistics. *Arabica* 48: 419–469.

——. [2006] 2009². *A linguistic history of Arabic*. Oxford: Oxford University Press.

Pickett, E. R., S. Blumstein, and M. Burton. 1999. Effects of speaking rate on the singleton/geminate consonant contrast in Italian. *Phonetica* 56: 135–157.

Port, R. F., S. Al-Ani, S. and S. Maeda. 1980. Temporal compensation and universal phonetics. *Phonetica* 37: 235–252.

Roman, André. 1977. Les zones d'articulation de la koinè arabe d'après l'enseignement d'Al-Halīl [Al-Khalil]. *Arabica* 24: 58–65.

Roman, André. 1981. De la langue arabe comme un modèle général de la formation des langues sémitiques et de leur évolution. *Arabica* 28: 127–161.

Ryding, Karin C. 2005. *A reference grammar of modern standard Arabic*. Cambridge, UK: Cambridge University Press.

Sara, Solomon. 2007. *Sībawayh on ʔimāla (Inclination). Text, translation, notes and analysis.* Edinburgh: Edinburgh University Press.

Scobbie, Jim. 2007. Interface and overlap in phonetics and phonology. In *The Oxford handbook of linguistic interfaces*, ed. Gillian Ramchand and C. Reiss, 17–52. Oxford: Oxford University Press.

Shahin, Kimary N. 1997. *Postvelar harmony: An examination of its bases and crosslinguistic Variation*. PhD diss., University of British Columbia, Vancouver.

Watson, Janet. 2002. *The phonology and morphology of Arabic*. Oxford: Oxford University Press.

Yeni-Komshian, Grace H., Alfonso Caramazza, and Malcom Preston. 1977. A study of voicing in Lebanese Arabic. *Journal of Phonetics* 5: 35–48.

Yeou, Mohamed. 1997. Locus equations and the degree of coarticulation of Arabic consonants. *Phonetica* 54: 187–202.

Yeou, Mohamed and Shinji Maeda. 2011. Airflow and acoustic modelling of pharyngeal and uvular consonants in Moroccan Arabic. In *Instrumental studies in Arabic phonetics*, ed. Zeki M. Hassan and Barry Heselwood, 141–162. Amsterdam: Benjamins.

Zawaydeh, Bushra A. 2003. The interaction of the phonetics and phonology of gutturals. In Phonetic interpretation. In *Papers in Laboratory Phonology, vol. 6*, ed. John Local, Richard Ogden, and Rosalind Temple, 279–292. Cambridge, UK: Cambridge University Press.

Zawaydeh, Bushra A. and Kenneth de Jong. 1999. Stress, phonological focus, quantity, and voicing effects on vowel duration in Ammani Arabic. In *Proceedings of the 14th International Congress of Phonetic Sciences*, Vol. 1, 451–454. Berkeley: University of California Press.

Zeroual, Chakir, Philip Hoole, Suzanne Fuchs, and John Esling. 2007. EMA study of the coronal emphatic and non-emphatic plosive consonants of Moroccan Arabic. In *Proceedings of 16th International Congress of Phonetic Sciences*, Saarbrücken, 397–400.

——. 2011. Contraintes articulatoires et acoustico-perceptives liées à la production de /k/ emphatisée en arabe marocain. In *La Coarticulation des indices à la representation*, ed. Mohamed Embarki, and Christelle Dodane, 227–40. Paris: L'Harmattan.

CHAPTER 3

PHONOLOGY

SAM HELLMUTH

3.1 Introduction

Phonology is the study of systematic patterning in the distribution and realization of speech sounds within and across language varieties. The phonology of Arabic features heavily in the work of the Arab grammarians, most notably in Al-Sībawayh's *Kitab* (Harun 1983). Sībawayh provides phonetic descriptions of the articulation of individual speech sounds [Embarki, "Phonetics"; Sara, "Classical Lexicography"], which are accompanied by an analysis of the patterning of sounds in Arabic that is indisputably phonological in nature. Sībawayh was thus among the first in a long line of phonologists to work on the phonology of Arabic, and in this chapter we set out some of the key strands in that research, highlighting the contribution made by the study of Arabic to our understanding of phonology itself.

It is relevant to ask in what sense Sībawayh is doing phonology, as it is understood today. For one thing, Sībawayh takes pains to carefully identify which consonants and vowels made up the phonological inventory of Arabic, classifying individual sounds ([ħuruuf] "letters") as either basic or "derived" (Al-Nassir 1993: 17–20). Some recent research in this area is discussed in Chapter 1 (Section 3.2.1).

Sībawayh quite clearly uses the concept of underlying forms, from which positional variants are derived in an orderly and predictable fashion, and carefully describes the operation of a number of named phonological processes. For example, in the case of *imaalah* "inclination" (raising/fronting of [a:]/[a]), he describes in detail the range of contexts that do or do not trigger the process and formulates it explicitly as derivational and iterative: a long vowel [a:] will raise/front (to [ie]; Owens 2006) when the preceding syllable contains a short front high vowel [i] *kasrah*, and the raised/fronted long vowel will itself then trigger *imaalah* in a following syllable (Al-Nassir 1993: 91–103).

The notion of markedness is applied indirectly in the work of the grammarians in all areas of the grammar (Owens 1988), and, in phonology, Sībawayh identifies *ṣaħiiħ* "strong" and *muʕtall* "weak" elements in many of the phonological oppositions that he proposes. For example, he distinguishes sounds as either *mutaħarrik* (CV, followed by a short vowel) or *saakin* (C, closing a syllable), and argues that the *mutaħarrik* is the strong member of the pair. Identification of syllable-initial (onset) position as strong and syllable-final (coda) position as weak is argued to account for the differing range of phenomena observed in each position (Al-Nassir 1993: 111), mirroring contemporary approaches to onset-coda asymmetries in general (e.g., Lombardi 1999) and directly matching claims made about the underlying syllabic structure of Arabic (Lowenstamm 1996; see Section 3.2.3).

Other phonological phenomena discussed by Sībawayh range from the optimal size of the verbal root (3–5 *ħuruuf*) (Al-Nassir 1993: 26) to variation in the realization of particular sounds or lexical items across definable groups of speakers (Al-Nassir 1993: 116–117; cf. Owens 2006: ch.7). We even find discussion of the potential phonological effects of word frequency ("they dare change what occurs more frequently in their speech"; Al-Nassir 1993: 117) that prefigure exemplar-based approaches to phonology (see Section 3.2.3).

A pattern we see in Sībawayh, repeated throughout phonological work on Arabic, is that Arabic proves to be an interesting object of study in two ways: (1) because the language has phonological features that are themselves typologically relatively unusual; and (2) because its phonological features vary, minimally but systematically, across different varieties of the language. The Arab grammarians would not have sought to compare the particular properties of Arabic with those of other languages; in the context of modern linguistics, however, the typologically unusual properties of Arabic present a genuine challenge to theories that have often been shaped for the most part by work on Indo-European languages. In turn, the fine-grained variation observed among spoken Arabic dialects has proved a rich seam of research, in particular in generative phonology, that seeks to model surface variation in terms of a limited set of underlying structural differences, whether parameters or ranked constraints. In Broselow's (1992: 7) words, "The dialects of Arabic provide an ideal testing ground..., since most of the dialects are similar enough to provide a basis for meaningful comparison, but taken as a whole they exhibit a wide range of variation."

In the main body of this chapter, we set out five important strands of phonological research on Arabic, taking in work on the language-particular phonological properties of Arabic as well as research that exploits fine-grained variation among spoken varieties of Arabic for theoretical gain. The discussion is structured to move from segmental phonology (the properties of individual speech sounds) to suprasegmental phonology (the properties of larger domains such as the syllable, word, or phrase).

3.2 State of the Art

3.2.1 Phonotactic Restrictions on Consonant Co-occurrence in Arabic Verbal Roots

The Arabic lexicon displays nonconcatenative (i.e., discontinuous) morphology. This has led some authors to analyze Arabic words in terms of a triliteral (three-term) consonantal root, with words generated from the lexical root by internal rearranging of the sequence of consonants and vowels (see [Ratcliffe, "Morphology"] for competing views of the structure of Arabic morphology):

(1)	katab	kutib	kita:b	kutub
	"he wrote"	"it was written"	"book"	"books"

In McCarthy's (1979) root + template analysis of Arabic morphophonology, consonantal features are represented on a separate tier (or plane) from vocalic features, and different grammatical classes are generated using fixed templates that define the sequence of consonantal and vocalic positions:

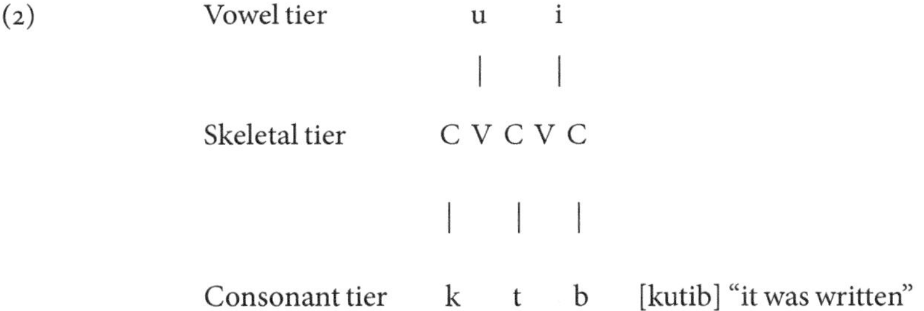

Since the majority of Arabic roots are composed of three consonants, one might expect the consonants in any particular lexical root to be selected at random from the consonantal inventory of Arabic and freely combined. This is not the case, however, and, apart from some mention by Arab grammarians of which consonants resist co-occurrence,[1] Cantineau (1946: 133–136) is first to note that not all possible combinations of consonants seem in fact to be observed. Building on this, Greenberg (1950) subjects the

[1] Greenberg (1950: n. 2) notes that lists of "incompatible consonants" are provided by Jalāl ad-Dīn Suyūṭī and Ibn Jinni.

possible combinations of consonants appearing in initial (C1), medial (C2), and final (C3) position to a systematic quantitative survey, in a corpus of 3775 Arabic verbal roots. The data were taken from two 19th-century Arabic dictionaries (by Western authors), with qualitative comparison to the facts of other languages within the Semitic family.

For Arabic (and for Semitic in general), Greenberg (1950) establishes two key patterns:

(3) Complete absence of roots with adjacent identical consonants in C1–C2 position *<*mmd*>, contrasting with no restriction on adjacent identical consonants in C2–C3 position <*mdd*>[2]

(4) Varying degrees of restriction on the occurrence of homorganic consonants, which share place of articulation, within a root (C1–C2, C2–C3, or C1–C3)

Working from the generalizations observed in (4), Greenberg motivates a grouping of the Arabic consonantal inventory into four "sections," or natural classes, shown in (5).[3] Within a single verbal root, Arabic consonants are seen to freely occur with those in other sections, which have a different place of articulation, but are subject to restrictions on co-occurrence with members of the same section. Although examples of verbal roots containing two consonants from the same section can be found, the number of such roots is relatively small.[4]

(5)	*Back*	*Liquids*	*Front*	*Labial*
	x ɣ ħ ʕ h ʔ k g q	l r n	θ ð t d ṭ ḍ s z ṣ ẓ ʃ	b f m

The generalizations expressed in (3) and (4) have each inspired a large body of research, which has proven significant for an accurate understanding of the phonology not only of Arabic but also of human language in general.

McCarthy (1979, 1981) proposes an explanation of the asymmetry inherent in (3) that combines a root + template morphological analysis of Arabic with the insights of autosegmental phonology (Goldsmith 1976, 1981). In autosegmental phonology,

[2] Identical consonants in C1–C3 position are relatively rare but nonetheless observed, for example, <*qlq*>.

[3] The table shows consonants only in the inventory of Arabic; Greenberg also includes consonants found in other Semitic languages, such as [p].

[4] In (5), and throughout this paper, the emphatic coronals are represented using symbols not from the International Phonetic Alphabet (IPA): [tˤ dˤ sˤ ðˤ] appear as [ṭ ḍ ṣ ẓ], respectively. Although current practice is to represent "emphasis" using the IPA uvularization diacritic [ˤ], the phonetic realization of emphasis varies more widely across dialects than this representation implies and is defined by a complex of articulatory gestures, only one of which is uvularization (see Section 3.2.2; also [Embarki, "Phonetics"]).

individual speech sounds are represented as (bundles of) features associated with syllabic structure. The surface realization of an underlying feature is determined by how it is linked to the prosodic structure. For example, a set of vocalic features will be realized as a short versus long vowel, depending on whether they are linked to one syllabic position only or are allowed to "spread" to two syllabic positions.

For McCarthy (1979, 1981), the ill-formedness of identical consonants in C1–C2 position versus the well-formedness of identical consonants in C2–C3 is due to two facts: (1) the strict observance in Arabic of the obligatory contour principle (OCP), which places a ban on adjacent identical segments; and (2) a requirement in Arabic that features spread autosegmentally only from left to right.[5] Underlyingly a verbal root such as <mdd> thus comprises two feature bundles only, representing <m> and <d>. The features of <d> spread left to right, filling the third syllabic consonantal position in the template and yielding surface forms analyzable as triliteral <mdd>. Since spreading proceeds only left to right, an empty syllabic position cannot be filled by leftward spreading of <m>, resulting in an absence of verbal roots such as *<mmd>. The analysis is illustrated in (6):

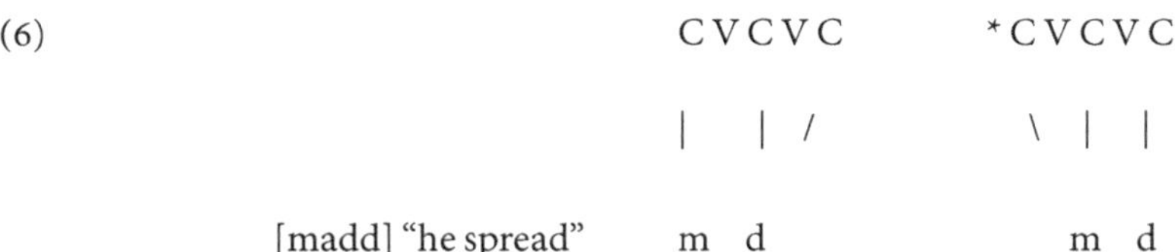

An analysis in terms of underlying forms is warranted because there is no ban on adjacent identical consonants in derived, morphologically complex forms; compare the lack of a verbal root *<ttk> with permitted forms such as [tatakallam] "you conversed" (McCarthy 1986: 209). Bohas (1997) proposes a more radical approach (cf. earlier work by Voigt 1988; Ehret 1989), suggesting that a biliteral root morpheme, called the "etymon," underlies all triliteral roots, not only those with identical C2–C3; each proposed etymon captures a regular form-meaning correspondence between a consonant pair and a semantic field. Other proposals that extend from the templatic nature of Arabic morphology include the claim that Arabic is a language in which all syllables are comprised of sequences of CV pairs (see Section 3.2.3).

The analysis in (6) has been challenged due to a nontrivial assumption it makes about the nature of phonology: namely, that some aspects of phonological knowledge—such as the ban in Arabic on adjacent, identical segments in C1–C2 position but not in C2–C3—are encoded as restrictions on possible underlying lexical representations (i.e., as *morpheme structure constraints*). McCarthy (1998, 2005) argues against his own earlier analysis for this reason. A core assumption of optimality theory (OT; Prince and

[5] Directionality of autosegmental spreading is usually argued to vary by rule and by language (see discussion in McCarthy 2004).

Smolensky 2004) is that all grammar, including phonology, determines surface realizations ("outputs") only. This claim is formulated in OT as the "richness of the base": the phonological grammar must generate all and only those forms observed on the surface of the language without stipulating restrictions on possible inputs to the grammar (i.e., on the properties of the lexicon). Greenberg's asymmetry in (3) represents a serious challenge to theories of this kind.

Solutions to this problem, in the OT literature, mostly appeal to the notion of paradigm uniformity, whereby surface forms are preferred if they bear structural resemblance to other surface forms in the same morphological paradigm (McCarthy 1998, 2005; Gafos 1998, 2001, 2003; Rose 2000). In some of these analyses (Gafos 1998; Rose 2000), the doubled final consonant in the surface form of a root like [madda] "he stretched" results from reduplication and is permitted because, in the OT framework, the OCP constraint can be outranked by other competing constraints. In another approach (Gafos 2001, 2003), the idea of separation of consonants and vowels onto different tiers is rejected, and the underlying form of all Arabic verbs is proposed to be a CVCC "stem," such as /madd/.[6]

What about Greenberg's other generalization in (4) that although there is no complete ban on adjacent homorganic consonants in C2–C3 position their occurrence is highly restricted? In a series of papers, McCarthy (1986, 1988, 1994) extended an OCP analysis to these facts also. In contrast to the categorical nature of the asymmetry in (3), the restrictions described in (4) are gradient in nature: the key fact to explain is why there are *some* roots containing homorganic consonants rather than none. McCarthy adopts feature geometry (Clements 1985; McCarthy 1988), in which the bundle of features that map onto an individual speech sound is represented as a hierarchically grouped tree structure rather than as an unordered matrix. For example, laryngeal features (e.g., [voice] or [spread glottis]) appear under a different node from place features (e.g., [labial], [coronal], or [dorsal]). McCarthy (1988) extends this idea by representing individual place features on separate tiers, as in (7). If the OCP (which bans adjacent identical elements) operates on individual tiers, then the place restrictions are explained.

(7)

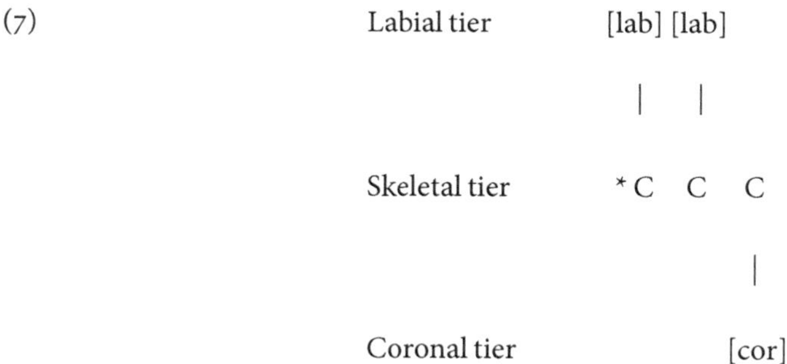

[6] See Ratcliffe ["Morphology"] for a discussion of root- versus stem- and word-based approaches to Arabic morphology.

This analysis predicts a complete ban on homorganic consonants within a single verbal root but cannot account for the small but nontrivial number of verbal roots that do contain homorganic consonants and that are too numerous to be treated as exceptions. An additional complication is that within the larger classes of consonants, such as the coronals (Greenberg's "front" section), consonants are observed to co-occur somewhat more freely than those within the smaller natural classes (Padgett 1995).

A competing approach (Pierrehumbert 1993; Frisch et al. 2004) addresses this problem by taking the gradient tendency in (4) as its starting point. The approach is based on a quantitative, probabilistic model of phonology, contrasting fundamentally with the categorical models of generative grammar embodied in the work of McCarthy and Gafos. The analysis in Frisch et al. (2004) is based on a corpus of 2674 verbal roots from a contemporary dictionary of Modern Standard Arabic (Cowan 1979). The distribution of roots is analyzed in terms of the ratio of *observed* consonant combinations to those that would be *expected* if consonants were allowed to occur freely in particular positions of the root (Pierrehumbert 1993). For example, given the frequency of occurrence of [d] in the C1 position and of [t] in the C2 position, Frisch et al. expect there to be 2.3 roots of the form <d t X> (where X is any consonant); in fact, there are no such roots, and the observed–expected (O–E) ratio is thus "0," which the authors describe as "the strongest degree of under-representation" (Frisch et al. 2004: 185). In contrast, there are four roots of the form <d g X>, where only 3.3 such roots are expected to occur, giving an O–E score of 1.21, a case of overrepresentation.

Frisch et al. (2004) argue that an adequate analysis of the gradient generalization described in (4) must capture both under- and over-representation of particular consonant co-occurrences. They propose that a principle of "similarity avoidance" operates productively in the Arabic lexicon. To model this principle, they calculate the degree of similarity between two consonants in the Arabic inventory in terms of the number of natural classes in which the two consonants share and do not share membership.[7] The metric thus encodes not only raw phonetic similarity (number of shared features) but also the relative size of the consonantal inventory at each place of articulation (cf. Padgett 1995). The analysis represents a hybrid approach in which the phonological knowledge of native speakers is claimed to combine traditional phonological factors (here, natural classes defined by place of articulation) with frequency effects: "the native speaker knows an abstract but gradient OCP-Place constraint... based on generalization over the statistical patterns found in the lexicon" (Frisch et al. 2004: 216). Frisch et al. suggest that a general cross-linguistic tendency to avoid repetition of similar sounds, based on a preference for maximally salient adjacent sounds (Boersma 1998), is heightened in Arabic since consonants are adjacent in lexical representations if a root-based analysis of Arabic morphology is assumed.

To prevent gradient similarity avoidance from applying in the case of roots with identical consonants in C2–C3—in the case of the generalization in (3)—Frisch et al. (2004)

[7] Similarity is calculated as the number of shared natural classes divided by the sum of the number of shared and unshared natural classes (Frisch et al. 2004: 198).

acknowledge that they must adopt some form of "categorical override." They noted that prior approaches to (3), whether autosegmental (McCarthy 1979, 1981, 1986) or paradigm-based (Gafos 2003), both treat the double consonant in a root like <mdd> as licensed by the appearance of a singleton consonant in a related form: the related form in the autosegmental approach is the underlying form (/md/); in a paradigm-based approach the related form is another surface realization of the same root ([madda] "he stretched" ~ [madadtu] "I stretched"). Frisch et al. thus proposed that some kind of "related form override" must account for C2–C3 identical roots.

Although Frisch et al. (2004) are formally agnostic about how related forms license geminate roots in Arabic, they cite a range of behavioral data that they suggest supports an analysis in terms of roots rather than stems. Frisch and Zawaydeh (2001) asked native speakers of Arabic to judge the relative well-formedness of nonsense words; roots with identical C1–C2 such as [tatafa] were universally rejected, but roots containing homorganic consonants in other positions and combinations, such as in C1–C2 in the nonsense word [tasafa], display the same variant restrictions as observed in the general Arabic lexicon. For Frisch et al., this confirms that similarity avoidance is a productive part of the phonological grammar for Arabic. Similarly, Davis and Zawaydeh (2001) argue that truncation patterns in Arabic hypocoristics (nicknames) display effects that can be explained only by appealing to the consonantal root in lexical representation. Finally, evidence from the speech errors of an aphasia patient who is bilingual in French and Arabic (Prunet et al. 2000; Idrissi et al. 2008) shows different patterns of errors in the two languages that are consistent with vowels being present in lexical representations in French but absent from lexical representations in Arabic. In contrast to Frisch et al., Gafos (2001) argue that psycholinguistic data of this kind provide evidence of root-based language *processing* (only) but maintain the claim that the *grammar* of Arabic is stem based (see Ratcliffe ["Morphology"]).

In conclusion, then, the patterning of consonants in Arabic verbal roots show both categorical and gradient effects (in the generalizations set out in (3) and (4), respectively), and theories of phonological knowledge need to be able to account for both types of effects. Arguably, therefore, a hybrid approach of some kind (e.g., Pierrehumbert 2006) is to be favored. It is worth noting, however, that almost all of the previously discussed analyses treat the distribution of consonants in verbal roots only and in Modern Standard Arabic. Studies of patterning of consonants in the nominal system (Faust and Hever 2010) or in spoken dialects are even more rare. An exception is Herzallah's (1990) study of phonetically velar sounds [k x ɣ] in Palestinian Arabic, which behave phonologically as uvular in their co-occurrence restrictions (cited in Davis 1995). Further, and broader, empirical work in this area may yet reveal a more complete picture for which phonological theory must account.

3.2.2 Postvelar Consonants and Emphasis

All varieties of Arabic share the property of having a small vowel inventory and a relatively large consonantal inventory (cf. Maddieson 2011). In particular, the consonant inventory has a large proportion of "guttural" consonants with postvelar place of articulation [q χ ʁ ħ ʕ h ʔ] and a set of "emphatic" coronal consonants that displays postvelar secondary articulation [ṭ ḍ ṣ ẓ] and contrasts with plain counterparts [t d s ð].[8] The postvelar(-ized) segments influence the phonetic realization of neighboring segments, both vowels and consonants. The most salient effect is backing (F2 lowering) of immediately adjacent vowels: compare [ta:b] "he repented" with [ṭɑ:b] "he recovered." In some dialects, other consonants, such as [r l m b], can also trigger the same effect in certain contexts. The domain of this "emphasis spread" is nonlocal in character, reaching the entire word in some spoken dialects and even beyond it into adjacent words in some cases. Emphasis spread is typologically unusual and is shared with only a few other language families.[9]

Work on emphasis represents a large proportion of both past and current research in Arabic phonology. Although the phonetics and phonology of emphatics are inextricably linked, the discussion here focuses on phonological issues.[10] The key phonological issues that have exercised the research community with regard to emphasis include what the nature—and name—of the phonological feature used to represent emphasis should be, whether this feature is a property of individual segments or larger domains, and how to explain the differing domain and directionality of emphasis spread observed in different dialects of Arabic (see Bellem 2007: 26–33 for a summary).

The Arab grammarians use a range of terms to describe the properties and effects of the emphatic and guttural consonants. Sībawayh describes the emphatic coronals [ṭ ḍ ṣ ẓ] as *muṭbaq* "covered, enclosed," contrasting with plain coronals such as [t d s], which are *munfatiħ* "open" (Al-Nassir 1993). The *muṭbaq* consonants are characterized by raising of the tongue dorsum toward *al-ħanak al-aʕlaa* "the roof of the mouth," with no mention of a role for the pharynx in the articulation (ibid.). Sībawayh also describes a class of seven consonants—the four *muṭbaq* emphatic coronals plus the three uvulars [q χ ʁ]—that share the feature of being *mustaʕlin* "elevated" and are identified as a natural class because they all block *imaalah* (see Section 3.1). Ibn Jinnī contrasts the seven *mustaʕlin* consonants with all other consonants, which are *munxafiḍ* "lowered" (ibid.). Sībawayh uses the term *mufaxxam* "made grand" to describe a raised and backed realization of /a:/ *alif* and /a/ *fatħa*, as [ɑ:] and [ɑ], respectively, in the context of a *mustaʕlin* consonant (ibid., 103).[11] Sībawayh thus does not categorize the pharyngeals [ħ ʕ] as eliciting *tafxiim*.

Watson (2002) analyzes "pharyngeal" gutturals and "pharyngealized" emphatics, in Cairene and San'aani, as a single group (cf. Broselow 1976), characterized

[8] Few varieties display the full set of emphatics; see Embarki ["Phonetics"] for discussion.

[9] Also found in some other Semitic languages, Caucasian, and languages of the Pacific North West (McCarthy 1994; Shahin 2003); the phonetic realization of the effect varies greatly across languages and dialects.

[10] See Embarki ["Phonetics"] for a detailed overview of research on the articulatory and acoustic properties of Arabic emphatics.

[11] Sibawayh also notes that *alif* is realized as [ɑ] in the Hijazi dialect (Al-Nassir 1993: 103).

phonologically by the feature [guttural][12] in a nonprimary position in the feature geometry. She sees the gutturals as pharyngealized counterparts of nonpharyngealized sounds, just as emphatic coronals are pharyngealized counterparts of plain coronals, as illustrated in (8) (ibid., 42–44). Watson describes emphasis spread as pharyngealization and notes that it is accompanied in some dialects by varying degrees of labialization:

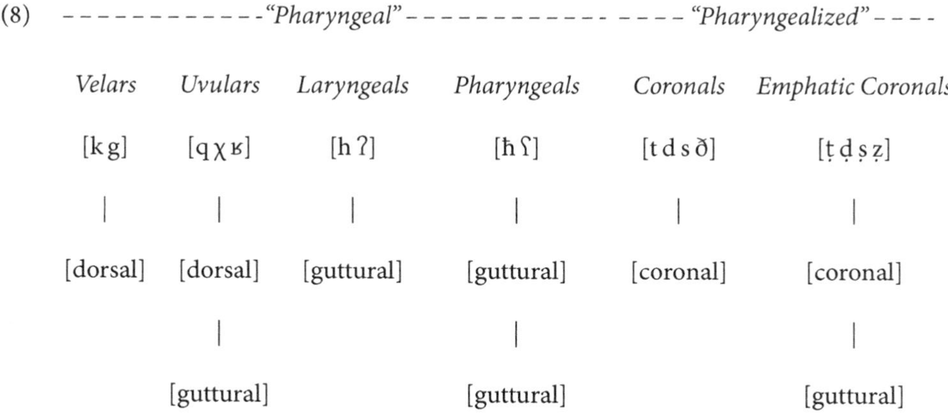

Watson (2002) analyzes pharyngeal and pharyngealized sounds with the same feature specification (nonprimary [guttural]) but argues that both the phonetic realization and the extent of pharyngealization will differ in each subgroup, due to the difference in the relationship between the primary and nonprimary features in each case. In pharyngealized coronals, the tongue dorsum realizes nonprimary [guttural] at the same time as the tongue tip/blade realizes primary [coronal]; the tongue is thus under tension, and it takes time for the articulators to move back to nonemphatic settings. This results in greater, more nonlocal spread of pharyngealization from the emphatic coronals than from the gutturals (Watson 2002: 273). Watson's featural representation can also explain the realization of Classical Arabic /q/ in spoken dialects: in Cairene, */q/ lost primary [dorsal] and nonprimary [guttural] was promoted, yielding /ʔ/ (Watson 2002: 45 n. 18).

In contrast, McCarthy (1994: 202–218) argues that the gutturals (Watson's *pharyngeal*) must receive a different featural analysis from the emphatic coronals (Watson's *pharyngealized*), because even though there is evidence for grouping gutturals and emphatic coronals together, in that they both block *imaalah* (ibid., 218–220), there is also ample evidence that the gutturals form a natural class to the exclusion of the emphatic coronals. Key evidence in Arabic for the natural class of gutturals comes from co-occurrence restrictions within lexical roots (see Section 3.2.1) and from

[12] This is a monovalent feature in Watson's analysis; monovalent features are either present or absent from the phonological representation of speech sound, with no binary ± settings.

vowel lowering and metathesis (*gahawah* syndrome) in the vicinity of gutturals (ibid., 202–218).

McCarthy (1994: 221) thus proposes a distinct feature representation for the various relevant classes of sound, as in (9). He uses the feature [pharyngeal], which is in most respects parallel to Watson's (2002) [guttural].[13]

(9)

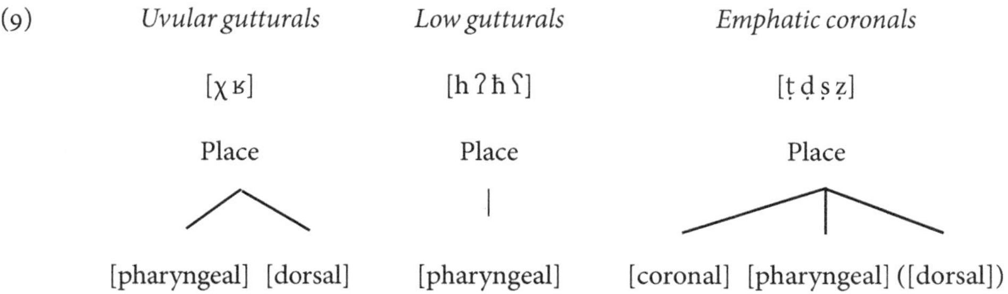

Other featural analyses of emphasis include Davis's (1995) treatment of two varieties of Palestinian Arabic (PA), in which a pharyngeal node is argued to host two features: [RTR] "retracted tongue root"; and [CP] "constricted pharynx." Davis argues on articulatory grounds that [RTR] is active in the uvular gutturals [χ ʁ], whereas [CP] is active in the pharyngeals [ħ ʕ]; the emphatic coronals have nonprimary [RTR]. In a study that compares data in PA and St'át'imcets Salish, Shahin (2003) argues for a cross-linguistic distinction between uvularization (spreading of nonprimary RTR, in PA from emphatic coronals) and pharyngealization (spreading of primary RTR, in PA from gutturals). In contrast to the articulatorily defined features described thus far, Bellem (2007) analyzes emphasis using a system of psychoacoustically defined features (after Harris and Lindsey 1995) that includes just three resonance features: A, I, and U. For Bellem, A spreading (emphasis spread) competes in the phonology with I spreading (*imaalah*) and U spreading (labialization).

A key area of variation across different varieties of Arabic is in the domain of emphasis spread. All of the spoken dialects studied thus far appear to share the asymmetry that leftward spreading is less restricted than rightward spreading and that spreading is greater from emphatic coronals than from gutturals. Spreading may be blocked by intervening palatal vowels or consonants in some dialects in one or both directions. Davis (1995) analyzes blocking of RTR spreading by high vowels and palatal consonants by means of a rule grounded in the natural antagonism between [RTR] (retracted) and a [+high] (advanced) tongue positions. Bellem (2007) suggests that variation in the domain of emphasis spread is better analyzed as blocking by intervening emphatics/gutturals of an active *imaalah* (palatalization) process than as blocking of *tafxiim* (emphasis) by intervening palatals.

[13] Both authors ascribe their use of [guttural]/[pharyngeal] to the proposal made in Hayward and Hayward (1989) for a feature [guttural], which is there argued to be more broadly defined in terms of the *zone of constriction*. Note that McCarthy treats /q/ separately from the uvular fricatives.

For most authors (e.g., McCarthy 1994; Watson 2002), emphasis spread is viewed as autosegmental spreading of a feature from a consonant to adjacent vowels and consonants. However, if separate V/C tiers are assumed, as in (2), the exact mechanism by which a spreading feature is able to spread not only to adjacent consonants but also to vowels is not fully spelled out. Working in OT, Shahin (2003) analyzes spreading using alignment constraints on surface (output) realizations. To a limited extent, this echoes Beeston's (1970: 19) view that *iṭbaaq* is a prosody (in the Firthian sense[14]) rather than a "component of the four velarized alveolar consonants" and, thus, a property of domains rather than of segments.

This brief summary includes only the most influential or innovative work on emphasis in Arabic phonology. A large number of studies of emphasis in individual spoken dialects exist (Bellem 2007 provides a recent survey), and only a few studies have attempted to analyze the patterns of emphasis across dialects or across Semitic in general (Hayward and Hayward 1989; McCarthy 1994; Bellem 2007). In particular, Bellem offers an analysis linking the relative strength of features in different dialects, and thus their capacity to participate in active feature spreading processes such as emphasis, with more general phonological properties of each dialect such as the number of laryngeal contrasts in the phonological inventory. It is comparative work of this kind that is most likely to reveal the full range of phonological representations underlying the surface phenomena collectively known as emphasis.

3.2.3 Syllabification and Syllable Structure

Cross-dialectal variation in syllabification across Arabic dialects is perhaps most clearly exemplified by the differing realization of sequences of three consonants (CCC). Such sequences commonly occur when a consonant-initial suffix such as [lu] "to him" is added to a CC final word, such as [qult] "I said."[15] Although a small number of dialects tolerate a surface CCC cluster (e.g., Moroccan [qultlu]), most dialects insert an epenthetic vowel to break up the CCC sequence, and dialects vary as to where the vowel is placed, CvCC versus CCvC: Iraqi [gəlitlu] but Cairene [ʔultilu]. The pattern is robust and is also reflected in the realization of CC-initial loanwords: "Fred" is [fi.rɛd] in Iraqi but [if.rɛd] in Cairene (Broselow 1983). The basic two-way distinction gives rise to an informal nomenclature of "gəlit" versus "qəltu" dialects (Blanc 1964), or, more recently, of VC versus CV dialects (Kiparsky 2003).

Two competing explanations of the VC ~ CV epenthesis facts emerged in the 1980s and 1990s. Ito (1989) proposed a directional difference between the dialects: Iraqi syllabifies from right to left, while Cairene syllabifies from left to right. Mester and Padgett

[14] See Firth (1948) or Lass (1984: 163–166) for a brief overview of Firthian prosodic analysis.

[15] Compare Classical Arabic [qult] "I said" with [qult] in Morocco, [gult] in Baghdad, and [ʔult] in Cairo.

(1994) offer an OT implementation of this directional approach but also notes its limitations, not least in explaining different syllabification patterns in word-initial CC clusters (as in the realizations of "Fred" already noted).

In contrast, Broselow (1992) proposes that a structural parameter determines the syllabic affiliation of stray consonants in different dialects, building on an earlier suggestion by Selkirk (1981) that "stray" consonants can be syllabified as "degenerate" (vowelless) syllables. Broselow suggests that Arabic dialects vary in how they treat the "stray" third consonant in a CCC sequence: in Iraqi, a stray consonant is syllabified into a (temporarily) vowelless rhyme; in Cairene, a vowelless rhyme is not permitted so the stray consonant is syllabified as an onset. Epenthesis fills in the empty vowel positions, inserting a vowel before a rhymal consonant and after an onset consonant. Broselow further argued that parallel variation across CV ~ VC dialects in the treatment of word-internal CVVC syllables is due to a similar structural parameter. In VC dialects, word-internal CVVC syllables are tolerated ([baab-ha] "her door"), despite breaching a more general preference in Arabic for bimoraic syllables;[16] in CV dialects, a word-internal CVVC sequence is not permitted at all and is instead repaired by closed syllable shortening (CSS; [bab-ha] "her door"). Broselow proposed that in VC dialects the final consonant in a CVVC word-internal syllable is incorporated into the preceding rhyme (satisfying the general preference for bimoraicity), by a process of Adjunction-to-Mora. This process applies exactly in dialects (the VC dialects) that permit syllabification of the stray consonant in a CCC sequence into the rhyme.

Kiparsky (2003) reframes Broselow's structural analysis as mora licensing. Dialects vary in whether they permit semisyllables, which contain a mora that is unlicensed (i.e., unaffiliated to any syllabic position, neither onset nor rhyme), and, if so, at what level of representation the unlicensed material is permitted. Kiparsky maintains a basic two-way divide, grouping C (Moroccan) dialects with VC (Iraqi) and contrasting them to CV dialects (e.g., Cairene).[17] The broad distinction is that VC dialects permit unlicensed moras, whereas CV dialects do not; the distinction between VC and C dialects is that VC dialects permit unlicensed moras at the lexical level but forbid them at postlexical level, whereas in C dialects unlicensed moras are permitted at all levels of representation, both lexical and postlexical. Kiparsky's account is formulated within OT in terms of ranked constraints: in VC dialects the constraint LICENSEμ (which requires a mora to be affiliated to syllabic structure) is low ranked, whereas in CV dialects it is highly ranked. Kiparsky assumes a stratified model of OT, allowing the VC ~ C dialects distinction to be modeled as promotion of the constraint LICENSEμ to a higher ranked position at the postlexical level in VC dialects (only).

[16] Broselow (1992) adopts a fairly standard moraic view of syllable structure, in which a mora, a unit of syllable weight, is assigned to rhymal constituents (vowels and coda consonants) but not to onset consonants. Arabic dialects display a general preference for bimoraic syllables, that is, with a heavy rhyme, either VC or VV.

[17] "C dialects" are those that, like Moroccan, allow surface CCC clusters.

Kiparsky (2003) suggests that variation in the position of the epenthetic vowel in CCC sequences covaries not just with availability of CSS (found in CV but not in VC, as argued by Broselow) but also with variation in a range of other syllabification phenomena, including metathesis (found in VC but not CV dialects) and the distribution of CC clusters (which occur only word finally in CV dialects and only word initially in VC dialects). Working from a typologically enlarged data set, Watson (2007) argues that the covariance between epenthesis and other syllabification patterns is not so clear-cut. The match is quite good for VC dialects, but a significant subset of CV dialects (as classified by epenthesis in CCC sequences) turns out to behave rather more like VC dialects, for example, by tolerating word-internal CVVC syllables. Watson thus argues for a further dialect group, the "Cv" dialects,[18] and incorporates Broselow's adjunction-by-mora parameter into Kiparsky's OT account as a NoSharedMora constraint. The constraint is low ranked in VC and Cv dialects, explaining shared patterns of behavior across the two groups.

A completely different approach to syllabification in Arabic, which happens to share the notion of vowelless syllables with Selkirk (1981), developed out of attempts during the 1990s to capture all and only the observed range of template shapes in Arabic verbal and nominal forms (Guerssel and Lowenstamm 1990; Idrissi 1997). In the resulting "CV-only" analysis (Lowenstamm 1996, 2003),[19] no consonants are syllabified as codas in Arabic at all, and instead every syllable-final consonant is analyzed as the onset of a vowelless syllable (cf. Yoshida 1993; Bellem 2007).

The somewhat atypical syllabification patterns observed in Moroccan Arabic (MA) have inspired their own strand of research. Along with other Maghreb dialects, MA permits a wider range of word-initial onset clusters than observed in other Arabic dialects, such as [kteb] "he wrote," [glih] "he grilled," and [qleb] "he knocked over" (Gafos et al. 2011: 30). These are analyzed as branching (complex) onsets by some authors (e.g., Benkirane 1998) but more commonly as sequences of simplex onsets separated by empty vocalic positions in both "standard" moraic syllable theory (Kiparsky 2003) and CV-only approaches (Boudlal 2001). Recent work by Shaw et al. (2009) and Gafos et al. (2010, 2011) within the broad model of articulatory phonology (Browman and Goldstein 1986) proposes a model of the mapping between syllabic structure and articulatory evidence (the fine-grained temporal alignment of the articulatory gestures of the two consonants) that favors analysis of MA word-initial clusters as sequences of simplex onsets. The authors remain agnostic as to which phonological representation of such sequences best matches the articulatory facts (though a formal analysis is proposed by Gafos 2002, 2006), but future work of this kind in MA and in other dialects may shed further light on the typology of syllabification in Arabic.

[18] The Cv dialects are mostly found in Yemen but also include Meccan.

[19] Lowenstamm's CV-only analysis for Arabic has its roots in government phonology, in which word-final codas are analyzed as the onset of a vowelless CV syllable (Kaye 1990), and has inspired strict-CV phonology, which extends the CV-only analysis to all languages (Scheer 2004).

Finally, recent work on variation in the rhythmic properties of different Arabic dialects suggests that the typology of variation in syllabification across all dialects may prove to be even more fine-grained. Work on cross-linguistic rhythmic typology has shown that a two-way divide between "stress-timed" and "syllable-timed" languages oversimplifies (Roach 1982; Nolan and Asu 2009). Instead, there appears to be a continuum of rhythmic variation across languages, arising from independent variables affecting syllabification, including incidence of vowel reduction and the syllabification phenomena discussed in the VC ~ CV literature outlined already. This rhythmic continuum is observed cross-dialectally in Arabic; although all dialects are stress timed, a comparison across six dialects displays that they move from more to less stress timed as one travels west to east from Morocco to the Levant (Ghazali et al. 2002, 2007). This surface variation correlates with the permitted syllabification patterns and syllable types observed in different dialects (Hamdi et al. 2005). Further investigation of the rhythmic properties of a wider range of dialects, employing the most stable rhythm metrics (Wiget et al. 2010) and perhaps also incorporating a survey of the incidence of vowel reduction (cf. Cantineau's differential vs. nondifferential parameter[20]), may reveal new avenues of research on Arabic syllabic structure and syllabification.

3.2.4 Word Stress and Metrical Theory

Arguably the most important contribution made by the study of Arabic dialectal variation to the advancement of phonological theory has been in the area of metrical phonology, which seeks to account for the position of word stress in words of different syllabic structures. The position of stress is predictable in all Arabic dialects and can usually be reduced to a simple stress assignment algorithm.

Although word stress received no attention in the work of the Arabic grammarians, probably because stress assignment is largely predictable (Watson 2011), there is a very rich body of research on Arabic word stress in contemporary linguistics. This has been fueled by an ample supply of data, in the form of good descriptions of the word stress patterns of a wide range of dialects (dating from the early 20th century onward), and by theoretical advances, which have led to continual reanalysis in the field, with some of the advances prompted by the facts of particular Arabic dialects. Watson provides a thorough survey of this literature and points out that much of the interest in the study of Arabic word stress lies in the fact that the surface stress patterns of Arabic dialects share many key properties but vary nontrivially in others (see also Kager 2009).

Stress assignment in all Arabic dialects is sensitive to syllable weight, that is, quantity sensitive. The basic stress algorithm for all Arabic dialects assigns stress to a final super-heavy syllable (CVVC or CVCC) or otherwise to a nonfinal (usually penultimate)

[20] In differential dialects, unstressed vowel deletion (syncope) targets only high vowels [i u], whereas in nondifferential dialects, syncope affects all short vowels, including [a] (Cantineau 1939).

Table 3.1 Stress assignment in words with varying syllabic structure, as realized in different dialects[21]

	Standard Arabic[22]	Palestinian Arabic	Lebanese Arabic	Cairene Arabic	Negev Bedouin	Gloss
a)	ka'tabt	ka'tabt	ka'tabt	ka'tabt	ki'tabt	I wrote
	ki'ta:b	ki'ta:b	ki'ta:b	ki'ta:b	ki'ta:b	book
b)	'maktab	'maktab	'maktab	'maktab	'maktab	office
	'ka:tib	'ka:tib	'ka:tib	'ka:tib	'ka:tib	writer
c)	'ʒamal	'ʒamal	'ʒamal	'gamal	ʒi'mal	camel
d)	'maktaba	'maktaba	'maktabi	mak'taba	'maktabah	library

heavy syllable (usually CVC or CVV).[23] A heavy syllable in word-final position does not attract stress, however. This pattern makes sense if we adopt the notion of consonant extrametricality, whereby a word-final consonant is excluded from calculations of syllable weight. The disjunction that a final super-heavy syllable attracts stress whereas a final heavy syllable does not has been observed in all Arabic dialects described to date, and most authors agree that some form of extrametricality holds in all dialects. A rare exception to the "stress a final super-heavy syllable" generalization is found in Sanaani Arabic in which a nonfinal heavy syllable (CVV or CVG) may attract stress away from a word-final super-heavy syllable (Watson 2002).

For the most part, then, cross-dialectal variation in stress assignment is seen in words without either a final super-heavy or a penultimate heavy. Table 3.1 gives data from Standard Arabic and four spoken dialects illustrating in (a)–(b) the shared properties observed in words containing a final super-heavy or penult heavy and in (c)–(d) the variation observed in two examples of words of other prosodic shapes.

The examples in (a) in Table 3.1 contain a final super-heavy CVCC or CVVC, which attracts stress in all of the dialects shown. In (b), stress falls on a heavy syllable (CVC or CVV) in the penultimate position, even if it is followed by a heavy syllable, in all dialects. Dialectal differences are seen in (c)–(d). The examples in (c) show stress assignment in a disyllable with a light penultimate, with Negev Bedouin Arabic the odd one out (stress on the final syllable rather than the first). In (d) we see stress assignment in a word with a heavy antepenultimate syllable followed by two light syllables ("HLL"), with Cairene Arabic the odd one out (stress on the light penultimate rather than the heavy antepenultimate).

[21] The algorithms for each dialect, as described in Hayes (1995), are applied to derive a parallel set of examples.

[22] These are "pausal" forms of the words, that is, as produced utterance-finally, without case-marking vowels.

[23] In Sanaani Arabic, only CVG (closed by geminate) and CVV count as heavy (Watson 2002).

Table 3.2 Summary of Hayes's (1995) metrical stress theory analysis of Arabic dialects

Dialect	Foot Type	Foot Construction	Extrametricality	Degenerate Feet
Classical	unbounded	left-headed	consonant	N/A
Bani Hassan[24]	moraic trochee	left-to-right	foot	permitted
Palestinian	moraic trochee	left-to-right	foot[25]	absolute ban
Cairene	moraic trochee	left-to-right	consonant	absolute ban
Lebanese	moraic trochee	right-to-left	syllable	absolute ban
Bedouin Hijazi	moraic trochee[26]	right-to-left[27]	syllable	absolute ban
Negev Bedouin	iamb	left-to-right	foot	permitted
Cyrenaican Bedouin	iamb	left-to-right	foot	absolute ban

The surface variation in cases like (c)–(d) in Table 3.1 can be ascribed to underlying structural variation, and different theoretical approaches propose different potential parameters of variation. A widely adopted approach is the metrical stress theory (Hayes 1995), which reduces surface variation in Arabic to underlying variation in foot type, in the direction of foot construction within the word, in the size of the prosodic constituent targeted by extrametricality (segment vs. syllable vs. foot), and in treatment of syllables that cannot be grouped into a foot of the preferred type (known as "degenerate feet" and linked to restrictions on the size of the minimal word; see Section 3.2.3). A summary of Hayes' analysis of a range of Arabic dialects is provided in Table 3.2.

A metrical foot is a grouping of one or more syllables in which one syllable is designated as the head. Classical Arabic has an unbounded foot (containing any number of unstressed syllables along with the head). The majority of dialects in Hayes' (1995) survey show a trochaic (left-headed) foot,[28] with just a few dialects of Bedouin origin displaying an iambic (right-headed) foot. The difference in foot type is seen clearly in disyllables (Table 3.1c): moraic dialects have initial stress [ˈʒamal]; iambic dialects have final stress [ʒiˈmal]. In fact, the iambic pattern is probably equally widely distributed,

[24] Bani Hassan Arabic is a Bedouin dialect spoken in northern Jordan (Irshied and Kenstowicz 1984).

[25] Jacobs (1990) analyzed Palestinian Arabic with syllable extrametricality rather than foot extrametricality.

[26] McCarthy (2003) reanalyzed Bedouin Hijazi as having iambic feet, in parallel with other Bedouin varieties.

[27] Hayes (1995: 181) suggests that Bedouin Hijazi could also be analyzed with left-to-right foot construction.

[28] Hayes distinguished two types of trochaic foot: the moraic trochee (comprising two mora); and the syllabic trochee (comprising two syllables). All the trochaic Arabic dialects use moraic trochees.

at least in geographic terms, as it is found in dialects in Chad, Cameroon, and also Nigeria.

All dialects of Arabic show extrametricality, but some of the surface variation can be ascribed to differences in the size of prosodic constituent which the stress algorithm treats as extrametrical. Hayes (1995) analyzes both Cairene and Palestinian Arabic as building trochaic feet left to right through the word, but they differ in how stress is assigned in a word that contains a heavy syllable followed by two light syllables, as in (d) in Table 3.1. Hayes attributes this difference to the operation of foot extrametricality in Palestinian Arabic [ˈmaktaba] (the final foot comprising two light syllables is ignored for the purposes of stress) versus consonant extrametricality only in Cairene Arabic [makˈtaba] (with no effect in this case). In a similar fashion, differences observed in words of different syllable structures are analyzed as evidence of variation in the direction of foot construction and in the treatment of degenerate feet (see ibid. for details).

Van der Hulst and Hellmuth (2010) point out that the minimal stress pairs that crucially distinguish one dialect from another are relatively infrequent, occurring only in words of certain prosodic shapes. This in turn means that, for the bulk of words, more than one set of parameters could account for the data, allowing for variation in which parameter settings language learners infer from them. These apparently minor surface differences between dialects have on occasion been instrumental in the development of metrical theory. For example, Watson (2011) describes how the particular patterns observed in morphologically complex words in Bedouin Hijazi Arabic (Al-Mozainy et al. 1985) led to the proposal of the bracketed metrical grid (Halle and Vergnaud 1987; Hayes 1995), a representation that encodes prosodic constituency at different levels. In a similar way, Arabic dialects show variation in the sensitivity of stress assignment to morphological structure (Brame 1973, 1974), and these facts were instrumental in developing theories such as lexical phonology (Kiparsky 1982) and stratal OT (Kiparsky 2000). Equally, the interaction of stress assignment with segmental processes is well-known in Arabic for giving rise to cases of opacity, in which the triggering context for a phonological process is not apparent in the surface form of the word. Such cases present a particular challenge to nonderivational theories of phonology, such as classic OT, and a sizeable body of literature has sought ways to analyze such cases of opacity (McCarthy 2003; Elfner 2009).

Finally, the literature includes one or two interesting cases of dialects in which citation form word stress assignment patterns are subject to variation in connected speech. In Sanaani Arabic, for example, stress may be attracted to the initial syllable of a word when it occurs in a postpausal (phrase-initial) position (Watson 2002). Similarly, in the Casablanca dialect of Moroccan Arabic, the word-stress algorithm observed in words in citation form appears to disappear in connected speech and is replaced by word-final stress on all words (Boudlal 2001). The interaction of word stress with phrasal stress and other suprasegmental phenomena is probably the least well-documented aspect of the metrical phonology of Arabic dialects and as such is likely to yield important results in future.

3.2.5 Intonation

Work on intonation in spoken Arabic dialects is an emerging field of research, and the body of literature discussed here is much smaller than that discussed in earlier sections of this chapter.

We define intonation here as comprising the following phenomena (Halliday 1967): the chunking of utterances into prosodic phrases (tonality); the distribution of prosodic prominences (tonicity); and the shape of the pitch contour observed on and around those prominences (tone). A range of competing theoretical positions exists to account for each of these (Gussenhoven 2004; Ladd 2008). For example, for some authors prosodic phrasing (tonality) is derived directly from syntactic structure, whereas for others it reflects an intervening level of representation, the prosodic hierarchy (Inkelas and Zec 1995). The autosegmental-metrical (AM) theory of intonation offers a formal phonological representation of intonation, in which the pitch contour is modeled as a series of high (H) or low (L) pitch targets, associated autosegmentally with either the heads or edges of prosodic ("metrical") constituents (Gussenhoven 2007).

As for all less widely researched languages, there is a descriptive gap in work on intonation in Arabic, since standard grammars generally lack detailed discussion of intonational properties. As a result, there are relatively few descriptions of the intonational phonology of individual Arabic dialects, and even fewer studies make comparisons across dialects. Chahal (2009) provides a secondary analysis of a number of descriptions of individual dialects. She concludes that all of the dialects studied to date display postlexical use of pitch only (no dialects of Arabic have lexical tone) and that in all cases the observed intonational patterns require analysis in terms of both prominence-lending and demarcative pitch events (pitch accents on stressed syllables and boundary tones at phrase edges, in AM terms). Chahal's survey finds that dialects do vary in the inventory of possible nuclear tones observed (the nuclear tone being the last and most prominent pitch accent in an intonational phrase, together with any following tonal configuration, such as a final rise or final fall). As in other areas of phonology, however, we might expect to find greater variation across dialects once more finely grained parameters of variation are identified. Cross-linguistic prosodic typology is as yet in its infancy but already suggests that the scope of cross-linguistic intonational variation is not limited to variation in the inventory of possible nuclear tone configurations (Jun 2005).

Ghazali et al. (2007) offer a very preliminary overview of intonational variation in Arabic based on qualitative analysis of a small sample of parallel data in six dialects.[29] More data and analysis informed by known cross-linguistic parameters of variation are likely to yield further insights. For example, intonational languages are known to vary in the distributional density of pitch accents (Vigario and Frota 2003; Jun 2005; Ladd 2008). This cross-linguistic variation is also observed cross-dialectally in Arabic: Lebanese Arabic shows at least one intonational pitch accent in every "intermediate" prosodic

[29] They also present the results of a larger, and more methodologically robust, quantitative study of rhythmic variation in Arabic dialects, which is discussed in Section 3.2.3.

phrase, whereas Egyptian Arabic displays an intonational pitch accent on every prosodic word; these two dialects also vary in whether they permit deaccentuation (Hellmuth 2007; Chahal and Hellmuth 2014). This parameter would match with the generalization observed by Ghazali et al. that "flat hat" patterns, with relatively sparse modulations in pitch across the utterance, were observed only in Eastern (Levantine) dialects and not in Western dialects (which included Egyptian Arabic).

In another potential parameter of prosodic variation, languages are known to vary in whether their intonational system uses both prominence-lending and demarcative pitch events (pitch accents and boundary tones) or demarcative (boundary tones) only (Jun 2005). Although Chahal's (2009) survey suggests that all Arabic dialects studied up to that point displayed both pitch accents and boundary tones, further descriptive work may reveal that the generalization is not correct. For example, the stress migration facts of Moroccan Arabic (Mitchell 1993; Boudlal 2001) are open to reanalysis as an intonational system that uses boundary tones only. Again, this is consistent with Ghazali et al.'s (2007) observation that North African dialects displayed a single rise + fall across each utterance (assuming partition of their utterances into two prosodic phrases each).

In intonational phonology, as in other areas of phonological investigation we have seen in this chapter, a range of competing theoretical frameworks is available so that similar surface facts are open to reanalysis. Rifaat (2005) argues, from analysis of Modern Standard Arabic used in Egyptian broadcast media, that the intonational phonology of Standard Arabic is typologically unusual in its simplicity compared with other languages. El Zarka (2011) develops Rifaat's analysis for colloquial Egyptian Arabic and suggests that different intonational configurations map directly to pragmatic functions such as focus and topic. Other work on the prosodic realization of pragmatic functions in Arabic includes work in functional grammar (Brustad 2000) and laboratory phonology (Hellmuth 2009, 2011). There is little work on the syntax–phonology interface in Arabic, with work on Egyptian Arabic being an exception (Hellmuth 2004, 2010, 2012).

As in all areas of Arabic phonology, then, good theoretical modeling depends on continuing availability of good descriptions of the empirical facts of a range of Arabic dialects. Unlike word stress, these suprasegmental issues did not escape the attention of the Arab grammarians, with discussion of both pre- and postpausal phenomena (Cantineau 1946) as well as the role of prosody in disambiguation (Al-Harbi 1991). These issues can be expected to yield further theoretical gains in the years to come, once descriptive data are available in a sufficiently wide range of varieties of Arabic.

3.3 Conclusion

The main body of this chapter outlines some of the most influential, or in our view important, areas of Arabic phonological research, and in all of these areas work is ongoing. Other aspects of Arabic phonology have received only limited attention to date and promise to be equally fruitful. One clear example is work on vowels, perhaps due in part to the small size of the vowel inventory of Arabic. This contrasts to Sībawayh, who treated the "*alifs* of *imaalah* and *tafkhiim*" with primary focus on *imaalah*; further research on the phonology of vowel fronting/raising in Arabic, within and across dialects, might serve to contextualize the extensive body of work that exists on emphasis (cf. Bellem 2007). Similarly, work on establishing the true size of the phonological vowel inventory of spoken varieties of Arabic is needed (cf. Youssef 2010).

The motivation for continued research in all areas of Arabic phonology is partly theoretical, with reanalysis of existing data triggered as new theories of phonology are proposed and developed. In other cases as we have seen, new data in Arabic have motivated theoretical innovation in the past and can be expected to do so again. The contribution made to Arabic phonological research by the availability of detailed descriptions of the phonetics and phonology of a range of Arabic varieties cannot be underestimated (Rosenhouse 2011), yet the facts of many aspects of the phonology of many varieties of Arabic are still unknown. Our understanding of Arabic phonology, and of phonology itself, will continue to benefit from fieldwork that adds descriptions of further dialects and registers of Arabic to the data set for which phonological theory must account.

References

Al-Harbi, L. 1991. *Formal analysis of intonation: The case of the Kuwaiti dialect of Arabic*. Edinburgh: Herriot-Watt University.

Al-Mozainy, Hamza, Robert Bley-Vroman, and John McCarthy. 1985. Stress shift and metrical structure. *Linguistic Inquiry* 16: 135–144.

Al-Nassir, A. A. 1993. *Sibawayh the phonologist: A critical study of the phonetic and phonological theory of Sibawayh as presented in his treatise Al-Kitab*. London: Kegan Paul International.

Beeston, A. F. L. 1970. *The Arabic language today*. London: Hutchinson University Library.

Bellem, Alex. 2007. *Towards a comparative typology of emphatics: across Semitic and into Arabic dialect phonology*. PhD diss. School of Oriental and African Studies, University of London.

Benkirane, T. 1998. Intonation in Western Arabic (Morocco). In *Intonation systems: a survey of twenty languages*, ed. D. Hirst and A. Di Cristo, 345–359. Cambridge, UK: Cambridge University Press.

Blanc, Haim. 1964. *Communal dialects in Baghdad*. Cambridge, MA: Harvard University Press.

Boersma, Paul. 1998. *Functional phonology*. The Hague: Holland Academic Graphics.

Bohas, Georges. 1997. *Matrices, etymons, racines*. Leuven: Peeters.

Boudlal, A. 2001. *Constraint interaction in the phonology and morphology of Casablanca Moroccan Arabic*. Rabat, Morocco: Université Mohammed V.

Brame, M. 1973. Stress assignment in two Arabic dialects. In *A festschrift for Morris Halle*, ed. S. Anderson and Paul Kiparsky, 14–25. New York: Holt, Rinehart & Winston.

——. 1974. The cycle in phonology: stress in Palestinian, Maltese and Spanish. *Linguistic Inquiry* 5: 39–60.

Broselow, Ellen. 1976. *The phonology of Egyptian Arabic.* Unpublished PhD diss., University of Massachusetts, Amherst.

——. 1983. Nonobvious transfer: On predicting epenthesis errors. In *Language transfer in language learning,* ed. S. Gass and L. Selinker, 269–280. Rowley, MA: Newbury House.

——. 1992. Parametric variation in Arabic dialect phonology. In *Perspectives on Arabic Linguistics IV: Papers from the 4th annual symposium on Arabic Linguistics,* ed. Ellen Broselow, Mushira Eid, and John McCarthy, 7–45. Amsterdam: John Benjamins.

Browman, C. and L. M. Goldstein. 1986. Towards an articulatory phonology. *Phonology Yearbook* 3: 219–252.

Brustad, Kristen. 2000. *The syntax of spoken Arabic: A comparative study of Moroccan, Egyptian, Syrian and Kuwaiti dialects.* Washington, DC: Georgetown University Press.

Cantineau, J. 1939. Remarques sur les parlers de sédentaires syro-libano-palestiniens. *Bulletin de la Société de Linguistique de Paris* 40: 80–88.

——. 1946. Esquisse d'une phonologie de l'Arabe Classique. *Bulletin de la Société de Linguistique de Paris* 126: 93–140.

Chahal, Dana. 2009. Intonation. In *EALL* 2, ed. Kees Versteegh. Associate Editors: Mushira Eid, Alaa Elgibali, Manfred Woidich, Andrzej Zaborski, 395–400. Leiden: Brill.

Chahal, Dana and Sam Hellmuth. 2014. The Intonation of Lebanese and Egyptian Arabic. In *Prosodic typology II,* Sun-Ah Jun (ed.), 365–404. Oxford: Oxford University Press.

Clements, G. N. 1985. The geometry of phonological features. *Phonology Yearbook* 2: 223–250.

Cowan, J. (ed.). 1979. *Hans Wehr: A dictionary of Modern Written Arabic.* Wiesbaden: Otto Harrassowitz.

Davis, Stuart. 1995. Emphasis spread in Arabic and grounded phonology. *Linguistic Inquiry* 26: 465–498.

Davis, Stuart and Bushra Zawayadeh. 2001. Arabic hypocoristics and the status of the consonantal root. *Linguistic Inquiry* 32: 512–520.

Ehret, Christopher. 1989. The origins of third consonants in Semitic roots: An internal reconstruction (applied to Arabic). *Journal of Afroasiatic Languages* 3: 109–202.

El Zarka, Dina. 2011. Leading, linking and closing tones and tunes in Egyptian Arabic—What a simple intonation system tells us about the nature of intonation. In *PAL: Papers from the annual symposia on Arabic Linguistics volume XXII-XXIII: College Park, Maryland, 2008 and Milwaukee, Wisconsin, 2009,* ed. Ellen Broselow and Hamid Ouali, 57–74. Amsterdam: John Benjamins.

Elfner, Emily. 2009. *Syllabification and stress-epenthesis interactions in harmonic serialism.* MS thesis, University of Massachusetts, Amherst.

Faust, Noam and Ya'ar Hever. 2010. Empirical and theoretical arguments in favor of the discontinuous root in Semitic languages. *Brill's Annual of Afroasiatic Languages and Linguistics* 2: 1–38.

Firth, J. R. 1948. Sounds and prosodies. *Transactions of the Philological Society* 1948: 127–152.

Frisch, Stefan and Bushra Zawayadeh. 2001. The psychological reality of OCP-Place in Arabic. *Language* 77: 91–106.

Frisch, Stefan, Janet Pierrehumbert, and Michael Broe. 2004. Similarity avoidance and the OCP. *Natural Language & Linguistic Theory* 22: 179–228.

Gafos, Adamantios. 1998. Eliminating long-distance consonantal spreading. *Natural Language & Linguistic Theory* 16: 223–278.

——. 2001. *The initial state and verbal stems in Arabic.* MS thesis, Utrecht Institute of Linguistics, OTS (Onderzoeksinstituut voor Taal en Spraak).

——. 2002. A grammar of gestural coordination. *Natural Language & Linguistic Theory* 20 269–337.

——. 2003. Greenberg's asymmetry in Arabic: a consequence of stems in paradigms. *Language* 79: 317–357.

——. 2006. Dynamics in grammar: A comment on Ladd and Ernestus and Baayen. In *Papers in Laboratory Phonology 8: Variaties of phonological competence*, ed. L. M. Goldstein, D. H. Whalen, and C. T. Best, 51–79. Berlin: Mouton de Gruyter.

Gafos, Adamantios, Philip Hoole, and Chakir Zeroual. 2011. Preliminary study of Moroccan Arabic word-initial consonant clusters and syllabification using electromagnetic articulography. In *Instrumental studies in Arabic phonetics*. Amsterdam, ed. Zeki Hassan and Barry Heselwood (eds.). *Instrumental studies in Arabic phonetics*, 29–45. Amsterdam: John Benjamins.

Gafos, Adamantios, Philip Hoole, Kevin Roon, and Chakir Zeroual. 2010. Variation in timing and phonological grammar in Moroccan Arabic clusters. In *Papers in Laboratory Phonology 10: Variation, detail and representation*, ed. Cécile Fougeron, Barbara Kühnert, Mariapaola D'Imperio, and Nathalie Vallée, 657–698. Berlin: Mouton de Gruyter.

Ghazali, S., R. Hamdi, and M. Barkat. 2002. Speech rhythm variation in Arabic dialects. Aix-en-Provence: Laboratoire Parole et Langage. In *Proceedings of the Speech Prosody 2002 Conference, 11–13 April 2002*, ed. B. Bel and I. Marlin, 127–132.

Ghazali, S., R. Hamidi, and K. Knis. 2007. Intonation and rhythmic patterns across the Arabic dialects continuum. In *PAL: Papers from the annual symposium on Arabic Linguistics volume XIX: Urbana, Illinois April 2005*, ed. Elabbas Benmamoun, 97–122. Amsterdam: John Benjamins.

Goldsmith, J. 1976. *Autosegmental phonology*. Bloomington: Indiana University Linguistics Club.

Greenberg, J. 1950. The patterning of root morphemes in Semitic. *Word* 6: 162–181.

Guerssel, Mohamed and Jean Lowenstamm. *1990*. The derivational morphology of the Classical Arabic verbal system. Ms.: Université du Québec à Montréal/Universite de Paris 7.

Gussenhoven, C. 2004. *The phonology of tone and intonation*. Cambridge, UK: Cambridge University Press.

——. 2007. The phonology of intonation. In *The Cambridge handbook of phonology*, ed. Paul de Lacy, 253–280. Cambridge, UK: Cambridge University Press.

Halle, Morris and Jean-Roger Vergnaud. 1987. *An essay on stress*. Cambridge, MA: MIT Press.

Halliday, M. A. K. 1967. *Intonation and grammar in British English*. The Hague: Mouton.

Hamdi, Rym, Salem Ghazali, and Melissa Barkat-Defradas. 2005. Syllable structure in spoken Arabic: A comparative investigation. In *Proceedings of Interspeech 2005*, 2245–2248.

Harris, John and Geoff Lindsey. 1995. The elements of phonological representation. In *Frontiers of phonology: Atoms, structures, derivations*, ed. Jacques Durand and Francis Katamba, 34–79. London: Longman.

Harun, 'Abd S. M. 1983. *Kitab Sibawayh: Tahqiq wa-sharh*. Beirut: 'Aalam al-Kutub.

Hassan, Zeki and Barry Heselwood (eds.). 2011. *Instrumental studies in Arabic phonetics*. Amsterdam: John Benjamins.

Hayes, Bruce. 1995. *Metrical stress theory: Principles and case studies*. Chicago: University of Chicago Press.

Hayward, Katrina and Richard Hayward. 1989. "Guttural": Arguments for a new distinctive feature. *Transactions of the Philological Society* 87: 179–193.

Hellmuth, Sam. 2004. Prosodic weight and phonological phrasing in Cairene Arabic. In *Proceedings of the 40th meeting of the Chicago Linguistics Society: The main session*. 97–111. Chicago: Chicago Linguistic Society.

——. 2007. The relationship between prosodic structure and pitch accent distribution: Evidence from Egyptian Arabic. *Linguistic Review* 24: 289–314.

——. 2009. The (absence of) prosodic reflexes of given/new information status in Egyptian Arabic. In *Information structure in spoken Arabic*, ed. Jonathan Owens and Alaa Elgibali, 165–188. London: Routledge.

——. 2010. Functional complementarity is only skin deep: Evidence from Egyptian Arabic for the autonomy of syntax and phonology in the expression of focus. In *The sound patterns of syntax*, ed. Nomi Erteschik-Shir and Lisa Rochman. Oxford: Oxford University Press.

——. 2011. Acoustic cues to focus and givenness in Egyptian Arabic. *Instrumental studies in Arabic phonetics*. Amsterdam, ed. Hassan, Zeki and Barry Heselwood (eds.). *Instrumental studies in Arabic phonetics*, 299–324. Amsterdam: John Benjamins.

——. 2012. Variable cues to phrasing: Finding edges in Egyptian Arabic. In *Prosody matters: essays in honor of Lisa Selkirk*, ed. Toni Borowsky, Shigeto Kawahara, and Mariko Sugahara, 237–279. London: Equinox.

Herzallah, Rukayyah. 1990. *Aspects of Palestination Arabic phonology: A non-linear approach*. Ithaca, NY: Cornell University.

Idrissi, Ali. 1997. Plural formation in Arabic. In *PAL, Papers from the annual symposium on Arabic linguistics, volume X*, ed. Mushira Eid and Robert Ratcliffe, 123–146. Amsterdam: John Benjamins.

Idrissi, Ali, Jean-François Prunet, and Renée Béland. 2008. On the mental representation of Arabic roots. *Linguistic Inquiry* 39: 221–259.

Inkelas, S. and D. Zec. 1995. Syntax-phonology interface. In *The handbook of phonological theory*, ed. J. Goldsmith, 535–549. Oxford: Blackwell.

Irshied, Omar and M. Kenstowicz. 1984. Some phonological rules of Bani-Hassan Arabic: A Bedouin dialect. *Studies in the Linguistic Sciences* 14: 109–148.

Itô, Junko. 1989. A prosodic theory of epenthesis. *Natural Language & Linguistic Theory* 7: 217–260.

Jacobs, Haike. 1990. On markedness and bounded stress systems. *Linguistic Review* 7: 81–119.

Jun, Sun-Ah. 2005. Prosodic typology. In *Prosodic typology: The phonology of intonation and phrasing*, ed. Sun-Ah Jun, 430–458. Oxford: Oxford University Press.

Kager, René. 2009. Stress. In *EALL*, vol. 4, ed. Kees Versteegh. Associate Editors: Mushira Eid, Alaa Elgibali, Manfred Woidich, Andrzej Zaborski, 344–353. Leiden: Brill.

Kaye, Jonathan. 1990. "Coda" licensing. *Phonology Yearbook* 7: 301–330.

Kiparsky, Paul. 1982. From cyclic phonology to lexical phonology. In *The structure of phonological representations*, ed. Harry van der Hulst and N. Smith, 131–175. Dordrecht: Foris.

——. 2000. Opacity and cyclicity. *Linguistic Review* 17: 351–367.

——. 2003. Syllables and mora in Arabic. In *The syllable in optimality theory*, ed. Caroline Féry and Reuben van de Vijver, 147–182. Cambridge, UK: Cambridge University Press.

Ladd, D. R. 2008. *Intonational phonology*. Cambridge, UK: Cambridge University Press.

Lass, R. 1984. *Phonology*. Cambridge, UK: Cambridge University Press.

Lombardi, Linda. 1999. Positional faithfulness and voicing assimilation in optimality theory. *Natural Language & Linguistic Theory* 17: 267–302.

Lowenstamm, Jean. 1996. CV as the only syllable type. In *Current trends in phonology, models and methods*, ed. Jacques Durand and Bernard Laks, 419–443. Salford: European Studies Research Institute.

——. 2003. À propos des gabarits. *Recherches linguistiques de Vincennes* 32: 7–30.

Maddieson, Ian. 2011. Consonant inventories. In *The world atlas of language structures online*, ed. Matthew Dryer and Martin Haspelmath. Munich: Max Planck Digital Library.

McCarthy, John. 1979. *Formal problems in Semitic phonology and morphology*. Cambridge, MA: MIT Press.

——. 1981. A prosodic theory of nonconcatenative morphology. *Linguistic Inquiry* 12: 373–418.

——. 1986. OCP effects: Gemination and antigemination. *Linguistic Inquiry* 17: 207–263.

——. 1988. Feature geometry and dependency: A review. *Phonetica: International Journal of Speech Science* 43: 84–108.

——. 1994. The phonetics and phonology of Semitic pharyngeals. In *Phonological structure and phonetic form: Papers in laboratory phonology III*, ed. P. Keating, 191–233. Cambridge, UK: Cambridge University Press.

——. 1998. Morpheme structure constraints and paradigm occultation. In *Proceedings of the Annual Meeting of Chicago Linguistic Society* 32, ed. Catherine Gruber, Derrick Higgins, Kenneth Olson, and Tamra Wysocki, 123–150. Chicago: Chicago Linguistics Society.

——. 2003. Sympathy, cumulativity, and the Duke-of-York gambit. In *The Syllable in optimality theory*, ed. Caroline Féry and Ruben van de Vijver, 23–76. Cambridge, UK: Cambridge University Press.

——. 2004. Headed spans and autosegmental spreading. Ms. University of Massachusetts, Amherst. Available at http and works.bepress.com/john_j_mccarthy/60.

——. 2005. Optimal paradigms. In *Paradigms in phonological theory*, ed. Laura Downing, Tracy A. Hall, and Renate Raffelsiefen, 170–210. Oxford: Oxford University Press.

Mester, Armin and Jaye Padgett. 1994. Directional syllabification in generalized alignment. In *Phonology at Santa Cruz* 3, ed. Jason Merchant, Jaye Padgett, and Rachel Walker, 79–85. Santa Cruz, CA: Linguistics Research Center.

Mitchell, T. F. 1993. *Pronouncing Arabic* 2. Oxford: Oxford University Press.

Nolan, Francis and Eva-Liina Asu. 2009. The Pairwise variability index and coexisting rhythms in language. *Phonetica: International Journal of Speech Science* 66: 64–77.

Owens, Jonathan. 1988. *The foundations of grammar: an introduction to medieval Arabic grammatical theory*. Amsterdam: John Benjamins.

——. 2006. *A linguistic history of Arabic*. Oxford: Oxford University Press.

Padgett, Jaye. 1995. *Stricture in feature geometry*. Stanford, CA: CSLI Publications.

Pierrehumbert, Janet. 1993. Dissimilarity in the Arabic verbal roots. *Proceedings of the North East Linguistics Society* 23: 367–381.

——. 2006. The next toolkit. *Journal of Phonetics* 34: 516–530.

Prince, A. and P. Smolensky. 2004. *Optimality theory: constraint interaction in generative grammar*. Malden, MA: Blackwell Publishing.

Prunet, Jean-François, Renée Béland, and Ali Idrissi. 2000. The mental representation of Semitic words. *Linguistic Inquiry* 31: 609–648.

Rifaat, Khalid. 2005. The structure of Arabic intonation: A preliminary investigation. In *PAL XVII-XVIII: Papers from the seventeenth and eighteenth annual symposia on Arabic linguistics*, ed. Mohammad Alhawary and Elabbas Benmamoun, 49–67. Amsterdam: John Benjamins.

Roach, P. 1982. On the distinction between "stress-timed" and "syllable-timed" languages. In *Linguistic controversies*, ed. D. Crystal, 73–79. London: Edward Arnold.

Rose, Sharon. 2000. Rethinking geminates: Long-distance geminates and the OCP. *Linguistic Inquiry* 31: 85–122.

Rosenhouse, Judith. 2011. Trends of development in Arabic dialectology in the 20th century: A survey. *Zeitschrift für arabische Linguistik* 54: 42–66.

Scheer, Tobias. 2004. *A lateral theory of phonology: What is CVCV, and why should it be?* Berlin: Mouton de Gruyter.

Selkirk, Elisabeth O. 1981. Epenthesis and degenerate syllables in Cairene Arabic. In *Theoretical issues in the grammar of Semitic language*, ed. Hagit Borer and J. Aoun, 209–232. Cambridge, MA: Department of Linguistics, MIT.

Shahin, Kimary. 2003. *Postvelar harmony*. Amsterdam: John Benjamins.

Shaw, Jason, Adamantios Gafos, Philip Hoole, and Chakir Zeroual. 2009. Temporal evidence for syllabic structure in Moroccan Arabic: Data and model. *Phonology* 26: 187–215.

van der Hulst, Harry and Sam Hellmuth. 2010. Word accent systems in the Middle East. In *A survey of word accentual patterns in the languages of the world*, ed. R. Goedmans and H. van der Hulst, 615–646. Berlin: Mouton de Gruyter.

Vigario, Marina and Sonia Frota. 2003. The intonation of Standard and Northern European Portuguese: A comparative intonational phonology approach. *Journal of Portuguese Linguistics* 2: 115–137.

Voigt, Rainer M. 1988. *Die infirmen Verbaltypen des Arabischen und das Biradikalismus-Problem*. Stuttgart: Steiner.

Watson, Janet C. E. 2002. *The phonology and morphology of Arabic*. Oxford: Oxford University Press.

——. 2007. Syllabification patterns in Arabic dialects: Long segments and mora sharing. *Phonology* 24: 335–356.

——. 2011. Word stress in Arabic. In *The Blackwell companion to phonology*, vol. 5, ed. Marc Oostendorp, Colin Ewen, Elizabeth Hume, and Keren Rice, 2990–3018. Oxford: Blackwell.

Wiget, Lukas, Laurence White, Barbara Schuppler, Izabelle Grenon, Olesya Rauch, and Sven L. Mattys. 2010. How stable are acoustic metrics of contrastive speech rhythm? *Journal of the Acoustical Society of America* 127: 1559–1569.

Yoshida, Shohei. 1993. Licensing of empty nuclei: The case of Palestinian vowel harmony. *Linguistic Review* 10: 127–159.

Youssef, Islam. 2010. Against underlying mid vowels in Cairene Arabic. *Zeitschrift für arabische Linguistik* 52: 5–38.

CHAPTER 4

MORPHOLOGY

ROBERT R. RATCLIFFE

4.1 General Issues

Morphology in general refers to the study of form. Hence, linguistic morphology can be loosely defined as the study of the form of words. But behind this deliberately vague formulation there is a world of controversy. Depending upon one's focus and theoretical point of view, morphology can be defined as the study of the internal structure of words, or as the study of the processes for forming words, or as the study of the formal similarities and interconnections among words. The study of Arabic morphology cannot be separated from these larger theoretical and definitional issues.

Broadly speaking, the history of morphology over the last century can be described as a shift from one of these three definitions to another, briefly as a trajectory from structure to process to relationship. Early 20th-century structuralism focused on analyzing words into minimal units of form and sense (signs), for which the term *morpheme* was coined. The structuralist approach can be characterized as analytical and reductionist.

The rise of generative grammar led to an emphasis on process. Unlike earlier structuralists, the generativists were explicitly interested in describing the mental behavior of speakers. It was thought that evidence for mental processes was most likely to be found in aspects of language that were productive (capable of producing novel forms) or regular (describable in terms of a rule). This led to a morphological theory centered on the notion of word formation rules (WFRs). McCarthy (2008: 297) says, "Morphology is the study of word formation."

In recent times, an alternative to the rule-based approach has emerged from neurocognitive linguistics, in the form of models based on a network of connections among words in a lexicon (Lamb 1998). This approach appears likely to converge with word-based and paradigmatic models that have developed organically from older generative and structuralist approaches. As Gafos (2009: 338) says, "...Linguistic morphology is primarily concerned with systems of relations between words."

If one were to characterize the earlier history of Arabic morphological theory in terms of these 20th- and 21st-century currents, it might be said that the medieval Arabic grammatical tradition was focused on process. The central concept of Arabic "ṣarf" (lit. "change," generally translated "morphology") is taṣriyf (lit. "causing something to change," generally translated "derivation" [Baalbaki, "ALT I"]). By contrast, the 19th-century comparative Semitic tradition, with antecedents in medieval biblical philology, focused on analysis of words into smaller units.

4.2 The Structuralist Approach and Its Antecedents

One of the great *idées reçues* in linguistics, often repeated in general textbooks and introductory grammars, is that words in Semitic languages are uniquely formed by combining a consonantal *root*, which indicates core meaning, and a syllabic-vocalic *pattern*, which indicates grammatical function [Hellmuth, "Phonology"]. No doubt this does have a basis in the way that most Arabic dictionaries have been organized since medieval times [Buckwalter and Parkinson, "Modern Dictionaries"]. Students of Arabic soon learn how to identify a root in a word to look it up in the dictionary.

However, as Larcher (1999, 2006) observes, the Arabic grammatical tradition, as opposed to the lexicographical tradition, does not make use of derivations of words from roots. The term *ʔaṣl* "root, source" as used in this tradition refers to a word form perceived to be the base for another, usually the *maṣdar* (verbal noun, lit. "source"). "Ġalāyīnī tells us that the imperative *uktub* 'write!' is derived from the imperfect *yaktub*, 'he writes, he will write' the imperfect *yaktub* from the perfect *katab*, and the perfect *katab* from the *maṣdar kitaaba*" (Larcher 2006: 575). Owens (1988: 89–124) makes it clear that the grammarians allowed analysis of words into smaller units only in the case where such units occurred in sequence. Thus, the 13th-century grammarian Astarabadhi analyzed a word like *muslimuuna* "Muslims" as consisting of two *kalima* ("words," but in this context perhaps "morphemes"): *muslim-* ("muslim") and *-uuna* (masc. pl. nom.). The same author, however, explicitly rejects the idea of analyzing a word like *kulayb* "small dog" (diminutive) into two *kalima* correlating with the root "dog" and the pattern "diminutive."

The tradition of rigorously analyzing all words into roots and patterns may well be rooted in medieval Hebrew comparative philology, which was in turn influenced by the Arabic lexicographical tradition (Maman 2004). For Biblical Hebrew and Aramaic, where conditioned sound changes have considerably complicated the surface synchronic phonology, the assumption that a three-consonant root necessarily underlies every surface word allowed for the discovery of regular phonological changes that might otherwise have remained unobserved. Because the history of comparative Semitics has been strongly shaped by researchers primarily interested in the Biblical languages, root-and-pattern (R&P) theory became the dominant model in comparative Semitics. From there it was adapted into reference and teaching grammars of the individual Semitic languages, including Classical Arabic (CA).

Exactly when the R&P theory became the orthodox approach to Arabic synchronic morphology is not clear. Larcher (1999) and other Francophone linguists (Bohas 1993) attribute the origin of the idea to Cantineau (1950a, 1950b). But the theory is already incorporated in textbooks in other European languages from the same period (e.g., Cowan 1958). The prosodic analysis of the London School linguists (e.g., Firth 1948; Palmer 1970) and the long component analysis developed within American structuralism (e.g., Harris 1944) assume an R&P model as the departure point for theories designed to extend the notion of morpheme to discontinuous sequences within a word. However, these theories were principally developed on the basis of Semitic languages other than Arabic.

As an explicit synchronic theory influenced by the structuralist ideal of maximal analytical reductionism, the attribution to Cantineau seems as good a starting point as any. Certainly Cantineau offers an explicit and maximally strong version of R&P theory:

> Les racines et les schèmes constituent deux grands systèmes croisés, enveloppant dans leur réseau toute la masse du vocabulaire sémitique.
>
> Cantineau (1956a, cited in Bohas 1993: 45)

> ...Tout mot est entièrement défini sans ambiguité par sa racine et son schème....
>
> Cantineau (1956b, cited in Bohas 1993: 45)

This theory works quite elegantly up to a point, as we can see by organizing the following basic verb forms into a *croisement*, or grid, as Cantineau suggests:

(1)			Imperfect	Perfect	Active PRT	Passive PRT
	pattern>		-CCuC	CaCaC	CaaCiC	maCCuuC
	root√					
	ktb	"write"	ya-ktub	kataba	kaatib	maktuub
	drs	"study"	ya-drus	darasa	daaris	madruus

From this point it is possible to further extend the reductionist analysis. One way is by looking for meaningful groups in consonantal strings shorter than the root. This is a

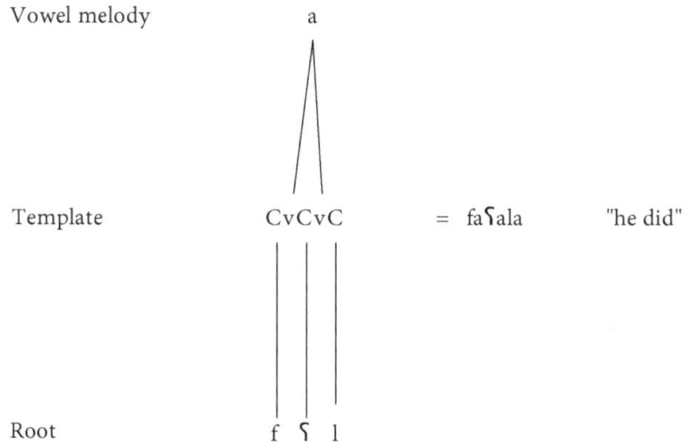

FIGURE 4.1 Root, template, vowel melody.

venerable tradition in Arabic and comparative Semitic linguistics (see Zaborski 1991), whose most recent variation is the etymon theory of Bohas (1997).

Another possibility is to further subdivide the pattern. This is the approach of the highly influential work of McCarthy (1979, 1981, 1983). McCarthy's aim is to adapt the analytical apparatus of autosegmental phonology, a theory developed for tonal phenomena, to the morphological analysis of Arabic. Although he essentially takes for granted the traditional R&P analysis, his particular innovation is to separate the traditional pattern into two parts, a vowel melody and a syllabic template (or CV skeleton), as shown in Figure 4.1.

Each of these three elements was said to be a morpheme on a separate tier. Words were formed through combining these morphemes through a process of tier conflation. And the "nonconcatenative" morphology of Arabic could be reanalyzed as morpheme based and combinatorial—although McCarthy (1981: 375) treats all of this as redundancy rules in a word-based lexicon.

One happy result of this analysis was that it brought out commonalities among patterns. Certain patterns like diminutive *kulayb* "little dog" and plural *kilaab* "dogs" (sg. *kalb*) share a CV skeleton (CvCvvC) but differ in vowel melodies. Derived verb stems II (yuCaCCiC) and III (yuCaaCiC) have different CV skeleta but share a vowel melody (u-a-i). Indeed the perfective of all the derived stems can be said to share a vowel melody, simply -a- with automatic spreading.

4.3 State of the Art: The Word-Based Turn

Since the mid-1980s the study of Arabic morphology has undergone something of a paradigm shift. Many students of Arabic morphology have reached the conclusion that a rigidly reductionist root-and-pattern analysis à la Cantineau is fundamentally inadequate as a descriptive tool. This has led to a variety of alternative models, which can be loosely grouped under the rubric of word-based or stem-based. All such models have in common the idea that many or all morphological regularities in Arabic can be best described in terms of derivational processes operating on words or stems rather than in terms of combinations of roots and patterns. No one would deny that forms like *yaktubu* and *kataba* are related. But there are various ways this relationship can be described without assuming derivation from a lexically listed root *k-t-b*.

There are several motivations for this shift. The most important has to do with technical problems of formal description. Many subsystems of Classical Arabic morphology that appear opaque or excessively complex within an R&P analysis (plurals, diminutives, tense/aspect and voice apophony, the derived verb system) yield to a much simpler and more rational analysis within a framework that incorporates the idea of word-to-word or stem-to-stem derivation (McCarthy and Prince 1990a, 1990b, 1995; McCarthy 1993; McOmber 1995; Ratcliffe 1997, 2003a, 2005; Benmanoun 1999, 2003; Ussishkin 2003). A second motivation, emphasized recently in work by Gafos (2003, 2009), Chekayri and Sheer (1996), and Chekayri (2007) but with antecedents reaching back to Schramm (1962, 1991), is that word-based derivation provides a better framework for exploring the relationship of phonology to morphology, especially the phonology of geminates and glides. A third motivation has to do with patterns of synchronic variation in dialectal spoken Arabic. Many descriptive linguists (see, e.g., Heath 1987; Holes 2004; Watson 2006) have concluded that the R&P framework is too restrictive to accommodate what speakers actually appear to be doing when they manipulate and innovate new word patterns. A fourth motivation, related to the previous, is diachronic change and analogy (Heath 1987; Carter 1996; Ratcliffe 1998, 2001a, 2003b, 2006). Many patterns in dialectal Arabic are not found in CA and therefore appear to be innovations. How do speakers create new patterns? A fifth motivation relates to meaning and semantic interpretation (Larcher 1995, 2006; Watson 2006). Simply put, if one expects that the meaning of a word can be determined by the meaning of its root combined with the meaning of its pattern, one is likely to be disappointed.

Against all of this, the principal critique has come from the side of psycholinguists, who argue that speakers seem to be aware of the relationships between words sharing a root (Boudelaa and Marslen Wilson 2005; Boudelaa 2006) and that speakers seem to be able to manipulate root consonants independently of vowels (Prunet, Beland, and Idrissi 2000).

4.3.1 Problems of Formal Description

McCarthy (1981: 375) observes that the traditional R&P analysis provides "no general treatment of relations between vowel patterns except as instantiated on a particular root." Within a framework that aimed "to capture significant generalizations," that is, to describe any sort of recurrent pattern in the data in terms of abstract rule-like statements, this situation was clearly unsatisfactory. As noted already, the division of patterns into CV skeletons and vowel melodies brought out commonalities among patterns that the traditional analysis ignores. Thus, paradoxically McCarthy's reductionism (dividing words into ever smaller pieces) led to a more holistic approach (recognition of regularities linking words or patterns across the lexicon).

But it quickly becomes apparent, or it became apparent to McCarthy and his collaborator Alan Prince, that other general patterns of cross-word regularity cannot be stated within a framework that assumes derivation from a root. This led them to propose a significant role for stem-based derivation, notably in the case of the so-called broken, or stem-internal, plurals, where they propose that "the stem rather than the root is the base of pluralization" (McCarthy and Prince 1990a: 251).

As an example of the sort of problem that motivated this shift consider the singular–plural pairs in (2).

(2)

SG	PL	
ʕaskar	ʕasaakir	"soldier"
maktab	makaatib	"office"
ḍamiir	ḍamaaʔir	"pronoun"
qaalab	qawaalib	"mold"

The plural forms in the second column all have the same syllable structure and vowel pattern. It is most economical to describe them as being formed on the same plural pattern, CaCaaCiC. But R&P theory does not allow this because the string of consonants that fills the pattern does not constitute a root in any but the first case. Under standard R&P analysis we are forced to recognize four different patterns: CaCaaCiC plus root *ʕ-s-k-r*; maCaaCiC plus root *k-t-b*; CaCaaʔiC plus root *ḍ-m-r*; and CawaaCiC plus root *q-l-b*. Furthermore, this analysis obscures the systematic relationship between singular and plural. The plural maCaaCiC always reflects singular with initial *m-*, CaawaCiC always reflects a singular with long vowel in the first syllable, and CaCaaʔiC always reflects a singular with a long vowel in the second syllable. Simply put, every onset and coda (every letter in the Arabic script, Ratcliffe 2001b) in the singular is mapped onto a C position in the plural. To put the problem another way, if we define a pattern as a vocalic-syllabic shape consistently associated with a meaning or grammatical function, then the plurals in (2) are clearly formed by combining a pattern with a consonantal string, but this consonantal string is not a root. If we insist that all words contain a root, then the residue does not fit the definition of the pattern.

Actually, the McCarthy and Prince (1990a) analysis goes beyond the patterns in (2). They suggest that plurals like those in (3) can also be accounted for by the same process as those in (2):

(3)

SG	PL	
qidħ	qidaaħ	"spear"
sulṭaan	salaaṭiin	"sultan"

In all these cases, the plural has an initial CvCaa sequence, and what follows this—C, CvC or CvvC—is determined by the syllable structure of the singular. McCarthy and Prince (1990a) propose to capture this generalizaton through the theory of prosodic circumscription: bracketing the first two-mora CvX sequence and mapping this to an iambic CvCaa.. template, with the syllabic residue carried over from singular to plural. As they acknowledge (1990a: 217–218), this analysis represents a radical break with R&P theory: "Although the defining iambic sequence has a clearly templatic character, the familiar resources of root-and-template morphology are quite inadequate to the task of representing it. The fault lies not in the notion of template but in its presumed dependence on the consonantal *root*; for the iambic plural systematically reflects aspects of the singular that the consonantal root does not determine."

McCarthy and Prince (1990b) and McCarthy (1993) propose a different, but also stem-based, mechanism for the verbal morphology. They derive stem II CaCCaC and stem III CaaCaC from the basic stem CaCaC through affixation of an empty mora (designated µ) after the intial Cv sequence <Ca>µCaC, which is then filled by spreading of either the preceding vowel yielding CaaCaC or of the following consonant yielding CaCCaC.

As Ratcliffe (1997, 2003a) and Benmamoun (2003) point out, these analyses are not contradictory. The decision to treat the verb one way and the noun another is quite arbitrary. If we take the imperfect form of the verb as basic and further assume word-based derivation, verbal and nominal morphology are surprisingly parallel. For the most frequent type of verbs and nouns, those with a three-consonant stem (CvCCun, yaCCvC-v), the most productive "internal" derivations in both nominal and verbal morphology involve the same core operation, which can be described either as mapping of a bimoraic CvX sequence to an iambic CvCvX template or as affixing of a vµ sequence to this same CvX base. Since prosodic circumscription explicitly allows reference to a phonologically, rather than morphologically, defined part of a word, the fact that the initial heavy syllable of verbs is heteromorphemic (person/number/gender prefix *ya*-, *ta*-, etc. + first consonant of stem CCVC) is not a problem. (The minimal freely occurring forms of CA nouns, indefinite (nominative), and verbs, jussive, are taken as the starting point.)

(4)

CvCCvC	>>	CvCvxCvC	
<CvX>	>>	<CvCvX>	
ya k t u b		yu k a t t i b	(I >> II) "cause to write"
ya k t u b		yu k aa t i b	(I >> III) "write to (s.o.)"
ka l b u n		k i l aa bun	(plural) "dogs"
ka l b u n		ku l ay bun	(diminutive) "little dog"

In fact, once we admit the principles of prosodic circumscription and moraic affixation into the analysis, we virtually eliminate the need for the idea of the fixed pattern. Ratcliffe (1997, 2003a) argues that all productive morphology appearing to be purely pattern based (not containing an additional affix) can be accounted for by the same rule of moraic affixation to a bimoraic base, interacting with other affixation processes. These include the active participle (CaaCiC), deverbal adjectives and nouns (CvCiiC, CvCuuC, CvCaaC), and the stem IX color verbs (iCCaCC, yaCCaCC) with stem final gemination:

(5) active participle

source:	aμ affixation	prefix deletion	coda filling
imperfective			
<yak>tub >>	<yvkaμ>tvb	>> kaμtib >>	kaatib "writer, having written"
deverbal nouns and adjectives			
source:	aμ affixation		coda filling
perfective			
<kat>ab >>	<katvμ>ab	>>	katiib, etc.
color verbs			
source:	aμ affixation	prefix addition	coda filling
color noun			
<zur>q >>	<zurvμ>q	>> ya<zVrvμ>q >>	yazraqq "become blue"

This analysis obviously depends upon what is taken as the source of the derivation, but the choice is not arbitrary. There is a logical connection between imperfective aspect and active (participles), as between perfective and passive (verbal adjectives). In the imperfective aspect since the action is ongoing, the agent must be present, although the patient—the effect or result of the action—may not yet exist. In active constructions the action is predicated of the agent (i.e., the agent is the subject). The focus in both categories is therefore on the agent or subject. In the perfective since the action is complete, the agent is no longer present, but the result or effect of the action remains. Likewise, in passive constructions the action of the verb is predicated of the patient (i.e., the patient is the subject). The focus here is on the patient or object. For the expression of color, nouns and adjectives are arguably more basic than verbs. The assumed direction of coda filling (rightward spread yielding a long vowel in nouns; leftward spreading yielding a geminate consonant in verbs II and IX) is consistent with other differences in the nominal and verbal morphology—nouns are predominately suffixing, verbs predominately prefixing.

Ussishkin (2003) argues that all the derived verb stems can be analyzed as formed by affixation, with no need for fixed templates. Adopting the idea that stems II and III involve affixation of an empty mora, he then uses an optimality theory (OT) analysis to argue that prosodic features of the derived stems, such as foot structure and stress placement, follow from interaction of phonological constraints applicable to all words. This is in contrast to McCarthy and Prince's (1990a, 1990b, 1995) hypothesis that morphological templates are defined in terms of units of prosody, which would imply that prosody is imposed (in some cases) by the morphology independent of the phonology.

Another technical problem where a word-based approach has promise is in the stem vowel alternations in the basic or stem-I verb. In an R&P analysis, these vowels can be analyzed only as having a direct referential value (or as being part of a pattern that has direct referential value). But there appears to be an implicational relationship between the vowel of the perfect and imperfect: the stem vowel of the imperfect is either the same as that of the perfect (*ya-ðha̱bu-ðaha̱ba* "go," *ya-kbu̱ru-kabu̱ra* "be big") or is different (*ya-ḍri̱bu-ḍara̱ba* "beat," *ya-ktu̱bu-kata̱ba* "write," *ya-lba̱su-labi̱sa* "wear"). If it is different, then one vowel is high (u,i) and the other is low (a). Alternation occurs about 75% of the time (McOmber 1995). The nonalternating types can be explained by phonological factors in the a-a case (presence of a postvelar consonant) and by semantic factors in the u-u case (stative meaning). Taking these factors into account, McOmber (1995) shows that the assumption of imperfect-to-perfect directionality gives 90+% predictability for the verbs in Wehr (1979) versus, at best, only 72% for the alternative perfect-based derivation. Ratcliffe (1997, 2003a) adopts this directionality on the basis of the argument that the imperfect stem shows a variety of (phonologically nonpredictable) syllabic shapes (-CvC, -CvvC, and -CCvC), consistent with the notion that it is a lexical entry, while the perfect shows a consistent (templatic) pattern (CvCvC-) (subject to regular phonological rules), which is consistent with the idea that this is a derived form whose shape can be predicted.

An alternative analysis follows the Arab grammatical tradition in taking the perfect as the base of derivation. Guerssel and Lowenstamm (1996) propose that the alternation follows an apophonic path Ø > i > a > u > u. This analysis requires the assumption that there is no underlying *a* in forms like *ḍar(a)ba, ya-ḍribu* but that there is one in *kataba, ya-ktubu* and ignores the *a-a* apophony. However, this pathway is supposedly a typological universal, found in other Afro-Asiatic and also Germanic languages (see Bendjaballah 2006 and references cited therein).

4.3.2 Interaction of Phonology and Morphology

R&P theory allows phonological explanations for morphological irregularity. For example, the observation that glide deletion in the environment *a_a* is a regular phonological process in Arabic [Baalbaki, "ALT I"] allows the inference that the 3rd sg. perfective *qaama* "he stood" reflects **qawama*—same pattern, CaCaC, as *kataba* "he wrote" (Voigt 1988). However, this sort of phonological interference in morphology is the only type of phonology–morphology interaction that is acknowledged.

A word-based approach permits a richer understanding of phonology–morphology interaction and offers a new solution to many old problems traditionally grouped under the label of "weak" or "biconsonantal roots." A central idea is that there may be morphological explanations for some kinds of phonological irregularity.

For example, there are a number of semantically basic nouns with only two consonants in the underived, singular form. These always acquire a third consonant (its quality determined by the surrounding vowels) in derived forms, such as broken plurals or denominal verbs: *dam* "blood," pl. *dimaaʔ* (pattern CiCaaC, with the final C filled by glottal stop); *ism* "name," pl. *ʔasmaaʔ* (pattern ʔaCCaaC); derived verb *samma(y)a, yusammiy* "to name" (pattern CaCCaC, yuCaCCiC, final C filled by /y/). By contrast, words with more than four consonants must lose a consonant to form broken plurals: *zanbarak* "(mechanical) spring," pl. *zanaabik*; *barnamij* "program," pl. *baraamij*. There is no phonological rationale for the absence of the glide or glottal stop in the underived forms in the first set of cases or for the absence of /m/ or /n/ in the derived forms in the second set of cases. Ratcliffe (1997, 2003a) explains these exceptions through the assumption that underived words are not formed on patterns while derived forms are. (Templatic constraints restricted to derived forms are indeed a phenomenon widely attested across world languages; Ratcliffe 2003a.) Thus, a word like *dam*, which has no further internal structure, must acquire a third consonant when mapped to a plural pattern. Since the pattern is by definition an invariant shape, composed of slots for a fixed number of consonants, it is the pattern that imposes or requires triliteralism (or quadriliteralism) and hence the "root." In other words, if a language uses fixed patterns to express morphological categories, the phenomenon of the "root" will emerge naturally as a result of derivational processes and need not be specified as a separate, independent morphological category.

Ratcliffe (1997, 2003a) extends this analysis to the verb and suggests that it explains the anomaly of the so-called 1-w verbs, like *waṣala, ya-ṣilu* "arrive." R&P theory forces the supposition that the imperfect reflects underlying **ya-wṣilu*, but as Voigt (1988) observed there is no phonological reason for deletion of *-w-* in these verbs. Not all verbs with *-w-* in the imperfect show absence of *-w-* in the perfect. Stem-initial *y-* in verbs never deletes. Under a word-based analysis, these verbs are the mirror image of biconsonantal nouns like *dam*: the imperfect two-consonant form is the basic, underived form, and the *-w-* of the perfect is a default consonant required to fill out the perfect template (as well as the templates of other derived forms such as participles and derived verbs). The insertion of the default to the left of the stem in verbs and to the right in nouns is consistent with the general directional bias of the two categories, as observed already. Some of these verbs even appear to be very old derivations from primitive biconsonantal nouns, for example, *wasama* "to mark" (cf. *ism* "name") (Ratcliffe 2001a).

For other so-called weak verbs, those assumed to have an underlying glide in second or third position, Chekayri's (2006: 168) conclusion is quite intriguing: "it has been shown that the distribution of [y] and [w] is predictable. That is, the glide appearance in some forms of a given verb is the output of a derivation originating in a lexical vowel." Simplifying somewhat for the purposes of exposition, the problem is that while R&P would predict two types each of 2nd and 3rd weak verbs (those with w and y, respectively) or perhaps six types (two glides times three possible stem vowels), what one finds is basically three types correlating with the lexical stem vowel of the imperfect (*yaquulu* "say," *yasiir* "go," *yanaam* "sleep"; *yadʕuu* "call," *yarmii* "throw," *yalqaa* "meet"). In particular, for verbs of the type *ya-naamu, naama*, it is difficult to make the case for an underlying "root glide." One would expect imperfective **ya-nwamu* or **ya-nyamu*, as there is no phonological restriction against such sequences (cf. the normal color adjectives *ʔaswad*, "black," *ʔabyaḍ* "white").

For verbs containing a geminate consonant, the R&P approach leads to an analysis of a verb like *yamuddu* "extend" as reflecting underlying **yamdudu*, with metathesis. Gafos (2003) shows that the alternations in this category can be explained most naturally in an approach that takes the surface geminated stem as the basic form.

The larger question in all of this is what speakers are actually doing when they identify a consonantal string for mapping to a template: identifying a root morpheme stored in the lexicon or extracting a phonologically defined string. A morpheme is standardly identified based on its recurrence in a set of words, like the *-mit* in English *permit, submit,* and *remit.* If the consonantal root is defined as a morpheme, then a root would be identifiable only where there was more than one word containing it. If the string is defined phonologically, however (such as "consonants in a word or stem"), a root is in principle extractable from any word. That speakers are identifying phonological strings rather than recurrent elements is supported by the fact that loanwords like *bank* "bank" (>>pl. *bunuuk*) or *sijill* "register" (<Latin *sigillum*), (>>*sajjal* "to register") have been integrated into the system. Bat-El (1994) first makes this argument for Hebrew.

If root extraction is approached as a problem of phonological parsing, we must ask what phonological features are relevant. Ratcliffe (2003a, 2004) proposes that the criterion for distinguishing a consonantal string for mapping purposes is relative sonority, as defined for Arabic by Angoujard (1990). Relative sonority, determines the potential occurrence of segments in different syllabic positions. (Nuclei must have a higher sonority, than onsets; codas must have a sonority, less than or equal to the nucleus.) And this in turn defines the distinction between consonants and vowels. Some relatively high sonority, segments (in Arabic the high vowels/glides u/w and i/y (IPA j)) can occur in both onset and nucleus position and hence are both consonants and vowels. Normally the stripping process will extract and carry over all segments with a sonority, lower than u/i. Thus, in *maʃruuʕ* >> pl. *maʃaariiʕ* "plan" the coda /u/ will not map to an onset in the output because there are already four lower sonority, segments in the input and no output template has more than four C slots. If the input has fewer than three segments below sonority, u/i, speakers have the option of raising the sonority bar to include vocalic codas. Thus, *ya-muut* "die" >> *yu-mawwit* "cause to die" the coda /u/ maps to an onset position (represented orthographically as w). If a word has more than four segments below sonority, of u/i, then the sonority bar can be lowered to further exclude high sonority, consonants such as approximants and nasals (as in the cases like *barnamij* >> pl. *baraamij*).

The theory predicts that problems will arise when the coda is maximum sonority /a/, which cannot be an onset. One solution is to map the coda /a/ to a default consonant, usually w (*qaalab* >> pl. *qawaalib* "mold," *baab* >> pl. *ʔabwaab* "door"). But there is abundant evidence that speakers have trouble processing CaaC type inputs, whether nominal or verbal, for purposes of derivation. About half of all noun stems with this pattern fail to undergo broken plural formation (Levy 1971). The total number of verbs with this stem shape in the imperfect is only around 30, versus over 200 with -CuuC and -CiiC (Chekayri 2007).

4.3.3 Variation in Dialectal Arabic

Heath's (1987: 12) treatment of Moroccan Arabic remains the most thorough attempt to describe a variety of Arabic without the assumption of derivation from a consonantal root: "underived noun, verb and other stems have a simple linear representation (or perhaps two or three slightly distinct ones, in the event of ambiguity). The linear representations include both Cs and Vs." Heath proposes three specific mechanisms for derivation: fixed template; template plus projection; and local rules (ibid., 3). The first mechanism accounts for cases where traditional R&P would also work, while the latter two roughly parallel (and prefigure) McCarthy and Prince's partial mapping and moraic affixation, respectively (1990a, 1990b, 1995).

Heath (1987: 5) offers various reasons for taking this stance, but one of the most important in retrospect is that it provides a framework for handling variation: "I often suggest that two or more distinct models... may have some degree of psychological validity for native speakers. Essentially I argue for the extension of variation models from the study of the social distribution of low-level surface forms... to the study of abstract representations and rules." Heath is in many cases able to elicit a variety of alternative output patterns of a given category from a single input, especially in cases where less frequently encountered words or less frequently employed derivations were involved. Owens (1998: 199–204) reports a similar result in his work on Nigerian Arabic. As one example of the sort of problems Heath uncovered, consider the two alternate diminutives for *kħəl* "black": *kʷħiħəl* and *kʷħiyəl* (153). In an R&P analysis, these forms would have to be described in terms of distinct patterns CCiyəC versus C̲C̲i̲C̲əC. However, Heath argues that they are better analyzed as different examples of the same pattern CCiCəC but with different strategies for mapping the input word to the pattern—spreading of a consonant versus insertion of a default consonant.

Another kind of variation emerges as a result of diachronic changes such as regular loss of phonemic glottal stop. Verbs like *ʔakala, yaʔkulu* "eat" can be analyzed unproblematically as containing a three-consonant root *ʔ-k-l* in CA. The Moroccan imperfect *yakel*, with stable /a /after the person/number prefix reflects the regular phonological development (*yaʔkul* >> *yaakul* >> *yakəl*). But elsewhere, the paradigm appears to incorporate two new roots: participle *wakəl* (like *waṣəl* "arriving," apparent root *w-k-l*), and perfective *kla* (3rd sg.) *klit* (1st sg.) (like *bda bdit* "began," with apparent root *k-l-y*). In other words, speakers seem to have resorted to various strategies for adding a third consonant to expand the inherited two-consonant sequence *k-l* to fill out the patterns of the derived forms. In so doing, they have created several new apparent "roots" from a single word (Heath 1987: 80, 168 n. 15).

On the other side of the Arabic dialect continuum, Holes (2004: 99) wrestles with the distinct strategies that speakers of Eastern Arabian dialects have for deriving quadriliteral verbs. Quadriliteral *gaṣgaṣ* means to "chop something up . . . into small pieces" (= intensive action), whereas theme II *gaṣṣaṣ* is "to do a lot of cutting" (= extensive over time), both verbs being derived from *gaṣṣ* "cut." Other examples such as *hajjal* and *hajwal,* both "to kick out," seem to show that speakers of this dialect too have alternative strategies for mapping a three-consonant input to a quadriliteral output. Watson (2006) describes a similar variety of strategies for forming quadriliteral verbs in San'ani.

Another area where one sees multiple strategies for deriving output patterns is in the hypocoristic formations in Palestinian and Levantine dialects described by Davis and Zawaydeh (1999, 2001).

(6)

Name	Hypocoristic
ʔanwar	nawwuur
diyma	damduum
dyaana	dayyuun
marwa	marmuur
raanya	rannuun

The hypocoristic is consistently CaCCuuC, but there appear to be a variety of ways for filling the C-slots. Recourse to an underlying root will work in the first case but not elsewhere. Ratcliffe (2004) shows that the variety of extraction strategies here can be rationalized in a sonority stripping analysis.

As the CaCCuuC hypocoristic illustrates, the dialects not only show various strategies for mapping input word to output patterns but also a variety of apparently innovative patterns (not found in CA). These include new patterns for old categories, such as the quadriliteral diminutives in Moroccan (Heath 1987: 113–132; Ratcliffe 2001), exemplified previously, the Moroccan nouns of profession CCaCCi (Heath 1987: 139–152) and new broken plural patterns from Iraq to Morocco (Ratcliffe 2003b). They also include new patterns for categories not found in CA, such as Moroccan diminutive verbs tCiCCeC (Heath 1987: 76), the presumably independent San'ani diminutive verbs (t)CayCaC (Watson 2006), new derived stems (e.g., CooCaC, tiCooCaC, CeeCaC, tiCeeCaC, yintiCaCCaaC) in Najdi (Ingham 1994), and the Levantine hypocoristics (Davis and Zewaydeh 1999, 2001), discussed above.

The mechanism by which speakers generate these innovative patterns are of tremendous interest for what they reveal about the creative aspects of language and mind. Yet a theory that says that words are formed exclusively by combination of preexistent roots and patterns cannot explain them.

4.3.4 Historical Change

When the dialects exhibit patterns, words, and roots that are not attested in CA, the most plausible assumption in most cases is that these forms were simply absent from the spoken forms of Arabic ancestral to the dialects during the period (8th–9th centuries) when the classical grammarians and lexicographers were active in codifying the language, that is, that such forms are innovations. Under this assumption two general trends can be said to characterize the historical morphology of Arabic (Carter 1996; Ratcliffe 2001a, 2003b, 2006).

First, most inherited biconsonantals are reanalyzed to have three consonants in all parts of the paradigm. For example, nouns like CA *ʃif-a* "lip" (pl. *ʃifaah, ʃifawaat*) often become geminated like Iraqi *ʃiffa* (pl. *ʃifaaf, ʃifaayif*); CA verbs like *ya-ṣil* generally acquire a stable glide as in Egyptian *yiwṣal*. When new biconsonantals emerge as a result of sound change, these too are reshaped on the triconsonantal pattern by adding defaults, sometimes creating multiple new "roots" from a single word, as in the Moroccan "eat" case.

Second, new patterns develop. One subtrend here is the generalization of quadriliteral patterns where CA has both triliteral and quadriliteral patterns, depending upon the structure of the input, as in the Moroccan diminutives (Ratcliffe 2001, 2006):

(7)	CA	Moroccan		
	kalb >> kulayb	kəlb	kliyəb	"dog"
	kitaab >> kutayyib	ktab	ktiyəb	"book"

These developments presuppose the operation of analogy, which requires reasoning over sets of words. They show that morphological patterns, and therefore roots, function as abstract structures rather than as concrete items or objects.

There is reason to think that similar processes of analogy and restructuring have given rise to new roots and patterns in the prehistory of Arabic. Larcher (2003: 576–577) presents a number of cases where words containing a long *-aa* have been reanalyzed to generate new apparent "roots." For example, *baal* "mind," where the tradition would expect a root *b-glide-l*, appears to be the source of *baalaa* "to mind" (stem III of root *b-l-y*). Also, *ʔiʃaara* "sign" (pattern ʔiCCaCa), verbal noun of *ʔaʃaara* (stem IV) "to indicate," root *ʃ-w-r*, seems to have been reinterpreted as pattern CiCaaCa from a root *ʔ-ʃ-r*, giving rise to a new form II verb *ʔaʃʃara* "to indicate." This type of reanalysis is a major source of apparent biconsonantal etyma (Zaborski 1991).

Ratcliffe (1998) argues in detail that most of the patterns of the Classical Arabic broken plurals are the result of analogic processes. The greatest degree of allomorphy is found for plurals of singulars containing a long vowel: CvvCvC and CvCvvC. Ambiguity in parsing long vowels would explain, for example, why one gets both triliteral (*ṭawiil*

>> *ṭiwaal* "tall") and quadriliteral (*ḍamiir* >> *ḍamaaʔir* "pronoun") plurals from inputs of the same stem shape.

4.3.5 Semantic Interrelationships

Finally, another critique of R&P analysis emerges from considerations of meaning and interpretation (Larcher 1995, 2006; Watson 2006). While it is often noted that words *kataba* "he wrote," *kitaab* "book," *maktab* "office, desk," and *maktaba* "library, bookstore" all have something to do with writing and all contain the "root" *k-t-b*, Larcher (1995) points out that the semantic connections among these forms is subtler and more precise. Both *maktab* and *maktaba* are nouns of place, but the former is a place where writing is done while the latter is a place where books are kept. In other words, *maktab* derives its meaning from *kataba* and *maktaba* from *kitaab*. There is no noun of place for the root *k-t-b*. Moreover, knowing that *kataba* means "write" would not allow one to predict that *kitaab* means "book." (Etymologically it should mean something like "letter.") When a word acquires a specific, nonpredictable meaning like this, standard morphological theory assumes that it must be lexically listed. But R&P theory prohibits words from having a lexical listing. Watson (2006: 7) makes a similar point about derivation in San'ani. For example, *taħaymar* "to act like a donkey" is semantically derived from *ħimaar* "donkey," not *ʔaħmar* "red."

4.4 The Psycholinguistic Critique

The principal critique of the word-based approach has come not in the form of offering alternative analyses of the technical problems that motivate this approach but rather in the form of arguments trying to prove the "legitimacy" or "psychological reality" of the consonantal root (see Prunet 2006 for a survey).

The fact that the debate has taken this turn reveals a deep philosophical problem in linguistics regarding the ontological status of the abstract terms we use to describe linguistic phenomena. Personally, I am convinced by arguments of neurocognitive linguists like Lamb (1998) that such terms as *root, morpheme*, or even *word* have no neurobiological reality and therefore no objective existence. They are convenient fictions, roughly analogous to the equally fictional units of measurement that scientists use to describe the physical world. One can debate whether feet or meters are more appropriate for measuring the height of Mt. Everest. One can debate the technical definition of such units. And one can make falsifiable statements about reality using such fictions ("Mt. Everest is higher than 7000 meters"). But logically, one cannot claim that the height of Mt. Everest provides evidence for the reality of the meter as opposed to the foot (or vice versa).

What many psycholinguists are actually doing is presenting data that they *analyze* in terms of a theory that root-morphemes are stored in a mental lexicon, but without showing that alternative theories cannot explain the same data as well or better. This is something like saying that since we have chosen to measure Mt. Everest in feet, feet are real and no alternative measurement is possible.

Nonetheless, this research raises a number of valid issues, notably:

1. Speakers seem to be aware of the relationship between words that share a root; see, for example, Boudelaa and Marslen-Wilson's (2005) priming experiments.
2. Speakers manipulate (root?) consonants independently of vowels; see Prunet, Beland, and Idrissi's (2000) discussion of aphasic errors.

Both of these points seem reasonable on the basis of other evidence as well. That speakers are aware of relationships instantiated through the root is apparent from the phenomenon of root-echo responses (Stewart 1996): *mabruuk* "congratulations" > *allah yibaarik fiik* "God bless you." That speakers can manipulate consonants independently of vowels is clear from language games involving consonantal inversion (McCarthy 1981; Heath 1987: 184–197). (However, Wolfer's [2011] survey of ludlings—secret languages made by changing words in systematic ways—shows that consonantal inversion is far from being the only way that speakers of Arabic dialects have to deconstruct and manipulate words.)

Boudelaa and Marslen-Wilson (2005: 232) propose to account for the first type of phenomena through "a morphological parsing process in which morphemic units are extracted and located at sub-lexical level." However, they argue that their experiments suggest a close link between words that share a purely phonological "root" (without semantic commonality) like *kitaab* "book," *katiiba* "regiment." This raises the question: Why not assume that parsing works on phonological principles (identifying consonants in a word) rather than by reference to a lexically listed "morphemic unit"? The standard reason for listing is that the relationship between form and meaning is arbitrary and hence must be learned. But if the root is simply a phonologically defined form without meaning, why does it need to be listed?

Prunet et al. (2000) argue that the domain of aphasic metathesis errors is the consonantal root. But as Ratcliffe (2004) points out, the domain of errors is not in fact the root as defined by lexicographical convention. Even the very small set of words in Prunet et al.'s sample exhibit the problems discussed in Sections 3.1 and 3.2. "Secondary" non-root consonants like the /w/ in plurals like *qawaalib* participate in metathesis errors. Glides participate only when there is a sonority contour present. Hypothetically underlying "root" glides do not participate. A sonority-based parsing analysis would seem to work as well or better here too.

While these new sources of data are welcome, the basic problems of description and analysis remain.

4.5 Future Prospects

There is probably much more to be said about the morphology of Arabic dialects—both in terms of basic documentation and diachronic explanation. Perhaps the most important impact of the word-based turn is that it has encouraged scholars to look for and try to analyze morphological phenomena in the dialects that cannot be easily explained in the R&P framework traditionally applied to CA.

There is also probably more to be said about Arabic morphology in typological perspective—beyond the comparative work on apophony discussed by Bendjaballah (2006) and the work on fixed-output effects in various languages cited in Ratcliffe (2003a). The point here is not that all languages have to be the same but rather that as linguists we want a theoretical apparatus that allows us to describe similar phenomena in different languages in the same way. Language-particular traditions of analysis, like R&P, tend to obscure such similarities.

No doubt there is quite a lot more to be said about Arabic morphology and mind. An important development in recent years has been the emergence of connectionism (Lamb 1998; Plaut and Gonnerman 2000). Connectionists argue that a grammar based on symbols and rules is not compatible with what is known about the brain and argue instead for a model of morphology as a network of interconnections analogous to a network of neurons.

R&P, if taken literally as a theory of mind, represents a particularly extreme version of the symbols and rules approach: the lexicon contains only abstract (unpronounceable) symbols, and all surface words must be derived by rules combining these symbols. Word-based approaches are less abstract, and some theorists like Gafos (2003, 2009) are already describing Arabic morphology in terms of relationships rather than rules.

But the main point of convergence is that both the word-based approach and connectionism eschew unique decompositionality and allow words to participate in multiple relationships:

> Traditional theories of lexical processing assume that... words are built out of discrete units called morphemes, and a given word either is or isn't decomposed into constituent morphemes at each stage of processing....
>
> Distributed connectionist modelling offers an alternative. Words are represented as alternative patterns of activity over multiple groups of units, and subpatterns of those patterns can exhibit varying degrees of stability and independence in a natural way. (Plaut and Gonnerman 2000: 478)

Compare: "Morphological rules may be able to reference various phonologically-defined parts of the input word whether syllables or strings of syllabic constituents such as consonants and vowels" (Ratcliffe 1997: 151–152). Replace Ratcliffe's "morphological rules" with "patterns of activity" and replace Plaut and Gonnerman's "subpatterns" with

Ratcliffe's phonological specifics, and the road toward a conciliation of these approaches lies open.

In the end, the success or failure of the word-based approach (as of any theoretical approach) must be evaluated not by such questions as "Is it true?" and "Should I believe it?" but by the questions "What (old problems) does it explain?" and "What (new problems) does it reveal?"

References

Angoujard, Jean-Pierre. 1990. *Metrical structure of Arabic.* Dordrecht: Foris.

Bat-El, Outi. 1994. Stem modification and cluster transfer in Modern Hebrew. *Natural Language and Linguistic Theory* 12: 571–596.

Bendjaballah, Sabrina. 2006. Apophony. In *EALL* I, ed. Kees Versteegh. Associate Editors: Mushira Eid, Alaa Elgibali, Manfred Woidich, Andrzej Zaborski, 119–123. Leiden: Brill.

Benmamoun , Elabbas. 1999. Arabic morphology: The central role of the imperfective. *Lingua* 108: 175–201.

——. 2003. Reciprocals as plurals in Arabic. In *Research in Arabic grammar II*, ed. Jacqueline Lecarme, 53–62. Amsterdam: John Benjamins.

Bohas, Georges. 1993. Diverses conceptions de la morphologie arabe. In *Développements récents en linguistique arabe et semitique*, ed. Georges Bohas, 45–59. Damascus: Institut français du Damas.

——. 1997. *Matrices, étymons, racines: éléments d'une théorie lexicologique du vocabulaire arabes.* Leuven: Peeters.

Boudelaa, Sami. 2006. Cognitive linguistics. In *EALL* I, ed. Kees Versteegh. Associate Editors: Mushira Eid, Alaa Elgibali, Manfred Woidich, Andrzej Zaborski, 421–427. Leiden: Brill.

Boudelaa, Sami and William Marslen-Wilson. 2005. Discontinuous morphology in time: Incremental masked priming in Arabic. *Language and Cognitive Processes* 20(1–2): 207–260.

Cantineau, Jean. 1950a. Racines et schèmes. In *Melanges W. Marçais*, 119–124. Paris: G.P. Maisonneuve et Cie.

——. 1950b. La notion de "schème" et son altération dans diverses langes sémitiques. *Semitica* 3: 73–83.

Carter, Michael. 1996. Signs of change in Egyptian Arabic. In *Understanding Arabic: Essays in honor of El-Said Badawi*, ed. Alaa Elgibali, 137–144. Cairo: American University of Cairo Press.

Chekayri, Abdellah. 2007. Glide. In *EALL*, II ed. Kees Versteegh. Associate Editors: Mushira Eid, Alaa Elgibali, Manfred Woidich, Andrzej Zaborski, 164–169. Leiden: Brill.

Chekayri, Abdellah and Tobias Sheer. 1996. The apophonic origin of glides in the verbal system of Classical Arabic. In *Studies in Afro-Asiatic grammar*, ed. Jacqueline Lecarme, Jean Lowenstamm, and Ur Shlonsky, 62–76. The Hague: Holland Academic Graphics.

Cowan, David. 1958. *Modern literary Arabic.* Cambridge, UK: Cambridge University Press.

Davis, Stuart and Bushra Adnan Zawaydeh. 1999. A descriptive analysis of hypocoristics in colloquial Arabic. *Langues et Linguistique* 3: 83–98.

——. 2001. Arabic hypocoristics and the status of the consonantal root. *Linguistic Inquiry* 32: 512–520.

Elgibali, Alaa (ed.). 1996. *Understanding Arabic: Essays in honor of El-Said Badawi*. Cairo: American University of CairoPress.
Firth, John R. 1948. Sounds and prosodies. *Transactions of the Philological Society 1948*, 127–152. Reprinted in Frank Palmer 1970, *Prosodic analysis*, 1–26. London: Oxford University Press.
Gafos, Adamantios. 2003. Greenberg's asymmetry in Arabic: A consequence of stems in paradigms. *Language* 79: 317–355.
——. 2009. Stem. In *EALL* IV, ed. Kees Versteegh. Associate Editors: Mushira Eid, Alaa Elgibali, Manfred Woidich, Andrzej Zaborski, 338–339. Leiden: Brill.
Guerssel, Mohand and Jean Lowenstamm. 1996. Ablaut in Classical Arabic measure I active verbal forms. In ed. Jacqueline Lecarme, Jean Lowenstamm, and Ur Shlonsky. *Studies in Afro-Asiatic grammar*, 123–34. The Hague: Holland Academic Graphics.,
Harris, Zellig. 1944. Simultaneous components in phonology. *Language* 20: 181–205.
Heath, Jeffrey. 1987. *Ablaut and ambiguity: Phonology of a Moroccan Arabic dialect*. Albany: State University of New York Press.
Holes, Clive. 2004. Quadriliteral verbs in the Arabic dialects of Eastern Arabia. In *Approaches to Arabic dialects*, ed. Martine Haak, Rudolph de Jong, and Kees Versteegh, 117–134. Leiden: Brill.
Ingham, Bruce. 1994. *Najdi Arabic*. Amsterdam: John Benjamins.
Kaye, Alan, ed. 1991. *Semitic studies in honor of Wolf Leslau*. 2 vols. Wiesbaden: Harrasowitz.
Lamb, Sydney M. 1998. *Pathways in the brain*. Amsterdam: John Benjamins.
Larcher, Pierre. 1995. Où il est montré qu'en arabe classique la racine n'a pas de sense et qu'il n y a pas de sens à dériver d'elle. *Arabica* 41: 291–314.
——. 1999. Vues "nouvelles" sur la dérivation lexicale en arabe classique. In *Tradition and innovation: Norm and deviation in Arabic and Semitic linguistics*, ed. Lutz Edzard and Mohammad Nekroumi, 103–123. Wiesbaden: Harrasowitz.
——. 2006. Derivation. In *EALL*, I, ed. Kees Versteegh, associate ed. Mushira Eid, Alaa Elgibali, Manfred Woidich, and Andrzej Zaborski, 573–579. Leiden: Brill.
Lecarme, Jacqueline, ed. 2003. *Research in Arabic grammar II*. Amsterdam: John Benjamins.
Lecarme, Jacqueline, Jean Lowenstamm, and Ur Shlonsky (eds.). 1996. *Studies in Afro-Asiatic grammar*. The Hague: Holland Academic Graphics.
Levy, Mary M. 1971. *The plural of the noun in Modern Standard Arabic*. PhD diss., University of Michigan.
Maman, Aharon. 2004. *Comparative Semitic philology in the Middle Ages*. Trans. David Lyons. Leiden: Brill.
McCarthy, John. J. 1979. *Formal problems in Semitic phonology and morphology*. PhD diss., Massachusetts Institute of Technology, Cambridge, MA.
——. 1981. A prosodic theory of non-concatenative morphology. *Linguistic Inquiry* 12: 373–418.
——. 1983. A prosodic account of Arabic broken plurals. In *Current trends in African linguistics*, ed. I. Dihoff, 289–320. Dordrecht: Foris.
——. 1993. Template form in prosodic morphology. In *Papers from the third annual formal linguistics society of Midamerica conference*, ed. L. Smith Stvan, 127–218. Bloomington: Indiana University Linguistics Club.
——. 2008. Morphology. In *EALL*, III, ed. Kees Versteegh, associate ed. Mushira Eid, Alaa Elgibali, Manfred Woidich, and Andrzej Zaborski, 297–307. Leiden: Brill.
McCarthy, John J. and Alan Prince. 1990a. Foot and word in prosodic morphology: The Arabic broken plural. *Natural Language and Linguistic Theory* 8: 209–283.

——. 1990b. Prosodic morphology and templatic morphology. In *PAL II*, ed. Mushira Eid and John McCarthy, 1–54. Amsterdam: Benjamins.

——. 1995. Prosodic morphology. In *The handbook of phonological theory*, ed. John Goldsmith, 318–366. Malden, MA: Blackwell.

McOmber, Michael L. 1995. Morpheme edges and Arabic infixation. In *PAL VI*, ed. Mushira Eid, 173–189. Amsterdam: Benjamins.

Owens, Jonathan. 1988. *The foundations of grammar: An introduction to medieval Arabic grammatical theory*. Amsterdam: John Benjamins.

——. 1998. *Neighborhood and ancestry: Variation in the spoken Arabic of Maiduguri, Nigeria*. Amsterdam: John Benjamins.

Palmer, Frank R. (ed.). 1970. *Prosodic analysis*. London: Oxford University Press.

Plaut, David and Laura Gonnerman. 2000. Are non-semantic morphological effects incompatible with a distributed connectionist approach to lexical processing? *Language and Cognitive Processes* 15: 445–485.

Prunet, Jean François. 2006. External evidence and the Semitic root. *Morphology* 16: 41–67.

Prunet, Jean François, Renee Beland, and Ali Idrissi. 2000. The mental representation of Semitic words. *Linguistic Inquiry* 31: 609–638.

Ratcliffe, Robert. 1997. Prosodic templates in a word-based morphological analysis of Arabic. In *PAL X*, ed. Mushira Eid and Robert Ratcliffe, 147–171. Amsterdam: Benjamins.

——. 1998. *The "broken" plural problem in Arabic and comparative Semitic: Allomorphy and analogy in non-concatenative morphology*. Amsterdam: John Benjamins.

——. 2001a. Analogy in Semitic morphology: Where do new roots and new patterns come from? In *New data and new methods in Afroasiatic linguistics: Robert Hetzron in memoriam*, ed. Andrzej Zaborski, 90–105. Paris: INALCO.

——. 2001b. What do "phonemic" writing systems represent: Arabic huruuf, Japanese kana and the Moraic principle. *Written Language and Literacy* 4: 1–14.

——. 2003a. Toward a universal theory of shape-invariant (templatic) morphology: Classical Arabic reconsidered. In *Explorations in seamless morphology*, ed. Rajendra Singh and Stanley Starosta, 212–269. London: SAGE.

——. 2003b. The historical dynamics of the Arabic plural system: Implications for a theory of morphology. In ed. Lecarme, 339–362.

——. 2004. Sonority-based parsing at the margins of Arabic morphology. *Al-Arabiyya* 37: 53–75.

——. 2005. Semi-productivity and valence marking in Arabic—the so-called "verbal themes." In *Corpus approaches to sentence structure*, ed. Toshiro Takagaki, Susumu Zaima, Yoichiro Tsuruga, Francisco Moreno Fernandez, and Yuji Kawaguchi, 179–190. Amsterdam: John Benjamins.

——. 2006. Analogy. In *EALL* I, ed. Kees Versteegh, associate ed. Mushira Eid, Alaa Elgibali, Manfred Woidich, and Andrzej Zaborski, 74–82. Leiden: Brill.

Schramm, Gene. 1962. An outline of Classical Arabic verb structure. *Language* 38: 360–375.

——. 1991. Semitic morpheme structure typology. In ed. Kaye, 1402–1408.

Stewart, Devin J. 1996. Root-echo responses in Egyptian Arabic. In ed. Alaa Eligbali, 157–180.

Ussishkin, Adam. 2003. Templatic effects as fixed prosody: The verbal system in Semitic. In ed. Lecarme, 511–530.

Voigt, Rainer.1988. *Die infirmen Verbaltypen und das Biradikalismus-Problem*. Stuttgart: F. Steiner.

Watson, Janet C. E. 2006. Arabic morphology: Diminutive verbs and diminutive nouns in San'ani Arabic. *Morphology* 16: 189–204.
Wehr, Hans. 1979. *A dictionary of modern written Arabic*. Ed. J. Milton Cowan. Wiesbaden: Harrasowitz.
Wolfer, Claudia. 2011. Arabic secret languages. *Folia Orientalia* 47: 7–49.
Zaborski, Andrzej. 1991. Biconsonantal roots and triconsonantal roots in Semitic: Solutions and prospects. In ed. Alan Kaye, 1675–1703.

CHAPTER 5

ARABIC LINGUISTIC TRADITION I

naḥw and ṣarf

RAMZI BAALBAKI

5.1 Introduction

The Arabic linguistic tradition (ALT, also termed Arabic grammatical tradition) is certainly the most extensive among the Arabic linguistic sciences. Although the distinction between the two groups referred to as *luġawiyyūn* and *naḥwiyyūn* is often artificial and simplistic, as in Zubaydī's (d. 379/989) *Ṭabaqāt al-naḥwiyyīn wa-l-luġawiyyīn*, the first group largely refers to philologists or lexicographers who, as of the 2nd/8th century, were concerned with collecting linguistic data and exploring the meaning of words in *ġarīb* (strange usage) material and dialectal variants. This trend in linguistic study, which has surely contributed to the early appearance of lexicons as well as lexical collections based on subject rather than root (e.g., plants, animals, human body organs, weapons, natural phenomena; [Sara, "Classical Lexicography"]), survived in works such as *al-Ṣāḥibī* by Ibn Fāris (d. 395/1004), *al-Muḫaṣṣaṣ* by Ibn Sīda (d. 458/1066), and as late as the 10th century *al-Muzhir* by Suyūṭī (d. 911/1505). In contrast, the term *naḥwiyyūn* refers to the grammarians par excellence, that is, scholars whose interest mainly lies in the realm of syntax, morphology (including morphophonology), and, to a lesser extent, phonetics. A third group of scholars is known as the *balāġiyyūn* (rhetoricians, [Larcher, "ALT II"]). In spite of the great affinity between their discipline and grammar so much that one of their most prominent authors, Ǧurǧānī (d. 471/1078), bases his whole theory of word order and semantic and syntactic interrelationships (i.e., *naẓm*) on the meanings that *naḥw* provides (*Dalāʾil* 64, 176, 282, 310, 403–404), the approach of the *balāġiyyūn* to linguistic analysis and their subject matter differ significantly from those of the *naḥwiyyūn* (Baalbaki 1983). To the exclusion of the fields of philology, lexicography, and rhetoric, this chapter deals with the two major branches of the grammatical tradition, namely, *naḥw* (which refers to grammar in general but more specifically to syntax) and *ṣarf* (morphology).

5.2 Early Grammar and the Origins of the Grammatical Theory

Most biographical sources attribute the founding of Arabic grammar to Abū l-Aswad al-Duʾalī (d. 69/688). Other early figures credited with laying the foundations of grammar include Naṣr b. ʿĀṣim (d. 89/708) and ʿAbdalraḥmān b. Hurmuz (d. 117/735) (Sīrāfī, *Aḫbār* 13; Zubaydī, *Ṭabaqāt* 21–27). But although these reports and the anecdotal material related to them can in no way be substantiated, they serve to highlight the link between early grammatical activity and the need to attend to the "corruption" of speech (*laḥn*) that was blamed on nonnative speakers of Arabic as a result of the *futūḥāt* (conquests). Furthermore, the subjects that were claimed to have captured the interest of these early scholars, namely, the three parts of speech and the particles that govern nouns and verbs, are strongly connected with *laḥn* and argue that early grammatical activity aimed primarily at adherence to "correct" usage and avoidance of error. An oft cited anecdote, for instance, has it that what prompted Abū l-Aswad to author a book (*waḍaʿa kitāban*) on grammar is that his daughter addressed him by saying:

(1)
mā *a-šadd-u* *l-ḥarr-i*
what EL-severer-NOM DEF-heat-GEN
"What type of hot weather is most severe"?

In fact, she wanted to exclaim over the hotness of the weather and should have used the exclamatory phrase:

(2)
mā *a-šadd-a* *l-ḥarr-a*
what EL-be severe DEF-heat-ACC
"How hot it is!"
(Sīrāfī, *Aḫbār* 19; cf. Zubaydī, *Ṭabaqāt* 21).

At this stage it is clear that there was no real distinction between the various linguistic disciplines and that early interest in syntax and morphology was strongly related to other areas of Islamic scholarship and, in particular, the *qirāʾāt* (Quranic readings), *ḥadīṯ* (prophetic tradition), *fiqh* (jurisprudence), and *tafsīr* (exegesis). It is noteworthy that most of the grammarians before Sībawayhi were readers (*qurrāʾ*) and that many of them narrated *ḥadīṯ* or were formally trained in it (Baalbaki 2008: 5). Sībawayhi (d. 180/796) himself comments on several *qirāʾāt* in his *Kitāb*, and, according to the biographical sources, an error he made in reciting a *ḥadīṯ* prompted him to seek a discipline that would guard against linguistic error, hence his pursuit of grammar and subsequent authorship of the *Kitāb* (Zubaydī, *Ṭabaqāt* 66; Ibn al-Anbārī, *Nuzha* 54–55). But it is the influence of *fiqh* and *tafsīr* on *naḥw* that has largely occupied scholars in the last few decades. Carter (1972) advanced the theory that the origins of Arabic grammar can be traced in the Islamic science of law and that "grammar has no meaning if it cannot be related to the practicalities either of Islamic doctrine or the power and influence of the grammarians in Islamic society" (Carter 1991: 9). His most compelling argument is that Sībawayhi's criteria of linguistic correctness are expressed by ethical terms such as *ḥasan* (good) and *mustaqīm* (right) and that a host of grammatical terms such as *badal* (substitute), *šarṭ* (condition), *ḥadd* (limit), *aṣl* (origin), and *niyya* (intention) can best be understood in the light of their employment in legal contexts. Carter's "legal thesis" contributes significantly to our understanding of the interrelatedness of grammar and law, but it should be pointed out that the grammatical terms he cites are predominantly methodological terms rather than categorical ones (cf. Versteegh 1993: 35).

Further clarification of the origins of grammatical terminology may be sought in the earliest extant Quranic commentaries. In this respect, Versteegh (1993: 196–197) demonstrates how several terms used by early exegetes constitute the link between everyday vocabulary and the later technical terminology. Examples include *ḫabar* (predicate), *naʿt* (attribute), *māḍī* (past tense), *ism* (noun), *istifhām* (question), *taʿaǧǧub* (admiration), and *iḍmār* (deletion). It should be borne in mind, however, that our knowledge of the terminological situation of early grammar is quite limited. Baalbaki (2006), for example, discusses the set of previously unknown outlandish morphological terms that Muʾaddib, a 4th-century grammarian, uses in his *Daqāʾiq al-taṣrīf* and argues that they belong to an earlier period. Whether or not these terms are peculiar to a group of scholars whose main preoccupation was morphological *ʿilal* (causes) remains an open question. But it is certain that a better understanding of early grammatical terminology—hopefully with the emergence of hitherto unknown texts such as Muʾaddib's—would have huge implications on our reconstruction of the beginning of grammatical activity, as many of the assumptions related to various aspects of early grammar (e.g., the Basran–Kufan polarization) rely heavily on our present knowledge of early terminology.

Theories that ascribe the genesis of Arabic grammar to foreign influence also rely in part on terminological evidence. Merx (1889) argues that Arabic grammar is based on the Greek model that was available to the Arabs in translation of Greek treatises. He thus traces the terms for the three parts of speech, *ism* (noun), *fiʿl* (verb), and *ḥarf* (particle) to *ónoma*, *rhèma*, and *súndesmos*, respectively, and he links *iʿrāb* (declension) and *ḫabar* (predicate) to *hellènízein/hellènismós* and *katègoroúmenon*, respectively.

According to Rundgren (1976), several basic grammatical terms, including *naḥw*, *ṣarf*, and *qiyās*, are direct translations of Greek terms or are inspired by Greek notions. The "Greek thesis" was harshly attacked by a number of scholars, most notably Carter, who convincingly argues that the absence of any reference to foreign influences in the indigenous accounts of Arabic grammar is a major flaw in the theory (Carter 1972: 72). Versteegh (1993: 25) proposes the possibility that the Arabs only borrowed some of the elements of Greek grammatical teaching since they "became acquainted with Hellenistic culture and scholarship in a watered down version as it was being taught in schools all over the Byzantine empire." As far as terminology is concerned, Troupeau (1981) demonstrates that, based on Ibn al-Muqaffaʿ's (d. 142/759) epitome of the *Hermeneutics*, there is no conformity between primitive Arabic grammatical terminology and terminology of Greek logic. In short, attempts to trace the emergence of Arabic grammar to foreign influence, be it Greek, Syriac, or Indian, have shown the existence of interesting parallels in terminology and grammatical categories between Arabic grammar and foreign traditions but have largely failed to demonstrate the existence of massive borrowing from foreign sources in the early period. That certain terms and notions might have been borrowed from other traditions is of relatively little importance given that the distinctive characteristics of the ALT—including its essential terminology of syntactic position and its fundamental notions of dependency, hierarchy, suppletive insertion (*taqdīr*), and original form or pattern (*aṣl*)—argue for predominantly native origins.

Most of our primary knowledge about the pre-Sībawayhi grammarians comes from the *Kitāb* itself. Sībawayhi makes no reference to the early figures who later biographical sources credit with the establishment of grammar (i.e., Abū l-Aswad and his contemporaries). He quotes, however, the views of several later authorities who were either his predecessors or his contemporaries. ʿAbdallāh b. Abī Isḥāq (d. 117/735) is quoted 7 times, ʿĪsā b. ʿUmar (d. 149/766) 20 times, Abū ʿAmr b. al-ʿAlāʾ (d. 154/770) 57 times, and Abū l-H̱aṭṭāb al-Aḫfaš al-Kabīr (d.177/793) 58 times. But the two scholars who had the greatest impact on Sībawayhi were Yūnus b. Ḥabīb (d. 182/798) and al-H̱alīl b. Aḥmad (d. 175/791). In fact, a note found in a copy of the *Kitāb* derived from Hārūn b. Mūsā (d. 401/1010) suggests, contrary to the biographical sources, that Yūnus and al-H̱alīl were the only two "real" teachers of Sībawayhi (*wa-muʿallimā Sībawayhi l-H̱alīl wa-Yūnus*; cf. Humbert 1995: 9). Yūnus is quoted 217 times in the *Kitāb*. From these, it is clear that he had a sophisticated system of grammatical analysis whose main features include (1) extensive use of *taqdīr* as an analytical tool, (2) formulation of grammatical "rules" of universal validity, (3) reliance on anomalous examples in drawing conclusions or formulating "rules," and (4) description of usage by employing terms that are characteristic of Sībawayhi's appraisal of his own data, such as *qabīḥ* (ugly), *qalīl* (infrequent), *ḫabīṯ* (repugnant), *kaṯīr* (frequent), and *waǧh* (correct or better usage) (Baalbaki 1995: 126–129, 2008: 14–16). For his part, al-H̱alīl was Sībawayhi's principal and most influential teacher. There are 608 references to al-H̱alīl in the *Kitāb*, and the amount of data that Sībawayhi reports on his authority is overwhelming indeed. Accordingly, it is practically impossible to examine the terminology and analytical tools and methods of either Sībawayhi or al-H̱alīl in isolation of one another. Al-H̱alīl's immense influence on Sībawayhi is highlighted in the tradition. Al-Faḫr al-Rāzī (d. 606/1210), for example, on the authority of Suyūṭī (*Iqtirāḥ* 205–206), is reported to have written that Sībawayhi put together (*ǧamaʿa*) in his book the data (*ʿulūm*, lit. sciences) that he derived (*istafādahā*) from al-H̱alīl.

Sībawayhi also mentions 21 times an anonymous group to which he refers as *naḥwiyyūn*. Views differ widely as to the exact meaning of the term (cf. Carter 1972: 76; Talmon 1982), but it is obvious that Sībawayhi almost invariably criticizes their views and at times even the views of Yūnus when he sides with them. The reason for this is most probably that he disapproves of their speculative approach and their keen interest in creating hypothetical forms and constructions that do not occur in speech in spite of their resemblance to attested usage. This may be corroborated by the fact that in his *Kitāb al-ʿAyn* al-H̱alīl mentions a similarly anonymous group of scholars whom he calls *naḥārīr* (pl. of *niḥrīr*, skillful or learned) and whom he explicitly accuses of creating words that do conform to Arabic word composition and patterns but that are neologisms that are not permissible (*lā taǧūz*) in actual usage (Baalbaki 2008: 20).

5.3 Early Works and Sībawayhi's *Kitāb*

It is evident that the *Kitāb* does not emerge from a vacuum but rather builds on previous grammatical activity that Sībawayhi himself, let alone the later sources, refer to. Sībawayhi's contemporaries as of the second half of the 2nd/8th century until the early 3rd/9th century (such as Aṣmaʿī, who is quoted in the *Kitāb* and died in 216/831 at the ripe age of 91) are reported in the biographical sources to have tirelessly collected linguistic data from the Bedouin—a process known as *ǧamʿ al-luġa* "collection of variants." There are no reports that Sībawayhi himself made any journey to the desert for data collection from the Bedouin, but his frequent references to them in statements like *samiʿnā l-ʿArab* (we heard the Arabs) or *min afwāh al-ʿArab* (from the mouths of the Arabs) strongly indicate that he had direct contact with native speakers whom he regarded as the ultimate source of the data he seeks, that is, *kalām al-ʿArab* (speech of the Arabs). Unlike the *Kitāb*, the extant sources authored by Sībawayhi's contemporaries mainly belong to the lexicographical tradition but incidentally touch upon grammatical issues. These sources include the two root-based lexica by al-H̱alīl, *Kitāb al-ʿAyn*, and by Abū ʿAmr al-Šaybānī (d. 206/821), *Kitāb al-Ǧīm*, and the thematically arranged lexicon of Abū ʿUbayd al-Qāsim b. Sallām (d. 224/838), *al-Ġarīb al-Muṣannaf*. In addition to several less extensive works on various aspects of lexicography—such as *laḥn al-ʿāmma* (common errors), *aḍdād* (words with two contrary meanings), *ištiqāq* (derivation particularly of proper nouns), *nawādir* (rare usage), and *amṯāl* (proverbs)—two groups of books deserve special attention (cf. Baalbaki 2008: 26). The first of these are three linguistically oriented exegetical works that include a sizable body of grammatical material. These are Farrāʾ's (d. 207/822) *Maʿānī l-Qurʾān*, Abū ʿUbayda Maʿmar b. al-Muṯannā's (d. 209/824) *Maǧāz al-Qurʾān*, and al-Aḫfaš al-Awsaṭ's (d. 215/830) *Maʿānī l-Qurʾān*. Being Quranic commentaries, these works are structurally different from the *Kitāb* since their grammatical content is determined by the text they interpret, none of them offering a comprehensive and systematic study of grammar. The second group comprises two grammatical works attributed to contemporaries of Sībawayhi's. The first, titled *al-Ǧumal fī l-Naḥw*, is erroneously attributed to al-Ḫalīl, whereas its real author is most probably Ibn Šuqayr (d. 317/929), as Tanūḫī (d. 442/1050) asserts (*Tārīḫ* 48). The other title is *Muqaddima fī l-Naḥw*, and its attribution to Ḫalaf al-Aḥmar (d. 180/796) is extremely doubtful and is not supported by the later grammatical or biographical sources. Even more doubtful is the attribution of grammatical works to pre-Sībawayhi grammarians, such as *Šarḥ al-ʿilal* to ʿAbdallāh b. Abī Isḥāq and *Ikmāl* and *Ǧāmiʿ* to Īsā b. ʿUmar.

One can safely conclude that the *Kitāb* is the first unquestionably authentic book on Arabic grammar. Whether its approach represents a departure from earlier grammar is open to question. Talmon (2003) compares the grammatical teaching of al-Ḫalīl and Sībawayhi with the extra-Kitābian linguistically oriented sources of the 2nd/8th and 3rd/9th centuries and concludes that the two grammarians considered their teaching distinct from the main grammatical theory up to their time. He calls this theory "The Old Iraqi School of Grammar," whose main exponent is the Kufan Farrāʾ. The theory was not restricted to the Kufan milieu since the two Basrans, Abū ʿUbayda and al-Aḫfaš al-Awsaṭ, also represent a grammatical tradition that is not identical with Sībawayhi's. Accordingly, Talmon speaks of the "innovations" and "reformation" or even "revolution," which al-Ḫalīl and Sībawayhi introduced to grammatical study. Baalbaki (2005: 413–416) points out that, although Talmon admits that the corpus of material presented in the sources is of "fragmentary character" and often talks of the "absence of concrete textual evidence" and of the data being "too meager for definite conclusions," his hypothesis claims a global interpretation of the grammatical activity and the relations among the grammarians in the early period of Arabic grammar. To be sure, the efforts of al-Ḫalīl and Sībawayhi represent a major development in the history of Arabic grammar, yet it is certainly an exaggeration to talk of a "revolution" that took place at their hands or to claim that the theoretical differences between them and other grammarians are due to the different grammatical "traditions" or "schools" at this stage. Whatever the case may be, the issues presented in the *Kitāb* dominated the grammatical tradition for centuries after Sībawayhi. Largely overshadowing other works, the *Kitāb* was viewed with a kind of sanctity and was often referred to as *Qurʾān al-naḥw* (the Quran of grammar; cf. Abū l-Ṭayyib, *Marātib* 106), in a rare instance of associating the word Quran with something other than the Revealed Book. To quote Versteegh (1997: 39), "Without exaggeration one could say that the entire linguistic tradition in Arabic is nothing but a huge commentary on the *Kitāb* Sībawayhi." With the surge in interest in Arabic linguistics over the last few decades, there has been increasing awareness of the centrality of the *Kitāb* to the ALT as a whole and consequently serious appreciation of the ALT itself in the history of linguistic ideas.

The bulk of the *Kitāb* comprises a large body of transmitted data that Sībawayhi reports and analyzes. This body of attested material generally known as *samāʿ* (lit. hearing) represents for him *kalām al-ʿArab* (speech of the Arabs), which falls under four major categories: the Quran; the prophetic traditions (*ḥadīṯ*); the speech of the Bedouin (including proverbs and speech patterns or idiomatic expressions); and poetry. There are, of course, methodological problems associated with each of these categories (cf. Baalbaki 2008: 35–47), but Sībawayhi is keen to accommodate the peculiarities of each type within his overall system of grammatical analysis. In the case of poetry, for example, he devotes an early chapter to poetic license (*Kitāb* I, 26–32) to highlight the inherent differences between *šiʿr* (poetry) and *kalām* (in the narrow sense of prose). He also refers repeatedly throughout the *Kitāb* to the difference between the two genres and discusses in separate chapters phenomena that are unique to poetic usage (ibid., I, 269–274; IV, 204–216). But Sībawayhi is not interested merely in reporting and describing attested linguistic phenomena; rather, he tries to justify them, to examine the relationships that exist among the constituents of structure, and to propose theoretical origins (*aṣl*, pl. *uṣūl*) from which forms and patterns might have developed. In this respect, he resorts to the notion of *ʿamal* (government) in interpreting various syntactical relations among the various constituents of structure and to the notion of *taqdīr* (suppletive insertion; also implied in contexts in which the terms *iḍmār* (suppression), *ḥaḏf* (elision), and *niyya* (intention) appear in ascribing various formal and semantic aspects of the utterance to elements that are not uttered but are essential in analyzing structure). A detailed examination of his analytical methods is beyond the present scope, but a glimpse at some of the more fundamental of these is essential for achieving an appreciation of the uniqueness of his approach in the tradition as a whole.

Sībawayhi adopts a number of methods and strategies in the analysis of his linguistic data. The distinction between norm and anomaly is obviously a vital preliminary step in the process of organizing the vast and often conflicting material at his disposal. His priority is to defend the norm, but since he almost universally accepts attested usage he also has to interpret and justify (at times even criticize but not dismiss) anomalous material. Commenting on the Tamīmī usage *ḏahaba ams-u* ("Yesterday-NOM has gone") instead of *ḏahaba amsi*, which occurs in all other dialects, he says that the norm in *ams* is to have a final *-i* (*kasra*), hence *amsi*. However, the Tamīmīs have modified this norm to make the word a triptote, and hence it takes nominative case in the Tamīmī usage when it is agent (*Kitāb* III, 283). In another instance, he describes the form *minhim* ("from them") in the dialect of Rabīʿa, instead of *minhum*, as bad usage (*luġa radīʾa*) but justifies its occurrence on phonological grounds (ibid., IV, 196–197). By adopting the concept of "basic rule" (cf. Baalbaki 2008: 134–152), which is implicit throughout the *Kitāb*, Sībawayhi ensures that the usage he considers to be most common or most representative of, for example, a form, pattern, or particle is recognized as the actual manifestation of accepted norm and is not undermined by attested material that does not conform to it. The recognition of "basic rules" allows Sībawayhi to make his data much more manageable than would have been the case had he adopted an indiscriminate approach that lends equal weight to the normal and anomalous.

The practical side to the distinction between norm and anomaly is that Sībawayhi allows the generation of material through *qiyās* (analogy) on the basis of the former but not the latter. His approach to the norm–anomaly dichotomy may be viewed as part of his overall effort to demonstrate the coherency of his data and consequently the ability of his analytical system to highlight this coherency. In this system that not only describes usage but also analyzes and interprets it, a *ʿilla* (cause) has to be sought for the major phenomena as well as for the minutest details of attested speech. A relatively small number of *ʿilal* are used to unveil what the later linguists refer to as the *ḥikma* (wisdom) that underlies *kalām al-ʿArab*. Among these *ʿilal* are *kaṯra* (frequency), *ḫiffa* (lightness), *ḥaml ʿalā l-akṯar* (analogy based on the more frequent usage), *saʿat al-kalām* (latitude of speech), and *ʿilm al-muḫāṭab bihi* (the addressee's knowledge of an implied element). For instance, *taḫfīf* (lightening) is cited as the reason for *tarḫīm* (euphonic elision), that is, the elision of the final parts of certain words, mainly in the vocative. An example of this is in the proper noun Ḥāriṯ, which may be changed to Ḥāri without the final consonant in *yā Ḥāri* "O Ḥāri"(*Kitāb* II, 239–241).

Until a few decades ago, early Arabic grammar, including Sībawayhi's *Kitāb*, was judged in the light of later sources and commentaries rather than the early sources themselves. An unfortunate consequence of this method is the assumption that Sībawayhi, like later authors, is largely preoccupied with *lafẓ* (form) at the expense of *maʿnā* (meaning). As scholars started to focus on examining the text of the *Kitāb*, there emerged an increasing awareness of the interrelatedness of form, *lafẓ* and meaning, *maʿnā* in Sībawayhi's method of analysis. Expressions of the type *maʿnā l-naṣb/al-fiʿl/al-fāʾ/al-tanwīn/al-taʿaǧǧub* (the meaning of the accusative/the verb/the conjunctive *fāʾ*/the nunation/the exclamation; *Kitāb* I, 320, 310; III, 68; II, 229; I, 328, respectively) clearly demonstrate the inseparability of form and meaning. A most telling example is the chapter on the *fāʾ*, which is followed by the subjunctive *Kitāb* III, 28–41). Sībawayhi proposes the construction

(3)	*lā*	*ta-ʾtī-nī*	*fa-tu-ḥaddiṯ-a-nī/*	*fa-tu-ḥaddiṯ-u-nī*
	not	you-come-me	and-you-converse-SBJ-me/	and-you-converse-INDC-me

and ascribes two possibilities of meaning to each of the subjunctive and indicative. In the subjunctive, the sentence means either "You do not visit me, so how can you converse with me"? or "You visit me often, but you do not converse with me," whereas in the indicative it means either "You neither visit me nor converse with me" or "You do not visit me, and you are conversing with me now" (cf. Baalbaki 2001). In an essentially experimental fashion, he then introduces various changes to the model sentence and illustrates how the case of the verb after *fāʾ* is linked to a specific meaning in each construction. For example, he discusses the meaning of both the subjunctive and indicative in each of the following related constructions:

(4a) *mā ta-'tī-nā fa-takallam-a/ fa-takallam-u illā*
not you-come-us and-you-speak-SBJ/ and you-speak-INDC except
bi-l-ğamīl-i
with-DEF-courtesy-GEN
"You never visit us and speak but courteously"

(4b) *lā ta-'tī-nā fa-tu-ḥaddiṯ-a-nā/ fa-tu-ḥaddiṯ-u-nā*
not you-come-us and-you-converse-SBJ-us/ and-you- converse-INDC-us
illā izdad-nā fī-ka raġbat-an
except increase-our in-you.M interest-ACC
"You never visit us and converse with us without us becoming more interested in you" and

(4c) *wadd-a law ta-'tī -hi fa-tu-ḥaddiṯ-a-hu/*
wished-he if you-come-him and-you-converse-SBJ-him/
fa-tu-ḥaddiṯ-u-hu
and-you-converse-INDC-him
"He wished that you would visit him so that you converse with him."

The claim that Sībawayhi's grammar lacks any systematic semantic component (Itkonen 1991: 148) is thus contradicted by the fact that *maʿnā* is inextricably linked to *lafẓ* in his analysis of structure. Furthermore, *maʿnā* in the *Kitāb* is directly related to the intention of the speaker (*mutakallim)* and the message he seeks to impart to his addressee or listener (*muḫāṭab*). The role of the linguist is thus to trace the mental operations that accompany the utterance and that dictate its formal and semantic characteristics. Sībawayhi's analysis of language as interaction between the speaker and the listener, that is, as social behavior that takes place in a specific context, is unmatched in the ALT. Successful communication becomes a type of social obligation whose fulfillment depends on the speaker's competence in deciding which utterance can best express his intentions as well as on the listener's competence in the analysis of the utterances he is addressed with and, if necessary, in responding to them correctly.

The issue of whether the theoretical frameworks proposed by Sībawayhi (and largely adopted by later grammarians; see Section 5.4) resemble certain modern linguistic theories has been hotly contested. From the typological point of view, for example, Bohas et al. (1990: 38) argue that Sībawayhi's grammatical system belongs to a class which analyzes utterances "in terms of operations performed by the speaker in order to achieve a specific effect on the allocutee." This is generally true of Sībawayhi's analysis of speech and its context of situation. It should be remembered, however, that he at times examines constructions of considerable complexity that he formulates (cf. *Kitāb* II, 404–406) but that certainly are not used and hence have absolutely no communicative value. One such example is as follows:

(5) *ayy-u* *man* *in* *ya-'ti-nā* *nu-'ṭi-hi* *nu-krim-u-hu*
which-NOM who if he-come.JSV-us we-give.JSV-him we-honor-INDC-him
(roughly translated as "Whom—if he comes to us we give him—shall we honor"?)

Scarce as they are, such constructions—which seem to be precursors of grammatical drills extensively used by Mubarrad (d. 285/898) and other later grammarians—are probably meant to illustrate the correct syntactical positions that the various components of the structure ought to occupy (Baalbaki 2008: 217) and hence do not negate Sībawayhi's general purpose of describing *kalām al-ʿArab* so that it can be replicated correctly.

In the later tradition, one finds pedagogical examples in which extended sentence structures are constructed showing a large panoply of governed and governing elements in their respective functions. In the following example from the 4th-/10th-century grammarian Ṣaymarī (*Tabṣira* I, 123), the verb is shown governing nine different clausal dependents, eight accusative and the nominative governance of the agent.

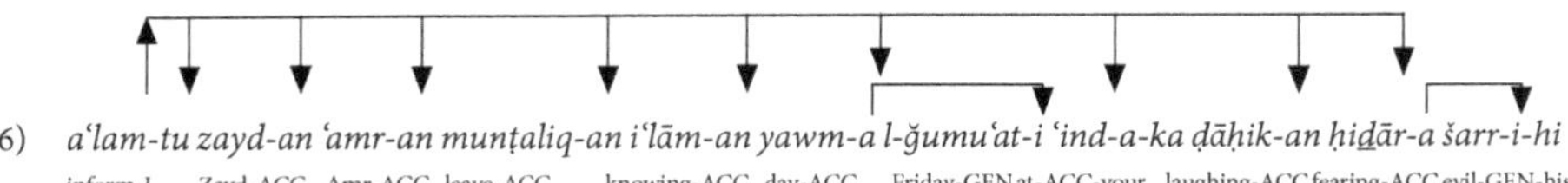

(6) *aʿlam-tu zayd-an ʿamr-an munṭaliq-an iʿlām-an yawm-a l-ǧumuʿat-i ʿind-a-ka ḍāḥik-an ḥiḏār-a šarr-i-hi*
inform-I Zayd-ACC Amr-ACC leave-ACC knowing-ACC day-ACC Friday-GEN at-ACC-your laughing-ACC fearing-ACC evil-GEN-his
"Friday at your place laughing, I seriously informed Zayd that Amr was leaving out of fear of his evil."

From a different perspective, Carter (1973) argues that Sībawayhi, in reducing the language to a set of functions, uses a method that has intrinsic similarities with immediate constituent analysis. Carter, however, insists that the parallels between Arabic grammar and Western linguistics—as in comparing reconstructed underlying forms and the ordered rules of deriving the passive verb in Arabic with notions of deep structure and transformation—are purely coincidental similarities between unrelated linguistic systems (Carter 1994: 386). For his part, Owens (1988) concludes that the Arabic grammatical theory of governance is based on a form of dependency grammar, although there are differences between the two.

Whereas interesting, at times even remarkable parallels do exist between the Arabic grammatical model and modern linguistics, the question is how relevant the latter is for understanding the former. For the purpose of ordering the Arabic linguistic theory among the many approaches known to linguistic description (cf. Owens 2000a: 119), comparison with modern linguistics can yield results that should interest any student of the history of linguistic ideas. The danger remains, however, that in looking for parallels with modern linguistics, researchers may be tempted to fully identify the Arabic grammatical theory with a particular Western approach and become oblivious to the unique sociohistoric context of Arabic grammar and the issues that are specific to the data on which it is based and to the Islamic disciplines to which it is related.

5.4 Grammar from the 3rd/9th Century Onward

Sībawayhi's basic analytical tools and methods were never really challenged throughout the tradition, except for Ibn Maḍāʾ's (d. 592/1196) unique attempt to refute some of the basic axioms of the grammatical theory, including *ʿamal* (government), *qiyās* (analogy), *taqdīr* (suppletive insertion), and the speculative type of *ʿilal*. There were, of course, questions on which individual grammarians did not see eye to eye with Sībawayhi, perhaps the most famous of which are the 134 *masʾala*s (issues) that Ibn Wallād (d. 332/944) in his *Kitāb al-Intiṣār* (cf. Bernards 1997) interprets as disagreement between the two Basran grammarians Sībawayhi and Mubarrad (d. 285/898). The Basran–Kufan divide is interesting in this respect. Although biographical and grammatical sources of the 4th/10th century onward often generalize the differences between two established *maḏhab*s ("schools"; cf. Carter 2000 for characteristics of schools), about a third of Ibn al-Anbārī's (d. 577/1181) *masʾala*s in his *Inṣāf* are actual points of disagreement between the Kufan grammarian Farrāʾ (d. 207/822) on one hand and the two main Basran figures, Sībawayhi and Mubarrad, on the other (Baalbaki 1981). This notwithstanding, Farrāʾ and the other Kufans use the same analytical tools and methods as the ones used by Sībawayhi. Thus, while they might differ with him or other Basrans on how rigorously in a certain case *qiyās* should be applied or *samāʿ* should be admitted, they never challenge the very use of *qiyās* or *samāʿ* and indeed any of the other tools of analysis—such as *taqdīr*, *ʿilla*, and *aṣl*—Sībawayhi so methodically applies in the *Kitāb*.

Grammarians after Sībawayhi viewed his *Kitāb* as the ultimate, often irrefutable source of truth in grammatical matters, but this does not mean that the ALT was static after Sībawayhi [Larcher, "ALT II"]. We propose here to highlight the major developments that took place after Sībawayhi, particularly in the realm of *naḥw*. *Ṣarf*, which witnessed relatively little change throughout the tradition, will appropriately be discussed in a separate section.

A marked development in approach, but always within the parameters of Sībawayhi's grammatical theory, is already obvious in the first major work after *Kitāb*, namely, Mubarrad's *Muqtaḍab*. Mubarrad generally relies more than Sībawayhi on *qiyās* and thus often dismisses as impermissible usage that is attested through *samāʿ* (e.g., *Muqtaḍab* I, 269–270; II, 146, 249, 336). He even dismisses *qirāʾāt* (Quranic readings) for being incompatible with *qiyās* and ridicules the *qurrāʾ* (readers) who introduced them (ibid., I, 123; II, 134, 316; IV, 105, 124–125, 195). Compared with Sībawayhi, furthermore, there is in Mubarrad's approach to the notions of *ʿamal* (government) and *taʿlīl* (causation) an increase in the level of "complexity" and "sophistication." His terminology related to *ʿamal* reveals a tendency to classify and describe the *ʿawāmil* (operants) and to refer to them as a class in its own right. His terms include *ʿawāmil al-afʿāl* (operants that govern verbs), *ʿawāmil al-asmāʾ* (operants that govern nouns), *taṣarruf al-ʿāmil* (plasticity of the operant), *al-ʿaṭf ʿalā ʿāmilayni* (here, elision of two operants after a conjunction), and *bāb al-ʿawāmil* (class of operants; ibid., II, 6, 10; IV, 195, 300,(cf. Mubarrad, *Kāmil* I, 287; III, 99), 317, respectively). Similarly, the term *ʿilla*, in addition to its original sense of "cause," acquires the sense of "quality" or "detail" (Baalbaki 2008: 246–247) and can thus be used to refer to linguistic phenomena rather than to their causes. Thus, an expression like *wa-hāḏā yušraḥ fī bāb ʿalā ḥiyālihi bi-ǧamīʿ ʿilalihi* (and this will be explained with all its details in a separate chapter; ibid., II, 275) shows how *ʿilal* become inseparable from the phenomena for which they are recognized as causes.

Kitāb al-Uṣūl fī l-naḥw, authored by one of Mubarrad's students, Ibn al-Sarrāǧ (d. 316/929), represents a remarkable departure from the *Kitāb*, not in terminology and content but in arrangement and style of presentation and argumentation. In the book's introduction, Ibn al-Sarrāǧ distinguishes between two types of *ʿilal*, the first of which comprises grammatical facts through which the speech of the Arabs is learned (e.g., that every agent is nominative), whereas the second—called *ʿillat al-ʿilla* (meta-*ʿilla*)—unveils the *ḥikma* (wisdom) embedded in that speech (e.g., for what reason is the agent nominative; *Uṣūl* I, 35). In a conscious effort at classifying grammatical material, he systematically separates the main or fundamental issues of a certain *bāb* or topic (hence, *uṣūl*) from the subsidiary or less essential questions or problems (hence, *furūʿ*). The distinction between *uṣūl* and *furūʿ* goes back to Mubarrad's teacher, Māzinī (d. 249/863), in his book on morphology called *Taṣrīf*. Mubarrad himself generalizes this distinction to the realm of syntax in his *Muqtaḍab*, but it is Ibn al-Sarrāǧ who opens the door wide for the systematic organization of the material according to the principle of *uṣūl* and *furūʿ*. In this sense one can appreciate the famous statement that, by applying his *uṣūl*, Ibn al-Sarrāǧ rationalized a previously "insane" grammar (*mā zāla l-naḥw maǧnūnan ḥattā ʿaqqalahu Ibn al-Sarrāǧ bi-uṣūlihi*; Yāqūt, *Muʿǧam* VI, 2535).

The interest that both Mubarrad and Ibn al-Sarrāǧ show in *taʿlīl* and *uṣūl* has surely contributed to the emergence of the two closely related genres of grammatical writing that, unlike the more widespread surveys of syntax and morphology, deal exclusively either with *ʿilal* assigned by the grammarians practically for every linguistic phenomenon or with the *uṣūl*, that is, the theoretical and methodological issues on which the discipline of grammar rests. One of the first books on *ʿilal* is authored by a Muʿtazilite, Zaǧǧāǧī (d. 337/949) and is titled *al-Īḍāḥ fī ʿilal al-naḥw* (cf. Versteegh 1995 for translation and comments). Zaǧǧāǧī distinguishes between three types of *ʿilal*, namely, *taʿlīmiyya* (pedagogical), *qiyāsiyya* (analogical), and *ǧadaliyya naẓariyya* (argumentational-theoretical; *Īḍāḥ* 64–66). The first type is descriptive and comprises the grammatical rules of Arabic such as might be used in classroom instruction. For example, in the construction *inna Zayd-an qāʾim-un* (Indeed Zayd is standing), the accusative in the noun of *inna* and the nominative in its predicate are both attributed to *inna* itself. The second type provides explanations for the rules, based on the principle of analogy (*qiyās*). Hence, the fact that *inna* causes its noun to be in the accusative is said to be due to its resemblance to transitive verbs that likewise cause the direct object to be in the accusative. Theoretical arguments related to grammatical debates are represented by the third type. One can thus debate here the nature of *inna*'s resemblance to transitive verbs and the reason for the occurrence of the accusative noun (*Zayd-an*) linearly before the nominative one (*qāʾim-un*).

Another Muʿtazilite, Ibn Ǧinnī (d. 392/1002), raises in his *Ḫaṣāʾiṣ* fundamental issues of methodology and epistemology and tirelessly tries to demonstrate the inherently organized and harmonious nature of Arabic and the *ḥikma* that underlies the speech of the Arabs in an almost unprecedented manner in the tradition (for the main features of *Ḫaṣāʾiṣ*, see Guillaume 2000: 276–279). He also argues that *ʿilal* of the grammarians are closer to those used by the theologians (*mutakallimūn*) than to those used by jurists (*mutafaqqihūn*; *Ḫaṣāʾiṣ* I, 48). In spite of the adherence of Zaǧǧāǧī and Ibn Ǧinnī to Muʿtazilite theology and logic, they both fully subscribe to the principle of the autonomy of grammar. In fact, Zaǧǧāǧī clearly demarcates the objectives of the logicians from those of the grammarians (*Īḍāḥ* 48), and Ibn Ǧinnī explicitly distinguishes between *taʿlīl* in grammar and jurisprudence but recognizes certain similarities between the two neighboring disciplines of grammar and logic with respect to the notion of *taʿlīl* on which they converge (Suleiman 1999: 66). Also worthy of mention under the genre of *taʿlīl* are Ibn al-Warrāq's (d. 381/991) *ʿIlal al-naḥw*, Ibn al-Anbārī's (d. 577/1181) *Asrār al-ʿArabiyya*, and ʿUkbarī's (d. 616/1219) *al-Lubāb fī ʿilal al-iʿrāb wa-l-bināʾ*, all of which exhaustively cite causes for the phenomena of *naḥw* and, to a lesser extent, *ṣarf*.

Much of the material known as *uṣūl al-naḥw* appears in the previously cited works on *taʿlīl*. Among the more famous works that specifically deal with *uṣūl* are Ibn al-Anbārī's *Lumaʿ al-adilla fī uṣūl al-naḥw* and *al-Iġrāb fī ǧadal al-iʿrāb* and Suyūṭī's (d. 911/1505) *al-Iqtirāḥ fī ʿilm uṣūl al-naḥw*. Both authors define *uṣūl al-naḥw* as a discipline that investigates the *adilla* (proofs) of grammar (*Lumaʿ* 80; *Iqtirāḥ* 27). According to Ibn al-Anbārī (*Lumaʿ* 81 ff.), the three *adilla* that make up *uṣūl al-naḥw* are *naql* (transmitted data), *qiyās* (analogy), and *istiṣḥāb al-ḥāl* (presumption of continuity; i.e., continuing to apply a certain *ʿilla* until it can be proven no longer applicable). To the other two components, *naql* (or *samāʿ*) and *qiyās*, Suyūṭī adds *iǧmāʿ* (consensus) on the authority of Ibn Ǧinnī. Accordingly, methodological issues related to these notions prevail in the *uṣūl* tradition, such as the following questions: What dialects are admissible to the corpus? What are the time limits for accepting transmitted data? Is consensus among grammarians an irrefutable proof of sound judgment? Should analogical extension apply to anomalous material? Which has precedence in case of conflict: *samāʿ* or *qiyās*? In addition to such issues, Suyūṭī identifies 24 types of *ʿilla* (*Iqtirāḥ* 115–119) and devotes a special section of his book to what he calls *masālik al-ʿilla*, that is, methods for establishing a *ʿilla*, such as reliance on explicit or implicit mention of a certain *ʿilla* by a trustworthy native speaker (ibid., 137–149; see detailed study in Suleiman 1999: 182–194).

To turn back to the 4th/10th century, it was clear by that time that grammar as a discipline was becoming increasingly speculative and that grammatical argumentation was impacted by the introduction of logic and philosophy to the linguistic sphere. A most striking example from the period is the Muʿtazilite grammarian Rummānī (d. 384/994), better known for his extensive commentary on the *Kitāb* in which he appears to be heavily influenced by logic. In his biography on Rummānī, Ibn al-Anbārī (*Nuzha* 233–235) notes that he, Rummānī, used to mix his writings with logic and cites Abū ʿAlī al-Fārisī (d. 377/987) as saying that his own grammatical teaching and Rummānī's cannot be the same thing.

The period from the 5th/11th century onward abounds with famous grammarians, some of whose works are still used today in some traditional institutions as textbooks for teaching grammar. Among these are Ibn Bābashād (d. 469/1077), Šantamarī (d. 476/1084), Zamaḫšarī (d. 538/1144), Ibn al-Dahhān (d. 569/1174), Ibn al-Anbārī (d. 577/1181), Suhaylī (d. 581/1185), Ibn Yaʿīš (d. 643/1245), Ibn al-Ḥāǧib (d. 646/1249), Ibn ʿUṣfūr (d. 669/1271), Ibn Mālik (d. 672/1274), Astarābāḏī (d. after 686/1287), Ibn al-Nāẓim (686/1287), Abū Ḥayyān (d. 745/1344), Ibn Hišām (d. 761/1360), Ibn ʿAqīl (d. 769/1367), Ušmūnī (d.*c.* 900/1495), and Suyūṭī (d. 911/1505). Broadly speaking, works from this period are characterized by a growing interest in formal (*lafẓī*) considerations at the expense of meaning. There was thus a considerable shift in focus, and Sībawayhi's originality and his approach to language as a social interaction between a speaker and a listener in a defined context gave way to a pedantic and largely uninspiring approach. Sībawayhi's terminology, analytical tools, and even his *šawāhid* (attested and often ascribed material) were largely preserved, but his insight into the pragmatic role he assigns to the speaker and listener and the delicate balance he establishes between form and meaning were no longer on the minds of most grammarians. The stereotypic nature of the basic grammars notwithstanding, some authors such as Ibn al-Ḥāǧib and Astarābāḏī did show significant interest in speech acts [Larcher "ALT II"], while others, notably Suhaylī, strove to demonstrate that meaning has a larger role in determining case endings than is normally admitted in the mainstream theory (Baalbaki 2008: 290–297).

5.5 Morphology

The terms *ṣarf* or *taṣrīf* (also *ʿilm al-ṣarf/al-taṣrīf*) designate the study of morphology in the ALT. Sībawayhi's *Kitāb* is in roughly two equal parts, with *naḥw* preceding *ṣarf*. Most grammar books follow the same arrangement (e.g. Zaǧǧāǧī's *Ǧumal* and Zamaḫšarī's *Mufaṣṣal*), although there are exceptions, such as Mubarrad's *Muqtaḍab*, which starts with *ṣarf* but does not fully separate chapters that deal with it from those that deal with *naḥw*. Early in the tradition, Māzinī (d. 249/863) devotes his book entitled *Kitāb al-Taṣrīf* to morphological topics in isolation of syntax. This practice survived along with the more prevalent practice of including both *naḥw* and *ṣarf* under the same title. Among the most well-known works that are exclusively devoted to *ṣarf* are as follows: Ibn Ǧinnī's (d. 392/1002) *Munṣif*, *Sirr ṣināʿat al-iʿrāb*, and *al-Taṣrīf al-Mulūkī*; Muʾaddib's (d. after 338/949) *Daqāʾiq al-taṣrīf*; Ibn al-Ḥāǧib's (d. 646/1249) *Šāfiya*; Ibn ʿUṣfūr's (d. 669/1271) *Mumtiʿ*; and Astarābāḏī's (d. c. 686/1287) *Šarḥ Šāfiyat Ibn al-Ḥāǧib*. Throughout the tradition, the study of *ṣarf* was much less susceptible than *naḥw* to controversy or to differences in approach or rule formulation among the grammarians. Indeed, the same methods of morphological analysis adopted by Sībawayhi and Māzinī are applied by the later grammarians to yield very similar results.

Ibn Ǧinnī (*Munṣif* I, 4) typically defines the domain of *ṣarf* as the fixed form of words (*anfus al-kalim al-ṯābita*) in contrast to *naḥw*, which deals with the changes that words undergo (*aḥwālihi l-mutanaqqila*) due to the effect that the operants have on their case endings. He illustrates this by citing the following three constructions:

(7a) *qāma Bakr-un*
stood up Bakr-NOM
"Bakr stood up."

(7b) *ra'ay-tu Bakr-an*
saw-I Bakr-ACC
"I saw Bakr."

(7c) *marar-tu bi-Bakr-in*
passed-I with-Bakr-GEN
"I passed by Bakr."

As far as *naḥw* is concerned, each of the three different operants causes a change in the case ending of Bakr. Yet as a word or lexical unit (*kalima*), Bakr remains the same throughout since it is otherwise unaffected by the various operants.

But there are instances where the boundaries between *naḥw* and *ṣarf* are difficult to delineate. One such case is that of the passive participle, which as a morphological pattern belongs to *ṣarf* but which also belongs to *naḥw* by virtue of its being an operant that governs the agent of a passive verb (*nā'ib ʿan al-fāʿil*). It is interesting, for example, to see how the chapter on the agent of a passive verb in commentaries on *Alfiyya* (cf. Ibn ʿAqīl, *Šarḥ* 219–225) straddles both perspectives from which passive participles are examined. At another level, no distinction is made between phonology and morphophonology. In fact, phonetics is introduced in conjunction with one aspect of morphophonology, namely, assimilation (*idġām/iddiġām*), as in the *Kitāb* (IV, 431; cf. Owens 2000b: 296; [Embarki, "Phonetics"]; [Hellmuth, "Phonology"]; [Edzard, "Philology"]). Hence, Sībawayhi dealt with the points and manner of articulation in order to explain how certain characteristics of articulation can cause gemination or prevent it (*Kitāb* IV, 436, ll. 15–17).

The study of morphology is generally divided into two parts, explicitly expressed in later works (e.g., Ibn ʿUṣfūr, *Mumtiʿ* I, 31–33; cf. Bohas and Guillaume 1984: 17; Bohas et al. 1990: 73). The first of these, *taṣrīf* (derivation), includes the total range of morphological patterns of verbs and nouns [Ratcliffe, "Morphology"]. Words are presumed to be derived from consonantal roots and belong to fixed patterns that often have semantic values. The pattern *mafʿūl*, for instance, is typically a passive participle, as in *maktūb* "written." Note that some monographs, such as works on *faʿala* and *afʿala*, deal specifically with the meanings of certain patterns: for example,

Aṣmaʿī's (d. 216/831) *Faʿala wa-afʿala* (form I and form IV verbs); Ṣaġānī's (d. 650/1252) *Kitāb al-infiʿāl* (form VII verbs). To express the relationship between a root and the various patterns derived from it, grammarians represent the root by the triliteral template *f- ʿ- l*, where the *f* stands for the first radical (*fāʾ al-fiʿl*), the ʿ for the second (*ʿayn al-fiʿl*), and the *l* for the third (*lām al-fiʿl*). The root is regarded as the "basic" component of a word, to which are added vowels and, at times, prefixes, infixes, and suffixes ([Hellmuth, "Phonology"] vs. [Ratcliffe, "Morphology"]). The notion of *mīzān ṣarfī* (morphological measure) is introduced to identify the patterns to which words belong. The *mīzān* takes into account the root of the word, its vowels, and, where applicable, its affixes. These 10 affixes, usually carrying morphemic value, are known as *ḥurūf al-ziyāda* (augmented consonants) and are combined in mnemonic phrases such as *al-yawma tansāhu* (Today you shall forget it), *saʾaltumūnīhā* (You asked me it), and *hawītu l-simān* (I loved the plump women). Accordingly, verbal and nominal patterns are identified based on the *mīzān*. For example, beginning with the form I verb "he hit," *ḍaraba, iḍ**ṭ**araba,* **ist***aḍraba, ḍ***ā***rib, ḍar***r***āb,* and **mun***ḍarib* belong to the patterns *faʿala, i**ft**aʿala,* **ist***afʿala, f***ā***ʿil, faʿʿāl,* and **mun***faʿil,* respectively, the added consonants indicated here in boldface. Numerous conventions also apply to the use of the *mīzān* (cf. Astarābāḏī, *Šarḥ* I, 10). For example, the fourth and fifth radicals in quadriliterals and quinqueliterals are expressed by reduplicating *lām*; hence, *jaʿfar* "brook" and *safarǧal* "quince" are of the patterns *faʿlal* and *faʿallal,* respectively. Another rule is that, if the augmented consonant is a reduplication, it is represented by the relevant consonant in the template *f- ʿ- l* and not by the actual consonant of the word itself. Hence, *qaṭṭaʿa* "to tear apart" from *qaṭaʿa* "cut," is of the pattern *faʿʿala* and not **faʿṭala*. In contrast, augmented consonants that are not reduplications are retained in the pattern, as in *mustaqbal* (future) and *ʿanbas* (lion), whose patterns are *mustafʿal* and *fanʿal,* respectively.

The second part of morphology comprises the morphophonological rules that account for the change words undergo from a supposed *aṣl* (origin) without an accompanying change in meaning. In many cases, the *aṣl* is posed to demonstrate the rules of vowel mutation (*iʿlāl*). For example, *qāma* and *yaqūmu* are said to have as their *aṣl* **qawama* and **yaqwumu*. The surface form *yaqūmu* is thus presumed to have been derived from **yaqwumu* through an intermediate stage involving metathesis, as in (8):

(8) **yaqwumu* = underlying form (*aṣl*)>
**yaquwmu* via metathesis *(naql)* of *u-w* >
yaqūmu = surface form

Although the likes of **qawama* and **yaqwumu* are almost never used as surface forms, their assumption, according to the grammarians, is based on analogy to their "sound" counterparts, such as *kataba* and *yaktubu*, which display no discrepancy in this instance between the basic (*aṣl*) and surface forms. It is further supported by the fact that the *wāw* surfaces in other derivatives such as *qawwama* "erect," *qāwama* "resist," and *taqāwama* "mutually resist." Similarly, the *aṣl* of *maqūl* and *mabīʿ* are **maqwūl and *mabyūʿ*, both on the analogy of the "sound" counterpart (e.g., *maktūb*), their surface form explicated by various morphophonological changes analogous to those in (8). Other than *iʿlāl*, these morphophonological processes include *ibdāl* (substitution), *ziyāda* (augmentation), *ḥaḏf* (omission), *idġām* (gemination), *qalb* (mutation of glides), *naql* (metathesis between glides and vowels; see (8)), and *waqf* (pause). As far as the historicity of the proposed *uṣūl* is concerned, Ibn Ǧinnī clearly stated (*Munṣif* I, 190–191) that when grammarians consider **qawama* to be the *aṣl* of *qāma* and **istaqwama* the *aṣl* of *istaqāma* they simply state that the proposed *aṣl* would have been expected had the norm applied and do not refer to any prior stage of the language.

Grammarians apply to *ṣarf* several of the strategies they employ in their study of *naḥw*. Section 5.3 pointed out that the notion of "basic rules" helps make the data more manageable, while at the same time anomalous material is usually interpreted and admitted to the corpus of acceptable linguistic usage. This is closely paralleled in *ṣarf* by the concept of *ilḥāq* (appending), which embraces extremely complex rules through which triliterals are said to be appended to quadriliterals and quinqueliterals and quadriliterals are appended to quinqueliterals (Baalbaki 2001–2002). For example, *ğadwal* "creek" of the triliteral root *ǦDL* is appended to *ğaʿfar* of the quadriliteral root *ǦʿFR*, and *ğaḥanfal* "thick-lipped" (*ǦḤFL*) is appended to *safarğal* (*SFRǦL*):

(9) Operation of *ilḥāq* on two words

	ğ	a	d	Ø	a	l	ğ	a	ḥ	a	Ø	f	a	l
attached to pattern represented by							*attached to pattern represented by*							
	ğ	a	ʿ	f	a	r	s	a	f	a	r	ğ	a	l
=	f	a	ʿ	l	a	l	f	a	ʿ	a	l	l	a	l
				⇓							⇓			
				yielding							*yielding*			
	ğ	a	d	w	a	l	ğ	a	ḥ	a	n	f	a	l

As a result, the number of the basic morphological patterns that are acknowledged within a closed system is reduced considerably as several patterns are condensed into one and rare or deviant examples are appended to the nearest frequent or "normal" pattern available. For example, *hammariš* "ill-tempered old woman," the only quadriliteral example of the pattern *faʿʿalil*, is appended to quinqueliterals of the type *qahbalis* "huge woman," *ğaḥmariš* "old woman," and *ṣahṣaliq* "vehement voice" (cf. Sībawayhi, *Kitāb* IV, 302, 330). It should be noted that appended consonants, such as *n* in *ğaḥanfal* and *m* in *hammariš*, are not individually morphemic in contrast to consonantal affixes (e.g., *m* and *t* in *mustaqbal*).

Beyond the spheres of *ištiqāq* and *ilḥāq*, Ibn Ǧinnī introduced a general principle for justifying morphologically deviant examples. He argued that such examples serve as an indication (*manbaha*) of the original from which preceded a change that took place in the pattern it represents (*Ḫaṣāʾiṣ* I, 159–163, 256–264; *Munṣif* I, 190–191). For example, the attested form *istarwaḥa* "breathe" is anomalous because, contrary to *qiyās*, it was not changed to *istarāḥa*. Its occurrence, however, according to Ibn Ǧinnī serves a specific purpose, namely, to indicate that the origin of verbs like *istaqāma* "stand erect" and *istaʿāna* "seek help" are **istaqwama* and **istaʿwana*. Through this interpretation, Ibn Ǧinnī not only exploited the occurrence of an anomaly to reinforce, rather than to undermine, the norm for the pattern involved but also highlighted the wisdom (*ḥikma*; cf. *Munṣif* I, 277) that characterizes Arabic in retaining anomalous forms. The notion of *ḥikma* is also strongly implied in the newly discovered genre of writing that deals exclusively with morphological *taʿlīl*. The publication of Muʾaddib's (d. after 338/949) *Daqāʾiq al-taṣrīf* brought to light the existence in the ALT of attempts that exhaustively provide justification for morphological phenomena (Baalbaki 2006). Muʾaddib's reference (*Daqāʾiq* 25, 343) to a group of scholars of morphology, whom he calls *aṣḥāb al-taṣrīf* (morphologists) or *mutaʿāṭū hāḏihi l-ṣināʿa* (practitioners of this craft), strongly suggests that by the early 4th/10th century *ṣarf* was increasingly gaining independence from *naḥw*, although it shared the key strategies of grammatical analysis.

Glossary: Technical Linguistic Terms Used in This Article

aḍdād	words with two contrary meanings
adilla (pl. of *dalīl*)	proofs
aḥwāl mutanaqqila	changes that words undergo due to the effect the operants have on their case endings
ʿamal	government
amṯāl (pl. of *maṯal*)	proverbs
aṣḥāb al-taṣrīf	morphologists
aṣl (sg. of *uṣūl*)	origin, original form, pattern; the main or fundamental issue of a certain *bāb* or topic
ʿaṭf ʿalā ʿāmilayni	elision of two operants after a conjunction
ʿawāmil	operants, governors
ʿawāmil al-afʿāl	operants that govern verbs
ʿawāmil al-asmāʾ	operants that govern nouns
badal	substitute (appositive)
balāġiyyūn	rhetoricians
fʿl	three root consonants representing basic morphological template
fiʿl	verb
fiqh	jurisprudence
furūʿ	subsidiary or less essential questions or problems, marked structures

futūḥāt	conquests
ǧamʿ al-luġa	collection of linguistic data
ġarīb	strange usage
ḥarf	particle (part of speech), letter, sound
ḥikma	wisdom
ḥurūf al-ziyāda	augmented consonants
ḫabīṯ	repugnant usage
ibdāl	substitution of one consonant for another
idġām/iddiġām	assimilation, gemination
iḍmār	deletion, suppression
iǧmāʿ	consensus, esp. consensus of experts
ilḥāq	appending, analytic morphophonological process deriving expanded form on basis of another existing pattern (*wazn*)
ʿilla (sg. of *ʿilal*)	cause, quality, explanation, detail; in phonology, conditioned change of long vowels
ʿillat al-ʿilla	meta-*ʿilla*
ʿilal ǧadaliyya naẓariyya	argumentational-theoretical explanation
ʿilal qiyāsiyya	explanation by analogy
ʿilal taʿlīmiyya	explanation for pedagogical purposes
iʿrāb	declension, case, and mode endings/categories
ism	noun
istifhām	question
istiṣḥāb al-ḥāl	presumption of continuity
ištiqāq	derivation
kalām	prose; in later usage, sentence
kalām al-ʿArab	speech of the Arabs
kalima	word, lexical unit, morpheme
kaṯīr	frequent usage
kaṯra	frequency (of use)
lafẓ	form
lafẓī	formal
laḥn	"corruption" of speech
laḥn al-ʿāmma	common errors, errors of common people
lā yaǧūz	not permissible
luġa radīʾa	bad usage
luġawiyyūn	philologists, lexicographers
maḏhab (sg. of *maḏāhib*)	school of thought/grammar
māḍī	past tense
maʿnā	meaning
manbaha	indication
masʾala (sg. of *masāʾil*)	issue
mīzān ṣarfī	morphological measure or form, including both vowels and consonants

muḫāṭab	addressee, listener
mustaqīm	right, correct
mutafaqqihūn	jurists
mutakallim	speaker
mutakallimūn	theologians
naḥārīr (pl. of *niḥrīr*)	skillful, learned
naḥw	grammar in general, more specifically syntax
naḥwiyyūn	grammarians
nāʾib ʿan al-fāʿil	agent of a passive verb
naql	transmitted data, irregular but sanctioned data; in phonology, metathesis between glides and vowels
naṣb	accusative (in nouns), subjunctive (in verbs)
naʿt	attribute, adjective
nawādir	rare usages
naẓm	theory of word order and semantic and syntactic interrelationships
niyya	intention
qabīḥ	ugly usage
qalb	metathesis; in phonology
qalīl	infrequent usage
qirāʾāt	Quranic readings
qiyās	analogy
qurrāʾ	Quranic readers
saʿat al-kalām	latitude of speech
samāʿ	(lit.) hearing, body of attested material heard directly from native speakers of Arabic
ṣarf	morphology, in particular lexically fixed form of words
šarṭ	condition, conditional sentence
šawāhid	attested and often ascribed material, esp. from poetry and the Quran
šiʿr	poetry
taʿağğub	admiration, astonishment
tafsīr	exegesis
taḫfīf	lightening (usually by phonological reduction)
taʿlīl	causation
tanwīn	nunation
taqdīr	suppletive insertion
tarḫīm	euphonic elision
taṣarruf al-ʿāmil	plasticity of the operant
ʿulūm	data, (lit.) sciences
wağh	correct, better usage
waqf	pause, pausal position
ziyāda	augmentation to basic morphological form

References

Primary Sources

Abū l-Ṭayyib, *Marātib* = Abū l-Ṭayyib ʿAbdalraḥmān b. ʿAlī al-Luġawī, *Marātib al-naḥwiyyīn*, ed. Muḥammad Abū l-Faḍl Ibrāhīm. 2nd ed. Cairo: Dār Nahḍat Miṣr, 1974.

Astarābāḏī, *Šarḥ al-Šāfiya* = Raḍī al-Dīn Muḥammad b. Ḥasan al-Astarābāḏī, *Šarḥ Šāfiyat Ibn al-Ḥāǧib*, ed. Muḥammad Nūr al-Ḥasan, Muḥammad al-Zafzāf and Muḥammad Muḥyī l-Dīn ʿAbdalḥamīd. 4 vols. Reprint from the Cairo edition. Beirut: Dār al-Kutub al-ʿIlmiyya, 1982.

Ǧurǧānī, *Dalāʾil* = Abū Bakr ʿAbdalqāhir b. ʿAbdalraḥmān al-Ǧurǧānī, *Dalāʾil al-iʿǧāz*, ed. Muḥammad Rašīd Riḍā. Reprint from the Cairo edition, Beirut: Dār al-Maʿrifa, 1981.

Ibn al-Anbārī, *Iġrāb* = Abū l-Barakāt ʿAbdalraḥmān b. Muḥammad al-Anbārī, *al-Iġrāb fī ǧadal al-iʿrāb*, ed. Saʿīd al-Afġānī. 2nd ed. Beirut: Dār al-Fikr, 1971.

Ibn al-Anbārī, *Inṣāf* = Abū l-Barakāt ʿAbdalraḥmān b. Muḥammad al-Anbārī, *al-Inṣāf fī masāʾil al-ḫilāf bayna l-naḥwiyyīn al-Baṣriyyīn wa-l-Kūfiyyīn*, ed. Muḥammad Muḥyī l-Dīn ʿAbdalḥamīd. 2 vols. Cairo: al-Maktaba l-Tiǧāriyya, 1955.

Ibn al-Anbārī, *Lumaʿ* = Abū l-Barakāt ʿAbdalraḥmān b. Muḥammad al-Anbārī, *Lumaʿ al-adilla fī uṣūl al-naḥw*, ed. Saʿīd al-Afġānī. 2nd ed. Beirut: Dār al-Fikr, 1971.

Ibn al-Anbārī, *Nuzha* = Abū l-Barakāt ʿAbdalraḥmān b. Muḥammad al-Anbārī, *Nuzhat al-alibbāʾ fī ṭabaqāt al-udabāʾ*, ed. Ibrāhīm al-Sāmarrāʾī. Baghdad: Maktabat al-Andalus, 1970.

Ibn ʿAqīl, *Šarḥ* = Bahāʾ al-Dīn ʿAbdallāh b. ʿAbdalraḥmān Ibn ʿAqīl, *Šarḥ Ibn ʿAqīl ʿalā Alfiyyat Ibn Mālik*, ed. Ramzī Munīr Baʿalbakī. Beirut: Dār al-ʿIlm li-l-Malāyīn, 1992.

Ibn Ǧinnī, *Ḫaṣāʾiṣ* = Abū l-Fatḥ ʿUṯmān Ibn Ǧinnī, *al-Ḫaṣāʾiṣ*, ed. Muḥammad ʿAlī al-Naǧǧār. 3 vols. Cairo: Dār al-Kutub al-Miṣriyya, 1952–1956.

Ibn Ǧinnī, *Munṣif* = Abū l-Fatḥ ʿUṯmān Ibn Ǧinnī, *al-Munṣif, šarḥ Kitāb al-Taṣrīf li-l-Māzinī*, ed. Ibrāhīm Muṣṭafā and ʿAbdallāh Amīn. 3 vols. Cairo: Muṣṭafā l-Bābī al-Ḥalabī, 1954–1960.

Ibn al-Sarrāǧ, *Uṣūl* = Abū Bakr Muḥammad b. Sahl Ibn al-Sarrāǧ, *al-Uṣūl fī l-naḥw*, ed. ʿAbdalḥusayn al-Fatlī. 3 vols. Beirut: Muʾassasat al-Risāla, 1985.

Ibn ʿUṣfūr, *Mumtiʿ* = Abū l-Ḥasan ʿAlī b. Muʾmin Ibn ʿUṣfūr, *al-Mumtiʿ fī l-taṣrīf*, ed. Faḫr al-Dīn Qabāwa. 4th ed. 2 vols. Beirut: Dār al-Āfāq al-Ǧadīda, 1979.

Muʾaddib, *Daqāʾiq* = Abū l-Qāsim Muḥammad b. Saʿīd al-Muʾaddib, *Daqāʾiq al-taṣrīf*, ed. Aḥmad Nāǧī l-Qaysī, Ḥātim Ṣāliḥ al-Ḍāmin, and Ḥusayn Tūrāl. Baghdad: al-Maǧmaʿ al-ʿIlmī al-ʿIrāqī, 1987.

Mubarrad, *Kāmil* = Abū l-ʿAbbās Muḥammad b. Yazīd al-Mubarrad, *al-Kāmil*, ed. Muḥammad Abū l-Faḍl Ibrāhīm, and al-Sayyid Šiḥāta. 4 vols. Cairo: Maktabat Nahḍat Miṣr, 1956.

Mubarrad, *Muqtaḍab* = Abū l-ʿAbbās Muḥammad b. Yazīd al-Mubarrad, *al-Muqtaḍab*, ed. Muḥammad ʿAbdalḫāliq ʿUḍayma. 4 vols. Cairo: Dār al-Taḥrīr, 1965–1968.

Sībawayhi, *Kitāb* = Abū Bišr ʿAmr b. ʿUṯmān Sībawayhi, *al-Kitāb*, ed. ʿAbdalsalām Muḥammad Hārūn. 5 vols. Cairo: al-Hayʾa l-Miṣriyya l-ʿĀmma, 1977.

Sīrāfī, *Aḫbār* = Abū Saʿīd al-Ḥasan b. ʿAbdallāh al-Sīrāfī, *Aḫbār al-naḥwiyyīn al-Baṣriyyīn*, ed. Fritz Krenkow. Beirut: Imprimerie Catholique, 1936.

Suyūṭī, *Iqtirāḥ* = Ǧalāl al-Dīn Abū l-Faḍl ʿAbdalraḥmān b. Abī Bakr al-Suyūṭī, *al-Iqtirāḥ fī ʿilm uṣūl al-naḥw*, ed. Aḥmad Muḥammad Qāsim. Cairo: Maṭbaʿat al-Saʿāda, 1976.

Ṣaymarī, *Tabṣira* = Abū Muḥammad ʿAbdallāh b. ʿAlī al-Ṣaymarī, *al-Tabṣira wa-l-taḏkira*, ed. Fatḥī Aḥmad Muṣṭafā ʿAlī al-Dīn. 2 vols. Makka: Umm al-Qurā University, 1982.

Tanūḫī, *Tārīḫ* = Abū l-Maḥāsin al-Mufaḍḍal b. Muḥammad b. Misʿar al-Tanūḫī, *Tārīḫ al-ʿulamāʾ al-naḥwiyyīn*, ed. ʿAbdalfattāḥ Muḥammad al-Ḥulw. Riyad: Maṭābiʿ Dār al-Hilāl, 1981.

Yāqūt, *Muʿǧam* = Šihāb al-Dīn Abū ʿAbdallāh Yāqūt b. ʿAbdallāh al-Rūmī al-Ḥamawī, *Muʿǧam al-udabāʾ*, ed. Iḥsān ʿAbbās. 7 vols. Beirut: Dār al-Ġarb al-Islāmī, 1993.

Zaǧǧāǧī, *Īḍāḥ* = Abū l-Qāsim ʿAbdalraḥmān b. Isḥāq al-Zaǧǧāǧī, *al-Īḍāḥ fī ʿilal al-naḥw*, ed. Māzin al-Mubārak. Cairo: Dār al-ʿUrūba, 1959.

Zubaydī, *Ṭabaqāt* = Abū Bakr Muḥammad b. al-Ḥasan al-Zubaydī al-Andalusī, *Ṭabaqāt al-naḥwiyyīn wa-l-luġawiyyīn*, ed. Muḥammad Abū l-Faḍl Ibrāhīm. 2nd ed. Cairo: Dār al-Maʿārif, 1973.

Secondary Sources

Baalbaki, Ramzi. 1981. Arab grammatical controversies and the extant sources of the second and third centuries A.H. In *Studia Arabica et Islamica: Festschrift for Iḥsān ʿAbbās on His Sixtieth Birthday*, ed. Wadād al-Qāḍī, 1–26. Beirut: American University of Beirut.

——. 1983. The relation between *naḥw* and *balāġa*: A comparative study of the methods of Sībawayhi and Ǧurǧānī. *ZAL* 11: 7–23.

——. 1995. The book in the grammatical tradition: Development in content and methods. In *The book in the Islamic world*, ed. George N. Atiyeh, 123–139. New York: State University of New York Press.

——. 2001. *Bāb al-fāʾ* [*fāʾ* + subjunctive] in Arabic grammatical sources. *Arabica* 48: 186–209.

——. 2001–2002. *Ilḥāq* as a morphological tool in Arabic grammar. *Journal of Arabic and Islamic Studies* 4: 1–25.

——. 2005. Review of R. Talmon's *Eighth-century Iraqi grammar: A critical exploration of pre-Ḫalīlian Arabic linguistics*. *Journal of Semitic Studies* 50: 413–416.

——. 2006. Unfamiliar morphological terminology from the fourth century A.H.: Muʾaddib's *Daqāʾiq al-taṣrīf*. In *Grammar as a window onto Arabic humanism: A collection of articles in honour of Michael G. Carter*, ed. Lutz Edzard and Janet Watson, 21–50. Wiesbaden: Harrassowitz.

——. 2008. *The legacy of the Kitāb: Sībawayhi's analytical methods within the context of the Arabic grammatical theory*. Leiden: Brill.

Bernards, Monique. 1997. *Changing traditions: al-Mubarrad's refutation of Sībawayh and the subsequent reception of the Kitāb*. Leiden: Brill.

Bohas, Georges and Jean-Patrick Guillaume. 1984. *Étude des théories des grammairiens arabes. I. Morphologie et phonologie*. Damascus: Institut Français de Damas.

Bohas, Georges, Jean-Patrick Guillaume, and Djamel Eddin Kouloughli. 1990. *The Arabic linguistic tradition*. London: Routledge.

Carter, Michael G. 1972. Les origines de la grammaire arabe. *Revue des études islamiques* 40: 69–97.

——. 1973. An Arab grammarian of the eighth century A.D. *Journal of the American Oriental Society* 93: 146–157.

——. 1991. The ethical basis of Arabic grammar. *al-Karmil* 12: 9–23.

——. 1994. Writing the history of Arabic grammar. *Historiographia Linguistica* 21(3): 385–414.

——. 2000. The development of Arabic linguistics after Sībawayhi: Baṣra, Kūfa and Baghdad. In *History of the Language Sciences*, vol. 1, ed. Sylvain Auroux et al., 263–272. Berlin: Walter de Gruyter.

Guillaume, Jean-Patrick. 2000. La nouvelle approche de la grammaire au IVe-Xe siècle: Ibn Ǧinnī (320/932–392/1002). *History of the Language Sciences*, ed. Sylvain Auroux et al., I, 273–280. Berlin and New York: Walter de Gruyter.

Humbert, Geneviève. 1995. *Les voies de la transmission du Kitāb de Sībawayhi*. Leiden: E.J. Brill.

Itkonen, Esa. 1991. *Universal history of linguistics: India, China, Arabia, Europe*. Amsterdam: J. Benjamins.

Merx, Adalbertus. [1889] 1966. *Historia artis grammaticae apud Syros*. Reprint, Nendeln, Liechtenstein: Kraus.

Owens, Jonathan. 1988. *The foundations of grammar: An introduction to medieval Arabic grammatical theory*. Amsterdam: J. Benjamins.

——. 2000a. On club membership: A reply to Kouloughli. *Histoire Épistémologie Langage* 22(2): 105–126.

——. 2000b. The structure of Arabic grammatical theory. In *History of the language sciences*, vol. 1, ed. Sylvain Auroux et al., 286–300. Berlin: Walter de Gruyter.

Rundgren, Frithiof. 1976. Über den griechischen Einfluss auf die arabische Nationalgrammatik. *Acta Universitatis Upsaliensis* 2: 119–144.

Suleiman, Yasir. 1999. *The Arabic grammatical tradition: A study in taʿlīl*. Edinburgh: Edinburgh University Press.

Talmon, Rafael. 1982. *Naḥwiyyūn* in Sībawayhi's *Kitāb*. *ZAL* 8: 12–38.

——. 2003. *Eighth-century Iraqi grammar: A critical exploration of pre-Ḫalīlian Arabic linguistics*. Winona Lake, IN: Eisenbrauns.

Troupeau, Gérard. 1981. La logique d'Ibn al-Muqaffaʿ et les origines de la grammaire arabe. *Arabica* 28: 242–250.

Versteegh, Kees. 1993. *Arabic grammar and Qurʾānic exegesis in early Islam*. Leiden: E.J. Brill.

——. 1995. *The explanation of linguistic causes: az-Zaǧǧāǧī's theory of grammar*. Amsterdam: J. Benjamins.

——. 1997. *Landmarks in linguistic thought III: The Arabic linguistic tradition*. London: Routledge.

CHAPTER 6

THE SYNTAX OF ARABIC FROM A GENERATIVE PERSPECTIVE*

ELABBAS BENMAMOUN AND LINA CHOUEIRI

6.1 Introduction

Research on Arabic varieties within modern syntactic approaches has tracked the debates that have preoccupied the field of generative linguistics in its different incarnations throughout the last six decades. The debates centered on the nature of linguistic categories, syntactic configurations and their constituents, syntactic alternations and processes that alter the order of constituents, and dependencies between members of the syntactic representations. The discussion focused on problems of word order and sentence structure, phrasal structure, agreement, tense, negation, questions, relative constructions, and clitic-left dislocation. Related to those specific issues are the questions about the nature of the linguistic system, its components and how they interface with each other, and its universal and language specific characteristics. Arabic has figured in the debates within generative linguistics in varying degrees, though the focus started with the syntax of Standard Arabic (SA) and has since been expanded to include the spoken varieties and, more recently, the processing and the acquisition of Arabic. While we cannot possibly do justice to all the research on Arabic syntax within the generative paradigm, we hope, in the pages to follow, to familiarize the reader with the main issues within Arabic syntax and the influential approaches that have been advanced.

* Elabbas Benmamoun's research for this paper was supported in part by National Science Foundation (NSF) grant BCS 0826672.

6.2 Phrase Structure and Word Order

Since the phrase marker plays a central role in deriving syntactic generalizations within generative syntactic paradigms, research on Arabic has focused extensively on this area. The differences that Arabic displays in this regard compared with, for example, Germanic and Romance languages and the different word orders available in the various Arabic varieties present challenges for theories of phrase structure and their quest for isolating universal aspects of language.

In that regard, one important challenge that Arabic varieties present for syntactic approaches has dominated the debate. This revolves around so-called verbless sentences such as (1) from SA, where nouns and predicates are marked for case, and Moroccan Arabic (MA), where nouns and predicates are not.[1]

(1)

a. ʔal-bayt-u kabiir-un
DEF-house-NOM big-NOM
"The house is big."

b. ʔar-ražul-u kaatib-un
DEF-man-NOM writer-NOM
"The man is a writer."

c. ʔar-ražul-u fii l-bayt-i
DEF-man-NOM in DEF-house-GEN
"The man is in the house."

(2)

a. ḍ-ḍar kbir-a
DEF-house big-F
"The house is big."

b. r-ražəl nəžžar
DEF-man carpenter
"The man is a carpenter."

c. r-ražəl f-ḍ-ḍar
DEF-man in-DEF-house
"The man is in the house."

In this respect, Arabic is quite different from English and French in having main sentences ostensibly without a verb. The equivalent constructions in English contain a verb

[1] In this respect, MA patterns with the modern spoken Arabic varieties, which also lack morphological case marking.

that seems to form a constituent with the predicate. In other words, there is a verbal constituent in (3) that seems to be missing in (1) and (2).

(3) a. The house is big.
b. The man is a teacher.
c. The main is in the house.

This is a classic case of language variation related to clause structure. Two broad approaches were contemplated by students of Arabic within the generative paradigm (Bakir 1980; Ayoub 1981; Jelinek 1981; Eid 1983, 1991; Moutaouakil 1987; Heggie 1988; Fassi Fehri 1993; Bahloul 1994; Benmamoun 2000; Aoun et al. 2010).[2] The first approach claims that there is indeed a verb in the structure but that it is phonologically null, that is, an abstract verb that is syntactically present but does not have phonological content. This approach tapped into the idea that has been well accepted within the generative paradigm that some categories may be phonologically null, either because they lack phonological content or because they have undergone a process of deletion. According to this approach, the main feature that distinguishes Arabic from, for example, English and French is that the copula verb can be null in main finite clauses such as (1) and (2). One reason that this may be plausible is that, in past tense and future tense clauses, the copula is overt, that is, has phonological content as illustrated in (4) and (5) from SA and (6) and (7) from MA.[3]

(4) a. kaana ʔal-bayt-u kabiir-an
be.PST DEF-house-NOM big-ACC
"The house was big."

b. kaana ʔar-ražul-u kaatib-an
be.PST DEF-man-NOM writer-ACC
"The man was a writer."

[2] There is also a debate about the status of the so-called pronominal copula found in contexts such as (i) from MA:

(i) ħna huma l-xəddama
we they DEF-workers
"We are the workers."

Notice that the pronoun *huma* "they" agrees with the subject pronoun *ħna* "we" only in number and gender. They obviously do not agree in person. The critical problem about this type of construction, found across Arabic varieties including SA, is the syntactic status of the pronoun. See Eid (1991) for an overview of its distribution and analysis.

[3] As is well-known, the nature of the temporal and aspectual systems of Arabic, and Semitic in general, is not settled. We will refer to the so-called perfective verb (*maaḍii* in the Arabic tradition) as past. With regard to generative approaches, the critical issue is whether there is a grammatical category that encodes tense and aspect and that interacts with nominals, such as the subject. This issue will be discussed in more detail later on.

c. kaana ʔar-ražul-u fi l-bayt-i
be.PST DEF-man-NOM in DEF-house-GEN
"The man was in the house."

(5) a. sa-ya-kuunu ʔal-bayt-u kabiir-an
FT-3-be DEF-house-NOM big-ACC
"The house will be big."

b. sa-ya-kuunu ʔar-ražul-u kaatib-an
FT-3-be DEF-man-NOM writer.acc
"The man will be a writer."

c. sa-ya-kuunu ʔar-ražul-u fi l-bayt-i
FT-3-be DEF-man-NOM in DEF-house-GEN
"The man will be in the house."

(6) a. ḍ-ḍar kan-ət kbir-a
DEF-house be.PST-F big-F
"The house was big."

b. r-ražəl kan nəžžar
DEF-man be.PST carpenter
"The man was a carpenter."

c. r-ražəl kan f-ḍ-dar
DEF-man be.PST in-DEF-house
"The man was in the house."

(7) a. ḍ-ḍar ɣadi t-kun kbir-a
DEF-house FT 3.F-be big-F
"The house will be big."

b. r-ražəl ɣadi ykun nəžžar
DEF-man FT be carpenter
"The man will be a carpenter."

c. r-ražəl ɣadi y-kun f-ḍ-ḍar
DEF-man FT 3-be in-DEF-house
"The man will be in the house."

Assuming a null copular verb in present tense sentences makes it possible to have one consistent structure for all copular sentences in Arabic regardless of the tense of the clause. It also makes Arabic look like English and French, reducing the variation between them to whether the auxiliary verb has phonological content. In other words, the variation is morphophonological and not syntactic and therefore does not require a different syntactic analysis of the clause structure of present tense copular sentences.

This is a desirable outcome since it minimizes the complexity of the syntactic apparatus. The main issue to be settled within this first approach is whether the copula was originally there and got deleted (Bakir 1980) or whether it has always been there with no phonological features that need to be spelled out (Fassi Fehri 1993).

When examined closely, the null copula and the copula deletion accounts are motivated only on conceptual grounds. As far as we know, no compelling empirical arguments have been advanced to demonstrate that a verb should be posited in those sentences. Moreover, the expectation is that the syntax of present tense copular constructions should work the same way as the syntax of past tense and future tense sentences.

A second approach is to treat present tense copular sentences as lacking a verbal copula altogether: they are true verbless sentences. The details of such accounts vary, but their main arguments, summarized in Benmamoun (2000), are as follows. First, the predicate in the context of the putative null copula in (1) does not carry accusative case, while it does in the context of the overt copula in the present and past tense (Déchaine 1993). If there were a null copula or an elided copula in (1), one would expect the predicate to also be marked accusative rather than the default nominative case sometimes associated with the absence of a syntactic case marker/licenser. Any attempt to explain the difference in case marking on the basis of the phonological nature of the copula (overt vs. covert) would seem ad hoc and lacking in explanatory force because the connection between the ability to assign case and phonological content is hard to make.[4]

Second, one characteristic of clause structure is that modals require verbs as dependents. This is also the case in Arabic, as illustrated in (8) from SA.[5]

(8)

a. qad ya-kuunu fi l-bayt-i
   may 3-be in DEF-house-GEN
   "He may be in the house."

b.* qad fi l-bayti
   may in DEF-house-GEN

In (8a), the modal is followed by a verbal copula. If the copula is absent, the sentence is ill formed (8b). The explanation is straightforward; the modal requires a verbal dependent, which is not available in (8b). The same explanation is not available under the first approach. Since the dependency between the modal and the verb is syntactic, whether

[4] For example, the English present tense is null, but it is associated with nominative case.

[5] Note that the modal in SA in (8) is a particle that does not inflect. In MA, for instance, the modal inflects for agreement with the subject (i).

(i)

a. yəqdər ykuun f-ḍ-ḍar
   may be in-DEF-house
   "He may be in the house."

b. *yəqdər f-ḍ-ḍar
   may in-DEF-house

the copula is overt or null/elided should not have any bearing on the grammaticality of the sentence, all else being equal. The simplest conclusion, then, is that there is no null copula in the representation of sentences such as (8b), which violates the dependency requirement of the modal.

Third, an interesting aspect of sentential syntax that has preoccupied the generative paradigm concerns the interaction between lexical categories and grammatical categories and the consequences of that interaction on word order. Thus, one explanation of the subject–auxiliary inversion phenomenon in matrix English questions is that the complementizer domain, which encodes clause type (interrogative in this instance), interacts with the tense domain, which encodes the temporal reference of the sentence. This interaction results in the complementizer attracting the temporal head and the elements it hosts, which results in subject–auxiliary inversion.[6] We will show that the same phenomenon is manifested in SA negation, but for now let us focus on how this is relevant to the status of the copula in present tense sentences in Arabic. Here, the syntax of MA provides the best argument. In MA, there are two main negatives: the discontinuous negative *ma-š*; and the nondiscontinuous negative *ma-ši*. The former occurs mainly in the context of verbs and the latter in the context of nonverbal predicates, as illustrated in (9):

(9)
a. ma-qra-š
NEG-read.3-NEG
"He didn't read."

b. ḍ-ḍar maši kbir-a
DEF-house NEG big-F
"The house is not big"

Interestingly, in Moroccan Arabic, nonverbal predicates can optionally occur in the context of the discontinuous negative (10):

(10)
ḍ-ḍar ma-kbir-a-š
DEF-house NEG-big-F-NEG
"The house is not big."

However, the nondiscontinuous negative option is not available if there is an overt copula verb, whether it is past tense or future tense:

[6] The same analysis extends to the interaction between tense and the verb in English. The tense needs to be merged with the verb, but that merger may be blocked by an intervening element such as negation, resulting in a repair mechanism, such as Do-support. This has been a mainstay of generative syntax since its inception. Putting aside the details and the merits of the analysis, the main point, which is not controversial, is that members of the sentence interact, and this may get disrupted if other elements intervene.

(11)

a. ḍ-ḍar ma-kan-ət-š kbir-a
DEF-house NEG-be.PST-3.F-NEG big-F
"The house was not big."

b. ḍ-ḍar ma-ɣadi t-kun-š kbir-a
DEF-house NEG-FT 3.F-be-NEG big-F
"The house will not be big."

When the copula verb is overt, the predicate cannot combine with negation; that is, the option in (10) is no longer available (12):

(12)

a. *ḍ-ḍar kan-ət ma kbir-a-š
DEF-house be-3.F NEG big-F-NEG

b. *ḍ-ḍar ɣadi tkun ma-kbir-a-š
DEF-house FT be NEG-big-F-NEG

The most plausible explanation for why the sentences in (12) are ill formed is that the copula is a closer host to negation than the predicate is. In generative syntactic terms, this is a typical case of minimality effects, whereby syntactic dependencies are sensitive to intervening material, which explains why some word order options are not allowed under some circumstances. But if this is the case, then (10) becomes problematic under the null copula account. That is, it is not clear why the putative null copula does not trigger a minimality effect and blocks the merger between negation and the nonverbal predicate. Again, the phonological status of the copula should not be critical since the dependency scans only the syntactic representation.[7] The issue is of course moot if there is no null or elided copula; no minimality effects would be expected to arise, a conclusion that is empirically well supported.

Other arguments have been provided against the null/elided copula analyses, but the previous discussion presents the typical line of attack within modern syntactic theories. The arguments clearly show that there is no null or elided copula, which means that the verbless sentences are true to their names, that is, devoid of any verb. The seriousness of the implications of such a conclusion cannot be underestimated. Most importantly, present tense verbless sentences are different from their past of future tense counterparts in fundamental ways that have to do with clause structure. Phrase markers of main finite clauses do not have to contain verbs; therefore, the requirement to have a verb in

[7] However, the argument may lose its force if it turns out that the merger between negation and the predicate takes place not in the syntax but in some postsyntactic component. Such a component would have the vocabulary and primitives to capture generalizations that are sensitive to the phonological content of the members of the syntactic phrase marker. At this stage, the nature of the postsyntactic component is still vague and cannot be properly subjected to scrutiny. At any rate, the fact that the minimality effects from the negative constructions align neatly with the arguments from modals and case is significant.

such constructions is not a universal. This, of course, leads to the next logical question, namely, the structure of sentences such as (1) and (2): they may not contain a verb, but is that the only property they lack compared with their counterparts in English? Here again, different proposals have been advanced.

Under one proposal, the sentences in (1) and (2) are small clauses that consist of the subject and the predicate only. Mouchaweh (1986) advances the small clause analysis for Arabic. However, as Benmamoun (2000) points out, it faces a number of challenges. For example, verbless sentences can contain adverbs that refer to tense (13) and can also contain grammatical categories such as negation (14):

(13)	ʔar-ražul-u	fi	l-bayt-i	l-ʔaana	*SA*
	DEF-man-NOM	in	DEF-house-GEN	DEF-now	

"The man is in the house now."

(14)	ḍ-ḍar	maši	kbir-a	*MA*
	DEF-house	NEG	big-F	

"The house is not big."

Under the assumption that temporal adverbs such as *ʔal-ʔaana* "now" must be anchored by tense, the clause in (14) must be bigger than a small clause, since small clauses are considered to be nonfinite with no independent tense of their own. That conclusion is inevitable in (14) because the clause contains sentential negation, which usually occurs in full finite clauses. Also, the sentence in (13) can be embedded under the SA complementizer that requires a dependent finite clause (15):[8]

(15)	ʔa-ʕtaqid-u	ʔanna	ʔar-ražul-a	fi	l-bayt-i	l-ʔaana
	1.SG-think-INDC	that	DEF-man-ACC	in	DEF-house-GEN	DEF-now

"I think that the man is in the house now."

The plausible assumption then is that the embedded constituent in (15) is not a small clause but a full clause. However, it cannot be a full clause like its English counterpart, which must contain a verb. While the proposals vary, they all agree that the structure of verbless sentences contain some grammatical category that expresses finiteness. Benmamoun (2000) refers to this clause as a tense phrase (TP) on a par with its counterpart in English and gives it the configuration in (16):

(16)

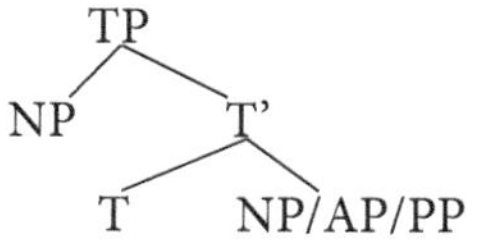

```
        TP
       /  \
     NP    T'
          /  \
         T   NP/AP/PP
```

[8] See Eisele (1988) for a detailed study of tense in Egyptian Arabic (EgA). See also Mughazy (2004) for a study of participles in EgA and the temporal and aspectual properties of the clauses they head.

Under this account, the embedded sentence in (15) has the representation in (17):

(17)

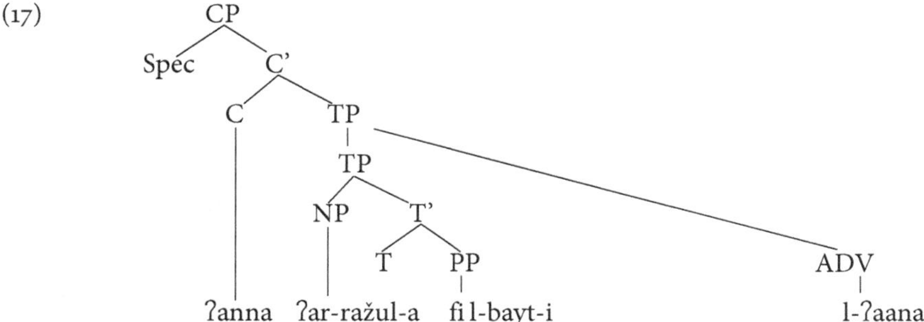

In (17) the complementizer dominates the finite TP, which in turn contains the subject and its predicate. The head of TP is the abstract present tense (represented by present tense features). That tense head anchors the temporal adverb adjoined to the TP.[9] The clause also includes a small clause, prepositional phrase (PP), which contains the subject and its predicate prior to the former moving to the [Spec,TP], a topic we will discuss in greater detail in Section 6.4.

The idea that verbless sentences are authentically verbless can be traced back to Jelinek (1981), who proposed the structure in (19) for the EgA verbless sentence in (18):

(18)

ir-raagil da waziir
DEF-man this minister
"This man is a cabinet minister."

(19)

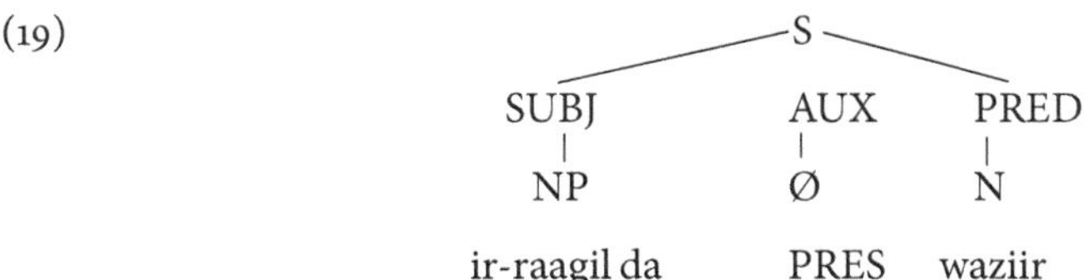

The main difference between the structures in (16) and (19) is the claim that the sentence displays an endocentric structure whose head is tense. The two analyses assume

[9] There is also disagreement about whether the vocalic melody on active verbs in SA carries tense or aspect. McCarthy (1979) assumes that it does, but Benmamoun (2000) and Ouali and Fortin (2007) adopt the opposite view. For Benmamoun (2000), the fact that in MA there is no discernable vocalic melody casts doubt on attributing any temporal or aspectual properties to vowels in Arabic in general. The other problem is that, even in SA, vocalic melodies differ for no temporal or aspectual reason. In addition, the vocalic melodies on singular nouns seem to have no grammatical content, which raises further suspicion about the vocalic melody in Arabic morphology in general. However, the vocalic melody in the passive verb and statives does seem to have semantic content but this is not the case in most of the modern dialects. Further research is obviously needed to understand the grammatical content of the vocalic patterns.

that there is no verbal element within the sentence, but they agree that there is a functional category that expresses tense.

While there are plausible and sometimes strong arguments for the structure in (16), it itself raises serious questions. The main question revolves around the nature of the present tense head. According to the structure in (16), the present tense head is abstract and is not associated with any lexical category.[10] This is not problematic for there are temporal categories that are expressed on auxiliaries or even grammatical categories such as negation and subordinators. What could be problematic is that no other category realizes these tense features, which are syntactically active, if the argument that they license temporal adverbs can be maintained. Within the generative paradigm, the problem is less serious if one could provide evidence for the syntactic presence of the abstract tense head. We have already discussed two arguments, namely, embedding under the complementizer that requires a finite embedded clause, and the occurrence of the adverb that needs to be anchored by tense. Additional arguments are discussed in Benmamoun (2000), two of which are particularly relevant. One has to do with the case on the subject in verbless sentences, particularly sentences where the subject is clearly not topicalized or left dislocated and therefore cannot be the recipient of default case marking. The other argument has to do with the possibility of allowing so-called expletive subjects in such constructions. Both arguments are illustrated in the sentence in (20):

(20)	hunaaka	ražul-un	fi l-bayti
	there	man-NOM	in DEF-house
	"There is a man in the house."		

The consensus within generative syntax is that case that is not default and not tied to a semantic relation (so-called inherent case; Chomsky 1986) is assigned by a grammatical category, which in the case of the subject is typically tense. In (20), the indefinite subject that is very likely not in a topicalized or dislocated position carries nominative case. This seems to suggest that nominative case comes from the abstract present tense in the verbless sentence. The presence of the expletive in (20) can also be taken to argue for the presence of tense in the sentence. The expletive cannot be licensed by the lexical predicate, which forms a cluster with the lexical subject. Again, within generative syntax, expletives are assumed to relate to some property of the temporal category in the sentence, which in (20) must be the present tense. The upshot of this discussion is that the theoretical apparatus within generative syntax has played a role in providing novel insights into the workings of Arabic. Arabic, in return, has provided fertile ground for putting some cherished assumptions of generative syntax under the microscope.

[10] Ouali and Fortin (2007) argue that the prefixes/proclitics found on imperfective verbs in MA carry tense. They also argue that when the auxiliary verb is present the sentence has a biclausal structure that contains two tense projections that dominate aspectual projections, which in turn dominate the main verbal projection.

The previous discussion neatly captures the evolution of generative approaches to the syntax of Arabic. The copula deletion rule (Bakir 1980) was developed at a time when transformations were allowed to be powerful to the point of radically altering the syntactic representation. In contrast, the null copula account (Fassi Fehri 1993) departed from the powerful deletion tool and adopted a widely popular approach in the 1980s and 1990s, namely, that some constituents can be phonologically null (e.g., pronominals, complementizers, verbs). On the other hand, Jelinek's (1981) approach shies away from the abstractness of the copula deletion approach but still adopts the idea that the category that realizes tense can be abstract. Benmamoun (2000) basically adopts the same idea but provides a headed binary structure with the sentence being a projection of tense. This again echoes the debate in the last 30 years about the nature of syntactic constituents and the nature of syntactic configurations. The consensus that has developed over the last three decades is that syntactic constituents are endocentric (headed) and that some elements may lack a phonological matrix. However, for them to be learnable one has to have independent evidence that they are present. With regard to verbless sentences, this amounts to showing that the putative abstract temporal or aspectual head is syntactically active. Of course, this only leads to another question: why does Arabic (and other languages with verbless sentences) lack an element that is overt in other languages? This is a question about syntactic variation between languages or what is usually refereed to within the generative tradition as parametric variation. Unfortunately, there is no convincing answer to this question. Benmamoun (2000) tries to attribute the absence of the verb to some nominal property of present tense sentences, but that proposal remains tentative.

6.3 The Syntax of the Noun Phrase

Generative approaches to the syntax of the noun phrase in Arabic have engaged important theoretical debates related to the syntactic configuration and constituency of the noun phrase, the structural parallelism between noun phrases and sentences, and importantly the issue of word order within the nominal domain.

2.1 Structure of the Simplex Noun Phrase

The Arabic noun phrase is known to have a complex structure.[11] For instance, while adjectives seem to generally follow the noun they modify, other modifiers,

[11] For a detailed description of the structure of the noun phrase in SA, see Ryding (2005) and references therein.

especially determiner-like elements, precede the noun they modify. This is exemplified in (21)–(24).

(21) a. ʔal-bayt-u ʔal-žamiil-u *SA*
DEF-house-NOM DEF-beautiful-NOM
"the beautiful house"

b. l-beet l-ħəlo *LA*
DEF-house DEF-nice
"the nice house"

In SA, as well as the other dialects of Arabic, adjectives follow the nouns they modify, agreeing with them in gender, number, and definiteness. In SA, the adjectives agree with the noun they modify in case as well:

(22) a. haaðaa l-bayt-u *SA*
this DEF-house-NOM
"this house"

b. haaðihi l-bint-u
this.F.SG DEF-girl-NOM
"this girl"

Like demonstratives, quantifiers and numerals (whether cardinal or ordinal) also typically precede the noun they modify ((23)–(24)):

(23) a. kull-u walad-in *SA*
every/each-NOM boy-GEN
"every/each boy"

b. kull-u l-ʔawlaad-i
every-NOM DEF-boys-GEN
"all the boys"

(24) a. θaaliθ-u walad-in
third-NOM boy-GEN
"the third boy"

b. θalaaθ-at-u ʔawlaad-in
three-F-NOM boys-GEN
"three boys"

However, demonstratives, as well as quantifiers and numerals can also appear postnominally, as illustrated in (25)–(27):

(25) a. ʔal-bayt-u haaðaa *SA*
DEF-house-NOM this
"this house"

b. ʔal-bint-u haaðihi
DEF-girl-NOM this.F.SG
"this girl"

When the quantified noun phrase is definite, the latter can precede the quantifier (26):[12]

(26) ʔal-ʔawlaad-u kull-u-hum
DEF-boys-NOM every-NOM-them
"all the boys" (lit. "the boys, all")

Similarly, when the number modifies a definite noun, the latter must precede the number word. This order is exemplified in (27):[13]

(27) ʔaθ-θalaaθ-at-u ʔal-ʔawlaad-u
DEF-boys-NOM DEF-three-F-NOM
"the three boys"

It is generally claimed in the generative tradition that the word order within noun phrases in Arabic is the result of movement (see, e.g., Mohammad 1988; Ouhalla 1988, 1996a; Fassi Fehri 1999; Benmamoun 2000). A debate in the recent literature on noun phrase structure has centered on whether the movement in question is that of the head noun (N-movement) or of the phrasal/XP-movement.

[12] In the Q__NP order, the noun phrase (NP) in SA appears with genitive case. In the NP __ Q order the quantifier carries a clitic agreeing with the NP in number and gender. In addition, the quantifier agrees in case with the preceding NP.

[13] While in some dialects of Arabic the order definite article-cardinal number-noun is acceptable, this is not possible in SA:

(i) a.* ʔaθ-θalaaθ-at-u ʔawlaad-in *SA*
DEF-three-F-NOM boys-GEN
"the three boys"

b. l-tleet wleed *LA*
DEF-three children
"the three children"

c.* l-teelit walad
DEF-third child
"the third child"

Given a basic skeletal structure for noun phrases in Arabic as in (28) (see Shlonsky 2004), N-movement directly accounts for the basic ordering of modifiers observed in (21)–(24):

(28) D....> ... NumP ....> ... AP ... > PP ...> ... N

Leaving some details aside, N-movement is assumed to be partial in (28), with a landing site below number phrase (NumP), the position that hosts numbers,[14] but above adjective phrase (AP). As Mohammad (1988) notes, (partial) N-movement within NP unifies the structure of noun phrases with that of sentences: N-movement within DP is thus parallel to V-movement within IP.[15]

It is, however, observed that N-movement makes the wrong predictions regarding the serialized ordering of postnominal adjectives (see Fass Fehri 1999; Shlonsky 2004). When multiple adjectives modify the same noun, they generally follow the strict ordering hierarchy given in (29) and illustrated in (30):[16]

(29) provenance < color < shape < size < quality

(30) a. ʔal-kitaab-u l-ʔaχḍar-u ṣ-ṣaɣiir-u
DEF-book-NOM DEF-green-NOM DEF-little-NOM
"the little green book"

b. šaay-un ṣiiniiy-un ʔaχḍar-u žayyid-un
tea-NOM Chinese-NOM green-NOM excellent-NOM
"an excellent green Chinese tea"

Interestingly, the ordering in (29) is the mirror image of the ordering of prenominal adjectives found in many of the world's languages (31) (see Sproat and Shih 1988; Cinque 1994; Rouveret 1994 and references cited therein).

(31) quality > size > shape > color > provenance

Assuming that Arabic generates adjectives, like other modifiers, in prenominal position in the order given in (31), the mirror image order in (29) cannot be obtained by N-movement.[17] The mirror image ordering of postnominal adjectives can be obtained only as a result of successive (cyclic) XP-movement to the left, a movement that

[14] NumP conflates ordinal and cardinal numbers. Shlonsky (2004) makes a distinction between the two, and our NumP corresponds to his Card#P, the projection that hosts cardinal numbers.

[15] The original argument for N-movement within the Semitic noun phrase can be found in Ritter (1988). There, N-movement was also motivated on the basis of unifying the syntax of simplex and complex noun phrases.

[16] The examples in (30) correspond to Fassi Fehri (1999: 107, (1)–(2)).

[17] For arguments that adjectival modifiers are indeed generated prenominally in Arabic, see Fassi Fehri (1999).

pied-pipes all the material to the right of XP. To see an instantiation of this movement, we provide the representations in (32)–(33):

(32) …[$_{AP_3}$ … žayyid-un… [$_{AP_2}$ … ʔaχḍar-u … [$_{AP_1}$ … ṣiiniyy-un … [$_{NP}$ … šaay-un]]]]

(33)

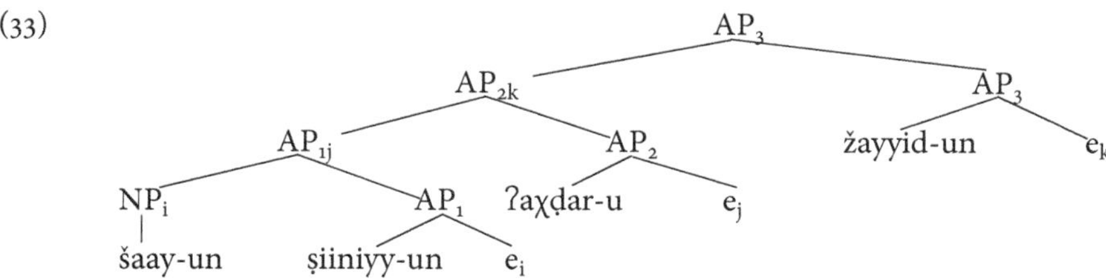

The main challenge for the previous analysis, which relies on phrasal movement, is that such movement does not seem to be well motivated, and neither are the projections that are posited as targets for that movement.[18] This remains a serious weakness of such highly abstract analyses.

2.2 The Construct State

One of the hallmarks of the Semitic noun phrase is the iḍaafa construction (henceforth, construct state). The characteristics of construct state nominals are well-known. However, the debate is still ongoing to provide an account for them;[19] it tackles not only issues of syntactic representation but also the interface between the syntactic and the morphological components of the grammar.

Benmamoun (2000) lists the characteristics of construct state nominals in (34) and illustrates them in (35):

(34) a. The members of the Construct State (CS) tend be adjacent.
b. The CS complex constitutes a single prosodic unit.
c. Only the last member of the CS can carry the marker of (in)definiteness.

[18] Shlonsky (2004) extended the XP-movement analysis previously outlined to account for the alternation between the pronominal and postnominal order of numerals and quantifiers, illustrated in (21)–(27) (see also Shlonsky 1991). In a study of the syntax of quantifiers in Arabic, Benmamoun (1999) argued, however, that the Q__NP ordering (23) and the NP__Q ordering (26) are radically different and that they involve different derivations. In that case, the prenominal order and postnominal order of modifiers would have two different syntactic sources, and the perceived alternation does not constitute evidence for XP-movement within the Arabic noun phrase.

Of course, the picture is more complicated than our discussion would lead one to believe: both Fassi Fehri (1999) and Shlonsky (2004) present arguments for the limitations of massive XP-movement within the Arabic NP. Our main point here is to show how the syntax of the noun phrase in Arabic weighs in on an important debate in the generative literature concerning movement within the noun phrase.

[19] For a more exhaustive list of properties, see Borer (1996), Mohammad (1999b), and Fassi Fehri (1999).

(35) a. ktab l-wəld *MA*
book DEF-boy
"the boy's book"

b. kitaab-u ṭ-ṭaalib-i *SA*
book-NOM DEF-student-GEN
"the student's book"

In contrast, free state nominals do not share any of the characteristics in (34) with construct state nominals:[20]

(36) lə-ktab dyal l-wəld *MA*
DEF-book of DEF-boy
"the boy's book"

Unlike the first member of the free state NP in (36), the first member of the construct state nominal cannot take the definite article (37):

(37) a.* lə-ktab l-wəld *MA*
DEF-book DEF-boy

b.* ʔal-kitaab-u ṭ-ṭaalib-i *SA*
DEF-book-NOM DEF-student-GEN

The analyses put forth for this generalization within the principles and parameters approach have focused on the idea that definiteness is a syntactic feature that requires pairing (or "checking") with a nominal category such as the noun. Despite the differences in their details, those analyses assume that the definiteness feature is located in D and that checking it involves either N-movement to D or XP-movement to [Spec, DP].

N-to-D movement provides a straightforward account for the absence of the definite article on the first member of the construct state nominal (see also Ritter 1988;

[20] The genitive marker varies from dialect to dialect. Brustad (2000: 72) provides the table in (i) showing the genitive exponents in four different dialects representing four major dialect groups (Maghreb, Egyptian, Levantine, and Gulf Arabic):

(i) Genitive Exponents

	Masculine	Feminine	Plural
Moroccan	dyal/d	–	–
Egyptian	bitaaʕ	bitaʕit	bituuʕ
Syrian	tabaʕ	–	(tabaʕul)
Kuwaiti	maal	(maalat)	(maalot)

Borer 1996; Fassi Fehri 1999; Benmamoun 2000): assuming that the definite article is an overt realization of the definiteness feature on D, its presence will block N-to-D movement.

Analyses of construct state nominals involving XP-movement (see Fassi Fehri 1999; Shlonsky 2004 and references therein) make the further assumption that a feature in a given functional projection FP is checked either via head adjunction to F or via Spec-Head agreement, but not both. Therefore, if construct state nominals involve movement to [Spec, DP], the definiteness feature in D will be checked and the presence of the definite article in D will be blocked. Interesting evidence is adduced showing that the position of construct state nominals is higher than that of other noun phrases (38) (Shlonsky 2004):

(38) a.* haaðaa ʔibn-u r-ražul-i
this son-NOM DEF-man-GEN
"this man's son"

b. ʔibn-u r-ražul-i haaðaa
son-NOM DEF-man-GEN this.M
"this man's son"

While we observed that demonstratives in Arabic can occur either before or after the noun they modify, when that noun is a construct state nominal the demonstrative must follow it. The contrast between (38a) and (22) indicates that the construct state nominal does not occupy the same position as noun construct state noun phrases. In fact, it must be higher.[21] Proponents of the XP-movement analysis as well as the N-movement analysis of construct state nominals advocate this. As Benmamoun (2000) points out, despite the different analyses, the accounts provided for property (34c) all rely on the configuration properties of DPs and the structural relations made available by the grammar (e.g., agreement or checking).

[21] The examples in (i) from LA are consistent with this generalization.

(i) a. l-χams kətub
DEF-five books
"the five books"

b.* l-χams kətub l-walad
DEF-five books DEF-child
"the five books of the child"

c. kətub l-walad l-χamse
DEF-books DEF-child DEF-five
"The five books of the child"

While in some dialects of Arabic the order definite article-cardinal number-noun is acceptable (see also footnote 13), this order is not available with construct state nominals. The only order possible in that case is the one where the cardinal number word follows the construct state nominal.

The prosodic properties of construct state nominals are well documented (see, e.g., Ritter 1988; Borer 1996; Kihm 1999; Mohammad 1999b; Benmamoun 2000; Siloni 2001 and references therein). For instance, construct state nominals display word-level phonological processes: Benmamoun (2000) illustrates this in MA. The feminine marker /*-at*/ surfaces mostly in construct state nominals (39) but not in other contexts (40):

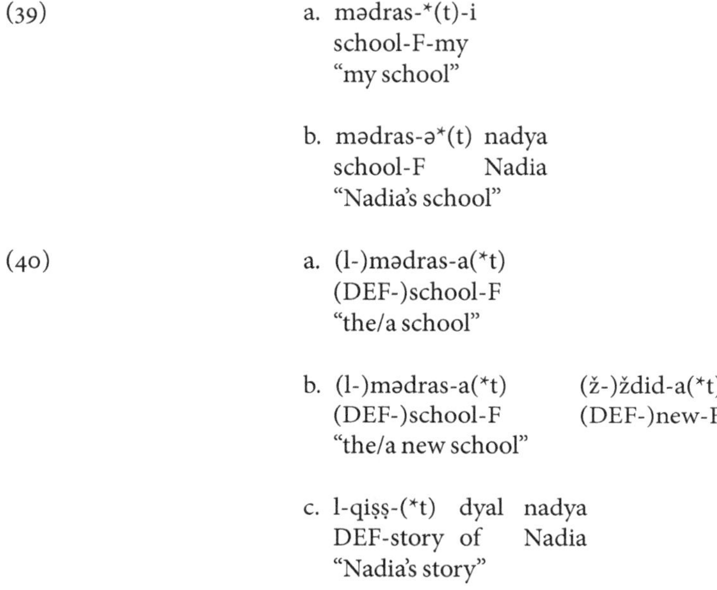

(39)
a. mədras-*(t)-i
school-F-my
"my school"

b. mədras-ə*(t) nadya
school-F Nadia
"Nadia's school"

(40)
a. (l-)mədras-a(*t)
(DEF-)school-F
"the/a school"

b. (l-)mədras-a(*t) (ž-)ždid-a(*t)
(DEF-)school-F (DEF-)new-F
"the/a new school"

c. l-qiṣṣ-(*t) dyal nadya
DEF-story of Nadia
"Nadia's story"

This property, which can be generalized to other dialects of Arabic, is then related to adjacency (34a). The phonological cohesion of members of the construct state has been analyzed as the result of merger of the two members of the construct state nominal (see Borer 1996; Benmamoun 2000; Siloni 2001). Borer (1996) argues that a syntactic merger of the two members of the construct state nominal is necessary to assign definiteness specification to the first member (N1) of the construct state. The merger of the two members, N1 and N2, takes place in the configuration in (41):

(41)

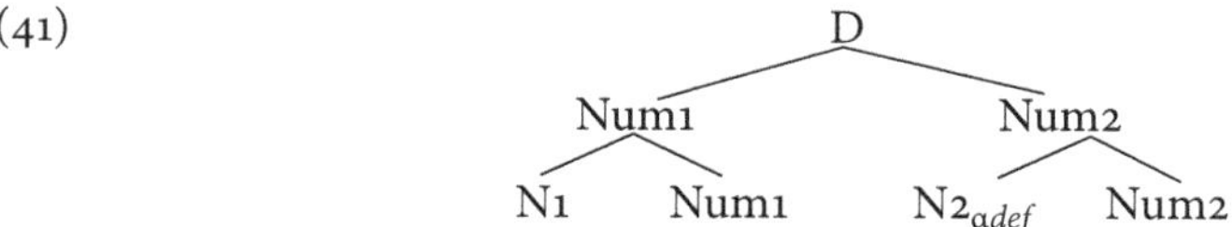

In (41), the definiteness feature, lexically associated with N2, percolates up and then down the tree to N1. Benmamoun (2000), while adopting Borer's insight that the properties of construct state nominals listed in (34) are linked to each other through merger, proposes an analysis that argues for a postsyntactic merger.[22]

In short, Benmamoun's (2000) analysis accounts for the properties in (34) as follows: a merger between the two members of a construct state nominal is a morphological process that is not sensitive to syntactic conditions. It is akin to word formation and is sensitive to morphological conditions, such as adjacency (34a)–(34b). Morphological merger also allows the second member of the construct state nominal to spell out the definiteness feature of the first member. This explains the absence of a marker of definiteness on the first member of the construct state nominal (34c).

As Benmamoun (2003) discusses, the absence of a definite marker on the first member of a construct state nominal parallels the absence of the number feature on the verb in a VS sequence (42):

(42) a. ʔakal-at ṭ-ṭaalib-aat-u
ate-3.F.SG DEF-student-F.PL-NOM
"The students ate."

b.* ʔakal-na ṭ-ṭaalib-aat-u
ate-3.F.PL DEF-student-F.PL-NOM
"The students ate."

As in construct state nominals, in the VS order, the verb and subject form a prosodic unit as a result of morphological merger. In that case, the subject noun phrase spells out the number feature of the verb.[23]

While the construct state has received extensive attention within generative syntax, many issues remain such as the status of adjectival constructs, the nature of the case assigned by the construct state, and the interplay between the construct state and the free state within the spoken dialects.

6.4 Subjects and Subject Agreement

The status of the subject remains one of the most contentious and unsettled issues in modern accounts of Arabic syntax. In fact, the debate appears to echo the

[22] Lexical merger, as Benmamoun (2000) discusses, can be quickly dismissed since members of the construct state nominal are syntactically and semantically compositional. For more on this issue, see Siloni (2001) and Borer (2008). Benmamoun (2000) provides, in addition, arguments against syntactic merger between the two members of a construct state nominal. Due to limited space, we will not discuss those arguments here.

[23] Benmamoun (2003) further investigates the nominal origins of the VS sequence that has led to this parallelism.

long-standing controversy within the Arabic linguistic tradition, particularly the disagreement between the so-called Basra and Kufa schools on the status of the preverbal position and nongenerative approaches.[24] The issue simply is whether the preverbal noun phrase in a sentence such as (43) can be analyzed as a subject on a par with its English counterpart:

(43) ʔar-ražul-u qaraʔa l-kitaab-a
DEF-man-NOM read.PST.3 DEF-book-ACC
"The man read the book."

Related to the status of the preverbal noun phrase in (43) is its correspondence with the sentence in (44) where the same noun phrase carrying the same case is in the postverbal position.

(44) qaraʔa ʔar-ražul-u l-kitaab-a
read.PST.3 DEF-man-NOM DEF-book-ACC
"The man read the book."

Many scholars argue that the preverbal NP in (43) is not a genuine subject but a topic or left-dislocated element (Bakir 1980; Ayoub 1981; Fassi Fehri 1981; Soltan 2007). The idea is that the preverbal noun phrase is in a clause peripheral position binding a pronoun that is the genuine subject. The agreement asymmetry illustrated in (42) in SA is taken as evidence for this analysis. As is well-known, in SA, the verb partially agrees with the subject when the latter is in the postverbal position but fully agrees with it when it is in the preverbal position:[25]

(45) a. daxala l-muhandis-uun
entered.3 DEF-engineer-NOM.M.PL
"The engineers came."

b. ʔal-muhandis-uun daxal-uu
DEF-engineer-NOM-M.PL entered-3.M.PL
"The engineers came."

[24] See Fassi Fehri (1993: 91).

[25] As pointed out by the traditional Arab grammarians, some speakers deployed full agreement in both orders, which is similar to the pattern we find in the modern spoken dialects. However, the asymmetry is a property of the language or at least the varieties studied by the grammarians and therefore is a legitimate topic of study. To claim otherwise would be to make Arabic appear to be different from any other language that displays variation among its speakers and dialects, which is an indication of change in progress that could be the result of a loss of property or the emergence of a new property (innovation). Incidentally, agreement asymmetries relative to word order are attested in a number of languages (e.g., participial agreement in French). Therefore, the situation in SA is not unique.

Fassi Fehri (1988) argues that the full agreement on the verb (*-uu*) in (45b) is a genuine pronominal that has been incorporated into the verb. Since a sentence can have only one subject, the preverbal noun phrase cannot be a subject. This analysis capitalizes on a popular account for similar patterns in Celtic languages where agreement is in complementary distribution with the lexical subjects. The same complementary distribution obtains in the context of object clitics:

(46)
a. qaraʔ-tu l-kitaab-a
Read-1.SG DEF-book-ACC
"I read the book."

b. qaraʔ-tu-hu
read-1.SG-3.M.SG
"I read it."

Thus, it is tempting to provide a unified analysis for the complementary distribution between the inflectional morphology that the verb hosts and its subject and object dependents. This is basically the approach that Fassi Fehri (1988) advances, and it is consistent with the principles of generative syntax, particularly the variants that allow syntax to generate complex words through syntactic processes of movement, such as incorporation (Baker 1988). Of course, one does not have to adhere to the incorporation account to maintain that the preverbal NP is not a genuine subject. One could alternatively assume that the full agreement on the verb is genuine agreement that licenses a null pronominal subject. The theory, particularly its preminimalist versions, allowed for such a null syntactic category to be present in the syntactic representation as long as it was licensed by agreement on the verb (Kenstowicz 1989). Thus, the null pronominal is possible in the context of agreement on the verb but not with agreement on the adjective or participle.

(47)
a. naam-uu
slept-3.M.PL
"They slept"

b. *naaʔim-uun
sleeping-M.PL

(47a) is a full sentence with a null pronominal licensed by the agreement on the verb, but (47b) is not because the adjective does not carry person agreement which is critical to licensing the null pronominal.[26]

[26] The picture is, of course, more complicated. So-called null pronominals can be licensed in rich discourse contexts where person agreement may not be present. However, absent such rich contexts, person agreement seems critical. It should be mentioned that the syntactic status of the category null pronominal remains undetermined within minimalist approaches. This in turn has something to

The view that the preverbal noun phrase is not a subject contrasts with the approach that Fassi Fehri (1993) and Benmamoun (1992, 2000) advocate.[27] This approach gets its theoretical motivation from the rise of the so-called VP-internal subject hypothesis (Koopman and Sportiche 1991). The idea is that the subject is generated within the lexical projection of the verb as in (48).

(48)

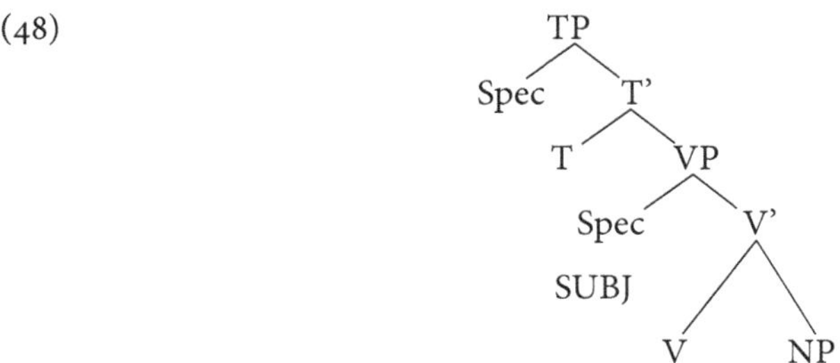

Mohammad (1988, 1999a) and Fassi Fehri (1993) argue for generating the subject within the lexical projection on very strong empirical and theoretical grounds. Theoretically, the subject is thematically dependent on the verb and not on tense. Empirically, the structure in (48) allows for a straightforward analysis of the VSO structure in Arabic. Prior to the insightful analyses in those studies, Arabic was considered a language that lacks a VP constituent that combines the verb and its complement and excludes the subject. The structure in (49) was typically adopted for VSO orders in languages such as Arabic, Berber, and Celtic families.

(49)

As convincingly shown by Mohammad (1988) and Fassi Fehri, the structure in (49) wrongly implies that there is no asymmetric relation between the subject and object. Such asymmetries abound. For example, the subject can corefer with the object but not vice versa (50). If there is both a subject and an object question phrase, it is easier to extract the subject than the object (51). Moreover, it is more likely to find a verb and an object forming an idiomatic expression in Palestinian Arabic (PA) and other varieties (Aoun et al. 2010) than a subject and verb (52).

do with the still unclear relation between thematic structure, the notion of subject, and the syntactic configuration. One reason for positing a null pronominal was the need to satisfy the thematic criterion or to the fulfill the subject requirement of clauses (so-called extended projection principle) in addition to providing binders for anaphors and place holders for circumventing island conditions in syntactic dependencies.

[27] See also Doron and Heycock (1999), who argue for two types of subjects for Arabic, the so-called broad subject and the so-called narrow subject.

(50) a. raʔaa xaal-u l-bint-i l-bint-a
saw.3 uncle-NOM DEF-girl-GEN DEF-girl-ACC
"The girl's uncle saw the girl."

b. *raʔ-at l-bint-u xaal-a l-bint-i
saw-3.F.SG DEF-girl-NOM uncle-ACC DEF-girl-GEN
"The girl saw the girl's uncle."

(51) a. man baaʕa maaðaa
who sold.3 what
"Who sold what?"

b. *maaðaa man baaʕa
what who sold.3
"*Who sold what?"

c. *maaðaa baaʕa man
what sold.3 who
"*Who sold what?"

(52) ʔeħmad ḍayyaʕ ʕagl-u
Ahmed lost.3 mind-his
"Ahmed went crazy."

This type of evidence and others (based on movement and coordination) have been generally consistent in languages that have been argued previously not to have a VP constituent. In fact, the analysis for Arabic VSO structure along the lines of the structure in (49) was developed almost concurrently with similar analyses for Celtic languages and Berber. It was part of a debate in the 1980s about the status of the subject, word order, and configurationality. In this respect, Arabic benefited greatly from the rich empirical research that was conducted within generative syntax particularly in the 1980s when a number of languages were discussed in greater detail but with an eye toward exploring issues of language variation and language universals. Arabic also contributed to that debate and helped advance it.

Now, the structure in (48) has empirical and conceptual support, but for it to work, one needs to account for the fact that, on the surface, the verb precedes the subject yielding the VSO order. The most plausible option that is consistent with the principles and parameters theory is that the verb undergoes movement from within the VP that it moves to the head of T. If the subject remains within the VP, the result is the VSO order. This is the analysis that Mohammad (1988, 1989), Benmamoun (1992) Fassi Fehri (1993), and Ouhalla (1994) argue for. Since movement can take an element to a position that is only hierarchically more prominent than its original position, the logical solution is that it is the verb that is raised to T rather than the subject moving to some lower position between the verb and the object. The movement of the verb in the VSO order echoes similar movement posited for other languages, including French, where the verb is assumed to raise to T but there is also movement of the subject from the Spec of VP to the Spec of TP, which yields the SVO order. Thus, the difference between languages could be due to verb movement without subject movement (Arabic) or verb movement and subject movement (French) or subject movement but no lexical verb movement (English).[28]

Once this assumption is made, a host of issues arise. For example, what drives verb movement? Does the subject stay within the VP, or is it in a higher position, which means that the verb itself maybe in an even higher projection? The first question relates to a fundamental issue within the principles and parameters framework about the nature of movement and its causes and has sparked a lively debate about clause structure (the types of functional categories and their nature) and the relation between grammatical categories and lexical categories and the implications of that relation on word order and syntactic dependencies such as case, agreement, polarity, and information structure. Arabic is part of this debate, as the recent work of Aoun et al. (2010), Soltan (2007), Shlonsky (1997), Ouhalla (2002), Doron and Heyock (1999), Choueiri (2002), among many others, shows. The debate has started off with SA and has expanded its scope to include a variety of spoken Arabic dialects.

Before closing this section let us revisit subject–verb agreement. It is one of the most contentious issues in Arabic syntax and also one of the properties of Arabic that has received great attention within the theory of principles and parameters at large. Two main facts about agreement have had this privilege. The first one, which we already mentioned, centers on the agreement asymmetry relative to word order. The second one has to do with another asymmetry that is relevant to word order but in the context of coordinated subjects.

With regard to the agreement asymmetry between a single NP subject and the verb, the focus has been exclusively on SA. Simply put, the main question is the following: If full and partial agreement are indeed genuine agreement features on the verb, how would one account for their distribution?[29] The critical factor here is word order. One

[28] The fourth option, namely, neither movement of the subject nor movement of the verb, may also be possible (see Borer 1995).

[29] If full agreement is the realization of a pronominal, the issue of the asymmetry dissolves, but then one must contend with the fact that full agreement is found in a variety of contexts where it would be hard to argue that it is a pronominal. For example, it can be found on both an auxiliary verb and a main verb when it seems that there is one source for the pronoun in the specifier of the lexical projection of the main verb.

(i) kun-**na** **ya**-ʔkul-**na**
be.PST-3.F.PL 3-eat-F.PL
"They were eating."

Also, a lexical subject in the same context fully agrees with the lexical verb and partially agrees with the auxiliary:

(ii) kaan-at ṭ-ṭaalib-aat-u **ya**-ʔkul-**na**
be.PST-3.F DEF-student-F.PL-NOM 3-eat-F.PL
"The students were eating."

It would be hard to maintain the claim that the full agreement in (ii) on the main verb is a pronoun given that there is already a subject between the verb and the auxiliary.

would need to find a way to relate word order to the presence versus absence of number agreement. The proposals have ranged from setting up different structural conditions on number agreement and person–gender agreement (Benmamoun 1992) to deriving full and partial agreement at different points in the derivation (Fassi Fehri 1993; Doron 1996) to relegating the problem to the morphology syntax interface (Benmamoun 2000; Benmamoun and Lorimor 2006). A convincing solution remains elusive, but any that is proposed also needs to explain why the same asymmetry does not obtain in the same way in the spoken dialects.[30] Thus, (45) markedly contrasts to (53) from MA, where no agreement asymmetry relative to word order arises.

(53)

a. wəqf-u lə-wlad
stood-3.PL DEF-children
"The children stood up."

b. lə-wlad wəqf-u
DEF-children stood.3.PL
"The children stood up."

c.* wəqf lə-wlad
stood.3 DEF-children

This contrast between SA and the modern spoken dialects provides a rich empirical source for engaging issues about variation and language change from a theoretical perspective.

Turning to agreement in the context of coordination, the main issue has been the fact that when the coordinated subject follows the verb the latter agrees with the leftmost conjunct as illustrated in (54a) from MA. This so-called close conjunct agreement is not possible when the coordinated subject precedes the verb, as indicated by the ungrammaticality of (54d). The full agreement option is available regardless of word order (54b)–(54c).

(54)

a. ža l-wəld w l-muʕəllim
came.3 DEF-boy and DEF-teacher
"The teacher and the boy came."

b. ža-w l-wəld w l-muʕəllim
came-3.PL DEF-boy and DEF-teacher
"The teacher and the boy came."

c. l-wəld w l-muʕəllim ža-w
DEF-boy and DEF-teacher came-3.PL
"The teacher and the boy came."

[30] Some spoken dialects, such as PA and LA, do display an agreement asymmetry relative to word order in the context of indefinite subjects (see Hallman 2000; Hoyt 2002).

d.	*l-wəld	w	l-muʕəllim	ža
	DEF-boy	and	DEF-teacher	came.3

Syntactic approaches can easily handle full conjunct agreement, which essentially entails extending the same account for agreement with simple plural noun phrases.[31] Close conjunct agreement resists those accounts because of its apparent sensitivity to linear order, but in one direction in Arabic (rightward). The challenge is to find a principled way of isolating the closest conjunct to the right of the verb. For Benmamoun (1992), the verb accesses the leftmost conjunct to its right because it governs the entire coordination and its specifier (assuming a specifier head complement structure of coordination). This assumes a purely syntactic account of close conjunct agreement. Munn (1999) and Soltan (2007) provide alternative accounts that also privilege the leftmost conjunct. On the other hand, Aoun et al. (1994) argue that close conjunct agreement is not special, because the coordination is in fact a coordination of sentences and not phrases. Under that scenario, close conjunct agreement is in reality agreement between the verb and one single NP subject. The other NP subject (second conjunct) is a subject of a sentence that contains a gapped verb. This account relies on a very abstract representation but is also in agreement with the other accounts in adhering to a purely syntactic account. Aoun et al. (1994) advance a number of arguments based on number sensitive items in favor of the gapping/biclausal account, but Munn (1999) and Soltan (2007) have challenged their conclusion.

Departing from a purely syntactic account, Benmamoun et al. (2010) argue on somewhat similar data from Hindi and Tsez (two head final languages that also display close conjunct agreement but in both directions) that adjacency and linear order are critical factors for any account of this phenomenon. The gapping analysis was shown to be inadequate for head final languages and also for Arabic. They argue that the output of syntax, which targets the entire coordination, can be spelled out differently under pressure from the morphophonological component. Essentially, they argue that close conjunct agreement is an interface problem that neatly highlights the interaction between the syntax component and the other components (morphology and phonology) that interpret and spell out its output. Usually, one would expect spell out to be fully faithful, but slight distortions might result due to performance and linear order pressures. However, this account does not fully resolve the distribution of number sensitive items in the context of coordinated subjects. These items, such as collective predicates and reciprocals, which require a plural subject, always seem to require plural agreement on the verb. In some languages, close conjunct agreement seems to be perfectly acceptable in the context of number sensitive items, but in Arabic they seem to require plural agreement on the verb. This contrast remains an open question.

[31] The structure of coordination and the computation of the features of its members must also be part of any analysis of agreement in the context of coordination. See in this connection Benmamoun (1992), Bahloul and Harbert (1993), Munn (1993), Harbert and Bahloul (2002), and Soltan (2007).

The debate about close conjunct agreement has now resulted in a full-blown discussion about the nature of agreement, the role of syntax in capturing and constraining agreement relations, and the interface issues that arise when other components come into play. Arabic and particularly spoken Arabic dialects are figuring prominently in this important debate, and the study of this phenomenon in Arabic has also greatly benefited from research on similar issues in other languages.

6.5 Negation

Negation is another area that has received extensive attention within generative approaches to Arabic syntax (Benmamoun 1992, 2000; Fassi Fehri 1993; Ouhalla 1993a, 1993b, 1994; Bahloul 1994; Soltan 2007). The issues that dominated the debate were the same issues that took center stage at the inception of the so-called minimalist program around the late 1980s and during the 1990s. The issues were whether functional categories such as negation occupy independent syntactic projections, where those projections are located, and how they interact with the temporal and verbal categories. The other issue that was somewhat specific to Arabic revolved around the variation observed between negative particles across varieties including SA and the difference between sentences with verbal predicates and sentences without verbal predicates.

With regard to the status of negation, the consensus has been that the negative particles in SA, particularly *laa*, *lam*, *lam*, and *laysa*, head a negative projection. This is easy to show by the fact that some of them, such as *lam* (55b) and *lan* (55c), carry temporal information, and *laysa* (55d) carries agreement features, which are all properties of heads:

(55)

a. ṭ-ṭullaab-u **laa** ya-drus-uu-na
DEF-students-NOM NEG 3-study-M.PL-INDC
"The students do not study."

b. ṭ-ṭullaab-u **lam** ya-drus-uu
DEF-students-NOM NEG.PST 3-study-M.PL
"The students did not study."

c. ṭ-ṭullaab-u **lan** ya-drus-uu
DEF-students-NOM NEG.FT 3-study-M.PL
"The students will not study."

d. lays-at fi l-bayt
NEG-3.F in DEF-house
"She is not in the house."

The controversy has been around the location of the negative projection: if we take another look at the representation in (48), the options are to locate negation above TP or below TP. Benmamoun (1992) and Ouhalla (1993a), for example, locate the negative phrase (NegP) between TP and VP, while Soltan locates it above TP.[32] All try to derive the temporal negatives through the interaction of TP and NegP. Locating negation between the tense head and the verb makes the negative a closer host of tense than the verb. This analysis deploys the theory of minimality within the principles and parameters framework that took shape during the 1980s and 1990s and was an important precursor to the so-called minimalist program (Chomsky 1995). Minimality simply means that dependencies are sensitive to the type of intervening element. For example, the relation between a displaced interrogative phrase and its original position (designated by a trace or copy) may be intercepted or disrupted by another interrogative phrase, if the latter occurs in the path of the chain formed by the moved element and its base position. Another related property of minimality is grounded in the economy of derivations and representations. Within the present context, the negative head is closer to tense and is a potential host, so it has priority over the verb. Soltan (2007), on the other hand, relies on feature checking theory, made popular during the 1990s and now widely adopted within minimalist approaches. The main idea is that the negative head, which is higher than the tense head, is also specified for tense features. The negative enters into a checking relation with tense (Benmamoun et al. Forthcoming), and, due to a condition that bans the spelling of features on the same two heads in a checking relation, tense surfaces on the negative only.[33] It does not surface on the verb, not because the latter does not contain the tense feature but because tense is already spelled out on the higher negative.

The same issues have been discussed in the context of syntactic research on negation in the spoken Arabic dialects (Benmamoun 1992, 2000; Halila 1992; Shlonsky 1997; Soltan 2007; Hoyt 2010). In the colloquial dialects, we usually find two types of negatives, though neither of them carries temporal information (Benmamoun et al. Forthcoming). We have a negative circumfix and an independent negative. The former usually occurs in the context of verbs and so-called pseudo-verbs.[34] The latter occurs usually in the context of nonverbal predicates.[35] The two sets of distributional facts are illustrated in (56):

(56)

a. ma-qra-š l-wəld
NEG-read-NEG DEF-boy
"The boy did not read."

b. huwa maši hna
he NEG here
"He is not here."

[32] Ouhalla (1993a) provides strong arguments that the negative *maa* in SA, which is associated with focus, is located in a higher projection specified for focus features.

[33] We are putting aside important details for lack of space. Soltan (2007) relies crucially on the notion that noninterpretable features on negation drive the checking relation. He assumes that there is a tense feature on negation that compels it to enter into a checking relation with the tense feature on the verb.

[34] See Brustad (2000).

[35] The picture is actually more complex. We do find the circumfix in the context of nonverbal predicates and the independent negative in the context of verbs and pseudo-verbs (Eid 1993; Brustad 2000; Soltan 2007).

Most syntactic approaches adopt the view that we are dealing with one single negative whose distribution varies according to whether it merges with a head. If it does, we get the circumfix, as in (56a); in the dialects without the enclitic -*š*, such as Kuwaiti, we get *maa* (57a). If it does not, we get the independent negative as in (56b) or the negative *muu* in Kuwaiti, Gulf, and some Levantine varieties (57b):

(57)

a.

maa	ʔa-dri	šlon	marr-at	s-sana
NEG	1.SG-know	how	went-F	DEF-year

"I don't know how the year went."

b.

r-rayyal	muu	min	l-kweet
DEF-man	NEG	from	DEF-Kuwait

"The man is not from Kuwait."

It is still an open question whether the negative circumfix is one single element or two independent elements that co-occur. In the latter case, the issue of where the two are located and their distribution becomes acute.

Due to space limitations we will not detail how tense interacts with negation and how the negative particles interact with negative polarity items and quantifiers (Benmamoun 1997, 2006). Another important question that is beginning to get some attention concerns the evolution of negation and the possible syntactic approaches to that evolution (van Gelderen 1996, 2008). Overall, the study of negation in SA and other modern Arabic dialects within the principles and parameters approach has contributed a great deal to the ongoing research on grammatical categories and their interaction with lexical categories. Needless to say, this research is still in its early stages and needs more in-depth study of similar facts in other varieties of Arabic and a study of the syntax and semantic interface in the context of negation.

6.6 Long A'-Dependencies

The study of (long) A'-dependencies features prominently in the investigation of displacement, a defining characteristic of human language, and of its properties, from both a derivational and representational perspective. The work recently done on A'-chains in Arabic tackles important questions related to those issues, such as the role of island conditions and reconstruction in defining movement A'-chains, the relation of resumptive chains to movement, and cross-linguistic syntactic variation.[36]

[36] There are many constructions that exhibit long A'-dependencies, including wh-interrogatives, restrictive relatives, free relatives, clefts, (clitic-)left dislocation, topicalization, tough-movement constructions, parasitic gaps, and comparative clauses, among others. In this chapter, we will focus on wh-interrogatives, illustrated in (58), restrictive relatives (ia), and clitic-left dislocation (CLLD) (ib).

6.6.1 Gaps and Resumptives: Distribution and Variation

The distribution of gaps and resumptive elements in A'-dependencies is not uniform across the different varieties of Arabic: dialects differ in whether they make use of the gap or resumptive strategy for a given A'-construction. Within a given dialect, on the other hand, the availability of the gap or resumptive strategy depends on the type of A'-construction and on the variable position within the sentence. While SA makes use of the gap strategy in forming constituent wh-questions (58a)–(58b), EgA seems to prohibit the use of this strategy in those contexts (59a)–(59b) (see Wahba 1984; Aoun, Benmamoun, and Choueiri 2010; Soltan 2011):[37]

(58) a. maaðaa žaraa e fii ʔižtimaaʕ-i l-qaahira
what happened.3 in meeting-GEN DEF-Cairo
"What happened at the Cairo meeting?"

b. maaðaa yumkinu-nii ʔan ʔu-ʕṭiya e ʔakθar
what be.possible-1.SG that 1.SG-give more
"What more can I give?"

(59) a.* miin ʔinta šuf-t e imbaariħ
who you.M.SG see-2.M.SG yesterday
"Who did you see yesterday?"

b.* eeh mona nis-it ti-ktib e
what Mona forgot-3.F.SG 3.F.SG-write
"What did Mona forget to write?"

Within a given variety, the availability of the gap and resumptive strategies to form long-distance A'-dependencies varies between construction types. In LA, for instance, the gap strategy is readily available for wh-interrogatives (60a) but not for restrictive

(i) a. haʔulaaʔ šurakaaʔ-u-na allaðiina kun-na na-dʕuu min duuni-ka
those partners-NOM-our that.M.PL were-1.PL 1.PL-invite without-you
"Those are our partners that we used to invite without you."

b. ʔinna **haaðaa l-xiṭaab** li-r-raʔiis Bush kaana yumkinu
COMP this DEF-speech to-DEF-president Bush was.3 be.possible.3
ʔan yaktuba-**hu** masʔuul-un fi al-Likud
that write-3.M.SG official-NOM in DEF-Likud
"This speech by President Bush, an official from the Likud Party could have written it."

[37] Adjunct wh-words in Egyptian Arabic can marginally appear in the left periphery related to a gap within the sentence (i):

(i) ?? fein/ʔimtaa/ʔizzaay/leih ʔaħmad ha-yi-saafir
where/when/how/why Ahmad FT-3-travel
"Where/When/How/Why will Ahmad travel?"

relatives (60b)–(60c), with the possible exception of relative clauses involving relativized subjects (see also Section 6.6.4).

(60) a. ʔayya mmassil šif-te e b-l-maṭʕam
which actor saw-2.F.SG in-DEF-restaurant
"Which actor did you see in the restaurant?"

b.* l-mmassil lli šif-te e b-l-maṭʕam miš mašhuur
DEF-actor that saw-2.F.SG in-DEF-restaurant NEG famous
"The actor that you saw in the restaurant is not famous."

c. **l-mmassil** lli šif-t-**i** b-l-maṭʕam miš mašhuur
DEF-actor that saw.2.F.SG-him in-DEF-restaurant NEG famous
"The actor that you saw in the restaurant is not famous."

Unlike LA (and several other varieties of Arabic including EgA (see also Brustad 2000) and PA (see also Shlonsky 1992)), SA (61) and MA (62) make use of the gap strategy alongside the resumptive strategy in restrictive relatives.

(61) a. ʔinna l-ʔamrikaan yu-ɣriq-uuna-ka fi l-ʔaxbaari llati yu-riid-uun e
COMP DEF-Americans 3-drown-M.PL-you.M in DEF-news that.F 3-want-M.PL
"The Americans drown you in the news that they want."

b. lakinna-hu fašila fii takraari **l-ʔinžaaz-i** llaði ħaqqaqa-**hu**
but-he failed.3 in repeating DEF-achievement-GEN that achieved.3–3.M.SG
fi haaðaa s-sibaaqi
in this DEF-race
"But he failed in repeating the performance that he had achieved in this race."

(62) žbar-t **lə-ktab** lli nsi-ti-(**h**) fi l-qism
found-1.SG DEF-book that forgot-2.F.SG-it in DEF-class
"I found the book that you forgot in the classroom."

Finally, the distribution of gaps and resumptives also varies with respect to the position of the variable within the sentence. Thus, in all varieties of Arabic, A'-dependencies that relate a wh-element or a relativized NP to the complement position of a preposition must terminate in a resumptive element. Gaps are not licensed as prepositional complements, as illustrated in (63) from SA:

(63) wa **junuudu roma** llaðiina ya-taħaddaθ-u ʕan-*(**hum**) l-bayati
and soldiers Rome that 3-talk-INDC about-*(them) al-Bayati
fi l-ʔabyat-i s-saabiqa ...
in DEF-verses-GEN DEF-preceding ...
"And the soldiers of Roma that Al-Bayati talks about in the preceding verses ..."

Table 6.1 Cross-dialectal availability of the gap and resumptive strategies in forming wh-questions

	Gap Strategy	Resumptive Strategy
Lebanese Arabic and Standard Arabic	YES	YES
Moroccan Arabic	YES	NO
Egyptian Arabic	NO	NO

Table 6.2 Variation in the availability of the gap and resumptive strategies based on type of A'-construction

	Gap Strategy	Resumptive Strategy
Lebanese Arabic	Wh-interrogatives	Wh-interrogatives Restrictive relatives
Moroccan Arabic and Standard Arabic	Restrictive relatives Wh-interrogatives	Restrictive relatives
Egyptian Arabic[38]		Restrictive relatives

The distributional facts briefly discussed so far show that the gap strategy and the resumptive strategy are not uniformly available across the various Arabic dialects. Table 6.1 represents the cross-dialectal difference in the availability of those strategies in forming wh-interrogatives.

Another observation we made is that, within a given variety of Arabic, the gap strategy or the resumptive strategy are not uniformly available in forming long A'-dependencies. Table 6.2 is a representation of this observation based on a sample of four dialect varieties.

Nouhi (1996) points out that resumptive pronouns are not possible in constituent wh-questions in MA (64):

(64) *ʔaš šaaf-**u** ʕli
what saw.3-it.M Ali
"What did Ali see?"

It is also important to note here that we do not know of any dialect of Arabic where restrictive relatives are formed using only the gap strategy.

[38] Soltan (2011) suggests that the constraint in (i) is at work in EgA:

(i) A'-positions must be resumed.

6.6.2 Constraints on Movement: Island Conditions

One of the most discussed issues in the syntax of A'-dependencies is their behavior in island contexts: gaps have been generally shown to be sensitive to island conditions, while resumptive elements seem to systematically violate them. This is true in the various dialects of Arabic.

While gaps can be related to an antecedent across clause boundaries (65), they are not allowed to occur within islands (see Aoun et al. 2010 and references cited therein). We illustrate this fact using relative-clause islands in LA (66) and wh-clause islands in MA (67):

(65) a. smaʕ-t ʔənno naadia ʔəl-te ʔənno raħ t-šuuf-e e bi-beeriz
heard-1.SG that Nadia said-2.F.SG that FT 2-see-F.SG in-Paris
"I heard that Nadia, you said that you will see in Paris."

b. miin ʔəl-t-o ʔənno raħ t-šuuf naadia e bi-beeriz
who said-2-PL that FT 3.F-see Nadia in-Paris
"Who did you say that Nadia will see in Paris?"

(66) a.* smaʕ-t ʔənno naadia b-ta-ʕrf-o l-mara yalli zeer-it e
heard.1.SG that Nadia INDC-2-know-PL DEF-woman that visited-3.F.SG
"I heard that, Nadia, you know the woman that visited."

b.* miin/ʔayya mariiḍ b-ta-ʕrf-o l-mara yalli zeer-it e
who/which patient INDC-2-know-PL DEF-woman that visited-3.F.SG
"Who/which patient do you know the woman that visited?"

(67)?? škun ka-t-saaʔal waš brahim ʕaaraf e e safer
who INDC-2-wonder whether Brahim knew.3 traveled.3
"Who do you wonder whether Brahim knew traveled?"

In contrast to A'-constructions involving gaps, resumptive A'-constructions in the various Arabic dialects demonstrate their immunity to island constraints. Using relative clause islands, we illustrate this fact in LA (68) and EgA (69):

(68) a. smaʕ-t ʔənno **naadia** b-ta-ʕrfo l-mara yalli zeer-it-**a**
heard-1.SG that Nadia INDC-2-know-PL DEF-woman that visited-3.F-her
"I heard that, Nadia, you know the woman that visited her."

b. **miin/ʔayya mariiḍ** b-ta-ʕrfo l-mara yalli zeer-it-**o**
who/which patient INDC-2-know-PL DEF-woman that visited-3.F.SG-him
"Who/which patient do you know the woman that visited him?"

(69) dah **l-beet** illi baba ye-ʕraf il-raagil illi ban-**ah**
this DEF-house that father 3-knows DEF-man that built.3-it.M
"This is the house that Father knows the man who built it."

The observations in (66)–(69) are enough to confirm that gap A'-constructions and resumptive A'-constructions in Arabic behave as expected with respect to island constraints. Assuming sensitivity to islands to be a diagnostic for wh-movement (Chomsky 1977), we can further add that A'-dependencies that terminate with a gap are generated by movement of the antecedent from the variable position to a position at the clause periphery leaving behind a gap, whereas A'-dependencies that terminate with a resumptive pronoun are not so generated.

6.6.3 The Nature of Resumptive Elements and Their Binding Properties

Chao and Sells (1983) and Sells (1984) argue that the resumptive strategy is not uniform: some languages make use of *resumptive pronouns*; others make use of *intrusive pronouns*, which are a saving device for constructions that would otherwise violate some grammatical principle, such as island constraints. Resumptive pronouns, on the other hand, are interpreted as variables bound by operators in A'-position. Based on this early distinction, Ouhalla (2001) proposes the definition in (70) for resumptive pronouns:[39]

(70) A pronoun P is resumptive if there exists an operator O such that O directly A'-binds P at S-structure.

(71) α directly A'-binds β iff α A'-binds β and there is no γ, γ a trace of α, such that γ c-commands β.

The definition in (70) helps to draw a distinction between resumptive pronouns and A-bound pronouns, an example of which can be seen in (72a):

(72) a. ʔayya walad$_i$ ʔakal təffeħt-o$_{i/j}$ *LA*
which child ate.3 apple-his
"Which child ate his apple?"

b. ʔayya walad$_i$ ʔakal-it naadia təffeħt-o$_{i/*j}$
which child ate-3.F.SG Nadia apple-his
"Which child did Nadia eat his apple?"

In (72a), the possessive pronoun may or may not have the bound variable reading: the pronoun can freely refer to someone in the discourse context (marked with the

[39] Ouhalla (2001) uses the term *pronoun*, since he discusses only strong and weak pronouns as resumptive elements. Due to space limitations, we will not extend the discussion to epithets. For an analysis of epithets as resumptive pronominals in Arabic see Aoun and Choueiri (2000) and Aoun, Choueiri, and Hornstein (2001).

Table 6.3 Third-person weak and strong pronouns in LA[40]

	Singular		Plural
	Masculine	Feminine	
Weak	-o	-a	-un
Strong	huwwe	hiyye	hənne

index *j* in (72a)). This is not the case in (72b), where the bound reading is the only available reading for the possessive pronoun. In (72a), unlike (72b), the trace of the subject wh-phrase *ʔayya walad* "which child" c-commands the possessive pronoun; therefore, the possessive pronoun in (72a) is not directly A'-bound by the operator at S-structure.

An interesting contrast is highlighted in Aoun and Choueiri (2000) between weak and strong pronouns regarding their ability to function as resumptive elements (see also Ouhalla 2001). Thus, while (72b) is acceptable in LA, the sentences in (73) are not:

(73) a.* miin$_i$ fakkar-t-o huwwe$_i$ b-l-beet
who thought-2-PL he in-DEF-house
"Who did you think he was at home?"

b.* χabbar-uu-kun ʔənno kəll walad$_i$ fakkar-na huwwe$_i$ b-l-beet
told-3.PL-you.PL that every boy thought-1.PL he in-DEF-house
"They told you that every boy we thought he was at home."

Third-person strong pronouns in LA and their weak counterparts are given in Table 6.3.

To account for the contrast between (72b) and (73), it is claimed that strong pronouns, unlike weak pronouns, are subject to an A'-disjointness requirement stated in (74) (see, e.g., Chao and Sells 1983; Borer 1984; Aoun and Li 1990, 1993a; McCloskey 1990; Ouhalla 1993b):

(74) *A'-disjointness requirement*
A strong or tonic pronoun cannot be linked to the most local operator.

The A'-disjointness requirement basically states that a strong pronoun cannot be too close to its antecedent, when the latter is an operator. This requirement provides an account for the unacceptability of the sentences in (73), where the resumptive strong

[40] Weak pronouns, which occur in all nonsubject positions, are affixed to heads, for example, V, N, or P (as seen in (72)); strong or tonic pronouns, which usually occur in subject positions, are free morphemes (as seen in (73)).

pronoun is linked to the most local operator, and for the acceptability of the sentences in (75):

(75) a. miin$_i$ tseeʔal-t-o ʔəza/ʔemtiin huwwe$_i$ rəbiħ žeeyze *LA*
who wondered-2-PL whether/when he won.3 prize
"Who did you wonder whether/when he won a prize?"

b. ʕrəf-t-o ʔənno kəll walad$_i$ tseeʔal-na ʔəza/ʔemtiin huwwe$_i$
knew-2-PL that every boy wondered-1.PL whether/when he
rəbiħ žeeyze
won.3 prize
"You learned that every boy we wondered whether he won a prize."

In (75), a wh-operator (*ʔəza/ʔemtiin* "whether/when") intervenes between the resumptive pronoun and its antecedent in the sentence. Therefore, linking each of the resumptive pronouns to their antecedent in those sentences does not violate the A'-disjointness requirement.

When the antecedent is not an operator, (74) does not apply. This explains the acceptability of (76):

(76) [ʔəxt-e]$_i$ (ʔaal-u-l-e ʔənno) hiyye$_i$ ribħ-it s-sabaʔ
sister-my (said-3.PL-to-me that) she won-3.F DEF-race
"My sister, (they told me that) she won the race."

While this version of the A'-disjointness requirement accounts for the distribution of strong pronouns as resumptive elements in LA, it does not seem to extend to all varieties of Arabic. Ouhalla (2001: 154) observes that "strong pronouns cannot function as resumptive pronouns in MA." This observation is attributed to the generalization in (77) and illustrated in (78).[41]

(77) A strong pronoun cannot be directly A'-bound in MA (Ouhalla's (12)).

(78) a. šmen ṭalib nsi-ti fin tlaqii-h (*huwwa)? *MA*
which student forgot-2.M.SG where met.2.M.SG-him (HIM)
"Which student have you forgotten where you met?"

[41] Following Roberts and Shlonsky (1996), Ouhalla (2001) assumes that nonsubject clitics in Arabic are agreement affixes, having the representation in (ib).

(i) a. šəf-t-/kteeb-/minn-o
saw-1SG-/book-/from-him/his
"I saw him/his book/from him."

b. X+cl [$_{DP}$ *pro*]

c. X+cl [$_{DP}$ *huwwa*]

b. šmen ṭalib saferti qblma y-ṭerd-u-h (*huwwa)?
which student travelled.2.M.SG before 3-expell-PL-him (HIM)
"Which student did you travel before they expelled?"

The position of the strong pronoun in (78) is directly A'-bound by the sentence initial wh-phrase, and therefore those sentences incur a violation of the generalization in (77). The main difference between (78) and (75) is that the status of the antecedent as operator is relevant in LA, whereas strong pronouns in MA cannot tolerate any local A'-antecedent, whether it is an operator or not.[42] Thus, the generalization in (77) is too strong for LA. It appears too strong for Jordanian Arabic (JA) as well. Thus, Guilliot and Malkawi (2006) present evidence that strong pronouns appearing as clitic doubles in JA can function as resumptive elements, as seen in (79):

(79) a. **kul** **bint** kariim gal ʔin-**ha** **(hi)** raħ ti-nžaħ *JA*
every girl Karim said.3 that-her (she) FT 3.F-succeed
"Every girl, Karim said that she will pass."

b. **kul** **zalamih** zʕil-t-u li-ʔannu-**uh** **(hu)** raaħ biduun ma yi-guul
every man upset-2-PL because-him (he) went without NEG 3-say
maʕ salaamih
goodbye
"Every man, you were upset because he left without saying goodbye."

More comparative research is needed to investigate the cross-dialectal variation that we have observed here with respect to the nature of resumptive elements and their binding properties. More specifically, to understand the lay of the land, future research needs to address the syntax of strong pronouns in Arabic more systematically.

6.6.4 Resumption and Movement

The standard assumption with respect to the syntax of resumption in the late 1970s and during the 1980s was that resumptive elements are not generated by movement. As discussed in Section 6.6.2, the immunity of resumptive constructions to island violations led to that conclusion. In light of theoretical developments within generative grammar, especially those pertaining to A'-movement, several approaches to the relation between

The enclitic pronominal, which can be manifested on the categories V, N, and P, as seen in (ia), is in fact an agreement affix identifying a null pronoun argument. In certain contexts, Ouhalla (2001) further claims, the null pronoun can be replaced by an overt strong pronoun, as illustrated in (ic). This analysis brings together strong pronouns appearing in object position with those that appear in subject position, since the latter usually co-occur with agreement morphemes on the verb.

[42] Here we are making the assumption that wh-words like *miin* "who" (in (73a) and (75a)) are operators, while wh-phrases like *šmen ṭalib* "which student" (in (78)) are not (see Pesetsky 1987 for a defense of such an assumption).

resumption and movement were developed to account for the complexity of the phenomenon in the various Arabic dialects.

Shlonsky (1992) proposes analyzing resumption as a last resort strategy: that is, he argues that resumptive pronouns appear only where movement fails to apply. Thus, in the relative clauses in (80) resumptive pronouns are obligatory; gaps are unacceptable.

(80) a. **l-bint** ʔilli šuf-ti-*(**ha**)
DEF-girl that saw-2.F-(her)
"the girl that you saw"

b. **l-bint** ʔilli fakkar-t-i ʔinno mona ħabb-at-*(**ha**)
DEF-girl that thought-2-F that Mona loved-3.F.SG-(her)
"the girl that you thought that Mona loved"

c. **l-bint** ʔilli fakkar-t-i fii-*(**ha**)
DEF-girl that thought-2-F in-(her)
"the girl that you thought about"

In (80c), the resumptive pronoun appears in a position from which A'-movement is traditionally unavailable (i.e., the prepositional complement). More interestingly, resumptive pronouns must appear in the highest and embedded direct object positions from which movement is generally thought to be available (80a)–(80b).[43] Shlonsky's (1992) analysis consists of showing that in all contexts where resumptive pronouns appear, the gap is illicit because it violates some independent constraint on movement. Without going into the details of the analysis, it is clear that it cannot be extended to wh-interrogatives, since several Arabic dialects, including PA, allow the gap strategy to alternate freely with the resumptive strategy.[44]

Another approach to the relation between resumption and movement is pioneered in Demirdache (1991) (see also Demirdache 1997). It relies on the distinction between overt and covert movement and argues for a covert movement analysis of resumption. Demirdache (1991) argues that resumptive pronouns are like null operators that appear in situ in overt syntax. This operator in languages like Arabic is signaled by spelling out its phi-features. The null operator moves covertly to establish the operator–variable chain necessary for its interpretation. This movement is the covert counterpart of the observed movement in cases like (81):

[43] Shlonsky (1992) observes that the only position where gaps are allowed and resumptives prohibited in PA is the highest subject position (HSR), as seen in (i):

(i) l-bint ʔilli (*hiy) raayħ-a ʕa-l-beet
DEF-girl that (*she) going-F.SG to-DEF-house
"the girl that is going home"

Aoun and Choueiri (1996) present evidence that HSR doesn't apply in LA restrictive relatives.

[44] See Shlonsky (1992) for a possible analysis of the alternation between the resumptive and gap strategies in SA restrictive relatives that relies on the agreement properties of the relative marker.

(81) ražaʕa r-ražul-u allaði ʔiyya-hu zur-tu *SA*
returned.3 DEF-man-NOM who that-him visited-1.SG
"the man that I visited returned."

In SA, the resumptive pronoun can be fronted to a clause initial position. In such cases, the weak pronoun requires the support of *ʔiyya-*, which does not contribute any semantic meaning. Under this approach, there is no incompatibility between movement and resumption.

Pursuing a similar line of thinking, Aoun and his colleagues explore, in a series of papers, the complex relation between resumption and movement. Relying mainly on reconstruction as a diagnostic for movement, Aoun and Choueiri (1996) and Aoun and Benmamoun (1998) show that restrictive relatives as well as clitic-left dislocation in LA display reconstruction effects, only when the resumptive pronoun is not separated from its antecedent by an island.[45] This is shown to be the case whether the resumptive pronoun is a weak pronoun as in (82) or a strong pronoun (83):

(82) a. šəf-t **ṣ-ṣuura** **tabaʕ** **ʔəbn-[a]$_i$** yalli [kəll mwazzaf-e]$_i$
saw-1.SG DEF-picture of son-her that [every employee.F]$_i$
(ʔaal-it ʔənno) badd-a t-ʕalləʔ-**a** bi maktab-a$_i$
(said-3.F.SG that) want-3F.SG 3.F-hang-it in office-her
"I saw the picture of her son that every employee (said that) she wants to hang in her office."

b.* šəf-t **ṣ-ṣuura** **tabaʕ** **ʔəbn-[a]$_i$** yalli zʕəl-to laʔanno [kəll
saw-1.SG DEF-picture of son-her that upset-2.PL because [every
mwazzaf-e]$_i$ badd-a t-ʕalləʔ-**a** bi-l-maktab
employee-F] want-3.F.SG 3.F-hang-it in-DEF-office
"I saw the picture of her son that you were upset because every employee wants to hang it in the office."

(83) a. **təlmiiz-[a]$_i$** **l-kəsleen** ma badd-na n-χabbir [wala mʕallme]$_i$ ʔənno
student-her DEF-bad NEG want-l.PL l.PL-tell no teacher that
huwwe zaʕbar b-l-faħṣ
he cheated.3 in-DEF-exam
"Her bad student, we don't want to tell any teacher that he cheated on the exam."

b.* **təlmiiz-[a]$_i$** **l-kəsleen** ma ħkii-na maʕ [wala mʕallme]$_i$ ʔablma
student-her DEF-bad NEG talked-1.PL with no teacher before
huwwe yuusal
he arrive.3
"Her bad student, we didn't talk to any teacher before he arrived."

[45] To illustrate the generalization, we are using here examples of adjunct islands. It is important, however, to note that the generalization extends to other types of islands (e.g., relative clause islands and wh-islands) as well.

To see how reconstruction for bound variable anaphora works, we provide schematic representations of the sentences in (82–83):

(84) a. *Reconstruction Available*
... $[_{Antecedent}$ .... $pron_i$ .... $]_j$ .... $([_{CP})$.......... QP_i .... $([_{CP})$ ..... RP_j ... (]) (]) ...

b. *Reconstruction unavailable*
* ... $[_{Antecedent}$ .... $pron_i$ .... $]_j$ ...... $([_{Island})$........ QP_i ... $([_{Island})$ .... RP_j ... (]) (]) ...

Resumption, it is concluded, is not a unitary phenomenon. It can be derived from two different sources: the first one, *true resumption* (see Aoun, Choueiri, and Hornstein 2001), has the antecedent base-generated in its surface position and related to a pronominal inside the sentence via some interpretive mechanism available in the grammar (85a). In the other derivation, termed *apparent resumption* (see ibid.), the antecedent is generated together with the resumptive element, and it undergoes movement to its surface position leaving a copy or trace in the base (85b):

(85) a. *True resumption*
$Antecedent_i$ .... RP_i

b. *Apparent resumption*
$Antecedent_i$ .... $\textit{Antecedent}_i$-RP

The bound variable reading obtains only when a sentence can be derived from the source in (85b). In that case, the lower copy of the antecedent contains a copy of the bound pronoun, which will be c-commanded by the quantifier phrase within the sentence—hence the bound variable reading. The representation in (85b) depends on the availability of movement: since movement from within islands is prohibited, the sentences in (82b)–(83b) cannot have such a representation. It is not surprising then, that the bound variable reading resulting from reconstruction is not available in those sentences.

Recent work by Guillot and Malkawi (2006) and Malkawi and Guilliot (2007) challenges the tight connection that Aoun, Choueiri, and Hornstein (2001) assume to exist between reconstruction and movement. For the latter, reconstruction is the result of interpreting the lower copy of a moved element. Malkawi and Guilliot (2007) use data from JA to show that reconstruction needs to be dissociated from movement. (86a) shows that reconstruction can take place inside strong islands in JA, and (86b) illustrates the fact that, despite the absence of islands, reconstruction is still not available:

(86) a. **ṭaalib-[ha]$_i$** **l-kassul** l-mudiira ziʕl-at laʔannu [kul mʕalmih]$_i$
student-her DEF-bad DEF-principal upset-3.F because every teacher
šaaf-at-**uh** **(hu)** ɣašš bi li- mtiħaan
saw-3.F-him he cheated.3 in DEF-exam
"Her bad student, the principal got upset because every teacher saw him cheating in the exam."

b. **ʕalamit kariim** b-it-fakkir ʔinnu lazim i-ɣayyar-**ha**
grade Karim INDC-2-think that must 3-change-it.F
"Karim's grade, you think that he must change (it)."

Assuming that bound variable anaphora requires a c-command relation between the quantifier phrase and the relevant pronoun, cases like (86a) clearly indicate that, even in the absence of movement, reconstruction must be available. Coreference between *kariim* and the embedded subject is possible in (86b). If reconstruction were forced, we would expect coreference to fail as a result of a principle C violation.[46] Since this is not the case, we can therefore conclude that reconstruction is not necessary even when movement is available.

Malkawi and Guilliot (2007) further argue that the contrast between the presence of reconstruction and its absence cannot be explained away by stipulating that reconstruction is merely optional. Such an assumption would not account for the contrast they observe between weak pronouns (86b) and strong pronouns (87) with respect to principle C effects:

(87)* **ʔaχu layla**$_i$ *pro*$_i$ gaal-at ʔinnu **hu** saafar
brother Layla said-3.F that he left.3
"The brother of Layla, she said that he/the idiot left."

In (87), coreference between *Layla* and the subject of the main clause is not possible, indicating that reconstruction of the clitic-left dislocated element has taken place and a principle C violation ensued. The pattern of reconstruction in resumptive contexts is even more complex in JA, but this suffices to show how it challenges a tight link between movement and reconstruction. Guilliot and Malkawi (2006) and Malkawi and Guilliot (2007) argue that reconstructed readings follow, not necessarily from movement, but from the operation COPY, which is independently available in the grammar of all languages. The interaction between COPY and the syntax of pronouns in JA accounts for the data in (86)–(87). The approach in Guilliot and Malkawi (2006) and Malkawi and Guilliot (2007) to the syntax of pronouns in Arabic differs from that set out in Ouhalla (2001). They assume that weak pronouns are definite determiners that can appear in two different structures: one where the definite determiner is followed by a NP that later undergoes deletion under identity with an antecedent (88a); and the other where the definite determiner is not branching (88b) (see Elbourne 2001):

(88) *Weak pronouns*
a. [the/it ~~NP~~] b. [the/it$_i$]

[46] Principle C of the binding theory (Chomsky 1981) blocks identity between a referential expression and a c-commanding pronoun (i).

(i) She said that Mary left. (She ≠ Mary)

It is the availability of both structures that accounts for the optional availability of reconstructed readings with weak pronouns (88). In (86a), the weak resumptive pronoun has the structure in (88a), with the NP being a copy of the clitic-left dislocated noun phrase that gets deleted. Thus, a copy of the pronoun contained within the clitic-left dislocated noun phrase is present in the resumption site for interpretation. This accounts for the availability of the bound variable reading in (86a). In (86b), the availability of the structure in (88b) accounts for the absence of principle C effects.

Malkawi and Guilliot (2007) follow Aoun, Choueiri, and Hornstein (2001) in assuming that strong pronouns are full DPs that can be adjoined to another DP resulting in constructions like (89):

(89) saami huwwe nəse l-mawʕad
Sami he forgot.3 DEF-appointment
"Sami, he, forgot the appointment."

In (87) then, the clitic-left dislocated phrase is initially generated in an adjunction structure with the strong pronoun and then moved to its sentence initial position. Therefore, a copy of the name *layla* is present in the resumption site, leading to the observed principle C effect.

The discussion of resumption in long A'-dependencies highlights the complexity of the syntactic microvariation that we observe between the various spoken dialects of Arabic. Needless to say, further research is required to understand what underlies this variation. Nevertheless, the investigation of resumption and its properties within the generative paradigm has led to an interesting discussion of the diagnostics of A'-movement. It has also raised questions regarding the nature of resumptive elements.

6.7 Wh-In Situ

Similar concerns have led students of Arabic syntax to examine wh-in situ constructions in the dialects where they are available. We have already observed that, unlike other Arabic varieties, EgA does not make use of the gap strategy in wh-questions (see Table 6.1). In fact, direct questions in EgA are generally formed by keeping the wh-word in situ. Soltan (2010) provides the sentences in (90) and (91) to illustrate the in situ strategy in EgA:

(90) a. ʔinta šuf-t miin ʔimbaarih
you.M.SG saw-2.M who yesterday
"Who did you see yesterday?"

b. ʔaħmad ha-yi-saafir fein/ʔimtaa/ʔizzaay/leih
Ahmad FT-3-travel where/when/how/why
"Where/When/How/Why will Ahmad travel?"

(91) a. (huwwa) ʔaħmad ʔal-l-ak ʔin mona ʔištar-it ʔeih
(he) Ahmad said.3-to-you.M that Mona bought-3.F what
"What did Ahmad tell you that Mona bought?"

b. (huwwa) ʔaħmad ʔal-l-ak ʔin mona safir-it fein
(he) Ahmad said.3-to-you.M that Mona traveled-3.F where
"Where did Ahmad tell you that Mona traveled?"

As seen in (90)–(91), argument as well as adjunct wh-pronouns can remain in situ in EgA. Interestingly, the wh-in situ can have matrix scope whether the wh-element occurs in the matrix clause (90) or the embedded clause (91).

Following initial observations in Wahba (1984), Soltan (2010) shows that wh-in situ interrogatives are not sensitive to island constraints in EA. The examples in (92) illustrate this generalization:

(92) a. ʔinta ʔabil-t ʔil-bint illi ʔitgawwiz-it miin
you met-2 DEF-girl that married-3.F who
"You met the girl who married who?" (="Who did you meet the girl that married?")

b. huda mišy-it ʔabl-ma ʔaħmad yi-ʔaabil miin
Huda left-3.F before Ahmad 3-meet who
"Huda left before Ahmad met who" (="Who did Huda leave before Ahmad met?")

Wahba (1984) and Soltan (2010) propose different accounts of wh-in situ interrogatives in EgA. Focusing on the interpretation of sentences like (90)–(91) as matrix questions, Wahba (1984) argues that in situ elements move covertly to the matrix Comp to mark the scope of the question. The acceptability of the sentences in (92) is attributed to the assumption that islands do not constrain LF movement (see, e.g., Huang 1982). Soltan (2010) criticizes this stipulation and claims that wh-in situ questions in EgA are generated without any movement and that they are interpreted via the mechanism of *unselective binding* (see Pesetsky 1987). Thus, a question like (90a) would have the representation in (93), where *Op*, a base-generated operator in the matrix clause, marks the scope of the wh-question:

(93) $[_{CP}$ Op_i $[_{TP}$ ʔinta šuft $miin_i$ ʔimbaariħ]]

Examining wh-in situ interrogatives across the various Arabic varieties complicates the picture substantially. SA and MA do not allow wh-in situ questions (Nouhi 1996; Al-Ghalayini 2003). LA and Iraqi Arabic (IA), on the other hand, are languages that allow optional wh-in situ, but unlike EgA they impose restrictions on those constructions. In fact, wh-in situ questions in those varieties are more constrained than questions involving wh-fronting, as illustrated in (94) from IA (see also Wahba 1991; Ouhalla 1996b):[47]

(94) a.* ʕurf-ut mona il-bint [illi ištar-at šeno]
knew-3.F mona DEF-girl that bought-3.F what
"What(x) Mona knew the girl who bought (x)?"

b.* tṣawwar-at mona [Ali ištara šeno]
thought-3.F Mona Ali bought.3 what
"What did Mona think Ali bought?"

c. šeno tṣawwar-at mona [Ali ištara e]
what thought-3.F Mona Ali bought.3
"What did Mona think Ali bought?"

In IA, unlike EgA, wh-phrases cannot appear within islands (94a). In fact, wh-in situ elements are also prohibited in an embedded tensed clause, when the question has matrix scope (94b). (94a) contrasts with (95), which involves wh-fronting from within a relative clause island but induces only a mild subjacency violation. This contrast in acceptability indicates that wh-fronting and wh-in situ in IA involve different derivations.

(95) ?? šeno ʕurf-ut mona il-bint [illi ištar-at e]
what knew-3.F Mona DEF-girl that bought-3.F
"What(x) Mona knew the girl who bought (x)?"

Ouhalla (1996b) proposes an analysis of IA wh-in situ questions that advances the two claims in (96):

(96) a. There are two types of wh-elements: the bare type and the compound type. The compound type shows overt phi-features.

b. Bare wh-elements are long distance A'-anaphors whereas compound wh-elements are local A'-anaphors.

(96a) underlies the contrast one observes between IA wh-words and EgA wh-words. Thus, in IA, the wh-words *meno* "who" and *šeno* "what" can be divided into two parts: one carries the wh-morpheme, i.e. *men-* and *šen-*, and the second carries phi-features (i.e., *–o*). The pronominal element found in wh-words in IA, functions also as an accusative pronoun in the language (97):

(97) šuf-t-o
saw-1.SG-him
"I saw him."

[47] For a discussion of wh-in-situ questions in LA, see Aoun and Choueiri (1999) and Aoun, Benmamoun, and Choueiri (2010).

In EgA, wh-words are bare in the sense of Ouhalla (1996b) since they do not carry phi-features. Being of the compound type, IA wh-words are local A'-anaphors (96b). This means that they must have an antecedent in the minimal tensed clause in which they occur. This requirement readily accounts for the unacceptability of (94b). In (94b), the domain in which the wh-word needs to have an antecedent is the embedded clause. However, the embedded Comp is not marked [+wh] in that sentence. Hence, the wh-word fails to have an antecedent in the minimal tensed clause in which it occurs and the resulting sentence is unacceptable. (94a) has a somewhat different explanation: the wh-word in situ there is related to a local antecedent in the minimal tensed clause in which it occurs. This is the embedded Comp, which is marked [+wh], in the case of relative clauses. Thus, the wh-word in (94a) cannot be related to the matrix Comp, and the sentence cannot have a matrix scope reading.

Ouhalla's (1996b) analysis of IA wh-in situ can be extended to EgA, where wh-pronouns are of the bare type. They are thus expected to behave as long distance A'-anaphors. This means that they need not have a local antecedent in the minimal finite clause in which they occur, and they need not be bound to the nearest potential antecedent. This accounts for the fact that, in EgA, wh-in situ can occur in embedded tensed clauses and inside islands as well. Such an analysis has the advantage of reducing this case of syntactic (micro)variation to the lexical properties of the wh-words themselves.

A systematic exploration of wh-in situ questions across Arabic dialects is still lacking. Some important theoretical issues remain open: what factors are responsible for the presence or absence of wh-in situ questions in some Arabic varieties? Ouhalla's analysis addresses the properties of wh-elements in situ independently of movement. However, the question remains regarding the relation between wh-in situ and wh-fronting.

6.8 Other Related Approaches to the Syntax of Arabic

Generative approaches to the syntax of Arabic have provided important generalizations to probe various aspects of the theoretical apparatus of the generative paradigm. The study of SA and various other Arabic dialects has made important contributions to the ongoing research on the computational component of the grammar, its properties, and how it interacts with other aspects of the grammar. The dialects that have particularly been the focus of attention represent four main linguistic groupings (Maghrebi, Levantine, Egyptian, and Gulf). However, many varieties within these regions remain underresearched, and other varieties of Arabic spoken by minorities in sub-Saharan Africa and Asia have yet to receive the same degree of attention within the generative paradigm.

In addition to the focus on synchronic syntactic phenomena, the field has also engaged issues related to the acquisition of language, language deficits and disorder, language change, and language contact, among many others. Recently, there has been increasing interest in the psycholinguistic and neurolinguistic aspects of Arabic syntax and morphology. In addition, research in syntax proper now increasingly relies on the use of a diverse set of research tools and data, including production and comprehension experiments, searchable electronic corpora, and of course elicited data and narratives from native speakers. The goal is to compare the acquisition of some syntactic and morphosyntactic patterns (e.g., the acquisition of inflectional morphology, questions, negation) in Arabic with the acquisition of similar patterns in other languages.

This kind of research is informed by recent developments in syntax and informs both syntactic research as well as the study of the cognitive aspects of language. For example, Aljenaie (2001, 2010) investigates the acquisition of the morphosyntax of Kuwaiti Arabic. She collected extensive data from Kuwaiti children over a long period of time. Her findings have so far confirmed that Kuwaiti children use the imperfective as a default form, which is consistent with recent proposals in Arabic syntax and morphology that have demonstrated that the imperfective does not carry any temporal or aspectual information and is rather a "nonfinite" form of the verb. Kuwaiti children improperly use the imperative form, an inflected form, in a way that is again consistent with the status of the imperative as a reduced form of the imperfective that is devoid of person agreement. Working with Saudi children with language impairment, Abdullah (2002) uncovered similar results.

Similarly, Lorimor (2007) undertook a sentence completion experiment to test how Lebanese speakers perform on agreement in the context of coordination, which is still generating a lively debate in syntax. Her findings were consistent with what descriptive studies of close conjunct agreement have shown, namely, that there is a tendency to have close conjunct agreement when the conjuncts follow the verb but not when they precede the verb. However, she also uncovered an interesting result that previous theoretical studies did not discuss. When Lebanese speakers are confronted with a situation where the two conjuncts must be between an auxiliary verb and another predicate, such as an adjective, there is a tendency to have close conjunct agreement with the auxiliary that precedes the two conjuncts and full agreement with the predicate that follows the two conjuncts. As discussed in Benmamoun et al. (2010), this finding has important implications for theoretical analyses of close conjunct agreement. The biclausal/gapping account advanced in Aoun et al. (1994) cannot be easily extended to these facts. Rather, the facts seem to argue for the effect of adjacency on agreement. This in turn has led to a different conception of the relation between syntax and morphology. This suitably illustrates how experimental work can inform and be informed by theoretical syntactic studies. The same can be said about corpus studies, field work-based studies, and studies that use the old fashioned but still critically relevant introspective data. It is encouraging that this type of research is being carried out on Arabic.

References

Abdullah, F. 2002. *Specific language impairment in Arabic-speaking children: deficits in morphosyntax*. PhD diss., McGill University, Canada.

Al-Ghalayini, Mustafa. 2003. *Žaamiʕu d-duruusi l-ʕarabiyyati*. Beirut: al-Maktaba al-ʕaṣriyya.

Aljenaie, Khawla. 2001. *The emergence of tense and agreement in Kuwaiti Arabic child language*. PhD diss., University of Reading, UK.

Aljenaie, Khawla. 2010. Verbal inflection in the acquisition of Kuwaiti Arabic. *Journal of Child Language* 37: 841–863.

Aoun, Joseph and Elabbas Benmamoun. 1998. Minimality, reconstructions, and PF-movement. *Linguistic Inquiry* 29(4): 569–597.

Aoun, Joseph, Elabbas Benmamoun, and Dominique Sportiche. 1994. Agreement and conjunction in some varieties of Arabic. *Linguistic Inquiry* 25: 195–220.

——. 1999. Further remarks on first conjunct agreement. *Linguistic Inquiry* 30: 669–681.

Aoun, Joseph, Elabbas Benmamoun and Lina Choueri. 2010. *The syntax of Arabic*. Cambridge, UK: Cambridge University Press.

Aoun, Joseph and Lina Choueiri. 1996. *Resumption and last resort*. Unpublished manuscript, University of Southern California, Los Angeles.

——. 1999. Modes of interrogation. In *PAL XII* ed. Elabbas Benmamoun, 7–26. Amsterdam: John Benjamins.

——. 2000. Epithets. *Natural Language and Linguistic Theory* 18: 1–39.

Aoun, Joseph, Lina Choueiri, and Norbert Hornstein. 2001. Resumption, movement, and derivational economy. *Linguistic Inquiry* 32: 371–403.

Aoun, Joseph and Yen-Hui Audrey Li. 1990. Minimal disjointness. *Linguistics* 28: 189–203.

——. 1993a. *Syntax of scope*. Cambridge, MA: MIT Press.

Ayoub, Georgine. 1981. *Structure de la phrase verbale en Arabe Standard*. PhD diss., Université de Paris VII, France.

Bahloul, Maher. 1994. *The syntax and semantics of taxis, aspect, tense and modality in Standard Arabic*. PhD diss., Cornell University, Ithaca.

Bahloul, Maher and Wayne Harbert. 1993. Agreement asymmetries in Arabic. In *Proceedings of WCCFL 11*, ed. Jonathan Mead, 15–31. Stanford, CA: CSLI.

Baker, Mark C. 1988. *Incorporation: A theory of grammatical function changing*. Chicago: University of Chicago Press.

Bakir, Murtadha. 1980. *Aspects of clause structure in Arabic. PhD diss.*, Indiana University, Bloomington.

Benmamoun, Elabbas. 1992. *Inflectional and functional morphology: Problems of projection, representation and derivation*. PhD diss., University of Southern California, Los Angeles.

——. 1997. Licensing of negative polarity in Moroccan Arabic. *Natural Language and Linguistic Theory* 15: 263–287.

——. 1999. The syntax of quantifiers and quantifier float. *Linguistic Inquiry* 30: 621–642.

——. 2000. *The feature structure of functional categories: A comparative study of Arabic dialects*. Oxford: Oxford University Press.

——. 2003. Agreement parallelism between sentences and noun phrases: A historical sketch. *Lingua* 113: 747–764.

——. 2006. Licensing Ccnfigurations: The puzzle of head negative polarity items. *Linguistic Inquiry* 37(1): 141–149.

Benmamoun, E., Abunasser, M., Al-Sabbagh, R., Bidaoui, A. & Shalash, D. Forthcoming. *The Location of Sentential Negation in Arabic Varieties*. Brill's Annual of Afroasiatic Languages and Linguistics.

Benmamoun, Elabbas and Heidi Lorimor. 2006. Featureless expressions: When morphophonological markers are absent. *Linguistic Inquiry* 37(1): 1–23.

Borer, Hagit. 1984. Restrictive relatives in Modern Hebrew. *Natural Language and Linguistic Theory* 2: 219–260.

——. 1995 The ups and downs of Hebrew verb movement. *Natural Language and Linguistic Theory* 13: 527–606.

——. 1996. The construct in review. In *Studies in Afroasiatic grammar*, ed. J. Lecarme, J. Lowenstamm, and U. Shlonsky, 30–61. The Hague: Holland Academic Graphics.
——. 2008. *Compounds: The view from Hebrew*. Unpublished manuscript, University of Southern California, Los Angeles.
Brustad, Kristen. 2000. *The syntax of spoken Arabic*. Washington, DC: Georgetown University Press.
Chomsky, Noam. 1977. On Wh-movement. In *Formal syntax*, ed. P. Culicover, T. Wasow, and A. Akmajian, 71–132. New York: Academic Press.
——. 1981. *Lectures in government and binding*. Drodrecht: Foris.
——. 1995. *The minimalist program*. Cambridge, MA: MIT Press.
Choueiri, Lina. 2002. *Issues in the syntax of resumption: Restrictive relatives in Lebanese Arabic*. PhD diss., University of Southern California, Los Angeles.
Cinque, G. 1994. On the evidence for partial N-movement in the Romance DP. In *Paths towards universal grammar: Essays in honor of Richard Kayne*, ed. G. Cinque, J. Koster, J.-Y. Pollock, and R. Zanuttini, 85–110. Washington, DC: Georgetown University Press.
Déchaine, Rose-Marie. 1993. *Predicates across categories*. PhD diss., University of Massachusetts, Amherst.
Demirdache, Hamida. 1991. *Resumptive chains in restrictive relatives, appositives, and dislocation structures*. PhD diss., Massachusetts Institute of Technology, Cambridge.
——. 1997. Dislocation, resumption, and weakest crossover. In *Materials on left dislocation*, ed. Elena Anagnostopoulou, Henk van Riemsdijk, and Frans Zwarts, 193–231. Amsterdam: John Benjamins.
Doron, Edith. 1996. The predicate in Arabic. In *Studies in Afroasiatic grammar*, ed. J. Lecarme, J. Lowenstamm, and U. Shlonksy, 77–87. Leiden: Holland Academic Graphics.
Doron, Edit and Caroline Heycock. 1999. Filling and licensing multiple specifiers. In *Specifiers*, ed. David Adger, Susan Pintzuk, Bernadette Plunkett, and George Tsoulas, 69–89. Oxford: Oxford University Press.
Eid, Mushira. 1983. The copula function of pronouns. *Lingua* 59: 197–207.
——. 1991. Verbless sentences in Arabic and Hebrew. In *PAL III*, ed. Bernard Comrie and Mushira Eid, 31–61. Amsterdam: John Benjamins.
——. 1993. Negation and predicate heads. In *Principles and prediction: The analysis of natural language*, ed. Mushira Eid and Gregory K. Iverson, 135–152. Amsterdam: John Benjamins.
Eisele, John. 1988. *The syntax and semantics of tense, aspect, and time reference in Cairene Arabic*. PhD diss., University of Chicago.
Elbourne, Paul. 2001. E-type anaphora as NP deletion. *Natural Language Semantics* 9: 241–288.
Fassi Fehri, Abdelkader. 1988. Agreement in Arabic, binding and coherence. In *Agreement in natural language: Approaches, theories, description*, ed. M. Barlow and C. Ferguson, 107–158. Stanford, CA: CSLI.
——. 1993. *Issues in the structure of Arabic clauses and words*. Dordrecht: Kluwer.
——. 1999. Arabic modifying adjectives and DP structures. *Studia Linguistica* 53: 105–154.
Gelderen, Elly van. 1996. Parametrising agreement features in Arabic, Bantu languages, and varieties of English. *Linguistics* 34: 753–767.
——. 2008. Negative cycles. *Linguistic Typology* 12: 195–243.
Guilliot, Nicolas and Nouman Malkawi. 2006. When resumption determines reconstruction. In *Proceedings of the 25th West Coast Conference on formal linguistics*, ed. Donald Baumer, David Montero, and Michael Scanton, 168–176. Somerville, MA: Cascadilla Proceedings Project.
Halila, Hafedh. 1992. *Subject specifity effects in Tunisian Arabic*. PhD diss., University of Southern California, Los Angeles.

Hallman, Peter. 2000. The structure of agreement failure in Lebanese Arabic. In *Proceedings of the 19th West Coast Conference on Formal Linguistics*, ed. Roger Billerey, 178–190. Somerville, MA: Cascadilla Press.

Harbert, Wayne and Maher Bahloul. 2002. Postverbal subjects in Arabic and the theory of agreement. In *Themes in Arabic and Hebrew syntax*, ed. U. Shlonsky and J. Ouhalla, 45–70. Dordrecht: Kluwer.

Heggie, Lorie. 1988. *The syntax of copular structures*. PhD diss., University of Southern California, Los Angeles.

Hoyt, Frederick. 2002. Impersonal agreement as a specificity effect in rural Palestinian Arabic. In *PAL XIII-XIV*, ed. Dil Parkinson and Elabbas Benmamoun, 111–141. Amsterdam: John Benjamins.

Huang, C. T. James. 1982. Move WH in a language without WH movement. *Linguistic Review* 1: 369–416.

Jelinek, Eloise. 1981. *On defining categories: Aux and predicate in Egyptian Colloquial Arabic*. PhD diss., University of Arizona, Tuscon.

Kenstowicz, Michael. 1989. The null subject parameter in Modern Arabic Dialects. In *The null subject parameter*, ed. Osvaldo Jaeggli and Ken Safir, 263–275. Dordrecht: Kluwer.

Kihm, Alain. 1999. *Towards a predication theory of Semitic construct state nominals*. Unpublished manuscript, CNRS, Paris.

Koopman, Hilda and Dominique Sportiche. 1991. The position of subjects. *Lingua* 85: 211–258.

Lorimor, Heidi. 2007. *Conjunctions and grammatical agreement*. PhD diss., University of Illinois at Urbana-Champaign.

Malkawi, Nouman and Nicolas Guilliot. 2007. Reconstruction and islandhood in Jordanian Arabic. In *PAL XX*, ed. Mustafa Mughazy, 87–104. Amsterdam: John Benjamins.

McCarthy, John. 1979. *Formal problems in Semitic phonology and morphology*. PhD diss., Massachusetts Institute of Technology, Cambridge.

McCloskey, James. 1990. Resumptive pronouns, Ā-binding and levels of representation in Irish. In *Syntax and semantics 23: Syntax of the modern Celtic languages*, ed. Randall Hendrick, 199–248. San Diego: Academic Press.

Mohammad, Mohammad. 1988. On the parallelism between IP and DP. In *Proceedings of WCCFL VII*, ed. Hagit Borer, 241–254. Stanford, CA: CSLI.

——. 1989. *The sentence structure of Arabic*. PhD diss., University of Southern California, Los Angeles.

——. 1999a. *Word order, agreement and pronominalization in Standard and Palestinian Arabic*. Amsterdam: John Benjamins.

——. 1999b. Checking and licensing inside DP in Palestinian Arabic. In *PAL XII*, ed. Elabbas Benmamoun, 27–44. Amsterdam: John Benjamins.

Mouchaweh, Lina. 1986. *De la syntaxe des petites prépositions*. PhD diss., Université de Paris VIII, Paris.

Moutaouakil, Ahmed. 1987. *min qaḍaayaa r-raabiṭ fii l-lugha l-'arabiyya*. Casablanca: 'Ocaadh.

Mughazy Mustafa. 2004. *Subatomic semantics and the active participle in Egyptian*. PhD diss., University of Illinois, Urbana-Champaign.

Munn, Alan. 1999. First conjunct agreement: Against a clausal analysis. *Linguistic Inquiry* 30(4): 643–668.

Nouhi, Youssef. 1996. *Wh-constructions in Moroccan Arabic*. MA thesis, University of Ottawa, Ottawa.

Ouali, H. and C. Fortin. 2007. The syntax of complex tense in Moroccan Arabic. In *PAL XIV*, ed. Elabbas Benmamoun, 175–190. Amsterdam: John Benjamins.

Ouhalla, Jamal. 1988. *The syntax of head movement: A study of Berber*. PhD diss., University College London.
——. 1993a. Negation, focus and tense: The Arabic *maa* and *laa*. *Rivista di Linguistica* 5: 275–300.
——. 1993b. Subject-extraction, negation, and the anti-agreement effect. *Natural Language and Linguistic Theory* 11: 477–518.
——. 1994. Verb movement and word order in Arabic. In *Verb movement*, ed. D. Lightfoot and N. Hornstein, 41–72. Cambridge, UK: Cambridge University Press.
——. 1996a. The construct state in Berber. In *Studies in Afroasiatic grammar*, ed. Jacqueline Lecarme et al., 278–301. The Hague: Holland Academic Graphics.
——. 1996b. Remarks on the binding properties of wh-pronouns. *Linguistic Inquiry* 27: 676–707.
——. 2001. Parasitic gaps and resumptive pronouns. In *Parasitic gaps*, ed. Peter Culicover and Paul Postal, 147–180. Cambridge, MA: MIT Press.
——. 2002. The structure and logical form of negative sentences in Arabic. In *Themes in Arabic and Hebrew syntax*, ed. J. Ouhalla and U. Shlonsky, 299–320. Dordrecht: Kluwer.
Pesetsky, David. 1987. Wh-in-situ: Movement and unselective binding. In *The representation of (in)definiteness*, ed. Eric Reuland and Alice ter Meulen. Cambridge, MA: MIT Press.
Ritter, Elizabeth. 1988. A head-movement approach to construct state noun phrases. *Linguistics* 26: 909–929.
Roberts, Ian and Ur Shlonsky. 1996. Pronominal enclisis in VSO languages. In *The syntax of the Celtic languages*, ed. Robert D. Borsely and Ian Roberts, 171–199. Cambridge, UK: Cambridge University Press.
Rouveret, Alain. 1994. *Syntaxe du Gallois.* Paris: CNRS Editions.
Ryding, Karin. 2005. *A reference grammar of Modern Standard Arabic.* Cambridge, UK: Cambridge University Press.
Sells, Peter. 1984. *Syntax and semantics of resumptive pronouns.* PhD diss., University of Massachussets, Amherst.
Shlonsky, Ur. 1991. Quantifiers as functional heads: A study of quantifier float in Hebrew. *Lingua* 84: 159–180.
——. 1992. Resumptive pronouns as last resort. *Linguistic Inquiry* 23: 443–468.
——. 1997. *Clause structure and word order in Hebrew and Arabic: An essay in comparative Semitic syntax.* Oxford: Oxford University Press.
——. 2004. The form of Semitic noun phrases. *Lingua* 114: 1465–1526.
Siloni, Tal. 2001. Construct States at the PF interface. *Linguistic Variation Yearbook* 1: 229–266.
Soltan, Usama. 2007. *On formal feature licensing in minimalism: Aspects of Standard Arabic morphosyntax.* PhD diss., University of Maryland.
——. 2010. *On licensing wh-scope: Wh-questions in Egyptian Arabic revisited.* Unpublished manuscript, Middlebury College, Vermont.
——. 2011. On strategies of question-formation and the grammatical status of the Q-particle huwwa in Egyptian Arabic Wh-questions. *University of Pennsylvania Working Papers in Linguistics* 1: Article 24. Available at http://repository.upenn.edu/pwpl/vol17/iss1/24.
Sproat, Richard and Chilin Shih. 1988. The cross-linguistic distribution of adjective ordering restrictions. In *Interdisciplinary approaches to language,* ed. C. Georgopoulos and R. Ishihara, 565–593. Dordrecht: Kluwer.
Wahba, Wafaa. 1984. *Wh-constructions in Egyptian Arabic.* PhD diss., University of Illinois, Urbana-Champaign.
——. 1991. LF-movement in Iraqi Arabic. In *Logical structure and linguistic structure,* ed. C.-T. J. Huang and R. May, 253–276. Dordrecht: Kluwer Academic Publishers.

CHAPTER 7

THE PHILOLOGICAL APPROACH TO ARABIC GRAMMAR

LUTZ EDZARD

7.1 Introduction

THE term *philology* can be narrowed down to the study of language in written historical texts, encompassing aspects of history, literary studies, and linguistics. The philological approach can be language specific or comparative and can also refer more specifically to the decipherment, edition, and preservation of texts. This chapter provides an overview over some important ideas in the Western philological tradition of the description of Arabic on its levels of phonology, morphology, syntax, and lexicon. Thereby, the term *philological* implies a data-based approach, not to the exclusion of linguistic approaches, as long as these are oriented at word lists and texts as opposed to exclusively linguistic theory. The philological approach to Arabic also considers comparative Semitic evidence and other comparative data. Indeed, a typological perspective is an important ingredient of the philological approach to grammar. Keeping in mind that the traces of the Western philological tradition are deeply rooted in both the Arab and the European Middle Ages (cf., e.g., Fück 1955; Bobzin 1992, 1995; Hamilton 2006), this chapter takes at its point of departure and *terminus post quem* the Arabic grammar by Sylvestre de Sacy dating from 1831 rather than the work of Petrus Venerabilis or other important figures in the Middle Ages (for a motivation of this divide, cf., e.g., Bobzin 1992: 155). In a European context, *philological* has also been understood as referring specifically to the philology of Greek and Latin ("Altphilologie"), or philology par excellence. Of course, the philological description of Arabic cannot be treated in isolation from the Classical tradition. Regarding the Arabic grammatical tradition, Versteegh

(1977) argues for strong influence of or dependency on the Greek tradition, pointing, for instance, to the same set of examples of prototypical nouns (ἄνθρωπος/*rağul* "man," ἵππος/*faras* "horse," and τεῖχος/*ḥāʾiṭ* "wall") in both the writings of Dionysios Thrax and the Arabic grammarians (Edzard 2001a). The evidence of Greek influence, usually transmitted via an intermediate Syriac–Aramaic stage, is even stronger in the realms of the sciences like philosophy, medicine, astronomy, and music theory.

The philological approach to Arabic grammar is, of course, only a small part of what can be considered Arabic philology in general. Noteworthy examples of anthologies covering aspects of Arabic philology include the *Cambridge History of Arabic Literature* (notably the 1990 volume *Religion, Learning and Science in the ʿAbbasid Period*) and the *Grundriß der Arabischen Philologie* (three volumes, 1982–1992 edited by Wolfdietrich Fischer and Helmut Gätje). The first volume of the latter series treats the whole history of the Arabic language, from pre-Islamic times up to the modern dialects, and examines special features of the lexicon and onomastics. The same volume also includes in-depth information on script history, epigraphy, numismatics, papyri, and features of Arabic manuscripts in general, areas that constitute indispensable tools for the diachronic and synchronic analysis of Arabic texts. The second volume in the series is devoted to Arabic literature, in a meaningful sequence that reflects both chronology and scholarly dependence on respective other genres of literature: poetry, the Quran, lexicography, grammatical theory, poetology, rhetorics and metrics, *ʾadab* literature, artificial prose, popular literature, and modern literature in general. Further chapters cover historiography and geography, religious literature, and scientific literature (philosophy, mathematical sciences, medicine, and other realms) and the development of subject-specific language and terminology (cf. notably Endress 1992). While the Quran is considered to be *sui generis* in the Muslim tradition [Larcher, "ALT II"] (even though it certainly has poetic features), the other genres bear witness to the mentioned scholarly dependency. Both lexicography and grammatical theory had to rely on poetry and the Quran as essential databases: poetology, rhetorics, and metrics obviously were dependent on all of the previous genres; all of the other genres depend on the former, reflecting the deeply entrenched intertextuality in Arabic culture. Finally, the genre of *ʾinšāʾ* literature is an important research area for philologists, relating to both form and style of Arabic administrative documents. The latter is closely linked to the field of Arabic papyrology, which has boomed in recent years and among whose major modern exponents are Werner Diem (e.g., Diem 2006), Simon Hopkins (e.g., Hopkins 1984), and Geoffrey Khan (e.g., Khan 2011).

As the philological approach is primarily concerned with a diachronic analysis, the definition of a *terminus post quem* for what constitutes Arabs and Arabic is important. According to Retsö (2003), the term *Arab* can for the first time be identified as one of the participants in the battle of Qarqar in Syria (853 BC). As far as written sources are concerned, the inscription of an-Namāra dating from 328 AD is often cited as one of the first documents with clearly identifiable Arabic features, such as the definite article *(ʾ)l-* in line two of the inscriptions: < ʾ l ʾ š d y n > "the two ʾŠD" (cf. Retsö 2003: 467–470; [Retsö, "Arabic?"]).

The present chapter is devoted to the philological analysis of selected features of Classical Arab and Modern Standard Arabic on one hand and selected features of Middle Arabic on the other; in principle, however, the philological approach could also be meaningful as applied to corpora of modern (or older) dialectal data in transcription. The following subchapters regarding the writing system and phonology as well as morphology are rather brief, as the aspect of cultural embeddedness seems to be less relevant in these realms of grammar. First and foremost, the following reflects a nonexhaustive overview of some cases or even *causes célèbres* in Arabic syntax and semantics, selected by the author. This chapter closes with a short philological analysis of a Middle Arabic (here Judeo-Arabic) text.

7.2 Writing System and Phonology

As stated already, proper decipherment and edition of texts is a cornerstone of philology, and this is no trivial endeavor in the case of early Arabic inscriptions and Arabic manuscripts in general. The Nabatean script (attested from c. 100 BC until 350 AD) counts as the genetic ancestor of the Arabic alphabet (for an overview, cf. Gruendler 2006). As the phonemic inventory of Classical Arabic is slightly larger than that of Aramaic, and, since the systematic use of diacritics (*naqṭ*) emerged only in the second half of the first century after the Hiǧra, a lot of ambiguities exist when it comes to the reading of early documents. A building inscription on a dam of Muʿāwiya (from the year 677 AD) and Quran manuscripts in Ḥiǧāzi script are among the first documents with consistent use of diacritical marks (ibid., 151).

Research on phonology, especially in the older stages of Arabic, obviously depends on a precise reading of the historical sources. For instance, the correct understanding of the opposition pair *maǧhūr* versus *mahmūs* or the historically voiced quality of both /ṭ/ and /q/ would not be known today. Neither would one be aware of lateral quality of /ḍ/ (e.g., compare Arabic *al-qāḍī* "the judge" as reflected in Spanish *alcalde* "mayor" with reanalysis of the Arabic definite article as part of the word) if not for the information contained in Chapters 565 through 571 of Sībawayhi's *Kitāb* and other historical sources (cf., e.g., Fleisch 1958a, 1958b; Al-Nassir 1993; Edzard 2001b).

Sībawayhi's declared rationale in Chapter 565 for providing extremely precise descriptions of pronunciation is to explain why certain consonants (can) undergo assimilation (*ʾidġām* or *iddiġām*; [Baalbaki, "ALT I"]) within and across words and why other consonants cannot. One of the points addressed by Sībawayhi are assimilation and resyllabification in forms V, VI, VII, and VIII. Sībawayhi quotes a number of alternative forms of the standard diatheses V, VI, VII, and VIII, all of which feature assimilation and resyllabification. In forms V and VI, haplological syllable ellipsis occurs in cases like *fa-lā (t)tanāǧaw!* "don't whisper to each other." Sībawayhi also quotes assimilated verbs of form VII (standard /inC_1aC_2aC_3a/) that are not part of the standard language, such as *immaḥā* "he was effaced." (1) gives derivations of the nonstandard examples of forms V, VI and VII:

(1) Derivation of nonstandard forms (V, VI, and VII)

tatamannawna "You (m. pl.) wish."	→	*tamannawna*
fa-lā tatanāǧaw! "Don't whisper to each other!"	→	*fa-lā (t)tanāǧaw!*
inmaḥā "He was effaced."	→	*immaḥā*

The situation in form VIII is more complex, as Sībawayhi cites an array of forms that exceeds the well-known cases of partial and total assimilation that may occur in this form. Example (2) presents an overview of the nonstandard output forms (masculine plural of perfect, imperfect, and participle) of the verb {q-t-l} "to kill" in form VIII ("to kill each other") that normally do not undergo any assimilatory change:

(2) Nonstandard assimilation and metathesis (VIII)

iqtatalū	→	*qittalū*
yaqtatilūna	→	{*yaqattilūna, yaqittilūna*}
muqtatilūna	→	{*muqattilūna, muqittilūna*}

The ordering in the set brackets indicates that people who say *yaqattilūna* will also say *muqattilūna*, and so on. Interestingly, these forms amount to an assimilation of the infixes (*-t-*) to the middle radical, as is also obvious in the participle form *murtadifūna* → *muruddifūna* "[they (m.) are] directly following," which also features vowel harmony with respect to *u*. The driving force behind these forms appears to be the wish to avoid a sequence of equal or similar CV syllables. As a result, the underlying form of the diathesis (VIII) is quite opaque in these cases. Forms with total phonological merger (progressive, regressive, or "reciprocal" assimilation, that is, "compromise" on a phonetically intermediate consonant) arise in the case of verbs whose first radical is a voiced or velarized sibilant or a voiced or velarized alveolar stop:

(3) Nonstandard progressive and regressive assimilation (VIII)

iṣṭabara "He was patient."	→	*iṣṣabara*
iḍṭaǧara "He was angry."	→	*iḍḍaǧara*
iẓṭalama "He suffered injustice."	→	*iṭṭalama*

The last output form clearly demonstrates that /ṭ/ historically was voiced [Embarki, "Phonetics"]; otherwise, the modern concept of partial regressive assimilation with respect to the feature [±voiced] would not make sense in this case.

Most of the forms cited by Sībawayhi are also attested in the Quran (for a collection of forms, cf. Vollers 1906: 111–122). A careful consideration of the *textus receptus* of the Cairene Quran edition also yields important information on other phonological features, both segmental and suprasegmental, of Classical Arabic, including assimilation and haplological syllable ellipsis. Special signs indicate partial or total assimilation to be observed in proper *tağwīd* "Quranic recitation." The following example illustrates both haplology and assimilation features with assimilated/elided positions in boldface:

(4) Haplology and assimilation in the Quran (Q 12:2)
*ʾin**n**ā ʾanzalnā-hu qurʾānan ʿarabīya **l**laʿalla-kum taʿlamūna* instead of
ʾinna-nā ʾanzalnā-hu qurʾānan ʿarabīyan laʿalla-kum taʿlamūna
"We [God] have indeed sent it [the Quran] down as an Arabic Quran; maybe you will know."

Also, special Quranic signs, that is, minuscule *wāws* and *yāʾs* above a word-final <h>, indicate that the possessive and object suffix of the third-person masculine singular <-h> is long after a short syllable (CV), that is, *-hū*/*-hī*, and short of a long syllable (Cv̄ or CvC), that is, *-hi*/*-hi*, a circumstance also known from Classical Arabic metrics.

Guttural phonology can also be mentioned as a realm, where a comprehensive evaluation of attested form is essential for coming to sound conclusions, for example, regarding the distribution of imperfect ("theme") vowels. McCarthy (1991) provides ample documentation for Arabic in this context.

7.3 Morphology

A philological approach, that is, a close evaluation of texts and forms in context, is indispensable in deciding on the status of a certain morphological category. As an example, the status of the so-called *pluralis paucitatis* (*ğamʿ al-qilla*), characterized by a prefixed *ʾa-* (e.g., Fischer 2006: 57 (= Nöldeke 1896)) has recently come under discussion. Relevant forms include *ʾaʿyun* "(few) eyes" instead of *ʿuyūn* "(more than a few) eyes."

A philological approach is also essential when it comes to detecting new morphological patterns and word-formation strategies (or the further development of preexisting ones) through careful examination of written sources. More recent developments in this context include compound formations such as the phenomenon of blends, where one or both of the constituting elements are shortened (e.g., Badawi et al. 2004: 58, 751). Relevant examples include substantives and adjectives with prefixes as well as structures with an internal appositional structure, such as *lā-nihāʾīya* "infinity," *šibh-rasmī* "semiofficial," or *šarq-ʾawsaṭī* "Middle Eastern." Blending is also productive in modern times (e.g., Versteegh 2001: 181–183) and surfaces in such forms as *kahraṭas* "electro-magnetism" (composed of *kahrabāʾ* "electricity" + *maġnāṭīs* "magnet").

Loan words for scientific vocabulary may be fully integrated in the Arabic nominal system or retain (part) of their original structure. An example of a fully integrated technical term is the neologism *raskala* "recycling" (/$C_1aC_2C_3aC_4a$/). An example of a partially integrated technical term is the neologism *kibrītīd* "sulfide," where a European-style suffix *-īd* is attached to the Arabic equivalent of "sulfur," *kibrīt* (cf. Badawi et al. 2004: 741). New patterns continue to emerge, such as the pattern

/$C_1awC_2aC_3a$/ for denominal verbs from nouns with a long first syllable: *ʿawlama* "globalization" from *ʿālam* "world" (cf. Badawi et al. 2004: 762). Some patterns have become prominent by way of *qiyās* [Baalbaki, "ALT I"], [Larcher, "ALT II"] through one word, such as /$C_1\bar{a}C_2\bar{u}C_3$/ for technical instruments, a pattern "triggered" most likely by the noun *ḥasūb* "computer" (cf. also Edzard 2007; [Newman, "Nahda"]; [Kossmann, "Borrowing"]).

Innovations can also be observed in the verbal system. A noteworthy example is the neologism *ʾaslama, yuʾaslimu* "to islamize" and its reflexive form *taʾaslama, yataʾaslamu* "to be(come) islamized," as opposed to *ʾaslama, yuslimu* "to render oneself [to God], to become a Muslim," resulting in the creation of a minimal pair *ʾa-slama* (/ʾa-$C_1C_2aC_3a$/) versus *ʾaslama* (/$C_1aC_2C_3aC_4a$/). The former verb is modeled in its surface structure after verbs like *ʾamraka* "to Americanize" and its reflexive form *taʾamraka* "to be(come) Americanized."

7.4 Syntax

7.4.1 Overview

Syntax is another realm of Arabic grammar that has seen considerable progress in the past decades. As far as the philological approach is concerned, Diem (1998, 2002, 2011) and Manfred Ullmann (1988, a detailed study on irreal conditional clauses) are two central authors in this respect. Peled (1992) attempts successfully to combine a philological with a (historical-)linguistic approach to Arabic syntax. As far as Diem's studies are concerned, their particular strength lies in the detailed reference to the types of verbs involved and their specific context (for Diem 1998, see Section 7.3.3). Diem (2002) investigates the precise distribution of verbs with double accusative ("translocative" in more recent grammatical terminology) throughout the history of Arabic (for verbs with two pronominal suffixes, see also Gensler 2003). The basic examples are as follows:

(5) Translocative constructions in Arabic

ʾaʿṭay-tu	*Zayd-ani*	*l-kitāb-a*
gave-I	Zayd-ACC	DEF-book-ACC
"I gave Zayd the book."		
ʾaʿṭay-tu	*l-kitāb-a*	*li-Zayd-in*
gave-I	DEF-book-ACC	to-Zayd-GEN
"I gave the book to Zayd."		

Diem (2002: 5) identifies the following semantic verb groups in this context (translocation of a thing from the translocator to the recipient or vice versa): (a) "to give" (e.g., *ʾaʿṭā* "to give"); (b) "to impose" (e.g., *ʾalzama* "to oblige s.o."); (c) "to transmit a message" (e.g.,

ʿarrafa "to inform"); and (d) "withdraw" (e.g., *saraqa* "to steal from s.o."). In his study on *kayfa* as a conjunction, for example, in sentences like *ʾa-lam tara kayfa faʿala rabbu-ka bi-ʾaṣḥābi l-fīli* "have you not seen how God has dealt with the owners of the elephant," Diem (2011) pursues a similar strategy. The relevant constructions are analyzed according to different verbal categories: (a) emotion; (b) perception; (c) communication; (d) intellect; and (e) affectual expressions.

In this context it is noteworthy that neither Classical nor Modern Standard Arabic constitutes a monolithic block. Willmsen (2010), for instance, raises the issue that object pronouns in Egyptian newspapers syntactically are treated differently from those in Syrian and Jordanian newspapers.

Syntax is a realm of grammar that especially warrants a typological perspective. Diem's (1986) work on alienable and inalienable possession in Semitic is an example of research that clearly owes its depth of insight to such a typological perspective. From a broader perspective, it is important to note that Classical Arabic in terms of linguistic word order universals (cf. Greenberg 1966) is a model of a verb–subject–object (VSO) language, exhibiting the following features (">>" signifies "implication"):

1) VSO >> prepositions
2) VSO >> prefixed (prespecifying) definite article
3) VSO >> adjectives, genitives, and relative clauses succeed head noun
4) VSO >> auxiliary before main verb
5) VSO >> standard of comparison after adjective

Here are some illustrating examples (6):

(6) Predicted morphosyntactic features of Classical Arabic, patterns (6a)–(6e):

a)

bi-l-bayt-i	*ʿalā*	*l-ʾarḍ-i*	*qabla*	*l-ġadāʾ-i*
in-DEF-house-GEN	on	DEF-earth-GEN	before	DEF-lunch-GEN
"in the house"	"on earth"		"before lunch"	

b)

al-bayt-u	*l-kabīr-u*
DEF-house-NOM	DEF-big-NOM
"the big house" (subject)	

c)

bayt-u-n	*kabīr-u-n*	*al-bayt-u*	*l-kabīr-u*
house-NOM-IDF	big-NOM-IDF	DEF-house-NOM	DEF-big-NOM
"a big house" (subject)		"the big house" (subject)	

bayt-u	*walad-i-n*	*bayt-u*	*l-walad-i*
house-NOM	child-GEN-IDF	house-NOM	DEF-child-GEN
"a child's house"		"the house of the child"	

walad-u-n	*ǧāʾa*	*al-walad-u*	*llaḏī*	*ǧāʾa*
child-NOM-IDF	he.came	DEF-child-NOM	who.MSG	he.came
"a child that came"		"the child that came"		

d)

ya-ksir-u	*ǧaʿala*	*ya-ksir-u*
he-breaks-INDC	he.made	he-breaks-INDC
"He breaks"	"He began to break"	

e) *ʾaṭwal-u* *min* *Muḥammad-i-n*
taller-NOM from Muḥammad-GEN
"taller than Muḥammad"
ʾaḥsan-u *min-hā*
more.beautiful-NOM from-her
"more beautiful than she"

Case marking (*ʾiʿrāb*) allows for a certain degree of syntactic variation, not in the (morpho-) syntax as outlined already but in the position of the basic components verb, subject, and object. Indeed, there has been discussion of whether word order in the history of Arabic allows one to determine at which point in history *ʾiʿrāb* was lost. Fück (1950: 2) adduces, *inter alia*, the following examples from the Quran, where the object appears before the subject and where a reading without *ʾiʿrāb* might give way to misunderstanding (7):

(7) Classical Arabic sentences with VOS word order:
ka-ḏālika ʾinna-mā yaxša llāha min ʿibādi-hī l-ʿulamāʾu (Q 35:28)
"Out of his worshipers, only the scholars love God."
wa-ʾiḏi btalā ʾibrāhima rabbu-hū bi-kalimatin (Q 2:124)
"when his Lord put Abraham to test"

On the other hand, Wehr (1952: 181) argues that the Egyptian colloquial also featured occasional VOS word order, without causing semantic problems. Thus, it appears that word order *per se* is no argument for deciding on a timeline for the loss of *ʾiʿrāb*. Philological research also has to take into consideration whether subject and object are animate or inanimate and other factors.

Verbal syntax and semantics continue to be an intriguing field in Arabic and Semitic linguistics. The difference between *mā faʿala* and *lam yafʿal*, has been a notorious problem, already treated by Wehr (1953), Larcher (1994), and Dahlgren (2006) [Benmamoun and Choueri, "Syntax"]. Early analyses tried to prove the existence of an aspectual opposition between *mā faʿala* (resultative) and *lam yafʿal* (past). Wehr (1953) makes a strong case that *mā* often expresses "affected" involvement of the speaker and is almost mandatory after oaths and the like. Birnstiel (forthcoming) argues that the primary function of the former is to negate a constituent, whereas the primary function of the latter is to negate the predicative relationship between subject and predicate (nexus negation). Examples (8a) versus (8b) illustrate the contrast:

(8) The opposition *mā faʿala* vs. *lam yafʿal*

a. *wa-**mā** kafara sulaymānu **wa-lākinna** š-šayāṭīna kafarū* (Q 2:102)
"For it was **not Solomon** who denied the truth, but it was the devils who disbelieved." (constituent negation)

b. *wa-sawāʾun ʿalay-him ʾa-**ʾanḏarta-hum** ʾam **lam tunḏir-hum** lā yuʾminūn* (Q 36:10)

"It is the same to them whether **you warn them** or **do not warn them**: they will not believe." (nexus negation)

The opposition hypothetical versus counterfactual in irreal conditional structures (cf. Peled 1992: 40) is another case in point in this context. This opposition is encoded not by means of different particles but by the use of tense. Hypothetical conditions (i.e., conditions that *can* be realized) can be reflected by a protasis with a verb in the prefix conjugation (imperfect). The protases of counterfactual conditional structures (i.e., structures whose conditions *cannot* be realized) regularly feature *kāna* + suffix conjugation. Examples of both cases are found in (9):

(9) The opposition factual vs. counterfactual in conditional clauses

a. *law našā'u ǧa'alnā-hu 'uǧāǧan* (Q 56:70)
"If we [really] wanted (factual-hypothetical), we would make it [the drinking water] bitter."

b. *law kuntum da'awtumū-nā 'aṭa'nā-kum*
"If you had called us (counterfactual), we would have obeyed you."

7.4.2 Case Study: Arabic *Mā* as an Interrogative Element and a Negator

In Classical Arabic, the status (*pars orationis*) of a given word may not always be clear, and a meticulous philological approach is essential when it comes to analyzing passages that defy an unambiguous interpretation. A famous passage in the *sīra nabawīya* concerns the interpretation of the particle *mā* in *mā 'aqra'u* (e.g., Brünnow and Fischer 2008: 41, Arabic text). According to the Ḥadīṯ tradition, this passage is to be understood as "I cannot/will not read/recite." The translations of both Weil (1864, vol. 1: 114) and Rotter (1976: 44) follow this interpretation; Guillaume (1955: 106), however, translates "What shall I read." Rubin (2005: 50) suggests that historically the Arabic interrogative pronoun *mā* has been grammaticalized as a negative marker. Instead of "grammaticalization," one could also speak of an "illocutionary transgression" in such cases. At any rate, one may well argue that the interpretation "I cannot/will not read/recite" does not necessarily differ logically from the interpretation "what shall I read." Generally speaking, the rhetorical statement "what can I do [in this matter]?" appears to be coextensive with the statement "I cannot do anything [in this matter]." Regarding the transmission of the report on Muḥammad's first revelation, Schoeler (2010: 70) carefully shows how the original ambiguous statement *mā 'aqra'u*, as transmitted by az-Zuhrī on the authority of 'Urwa, was later in Muslim tradition turned into the comparatively unequivocal statement *mā 'anā bi-qāri'in* "I am not one to recite." Wehr (1953: 36) adduces more examples from the Quran that are *a priori* ambiguous with respect to the understanding of *mā* (10):

(10) Ambiguous examples (interpretation of *mā*) from the Quran:
mā 'aġnā 'an-hu mālu-hū wa-mā kasab (Q 111:2)
"What was the benefit of his wealth for him and what did he acquire?" or

"His wealth did not benefit him and he did not acquire."
wa-mā yubdi'u l-bāṭilu wa-mā yu'īdu (Q 34:49)
"And what does the wrong produce and what does it help?" or
"And the wrong does not produce anything, nor does it help."

The basic question to ask is whether these commonalities are only of a superficial phonological nature or of a deeper semantic nature. Even some book titles seem to imply a logical connection between these two categories, such as Bergsträsser's (1914) *Verneinungs- und Fragepartikeln und Verwandtes im Ḳur'ān. Ein Beitrag zur historischen Grammatik des Arabischen*. Nekroumi (2003: 72) also highlights the distributional, or logical parallels, between interrogation and negation (11):

(11) Distributional parallels between interrogation and negation

hal ǧā'a	*Zayd-un*	*rākib-an*	*'amsi*
Q came	Zaud-NOM	riding-ACC	yesterday

"Did Zayd come yesterday by horse?"

mā ǧā'a	*Zayd-un*	*rākib-an*	*'amsi*
not came	Zayd-NOM	riding-ACC	yesterday

"Zayd did not come yesterday by horse."

In logical grammar, both interrogations and negations are simply defined as "modified forms of the affirmative/declarative sentences" and thus form a semantic group. The most intuitive construction in this context is probably found in Wehr (1953: 36), who argues convincingly that one can hardly, if at all, distinguish interrogation from negation in negated exceptive clauses (12):

(12) Interrogation or negation in negated exceptive clauses
mā wa'ada-nā llāhu wa-rasūlu-hū 'il-lā ġurūran (Q 33:12)
"What have God and his apostle promised us except deception?" =
"God and his apostle have promised us nothing but deception"

Another example concerns the grammarian Muḥammad ibn al-Mustanīr (Quṭrub), who used to visit Sībawayhi early in the morning and to whom Sībawayhi would say (13):

(13) Interrogation or negation in negated exceptive clauses
mā 'anta 'illā quṭrubu laylin
"What are you except a night-*quṭrub*." =
"You are nothing but a night-*quṭrub*."

7.4.3 Case Study: Subject and Predicate in Arabic Sentences

It is elucidating, for instance, to compare the approach of modern grammar to the sentence types of Arabic with that of native Arab(ic) grammar. Peled (2009) analyzes, *inter alia*, the following two sentence types, which were identical for many of the Arab grammarians (14):

(14) Subject and predicate in Arabic sentences

a. *ʿAbd-u-llāhi* *ḍaraba* *zayd-an*
ʿAbd-NOM- llāh hit zayd-ACC
"ʿAbdullāh hit Zayd."

b. *Zayd-un* *ḍarab-tu-hū*
Zayd-NOM hit-I-him
"I hit Zayd." ("Zayd I hit him.")

Whereas a "Western" analysis would classify (14b) as a topicalized ("left-dislocated") variant of *ḍarabtu zaydan*, the majority of Arab grammarians classified (14b) as structurally identical with *zaydun munṭaliqun* "Zayd departs ["is departing"]" ("Zayd is somebody, whom I hit"), that is, *ḍarabtu-hū* in (14b) was treated as predicate, and not *zaydun* as left-dislocated topic. Peled (2009: 105) argues that the modern description of (14b) can either follow the left-dislocation or topicalization model (e.g., Holes 1995: 205–209) or the native Arabic approach without necessarily abandoning the concept of topicalizion. Badawi, Carter, and Gully (2004: 346) take a comparable position in their grammar of modern written Arabic. The following quotation, which refers to *ḍarabtu zaydan* "I hit Zayd" vs. *Zaydun ḍarabtu-hū* "idem" ("Zayd, I hit him"), is instructive:

> What happens to be inversion of the agent and verb [cf. (14a)] is actually a variety of topic-comment sentence, in which the topic, the agent of the comment-verb and the binding pronoun all happen to be identical (coreferential). In other words, there is no true inversion of agent and verb on the western pattern. This is confirmed by the fact that the verb + agent sequence contains only two elements while its apparent conversion contains three, a noun (= topic), a verb, and a pronoun agent (acting as both logical agent and binding pronoun).

7.4.4 Case Study: The *ʾIḍāfa Ġayr Ḥaqīqīya* and the *Naʿt Sababī* Construction

Another case in point for an approach that combines an investigation of native Arabic grammatical theory and a modern philological-linguistic perspective is the improper annexation (*ʾiḍāfa ġayr ḥaqīqīya*) and the semantically linked qualifier (*naʿt sababī*), both of which have no direct equivalent in modern European languages. Already the grammar by de Sacy (1831, vol. 2: 275–280) provided a useful analysis. Here are examples of the *ʾiḍāfa ġayr ḥaqīqīya* in Classical Arabic (15):

(15) The *ʾiḍāfa ġayr ḥaqīqīya* in Classical Arabic

a. *ḍāribu ʾaxī-hi*
"one who beats (or: has beaten) his brother"

aḍ-ḍāribu ʾaxī-hi
the one who beats (or: has beaten) his brother"

b. *rağulun karīmu n-nasabi*
"a man of noble descent"
ar-rağulu l-karīmu n-nasabi
"the man of noble descent"

Whereas type (15a) is statistically rarer, one *does* find examples such as *[a]l-muqīmī ṣ-ṣalāti* "the ones who perform prayer" (Q 22:35) or *[a]š-šātimay ʿirḍ-ī* "the two who are smearing my reputation" (verse 74 of the *Muʿallaqa* of ʿAntara). As Diem (1986: 248f.) has shown, European Arabists have referred to type (15b) only as "improper annexion," while native Arab grammatical theory (notably az-Zamaxšarī, *Mufaṣṣal*, § 111) classifies both type (15a) and type (15b) as *ʾiḍāfa lafẓīya* "(purely) formal annexation" or *ʾiḍāfa ġayr ḥaqīqīya*—as opposed to the *ʾiḍāfa maʿnawīya*, the "proper annexation."

The second related type, the semantically linked qualifier (*naʿt sababī*), exhibits the same rules regarding determination as can be observed in the *ʾiḍāfa ġayr ḥaqīqīya* (e.g., Fischer 2006: 194, 210). In addition, the phenomenon of "case attraction" is remarkable in this context (16), where *ḥasan-an* is linked morphologically through the agreeing accusative *-an* to the preceding noun, though it is semantically a predicate to the following *wağh*:

(16) The *naʿt sababī* construction in Arabic

raʾay-tu	*mraʾat-a-n*	*ḥasan-a-n*	*wağh-u-hā*
saw-I	woman-ACC-IDF	beautiful-ACC-IDF	face-NOM-her

"I saw a woman with a beautiful face."

raʾay-tu	*l-mraʾat-a*	*l-ḥasan-a*	*wağh-u-hā*
saw-I	DEF-woman-ACC	DEF-beautiful-ACC	face-NOM-her

"I saw the woman with the beautiful face."

The diachronical derivation of this type of construction, according to Diem (1998: 10, following Reckendorf 1898), can be represented as follows (17):

(17) Derivation of the surface of a *naʿt sababī* structure,

(an-nāsu) *l-qāsiyatu*		*qulūbu-hum* (Q 39: 22) →
nās-un *qulūb-u-hum*		*qāsiyat-u-n*
people-NOM hearts-NOM-their		hard-NOM-IDF
"people whose hearts are hard"		
(inversion within the relative clause)		→
nāsun qāsiyatun qulūbu-hum		→ (determination/*naʿt sababī*)
an-nās-u	*l-qāsiyat-u*	*qulūb-u-hum*
DEF-people-NOM	DEF-hard-NOM	hearts-NOM-their
"the people with hard hearts"		→ (deletion of *an-nāsu*)
("the hard-of-heart people")		
(*naʿt sababī*)		

al-qāsiyat-u	*qulūb-u-hum*
DEF-hard-NOM	hearts-NOM-their

"those whose hearts are hard"
("the hard of heart")

Typologically, the *naʿt sababī* structure continues to be hard to capture. Edzard (2011) represents an attempt to compare this type of construction with the stylistic figure *enallagé* (or *hypallagé*) *adjectivi*. Examples include the quotation from Shakespeare's *Hamlet* (1, 1, 48), *the majesty of buried Denmark*, properly meaning "the buried majesty of Denmark," or the quotation from Schiller's *Der Ring des Polykrates* (6), *der Schiffe mastenreicher Wald* "the ships' mast-rich forest," meaning "the forest of mast-rich ships." A tentative derivation comparable to the foregoing could look as follows (18):

(18) Derivation of the surface structure of an *enallagé (hypallagé) adjectivi*
"deep structure": *der Wald der mastenreichen Schiffe*
extraposition of the genitive: *der mastenreichen Schiffe Wald*
enallagé (hypallagé) adjectivi: *der Schiffe mastenreicher Wald*

Obviously, "deep structure" is understood here in a strictly synchronic sense. The *enallagé (hypallagé) adjectivi* differs from the *naʿt sababī* structure in that is cannot be analyzed as the result of the nominalization of a relative clause, but the structurally parallel form is still striking.

7.5 Lexicon

Hans Wehr's (1961) *Dictionary of Modern Written Arabic* continues to be of utmost importance, also for the reading of Classical Arabic texts. Edward Lane's (1863) large-scale Arabic–English Dictionary, which transmits the information contained in the Classical Arabic dictionaries such as *Lisān al-ʿarab* and *Tāǧ al-ʿarūs* (az-Zabīdī), was followed up in the 20th century by the *Wörterbuch der klassischen arabischen Sprache* (*WKAS*) initiated by Manfred Ullmann (1970), who decided to start with the letter *kāf*, that is, at the place in the alphabet, where Lane's dictionary no longer is exhaustive. So far, the letters *kāf* and *lām* have been completed in the large-scale *WKAS*, but the continuation of the project is not yet secured. Reinhard Dozy's *Supplément aux dictionnaires arabes* (1927) still can be considered a useful tool in addition to the previously mentioned works. (For an overview of Classical Arabic lexicography, see Carter 1990.)

7.5.1 Case Study: *Quṭrub*

One of the most impressive and detailed lexicographical studies is certainly Ullmann's (1976) article on the Arabic "ghost word" *quṭrub* "wer(e)wolf." The *Lisān al-ʿarab* and the *Tāǧ al-ʿArūs* give a host of meanings, taking up many sources, such as *duwaybbatun kānat fī l-ǧāhilīya ... laysa la-hā qarāruni l-batata* "a little animal that existed in the Jahiliya ... which does not ever have a period of rest," *ḏakaru l-ġīlāni* "the male ghul" (desert demon), *aṣ-ṣaġīru mina l-kilābi* "the whelp" ("the little one of the dogs"), *al-liṣṣu l-fārihu fī l-luṣūṣīya* "the swift thief" ("the thief who is agile in theft"), as well as others. The term *quṭrub* is also cited as the nickname of the grammarian Muḥammad ibn al-Mustanīr (cited in Section 7.3.2), who used to visit Sībawayhi early in the morning and to whom Sībawayhi then would say *mā ʾanta ʾillā quṭrubu laylin* "you are just the night-*quṭrub*." The dictionary closes with the formula *wa-llāhu ʾaʿlam* "God is all-knowing," that is, the author and compiler of the dictionary did not know himself.

The meaning "wer(e)wolf" can be derived from the Greek word λυκάνθρωπος, a compound consisting of the elements λῦκος *lykos* "wolf" and ἄνθρωπος *anthrōpos* "man," which underlies the Arabic word *quṭrub*. In the *Qānūn*, a medical dictionary by Ibn Sīnā, the term *quṭrub* is explained as *nawʿun mina l-mālanxūliyā* "a sort of melancholy," which is characterized by some of the previously listed qualities, such as roaming around by night and having no rest. In the Greek history of medicine, this disease was known as "lycanthropy." The word made its way into Arabic via an intermediate Syriac form *qanṭropos*. Ullmann points out plausibly that the ultimate Arabic form was triggered by the /$C_1uC_2C_3uC_4$/ pattern, which holds for animals such as *furʿul* "young hyena," *qunfuḏ* "hedgehog," and *ǧundub* "locust." Of special interest is the semantic transition from a concrete term to an abstract one (designating a malady). While one would have expected an Arabic term for the malady such as *dāʾ al-quṭrub*, comparable to *dāʾ aṯ-ṯaʿlab* "alopecia," the form *quṭrub* can, according to Ullmann, be traced back to a Greek manuscript, which in a list of maladies had the Greek wording περὶ λυκανθρώπου *peri lykanthrōpou* "about the wer(e)wolf" (instead of expected περὶ λυκανθρωπίας *peri lykanthrōpias* "about the lycanthropy"). Hence, the Arabic translators faithfully rendered the term for this disease as *quṭrub*. Clearly, Ullmann's analysis constitutes a model example of sound philological work.

7.5.2 Case Study: The "Virgins of Paradise" and the "Luxenberg" Hypothesis

In 2000, a Christian Lebanese scholar operating under the pen name of "Luxenberg" set out to re-interpret "obscure" passages in the Quran (Q). The most notorious lexical item in this connection was the noun phrase *ḥūr(un) ʿīn(un)*, approximately "round white-eyed ones" ("houris"), which is commonly understood in Classical Arabic as a metaphor for "beautiful (young) women" and which Luxenberg (2000) tried to reinterpret as a metaphor for "grapes," apparently with a view to providing a more "Victorian" image of the Quran. The common opinion is that *ḥūr* is to be interpreted as the plural of feminine singular *ḥawrāʾ* "having eyes in which the contrast between black and white is very intense," and *ʿīn* as the plural of feminine singular *ʿaynāʾ* "wide-eyed." Against this,

Luxenberg suggested interpreting *ḥūr* as an adjective derived from the Aramaic verb *ḥwar* "to be white," and *ʿīn* as an Arabicized pausal form of Aramaic *ʿaynē* "jewels."

A philological approach, as already defined, is indispensable for passing judgment on such a dispute. Two quotations from the Quran are central in this context: Q 44:54 and Q 52:20, both featuring the passage *wa-zawwağnā-hum bi-ḥūrin ʿīnin* ... "And we [God] shall wed them to wide-eyed houris...." To maintain the assumed meaning "grapes," Luxenberg emended *wa-zawwağnā-hum* "and we [God] will marry them to ..." to *wa-rawwaḥnā-hum* "and we [God] will provide them with ...," based on the similar consonantal *rasm*, even though such a form is otherwise unattested in Classical Arabic. Wild (2010) successfully debunks Luxenberg's proposals, not only by adducing relevant passages in the Quran describing the pleasures of paradise (notably Q 37:48–49, Q 44:51–56, Q 52:19–24, Q 55:56–58, Q 55:62–74, Q 56:15–38, and Q 78:31–34) but also by pointing to the description of the attributes of a banquet in pre-Islamic poetry (19):

(19) Excerpt (banquet description) of a poem by the pre-Islamic poet al-ʾAʿšā Maymūn

wa-miskun wa-rayḥānun wa-rāḥun tuṣaffaqu	"And musk and basil and wine mixed with water,"
wa-ḥūrun ka-ʾamṯāli d-dumā wa-manāṣifu	"And big-eyed beauties like statues, and servants,"
wa-qidrun wa-ṭabbāxun wa-kaʾsun wa-daysaqu	"And a cooking pot, a cook, a goblet, and a plate."

In sum, a proper philological analysis of this highly publicized issue has to point out at least the following flaws in Luxenberg's analysis, according to Wild (2010): the unclear definition of a "Syro-Aramaic" substratum in 7th-century Arabic; the disregard of other important philological witnesses (notably pre-Islamic poetry); and the projection of a Victorian world image (transferred to paradise) on Islam. Other controversial points for which Luxenberg has been criticized include the unsystematic tampering with the consonantal text (*rasm*), the resulting relativism (i.e., an overproduction of results) due to the previous problem, the disregard of the role of oral transmission of the text, the lack of an explanation for the emergence of the *textus receptus* of the Quran, and the unclear (selective) and normative definition of "obscure" passages in the Quran.

7.6 Case Study: Philological Analysis of a Judeo-Arabic Document

The philological approach can be devoted to individual realms of grammar and lexicon, as in the preceding cases. In the case of documents in a nonstandard variety of Arabic, like Judeo-Arabic, it may be interesting to apply the philological approach wholesale to all of the realms previously treated individually and to attempt to come up with a "mini grammar" of the respective text. The following remarks are based on a recent study by the author on an Iraqi Judeo-Arabic version of the Joseph story, representing the *qiṣaṣ al-ʾanbiyāʾ* genre (Ben Porat 1924. cf. Edzard, 2012), and cover features of phonology, morphology, syntax, lexicon, and style. The text has many typical features of Iraqi Arabic, in some cases specifically of the "qəltu" dialect, as exemplified in the following.

The Hebrew orthography of the text under investigation is phonetic as a tendency, especially as far as the use of vowels is concerned. Due to the loss of the dental fricatives in urban dialects, as also happened in the Baghdad region, the only occasional and unsystematic marking of the dental fricatives /ḏ/ and /ṯ/ is expected. The same holds for the dialectal merger of classical /ḍ/ and /ẓ/. The text offers rich documentation of the phenomena of *tafxīm* and *tarqīq*. Examples of the former process, that is, suprasegmental assimilation with respect to velarization, or advanced tongue root (ATR) include forms like <ṭmṣw>, from *ṭamasū* "they effaced."

One of the shibboleths of Iraqi Arabic dialects is the indefinite article (or indeterminacy marker) *fadd* or *fard*, which can also stand before nouns in the dual or in the plural (e.g., Blanc 1964: 118), for example, in <lʾgh frd ʿrby yswq frd nʾgh> "he met a Bedouin leading a camel." Some verb forms found in the text may be interpreted as being clearly indicative of the Jewish Baghdadi variety, such as <gbtw> "I brought" or <nʾdytwk> "I called you for help," where the final *-u* (i.e., of *–tu*) is spelled out (cf. Blanc 1964: 107).

The hypercorrect use of *lam* with the suffix conjugation ("perfect") is noteworthy in the text. Examples include <wlm frstw frysh> "and I did not became prey." This example also shows the combination of a hypocorrect construction with a "high" stylistic figure, that is, paronomasia (or figura etymologica—*mafʿūl muṭlaq*). A further feature is the marking of the definite direct (accusative) object with either *li-* or hypercorrect *ʾilā*, such as <yḥb ʾl ywsp> "he loves Joseph" (e.g., Hary 1991). Definiteness on noun–adjective phrases is usually marked only at the qualifying adjective, for example, <tʾg'r ʾl ʿrb> "the Arab (Bedouin) merchant."

The Judeo-Arabic text of the Joseph story contains a fair number of colloquial words, some of which are common to the Arabic *koiné* and some of which are specific to either Jewish or Muslim Baghdadi Arabic or even shared in both varieties. The verb <šʾp> is the most obvious example of the first category. Likewise, <pʾt> is used instead of Classical *daxala* "to enter." Another shibboleth of Iraqi Arabic, namely, the existence marker *aku*, is also found occasionally in the text, for example, <yʾ ʿrby ʾkw šgrh ʾṣlhʾ tʾbt> "O Bedouin, there is a tree with a firm trunk."

Stylistically, the oral character of this Judeo-Arabic version of the Joseph story can clearly be associated with the storyteller or *ḥakawātī* genre. There are several stylistic allusions to the fairy tale genre, as becomes evident, for instance, in the following formulation <ywm mn ʾl ʾyyʾm wsʾʿh mn ʾl zmʾn šʾp ywsp ḥlm> "on one day ('eines schönen Tages') at a certain hour Joseph had ('saw') a dream." It is also remarkable that this Judeo-Arabic text destined for a Jewish audience sets out with the *basmala* and in this way establishes a quasi-Muslim setting (on this issue, cf. Cohen 2007: 20):

(20) Example of Muslim textual elements in Jewish context
<bʾsm ʾllh ʾl rḥmʾn ʾl rḥym ʾyyʾhw nʿbdhw wbyh nstʿyn ʿlʾ qwm ʾl ṣʿʾlmyn>

"In the name of God the merciful the Compassionate; Him we venerate and to Him we seek refuge from the evil people"

7.7 Conclusion

In principle, the concepts *linguistic* and *philological* cannot and should not be separated in the first place. In practice, these two approaches at times have been drifting apart in recent research. Aoun et al. (2010), for instance, provide an exclusively formal linguistic study, without any philological ingredient. However, there is still room for carefully combining insight presented by the native Arab grammarians and modern linguistic theory on one side and insight gained by philological text-based research on the other. Indeed, only the empirical approach based on large diachronic and synchronic data is apt to yield results as presented, say, in the work of Joshua Blau, Werner Diem, Simon Hopkins, Geoffrey Khan, Pierre Larcher, Manfred Ullmann, and Stefan Wild.

References

Primary Sources

Ben Porat, Josef. 1924. *Qiṣṣat Yosef ha-ṣadiq ʿalav ha-šalom*. Baghdad: Maṭbaʿat al-Waṭanīya al-Yisrāʾilīya.

Ibn Manẓūr, Muḥammad ibn Mukarram. *Lisān al-ʿarab*. Beirut: Dār ʾiḥyāʾ at-turāṯ al-ʿarabī. 1988.

Ibn Sīnā. *al-Qānūn fī ṭ-ṭibb*. Bulaq. 1877.

Sībawayhi. *Kitāb Sībawayhi*. Ed. Muḥammad ʿAbd al-Salām Hārūn. 5 vols. Cairo, 1968–1977; 2nd ed. Cairo. 1977.

az-Zabīdī, Muḥammad Murtaḍā. *Tāǧ al-ʿarūs min ǧawāhir al-Qāmūs*. Kuwait: Maṭbaʿat ḥukūmat al-Kuwayt. 1965.

az-Zamaxšarī. *Kitāb al-Mufaṣṣal li-z-Zamaxšarī. Opus de re grammatica arabicum*. Ed. J.P. Broch. Christianiae: Libraria P. T. Mallingii. 1879.

Secondary Sources

Al-Nassir, A. 1993. *Sībawaih the phonologist: A critical study of the phonetic and phonological theory of Sībawaih in his treatise "Al-Kitāb."* London: Kegan Paul International.

Aoun, Joseph E., Elabbas Benmamoun, and Lina Choueiri. 2010. *The syntax of Arabic*. Cambridge, UK: Cambridge University Press.

Badawi, Elsaid, Michael G. Carter, and Adrian Gully. 2004. *Modern written Arabic: A comprehensive grammar.* London: Routledge.

Bergsträsser, Gotthelf. 1914. *Verneinungs- und Fragepartikeln und Verwandtes im Ḳurʾān. Ein Beitrag zur historischen Grammatik des Arabischen.* Leipzig: J.C. Hinrichs'sche Buchhandlung.

Birnstiel, Daniel. 2011. *Selected features of Arabic syntax in the Quran.* PhD diss., University of Cambridge.

Blanc, Haim. 1964. *Communal dialects in Baghdad.* Cambridge, MA: Harvard University Press.

Blau, Joshua. 1965. *The emergence and linguistic background of Judaeo-Arabic: A study of the origins of Middle Arabic.* Oxford: Oxford University Press.

Bobzin, Hartmut. 1992. Geschichte der Arabischen Philologie in Europa bis zum Ausgang des achtzehnten Jahrhunderts. In *Grundriß der arabischen Philologie. Band III: Supplement*, ed. Wolfdietrich Fischer, 155–187. Wiesbaden: Dr. Ludwig Reichert Verlag.

——. 1995. *Der Koran im Zeitalter der Reformation. Studien zur Frühgeschichte der Arabistik und Islamkunde in Europa.* Stuttgart: Steiner.

Brünnow, Rudolf-Ernst and August Fischer. [1895] 2008[8]. *Chrestomathy of Classical Arabic prose literature.* 8th rev. ed. Ed. Lutz Edzard and Amund Bjørsnøs. Wiesbaden: Harrassowitz.

Carter, Michael G. 1990. Arabic lexicography. In *Cambridge history of Arabic literature: Religion, learning and science in the ʿAbbasid Period*, ed. M. J. L. Young et al., 106–117. Cambridge, UK: Cambridge University Press.

Cohen, Mark R. 2007. On the interplay of Arabic and Hebrew in the Cairo Geniza letters. In *Studies in Hebrew and Arabic letters in honour of Raymond P. Scheindlin*, ed. Jonathan P. Decter and Michael Rand, 17–35. Piscataway, NJ: Gorgias Press.

Dahlgren, Sven-Olof. 2006. Sentential negation in Arabic. In *Current issues in the analysis of Semitic grammar and lexicon II*, ed. Lutz Edzard and Jan Retsö, 64–78. Wiesbaden: Harrassowitz.

Diem, Werner. 1986. Alienable and inalienable possession in Semitic *ZDMG* 136: 227–291.

Diem, Werner. 1998. *Fa-waylun li-l-qāsiyati qulūbuhum. Studien zum arabischen adjektivischen Satz.* Wiesbaden: Harrassowitz Verlag.

——. 2002. *Translokative Verben im Arabischen. Eine diachronische Studie.* Wiesbaden: Harrassowitz.

——. 2006. Philologisches zu den arabischen Papyri der Hamburger Staats- und Universitäts-Bibliothek. *ZAL* 45: 7–54.

——. 2011. *Arabisch* kayfa *"wie" als Konjunktion. Ein Beitrag zur Geschichte der arabischen Syntax.* Wiesbaden: Harrassowitz.

Dozy, Reinhard. 1927. *Supplément aux dictionnaires arabes.* 2 vols. Leiden: Brill.

Edzard, Lutz. 2001a. Grammatical systems in indigenous and in foreign perspective: The case of Arabic. In *Indigenous grammar across cultures*, ed. Hannes Kniffka, 317–345. Frankfurt a.M.: Peter Lang.

——. 2001b. Sībawayhi's observations on assimilatory processes and re-syllabification in the light of optimality theory. *Journal of Arabic and Islamic Studies* 3(2000): 48–65.

——. 2007. Noun. In *Encyclopedia of Arabic language and linguistics*, Vol. 2, ed. Kees Versteegh, Associate Editors: Mushira Eid, Alaa Elgibali, Manfred Woidich, Andrzej Zaborski, 422–428. Leiden: Brill.

——. 2011. Die *ʾiḍāfa ġayr ḥaqīqīya*, der *naʿt sababī* und die *enallagé (hypallagé) adiectivi*: ein typologischer Vergleich. In *Orientalistische Studien zu Sprache und Literatur. Festgabe zum 65. Geburtstag von Werner Diem*, ed. Ulrich Marzolph, 9–20. Wiesbaden: Harrassowitz.

——. 2012. Linguistic and cultural features of an Iraqi Judeo-Arabic text of the *qiṣaṣ al-ʾanbiyāʾ* genre. In *Mixed Arabic: Diachrony and synchrony*, ed. Liesbeth Zack, 83–94. Leiden: Brill.

Endress, Gerhard. 1992. Die wissenschaftliche Literatur. In *Grundriß der Arabischen Philologie*. Band III: Supplement, ed. Wolfdietrich Fischer, 3–152. Wiesbaden: Dr. Ludwig Reichert Verlag.

Fischer, Wolfdietrich (ed.). 1982. *Grundriß der Arabischen Philologie. Band I: Sprachwissenschaft*. Wiesbaden: Dr. Ludwig Reichert Verlag.

——. 1992. *Grundriß der Arabischen Philologie. Band III: Supplement*. Wiesbaden: Dr. Ludwig Reichert Verlag.

Fleisch, Henri. 1958a. La conception phonétique des Arabes d'après le Sirr *Ṣināʿat al-Iʿrāb* d'Ibn Ǧinnī. *ZDMG* 108: 74–105.

Fleisch, Henri. 1958b. *Mağhūra, mahmūsa*: examen critique. *Mélanges de l'Université Saint-Joseph* 35:193–210.

Fück, Johann. 1950. *Arabiya. Untersuchungen zur arabischen Sprach- und Stilgeschichte*. Berlin: Akademie-Verlag.

——. 1955. *Die arabischen Studien in Europa bis in den Anfang des 20. Jahrhunderts*. Leipzig: O. Harrassowitz.

Gätje, Helmut(ed.). 1987. *Grundriß der Arabischen Philologie*. Band II: Literaturwissenschaft. Wiesbaden: Dr. Ludwig Reichert Verlag.

Gensler, Orin. 2003. Object ordering in verbs marking two pronominal objects: Non-explanation and explanation. *Linguistic Typology* 7: 187–231.

Greenberg, Joseph H. 1966. Some universals of grammar with particular reference to the order of meaningful elements. In *Universals of language* ed. Joseph Greenberg, 577–587. Cambridge, MA: MIT Press.

Gruendler, Beatrice. 2006. Arabic alphabet: Origin. In *EALL*, I. ed. Kees Versteegh et al., 148–165.

Guillaume, Alfred. 1955. *The life of Muḥammad: A translation of Isḥāq's* Sīrat rasūl allāh. London: Oxford University Press.

Hamilton, Alastair. 2006. Arabic studies in Europe. In *Encyclopedia of Arabic language and linguistics*, Vol. 1, ed. Kees Versteegh, associate ed. Mushira Eid, Alaa Elgibali, Manfred Woidich, Andrzej Zaborski, 166–172. Leiden: Brill,

Hary, Benjamin. 1991. On the use of *ʾilā* and *li* in Judeo-Arabic texts. In *Semitic studies in honor of Wolf Leslau on the occasion of his eighty-fifth birthday*, ed. Alan Kaye, 595–608. Wiesbaden: Harrassowitz.

Holes, Clives. 1995. *Modern Arabic: Structures, functions and varieties*. London: Longman.

Hopkins, Simon. 1984. *Studies in the grammar of Early Arabic based upon papyri datable to before 300 A.H./912 A.D.* Oxford: Oxford University Press.

Khan, Geoffrey. 2011. Vocalised Judeo-Arabic manuscripts in the Cairo Geniza. In *From a sacred source: Genizah studies in honour of Stefan C. Reif*, ed. B. Outhwaite and S. Bhayro, 201–218. Leiden: Brill.

Lane, Edward. 1863. *An Arabic-English lexicon: Derived from the best and the most copious Eastern sources*, Book I, Part 1. London: Williams and Norgate.

Larcher, Pierre. 1994. *mā faʿala* vs. *lam yafʿal*: une hypothèse pragmatique. *Arabica* 41: 388–415.

Luxenberg, Christoph (pen name). 2000. *Die syro-aramäische Lesart des Koran: Ein Beitrag zur Entschlüsselung der Koransprache*. Berlin: Das Arabische Buch.

McCarthy, J. 1991. Guttural phonology. In *Perspectives on Arabic linguistics III: Papers from the third annual symposium on Arabic linguistics*, ed. Bernard Comrie and Mushira Eid, 63–92. Amsterdam: Benjamins.

Nekroumi, Mohammed. 2003. *Interrogation, polarité et argumentation: Vers une théorie structurale et énonciative de la modalité en arabe classique.* Schenefeld: EB-Verlag.

Nöldeke, Theodor. [1896] 2006⁴. *Grammatik des Klassischen Arabisch.* 4th rev. ed. Ed. Wolfdietrich Fischer. Wiesbaden: Harrassowitz.

Peled, Yishai. 1992. *Conditional structures in Classical Arabic.* Wiesbaden: Harrassowitz.

——. 2009. *Sentence types and word order patterns: Medieval and modern perspectives.* Leiden: Brill.

Reckendorf, Herrmann. 1898. *Die syntaktischen Verhältnisse des Arabischen.* Leiden: Brill.

Retsö, Jan. 2003. *The Arabs in antiquity: Their history from the Assyrians to the Umayyads.* London: Routledge.

Rotter, Gernot. 1976. *Ibn Ishâq. Das Leben des Propheten.* Tübingen: Horst Erdmann Verlag.

Rubin, Aaron D. 2005. *Studies in Semitic grammaticalization.* Winona Lake, IN : Eisenbrauns.

Sacy, Sylvestre de. 1831. *Grammaire arabe à l'usage des élèves de l'École spéciale des langues orientales vivantes.* Paris: Imprimerie royale.

Schoeler, Gregor. 2010. *The biography of Muḥammad: Nature and authenticity*, ed. James Montgomery. Trans. U. Vagelpohl. London: Routledge.

Ullmann, Manfred. 1970–. *Wörterbuch der klassischen arabischen Sprache.* Wiesbaden: Harrassowitz.

——. 1976. Der Werwolf. Ein griechisches Sagenmotiv in arabischer Verkleidung. *Wiener Zeitschrift für die Kunde des Morgenlandes* 68: 171–184.

——. 1988. *Sätze mit lau. Beiträge zur Lexikographie des Klassischen Arabisch 14.* Munich: Bayerische Akademie der Wissenschaften.

Versteegh, Cornelis H. M. 1977. *Greek elements in Arabic linguistic thinking.* Leiden: Brill.

Versteegh, Kees. [1997] 2001². *The Arabic language.* Edinburgh: Edinburgh University Press.

Vollers, Karl. 1906. *Volkssprache und Schriftsprache im alten Arabien.* Strassburg: Trübner.

Wehr, Hans. 1952. Review of Fück 1950. *ZDMG* 102: 179–186.

——. 1953. Zur Funktion arabischer Negationen. *ZDMG* 193: 27–59.

——. [1961] 1994. *A dictionary of modern written Arabic*, 4th ed. Ed. J. Milton Cowan. Wiesbaden: Harrassowitz.

Weil, Gustav. 1864. *Das Leben Mohammed's nach Mohammed Ibn Ishâk bearbeitet von Abd el-Malik Ibn Hischam.* Stuttgart: Verlag der J. B. Metzler'schen Buchhandlung.

Wild, Stefan. 2010. Lost in philology? The virgins of paradise and the Luxenberg hypothesis. In *The Qur'ān in context: Historical and literary investigations into the Qur'ānic milieu*, ed. Angelika Neuwirth, Nicolai Sinai, and Michael Marx, 625–647. Leiden: Brill.

Willmsen, David. 2010. Dialects of written Arabic: Syntactic differences in the treatment of object pronouns in Egyptian and Levantine newspapers. *Arabica* 57: 99–128.

CHAPTER 8

ARABIC LINGUISTIC TRADITION II

pragmatics

PIERRE LARCHER

8.1 Introduction: From the Grammatical Tradition to the Linguistic Tradition

The idea that grammar is nothing more than one of the linguistic disciplines is found in the Arabic tradition itself. We can cite at least two works in evidence. The first is the *Miftāḥ al-ʿulūm* (The key to the sciences) by Sakkākī (d. 626/1229). This work is divided into three parts. The first part is dedicated to morphology (*ʿilm al-ṣarf*), the second to syntax (*ʿilm al-naḥw*), and the third to the "two sciences of meaning and of expression" (*ʿilmā al-maʿānī wa-l-bayān*), or rhetoric (*Miftāḥ*, 3:25–27).

A little earlier, however, Sakkākī had presented syntax as having as its "complement" (*tamām*) rhetoric and the first part of rhetoric as having as its "complement" the "two sciences of definition and of argumentation" (*ʿilmā al-ḥadd wa-l-istidlāl*), in other words logic. Rhetoric in turn was presented as bipartite, to the extent that it is used and practiced in the two arts of prose (*nathr*) and versification (*naẓm*), as needing, for the latter, the "two sciences of prosody and of rhymes" (*ʿilmā al-ʿarūḍ wa-l-qawāfī*), in other words poetics (*ʿilm al-shiʿr*). Sakkākī indicates that he deals with all of this because it is a matter "of several species of belles-lettres" (*ʿiddat ʾanwāʿ al-ʾadab*), "taking each one from the other" (*mutaʾākhidha*), in other words forming a coherent whole. He explicitly excludes lexicography from his structure, however (*ʿilm al-lugha*) (*Miftāḥ*, 2:20–21; 3:1–12).

The contents of the *Miftāḥ* would thus be better described as a veritable encyclopedia of the sciences of language combining grammar, rhetoric, logic, and poetics, with each part

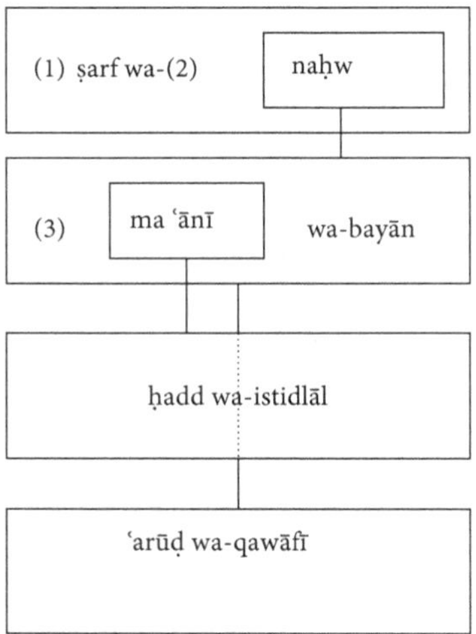

FIGURE 8.1 The science of language.

presented as a binary structure: the phrase *ʿilmā l-ṣarf wa-l-naḥw* appears at 3:33–34; it is parallel, as seen already, to those Sakkākī uses for the other three disciplines.

There is no contradiction between these two perspectives. The tripartite presentation is foreshadowed by the quadripartite presentation, in the sense that a distinction is made by the latter between what might be called the basic core and the expansions. The basic core comprises grammar and rhetoric, because these are the only disciplines that have expansions. To be sure, rhetoric is presented as an expansion of one of the two parts of grammar, but, in turn, it has for expansions logic, for the first of its two parts, and poetics for its two parts. The complex relationships among the various parts of this whole can be represented as shown in Figure 8.1.

The second work is the *Muqaddima* of Ibn Khaldūn (d. 808/1406). As its name indicates, it is the "introduction" to his great work of history, the *Kitāb al-ʿibar* (Book of lessons), Book I of the tome. The *Muqaddima* itself is divided into six chapters (*bāb*), which are subdivided into sections (*faṣl*). The sixth chapter is a veritable encyclopedia of the sciences, which contains a chapter entitled *fī ʿulūm al-lisān al-ʿarabī* (On the sciences of the Arabic language, no. 45) (*Muqaddima*, 1055–1070). Ibn Khaldūn enumerates four of them, in this order: grammar (*ʿilm al-naḥw*); the science of the lexicon (*ʿilm al-lugha*); rhetoric (*ʿilm al-bayān*); and the science of belles-lettres (*ʿilm al-ʾadab*).

Comparison between the two works is very instructive. First, the two structures have two disciplines in common, grammar and rhetoric, even though the two authors use different terminologies. Sakkākī uses *naḥw* in opposition to *ṣarf* to refer specifically to syntax. In contrast, Ibn Khaldūn uses *naḥw* in the general sense of grammar. Likewise, Sakkākī uses *bayān* as the name of one of the two parts of rhetoric, while Ibn Khaldūn uses it to name the entirety. But the presence of these two disciplines within the two structures confirms that they did indeed constitute the "basic core" of the Arabic linguistic tradition [Baalbaki, "ALT I"].

Second, Sakkākī excludes from his structure the ʿ*ilm al-lugha* that Ibn Khaldūn, conversely, does include. Even though neither of the two authors explains his choice to include or exclude it, the reason can be inferred on the basis of a remarkable passage in the *Sharḥ al-Kāfiya* (I:5) by the grammarian Raḍī al-dīn al-Astarābadhī (d. 688/1289) (Larcher 2000). There he defines the specific "objects" of the ʿ*ilm al-lugha*, the ʿ*ilm al-ṣarf* (*taṣrīf*, as he calls it), and the ʿ*ilm al-naḥw*. He does so through the concept of *waḍ* ʿ, which is inherited from *falsafa* (Greek *thesis*, Latin *impositio*, modern "institution") and which itself in the post-classical period will become the object of its own discipline, the ʿ*ilm al-waḍ*ʿ (Weiss 1976). For Astarābadhī, these objects were instituted either as "determinate expressions" (ʾ*alfāẓ mu*ʿ*ayyana*), which he describes as *samā*ʿ*iyya* (lit. relating to *samā*ʿ "hearing"), dealt with in the ʿ*ilm al-lugha*, or a "general rule" (*qānūn kullī*), through which one knows *qiyāsiyya* expressions (lit. relating to *qiyās* or "measure"). If the latter term is translated as "regular," then *samā*ʿ*ī* will be "irregular." Regular expressions can be simple (*mufradāt*) or complex (*murakkabāt*). Regular simple expressions and some regular complex expressions (e.g., the relative adjective or the imperfect verb) relate to the ʿ*ilm al-taṣrīf*: the relative adjective and the imperfect verb are formally complex, comprising a stem with a suffix in the first case and a prefix in the second, but do not function any less as units [Ratcliffe, "Morphology"]. The other regular complex expressions (phrases and sentences) relate to the ʿ*ilm al-naḥw*. All this can easily be translated into contemporary linguistic terms. A language on the whole comprises a grammar on one hand and a lexicon on the other. Grammar in turn includes a phonology, a morphology (*ṣarf*/*taṣrīf* including both phonology and morphology), and a syntax. The *ṣarf*/*taṣrīf* and the *naḥw* deal with the entirety of grammar, so it is only logical that a specific component deals with the lexicon. But the lexicon of a language consists of two parts: a regular part and an irregular part. Of course the regular part of the lexicon—that is, the rules of formation and interpretation of words—is in fact already treated in the *ṣarf* and, more specifically, the *ishtiqāq* ("derivation"). Thus, what is left over is the irregular part of the lexicon, which is likely to interest the lexicographer but not someone so concerned about systematization as is Sakkākī.

Third and last, Sakkākī considers the four disciplines he deals with to relate to an entirety that is the ʾ*adab* (*Miftāḥ*, 3:12), though Ibn Khaldūn, conversely, considers the ʾ*adab* to be a part of the entirety! This is explained by the difference in perspective of the two authors. Sakkākī is known as the systematizer of rhetoric (Smyth 1995). This is no accident. Rhetoric is central in his structure; it is the only discipline that is an expansion of another discipline, grammar, and that has, with logic and poetics, its own expansions. By including the various disciplines he deals with in an entirety relating to ʾ*adab*, Sakkākī marks out his perspective as essentially literary. Ibn Khaldūn's is quite different. He is known as a historian, but his profession was magistrate (*qāḍī*). He displays this perspective immediately after naming the four "pillars" (ʾ*arkān*) of the "sciences of the Arabic language" (*Muqaddima*, 1055):

> Knowledge of them all is necessary for religious scholars, since the source of all religious laws is the Qur'ān and the Sunnah, which are in Arabic. Their transmitters, the men around Muḥammad and the men of the second generation, were Arabs. Their difficulties are to be explained from the language they used. Thus, those who want to be

religious scholars must know the sciences connected with the Arabic language. (trans. Rosenthal, abr. ed. 433)

ومعرفتها ضرورية على أهل الشريعة اذ مأخذ الأحكام الشرعية كلها من الكتاب والسنة وهي بلغة العرب ونقلتها من الصحابة والتابعين عرب وشرح مشكلاتها من لغتهم فلا بد من معرفة العلوم المتعلقة بهذا اللسان لمن أراد علم الشريعة.

Ibn Khaldūn's perspective is clearly hermeneutic. Comparing the two works will thus remind us that the Arabic linguistic tradition has two aspects: one literary and the other hermeneutic. On its hermeneutical side, it thus intersects with the religious (i.e., theologico-juridical) sciences *(e.g., fiqh, ʾuṣūl al-fiqh, tafsīr, kalām)*.

This chapter deals essentially with two topics:

1) Rhetoric, as one of the two *sectors* of the basic core of the Arabic linguistic tradition (for overviews, see Heinrichs 1987, 1998; Halldén 2006; Larcher 2009). Since the tradition was not definitively constructed until the postclassical period, I use the *Talkhīṣ* of Qazwīnī (d. 739/1338), the most famous "epitome" of the rhetorical part of the *Miftāḥ* of Sakkākī, which itself is based on the two works of ʿAbd al-Qāhir al-Jurjānī (d. 471/1078), *Asrār al-ʿarabiyya* and *Dalāʾil al-Iʿjāz*. The *Talkhīṣ* owes its fame to the fact that it is a textbook (Smyth 1993), the object of many commentaries and supercommentaries, some of them collected in the *Shurūḥ al-Talkhīṣ* and widely used, until quite recently, in teaching and also used by Western scholars (Mehren 1853; Jenssen 1998).

2) Given the central nature of rhetoric, its *intersections* with the other parts of this tradition: one of them linguistics proper (i.e., grammar); the other not linguistics proper (i.e., the theologico-juridical sciences).

8.2 Rhetoric

8.2.1 Structural and Terminological Uncertainty

Qazwīnī's *Talkhīṣ* calls rhetoric *ʿilm al-balāgha* and divides it into three parts: *ʿilm al-maʿānī*, *ʿilm al-bayān*, and *ʿilm al-badīʿ*. After briefly presenting the subject of each, he concludes (*Talkhīṣ*, 36–37): "but many call the entirety *ʿilm al-bayān*, whereas some call the first *ʿilm al-maʿānī* and the other two *ʿilm al-bayān* and all three *ʿilm al-badīʿ*" (وكثير يسمي الجميع علم البيان وبعضهم يسمي الأول علم المعاني والآخرين علم البيان والثلاثة علم البديع). The first set of terms is, for example, that of Ibn Khaldūn, who gives the name *ʿilm al-bayān* to both the entirety and the second part of the entirety and the name *ʿilm al-balāgha* to the first part. It is also Ḍiyāʾ al-Dīn Ibn al-Athīr's (d. 637/1239). His work *al-Mathal al-sāʾir* gives the name *ʿilm al-bayān* to the entirety, dividing the content into an "introduction" and two "discourses" (*maqāla*), dealing, respectively, with "technique relating to the *lafẓ*" (*ṣināʿa lafẓiyya*) and with "technique relating to the meaning" (*ṣināʿa maʿnawiyya*).

The second set of terms is Sakkākī's (*ʿilmā al-maʿānī wa-l-bayān*), although he does not give a name to the entirety. I do not know whether the name *ʿilm al-badīʿ* was ever given to the entirety. But if it was, this might be compared with Ibn Khaldūn's remark that some rhetoricians, basically Maghrebi, favored this part, his example being the *ʿUmda* of Ibn Rashīq (d. 456/1063–1064) (*Muqaddima*, 1068). I will follow the division and terminology of Qazwīnī, always keeping in mind the structural and terminological uncertainties of the field in the Arabic tradition.

8.2.2 *ʿIlm al-Maʿānī*

The *ʿilm al-maʿānī* or "science of meanings" in its very name identifies itself as a *semantics*. In the definition given of it, however, the word "*maʿnā*," of which *maʿānī* is the plural, does not appear, but rather the word paired with it in the Arabic tradition (*Talkhīṣ*, 37): "it is a science by which the states of Arabic expression become known, appropriate to the needs of the situation" (وهو علم يعرف به أحوال اللفظ العربي التي بها تطابق مقتضى الحال). Other than *lafẓ*, the important word here is *ḥāl*, which appears twice, once in the singular and once in the plural. Such a definition posits the existence of a *correlation* between the *variation* (the "states") in the expression and the *situation* (the "state"). It is a semantics, the point of view adopted being *semasiological* (i.e., going from the expression to the *maʿnā*), and, more specifically, a *contextual* semantics.

Further elements of an answer can be drawn from the examination of the sections that make up the *ʿilm al-maʿānī* and the justification for this division (*Talkhīṣ*, 37–38). It is divided into eight sections: (I) states of the assertive predication; (II) states of the "support"; (III) states of the "supported" (lit. "that which is leaned"); (IV) states of the complements of the verb; (V) restriction; (VI) performative; (VII) conjunction and disjunction; and (VIII) concision, prolixity, and equilibrium. This division is justified by a set of six propositions.

The first proposition is as follows: "The utterance, in fact, is either statement or performative, because if its relationship has a referent, to which it is appropriate or not, it is a statement and, if not, a performative."

الكلام اما خبر أو انشاء لأنه ان كان لنسبته خارج تطابقه او لا تطابقه فخبر والا فانشاء.

The first proposition justifies sections I and VI and suggests that this semantics is primarily a semantics of the utterance. It repeats in fact the classification of utterances into *khabar* and *ʾinshāʾ* (Larcher, 1980, 1991), which was established conclusively in the 7th/13th century but which represents the outcome of a long tradition, the *maʿānī al-kalām* "meanings of the utterance," to use the title of a chapter of Ibn Fāris' *Ṣāḥibī* (d. 395/1004) (Frank 1981; Buburuzan 1995; Versteegh 2004). If the *khabar* is defined positively as a referential utterance, in other words an assertion, the *ʾinshāʾ* is here defined simply in a negative way, as a nonreferential utterance. But its name (lit. "creation") and examination of the sources show that it can be defined positively as a self-referential utterance, identifiable both by extension and by intension with Austin's (1962) category of performative (vs. constative). The *'inshā'* is at first added to a preexisting classification of utterances into *khabar* "statement" and *ṭalab* "request, demand" (= Fr. "jussion" and related adjective "jussive") designating only juridical performatives (*siyagh al-ʿuqūd wa-l-fusūkh* "contractual and renunciative formulas"). Then, at a later time, *ṭalab* was subsumed under *'inshā'*. A trace of this history remains in the commentators on Sakkākī. Sakkākī knows only a classification of utterances into *khabar* and *ṭalab*. His commentators adopt the new classification into *khabar* and *'inshā'* but subdivide the latter into *ṭalabī* "requesting, demanding" and *ghayr ṭalabī* "not requesting, demanding." If the *ʿinshā' ṭalabī* has the same extension as Sakkākī's *ṭalab*, the *'inshā' ghayr ṭalabī* includes, along with the juridical performatives, sometimes called *'īqāʿī* "operatives," all utterances that are neither assertions nor requests, such as the exclamations (see Section 8.3.5).

The second proposition is, "The statement requires a support, a supported, and a predication."

والخبر لا بد له من مسند اليه ومسند واسناد

This alludes to the fact that every utterance, whether statement or not, is a clause (*jumla*) and every clause a set (literal meaning of the word *jumla* in Arabic) of two elements (*juz'*) linked by a relationship (*nisba*) of predication (*'isnād*). Because *'isnād* is the *maṣdar* of a verb *'asnada* construed with two objects, a direct one and an indirect one introduced by the preposition *'ilā*, these two elements are called in Arabic *musnad* and *musnad 'ilayhi* and should logically be called predicate and subject. These two terms, however, hardly suit the verb (= *fiʿl*) and the subject (= *fāʿil*) of the verb, corresponding to *musnad* and *musnad ilayhi*, of the verbal clause, which is a *linked* clause, in the sense of the Swiss linguist Charles Bally ((1865–1947) (Bally 1965)), where the verb governs its arguments. They are even less appropriate for the terms "topic" (*mubtada'*) and "comment" (*khabar*), respectively, the *musnad 'ilayhi* and *musnad* of the nominal clause, which is a *segmented* clause, in the sense of Bally (ibid.). The verb *'asnada* literally means "to lean s.t. on" (*'ilā*); the derived passive participles *musnad* "supported" and *musnad 'ilayhi* "leaned on" designate the two obligatory parts of a predication, which I will translate as "supported" and "support" (Guillaume 1986; Larcher 2000). This second proposition justifies II and III and shows that this semantics concerns not only the utterance but also its constituents, in their major species.

The third proposition states: "The supported can have complements, if it is a verb or an element having the meaning of one."

و المسند قد يكون له معلقات اذا كان فعلا او في معناه

This proposition justifies IV and shows that this semantics concerns the minor as well as the major constituents.

The fourth proposition is as follows: "Each of the two relationships, predicative and verbal complements, can be made with or without restriction."

وكل من الاسناد والتعلق اما بقصر او غير قصر

This justifies V. Even though the restriction is presented as bearing on the constituents, whether major or minor, one finds here no less the utterance and even the semantically complex utterance.

The fifth proposition states: "Every clause is connected to another, whether coordinated with it or not."

وكل جملة قرنت بأخرى اما معطوفة عليها أو غير معطوفة

This proposition justifies VII and shows that this semantics also goes beyond the utterance, concerning the way one clause links with another, in other words, the formally complex utterance or discourse.

The sixth proposition is as follows: "The efficient utterance either considerably exceeds what is fundamentally intended, otherwise not."

والكلام البليغ اما زائد على أصل المراد لفائدة أو غير زائد

If it is too much, there is "prolixity" (*'iṭnāb*); if there is too little, there is "concision" (*'ījāz*). If there is no excess, it is "equilibrium" (*musāwāt*). In this sixth and last proposition, which justifies VIII, the term *balīgh* appears. This is the adjective corresponding to the verb *balugha*, whose verbal noun, *balāgha*, is, within the field of *ʿilm*, the term for rhetoric in Qazwīnī. *Balugha* perhaps understood as the stative–resultative voice of a verb of which *balagha* "arrive, reach" is the active voice. A *balīgh* discourse is thus a discourse that has achieved its purpose; in other words, it is efficient. The *balāgha* presupposes *faṣāḥa*, but not vice versa. *Faṣāḥa* is the verbal noun of the stative verb *faṣuḥa*, to which the adjective *faṣīḥ* corresponds. The elative *'afṣaḥ* that appears in the Quran (28:34) clearly designates the *faṣāḥa* as Aaron's fluency of speech as opposed to Moses' speech impediment. Something of the Quranic usage remains in rhetoric, where the term might be translated as "eloquence." Before postclassical rhetoric finally got rid of the two terms, *faṣāḥa* also appears in the titles of works of rhetoric, the most famous being the *Sirr al-faṣāḥa* of al-Khafājī (d. 466/1074). Outside of rhetoric, *faṣāḥa* can be used in the sense of "grammatical correctness," focusing on the matter of case and mood suffixes (*'iʿrāb*) (on *balāgha* and *faṣāḥa*, see Ghersetti 1998).

While centering on the utterance, this semantics sometimes deals with sub-utterance elements, taking an interest in its constituents, both major and minor, and sometimes goes beyond it, taking an interest in the connection of utterances among themselves. It is thus not possible to find in the rank of the expression (i.e., the utterance) the characteristics of this semantics.

The following sections go into more detail.

8.2.2.1 *The Khabar*

This section begins with a distinction between two uses of a statement: *fā'idat al-khabar* ("information provided by a statement"); and *lāzim fā'idat al-khabar* ("what it implies"). The first occurs when a speaker (*al-mukhbir*) wants to make the hearer know about a state of affairs (*al-ḥukm*), and the second happens when the speaker wants to make the hearer aware of what the speaker knows (*Talkhīṣ*, 40–41). Qazwīnī, unfortunately, gives no examples. Sakkākī (*Miftāḥ*, 72) gives, as an example of the first, *Zaydun ʿālimun* ("Zayd is a scholar"), when it is said to someone who was not aware of the fact, and, as an example of the second, *qad ḥafiẓta al-Tawrāh* ("you know the Bible by heart"), when it is said to someone who knows the Bible by heart.

It is followed (*Talkhīṣ*, 41–42) by a second distinction, so famous that in Ibn Khaldūn (*Muqaddima*, 1065) it becomes one of the symbols of the *ʿilm al-maʿānī*. This is a distinction of three types of statements: *ibtidāʾī* (lit. "initial"); *ṭalabī* (lit. "requesting, demanding"); and *ʾinkārī* (lit. "denying"). The first is addressed to someone who does not have an idea (*khālī al-dhihn*, lit. "empty mind") of the content of the statement. Its name comes from the fact that, purely informative, it is found at the beginning of the discourse. The second is addressed to someone with an attitude of hesitation or questioning with respect to the content. The last is addressed to someone with an attitude of denial with respect to the content. They thus take their names from what constitute *reactions* (Simon, 1993) to the attitude of the hearer and can take place only in dialogue. Ibn Khaldūn gives grammatical examples: *Zaydun qāʾimun* ("Zayd is standing") for the first; *ʾinna Zaydan qāʾimun* ("Yes, Zayd is standing") for the second; *ʾinna Zaydan la-qāʾimun* ("Yes, Zayd really is standing") for the third.

Simply comparing these two paragraphs allows us to further our understanding of what *ʿilm al-maʿānī* is. In the first case, the meaning of the statement depends not only on the intention (*qaṣd*) of the speaker, as Qazwīnī has it, but also on what the hearer does or does not know, as noted by Sakkākī. In other words, the *calculation* of the meaning of the utterance depends narrowly on the situation of utterance and, more specifically, on the participants. This alone suffices to call this semantics a *pragmatics*, in the sense of the American semiotician Charles Morris (1901–1979). In the second case, the calculation of the meaning is no less pragmatic in nature, but it relies on objective markers that this situation of utterance leaves in the utterance: the reinforcement *ʾinna* in the second example; and the reinforcements *ʾinna* and *la-* in the third.

It is this last case that confirms the definition given of *ʿilm al-maʿānī*, a variation in the expression as a function of the situation of utterance, and explains the interpretation that has been given of *maʿānī* as *maʿānī al-naḥw*: a "semantics of syntax" (*EI*², s.v. *al-maʿāni wa-l-bayān*). The expression *maʿānī al-naḥw* appears elsewhere, if not in the *Talkhīṣ*, at least in the other epitome of the *Miftāḥ* made by Qazwīnī, the *ʾĪḍāḥ* (in *Shurūh al-Talkhīṣ*, vol. 1:132). It originated in the *Dalāʾil* of Jurjānī (Heinrichs 1987, Ghersetti 2002). It suffices to read Qazwīnī further to see that this interpretation is reductive. He gives not a grammarian's example but a Quranic one (36:14–16), that of the two envoys (identified by the Islamic tradition as the apostles) to the inhabitants of a city (identified as Antioch). After initially being treated as liars, they said, reinforced by a third apostle: *ʾinnā ʾilaykum mursalūn* "Yes, to you we have been sent" and, after being treated a second time as liars, they said: *rabbunā yaʿlamu ʾinnā ʾilaykum la-mursalūn* "Our Lord knows it: yes, to you we have indeed been sent." As a result, Qazwīnī believes that the "reinforcement" (*taqwiya*) of the utterance, while it is "a good thing" (*ḥasuna*) in the case of *khabar ṭalabī*, is "obligatory" (*wajaba*) only in the case of *khabar ʾinkārī*. The single and double reinforcements of the utterance do not make the difference here between *khabar ṭalabī* and *khabar 'inkārī* but between two *retorts*, to a first and a second *denial*.

Thus, a one to one relationship cannot be established between interpretation of the utterance and presence or absence of markers in the utterance, since these can be optional. No less, moreover, can it be established that it is always possible to give the hearer a role that is not his, as in Quran 11:37 and 23:27 لا تخاطبني في الذين ظلموا انهم مغرقون ("Do not speak to me of those who are unjust: they will be swallowed up"): here *'inna* is not a reponse to an actual question of the hearer's but anticipates and forestalls a possible question on his part ("you will ask me: *what* of the unjust? I reply to you, ..."). Likewise, dealing with the first distinction, the speaker can perfectly do as if the hearer, knowing *p* (the statement) and knowing that the speaker knows it does not know the two things, for example, by saying to someone who is not praying *al-ṣalāt wājiba* ("prayer is obligatory"): it is then a third meaning that is engendered, of recall and even recall in order (*Shurūḥ al-Talkhīṣ*, vol. 1:199).

The term "calculate," emphasized already, is essential because it can be formalized. One would then have, in the case of the first distinction: if speaker A says to hearer B *p* and that B does not know *p*, then A causes B to know *p*; if A says to B *p* and that B knows *p*, then A causes B to know not *p*, but that *he* knows *p*; if A says to B *p* and that B knows both *p* and that A knows *p*, then A *reminds* B of *p*.

8.2.2.2 *The 'inshā'*

It is a pragmatic calculation of this type that is found in the chapter on the *'inshā'*. Qazwīni treats under this name what Sakkākī treats under *ṭalab*. Like Sakkākī, he subsumes five species under it. But, unlike Sakkākī, he does not take the trouble to show how these five species derive from a single type. This derivation, which has been studied by Moutaouakil (1982, 1990), is basically logical, in both form (Porphyrian tree) and vocabulary. A request requires an object (*maṭlūb*) that does not exist at the moment of the request (*ghayr ḥāṣil waqt al-ṭalab*). This object is realizable (*'imkān al-ḥuṣūl*) or not. If it is not, it is a wish (*tamannī*) (on which see now Zysow 2008). If it is, it is "in the mind" (*fī l-dhihn*) or "in the external world" (*fī l-khārij*). In the first case, it is interrogation (*istifhām*). In the second, it is a matter of "representation" (*mutaṣawwar*), whether negative (*intifā'*) or positive (*thubūt*). In the first case, it is an interdiction (*nahy*), e.g., *lā tataḥarrak* ("do not move"), and in the second it is an order (*'amr*), e.g., *qum* ("get up") and a vocative (*nidā'*), e.g., *yā Zaydu* ("Zayd!").

On the other hand, the result is typically pragmatic. For each of these species "expressions" are "instituted," for example *layta* for the wish, *hal* and *'a* for interrogation, etc. But all "can be used in another sense than their own" (*qad yustaʿmal fī ghayr maʿnāhu*). Each of the five paragraphs of this chapter, then, studies how, beginning with these "primary" (*'aṣliyya*) meanings, a certain number of "secondary" (*farʿiyya*) meanings "are engendered" (*yatawallad*) situationally. Just one example (*Talkhīṣ*, 170–171): for the interdiction only one particle exists, the *lā* governing the apocopated form, the interdiction being the counterpart of the order, as regards the superiority [of the speaker over the hearer] (*istiʿlā'*). But it can be used for other things than "to require not to do" (*ṭalab al-kaff ʾaw al-tark*), for example threat (*tahdīd*), as when one says to a slave who does not obey: "Do not obey me!" (*lā tamtathil ʾamrī*, lit. "do not conform to my order"). As specified by Sakkākī (*Miftāḥ*, 132), in this context, "It cannot be a matter of a requirement of disobedience, if such a thing existed: it is oriented toward something that does not exist..., and what finds itself engendered, aside from itself, is a threat" (امتنع طلب ترك الامتثال لكونه حاصلًا وتوجه الى غير حاصل ... وتولد منه التهديد) (on this concept of "engendering," Firănescu 2011).

It does no harm to recognize here what Searle (1975) calls an "illocutionary derivation." Similarly, we can recognize more generally in the *ʿilm al-maʿānī* what Berrendonner (1981) calls a "semantics in Y": the meaning here appears in fact as the *result*, symbolized by the stem of the Y, of a calculation operating on two components, symbolized by the arms of the Y, one linguistic (the "institution") and the other "rhetorical" (the "use").

8.2.2.3 *The qaṣr or restriction: The semantically complex utterance*

In this section, Qazwīnī studies the utterances that might be called "restrictive" and the various syntactic mechanisms put into effect to express restrictiveness: negation and exception (*nafī wa-istithnāʾ*), coordination (*ʿaṭf*), preposing (*taqdīm*),[1] *ʾinnamā*.... On the semantic level, the classification he proposes "crosses" two distinctions. One is logical. It can either restrict the subject (*mawṣūf*) to the attribute (*ṣifa*), e.g., *mā Zaydun ʾillā kātibun* ("Zayd is nothing but a prose writer," "Zayd is only a prose writer"), or the attribute to the subject, e.g. *mā fī l-dāri ʾillā Zaydun* ("There is only Zayd in the house," "Only Zayd is in the house"). The other is pragmatic. Here the restriction is called "singularization" (*ʾifrād*), "inversion" (*qalb*), or "specification" (*taʿyīn*), according to the belief of the hearer to which it reacts. Thus, the first utterance is addressed to someone who believes that Zayd is both (*sharika*) prose writer and poet. But the utterance *Zaydun qāʾimun lā qāʿidun* ("Zayd is standing, not seated"), with the syntactic process of coordination (*ʿatf*), is addressed to someone who believes either the opposite ("Zayd is seated") or one or the other ("Zayd is seated or standing").

8.2.2.4 *Al-waṣl wa-l-faṣl, or conjunction and disjunction: The formally complex utterance*

"Conjunction" and "disjunction" are the two types of "connection" of one clause to another. Conjunction is defined as the coordination (*ʿaṭf*) of the first to the second and "disjunction" as its absence. This last thus corresponds to what is called, in our tradition, asyndesis or parataxis. Generally speaking, what rules "conjunction," basically, is

[1] *Taqdīm* and *taʾkhīr* ("postposing")—that is, order, pragmatically conditioned, of the constituents of the clause—treated in a dispersed fashion in the *Talkhīṣ*. Conversely, it occupies a special section in the *Dalāʾil* (83) of Jurjānī, studied by Owens (1988). Ibn Khaldūn (*Muqaddima*, 1065) includes it as the first theme of his *ʿilm al-balāgha* (= *ʿilm al-maʿānī*).

the semantic and formal homogeneity of "conjoined" utterances, and "disjunction" the semantic and/or formal heterogeneity of "disjoint" utterances. Turning to the details, the first opposition encountered is *khabar/'inshā'*. They cannot in fact be coordinated with each other, for example, *māta fulānun raḥima-hu llāhu*: even if the two utterances are formally declaratives, only the first of them is semantically one ("So-and-so is dead"), the second being in fact semantically optative ("May Allah take pity on him!"). But phenomena are also found that are typically "enunciative," e.g., Quran 2:14–15: 'But when they are alone with their evil ones, they say, "Indeed, we are with you; we were only mocking". (But) God mocks at them.' (و اذا خلوا الى شياطينهم قالوا ان معكم انما نحن مستهزئون/الله يستهزئ بهم), where the disjunction of *Allah yastahzi'u bihim* is justified by the fact that "it does not belong to what they say" (*laysa min maqūlihim*), in other words by the change of utterer. Especially remarkable is the case of "disjunction" called "resumption" (*isti'nāf*), because the second clause is to be understood as a response (*jawāb*) to an implicit question (*su'āl*) suggested by the first, as in the following verse: *qāla lī kayfa 'anta qultu ʿalīlū/saharun dā'imun wa-ḥuznun ṭawīlū* ("'How are you?' he asked me. 'Unwell! Permanent insomnia and prolonged melancholy!' I replied"); *saharun dā'imun wa-ḥuznu ṭawīlū* responds in fact to a question like *mā bāluka ʿalīlan* ("What maladies do you have?") or else *mā sababu ʿillatika* ("What is the cause of your malady?"). We see, from these few examples, that if "conjunction" is defined as a *syntactic* coordination, then "disjunction" could be interpreted as a *semantic* coordination, in the sense of Bally (1965): the two disjoint clauses are in the semantic relation of topic to comment and the comment implicitly makes reference to the topic: "He is dead (and, because he is dead,) may Allah take pity on him!"; "(They say that they do nothing but mock, but) it is Allah who mocks them; [I am] sick; (you are going to ask me from what): from permanent insomnia and prolonged melancholy."

8.2.3 The ʿ*ilm al-bayān*

If the *ʿilm al-maʿānī* designates itself by its very name as a semantics, the *ʿilm al-bayān* appears from the definition given by Qazwīnī to be a *stylistics* (*Talkhīṣ*, 235–236): "It is a science by which is recognized the communication of one and the same intention by different means in what concerns the clarity of its meaning" (وهو علم يعرف به ايراد المعنى الواحد بطرق مختلفة في وضوح الدلالة عليه).

In the synchrony of postclassical rhetoric, the *ʿilm al-bayān* represents a point of view simultaneously complementary to and symmetrical with that of the *ʿilm al-maʿānī*: a point of view that can be called *onomasiological*, in that it goes from *maʿnā* "meaning" to *lafẓ* "form". But in the diachrony of the discipline, it represents in fact an older point of view. The term *bayān*, which has Quranic resonances, it formally the *maṣdar* of the verb *bāna–yabīnu* "to be distinct." It appears in the title of the founding work of Arabic rhetoric, the *Kitāb al-bayān wa-l-tabyīn* ("to be and to make distinct") of al-Jāḥiẓ (d. 255/868) (Montgomery 2006). And we have seen *ʿilm al-bayān* competing with *ʿilm al-balāgha* as the name of the entire discipline.

These "means" are not beyond counting. To count them, Qazwīnī (*Talkhīṣ*, 236–238) uses the concept, which we have already met, of *waḍ'* ("institution"), which governs the relation of meaning (*dalāla 'alā ma'nā*), *lafẓ* and *ma'nā* being called, under this relationship, *al-mawḍū'* ("that which is instituted") and *al-mawḍū' lahu* ("that for which one institutes it"). This meaning is precisely "institutional" (*waḍ'iyya*), when the expression signifies "the entirety of that for which it is instituted" (*tamām mā wuḍi'a lahu*). It is also called in this case "adequacy" (*muṭābaqa*). It is "logical" (*'aqliyya*) when the expression means either a "part" (*juz'uhu*) of that for which it is instituted or something "external" (*khārij 'anhu*). The first case is called *taḍammun* ("comprehensiveness," "inclusion") and the second *iltizām* ("implication"). It is only this last that interests the rhetorician. Linguistically speaking, one would say *implicit* meaning, but the linguistic term should not make us forget its logical origin (Lat. *implicitus* < *implicare*). The "expression by which one aims at that which implies that for which it is instituted" (*al-lafẓ al-murād bihi lāzim mā wuḍi'a lahu*), in other words its implicit meaning (and not its explicit one), is called *majāz* if there is a "connection" (*qarīna*) indicating that the explicit meaning is not aimed at, and, if not, *kināya* ("metonymy"): this is in fact defined (*Talkhīṣ*, 337) as "the expression by which one aims at that which implies its meaning, with the possibility of aiming at this at the same time" (الكناية لفظ أريد به لازم معناه مع جواز ارادته معه). Finally, the *majāz* can be based on a comparison (*tashbīh*, on which see especially Smyth 1992), hence the three sections of the *'ilm al-bayān*: (1) *tashbīh*; (2) *ḥaqīqa wa-majāz*; and (3) *kināya*.

Here we cannot go into detail on these three sections and must be satisfied with a few remarks. First, *majāz* and *ḥaqīqa* do not at all refer, as has often been said, to the literal meaning or proper sense and the figurative meaning, but in fact to the expression used in its literal meaning and to the expression used in its figurative meaning. This confirms the onomasiological point of view (on this contrast, see Heinrichs 1984). Second, to the extent that *majāz* is opposed to *kināya*, it refers not to every figurative expression but more specifically to metaphorical expression. Third, because the *majāz* includes comparison, it refers in fact, for the most part, to figurative expressions based on what there is in common between metaphor and comparison, namely, resemblance (*mushābaha*). As in our tradition, metaphor is seen as a truncated comparison, see Qazwīni, citing Sakkākī (*Talkhīṣ*, 330): "He divided the lexical *majāz* into metaphor and other and defined metaphor as the fact of mentioning one of the two terms of the comparison, aiming, by it, at the other" (وقسم المجاز اللغوي الى الاستعارة وغيرها وعرف الاستعارة بأن تذكر أحد طرفي التشبيه وتريد به الآخر).

Ibn Khaldūn (*Muqaddima*, 1065–1066), for his part, holds resolutely to two "means," *isti'āra* and *kināya*, which he differentiates logically. He presents the first as a passage from the "antecedent" (*malzūm*) to the "consequent" (*lāzim*), e.g. *Zaydun 'asadun* ("Zayd is a lion": if Zayd is a lion, then he is courageous), and the second as a passage from the consequent to the antecedent, e.g. *Zaydun kathīru ramādi l-qudūr* ("Zayd has many ashes under his pots": if Zayd has many ashes under his pots, it is because he is very hospitable). This last example is known from Qazwīnī (*Talkhīṣ*, 340–341), who includes it in the metonymy of one *ṣifa* (attribute) for another, but "distant" (*ba'īda*), because it happens "through an intermediary" (*bi-wāsiṭa*). Qazwīnī reconstructs the chain of inferences leading from one to the other: "many ashes" (*kathīr al-ramād*), thus "much wood burned under the pots" (*kathra 'iḥrāq al-ḥaṭab taḥt al-qudūr*), thus "many cooked dishes" (*kathrat al-ṭabā'ikh*), thus "many eaters" (*kathrat al-'akala*), thus "many hosts" (*kathrat al-ḍīfān*). The logical criterion is known from Sakkākī (*Miftāḥ*, 170) and, following him, Qazwīnī, but criticized by the latter, on the grounds that one cannot be transferred from the consequent, because there is no antecedent!

Whatever criterion is employed, the Arab rhetoricians could not get very close to the idea because they had, at base, only two fundamental figures: metaphor and metonymy. In modern Western linguistics, Roman Jakobson (1896–1982) did. As we know, he proposed a correlation between metaphor and similarity, metonymy and contiguity, and, as a result, distributed them on the axes, respectively paradigmatic and syntagmatic, of language (Jakobson, 1956).

One last word: Qazwīnī here limits *majāz* to *majāz lughawī* ("lexical"). But Sakkākī (*Miftāḥ*, 166f.) treats both in the *'ilm al-bayān* of the *majāz 'aqlī* ("logical"). The latter concerns the utterance, notably when its two terms are metaphorical, e.g., *'aḥyā l-'arḍa shabābu l-zamāni* "The youth of time [= spring] has revived the earth [= has produced vegetation]." Qazwīnī is not unaware of this, but he treats it in the *'ilm al-ma'ānī*, section I (*Talkhīṣ*, 45f.). This suggests that the rank of the expression ends up competing with the point of view. Ultimately, rhetoric appears as nothing but a contextual semantics: of the utterance and its constituents in the context of the discourse for the *'ilm al-ma'ānī*, of the word in the context of the clause for the *'ilm al-bayān*.

8.2.4 The *'ilm al-badī'*

The *'ilm al-badī'* comes simultaneously from very close and very far.

From very close, because, as the third part of rhetoric, it is a recent innovation, due to Badr al-dīn Ibn Mālik (d. 686/1287), the son of the famous grammarian Ibn Mālik (d. 642/1274), in his work on rhetoric called *al-Miṣbāḥ*. For Sakkākī, it is not yet anything but a simple ornamental tailpiece to *'ilm al-bayān*. Qazwīnī gives the following definition (*Talkhīṣ*, 347): "It is a science through which the manners of embellishing discourse become known, after observing the adequacy [of the expression for what the situation requires] and the semantic clarity" (وهو علم يعرف به وجوه تحسين الكلام بعد رعاية المطابقة ووضوح الدلالة). In this definition not only are the very words of Sakkākī found, but also the memory of a tailpiece ("after") is preserved, even if, due to the fact of its assumption to the rank of part, a tailpiece no longer to the *'ilm al-bayān*, but to the *'ilmā al-ma'ānī wa-l-bayān*.

And from very far, because the term appears in one of the first works of rhetoric that we have, the *Kitāb al-badī'* of the poet (and caliph for a day) Ibn al-Mu'tazz (d. 296/808), who was assassinated the very day of his enthronement. The *Kitāb al-badī'* or book of the "new [style]" takes its name from its polemical aim, namely to show that the style of the poets called "modern" (*muḥdathūn*), such as Bashshār b. Burd (d. 167 or 168/784–5), Muslim b. al-Walīd (d. 208/823), or Abū Nuwās (d. between 198/813 and 200/815), is not so very "new" and that none of its features was not anticipated in the Quran, the traditions of Muḥammad and his companions, and old poetry. As for the rest, the *Kitāb al-badīʿ* presents itself as a simple catalogue of figures, five basic ones, including metaphor (*istiʿāra*), to which Ibn al-Muʿtazz adds twelve "ornaments" (*maḥāsin*) of discourse, in prose (*kalām*) or poetry (*shiʿr*), or a total of seventeen figures.

Through the centuries, the *ʿilm al-badīʿ* remained what it had been since the beginning: a *tropology*. The resemblance of the *ʿilm al-badīʿ* to what in our own tradition is called "rhetoric restricted to figures" is accentuated by the fact that Qazwīnī, following Sakkākī, divides them into two types (*ḍarbān*): "semantic" (*maʿnawī*) and "formal" (*lafẓī*). In this division the similarity must be recognized to what we call in our tradition "figures of thought" and "figures of expression." Of the 37 figures named by Qazwīnī, 30 belong to the first type versus 7 to the second. It will suffice here to present the first of each of the two types of figures. The *ṭibāq* is defined (*Talkhīṣ*, 348) as "the union of two contraries, that is, of two opposed meanings, in the clause" (*al-jamʿ bayna mutaḍāddayn ʾay maʿnayayni mutaqābilayni fī al-jumla*), for example *taḥsubuhum ʾayqāẓan wa-hum ruqūd* ("you believe them awake, even though they are abed"). It is antithesis. The *jinās* (*Talkhīṣ*, 388) is defined as the "formal resemblance of two terms" (*tashābuhuhumā fī al-lafẓ*). According to their degree of proximity, this figure varies from simple paronomasia to repetition pure and simple.

8.2.5 *Balāgha* vs. *khaṭāba*

ʿIlm al-balāgha is usually translated as "rhetoric." This leads to the question of its relationship with what we call "rhetoric" in our own tradition. The question is not empty. Aristotle's *Rhetoric* was translated into Arabic under the name *al-khaṭāba*. "Rhetoric" reveals itself etymologically to be an "[art] of oratory" (*rhetorikè technè*). *Khaṭāba* is the *maṣdar* of the verb *khaṭuba* "to be eloquent" (*khaṭīb*). The eloquent man having been chosen as spokesman of his tribe, the same word designates, by metonymy, the orator, and *khaṭaba* itself passes from the quality (eloquence) to the activity (office of *khaṭīb*), whence the reading **khiṭāba*.

Genetically, there is essentially no relationship between *ʿilm al-balāgha* and Aristotelian rhetoric, even if there might have been, marginally, contacts. In the Arabic tradition, in fact, which is heir on this point to a late Alexandrian tradition, Aristotle's *Rhetoric* (and *Poetics*) are part of the Organon, in other words they are works of logic. Consequently, it is in the framework of *falsafa* that they are commented on, like the other works of the First Master, by the great *falāsifa*: al-Fārābī (d. 339/950), Ibn Sīna (d. 428/1037), Ibn Rushd (d. 595/1198) (Aouad 1989, Black 1990, Würsch 1991). Which is not to say that "Hellenizing" works of poetics or rhetoric cannot be found even outside *falsafa* (see for an overview Larcher 1998a): for the classical period and the Mashriq, we may mention the *Naqd al-shiʿr* ("criticism of poetry") of Qudāma ibn Jaʿfar (d. 337/948?) and the *Burhān fī wujūh al-bayān* of Ibn Wahb (4th/10th century), initially published under the title *Naqd al-nathr* ("criticism of prose") and falsely attributed to Qudāma; for the postclassical period and the Maghreb, the *Minhāj al-bulaghāʾ wa-sirāj al-udabāʾ* of

Ḥāzim al-Qarṭājannī (d. 684/1285), which is actually, despite its title, a Hellenizing work of poetics, studied as such by Heinrichs (1969).

But logic (*manṭiq*) having become in the 11th century a scholastic discipline, the entire Arabic tradition knows *al-khaṭāba* and *al-shiʿr* as excessively abbreviated names for the rhetorical syllogism (*al-qiyās al-khaṭābī*), i.e., enthymeme, and the poetic syllogism (*al-qiyās al-shiʿrī*), that is, premisses that are not merely "uncertain" (*ghayr yaqīniyya*) but actually "producers of imagination" (*mukhayyila*) (on the poetic syllogism see Schoeler 1983). This clearly shows the double reduction undergone by Aristotelian rhetoric in passing from the Greek world to the Muslim world and, within that, from *falsafa* to scholasticism. We may note meanwhile the existence in *falsafa* of a specific development: the theory of the "prophet-legislator." We may also mention the criticism of the rhetoric and poetics of the philosophers (*mutafalsifūn*) made by Ibn al-Athīr in the *Mathal al-sā'ir* (I, 310–312), who quotes the *Shifā'* of Ibn Sīnā.

Typologically, there are large differences between *ʿilm al-balāgha* and Greek rhetoric. Two deserve attention. Greek rhetoric, it is said, is an oratorical art. The *ʿilm al-balāgha*, in contrast, does not deal with a specific genre, but with all. This explains that the poetics of Sakkākī only deals with strictly technical aspects (meter and rhyme) of poetry. The rest, that is, the basics, the stylistic and thematic aspects, are a matter for *ʿilm al-balāgha* as they are for the other genres. Even the works that appear to be dedicated to specific genres, such as the *Kitāb al-ṣināʿatayn fi-l-kitāba wa-l-shiʿr* ("The book of the two arts: the art of the secretary of the chancellery and poetry") of Abū Hilāl al-ʿAskarī (d. after 395/1005) actually deal with all of them. Greek rhetoric defines itself as an "art of persuasion," in other words places at its heart *perlocutionary* acts (Austin 1962). Conversely, the *ʿilm al-balāgha*, via the concept of *'inshā'*, places at its heart illocutionary acts.

This double difference is easily explained if one "recontextualizes" Greek rhetoric and *ʿilm al-balāgha*. Aristotle's *Rhetoric* is intimately linked to the judicial and political institutions of Athens, exactly, moreover, as his *Poetics* is linked to the cultural institutions (theater) of the Attic city. Not one of these institutions exists in the Islamic *umma*. On the other hand, it places one "word" above all the others, which it respects as the word of Allah (*kalām Allāh*), "revealed" (*tanzīl*) to Muḥammad, "transmitted" (*tablīgh*) by him, and transcribed in the Quran. Its addressee is not a spectator, who praises and blames, as in the ceremonial genre of Aristotelian rhetoric, and still less a judge to be persuaded, as in the judicial and deliberative genres of the same. But, once persuaded, he is in fact an interpreter. We are now approaching the hermeneutical side of the *ʿilm al-balāgha*.

Let us note, however, that there exists, in the world of Islam, a form of institutionalized eloquence: this is the sermon (*khuṭba*) that the preacher (*khaṭīb*) gives in the pulpit (*minbar*) on Fridays. His art, which is oratory, obviously bears the same name as Aristotle's *Rhetoric*: *al-khaṭāba*. This homonymy is the source of much confusion among scholars with insufficient cultural background. To avoid confusion, we call the first, with Heinrichs (1987), "philosophical" rhetoric, and the second, with Larcher (1998), homiletics (for an overview of which see Halldén 2005, 2006 and, for the *khuṭba* in Jāḥiẓ, Soudan 1992, Avril 1994).

8.3 Intersections

8.3.1 *ʿIlm al-balāgha* and *ʾiʿjāz*

As the title of one of ʿAbd al-Qāhir al-Jurjānī's works reminds us, rhetoric is here included in a specifically Islamic context, where it has an apologetic aim: to "prove" (*dalāʾil*) "the inimitability of the Quran" (*ʾiʿjāz al-Qurʾān*). The *ʾiʿjāz al-Qurʾān* has become the object of a considerable literature, among which the most famous work is that of Bāqillānī (d. 403 or 404/1013). As a result, it has also become the object of a considerable literature on the part of Arabists (s.v. *ʾiʿjāz* in *EI*[2] and Inimitability in *EQ*, Audebert 1982). Everything that is necessary and sufficient to know on the subject will be found there. The *ʾiʿjāz al-Qurʾān* was not definitively established as dogma until the 4th/10th century. Its basis is the verses of the Quran called "challenge" (*taḥaddī*: 10:39; 11:16; 17:90), in which the adversaries of Muḥammad are challenged to produce something similar to the Quran (*min mithlihi*), what in technical terms is called a *muʿāraḍa* or "replica." The fact that the challenge was not met proves the "miraculous" (*muʿjiz*) character of the Quran, lit. "it renders incapable" of a replica, in other words leaves its adversaries speechless. The concept is thus clearly polemical. As often in Arabic, the term that designates it is only the most important of a series of collocations. It is the collocation and not the term itself that European languages interpret with the word "inimitability (of the Quran)." The *mithli* of the Quranic text can be interpreted as "similar to the Quran, from the point of view of *maʿnā* and/or *lafẓ*." As a result, we distinguish a "thematic" *ʾiʿjāz* from a "stylistic" *ʾiʿjāz*. It is this last that has prevailed. The link between *ʾiʿjāz* and *balāgha* (as a quality) is recognized by Rummānī (d. 384/994), the author of one of the first works on the subject that we have: "what is at the highest degree of *balāgha* is *muʿjiz* and it has to do with the *balāgha* of the Qurʾān" (ان ماكان في أعلاها (طبقات البلاغة) معجز وهو بلاغة القرآن).[2] As a result, a significant advance was made in the domain of *balāgha*, i.e. rhetoric. The close connection between rhetoric, in its two basic components, and literature of the *ʾiʿjāz* did not escape Ibn Khaldūn, even though he, writing long after, attempted to put the relationship in the opposite order (*Muqaddima*, 1068):

> The fruit of this discipline is understanding of the inimitability of the Qurʾān. This consists in the fact that the (language of the Qurʾān) indicates all the requirements of the situations (referred to), whether they are stated or understood. This is the highest stage of speech. In addition, (the Qurʾān) is perfect in choice of words and excellence of arrangement and combination. (tr. Rosenthal, abr. ed. 437)
>
> واعلم أن ثمرة هذا الفن انما هي فهم الاعجاز من القرآن لأنَّ اعجازه في وفاء الدلالة منه بجميع مقتضيات الأحوال منطوقة ومفهومة وهي اعلى مراتب الكمال مع الكلام فيما يختص بالألفاظ في انتقائها وجودة رصفها وتركيبها

[2] Quoted by Aḥmad Ṣaqr in the introduction (11) to his edition of the *ʾIʿjāz al-Qurʾān* of Bāqillānī.

8.3.2 ʿ*Ilm al-balāgha* and *tafsīr*

Immediately after Ibn Khaldūn's discussion of relation between rhetoric and the *'iʿjāz al-Qur'ān*, he adds (*Muqaddima*, 1068): "This discipline is needed most by Qur'ān commentators" (وأحوج ما يكون الى هذا الفن المفسرون). But he says, "Most ancient commentators (*tafāsīr*) disregarded it, until Jār-Allāh az-Zamakhsarī (d. 538/1144) appeared" to provide a detailed rhetorical commentary on the Quran. Ibn Khaldūn does not conceal his admiration for this commentary, but he is embarrassed by the fact that its author is catalogued as "heterodox" (*'ahl al-bidaʿ*), hence his rejection by most of the "orthodox" (*'ahl al-sunna*). He then devotes the entire rest of the chapter on rhetoric to a justification of being at the same time both perfectly "orthodox" and a reader of Zamakhsharī, taking into account the profit that can be drawn from his work for this discipline overall and the *'iʿjāz al-Qur'ān* in particular. In the process, Ibn Khaldūn implicitly reminds us that Zamakhsharī was a Muʿtazilite and that Muʿtazilism, condemned for its thesis called "Qur'ān created (by Allah)" (vs. "uncreated," i.e. eternal), nonetheless played a considerable role in the elaboration of the dogma of the *'iʿjāz al-Qur'ān* and, as a result, in the development, and also reorientation, of rhetorical studies. If we now turn to the actual introduction that Zamakhsharī wrote to his commentary, we see that he unequivocally adumbrates his point of view. Reviewing all the Quranic specialists, both by background—jurist (*faqīh*), theologian (*mutakallim*), narrative expert (*ḥāfiẓ al-qiṣaṣ wa-l-'akhbār*), preacher (*wāʿiẓ*)—and by form—grammarian (*naḥwī*), lexicographer (*lughawī*)—he concludes that (*Kashshāf*, 16):

> There is no one among them who can present himself to follow the [Qur'ānic] ways nor anyone who can immerse himself into [Qur'ānic] realities, other than a man who has excelled in two specific Qur'ānic sciences, namely the science of the *maʿānī* and the science of the *bayān*.
>
> لا يتصدى منه أحد لسلوك تلك الطرائق ولا يغوص على شئ من تلك الحقائق الا رجل قد برع في علمين مختصين بالقرآن وهما علم المعاني وعلم البيان

Here we see an occurrence of the expression, repeated exactly on p. 20, ʿ*ilmā l-maʿānī wa-l-bayān*, which *EI*[2] (s.v. *al-maʿānī wa-l-bayān*) claims first appeared in Sakkākī, nearly a century later. And we also see that, in Zamakhsharī's view, there is no rhetoric but Quranic ....

8.3.3 ʿ*Ilm al-balāgha*, ʿ*ilm al-fiqh*, and ʿ*ilm uṣūl al-fiqh*

Less well-known are the relationships between linguistic and juridical disciplines. They are, nonetheless, perfectly well recognized by Ibn Khaldūn, in a general way in the passage quoted in the Introduction above and in a specific way in another passage of the *Muqaddima* (61). Wishing to distinguish *khabar*, in the historical sense (the plural

ʾakhbār is one of the words for history in Arabic) from *khabar* in the juridical sense (in this sense *khabar* is a synonym of *hadith*), he articulates the difference by means of the linguistic opposition *khabar/ʾinshāʾ*: the historical *khabar* is a statement, true or false, but "most legal *ʾakhbār* are performative prescriptions that the Legislator made obligatory to be put into practice"

معظمها(الأخبار الشرعية) تكاليف انشائية أوجب الشارع العمل بها
(Larcher 1993).

The *khabar* or *ḥadith* constitutes, after the Quran, the second of the "sources" (*ʾuṣūl*) of jurisprudence (*fiqh*) in Islam. It takes its name from the fact that it transmits the Sunna, that is, the entirety of what was said, done, or endorsed by Muḥammad. This transmission takes the following form: *ʾakhbaranī* (or *ḥaddathanī*) *fulān ʿan fulān ʿan fulān... qāl...* ("So-and-so told me after So-and-so, who had it from So-and-so..., as follows: ..."). But since most of what is transmitted consists of speech, the term *hadith* itself has become synonymous with "said" by Muḥammad.

Of course, if one is interested in the mechanism of juridical interpretation of the Quran and the Sunna, one soon discovers that it is rhetoric, in the sense defined above—that is, pragmatics. The *ʾuṣūliyyūn*, moreover, do not speak of the utterance (*kalām*), but of the address (*khiṭāb*). The *khiṭāb*, for the case where one might not have understood, is defined by the encyclopedist Kafawī (d. 1094/1683) as "the utterance oriented toward another, in order to cause to understand" (*al-kalām al-muwajjah naḥw al-ghayr li-l-ʾifhām*) (*Kulliyāt*, s.v. *khiṭāb*). *ʾIfhām* is a direct echo of *mafhūm* (vs. *manṭūq*), the name for implicit (vs. explicit) meaning among the *ʾuṣūliyyūn*, which we met in 8.3.1 in the quotation from Ibn Khaldūn: the juridical meaning of the utterance (Quranic verse or saying of Muḥammad) becomes "intelligible" only when one considers the utterance not for itself, but as an "address" from the Legislator (Allah or his prophet) to the faithful Muslim, who in this context is called *mukallaf.*

Likewise, whereas the other disciplines divide the utterance into *khabar* and non-*khabar*, the *ʾuṣūliyyūn* divide the address into *ṭalab* and non-*ṭalab*, a sign of the preeminence of the former over the latter. According to the *ʾIḥkām* (I, 91) of ʾĀmidī (d. 631/1233), the *ṭalab*, according to which he "imposes" (*ʾiqtiḍāʾ*) to "do" (*fiʿl*) or "not do" (*tark*), "categorically" (*jāzim*) or "uncategorically" (*ghayr jāzim*), is realized as "obligation" (*ʾījāb*) and "prohibition" (*taḥrīm*), "recommendation" (*nadb*) and "condemnation" (*karāhiya*). The non-*ṭalab* either "gives the choice" (*takhyīr*) between doing and not doing (it is a "permission" *ʾibāḥa*) or "declares" (*ikhbār*) that such a thing is valid or not, cause, condition, or obstacle to some other, "to become a (rigorous) duty" (*ʿazīma*) or "tolerance" (*rukhṣa*) (Weiss 1992, Larcher 1992).

These six legislative acts (*sharʿ*) constitute the *ʾaḥkām sharʿiyya* (that is, standards), "prescriptive" (*taklīfiyya*) for the first five and "ascriptive" (*waḍʿiyya*) for the sixth (Kafawī, *Kulliyyāt*, s.v. *khiṭāb*). Just one example: *al-ṣalāt wājiba* ("the canonic prayer is obligatory") is the *ḥukm sharʿī* that can be derived from a Quranic utterance such as *ʾaqim/ʾaqīmū l-ṣalāta* ("complete [sg./pl.] the prayer"), which is linguistically an "order" (*ʾamr*), "rendering obligatory," juridically, this act.

The "prescriptive" *aḥkām sharʿiyya*—the most important—are organized, as we have just seen, on two levels: the *ṭalab* and the *takhyīr*. But the *ṭalab* level is in turn organized as a "logic square" of deontic modalities: *wājib* ("obligatory (to do)") and *ḥarām* ("forbidden," understood as obligatory to not do) are opposites; *mandūb* ("recommended (to do)" and *makrūh* ("reprehensible," understood as recommended to not do) are subcontraries. Thus, *wājib* and *ḥarām* imply *mandūb* and *makrūh* while *wājib* and *makrūh*, on the one hand, and *ḥarām* and *mandūb*, on the other, are in a relation of contradiction. If we add that the *takhyīr* is understood as the disjunction "do or not do" and, as a result, the modality that follows from it, that of "permission" (*'ibāḥa*), as bilaterally permission to do or not do, the *'aḥkām sharʿiyya* must not be represented on a linear axis, from good to bad, but as an inverted pyramid (Kalinowski 1976). The four quadrants represent the modalities that are a matter of *ṭalab*, the point is the *mubāḥ*, and the edges are the relations between it and them (Larcher 1992). Obviously the agreement in number (five) of the *'aḥkām sharʿiyya* "prescriptions" among the *'uṣūliyyūn*, and the species of *ṭalab* among the rhetoricians, has been noted. The connection between *ṭalab* and *takhyīr* among the former finds its parallel among the latter (*Talkhīṣ*, 169): "the form introduced for an order can be used for something else, such as permission, thus 'Sit beside al-Hasan or Ibn Sīrīn'"

وقد تستعمل لغيره كالاباحة نحو جالس الحسن او ابن سيرين

That is not the only influence of logic. From primary standards, derived pragmatically, can be derived secondary ones, logically, i.e., by reasoning (*qiyās*), another source of jurisprudence (at least for those juridical schools that recognize it). Juridical logic has often been distinguished from the logic of logicians by the type of reasoning that is at the heart of each (analogy vs. syllogism), but forgetting that in Arabic they are homonyms. In the postclassical period, the *'uṣūl al-fiqh* recuperated syllogistics but distorted it, as is shown by the following very well known example: *al-nabīdh muskir* ("wine is an intoxicating beverage"); *kull muskir ḥarām* ("every intoxicating beverage is forbidden"); *al-nabīdh ḥarām* ("wine is forbidden"). What makes the specificity of this syllogism is not its form. If we refer to the logical part, and one cannot get more classic than this, of the *Miftāḥ* of Sakkākī, we will confirm that this is a syllogism of the first figure, one of the two affirmative modes, the analogue of our *Darii* (except that, following the Arab tradition, the minor premise is stated before the major). What creates its specificity is that it links descriptive and prescriptive utterances: the character as a standard of the major premise (which is a "saying" of Muḥammad) and of the conclusion is attested by the fact that *x is ḥarām* ("x is forbidden") can be replaced by the performative *ḥarramtu x* ("I forbid x"), see 'Āmidī, *'Iḥkām*, I:12 and IV:48 (on juridical logic see *EI*² s.v. Manṭiq, Brunschvig 1970, Weiss 1992, Larcher 1992, Hallaq 1994).

Indeed, *faʿaltu* is the most usual form of juridical performatives, the *ṣiyagh al-ʿuqūd wa-l-fusūkh* ("contractual and renunciative formulas") of the Arab tradition, that is, utterances used to tie or untie juridical bonds. It suffices, to be convinced, to open one of the great treatises of *fiqh* of the postclassical period, such as the *Bādā'iʿ* of Kāsānī

(d. 587/1189). These treatises are organized in two parts: *al-ʿibādāt* ("worship"), governing the duties of the believer toward the divinity, and *al-muʿāmalāt* ("transactions"), governing relations among individuals. In this last part, for example in the book of contracts (*al-buyūʿ*) or the chapter on repudiation (*ṭalāq*) or manumission (*ʾiʿtāq*), it is confirmed that the performatives of these acts are in order of priority of occurrence: *biʿtu* ("I sell") and *ishtaraytu* ("I buy"), *ṭallaqtu-ki* ("I repudiate you"), *ʾaʿtaqtuka* or *ḥarrartuka* ("I manumit you or I free you"), etc.

8.3.4 A *balāgha* integrated into *naḥw*: Raḍī al-dīn al-Astarābādhī

All this is found in grammar itself, in particular in the *Sharḥ al-Kāfiya* of Astarābādhī (Larcher 1990, 1992, 1998b, 2000, 2007). As its title indicates, it is actually a commentary on the *Kāfiya*, a brief introduction (*muqaddima*) to syntax, by Ibn al-Hājib (d. 646/1249). Ibn al-Hājib was also a Malekite *ʾuṣūlī*, author of two works on the matter, the *Muntahā* and the *Mukhtaṣar*, the latter the object of many commentaries. Ibn al-Hājib seems moreover to be the first grammarian to make explicit use of the category of *ʾinshāʾ*. But although he was *ʾuṣūlī*, Ibn al-Hājib did not truly make *ʾinshāʾ* a self-referential and performative conception. He conceived it more readily as the subjective mode of discourse (as opposed to the *khabar*, objective mode), or again, semiotically, as the mode of signifying "expression" (*Ausdruck*) a psychological event that the statement "represents" (*Darstellung*), using an opposition due to Karl Bühler (1879–1963). In this last conception, one does not state one's intention, one "signals" (*tanbīh*) it. This is the term, coupled with *ʾinshāʾ* in his successors, that in the *Maḥṣūl* (I, 1, 317–318) of Fakhr al-dīn al-Rāzī (d. 606/1209) designates utterances that are neither statements nor requests. Conversely, Astarābadhī, although he was a logician, is not at all a logicist. He dedicates considerable space to the category of *ʾinshāʾ*. If we gather all the passages where he mentions it, we can actually extract from the *Sharḥ al-Kāfiya* a veritable "pragmatic theory." It appears as a diptych, where the category of *ʾinshāʾ* constitutes the conceptual panel and the performative *faʿaltu* the formal panel. The elementary propositions can be stated as follows:

(1) *Kalām* is everything the utterance of which constitutes an "act of the utterer" (*fiʿl al-mutakallim*).

The priority given to the semantico-pragmatic criterion over the formal criterion (*jumla*) first of all permits Astarābadhī to understand the category of *ʾinshāʾ* as the totality of utterances. He uses *ʾinshāʾ* in two ways: both in opposition to *khabar* and *ṭalab* as the specific name of the juridical performative (*Sharḥ al-Kāfiya*, I, 8); and in opposition to *khabar* alone as the generic name for nondeclarative utterances, but subdividing them into *ṭalabī* ("requesting, demanding") and *ʾīqāʿī* ("operatives" = juridical performatives) (*Sharḥ al-Kāfiya*, II, 221). This double classification confirms that the category of *ʾinshāʾ*

is indeed the product of a generalization from performatives that are both explicit and juridical. But he also continues a reflection that was begun by Ibn al-Hājib on mixed utterances, of the exclamatory type, "susceptible of being both assertive and performative" (*yaḥtamil al-'ikhbār wa-l-'inshā'*) (*'Amālī* IV, 149–150), and then was continued by Ibn Mālik under the name *khabar 'inshā'ī* (*Sharḥ al-Tashīl* III, 33). Astarābādhī gathers them under the name *'inshā' juz'u-hu l-khabar* (*Sharḥ al-Kāfiya* II, 93 and 311). There one finds the *kam* called "assertive" ("How...!"), as opposed to the interrogative *kam* ("How...?"), *rubba* ("A little of...!"), the "verbs of praise and blame" (*'af'āl al-madḥ wa-l-dhamm*), and the "verb of admiration" (*fi'l al-ta'ajjub*). Astarābādhī thus opens the door to the interpretation of the "element" (*juz'*) *khabar*, not as posited, but as presupposed. This interpretation is made explicitly, in the commentary in the margin (*Ḥāshiya*) of the *Sharḥ al-Kāfiya* (II, 311), by his own commentator ʿAlī b. Muḥammad al-Jurjānī (d. 816/1413) under the name *lāzim ʿurfī* ("empirical implication"). This last thus characterizes the element *Zaydun ḥasanun* ("Zayd is good") in relation to the performative of "admiration" *mā 'aḥsana Zaydan* ("How good Zayd is!").

Furthermore, Astarābādhī turns to ascriptive statements, of the type *Zaydun 'afḍalu min ʿAmrin* ("Zayd is superior to ʿAmr"). He says in fact that the uttering of this declaration performs an act of *tafḍīl*. His own commentator (*Ḥāshiya*, in *Sharḥ al-Kāfiya*, II, 311) defines this not as "to make superior" (*ja'lu-hu 'afḍal*), but as "to call superior" (*al-'ikhbār ʿan kawnihi 'afḍal*). In other words, he gives the verb *faḍḍala*, of which *tafḍīl* is the *maṣdar*, not a "factitive" interpretation, but, following the terminology of the French linguist Emile Benveniste (1902–1976), "delocutive" (Benveniste 1958). Astarābādhī finally arrives at purely *descriptive* statements, of the type *Zaydun qā'imun* ("Zayd is standing"), of which he says that the utterance performs an act of assertion (*'ikhbār*).

The same criterion, of *kalām* defined by the act of the utterer, moreover allows Astarābādhī to extend the very concepts of *kalām* and *'inshā'* both below and beyond the classical "utterance" defined formally as *jumla*.

Below, as in the case of the *'asmā' al-'af'āl*. This is what the Arabic grammarians call "nouns," the denominal of which (*musammā*) are verbs, in other words have the same semantic value as them, and which correspond to what we in our tradition call interjections. But whereas the other grammarians paraphrase *'uff* ("Bah!") and *'awwah* ("Alas!") with *'ataḍajjaru* ("I am disgusted") and *'atawajja'u* ("I am distressed"), which they consider to be statements, Astarābādhī paraphrases them with *taḍajjartu* and *tawajja'tu*, which are explicitly called *'inshā'ī* (*Sharḥ al-Kāfiya* II, 65).

Beyond, as in the case of the pragmatic connectives *p lākinna q* and *p 'inna q*, or *p* and *q* are utterances. Of the first (*Sharḥ al-Kāfiya*, II, 346), Astarābadhī says that "in *lākinna*, there is the sense of *istadraktu*" (*wa-fī lākinna ma'nā istadraktu*). He describes it using the example *jā'anī Zaydun lākinna ʿAmran lam yaji'* ("Zayd came to me, but [as for] ʿAmr, did not come"), as carrying out an act of preemptive rectification (*istidrāk*) by *q*, of the false conclusion *r* ("thus ʿAmr came also") that is in danger of being drawn from *p* by the hearer, who is aware of the close relationship between Zayd and ʿAmr. Of the second (*Sharḥ al-Kāfiya* II, 349), Astarābādhī says that "placed in the middle of a *kalām*, but being the beginning of a new *kalām*" (*kāna fī wasṭ kalām lākinnahu ibtidā' kalām 'ākhar*), for example *'akrim Zaydan 'innahu fāḍil* ("Honor Zayd: (for) he has merit"), he presents a "justification" (*ʿilla*) of *p* by *q*. In other words, for him, there are here three *kalām*: the two *utterances p* and *q* and the *discourse p 'inna q*. The justification, like pre-emptive rectification, is an act of the utterer, which operate not at the level of the utterance, but at the level of discourse—that is, of the articulation of the utterances among themselves. We may observe that Astarābādhī calls *'inna-hu fāḍil* a "*kalām musta'naf*" ("resumption"), very certainly in the sense of the rhetoricians (cf. 8.2.2.4), that is, constituting an answer to the implicit question suggested by the preceding utterance: "I say to you *p*. You are going to ask me why. I answer you *q*." The very etymology of French *car* ("for") (< Lat. *quare* "why?") recalls the movement.

(2) This "act of the utterer" can be represented by a performative *faʿaltu*.

Formally, this is a *jumla*. But if we adopt the formalism of the linguistic philosophers (Searle 1969), namely, F(p), where F is an illocutionary force and *p* a proposition, *faʿaltu* obviously represents F and not *p*, a *modus*, not a *dictum*. We might just as well adopt the formalism of the logicians, namely f(x), where *f* is a function and *x* the argument that this function is going to saturate. If, then, we assimilate F to f, the illocutionary force to a function, *faʿaltu* appears in the following cases: (1) it is a function that is not going to saturate any explicit argument: this is the case for interjections, which constitute a comment on an implicit topic; and (2) it is a function whose argument is (a) a term *n*: this is the case of the vocative, or (b) the term *n* of an incomplete proposition: this is the case of exclamations, or (c) a proposition *p*: this is the case of classical utterances, or (d) two or more explicit or implicit utterances: this is the case of pragmatic connectives.

(3) This representation is either purely semantic or semantico-syntactic, according to whether it does not or contrariwise does play a role in the derivation of sentences.

It plays no role in the case of interjections or pragmatic connectives. To say that *'uff* or *'awwah* has the meaning of *taḍajjartu* or *tawajjaʿtu*, called *'inshā'ī*, in effect says that these expressions really have as their meaning a behavior (*taḍajjar-*, *tawajjaʿ-*) of the one who speaks (*-tu*), but that this behavior is not asserted, but "played" by the utterance of the interjection. It does, on the other hand, play one in the case of the vocative *yā Zaydu* ("Zayd!"), which Astarābādhī derives from *nadaytu/daʿawtu Zaydan* ("I call Zayd") (*Sharḥ al-Kāfiya*, I, 132). This derivation makes the vocative, on the syntactic level, look like the object complement of an understood verb: the grammarians argue that the vocative always has the marker of the accusative, except in the case illustrated by *yā Zaydu*, that is, in the case where it refers to an expression that is both simple (*mufrad*) and definite (*maʿrifa*) and where an undeclinable ending (*-u*) appears. The best grammarians themselves recognize that this representation is not entirely satisfactory on the semantic level: it conceals the fact that the vocative transforms a term of reference into a term of address. Whence the remark that this verb is necessarily understood and cannot appear, replaced as it is by the particle *yā*. It also plays a role in the case of *Zaydun qā'imun ḥaqqan* "Zayd is standing, truly," which Astarābādhī derives from *qultu Zaydun qā'imun qawlan ḥaqqan* "I say 'Zayd is standing' with a true saying" (*Sharḥ al-Kāfiya* I, 124). This derivation makes *ḥaqqan* appear, on the syntactic level, as the "resultative complement" (*mafʿūl muṭlaq*), of the "specificatory" type (*li-bayān al-nawʿ*), of an understood verb, which justifies its accusative inflection. And it makes it appear, on the semantic level, as qualifying the speech act (the act of assertion) as veridical, and not the thing said (the fact declared) as true, in other words the equivalent of a sentence adverb, but with enunciative effect.

(4) Finally, this representation is abstract.

It is abstract in the sense that there does not necessarily exist an explicit performative corresponding to the illocutionary act or that, if it exists, does not necessarily have the form *faʿaltu*. The first case is represented by the paraphrase of the interjections, which, for Astarābādhī, looks like nothing but a pure invention by the grammarians. The second case is represented by the vocative. Whereas Ibn Mālik understands the verb in the form *'afʿalu*, while considering it a performative (*Sharḥ al-Tashīl* III, 385), Astarābādhī prefers explicitly, in this role, the form *faʿaltu*, which he justifies as follows (*Sharḥ al-Kāfiya* I, 132):

> The verb has as its object the performance: and therefore it is better to understand it in the form of the past, i.e. *daʿawtu* or *nādaytu*, the performative verbs appearing most often in this form
>
> الفعل المقصود به الانشاء فالأولى أن يقدر بلفظ الماضي أي دعوت أو ناديت لأن الاغلب في الأفعال الانشائية مجيئها بلفظ الماضي

Faʿaltu is thus chosen for its expressive power and is thus equivalent to a real *formalization*.

8.4 Conclusion

With the grammarian Raḍī al-dīn al-Astarābadhī, we attain an extreme degree of sophistication that has no equivalent anywhere except, perhaps, in posterity, essentially Turko-Irano-Indian, of the *Kāfiya*, the commentators of it keeping an eye on Astarābādhī's commentary. Its very sophistication militates against and continues to militate against an appreciation of the work. Nonetheless, if, as done here, we contextualize it, we observe that it simply leads in the same direction, but farther than the entire Arab linguistic tradition in the postclassical period: the direction of a strong and original bond, essentially pragmatic in nature, between the various disciplines, entirely or partially linguistic, that constitute this tradition.

Primary Sources

'Āmidī, *'Iḥkām* = Sayf al-dīn Abū l-Ḥasan ʿAlī b. Abī ʿAlī b. Muḥammad al-'Āmidī. *Al-'Iḥkām fī 'uṣūl al-'aḥkām*. Cairo, Mu'assasat al-Ḥalabī, 1487/1967.

ʿAskarī, *Kitāb al-ṣināʿatayn* = Abū Hilāl al-Ḥasan b. ʿAbd Allāh b. Sahl al-ʿAskarī, *Kitāb al-ṣināʿatayn fī l-kitāba wa-l-shiʿr*, 1st édition, Istanbul, 1320/1902.

Astarābādhī, *Sharḥ al-Kāfiya* = Raḍī al-dīn Muḥammad b. al-Ḥasan al-Astarābādhī, *Sharḥ Kāfiyat Ibn al-Ḥājib*. 2 vols. Istanbul: Maṭbaʿat al-sharika al-ṣiḥāfiyya al-ʿuthmāniyya. 1275/1858 and 1892. [Répr. Beirut: Dār al-kutub al-ʿilmiyya, s.d.].

Badr al-dīn Ibn Mālik, *Miṣbāḥ* = Badr al-dīn Ibn Mālik *al-Miṣbāḥ fī l-maʿānī wa-l-bayān wa-l-badīʿ*, ed. Ḥusnī ʿAbd al-Jalīl Yūsuf. Cairo: Maktabat al-'Ādāb, 1989.

Bāqillānī, *'Iʿjāz* = Abū Bakr Muḥammad b. al-Ṭayyib al-Bāqillānī *'Iʿjāz al-Qur'ān*, ed. Aḥmad Ṣaqr, coll. Dhaḥā'ir al-ʿArab 12. Cairo: Dār al-maʿārif, 1963.

Jāḥiẓ, *Bayān* = Abū ʿUthmān ʿAmr b. Baḥr al-Jāḥiẓ, *Kitāb al-bayān wa-l-tabyīn*, ed. ʿAbd al-Salām Muḥammad Hārūn, 4 parts in 2 vol., Cairo, Maktabat lajnat al-ta'līf wa-l-tarjama wa-l-nashr, 1367/1948.

Jurjānī, *'Asrār al-balāgha* = ʿAbd al-Qāhir al-Jurjānī, *'Asrār al-balāgha*, ed. Hellmut Ritter, Istanbul, Government Press, 1954.

Jurjānī, *Dalā'il al-'Iʿjāz* = ʿAbd al-Qāhir al-Jurjānī, *Dalā'il al-'Iʿjāz fī ʿilm al-maʿānī*, ed. Muḥammad Rashīd Riḍā. Beirut: Dār al-maʿrifa, 1402/1982.

Jurjānī, *Ḥāshiya* = ʿAlī b. Muḥammad, al-sayyid al-sharīf, al-Jurjānī *al-Ḥāshiya ʿalā sharḥ al-Kāfiya*, cf. Astarābādhī.

Khafājī, *Sirr al-faṣāḥa* = Abū Muḥammad ʿAbd Allāh b. Muḥammad b. Saʿīd b. Sinān al- Khafājī al-Ḥalabī *Sirr al-faṣāḥa*. Cairo: Maktabat Muḥammad ʿAlī Ṣubayḥ, 1389/1969.

Ibn al-'Athīr, *al-mathal al-sā'ir* = Abū l-Fatḥ Ḍiyā' al-dīn Naṣr Allāh b. Muḥammad b. Muḥammad b. ʿAbd al-Karīm al-maʿrūf bi-Ibn al-'Athīr al-Mawṣilī, *al-Mathal al-sā'ir fī 'adab al-kātib wa-l-shāʿir*, ed. Muḥammad Muḥyī al-dīn ʿAbd al-Ḥamīd, 1 vol. in 2 parts, Cairo, Mustafa al-Bābī al-Ḥalabī, 1358/1939.

Ibn Fāris, *Ṣāḥibī* = Abū l-Ḥusayn Aḥmad Ibn Fāris *al-Ṣāḥibī fī fiqh al-lugha wa-sunan al-ʿarab fī kalāmihā*, éd. Moustafa El-Chouémi, Coll. Bibliotheca philologica arabica, published under the direction of R. Blachère and J. Abdel-Nour, vol. 1. Beirut: A. Badran & Co. 1383/1964.

Ibn Khaldūn, *Muqaddima* = Walī l-dīn ʿAbd al-Raḥmān b. Muḥammad Ibn Khaldūn. *al-Muqaddima*, vol. I of *Kitāb al-ʿibar*. Beirut: Maktabat al-madrasa and Dār al-kitāb al-lubnānī, 1967.

Ibn al-Ḥājib, *'Amālī* = Jamāl al-dīn Abū ʿAmr ʿUthmān b. ʿUmar dit Ibn al-Ḥājib, *al-'Amālī al-naḥwiyya*. Ed. Hādī Ḥasan Ḥammūdī. 4 parts in 2 vols. Beirut: ʿĀlam al-kutub et Maktabat al-Nahḍa al-ʿarabiyya, 1405/1985.

Ibn al-Ḥājib, *Kāfiya* = *al-Muqaddima al-kāfiya fī l-naḥw*, cf. Astarābādhī.

Ibn Mālik, *Sharḥ al-Tashīl* = Jamāl al-dīn Muḥammad b. ʿAbd Allāh b. ʿAbd Allāh al-Ṭā'ī al-Jayyānī al-Andalusī Ibn Mālik *Sharḥ al-Tashīl*, ed. ʿAbd ar-Raḥmān and al-Sayyid Muḥammad al-Makhtūn. 4 parts in 2 volumes. Gizeh: Hajr li-ṭibāʿa wa-l-nashr wa-l-tawzīʿ wa-l-'iʿlān, 1410/1990.

Ibn al-Muʿtazz, *Kitāb al-badīʿ*, ed. Ignatius Kratchkovsky, E.J.W. Gibb Memorial Publications, New Series, X, 1935.

Ibn Rashīq, *ʿUmda* = Abū ʿAlī al-Ḥasan Ibn Rashīq al-Qayrawānī al-'Azdī *al-ʿUmda fī maḥāsin al-shiʿr wa-'ādābihi wa-naqdihi*, ed. Muḥammad Muḥyī al-dīn ʿAbd al-Ḥamīd. Beirut: Dār al-Ğīl, 1972.

Ibn Wahb, *al-Burhān fī wujūh al-bayān*, ed. Aḥmad Maṭlūb and Khadīja al-Ḥadīthī, Baghdad 1387/1967.

Kafawī, *Kulliyyāt* = Abū al-Baqā' 'Ayyūb b. Mūsā al-Ḥusaynī al-Kafawī. *Kulliyyāt al-'ulūm*. Ed. 'Adnān Darwīsh and Muḥammad al-Maṣrī, 5 vols. Damascus: Wizārat al-Thaqāfa wa-l-Irshād al-Qawmī, 1981.
Kāsānī, *Badā'i'* = Abū Bakr b. Mas'ūd al-Kāsānī *Kitāb Badā'i' al-ṣanā'i' fī tartīb al-sharā'i'*, 7 vols. Cairo: Maṭba'at al-Jamāliyya, 1327–1328/1909–1910.
Qarṭājannī, *Minhāj* = Abū l-Ḥasan Ḥāzim al-Qarṭājannī *Minhāj al-bulaghā' wa-sirāj al-'udabā'*, éd. Muḥammad al-Ğabīb Ibn al-Ḫawja, 3rd ed. Beirut, Dār al-Gharb al-'islāmī, 1986 [first ed. Tunis, 1966].
Qazwīnī, *'Īḍāḥ* = Jalāl al-dīn Muḥammad b. 'Abd al-Raḥmān al-Qazwīnī, *al-'Īḍāḥ fī sharḥ Talḫīṣ al-Miftāḥ*. Cf. *Shurūḥ al-Talḫīṣ*.
Qazwīnī, *Talkhīṣ* = Jalāl al-dīn Muḥammad b. 'Abd al-Raḥmān al-Qazwīnī *Talkhīṣ al-miftāḥ fī 'ulūm al-balāgha*. Ed. 'Abd al-Raḥmān al-Barqūqī. Cairo, al-Maktaba al-tijāriyya al-kubrā, n.d.
Qudāma ibn Ja'far, Naqd al-shi'r,ed. by S.A. Bonebakker, Leiden: Brill, 1956.
Rāzī, *Maḥṣūl* = Fakhr al-dīn al-Rāzī *al-Maḥṣūl fī 'ulūm 'uṣūl al-fiqh*. Ed. Ṭaha Jābir Fayyād al-'Ulwānī. Imām Muḥammad b. Sa'ūd University, 1399/1979.
Sakkākī, *Miftāḥ* = Abū Ya'qūb Yūsuf b. Abī Bakr Muḥammad b. 'Alī al-Sakkākī, *Miftāḥ al-'ulūm*. Cairo: Matba'at al-taqaddum al-'ilmiyya, 1348/1929. [répr. Beirut, Dār al-kutub al-'ilmiyya, n.d.].
Shurūḥ al-Talkhīṣ, 4 vols. Cairo, Maṭba'at 'Īsā al-Bābī al-Ḥalabī. 1937.
Zamakhsharī, *Kashshāf* = Abū l-Qāsim Jār Allāh Maḥmūd b. 'Umar al- Zamakhsharī *al-Kashshāf 'an ḥaqā'iq al-tanzīl wa-'uyūn al-'aqāwīl fī wujūh al-ta'wīl*, Cairo, Muṣṭafā al-Bābī al-Ḥalabī, n.d.

Secondary Sources

Aouad, Maroun. 1989. La *Rhétorique*. Tradition syriaque et arabe. In *Dictionnaire des philosophes antiques*, vol. 1, ed. Richard Goulet, 455–472. Paris: Editions du CNRS.
Arnaldez, A. Manṭiq. In *Encyclopedia of Islam/Encyclopédie de l'Islam, new edition,* Vol. 6, 427–38. Leiden: Brill.
Audebert Claude-France. 1982. *Al-Khaṭṭābī et l'inimitabilité du Coran. Traduction et introduction au* Bayān 'I'jāz al-Qur'ān. Damascus: Institut Français d'Etudes Arabes.
Austin, John. 1962. *How to do things with words*. London: Oxford University Press.
Avril, Marie-Hélène. 1994. Généalogie de la *khuṭba* dans le *Kitāb al-bayān wa-l-tabyīn* de Jāḥiẓ. *Bulletin d'Etudes Orientales* 46: 197–216.
Bally, Charles. 1965. *Linguistique générale et linguistique française*, 4th rev. ed. Berne: Francke.
Benveniste, Emile. 1958 [1966]. Les verbes délocutifs. In *Studia Philologica et litteraria in honorem L. Spitzer*, ed. Anna G. Hatcher and K. L. Selig, 57–63. Berne: Francke [repr. in *Problèmes de linguistique générale*, I, 277–285. Paris: Gallimard. 1966].
Bernard, M. Mu'āmalāt. In *Encyclopedia of Islam/Encyclopédie de l'Islam, new edition,* 1960–2005, Vol. 7, 25–59. Leiden: Brill.
Berrendonner, Alain. 1981. *Eléments de pragmatique linguistique*. Paris: Minuit.
Black, Deborah L. 1990. *Logic and Aristotle's* Rhetoric *and* Poetics *in Medieval Arabic philosophy*. Leiden: Brill.
Bonebakker, S. Ma'ānī wa l-bayān. In *Encyclopedia of Islam/Encyclopédie de l'Islam, new edition,* Vol. 5, 904–08. Leiden: Brill.
Brunschvig, Robert. 1970. Logic and law in Classical Islam. In *Logic in Classical Islamic culture*, ed. G.E. von Grunebaum, 9–20. Wiesbaden: Harrassowitz.
Buburuzan [Firănescu], Rodica. 1995. Significations des énoncés et actes de langage chez Ibn Fāris. In *Proceedings of the colloquium on Arabic linguistics, Bucharest August 29–September 2, 1994*, vol. 1, 103–114. Bucarest: University of Bucharest, Center for Arab Studies.

Firănescu, Daniela Rodica. 2011. Readings notes on Sakkākī's concept of 'semantic engendering.' In *A Festchrift for Nadia Anghelescu*, ed. Andrei A. Avram, Anca Focşeneanu, and George Grigore, 215–233. Bucarest: Editura Universităţii din Bucureşti.

Frank, Richard. 1981. Meanings are spoken of in many ways: The earlier Arab grammarians. *Le Muséon* 94: 259–319.

Ghersetti, Antonella. 1998. Quelques notes sur la définition canonique de *balāgha*. In *Philosophy and arts in the Islamic World, Proceedings of the eighteenth congress of the Union Européenne des Arabisants et Islamisants held at the Katholieke Universiteit Leuven (Septembre 3–Septembrer 9, 1996)*, ed. U. Vermeulen et D. De Smet, 57–72. Leuven: Peeters.

——. 2002. La définition du *khabar* (énoncé assertif) dans la pensée rhétorique de 'Abd al-Qāhir al-Jurjānī. In *Studies in Arabic and Islam, Proceedings of the 19th Congress, Union Européenne des Arabisants et Islamisants, Halle 1998*, ed. S. Leder with H. Kilpatrick, B. Martel-Thoumian, and H. Schönig, 367–77. Louvain: Peeters.

Guillaume, Jean-Patrick. 1986. Sibawayhi et l'énonciation: une proposition de lecture. *Histoire Epistémologie Langage* 8: 53–62.

Hallaq, Wael. 1994. *Law and legal theory in Classical and Medieval Islam*. Aldershot: Variorum.

Halldén, Philip. 2005. What is Arab Islamic rhetoric? Rethinking the history of Muslim oratory art and homiletics. *International Journal of Middle East Studies* 37: 19–38.

——. 2006. Rhetoric. In *Medieval Islamic Civilization*, ed. Josef Meri, 679–681. New York: Routledge.

Heinrichs, Wolfhart. 1969. *Arabische Dichtung und griechische Poetik. Ḥāzim al-Qarṭājannī's Grundlegung der Poetik mit Hilfe aristotelischer Begriffe*, Beiruter Texte und Sudien, Band 8. Beirut: Orient Institut & Wiesbaden: Steiner.

——. 1984. On the genesis of the *ḥaqīqa-majāz* dichotomy. *Studia Islamica* 59: 111–140.

——. 1987. Poetik, Rhetorik, Literaturkritik, Metrik und Reimlehre. In *Grundriss der arabischen Philologie*, Band II Literaturwissenschaft, ed. H. Gätje, 177–207. Wiesbaden: Reichert.

——. 1998. Rhetoric and poetics. In *Encyclopedia of Arabic literature*, ed. Julia Meisami and Paul Starkey, 651–656. London: Routledge.

Jakobson, Roman. 1956. Two aspects of language and two type of aphasic disturbances. In Roman Jakobson and Morris Halle, *Fundamentals of language*, Part II, 55–82. The Hague: Mouton & Co.

Jenssen, H. 1998. *The subtleties and secrets of the Arabic language: Preliminary investigations into Al-Qazwīnī's* Talkhīṣ al-Miftāḥ. London: Hurst.

Kalinowski, George. 1976. Un aperçu élémentaire des modalités déontiques. *Langages* 43: 10–18.

Khalafallah, M. Badī'; In *Encyclopedia of Islam/Encyclopédie de l'Islam, new edition*, Vol. 1, 881–82. Leiden: Brill.

Larcher, Pierre. 1980. *Information et performance en science arabo-islamique du langage*. PhD diss., Université de Paris III.

——. 1990. Eléments pragmatiques dans la théorie grammaticale arabe post-classique. In *Studies in the history of Arabic grammar*, vol. 2, ed. Kees Versteegh and Mike Carter, 193–214. Amsterdam: Benjamins.

——. 1991. Quand, en arabe, on parlait de l'arabe... (II) Essai sur la catégorie de *'inshā'* (vs *khabar*). *Arabica* 38: 246–273.

——. 1992. Quand, en arabe, on parlait de l'arabe... (III) Grammaire, logique, rhétorique dans l'islam postclassique. *Arabica* 39: 358–384.

——. 1993. Les arabisants et la catégorie de *ʾinshāʾ*. Histoire d'une "occultation." *Historiographia Linguistica* 20: 259–282.

——. 1998a. Eléments de rhétorique aristotélicienne dans la tradition arabe hors la *falsafa*. In *La Rhétorique d'Aristote: traditions et commentaires de l'Antiquité au XVIIème siècle* (La Baume lès Aix, 10–12 Juillet 1995), ed. Gilbert Dahan et Irène Rosier-Catach, 241–256. *Traditions de l'Antiquité classique*. Paris: Vrin.

——. 1998b. Une pragmatique avant la pragmatique: "médiévale," "arabe" et "islamique." *Histoire Epistémologie Langage* 20: 101–116.

——. 2000. Les relations entre la linguistique et les autres sciences dans la société arabo-islamique. In *History of the language sciences*, vol. 1, ed. E. F. K. Koerner, Sylvain Auroux, Hans-Josef Niederehe, and Kees Versteegh, 312–318. Berlin: Walter de Gruyter & Co. [English translation: Relationships between linguistics and the other sciences in Arabo-islamic society. In *The Early Islamic Grammatical Tradition*, ed. Ramzi Baalbaki, 337–348. The Formation of the Classical Islamic World 36. Aldershot: Ashgate Publishing Limited. 2007].

——. 2007. 'Inshā'. *Encyclopedia of Arabic Language and Linguistics*, vol. 2, Eg–Lan, 358–361. Brill: Leiden.

——. 2009. Mais qu'est-ce donc que la *balāgha*?. In *Literary and philosophical rhetoric in the Greek, Roman, Syriac and Arabic worlds*, ed. Frédérique Woerther, 197–213. Europaea Memoria. Hildesheim: Olms.

Martin, Richard. 2002. Inimitability. In *The Encyclopaedia of the Qur'ān*, Vol. 2. ed. J.D. McAuliffe, 526–36. Leiden, Brill.

Mehren, A. 1853 [1970]. *Die Rhetorik der Araber*. Kopenhagen: Otto Schwarz & Wien: Kaiserl. Königl. Hof- und Staatsdrückerei. (Repr. Hidelsheim: Georg Olms Verlag.)

Montgomery, James. 2006. Al-Jāḥiẓ's *Kitāb al-Bayān wa-l-Tabyīn*. In *Writing and representation in Medieval Islam*, ed. Julia Bray, 91–152. Muslim Horizons. London: Routledge.

Moutaouakil, Ahmed. 1982. *Réflexions sur la théorie de la signification dans la pensée linguistique arabe*. Rabat: Publications de la Faculté des Lettres et des Sciences Humaines.

——. 1990. La notion d''actes de langage' dans la pensée linguistique arabe ancienne. In *Studies in the history of Arabic Grammar*, vol. 2, ed. Kees Versteegh and Mike Carter, 229–238. Amsterdam: Benjamins.

Owens, Jonathan. 1988. *The foundations of grammar: An introduction to Medieval Arabic grammatical theory*. Amsterdam: Benjamins.

Schaade, A. Balāgha. In *Encyclopedia of Islam/Encyclopédie de l'Islam, new edition*, Vol. 1, 1012–13. Leiden: Brill.

Schoeler, Gregor. 1983. Der poetische Syllogismus. Ein Beitrag zum Verständnis der 'logischen' Poetik der Araber. *Zeitschrift der deutschen morgenländischen Gesellschaft* 133: 44–92.

Searle, John. 1969. *Speech acts: An essay in the philosophy of language*. Cambridge, UK: Cambridge University Press.

——. 1975. Indirect speech acts. In *Syntax and semantics*. Vol. 3, *Speech acts*, ed. P. Cole and J. L. Morgan, 59–82. New York: Academic Press.

Simon, Udo. 1993. *Mittelalterliche arabische Sprachbetrachtung zwischen Grammatik und Rhetorik:* ʿilm al-maʿānī *bei as-Sakkākī*. Heidelberg: Heidelberger Orientverlag.

Smyth, William. 1992. Some quick rules *ut pictura poesis*: The rules for simile in *Miftāḥ al-ʿulūm*. *Oriens* 33: 215–229.

——. 1993. The making of a textbook. *Studia Islamica* 76: 99–115.

——. 1995. The Canonical formulation of *ʿIlm al-balāghah* and al-Sakkākī's *Miftāḥ al-ʿulūm. Der Islam* 72: 7–24.

Soudan, Françoise. 1992. L'éloquence arabe aux premiers temps de l'islam d'après le *Kitāb al-bayān wa-l-tabyīn* d'al-Ǧāḥiẓ, *Annales islamologiques* 26: 19–46.

Versteegh, Kees. 2004. Meanings of speech: The category of sentential mood in Arabic grammar. In *Le Voyage et la langue, Mélanges en l'honneur d'Anouar Louca et André Roman*, ed. Joseph Dichy and Hassan Hamzé, 269–287. Damascus: Institut Français du Proche-Orient.

Von Grunebaum, G. Bayān. In *Encyclopedia of Islam/Encyclopédie de l'Islam, new edition,* Vol. 1, 1147–1150. Leiden: Brill.

——. 'Iʿjāz. In *Encyclopedia of Islam/Encyclopédie de l'Islam, new edition,* Vol. 3, 1044–1046. Leiden: Brill.

——. Faṣāḥa . In *Encyclopedia of Islam/Encyclopédie de l'Islam, new edition* Vol. 2, 843–846. Leiden: Brill.

Weiss, Bernard. 1976. A Theory of the parts of speech in Arabic (Noun, verb and particle): A study in *ʿilm al-waḍʿ*. *Arabica* 23: 23–36.

——. 1992. *The search for Gods law. Islamic jurisprudence in the writings of Sayf al-Dīn al-Āmidī.* Salt Lake City: University of Utah Press.

Würsch, Renata. 1991. *Avicennas Bearbeitungen der aristotelischen Rhetorik. Ein Beitrag zum Fortleben antikes Bildungsgutes in der islamischen Welt.* Berlin: Klaus Schwartz Verlag.

Zysow, Aron. 2008. *Tamannī.* If wishes were...: Notes on wishing in Islamic texts. In *Classical Arabic humanities in their own terms: Festschrift for Wolfhart Heinrichs on his 65th birthday presented by his students and colleagues*, ed. Beatrice Gruendler, asst. Michael Cooperson, 522–567. Leiden: Brill. (Trans. from French Peter T. Daniels.)

CHAPTER 9

ISSUES IN ARABIC COMPUTATIONAL LINGUISTICS

EVERHARD DITTERS

9.1 Introduction

At a meeting in Doha (Qatar 2011), experts discussed the challenges for Natural Language Processing (NLP)[1] applied to (and, if possible, in) Arabic, concerning technologies, resources, and applications in cultural, social, educational, medical, and touristic areas, in the region concerned, for the near future. Interestingly enough, there was a consensus (by majority of votes)[2] about more focus on large-scale caption of written Arabic (OCR) in view of preservation and the accessibility of the Arabic and Islamic cultural heritage; the spoken varieties of Arabic in view of the development of all kinds of conversion and answering systems (AS) to and from a standard, speech-to-speech[3] (STS) as well as to speech-to-text (STT) and text-to-speech (TTS)[4] conversion; and,

[1] The Appendix at the end of the chapter lists some abbreviations and technical terms (frequently) used not only in this field in general but also in the current of this contribution, together with some paraphrasing of terms used in this contribution.

[2] I would like to have had some more attention for equally socially relevant matters like pure linguistics.

[3] Cf. Bouillon et al. (2007).

[4] On the program of the annual ALS symposium on Arabic linguistics (2011), more than half of the presentations (17 of 31) dealt with Arabic colloquials, the diglossia situation, and the application of general linguistic theories for the description of Arabic colloquials. Beginning in 1990, this trend can be found in all the issues of *Perspectives on Arabic Linguistics*. For a while, the Moroccan Linguistic Society had a similar development.

finally, on multisimultaneous signal processing (subtitling, visualization, and instant translation),[5] if possible, with event (EE) or factoid (FE) extraction for information retrieval (IR), document routing (DR), archiving purposes, mass storage, *Aboutness* suggestions, and different forms of retracing facilities.

NLP overlaps to a large degree with computational linguistics (CL), especially when both are applied to standard Arabic or spoken varieties. The former (NLP) usually centers on the interaction between man and machine, deals with "processing" and "automated processes," and is as exact as possible in nature. It therefore remains measurable and verifiable (NLP is eager for applications). The latter (CL) concentrates exclusively on linguistic theory and language modeling, while using any computational means it can exploit, for an adequate, coherent, and consistent linguistic description or language model.

CL is usually characterized as a subsection of artificial intelligence (AI). However, I would like to underline its *communicative* (action and reaction) perspective against a purely *cognitive* environment of AI. Moreover, the communicative aspect of CL points to a *reference to reality*. Even when formalized and in its most abstract and logically implemented form, semantics still remains an open domain. Moreover, I would like to underline two complementary aspects of CL concerning Arabic, one the application of computer sciences to Arabic; and the otherArabic linguistics making as much use as possible of computational as well as linguistic means and techniques. The former is more striking, and the latter is more basic.

For information on relevant trends in Arabic NLP and CL, we do not need to start from scratch. General trends in NLP are adequately described in Manning and Schütze (2003) and Jurafsky and Martin (2009);[6] for Arabic NLP, see Habash (2010) and the references therein. For CL in general, one should certainly consult Bunt et al. (2004, 2010).[7] Soudi et al. (2007) and Farghaly (2010) offer valuable contributions in the field of Arabic CL but also deal with Arabic NLP. Levelt (1974) is a must for formal grammars (and psycholinguistics). On (more linguistically oriented) main and subentries, there is valuable information in Versteegh (2006–2009).[8] Needless to say, the Internet is always a good, if not the best, starting point for a literature search.

The main topic of interest here is the current state of affairs in the field of Arabic CL. Relevant trends in phonetics and phonology, morphology, syntax, lexicology, semantics, and stylistics and pragmatics will be briefly examined. Then changes or special accents within the field of interest, namely, formal Arabic syntax, will be noted. After some evaluative remarks about the approach of this chapter, it continues with a linguistic description of MSA for analysis purposes as well as an introduction to a formal description. Some early results will be highlighted. Further perspectives are then

[5] If possible, together with a deaf window as well as a form of simultaneous (Arabic) Braille output.

[6] See also Ali (2003).

[7] The end of this chapter offers suggestions for further reading.

[8] For the main topics of this chapter, see Chenfour (2006) and Ditters (2006). Subtopics and references will be referred to in the body of the text.

offered for ongoing research and possible spinoffs such as a formalized description of Arabic syntax in formalized dependency rules as well as a subset thereof for IR purposes. Appendix 1 contains a list of acronyms frequently encountered in NLP and CL. Appendix 2, found only in the online version, gives a glossary of frequently-used terms in NLP and CL.

9.2 ARABIC CL

Defined as a *statistical or rule-based modeling of natural language from a computational point of view*,[9] CL should always contain a linguistic dimension in the form of a specific theory combined with a descriptive model together with a formal implementation in which that linguistic theory about a natural language or its adequate, coherent, and consistent description is entered in a processing environment for analysis or synthesis purposes. Jurafsky and Martin (2009) adequately describe a modern "toolkit" for CL, but we limit ourselves here mainly to rule-based modeling by means of a relational programming algorithm using a nondeterministic formalism of two interwoven context-free grammars, resulting in a bottom-up unification-based parser for Arabic.[10] Levelt (1974) provides a descriptively and didactically good introduction in the field of *Formal Grammars and Psycholinguistics*.

Arabic CL thus combines a linguistic and a computational part. The linguistic part exploits the most recent developments in the field of adequate, coherent, and consistent language description. The formal part tests the (natural or programming) language description concerned with computational viability. Nowadays, linguistic description testing usually takes place in the framework of corpus linguistics (CoL) using large collections of authentic language data, as such serving as a reliable test bed and learning model for refining the linguistic description. Nowadays, the formal part of such a linguistic implementation can be tested using personal computers.

Authentic text data contain both stylistic and pragmatic elements. Then we are dealing with a form of semantics, hidden in structured combinations (syntax) of lexical elements (lexicon). Relations and dependencies between elements may be underlined with morphemes (morphology) that should be accounted for in a description of the language concerned. Such a description comprises the inventory of the smallest unit of linguistic description, which is called the *phoneme* (phonology), or its orthographic, the *grapheme* (orthography). In this way, authentic (Arabic) data represent single multiple-layer *syntax*, distinguished in modules only for practical reasons.

[9] The source here is Wikipedia; see also Ditters (2006).

[10] For a paraphrase of descriptive terms, see Appendix 9.2.

9.2.1 Computational Phonetics and Phonology

Here the term *phonetics* indicates the study of the physical properties of the smallest units of linguistic description in the Arabic language (i.e., phonemes), whether for analysis (recognition) or synthesis (generation) purposes.[11] At an early stage, this study was extended with the study of its graphic counterpart, the grapheme. Later, research started on the development of all kinds of remedial support such as Arabic Braille (AB), text-to-speech, and speech-to-text conversion, or combinations thereof (for blind, deaf, and dumb).

Phonology, on the other hand, is more concerned with the generalized, grammatical characterization of the Arabic phoneme and grapheme inventory of the language system. Computational phonology is the use of models in phonological theory. For the description of the typical nonconcatenative root and pattern system of Semitic languages in general and Arabic phonology and morphology in particular, McCarthy (1981) proposes a representation of different layers, further developed by Kay (1987), Beesley (1996), Kiraz (1994, 1997), Kiraz and Anton (2000, 2001), and Ratcliffe (1998) [Ratcliffe, "Morphology"]. More recent developments go in the direction of optimality theory (OT; Prince and Smolenski 2004) and syllabification (Kiraz and Möbius 1998). There already are some specialized studies in this field on Arabic phonology [Hellmuth, "Phonology"].

Müller (2002) adds an NLP flavor with his probabilistic context-free grammars for phonology.[12] Computational phonology is the basis of many NLP applications, such as the previously mentioned AS systems and STT, TTS, and STS conversion and others such as Arabic speech recognition (SR), OCR, and text-to-text conversion (TTT) or machine translation (MT).[13]

In computational phonetics and phonology, we are confronted with terms such as tiers, distinct layers of representation (two-four, three), finite-state automata (FSA or FSM), transducers, programming languages, tables, tagging, ± deterministic, and a few other technical terms. Sometimes, a decisive discussion about progression in the field of research concerned is worded using general (Arabic) linguist terms, but for certain entries in Appendix 9.2 it was necessary to employ less frequently used linguistic terms.

9.2.2 Arabic Computational Morphology

As Richard Sproat correctly mentioned (Soudi et al. 2007: viii), Kaplan and Kay (1981) and Kay (1987), in line with Koskenniemi (1983), paved the way for Kenneth Beesley's

[11] There is a difference in interest between the computational subword (phonetics) and the computational word (phonology) level and beyond. This chapter is concerned with remedial and commercial applications.

[12] See also Coleman and Pierrehumbert (1997) on stochastic phonological grammars and acceptability.

[13] Cf. Farghali (2010: chapters 3 and 4) and Habash (2010: chapter 8 and Appendix 9.2).

(1989) research on Arabic computational morphology, which led to the work of many others as well as to the development of applications in the field of Arabic morphology.

One of the pioneers in computational Arabic morphology, Tim Buckwalter, developed *BAMA*, an Arabic morphological analyzer (Buckwalter 2010). Initially, his research was oriented toward automated corpus-based Arabic lexicology. Later, three lexicons, compatibility scripts, and an algorithm in the feature-rich *dynamically typed*[14] programming language called Perl were combined in a software package for the morphological analysis of Arabic words (Buckwalter 2002, 2004), used, inter alia, for morphological and part-of-speech (POS, part of speech) tagging as well as for syllabification of authentic data in existing Arabic Treebanks[15] (Maamouri and Bies 2010; Smrž and Hajič 2010) for morphological or syntactic annotation.

It is not surprising that research on Arabic computational morphology is easily adopted, adapted, and incorporated into general approaches to computational phonetics, phonology, and morphophonemics. Al-Sughaiyer and Al-Kharashi (2004) classify a number of Arabic morphological analyzers (analyzers) and synthesizers (generators) according to the approach employed regarding table lookup, linguistic (two-level, FSA or FSM, traditional applications), combinatorial, and pattern-based approaches. As Köprü and Miller (2009) point out, "Very few of the available systems are evaluated using systematic and scientific procedures." This is perhaps a bit too harsh a criticism. However, it is always worthwhile to scrutinize and evaluate the advantages and disadvantages as well as the adequacy, coherency, and consistency of a chosen approach.

Evaluating 20-odd Arabic morphological analyzers and synthesizers, Al-Sughaiyer and Al-Kharashi (2004: 198, Table 4) mention their algorithm name and type: some "brand" names and even one "Sebawai";[16] many "linguistics"; and one "rule based." Smrž (2007: 5–6) qualifies Beesley (2001), Ramsay and Mansur (2001), and Buckwalter (2002) as "lexical" in nature. Habash (2004) calls his own work "lexical-realizational" in nature. Finally, Cavalli-Forza et al. (2000), Habash et al. (2005), Dada and Ranta (2006), and Forsberg and Ranta (2004) are rather "inferential-realizational."

For his ElixirFM, Smrž (2007: 2) emphasizes its implementation within the Prague framework of function generative dependency (FGD) in functional programming (*Haskell*), contrasting with the dynamic programming (*Perl*) of Buckwalter (2002) and resulting in "a yet more refined linguistic model."

Partly based on the operational tagging system of Buckwalter's BAMA morphological analyzer for Arabic, Otakar Smrž developed "description of [Arabic] surface syntax in the dependency framework" (Smrž and Hajič 2010). This brings us to the doorstep

[14] Here in contrast with *statically typed*. Computer science presently has four main branches of programming languages: imperative oriented; functional oriented; logical oriented; and object oriented. For our purposes this information will be enough.

[15] Wikipedia paraphrases *treebank* as a text corpus in which each sentence has been parsed, that is, annotated with syntactic structure, which is commonly represented as a tree.

[16] I appreciate Darwish's (2002) reference to Sībawayhi in his account of "a one-day construction of a shallow Arabic morphological analyzer."

between Arabic phonology–morphology and Arabic computational syntax at least as far as the representation of the analysis results in the form of dependency trees is concerned. These results are obtained on the basis of a pretagged corpus. The Prague linguists opted for a functional dependency grammar approach. Nonetheless, also for the computational description of Arabic morphology and syntax, a programming language, *Haskell*,[17] is being used.[18] There is an important difference between the use of a programming language and a formalism for implementable and operational descriptions of a natural language.[19]

9.2.3 Arabic Computational Syntax

Syntax is the description of the overall organization of a natural language in which different complementary building blocks such as phonology, morphology, lexicology, semantics, stylistics and pragmatics come together to convey a particular message between an *A* and a *B*. To describe the general structure of this organization for natural languages in general or for a specific language such as Arabic is the objective of the linguistic part of the description. To find an implementable formal model for such a description is the objective of the computational part of that description.

9.2.3.1 *Linguistic Part*

For a historical overview of language description, I refer to HSK 18.3 (2006). Here we limit ourselves to the century of the dominance of immediate constituency (IC) and the rise of many other linguistic theories and descriptive models such as dependency grammar, of importance or used for the linguistic description of Standard and spoken Arabic varieties.

It is evident that the splitting up of a natural language system into its largest and smallest units of linguistic description, as well as the description of mutual relationships and

[17] Wikipedia paraphrases: *Haskell* is a standardized, general-purpose purely functional programming language, with nonstrict semantics and strong static typing.

[18] Quoting Smrž and Hajič (2010, 140): "these systems misinterpret some morphs for bearing a category, and underspecify lexical morphemes in general as to their intrinsic morphological functions." I come back on this point while discussing the automated linguistic description of Arabic by means of programming languages or computational formalisms.

[19] A programming language describes a dynamic and deterministic process. It is dynamic because there is a beginning and a series of steps to be taken leading inevitably to an end. It is deterministic because the computer is explicitly being told from the very beginning, how to start, where to find what it needs for the execution of the program, what to do with it, what the next step will be, and when its activity will come to an end. A formalism also is an artificial, formal language but is designed as a medium for the definition or the description of static structures. Such an approach is declarative because in the formal grammar only structures are defined and described. There is a beginning, a series of rules and an end, but there is no logical link between beginning and end. Not the computer but it is the machine-readable data that determine whether a match should occur or not; that is, the parser is dependent on the input string for deciding whether or not its structure can be recognized as defined or described in the formal grammar.

dependencies between these units, form an excellent starting point for any research on the fundamentals of human communication in general, and of the organisation of a specific natural language system in particular (Habash 2010: chapter 6). Computational linguistics (cf. Winograd 1983) started with the annotation (POS tagging) of formal (e.g., parts of speech; word and phrasal categories, sentences, sections, chapters, volumes, and the marking of nontextual insertions);[20] functional elements (e.g., cases, clitics, determiners, heads and modifiers, slots and fillers) in authentic text data (CoL); and continued later in the presentation of derivation trees or labeled bracketing, extracted from this (earlier inserted) information.

9.2.3.2 *Formal part*

For a historical overview of computational language description in general, I refer to Winograd (1983). Here we speak about the current state of syntactic parsing of Arabic text data wherein different steps can be distinguished. Usually, they are labeled with terms such as tokenization, diacritization, POS tagging, morphological disambiguation (Marton et al. 2010), base phrase chunking, semantic role labeling, lemmatization, stemming, and the like (cf. Appendix 9.2; cf. also Mesfar 2010). Most of these processes have been automated by now, but all the existing collections of syntactically analyzed Arabic text data (Habash 2010: section 6.2) such as the Penn Arabic Treebank (Maamouri et al. 2004), the Prague Arabic Dependency Treebank (Hajič et al. 2001), and the Columbia Arabic Treebank (Habash and Roth 2009) have been manually checked. This "forest of treebanks" (Habash 2010: 111) can now be used as learning models for the development of new statistical parsers, evaluating parsers and general Arabic parsers.

9.2.4 Arabic Computational Lexicology

Computational lexicology is the branch of linguistics, which is concerned with the use of computers in the study of machine-readable dictionaries (lexicon). Sometimes this term is synonymous with computational lexicography, though the latter is more specifically for the use of computers in the construction of dictionaries (Al-Shalabi and Kanaan 2004).[21]

Piek Vossen, a well-known computational lexicologist, founder and president of the Global Wordnet Association, worked on the first WordNet project (Fellbaum 1998) and supervised parallel projects such as EuroWordNet (Vossen 1998) and Arabic WordNet (Black et al. 2006; Elkateb et al. 2006). He is thinking in terms of (multi)lingual lexical

[20] For Arabic, Sībawayhi (d. 798, *kitāb*) described nouns (N), verbs (V) and non-noun non-verb particles (-N-V) as the basic word categories. He also hinted at greater constituents with an element of one of those categories as head, but the labeling into NPs, VPs, and PaPs here is mine.

[21] See, for example, also the objectives of The Arabic Language Computing Research Group (ALCRG), King Saud University (http://ccis.ksu.edu.sa/ar/en/cs/research/ALCRG).

databases with lexical semantic networks. We come close to a distinction in form, function, meaning, and contextual realization of a lexical entry. Besides this distinction we always have the linguistic and the formal part.

Linguistic part

Relevant here are studies such as those of Dévényi et al. (1993) on Arabic lexicology and lexicography as well as other research with valuable bibliographical references (Bohas 1997; Bohas and Dat 2008; Hassanein 2008; Hoogland 2008; Seidensticker 2008). Moreover, one should include the studies about affixes, features (Dichy 2005; Ditters 2007), or parameters hinting at theta, thematic, or semantic roles.

Formal part

On the formal side I would like to mention the tag sets (Habash 2010: 79–85; Maamouri et al. 2009; Diab et al. 2004; Diab 2007; Kulick et al. 2006; Habash and Roth 2009; Khoja et al. 2001; Hajič et al. 2005) used for the annotation of the corpora of Arabic text data as well as the by then enriched corpora (treebanks) from which all kinds of relevant information can be extracted. Here should also be included studies on Arabic semantic labeling (Diab et al. 2007) and Arabic semantic roles (Diab et al. 2008).

9.2.5 Arabic Computational Semantics, Stylistics, and Pragmatics

Computational syntax, at the academic level, is still not common practice. Computational semantics, stylistics, and pragmatics are even at a more rudimentary stage,[22] not only as far as the Arabic language is concerned but also even for more intensively studied natural languages. It is worthwhile here to refer to the HSK volumes on dependency and valency (HSK 25, 2003–2006), and in particular to contributions of interest for our discussion[23] (Owens 2003; Msellek 2006; Bielický and Smrž 2008, 2009).

According to Wikipedia:[24]

> Computational semantics is the study of how to automate the process of constructing and reasoning with meaning representations of natural language expressions. It consequently plays an important role in natural language processing and computational linguistics. Some traditional topics of interest are: semantic analysis, semantic

[22] Carter (2007: 27) discusses an earlier form of pragmatics in Larcher's approach of *ʾinšāʾ* (ibid., 28). See also Larcher (1990).

[23] Cf. Bangalore et al. (2003), Bröker (2003), Fillmore (2003), Hajičová and Sgall (2003), Hellwig (2003), Hudson (2003), Kahane (2003), Maxwell (2003), Mel'čuk (2003), Oliva (2003), Starosta (2003), Busse (2006), Hellwig (2006), Horacek (2006), and Schubert (2006).

[24] See also Jurafsky and Martin (2009, section 3) and Eijck and Unger (2010).

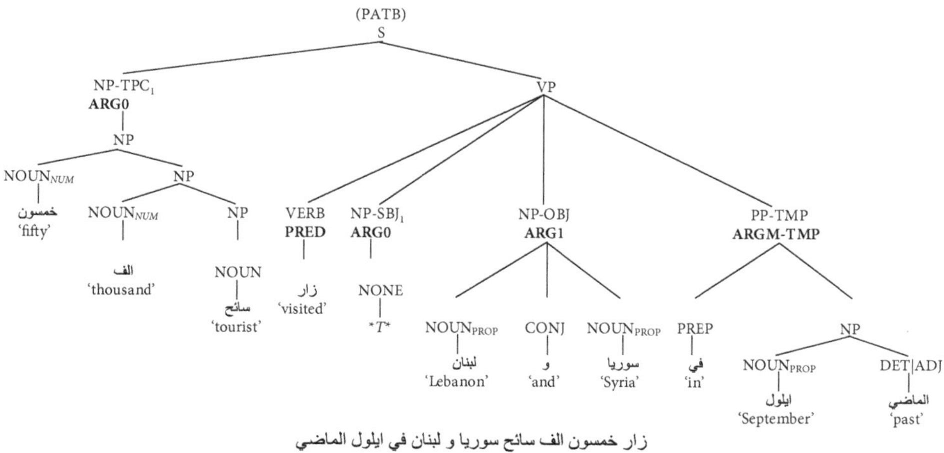

FIGURE 9.1 An example from the Arabic Propbank (Habash 2010, 115).

underspecification, anaphora resolution, presupposition projection, and quantifier scope resolution. Methods employed usually draw from formal semantics or statistical semantics.

In a note on Arabic semantics, Habash (2010: chapter 7) mentions the Arabic Proposition Bank (Propbank) and Arabic WordNet. A propbank (Palmer et al. 2005) is, in contrast with a treebank, a semantically annotated corpus. On the basis of predicate–argument information of the complement structure of a verb so-called frameset definitions (Baker et al. 1998) are associated with each entry of the verbal lexicon (Palmer et al. 2008). The description of the nature, number, and role of the arguments can be as detailed and specific as a linguistic description of the semantics of a language allows. It may be clear that here lies the greatest challenge in the development of adequate, coherent, and consistent parsers for any natural language text data, MSA, and spoken varieties of Arabic included.

Figure 9.1 presents information about the linguistic unity of description (S), type of sentence (NP-TPC$_1$), with a verb phrase (VP) as comment. The topic (ARG0) is realised by a noun phrase (NP). The comment, which may be termed "predicate" is realized by a finite transitive verb (PRED) with an implicit subject (ARG0), a direct object noun phrase (ARG1), and a prepositional time adverbial (ARGM-TMP). There is a form of subcategorization at the phrasal level (NP-TPC$_1$, NP, NP-SBJ$_1$, NP-OBJ). Nouns are by subscripts divided into common nouns and subcategories. There is some form of description in terms of functions and categories, but it is not maintained in a consistent and coherent way until the final lexical entries have been reached.

Arabic WordNet has been mentioned earlier in relation to computational lexicology (§1.4). Here I want to explicitly underline the importance of electronically available collections of text data and nowadays also parallel corpora, for linguistic research (Col = corpus linguistics). In the following section I defend a purely linguistic approach of Arabic language description exploiting as much computational means as possible on the basis of authentic data and within a long-standing linguistic Arabic grammatical tradition.

Other studies in the fields of semantics,[25] dialogue (Hafez 1991), discourse,[26] stylistics (Mitchell 1985; Mohammad 1985; Somekh, 1979, 1981), and pragmatics[27] remain mainly theoretical. Little can be found on heuristics. Something like a dialogue act annotation system allowing the ranking of communicative functions of utterances in terms of their subjective importance (Włodarczak 2012) for Arabic has still to be written. Computational semantics has points of contact with the areas of lexical semantics (word sense disambiguation and semantic role labeling), discourse semantics, knowledge representation, and automated reasoning (in particular, automated theorem proving).

9.3 A Formalized Linguistic Description of Arabic Syntax

There are, in my opinion, some basic concepts and rules important for long-term linguistic research. The first point is that *syntax* encompasses a number of subfields, including phonology, morphology, lexicology, semantics, stylistics, pragmatics, and heuristics, together with their respective branches, including the use of computational tools. Moreover, linguistic research should positively and negatively *improve* the field: positively in the sense of enriching the discipline as well as socially relevant; and negatively in the sense of convincingly demonstrating that a specific approach did not and will not lead to any useful results or meaningful research.

A rather important rule is that any account of linguistic research, with *some* additional information and footnotes, should be readable and understandable foras well as verifiable by colleagues. Finally, scientific linguistic research should not be presented encoded in machine language or a programming language printout or even in PDF form and, moreover, should not be superficial, as are many of the presentations of commercial researchers and product developers.

[25] The references are slightly dated: Al-Najjar (1984), Bahloul (1994), Blohm (1989), DeMiller (1988), Eisele (1988), Gully (1992), Justice (1981, 1987), Mohammad (1983), Ojeda (1992), and Zabbal (2002).

[26] Most references are a bit dated but concern colloquial varieties as well as Standard Arabic: Abu Ghazaleh (1983), Abu Libdeh (1991), Alfalahi (1981), Al-Jubouri (1984), Al-Shabab (1987), Al-Tarouti (1992), Bar-Lev (1986), Daoud (1991), Fakhri (1995, 1998, 2002), Fareh (1988), Ghobrial (1993), Hatim (1987, 1989), Johnstone (1990, 1991), Khalil (1985), Koch (1981), Mughazy (2003), Russell (1977), Ryding (1992), Salib (1979), and Sawaie (1980).

[27] Cf. Dahl and Talmoudi (1979), Ghobrial (1993), Mahmoud (2008), Moutaouakil (1987, 1989), Mughazy (2008), and Suleiman (1989).

The description of the syntactic structure[28] of Standard Arabic, readable and understandable foras well as verifiable by colleagues, may have the form of a hypothesis, to be tested against authentic language data. After refining and renewed testing, this leads to a theory about the syntactic structure of the same layer of data of Standard Arabic as tested in the data. The same approach can be followed by further research on other Arabic text data.

Earlier, a listing was made of useful and (moreover) operational computational instruments, including machine-readable resources of all kinds, for the automated linguistic research on Arabic. We discussed the difference between Arabic NLP and Arabic CL, underlining the independence of the linguistic and formal parts in this research, while acknowledging a bias in favor of the linguistic part. Here I will defend an approach to an adequate, consistent, and coherent description of, in this case, MSA for the automated analysis[29] of authentic Arabic text data.

First, we position this section in Arabic NLP history (9.3.1). Then I say something about linguistic and formal concepts for language description within the Arabic grammatical tradition (9.3.2). Finally, I present a sample of a linguistic (9.3.3) and a formal part (9.3.4) of a description of MSA. Finally (9.4), I say something about perspectives on the basis of options chosen.

9.3.1 Evaluating Remarks about the Approach Opted For

When Smrž (2007: 68) says, "The tokens[30] with their disambiguated grammatical information enter the annotation of analytical syntax," we are in the linguistic part of our discussion about computational Arabic syntax. The same is the case with *Topologische Dependenz-grammatik fürs Arabische* (Odeh 2004). In both, the results of the analysis of some interesting syntactic peculiarities of the Arabic language, processed in a language-independent dependency-oriented environment (Debusmann 2006), are presented in the form of unambiguous, rather very nice tectogrammatical dependency trees on the basis of an analytical representation in the case of Smrž (2007), and, except for the labeling, in almost identical ID (immediate dominancy) and LP (linear precedence) representations (Odeh 2004).[31]

[28] Accounting for all the aforementioned branches of *syntax*, including an opening to a semantic description of language properties.

[29] A similar linguistic (and not heuristic thus pragmatic) description for generation purposes is not yet within reach.

[30] The results of his formal system and the implementation of functional Arabic morphology (Smrž 2007b: 69) are presented in the form of unambiguous dependency trees.

[31] Here is not the most appropriate place to initiate a discussion about the processing of a nondeterministic formal description of a natural language, for instance, in CFG terms, and the processing of a deterministic (each programming language) formal description of a natural language, whether or not the results are presented in IC, DG, HPSG, or any other form.

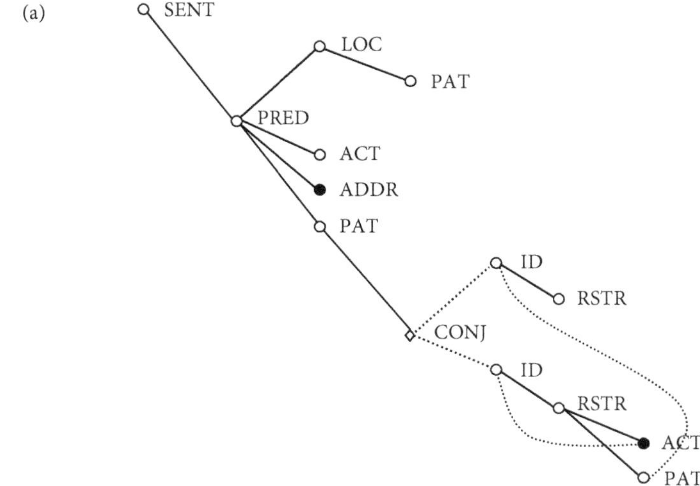

FIGURE 9.2a Tectogrammatic representation of the analysis of a sentence (Smrž 2007b, 73).

The sentence can be interpreted as containing a predicate (PRED) with an agent (ACT), no expressed addressee (ADDR), and an object (PAT). This object consists of two coordinated topics (ID), both further specified by an attributive modifier (RSTR). The second modifier does not have an agent but does govern an object (PAT). A positional apposition (LOC) plays the role of sentence adverbial. The second part of Figure 9.2b lists the Arabic word and its English translation as well as the tags used for the analytical representation (column 1). Column 2 lists the values for some variables used in the analysis. The third column (3) gives the values (in upper case) and representation of the variables (in lower case) I use in my approach of two-level description of the same target language.

Odeh (2004: Figure 9.3) presents the ID and the LP representation of a sentence with a finite verb form in first position. The abbreviations in Figure 9.3a are self-evident. Those in Figure 9.3b refer to the topological fields: sentence field (sf) and article field (artf).[32]

Notwithstanding the vagueness of the dismissal (Smrž 2007: 6), we like to comment on:

> The outline of formal grammar (Ditters, 2001), for instance, works with grammatical categories like number, gender, humanness, definiteness, but one cannot see which of the existing systems could provide for this information correctly, as they

[32] Duchier and Debusmann (2001) describe a new framework for dependency grammar with a modular decomposition of immediate dependency and linear precedence. Their approach distinguishes two orthogonal yet mutually constraining structures: a *syntactic dependency tree*; and a *topological dependency tree*. The former is nonprojective and even nonordered, while the latter is projective and partially ordered.

(b)

		1	2	3
مِلَفّ	collection	N---2R	Masc.Sing.Def	MASC,SING,DEF,GEN
أَدَب	literature	N--2D	Masc.Sing.Def	MASC,SING,DEF,GEN
طَرَح	to present	VP-A-3FS-	Ind.Ant.Act	I,PAST,ACT,THIRD,FEM,SING
مَجَلَّة	magazine	N---FS1D	Fem.Sing.Def	FEM,SING,DEF,GEN
هُوَ	someone		GenPronoun	FEM,SING,THIRD,NOM
قَضِيَّة	issue	N---FS4R	Fem.Sing.Def	FEM,SING,DEF,ACC
لُغَة	language	N---FS2D	Fem.Sing.Def	FEM,SING,DEF,GEN
عَرَبِيّ	Arabic	A---FS2D	Adjective	FEM,SING,DEF,GEN
وَ	and	C---	Coordination	CUM
خَطَر	danger	N--2D	Masc.Plur.Def	MASC,PLUR,DEF,ACC
هَدَّد	to threaten	VIIA-3FS-	Ind.Sim.Act	II,,INDIC,ACT,THIRD,FEM,SING
هِيَ	it	S---3FS4-	PersPronoun	FEM,SING,THIRD,NOM
هِيَ	it	G---	PersPronoun	FEM,SING,THIRD,NOM

FIGURE 9.2b The analyzed sentence: وَفِي مِلَفِّ الأَدَبِ طَرَحَت المَجَلَّة قَضِيَّةِ اللُغَةِ العَرَبِيَّةِ وَالأَخْطَارَ الَّتِي تُهَدِّدُهَا. 'and in the section on literature, the magazine presented the issue on the Arabic language and the dangers that threaten it.' (Smrž 2007b, 72–73).

misinterpret some morphs for bearing a category, and underdetermine lexical morphemes in general as to their intrinsic morphological functions.[33]

This is a correct remark, as far as Ditters (2001) is concerned. I am working with a description in terms of grammatical functions and categories, final lexical entries, dependency relations, and, additionally, an opening toward a description of semantic features as well.[34]

Grammatical in this context involves, as said earlier, the phonological, morphological, structural, and lexical modules for language description with rudimentary extensions to semantics, stylistics, and pragmatics as well as. It is necessary to remain understandable for and verifiable by colleagues. Serious semantic extensions are awaiting further computationally more coordinated research under supervision of the linguistic twin part in this kind of research. Let us continue with some words about *the outline of formal grammar*.

---

[33] It is, unmistakingly, my fault not to have been clear enough to explain the basic principles of my approach to language description: the analysis of a linguistic unit in terms of alternating layers of functions and categories until final (lexical) entries have been reached.

[34] For an example, see §2.3.

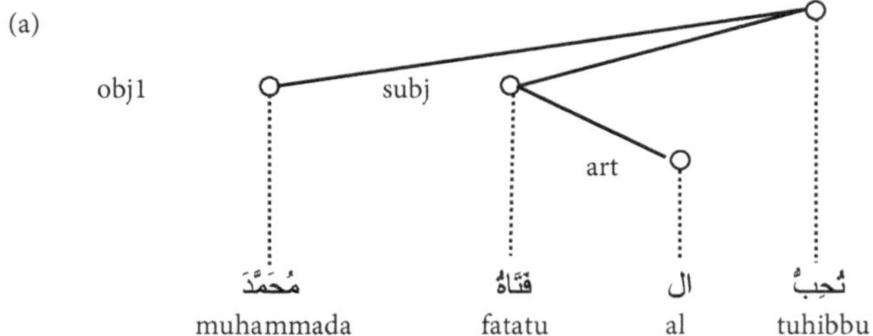

FIGURE 9.3a Immediate dominance (ID) representation.

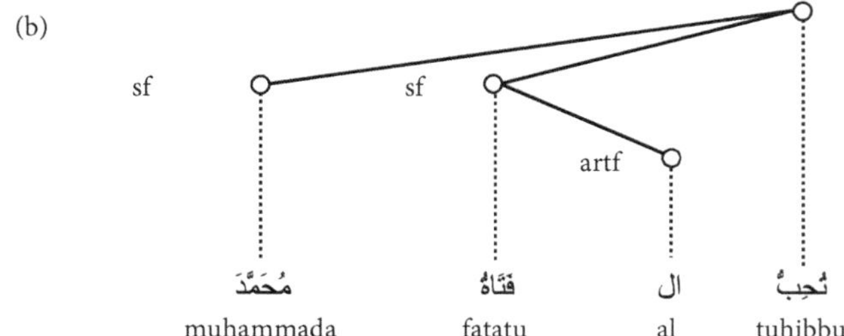

FIGURE 9.3b Linear precedence (LP) representation.

Computational means can be used to test a hypothesis about the linguistic structure of MSA sentences[35] in an efficient but linguistically understandable wording of nonterminals and terminals, applying only a context-free grammar formalism (with room for some additional context-free layers in the second level of description for semantics) but considering the availability of compilers for one, two, or more levels of context-free attribute grammar formalisms. Until now this approach has proved to be promising.

9.3.2 Linguistic and Formal Concepts about Language Description in the Arabic Grammatical Tradition

Immediate constituency (IC) has dominated descriptive linguistics for a long time. Dependency grammar (DG) concepts were already (according to Carter 1973, 1980; Owens 1988) familiar to Arab and Arabic grammarians and became a welcome, and needed, addition to an implementable descriptive power for natural languages in general and MSA in particular. Moreover, one can always explore other valuable suggestions.

[35] Maybe, for Arabic, we are not yet ready to think in terms of a linguistic and implementable paragraph, section, text, volume, and, generally applicable, syntax description of MSA or colloquial varieties of Arabic.

The basis for the description of parts of speech, functions, and categories in phrasal categories in MSA can be found in the *Kitāb* of Sībawayhi (d. 798).[36] Carter (1973: 146)[37] calls it "a type of structuralist analysis unknown to the West until the 20th century." He ends his abstract with:

> Utterances are analysed not into eight Greek-style "parts" but into more than seventy function classes. Each function is normally realized as a binary unit containing one active 'operator' (the speaker himself or an element of his utterance) and one passive component operated on (not "governed") the active member of the unit. Because every utterance is reduced to binary units, Sībawayhi's method is remarkably similar to immediate constituent Analysis, with which it shares both common techniques and inadequacies, as is shown.

As a first example of such a class of functions, Carter (1973: 151) presents the triad of "grammatical effect" (*ʿamal*), comprising a "grammatically affecting" (*ʿāmil*) and a "grammatically affected" (*maʿmūl*) component. Similar triads (possibly considered as dependency rules) can be drafted from the other function classes listed. Moreover, the function classes could be arranged in subcategories, for example, accounting for relationships between constituents, sentence types, or word formation. Other function classes deal with phonology and morphology, have discourse functions, or are related to stylistics. Finally, on the basis of Sībawayhi's comprehensive (exhaustive?) description of Arabic syntax, the function classes could easily be extended with more of this kind of "dependency rules," for example, with triads accounting for transitivity, or the subject–object–predicate relations.

Owens' (1988) historical overview with an apparent DG related perspective is broader. In section 2, all the relevant issues are discussed: constituency (IC) in Arabic theory (§2.9); dependency (DG) (§2.9.2); and *dependency* in Sībawayhi (§2.9.3). There are also chapters about markedness in Arabic theory (§8) and syntax, semantics, and pragmatics (§9).

9.3.3 Linguistic Description of MSA for Analysis Purposes[38]

An ideal compromise between IC and DG seems to be, for me, a context-free grammar description of MSA in IC terms accounting for the horizontal sequential order, enriched with a second, context-free grammar level attached to the nonterminals (Appendix 9.2) of the first level, accounting for relationships and dependencies (DG) in the vertical relational order between elements of a constituent or between constituents of one of the two sentence types (nominal and verbal). A third context-free grammar layer, only

[36] See for an overview of Arabic literature in general, among others, Sezgin (1967–2000), in particular volume 8 (lexicology) and 9 (syntax).

[37] Cf. in this perspective also Baalbaki (1979).

[38] See Appendix 9.2 for a paraphrase of technical terms used.

describing semantic extensions and properties, proved to be locatable (for the moment) within the two-layer context-free grammar frame.[39]

Working with two semantically and therefore also syntactically different sentence types in MSA, for both types one can distinguish categorial and functional nonterminals, categorial and functional terminals, lexical terminals, dependencies, and relationships between elements of a constituent and between constituents at sentence level. The syntactic consequences of a semantic property of a lexical entry will, of course, be of importance for the analysis and generation of text data of the language concerned.[40]

The *syntax* of sentence types in MSA, S^n, and S^v is described by means of alternating layers of categories, functions, and categories until terminals (here: lexical entries) have been reached. In the S^n, we distinguish two obligatory slots: a topic and a comment. The filler for a topic function characteristically belongs to the class of N's (here: head) or to the category NP's (optionally also containing modifiers to the head). In the S^v, we are dealing with a single obligatory slot, a predicate. The filler of a predicate function typically belongs to the class of V's (head) and is usually realized by a VP (optionally also containing modifiers to the head). The comment function in the S^n as well as optional slots, in both the S^n and the S^v, may be filled with entries of the different classes or with different phrasal categories.

In line with the first words of the *Kitāb* of Sībawayhi, as parts of speech we distinguish elements of the open word classes nouns (N) and verbs (V) and the closed class of particles (P).[41] Elements of these classes realize the head function in phrasal constituents such as noun phrases (NP), verb phrases (VP), and particle phrases (PP) as well as properties of elements of the word classes (N, V, and P), including morphological, syntactic, and semantic features (valency indications) and some pragmatic ones as well.[42] The following section introduces a simple sample implementation.

9.3.4 The Formal Description of MSA

For an adequate, coherent, and consistent description of MSA I examined different linguistic theories and models (Ditters 1992) for the best products, implementable in a processing environment for analysis purposes. For example, generalizations in the form of transformations in a transformational generative framework (TG) are too powerful a tool for an overall linguistic description;, when a simple machine like a computer failed to decide in a finite time whether or not a certain TG structure was described in the formal implementation of that linguistic description, I opted for a different formalism (AGFL)[43] to implement a description (Ditters 2001, 2007, 2011) in terms of a combination of IC and DG.

[39] See §2.3.

[40] I am exclusively working in an analysis perspective of authentic MSA text data.

[41] Superscripts to a nonterminal symbol, such as S, N, V, P, NP, VP, and PP point to categorial distinctions at the first level of description. Subscripts point to categorial, functional, or semantic characteristics at the second level of description.

[42] See §2.3.

[43] Cf. www.agfl.ru.cs.nl.

In contrast to a programming language (dynamic, functional, or relational in nature), a formalism (Ditters 1992: 134) is exclusively for the static, nondeterministic, and declarative description of structures such as programming languages (e.g., Algol-68, Affix- Attribute- Feature- Logical Grammars), also suited for the description of natural languages (e.g., Arabic, Dutch, English, Hebrew, Latin, Spanish). The objective is to test such a hypothetical description of, in our case, lMSA syntax structure on real data, for example, an Arabic text corpus. It is the machine-readable text data that determine whether a match should occur or not. Once tested, corrected, and refined, the hypothesis has become a theory, certainly for the language structure represented in the test bed in the form of a new hypothesis to be tested on other Arabic text corpora. Briefly, AGFL is an interwoven two-level context-free grammar formalism[44] with almost context-sensitive properties.[45]

On the Chomskian hierarchy of grammars (Levelt 1974) scale, context-free grammars are, for the description and automated testing of natural language descriptions, really rather nonproblematic. As a matter of fact, Chomsky qualified a context-free grammar as an inadequate descriptive tool for natural languages. However, he never showed, as far as I know, any interest in a combination of two (or even more) context-free grammars (with an almost context-sensitive descriptive power),[46] enough to describe, for example, most of Standard Arabic, including at least parts of its semantic richness. Furthermore, he never tested, as far as I know, his linguistic hypotheses and theoretical models practically by computational means.

A rule-based context-free grammar rewrites one single nonterminal at the left-hand side into one or more nonterminals or lexical entries on the right-hand side. AGFL, successor of EAG (Appendix 9.1), is a formalism for the description of programming languages or natural languages in which large context-free grammars can be described in a compact way. Along with attribute grammars[47] and DCGs, AGFLs belong to the family of two-level grammars, the first, context-free level, which accounts for the description of sequential word order of surface natural language elements, is augmented with set-valued features for expressing agreement between constituents and between elements of a constituent as well as linguistic properties (including semantic features). AGFL is implemented in *CDL3* and *C*.[48]

Notational AGFL conventions include the rewrite symbol (:), the marking of alternatives (;), the separation of sequences (,), the end of a rule (.), the layout of nonterminals and terminals of the first level and of the nonterminals and final values of variables of the second level of description in terms of lower- and uppercase representation.

[44] The main advantage of a formal description above a formalism, a computer or a programming language is that a linguist is able, after a simple introduction, to read, understand, and comment on your description without first becoming a mathematical, logical, or computational linguist or scientist.

[45] It is important to repeat that I exclusively use the formalism for analysis purposes. This means that the description may really be "liberal." For synthesis objectives it is quite a different story.

[46] 1 context-free grammar + 1 context-free grammar ≡ 2 context-free grammars ≠ 1 context-sensitive grammar.

[47] Koster, 1971, 1991.

[48] *CDL* refers to Compiler Description Language. CDL and C are, both, imperative programming languages, but in CDL3 the notational conventions are more suited for *AGFL*-formatted natural language descriptions to be tested.

Besides that, there is no longer any capacity problem for the storage of electronic data. Therefore, the choice of names and terminal values for the elements of the first and second level of description of, for example, MSA, may be as linguistically recognizable as one prefers.

We use four types of rules within the AGFL formalism: the so-called hyperrules; metarules; predicate rules; and lexical rules:[49]

- Hyperrules formally describe the occurrence of elements of word classes, in single or phrasal form. Variation in the sequence of those elements is dealt with by the formalism.
- Metarules define the nonterminals of the second level of description to a finite set of terminal values.
- Predicate rules describe and, if needed, condition relationships and dependencies between phrasal constituents or between elements of a constituent.
- Lexical rules describe final or terminal values of the first level of description, if possible with semantic features, some colocational information (including additional remarks about nonregular and unexpected occurrences in compositional semantics).

However, as is well-known, natural languages go further than the addition of the meaning of individual elements for capturing the real meaning of the linguistic data concerned.[50]

In Figure 9.4, Jaszczolt (2005) illustrates the process of utterance interpretation within the compositional theory of default semantics. It may be clear that the meaning of an utterance does not equal the sum of the meaning of its constituents.

The following presents a sample grammar[51] of a two-level context-free rewrite AGFL[52] for Modern Standard Arabic:[53]

[49] For detailed information about probabilistic and frequency accounting properties of the AGFL formalism, I refer to the aforementioned AGFL site.

[50] For more details see the aforementioned references.

[51] A *formal two-level context-free rewrite grammar* means one describes one and only one nonterminal on the left-hand side and rewrites it into one or more nonterminal or terminal values from the lexicon on the right-hand side. However, this action will take place at the first and second level of description. The second level of description is included between parentheses (()), attached, if desirable this has been considered, to nonterminals of the first level.

[52] AGFL stands for affix grammar over finite lattices. Cf. www.agfl.cs.ru.nl; Koster (1971, 1991).

[53] Notational conventions: a hash (#) introduces a comment line; a double colon (::) rewrites the left-hand side of a nonterminal of the second level of description into one or more final values or another nonterminal of the second level of description; a vertical bar (|) separates alternatives on the right-hand side of the second level of description; a colon (:) rewrites the nonterminal at the left-hand side of the first level of description into one or more nonterminals or terminal values; a comma (,) separates successive elements on the right-hand side; a semicolon (;) separates alternatives on the right-hand side; an addition sign (+) tells the machine to ignore all spaces; a dot (.) ends each rule, with the exception of lexical rules. Nonterminals of the second level are written in uppercase. Terminal values of the second level are written in lower case. Terminal values of the first level are enclosed in double quotes ("").

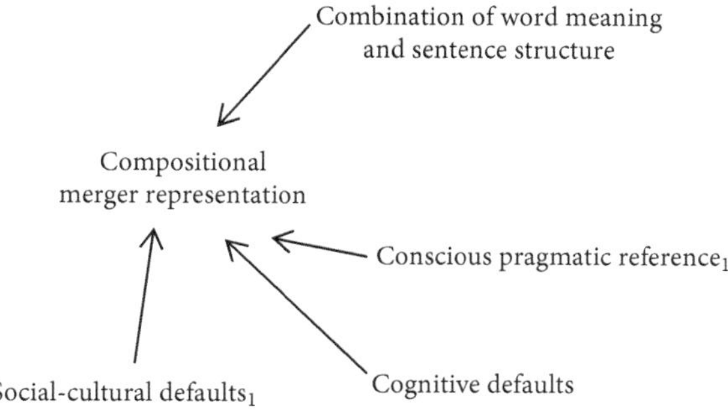

FIGURE 9.4 Utterance interpretation in default semantics (Jaszczolt 2005, 73).

GRAMMARsentence.
ROOT sentence(topic).
1 Meta rules
These define the finite domain of values for non-terminals of the second level of description.
This second level enables accounting for relationships and dependencies.
CASE::acc|gen|nom|invar.
DECLEN::defec|dipt|CASE.
DEFNESS::def|indef.
GENDER::fem|masc.
HEADREAL::com|pers|prop.
MODE::nominal|verbal.
MOOD::imper|indic|juss|subj.
NUMBER::coll|dual|PLUR|sing.
ORDER::topic|elliptic_topic.
PERSON::first|second|third.
PLUR::explu|inplu.
TENSE::perfect|MOOD.
TYPES::direc|finalintr|place|timeprep.
VOICE::active|passive.

2 Hyper rules
They describe functions and categories of non-terminals at the first level of description,

```
# until lexical values have been reached. This level enables accounting, in an efficient
  way,
# for the generalization of word order and sentence structure.[54]
sentence(topic):
   topic(GENDER,NUMBER),
      topic comp(GENDER,NUMBER).
topic(GENDER,NUMBER):
   nounphrase(def,GENDER,NUMBER,PERSON,nom|invar);
   prep(finalintr),
      np(HEADREAL,def,GENDER,NUMBER,PERSON,gen);
   bound prep(finalintr) +
      np(HEADREAL,def,GENDER,NUMBER,PERSON,gen).
topic comp(GENDER,NUMBER):
   predicate(MODE,DEFNESS,third,GENDER,NUMBER);
   np(HEADREAL,DEFNESS,GENDER,NUMBER,PERSON,nom);
   adjp(DEFNESS,GENDER,NUMBER,CASE);
   ap;
   pp.
nounphrase(def,GENDER,NUMBER,PERSON,nom|invar):
   np(HEADREAL,def,GENDER,NUMBER,PERSON, nom|invar).
np(HEADREAL,def,GENDER,NUMBER,PERSON,CASE):
   head(HEADREAL,DEFNESS,GENDER,NUMBER,PERSON,CASE),
      DEF is(HEADREAL,DEFNESS).
predicate(verbal,DEFNESS,third,GENDER,NUMBER):
   vp(TENSE,PERSON,GENDER,NUMBER).
predicate(nominal,DEFNESS,PERSON,GENDER,NUMBER):
   np(HEADREAL,DEFNESS,GENDER,NUMBER,PERSON,nom),
   headreal is(HEADREAL).
head(HEADREAL,DEFNESS,GENDER,NUMBER,PERSON,CASE):
   noun(DECLEN,GENDER,NUMBER).
noun(DECLEN,GENDER,NUMBER):
   common noun(DECLEN,GENDER,NUMBER);
   pers pronoun(GENDER,NUMBER,PERSON,CASE);
   proper noun(DECLEN,DEFNESS,GENDER,NUMBER).
vp(TENSE,PERSON,GENDER,NUMBER):
   verb(TENSE,VOICE,PERSON,GENDER,NUMBER).

# 3 Predicate rules
# They describe, or even determine, relations and dependencies between values of
  elements
```

[54] The listing of meta-, hyper-, predicate, or empty and lexical rules in reality is slightly longer.

```
# of the second level of description by means of the conditioning of specific values.
# This type of rules sometimes is called "empty rules."
# DEF is(HEADREAL,DEFNESS).
DEF is(com,DEFNESS):.
DEF is(pers,def):.
DEF is(prop,def):.

#Headrealis(HEADREAL).
headreal is(com):.
headreal is(pers):.
headreal is(prop):.

# 4 Lexical rules
# They describe the final or lexical value of entries in the lexicon.
# Adjp(DEFNESS,GENDER,NUMBER,CASE) and ap.
"adjp" adjp(DEFNESS,GENDER,NUMBER,CASE)
"ap"          ap

# Common noun(norm,masc,sing), including pronouns and proper nouns.
"rağul"       common noun(norm,masc,sing)
"riğāl"       common noun(norm,masc,inplu)
"bint"        common noun(norm,fem,sing)
"banāt"       common noun(norm,fem,inplu)

# Perspronoun(fem|masc,sing,first,nom).
"'anā"        perspronoun(fem|masc,sing,first,nom)
"naḥnu"       pers pronoun(fem|masc,inplu,first,nom)
"ī"           pers pronoun(fem|masc,sing,first,gen|acc)
"nī"          pers pronoun(fem|masc,sing,first,gen|acc)
"nā"          pers pronoun(fem|masc,inplu,first,gen|acc)

# Proper noun(dipt,def,masc,sing).
"'aḥmad"      proper noun(dipt,def,masc,sing)
"muḥammad"    proper noun(norm,def,masc,sing)
"fāṭimat"     proper noun(norm,def,fem,sing)

# Prep(TYPES).
"la"          bound prep(finalintr)
"la"          prep(finalintr)
"pp"          pp

# Verb(TENSE,VOICE,PERSON,GENDER,NUMBER).
"kataba"      verb(perfect,active,third,masc,sing)
```

"kutiba" verb(perfect,passive,third,masc,sing)
"yaktubu" verb(indic,active,third,masc,sing)
"yuktabu" verb(indic,passive,third,masc,sing)

Remark[55]

9.4 Perspectives for Further Linguistic and Formal Research on Arabic Syntax

In a joint contribution to the Nemlar conference (Ditters and Koster 2004),[56] we explored the potentiality of the existing approach to MSA syntax for other, socially equally relevant, spinoffs of my description of Arabic for corpus-linguistic analysis purposes. I prefer to finish testing the current implementation hypothesis about MSA *syntax* on Arabic text data. Second, I should like to refine the verified theory by means of a formal description of MSA *syntax* for generative purposes. Dependency grammar worded implementation could be extracted from such research. Finally, I like to make an, within the AGFL processing environment, implementable subset of DG rules for research on aboutness[57] in Arabic text data.

Appendix: Frequently used abbreviations

Symbol	Meaning
A	Aboutness
AB	Arabic Braille
ABP	Arabic proposition bank
AC	Automatic correction
AGFL	Affix grammar over finite lattices
AI	Artificial intelligence
AS	Answering system
ASL	Arabic Sign Language
ASR	Automatic speech recognition
BP	Base phrase
CALL	Computer-assisted language learning

55 In this sample grammar some alternatives of metarule rewritings of nonterminals at the second level of description occur only for elucidating purposes.

56 At the AGFL site mentioned as: *AP4IR* (Arabic [Dependency] Pairs for Information Retrieval).

57 Words from the open categories (nouns, verbs, and to a lesser extent adjectives and modifiers) carry the aboutness of a text, the others are in fact stop words. Similarly, only triples whose head or modifier are from an open category carry the aboutness of a text, and any other triples can be discarded as stopwords (Koster, 2011).

(*Continued*)

Symbol	Meaning
CFG	Context-free grammar
CL	Computational linguistics
CoL	Corpus linguistics
DM	Data mining
DR	Document routing
EAG	Extended affix grammar
EBL	Example-based learning cf. MBL
EE	Event extraction
FE	Factoid extraction
FGD	Function generative dependency
FSA	Finite state automaton
FSM	Finite state machine
FST	Finite state transducer
HR	Handwriting recognition
IBL	Instance-based learning cf. MBL
IC	Immediate constituency
ID	Immediate dominancy
IR	Information retrieval
LL	Lazy learning cf. MBL
LM	Language modeling
LP	Linear precedence
MBC	Morphological behavior class
MBL	Memory-based learning
MFH	Morphological form harmony
MLA	Machine learning approach
MSA	Modern Standard Arabic
MT	Machine translation
(S)MT	(Statistical) MT
NER	Named entity recognition
NET	Named entity translation
NL	Natural language
NLP	Natural language processing
OCR	Optical character recognition
OT	Optimality theory
ON	Orthographic normalization
POS	Parts of speech
POS-T	POS tagging
QAS	Question answering system
RBA	Rule-based approach
SA	Statistical approach
SBA	Stem-based approach
SC	Spelling correction
SG	Speech generation
SLA	Supervised learning approach
SP	Signal processing
SP	Speech processing
SR	Speech recognition
STS	Speech-to-speech
STT	Speech-to-text
SVM	Support vector machines

(*Continued*)

Symbol	Meaning
TC	Text categorization
TDT	Topic detection and tagging
TG	Text generation
TM	Text mining
TP	Text processing
TTS	Text-to-speech
TTT	Text-to-text
ULA	Unsupervised learning approach

Selected Bibliography[58]

Al-Shalabi, Riyad, and Ghassan Kanaan. 2004. Constructing an automatic lexicon for Arabic language. *International Journal of Computing and Information Sciences* 2: 114–128.

Al-Sughaiyer, Imad A., and Ibrahim A. Al-Kharashi. 2004. Arabic morphological analysis techniques: A comprehensive survey. *Journal of the American Society for Information Science and Technology* 55(3): 189–213.

Baker, Collin, Charles Fillmore, and John Lowe. 1998. The Berkeley FrameNet project. *(COLING-ACL'98): Proceedings of the University of Montréal Conference*, 86–90.

Beesley, Kenneth R. 1989. Computer analysis of Arabic morphology: A two-level approach with Detours. In *Perspectives on Arabic linguistics III: Papers from the 3rd annual symposium on Arabic linguistics*, ed. Bernard Comrie and Mushira Eid, 155–172. Amsterdam: John Benjamins.

——. 1996. Arabic finite-state morphological analysis and generation. In *Proceedings of the 16th international conference on computational linguistics (COLING-96)*, Copenhagen, Denmark, 89–94. Copenhagen: Center for Sprogteknologi.

——. 2001. Finite-state morphological analysis and generation of Arabic at Xerox research: Status and plans in 2001. In *Proceedings of the EACL workshop on language processing: Status and prospects*. Toulouse, France, 1–8. Available at: www.xrce.xerox.com/content/download/20547/147632/file/

Bielický, Viktor, and Otakar Smrž. 2008. Building the valency lexicon of Arabic verbs. In *Proceedings of the 6th international conference on language resources and* evaluation (LREC), Marrakech, Morocco.

——. 2009. Enhancing the ElixirFM lexicon with verbal valency frames. In *Proceedings of the 2nd international conference on Arabic language resources and tools*, ed. Khalid Choukri and Bente Maegaard. Cairo: The MEDAR Consortium.

Black, William, Sabri Elkateb, Horacio Rodriguez, Musa Alkhalifa, Piek Vossen, Adam Pease, and Christiane Fellbaum. 2006. Introducing the Arabic WordNet project. In *Proceedings of the 3rd international WordNet conference*, Jeju Island, Korea.

Bohas, Georges. 1997. *Matrices, étymons, racines: Éléments d'une theorie lexicographique du vocabulaire arabe*. Leuven: Peeters.

[58] Only titles that appear in the main text (not the footnotes) are included in the bibliography. A complete bibliography can be found in the online chapter of the *Handbook*.

Bohas, Georges, and Mihai Dat. 2008. Lexicon: Matrix and etymon model. In *EALL* vol. 3, ed. Kees Versteegh, Associate Editors: Mushira Eid, Alaa Elgibali, Manfred Woidich, Andrzej Zaborski, 45–52. Leiden: Brill.

Buckwalter, Timothy. 2002. *Arabic morphological analyzer version 1.0*. Philadelphia: Linguistic Data Consortium.

——. 2004. Issues in Arabic orthography and morphology analysis, in *Proceedings of the workshop on computational approaches to Arabic script-based languages, (COLING 2004)*, Geneva, Switzerland. ed. M. Farghaly and K. Megerdoomian, 31–34. Stroudsburg: Association for Computational Linguistics.

——. 2010. The Buckwalter Arabic morphological analyzer, in ed. Farghaly, 85–101.

Bunt, Harry, John Carroll, and Giorgio Satta (eds.). 2004. *New developments in parsing technology*. Dordrecht: Kluwer Academic Publishers.

Bunt, Harry, Paola Merlo and Joakim Nivre. 2010. *Trends in parsing technology*. Springer: Dordrecht.

Carter, Michael G. 1973. An Arab grammarian of the eight century A.D.: A contribution to the history of linguistics. *Journal of the American Oriental Society* 93: 146–157.

——. 1980. Sibawayhi and modern linguistics. *Histoire Épistémologique* 2(1): 21–26.

Cavalli-Sforza, Violetta, Abdelhadi Soudi, and Teruko Mitamura. 2000. Arabic morphology generation using a concatenative strategy. In *Proceedings of the 1st meeting of the North American Chapter of the Association for computational linguistics (NAACL 2000)*, Seattle, WA, 86–93.

Dada, Ali, and Aarne Ranta. 2006. Arabic resource grammar. In *Proceedings of the Arabic language processing conference (JETALA)*, Rabat, Morocco: IERA.

Debusmann, Ralph. 2006. *Extensible dependency grammar: A modular grammar formalism based on multigraph description*. PhD diss., Saarland University.

Dévényi, Kinga, Tamás Iványi, and Avihai Shivtiel (eds.). 1993. *Proceedings of the colloquium on Arabic lexicology and lexicography (C.A.L.L.): Budapest 1–7 September. Part one: Papers in European languages. Part two: Papers in Arabic*. Budapest: Eötvös Loránd University Chair for Arabic Studies.

Diab, Mona T. Kadri Hacioglu, and Daniel Jurafsky. 2004. Automatic tagging of Arabic text: From raw text to base phrase chunks. In *Proceedings of the 5th meeting of the North American chapter of the Association for computational linguistics/human language technologies conference (HLT-N/LICL04)*, Boston, MA, 149–152.

——. 2007. Towards an optimal POS tag set for modern standard Arabic processing. In *Proceedings of recent advances in natural language processing (RANLP)*, Borovets, Bulgaria.

Diab, Mona, Alessandro Moschitti, and Daniele Pighin. 2008. Semantic role labeling systems for Arabic language using Kernel methods. In *Proceedings of ACL-08: HLT*, Columbus, Ohio, 798–806.

Diab, Mona, Musa Alkhalifa, Sabry ElKateb, Christiane Fellbaum, Aous Mansouri, and Martha Palmer. 2007. Arabic Semantic Labeling. In *Proceedings of the 4th International Workshop on Semantic Evaluations (SemEval-2007 18)*, Prague, Czech Republic, 93–98.

Dichy, Joseph. 2005. Spécificateurs engendrés par les traits [±animé], [±humain], [±concret] et structures d'arguments en arabe et en français. In *De la mesure dans les termes. Actes du colloque en hommage à Philippe Thoiron*, ed. Henri Béjoint and François Maniez, 151–181. Travaux Centre de Recherche en Terminologie et Traduction (CRTT), Lyon: Presses Universitaires de Lyon.

Ditters, Everhard. 1992. *A formal approach to Arabic syntax: The noun phrase and the verb phrase*. PhD diss., Nijmegen University.

——. 2001. A formal grammar for the description of sentence structure in modern standard Arabic. In *EACL 2001 Workshop Proceedings on Arabic language processing: Status and prospects*, Toulouse, France, 31–37.

——. 2006. Computational linguistics. In *EALL* I, ed. Kees Versteegh et al., 511–518.

——. 2007. Featuring as a disambiguation tool in Arabic NLP, in Ditters and Motzki (eds.), 367–402.

——. 2011. A formal description of sentences in Modern Standard Arabic. In *Studies in Semitic languages and linguistics*, ed. T. Muraoka, A. Rubin, and C. Versteegh, 511–551. Leiden: Brill.

Ditters, Everhard, and Cornelis H. A. Koster. 2004. Transducing Arabic phrases into head-modifier (HM) pairs for Arabic information retrieval. In *Proceedings of the NEMLAR 2004 international conference on Arabic language resources and tools*, September 22–23, Cairo, 148–154.

Duchier, Denys and Ralph Debusmann. 2001. Topological dependency trees: A constraint-based account of linear precedence. In *Proceedings of the Association for Computational Linguistics*. Toulouse, France. 180–187. http://www.aclweb.org/anthology-new/P/P01/P01-1024.pdf

Elkateb, Sabri, William Black, Horacio Rodríguez, Musa Alkhalifa, Piek Vossen, Adam Pease, and Christiane Fellbaum. 2006. Building a WordNet for Arabic. In *Proceedings of the 5th international conference on language resources and evaluation (LREC 2006)*, Genoa, Italy.

Farghaly, Ali, and Karine Megerdoomian (eds.). 2004. *Proceedings of the workshop on computational approaches to Arabic script-based languages, (COLING 2004)*, Geneva, Switzerland. Stroudsburg: Association for Computational Linguistics.

—— (ed.). 2010. *Arabic computational linguistics*. Stanford: CSLI Publications.

Fellbaum, Christiane (ed.). 1998. WordNet: An electronic lexical database. Cambridge, MA: MIT Press.

Forsberg, Markus, and Aarne Ranta. 2004. Functional morphology. In *Proceedings of the 9th ACM SIGPLAN international conference on functional programming, ICFP 2004*, ACM Press, 213–223.

Habash, Nizar. 2004. Large scale lexeme based Arabic morphological generation. In *Proceedings of traitement automatique des Langues Naturelles (TALN-04)*, Fez, Morocco, 271–276.

——. 2010. *Introduction to Arabic natural language processing*. San Raphael, CA: Morgan & Claypool Publishers.

Habash, Nizar, and Ryan Roth. 2009. CATIB: The Colombia Arabic treebank. In *Proceedings of the ACL-IJCNLP 2009 conference Short Papers*, Suntec, Singapore, 221–224.

Habash, Nizar, Owen Rambow, and George Kiraz. 2005. Morphological analysis and generation for Arabic dialects. In *Proceedings of the Workshop on computational approaches to Semitic languages at 43rd meeting of the Association for computational linguistics (ACL'05)*, Ann Arbor, MI, 17–24.

Hafez, Ola M. 1991. Turn-taking in Egyptian Arabic: Spontaneous speech vs. drama dialogue. *Journal of Pragmatics* 15: 59–81.

Hassanein, Ahmed T. 2008. Lexicography: Monolingual dictionaries. In *EALL* III, ed. Kees Versteegh et al., 37–45.

Hoogland, Jan. 2008. Lexicography: Bilingual dictionaries. In *EALL* III, ed. Kees Versteegh et al., 21–30.

Jaszczolt, Katarzyna M. 2005. *Default semantics: Foundations of a compositional theory of acts of communication*. Oxford: Oxford University Press.

Jurafsky, Daniel, and James H. Martin. 2009. *Speech and language processing: An introduction to natural language processing, computational linguistics, and speech recognition*. Upper Saddle River, NJ: Prentice Hall.

Kaplan, Ronald, and Martin Kay. 1981. Phonological rules and finite-state transducers. In *Linguistic Society of America Meeting Handbook, 56th Annual Meeting*. New York.

Kay, Martin. 1987. Noncatenative finite-state morphology. In *Workshop on Arabic morphology*. Stanford: Stanford University Press, 2–10.

Khoja, Shereen, Roger Garside, and Gerry Knowles. 2001. A tagset for the morphosyntactic tagging of Arabic. In *Proceedings of corpus linguistics 2001*. Lancaster, UK, 341–353.

Kiraz, George Anton. 1994. Multi-tape two-level morphology: A case study in Semitic non-linear morphology. In *Proceedings of 15th international conference on computational linguistics (COLING-94)*, Kyoto, Japan, 180–186.

——. 1997. Compiling regular formalisms with rule features into finite-state automata. In *ACL/EACL-97*, Madrid, Spain, 329–336.

Kiraz, George Anton, 2000. Multi-tiered nonlinear morphology using multi-tape finite automata: A case study on Syriac and Arabic. *Computational Linguistics* 26: 77–105.

— 2001. Computational nonlinear morphology with emphasis on Semitic languages. *Studies in natural language processing*. New York: CUP.

Kiraz, George Anton, and Bernd Möbius. 1998. Multilingual syllabification using weighted finite-state transducers. In *Proceedings of the 3rd ESCA workshop on speech synthesis*, Jenolan Caves, Australia, 71–76.

Köprü, Selçuk, and Jude Miller. 2009. A unification based approach to the morphological analysis and generation of Arabic. In *3rd Workshop on computational approaches to Arabic script-based languages, Computational Approaches to Arabic Script-based Languages* (CAASL3). Available at http://mt-archive.info/MTS-2009-Kopru.pdf.

Koskenniemi, Kimmo. 1983. *Two-level morphology: A general computational model for word-form recognition and production*. Publication 11. Helsinki: Department of General Linguistics, University of Helsinki.

Kulick, Seth, Ryan Gabbard, and Mitch Marcus. 2006. Parsing the Arabic treebank: Analysis and improvements. In *Proceedings of the Treebanks and Linguistic Theories Conference*. Prague, Czech Republic, 31–42.

Levelt, Willem J.M. 1974. *Formal grammars in linguistics and psycholinguistics: An introduction to the theory of formal languages*. 3 vols. Den Haag: Mouton.

Maamouri, Mohamed, Ann Bies, and Seth Kulick. 2009. Creating a methodology for large-scale correction of treebank annotation: The case of the Arabic treebank. In *Proceedings of MEDAR international conference on Arabic language resources and tools*. Cairo: Medlar.

Maamouri, Mohamed, Ann Bies, Timothy Buckwalter, and Wigdan Mekki. 2004. *The Penn Arabic Treebank: Building a large-scale annotated Arabic corpus*. Paper presented at the NEMLAR International Conference on Arabic Language Resources and Tools, September 22–23, Cairo.

Maamouri, Mohamed, and Ann Bies. 2010. The Penn Arabic treebank, in ed. Farghaly, 103–135.

Manning, Christopher D., and Hinrich Schütze. 2003[6] [1999]. *Foundations of statistical natural language processing*. Cambridge, MA: MIT Press.

Marton, Yuval, Nizar Habash, and Owen Rambow. 2010. Improving Arabic dependency parsing with lexical and inflectional morphological features. In *Proceedings of the NAACL HLT 2010 1st workshop on statistical parsing of morphologically-rich languages*. Los Angeles, CA, 13–21.

McCarthy, John. 1981. A prosodic theory of non-concatenative morphology. *Linguistic Inquiry* 12: 373–418.

Mesfar, Slim. 2010. Towards a cascade of morpho-syntactic tools for Arabic natural language processing. In *Computational linguistics and intelligent text processing: Proceedings of the 11th international conference CICLing 2010*, Iaşi, Romania, ed. Alexander Gelbukh. 150–162. Berlin: Springer.

Mitchell, Terence F. 1985. Sociolinguistic and stylistic dimensions of the educated spoken Arabic of Egypt and the Levant. In *Language standards and their codification: Process and application*, ed. J. Douglas Woods, 42–57. Exeter: University of Exeter.

Mohammad, Mahmud D. 1985. Stylistic rules in classical Arabic and the levels of grammar. *Studies in African Linguistics* 9:228–232.

Msellek, Abderrazaq. 2006. Kontrastive Fallstudie: Deutsch—Arabisch. *HSK* 25(2):1287–1292.

Müller, Karin. 2002. Probabilistic context-free grammars for phonology. In *Proceedings of ACL SIGPHON*, Association for Computational Linguistics, PA, 70–80.

Odeh, Marwan. 2004. *Topologische Dependenzgrammatik fürs Arabische*. Abschlussbericht FR6.2-Informatik, Universität des Saarlandes.

Owens, Jonathan. 1988. *The foundations of grammar: An introduction to medieval Arabic grammatical theory*. Amsterdam: John Benjamins.

——. 2003. Valency-like concepts in the Arabic grammatical tradition. *HSK* 25(1): 26–32.

Palmer, Martha, Dan Gildea, and Paul Kingsbury. 2005. The proposition bank: An annotated corpus of semantic roles. *Computational Linguistics* 31: 71–106.

——, Olga Babko-Malaya, Ann Bies, Mona Diab, Mohamed Maamouri, Aous Mansouri, and Wajdi Zaghouani. 2008. A pilot Arabic propbank. In *Proceedings of the Sixth International Conference on Language Resources and Evaluation (LREC'08)*, ed. By Nicoletta Calzolari, 3467–3472. Marrakech, Morocco.

Prince, Alan, and Smolensky, Paul. 2004. *Optimality theory: Constraint interaction in generative grammar*. Oxford: Blackwell.

Ramsay, Alan, and Hanady Mansur. 2001. Arabic Morphology: A categorical approach. In *EACL workshop proceedings on Arabic language processing: Status and prospects*. Toulouse, France, 17–22.

Ratcliffe, Robert R. 1998. *The "broken" plural problem in Arabic and comparative Semitic: Allomorphy and analogy in non-concatenative morphology*. Amsterdam: John Benjamins.

Seidensticker, Tilman. 2008. Lexicography: Classical Arabic, In *EALL* III, ed. Kees Versteegh et al., 30–37.

Sībawayhi (d. 798). *Al-Kitāb*. 2 vols. Būlāq 1316 A.H. Reprint Baghdad: al-Muṯannā n.d.

Smrž, Otakar. 2007. *Functional Arabic morphology: Formal system and implementation*. PhD diss., Charles University, Prague, Czech Republic.

Smrž, Otakar, and Jan Hajič. 2010. The other Arabic treebank: Prague dependencies and functions. In ed. Farghaly, 137–168.

Somekh, Sasson. 1979. The emergence of two sets of stylistic norms in the early literary translation into modern Arabic prose. *Ha-Sifrut-Literature* 8(28): 52–57.

——. 1981. The emergence of two sets of stylistic norms in the early literary translation into modern Arabic prose. *Poetics Today* 2: 193–200.

Soudi, Abdelhadi, Antal van den Bosch, and Günter Neumann (eds.). 2007. *Arabic computational morphology: Knowledge-based and empirical methods*. Dortrecht: Springer.

Vossen, Piek. 1998. *EuroWordNet: A multilingual database with lexical semantic networks*. Dordrecht: Kluwer.

Winograd, Terry. 1983. *Language as a cognitive process*. Vol. 1: *Syntax*. Reading MA: Addison-Wesley.

Włodarczak, Marcin. 2012. Ranked multidimensional dialogue act annotation. *New Directions in Logic, Language and ComputationLecture Notes in Computer ScienceVolume* :ed. By Daniel Lassiter and Marija Slavkovik, 67–77. Berlin: Springer.

CHAPTER 10

SOCIOLINGUISTICS

ENAM AL-WER

10.1 Introduction

The beginnings of sociolinguistics as an independent discipline within linguistics is marked by William Labov's (1963) publication "The Social Motivation of a Sound Change," in which he showed that the relationship between social and linguistic variables could be studied systematically (see also Fisher 1958). Reporting on his sociolinguistic research on Martha's Vineyard, Massachusetts, Labov set forth methods of investigating language use in natural social settings within the speech community—hence the popular designation of sociolinguistics as the study of language in its social context. Most sociolinguists would consider the subject of their expertise to be simply a way of doing linguistics that shares with formal linguistics the objective of formulating a linguistic theory to account for the linguistic data. Where sociolinguistics diverges from formal linguistics is in its emphasis that language as a form of social behavior can be studied only in its natural setting, namely, society.[1]

Sociolinguistics is in various ways connected with most other subdisciplines in linguistics as well as with the other social sciences (especially at the level of interpretation). The most important challenge for sociolinguistics is the study of language change, the subject matter of historical (or diachronic) linguistics. However, whereas the analysis in historical linguistics begins with the *outcome* of change, sociolinguistic analysis deals with language change from inception through to propagation and completion.

In this chapter, I provide a critical overview of the application of sociolinguistic principles, methods, and analysis to Arabic data with reference to the research conducted over the past three decades or so in various Arabic-speaking societies. The focus will be

[1] For further elaboration on this point, see the discussion in Labov (1970: 30).

on linguistic variation and change, the major concerns of (variationist) sociolinguistics. I begin with an outline of the relationship between traditional dialectology and sociolinguistics, the ways dialectological data are incorporated into sociolinguistic analysis, and the benefits of maintaining the link between the two disciplines. Then an outline is given of the basic principles of the variationist paradigm, which are intricately bound up with sociolinguistic methodology and theory; where relevant, research practices in studies on Arabic will be cited. The chapter then critically reviews the "diglossia" model as an approach to the analysis of variation in Arabic. In the final part, I set out an alternative and up-to-date model of analysis, with illustration of case studies from recent research.

10.2 Dialectology as a Resource for Sociolinguistics

Both dialectology and sociolinguistics focus on linguistic variability in empirically collected data. But, whereas traditional dialectology is more interested in rural communities and, as far as possible, teases out variations in the speech sample by gathering data preferably from the oldest and least mobile members of the community,[2] sociolinguistics is interested in all types of speakers and all types of communities and has devised methods to analyze social as well as linguistic variables and to correlate the social and the linguistic variables in a systematic way.

Notwithstanding differences in sampling and analytical techniques, sociolinguistics clearly has its roots in traditional dialectology, and where dialectological data are available sociolinguistic research anchors its findings to previous dialectological findings. To demonstrate the ways dialectological data have benefited sociolinguistic analysis, some examples are cited.

In Labov's very first sociolinguistic research on Martha's Vineyard in 1962, he noted a particular way of pronouncing the diphthongs /ay/ ("price") and /aw/ ("house") with a centralized first element of the diphthongs. Beginning with the records of earlier dialectological studies, he traced the centralized variants from as early as the 16th and 17th centuries, right through to the first decades of the 20th century in various parts of North American English. Importantly for Labov's Martha's Vineyard study, *The Linguistic Atlas of New England* (Kurath et al. 1941) recorded an open, rather than a centralized, pronunciation of these diphthongs for Martha's Vineyard. On the basis of this record and the earlier historical records, Labov was able to establish that the centralization of /ay/ and /aw/ in Martha's Vineyard was an old pronunciation whose use decreased during the 1930s and in the 1960s was being revived by a particular group of speakers on

[2] The ideal speaker in traditional dialectological research is described as a nonmobile old rural male (NORM) since much of the very early work in the field typically preferred such speakers.

the island. The reintroduction of the traditional centralized pronunciation coincided with an influx of wealthy summer visitors from the mainland who were buying up property on the island. Some Vinyarders showed resentment toward these outsiders. Labov showed that centralization of the diphthongs was strongest among the speakers who showed most resistance to outside pressure, thus demonstrating the effect of social factors on linguistic structure.

The practice of drawing on earlier records where available has proven to be an invaluable resource, especially since most sociolinguistic studies are investigations in *apparent time*, where the symptoms of change are gleaned from the patterns of variation rather than from a comparison of the state of language at more than one point in real time. A case in point is the relatively recent discovery of recordings that were hidden in the archives of the New Zealand National Broadcasting Corporation of interviews conducted with the first generation of New Zealand–born Anglophones. Not only have these recordings provided empirical foundations for the study of the formation of New Zealand English (Gordon et al. 2006), but they have also modified previous assumptions regarding a number of innovations in British English, such as the approximate date of the loss of nonprevocalic /r/ in England (see Trudgill 2004).

With the exception of a few shining examples,[3] early Arabic sociolinguistics and Arabic dialectology have proceeded almost totally independently of each other, although dialectological descriptions of various Arabic dialects have been available since the second half of the 19th century, and, until the advent of sociolinguistics, dialect descriptions and dialect geography were the only sources of data about modern Arabic dialects.[4] This situation has nonetheless improved considerably especially since the 1990s and in both directions. A particularly interesting and significant case of reanalysis of dialectological data is one recently undertaken by Manfred Woidich and Liesbeth Zack concerning the history of *Jim* in Egyptian Arabic in which the social history of Egypt as well as insights from sociolinguistic theory and modern dialect geography are incorporated into the analysis (Woidich and Zack 2009). The thesis they examined is whether [g], the Egyptian realization of *Jim*, is indeed an innovation, as has been suggested by Blanc (1969) and later supported by Hary (1996). They conclude that, contrary to the earlier analysis, Egyptian [g] may be a direct derivation from an older variety of Arabic that had preserved Semitic /g/ (the antecedent to the Arabic *Jim*) (Woidich and Zack 2009: 56–57). This is a significant conclusion insofar as Egyptian Arabic is concerned and has an impact on the dialect geography of Arabic in general since it places Egyptian Arabic alongside dialects at the periphery of the Peninsula (South Yemen and Oman) in which this relic feature ([g]) continues to exist.[5]

[3] A notable exception in this context is the research conducted by Clive Holes (1987) during the 1970s (Holes 1987) in Bahrain, which draws on all available resources from dialectology.

[4] Of the published material during the early decades of the 20th century the works by Bergsträsser (1915) and Cantineau (1936, 1937, 1940) are worthy of mention. For a comprehensive bibliography on Egyptian Arabic, see Woidich (1993).

[5] Further important cases of reanalysis incorporating insights from sociolinguistics can be found in Jonathan Owens (2009).

10.3 Basic Principles and Methodological Practices in Sociolinguistics

Language variation and language change are the most important concerns of sociolinguistics. They represent two interrelated properties of language: the fact of variability and the fact of change. Change is always preceded by variation; it would be inconceivable for form A to change into form B without going through a stage where both forms, A and B, are used variably by members of the speech community. Therefore, understanding the intervening stages of the progression (variation) is a prerequisite to understanding the outcome of the process of change.

Sociolinguistics has shown that linguistic variability is not random but is structured by linguistic and social constraints; hence, the first task of sociolinguistic research is to identify and isolate these constraints through analyzing representative empirical data [Holes, "Orality"].[6] However, obtaining samples from the vernacular, or the way people normally speak when they are not being observed, is not an easy task, and sociolinguistic methodology has gone through a great deal of reformulation to improve this vital part of the procedure.[7]

In the next section, I consider some of the methodological issues that pertain to Arabic in particular.

10.3.1 Methodological Issues in Arabic Sociolinguistics

Since the early days of research in Arabic sociolinguistics, considerable methodological strides have been made toward obtaining data that represent natural speech as far as possible, from recording speech in more than one context (e.g., Owens 1998) to enlisting in-group members of the community as field-workers (e.g., Miller 2005). However, what constitutes the vernacular and how techniques can be improved to elicit natural speech in the context of Arabic-speaking societies are questions that are yet to be addressed directly by sociolinguists working with Arabic data. By way of highlighting some of the important methodological issues in Arabic research, I shall discuss two of the independent variables: how they were isolated and how they were employed in research.

[6] This is not to say that sociolinguists are not interested in samples of formal or semiformal speech, but such samples normally show irregular patterns as a result of conscious self-correction on the part of speakers and are, therefore, not the ideal source of information to determine the course of language change. On the other hand, samples of unmonitored speech show "more systematic speech, where the fundamental relations which determine the course of linguistic evolution can be seen most clearly" (Labov 1970: 46).

[7] See Labov (1970: 47) on the observer's paradox; see Milroy and Gordon (2003) on methodology.

10.3.1.1 *Style*

Generally speaking, stylistic variation is understood to involve variation in the speech of the individual speaker according to the task they are performing (speaking vs. reading), the context (e.g., interlocutors at home vs. work; interacting with family members, work colleagues, superiors), and topic of conversation.[8] In the early Labovian methodology, style was related to the use of more or less standardized speech and different styles that triggered different degrees of standardization were arranged along a scale that ranged from the casual to the most formal styles. Elicitation of the most formal styles has normally been achieved through reading tasks (passage and word lists), where the speakers are said to pay most attention to their speech and hence monitor it carefully. For languages such as English, where status and prestige are attached to linguistic features that are characteristic of the dialects spoken by the higher social classes and often coincide with the features found in the standard variety, the early Labovian methodology of quantifying style and correlating it with linguistic usage has yielded systematic results and interpretations. In this domain, it was found that the more attention speakers paid to their speech the more they approximated to standard or prestigious speech.[9] For a language like Arabic, where the speakers are confined by the normative and prescribed rules of Standard Arabic in reading tasks the Labovian methods of eliciting stylistic variation would not yield a comparable set of data to those obtained from research on English.[10]

By and large, stylistic variation in Arabic studies has been treated as constituting a binary choice between standard and colloquial features. A number of Arabic studies elicited this particular type of stylistic variation by manipulating the topic of discussion.[11] The underlying principle is as follows. Topics normally discussed in the public domain and in the media are deemed serious topics and thus trigger the use of standard Arabic linguistic features, whereas everyday ordinary topics trigger the use of colloquial features. For example, in Al-Khatib's (1988) study in Irbid (Jordan), the serious topics included "role of women in society" and "educational policy"; the informants' linguistic behavior

[8] On the use of "style" in sociolinguistic research, see Eckert and Rickford (2001) and Schilling-Estes (2002).

[9] This was found to be true for a wide range of variables in North American English (Labov 1972; Wolfram 1969), British English (Trudgill 1974), Australian English (Horvath 1985), and New Zealand English (Gordon and Deverson 1998).

[10] Notwithstanding the obvious flaws in following this method in research on Arabic, some researchers have in fact resorted to reading tasks and contrasted them with speaking styles along the same stylistic continuum (e.g., Shorab 1982; Al-Khatib 1988), while Abdel-Jawad (1981) had the foresight not to use this method, reasoning that in reading tasks Arabic speakers are confined to choosing standard Arabic pronunciations, which, of course, is correct.

[11] Topic was also used by Labov to manipulate style. Elicitation of different styles through change of topic and context (formal speeches delivered on TV or to the public) was used by Abdel-Jawad (1981) in Amman, by Schmidt (1974) in Cairo, by Al-Jehani (1985) in Mecca, and by Al-Amadidhi (1985) in Qatar, among others.

in discussing these topics was considered to reflect a formal style. To elicit casual style, the speakers were encouraged to discuss "lighter topics" such as hobbies and recreational activities and to tell jokes.[12] In Al-Khatib's study, as in others' that followed this method, the change in "style" thus measures only the use of the standard variant and neglects variation within the nonstandard variants (in variables with more than one colloquial variant). By way of illustration, in Al-Khatib's (1988) study, the variable (Q) has three colloquial variants, [g], [k], [ʔ], and Standard [q]. Covariation with style is calculated for the Standard variant only: 62%, 100%, 100% in formal style (discussing serious topics), reading passage, and word lists (Al-Katib 1988: 264), respectively. Predictably, in the two reading tasks the speakers used [q] consistently, but in the discussion of serious topics they varied between the standard and nonstandard variants. No statistics are given for the colloquial variants separately, giving the impression that variation at this level is irrelevant or that variation in the use of the colloquial variants (the vernacular) is not constrained by social or stylistic factors. On the contrary, as shown in Al-Khatib's study (as well as in all other studies on Jordanian Arabic), the use of one or the other of the *Qaf* colloquial variants is highly constrained by the social and contextual (interlocutor) factors, while the use of standard [q] is predictable. Furthermore, the frequency of the occurrence of [q] does not affect the sociolinguistic correlations of the colloquial variants, nor does it affect the course of change in *Qaf* or the structure of variation in the vernacular.[13]

Manipulating modes (speaking versus reading) and topics of discussion are clearly inadequate methods for style elicitation in Arabic vernaculars.[14]

The significance of the independent variables, including style, as constraints on linguistic behavior can be interpreted only if they are analyzed in relation to the social context from which they derive; the same variables can mean different things in different societies. Clearly, there is much to be done in this area in sociolinguistic investigations of variation in Arabic.

In the next section, I discuss "education" as a widely used but poorly understood social variable in Arabic studies.

10.3.1.2 *Education as a Speaker Variable*

Education has been used very widely as a major sampling criterion in Arabic studies, almost analogously to the way socioeconomic class has been used in studies in North America and the United Kingdom.[15] In most studies, speakers were classified according

[12] The telling of jokes here seems to mimic Labov's "danger of death" question, which was meant to elicit narratives that would engage the speaker emotionally. Al-Khatib, however, did not make a distinction within the range of the light topics he used.

[13] There are sound grounds for discounting [q] in Jordan as a variant of the same phonological unit as the colloquial variants since its occurrence is lexically conditioned to a high degree.

[14] There seems to be a tacit agreement about the inadequacy of such methods for Arabic; to my knowledge they have not been used in Arabic studies for quite some time.

[15] In addition to the previously mentioned studies, Al-Wer (1991) uses level of education as a variable. A notable exception is Haeri (1996), who classifies her speakers in Cairo according to social class, but she also uses education as a variable to refer to "type of schooling."

to "level of education." The results appeared to show regular and strong correlations between level of education and linguistic behavior.[16] However, these same results are paradoxical, or so they appeared, in that while the group of speakers with the highest educational level showed the highest rate of usage of standard Arabic features for some variables they were in the lead of innovations away from standard features for other variables. For example, in Abdel-Jawad (1981), the highest educational group used standard [q] most. For the second variable, (k), Abdel-Jawad also concluded that the same group standardized their speech most by using [k] rather than the affricated variant [tʃ]. In Al-Khatib (1988), the highest educational group used [q] most often, but for the variable *Jim* they used fricative [ʒ] rather than the standard affricate variant [dʒ] more than any other group.[17] In Al-Wer (1991) the highly educated group used [q] more frequently than the lower educational groups, but they also led all other groups in using three nonstandard innovative features, (θ): [t], (ð): [d] and (dʒ): [ʒ]. To resolve this prima facie paradox, two issues will be addressed. First, we need to analyze the significance of "education" as a speaker variable in Arabic-speaking societies. Second, the role of the standard variety in variation and change in spoken Arabic needs to be discussed in the light of the empirical data available from variationist research. In the remainder of this section I will discuss the first point, while the second issue forms part of the discussion in Section 10.4.

In Al-Wer (2002), I argue that education may be a *proxy* variable acting on behalf of other less conspicuous variables such as the speakers' relationships with their local community and the sums and types of relationships they have maintained with the local and outside communities (i.e., their social networks). A further possibility is that the underlying factors are related to their personal ambitions, orientations, and attitudes toward the local community as reflected in their daily activities, future plans for themselves and their children, place of residence in the town (inner-city vs. suburban residence), and participation in local politics (e.g., municipality elections, voluntary social work). The hypothesis that it is not education per se that correlated with linguistic behavior arose as a result of the overall conclusions about the trajectory of linguistic change in three Jordanian cities (Al-Wer 1991). The results showed that change may be in progress with respect to the following features: [θ] > [t]; [ð] > [d]; [ḍ] > [ḍ]; [dʒ] > [ʒ]. The changes altogether represent divergence from the traditional local dialects toward a nonlocal and at the same time a supralocal norm at the level of the Levant region.[18] In the case of the plain interdental sounds, the changes involve mergers spreading at the

[16] Abdel-Jawad (1981: 268) and Al-Khatib (1988: 130) are so impressed by these results that they even suggest replacing "age" by "education" as an indicator of change in apparent time. Not many linguists would take this suggestion seriously.

[17] Al-Khatib does not comment on this result although it represents an anomaly within the argument he advocates, namely, that the highest educated group overall standardize their speech most.

[18] James Milroy and Lesley Milroy introduce the notion of *supralocal* to sociolinguistic research and use it to explain the results in the Tyneside research with respect to glottalisation–glottal replacement of voiceless stops; see James Milroy et al. (1994).

expense of differentiated sounds. These two linguistic developments—preference for supralocal variants and spread of mergers—are in keeping with universal tendencies of the direction of change as demonstrated in sociolinguistic research. The local traditional Jordanian variants [θ ð dʒ] are at the same time characteristic features of standard Arabic. The emphatic interdental sound has two counterparts in the standard variety: an interdental sound, as in the local dialects; and an emphatic stop sound.[19] Therefore, another way we can summarize the changes in this case is that the educated speakers lead change away from the standard variety or that there is an inverse correlation between level of education and the use of standard features. At the same time, the highest educated group used the glottal stop variant [ʔ] variably with the local variant [g]. Very little variation was found between these sounds, but all of the speakers who used it consistently (5 speakers of 116) or variably (4 of 116) belonged to the highest educational group. At the time of research (1987) there was definitely no change in progress from [g] to [ʔ]; rather, the little variation attested was interpreted as an innovative linguistic behavior that was confined to a few speakers and involved the use of a supralocal feature at the expense of the localized feature [g], since the glottal stop realization is also characteristic of the major city dialects in the region. This then substantiates the findings about the direction of change being toward supralocal features. Predictably, for Qaf, the highest educational group used the highest proportion of lexical items that contained the standard variant [q], which may be explained with reference to their level of education. That is, their *functional* knowledge of the standard variety is higher than the knowledge of the less educated, and they are therefore able to integrate learned lexical items into their speech; however, obviously no sound change toward [q] (away from [g]) is involved.[20] In sum, the empirical results show that longer exposure to and better knowledge of the standard do not result in convergence toward standard features. On the contrary, where the localized features are identical to the standard features and change is in progress toward supralocal features, the educated speakers diverge most frequently from the standard and localized features and lead the change in the direction of supralocal features. What determines the course (and success) of a language change is not how similar the feature is to a standard form. It therefore follows that proficiency in the standard variety and its determinants, such as formal education, is not the best parameter of speaker categorization. At the same time, since education has been shown to correlate with linguistic usage it must be the case that it denotes something of relevance to linguistic usage.

[19] The emphatic interdental and stop sounds have a different historical development. In Al-Wer (2003) I argue that, unlike the plain interdental and stop sounds, no mergers are involved in moving from emphatic interdental to the emphatic stop counterpart and that this development should be analysed as a straightforward case of sound change from interdental to stop (rather than merger) in the modern dialects.

[20] By using these lexical items they do not of course change their phonology in the direction of the standard variety. On the contrary, their phonology was in fact changing in a direction away from the standard variety. Similar findings are found in Holes (1987); Abdel-Jawad & Suleiman (1990); Haeri (1996).

Table 10.1 [θ] variation in Amman

	[t]	N
High	59%	284
Middle	34%	164
Low	7%	34

I have suggested that education may be a proxy variable that acts on behalf of the degree of closeness or openness of individuals' social networks and the range of contacts they have contracted within and outside the community. The reason that sampling the speakers according to level of education has provided some neat correlations in the past is because it so happened that, in these Arabic-speaking communities that were investigated, the highly educated individuals and the most mobile individuals are the same people. In my research in Jordan, for instance, all of the highly educated individuals in the older age groups (above 50 years) were educated abroad since no institutions of higher education were available in the country; among the younger generations, all of the highly educated (university level) had to leave their hometowns to go to university.

To test this hypothesis, I reanalyzed parts of the data collected in 1987 from the city of Sult (Jordan) (Al-Wer 1991) and examined 42 speakers individually with respect to their use of the variable (θ). The linguistic data were correlated with the speakers' network of contacts inside the town, contact with the community of the nearby capital city of Amman, their backgrounds, activities, and socialization habits.[21] The results of this reanalysis (Al-Wer 2002) provide convincing evidence that amount of contact with the community of Amman (where the use of the innovative feature [t] is at an advanced stage), integration in the local community, and engagement in local issues and future plans are important factors that correlated with linguistic usage. Following are some details about these results.[22]

The overall statistics for the three educational groups—high (university), middle (high school), and low (elementary)—with respect to their use of the innovative variant [t] in words with etymological [θ] (e.g., θgiil "heavy") are presented in Table 10.1 (100% = [t], 0% = [θ]).

In the first group, the highly educated, the individual scores of the 18 speakers in this group vary considerably. At the polar ends, there was one speaker who used [t] consistently and two speakers who did not use it at all. Most speakers were clustered between 54% and 81% use of [t]. Toward the top end, in addition to the speaker who used [t] consistently, there are two further speakers whose scores are 95% and 81%. These three

[21] Of course this is not an ideal situation as far as methodological rigor goes but was worth exploring. In hindsight, social network should have been integrated and quantified as a method of sampling from the start.

[22] See Al-Wer (2002) for the full details of these results and their analysis.

speakers are most responsible for skewing the group's score upward. All three of them were educated at Arab universities abroad, two of them lived in the suburbs, one of them was a daily commuter to Amman, and her children also went to schools in Amman. Two of them were close friends and mostly socialized together. All three were very critical of the local community; they neither enjoyed living there nor appreciated the benefits of living in a close-knit community. None of them participated in voluntary work or voted in the local elections.

In the middle educational group (14 speakers), 4 young speakers did not use [t] at all, thus maintaining a consistent usage of the local variant [θ]. This subgroup of speakers had known one another since childhood and had been working together in the local post office. Outside work, they had a regular weekly get-together. Their network was based on shared interests, beliefs, outlook, and lifestyle as well as similar social backgrounds. In L. Milroy's terms, this group represents a (locally oriented) tight-knit social network, which protects and supports its members and acts as a mechanism that enforces the local norms of social behavior, including the local linguistic norm. A social network analysis of these data thus provides important information not only about the use of innovative features but also about the maintenance of local features.[23]

In Arab societies in a transitional phase to a modern type of society in economy and lifestyle, education tends to be the main channel through which upward social mobility can be achieved for the majority of the population. Individuals striving to attain higher education tend to expand their outside contacts. Thus, we often find that the speakers in the lowest educational group generally have limited outside contact. In the Sult sample, for example, the speakers in the lowest educational group (10 speakers) were the most conservative, in the sense that they used the local features most often (of all variables not just (θ)). Most of these speakers were also unemployed and rarely traveled outside the town. However, one speaker in this group stands out clearly as an innovator: she scored 72% of [t], 70% of [ʒ] (for local [dʒ]), and 45% of [d] (for local [ð]). At the time of the research, she was 21 years old and was employed as a caretaker at a college on the outskirts of Sult. Compared with the other speakers in this group, she had more opportunity for access to (trendy) linguistic innovations through daily interactions with the young college students. In a model based on access to the target features and contact, rather than educational level, this speaker would not be exceptional; there is a meaningful correlation between amount of variation in her speech and her social characteristics.

Education is clearly a simple, almost ready-made model of speaker classification. However, although it appears to correlate with linguistic usage, its usefulness as a speaker sampling tool in Arabic research may be only temporary as a result of ongoing social change. We might expect that once the developmental phase in these societies is

[23] Lesley Milroy's (1987) research in Belfast in the late 1970s is concerned precisely with maintenance of inner-city working-class Belfast linguistic features. To my knowledge, among studies of variation in Arabic, only Muhamad Jabeur's (1987) study in Rades, Tunisia, employs the social network approach as a sampling technique as well as an analytical tool.

completed and education is not the only channel via which contact and upward social mobility can be achieved, as a speaker variable "education" will run its course of utility.[24]

The methodological and analytical problems outlined in this and the previous sections are concomitants of an approach that is premised upon "diglossia" and proceeds in a *top-down* fashion toward analyzing variation in Arabic as an opposition between standard and nonstandard features, thus relegating sociolinguistic research to a confirmatory rather than an exploratory role. The following section discusses the validity and repercussions of this approach.

10.4 The "Diglossia" Model and Its Implications for the Study of Variation in Arabic

Almost four decades have passed since the first appearance of studies on variation in Arabic, yet we find that Arabic data play no role in the formulation of generalizations or theoretical frameworks in sociolinguistics. If Arabic data are mentioned in texts, they are cited as rather irksome anomalies. The failure to make an impact is a symptom that these data are gathered, analyzed, and presented in a fashion that is unsuited to the objective scientific study of language. In my view the fundamental problem lies in one of the most pervasive traditions in Arabic sociolinguistic research, which starts with diglossia as a framework for the analysis of variation in Arabic. For one thing, this approach has severed the natural connection between Arabic dialectology and Arabic sociolinguistics and has presented variation in Arabic as a case of opposition between standard and nonstandard features. The problem pointed out in this context is not concerned with investigations whose aim is to look at the ways the diglossic situation is functionalized as a stylistic resource by certain groups of speakers for specific purposes, but with the assumption that this circumstance is the key to understanding *variation* in Arabic or that this subset of data envelops the structure of variation in Arabic. The most serious misconceptions that emanate from this approach are explained as follows.

10.4.1 Dimensions of Variation Are Uniform

Since diglossia is prevalent in all Arabic-speaking societies, taking the diglossic situation as the starting point of sociolinguistic analyses is tantamount to assuming that

[24] It is also worth noting that the vast majority of research studies on Arabic use adult speakers only in cases where it was practically possible to use educational level as a way of speaker selection. In more recent studies where children and teenagers are included in the sample the results show them to be the most innovative groups; see, for instance, the results in Al-Qouz (2009) and Al-Wer (2007).

the structure of linguistic variation in different Arabic-speaking societies is invariant. Thus, there is no need to supply the social context, and the independent variables can be treated as abstract notions that do not relate to the life of the community. One aspect of this practice is the tendency to generalize patterns that were found in a particular community to Arabic in general without reason to believe that this one case is representative. On the contrary, the data show that, in Arabic as in all other languages, linguistic variation and change are structured by an interaction between linguistic and social variables, and both types of constraints are peculiar to each dialect and each community. Importantly, the linguistic constraints on variation are dictated by the respective native Arabic dialects of each community, not by structures or features found in the standard variety. The failure to factor these basic facts into the analysis leads to all sorts of misleading conclusions. For instance, in studies that used samples of speakers from different dialectal background, the linguistic characteristics of the native dialects of the speakers are not factored into the analysis, and the speakers of different Arabic dialects are treated as standing at equal distance from standard Arabic features regardless of their native grammars (the linguistic characteristics of their native dialects). It is thereby tacitly assumed that all native speakers of Arabic have an invariant grammar, that of the standard variety, from which they derive whatever dialectal forms they happen to use in daily interactions. For instance, Abdel-Jawad and Awwad's (1989) investigation of the use of the interdental sounds, the sample consists of speakers of different dialects from Jordan, Syria, and Egypt. The statistical analysis begins by calculating the average usage of the interdental realizations, which are referred to as *standard variants* even though all of the local Jordanian dialects have the same sounds. No information is supplied about the dialectal backgrounds of the Jordanian speakers; they are labeled as speakers of urban Jordanian dialects. The use of interdental versus stop sounds in Jordan's urban centers is variable, but it is constrained by the speakers' dialectal background: those whose native dialects are indigenous Jordanian dialects or rural Palestinian dialects have interdental sounds; and those whose native dialects are urban Palestinian or urban Syrian do not have the interdental sounds. These important constraints on variation are not factored into the analysis (see Abdel-Jawad and Awwad 1989: 263–265). The same method of analysis is used to make conclusions about the distribution of the use of the variants by sex. It is concluded that "men use the standard variants [i.e., the interdental sounds] more often than women do, whereas women use the socially prestigious forms... more often than men do" (ibid., 264). Here, the problem emanating from the failure to take account of the dialectal backgrounds of the speakers is compounded by using what was in the first place a misleading description (labeling the interdental sounds as the standard variants without accounting for the fact that these sounds are at the same time characteristic of the local dialects) as a basis for the description of a different level of variation: sex differentiation. Naturally, these speakers (men and women) could have simply been maintaining their normal realization of these sounds rather than approximating to or diverging from the standard. More problems arise when inter-dialectal comparisons are made (Jordanian–Syrian–Egyptian). In these results (ibid., 267, Table 10) the Jordanians were found to use the interdental sounds of all variables more frequently than using the stop or sibilant sounds and more than the Syrian and Egyptian speakers. This is obviously a highly predictable result given that the Jordanians have a native facility toward the use of these sounds, which is unavailable to the speakers of Damascus and Cairo Arabic.

Similarly, misleading conclusions can arise by failing to take account of the fact that the social constraints on variation in Arab communities vary quite considerably, even in geographically adjacent and culturally very similar societies.

10.4.2 Standard Features Have the Highest Rate of Approval and Enjoy Unquestionable Prestige

This is an assumption without empirical evidence. In fact, the linguistic evidence that is available can be read as an antithesis to this assumption since the empirical data show that many dialectal features are abandoned even though they are identical to standard features. For example, at the level of segmental phonology, in Levantine dialects the standard features [q θ ð dʒ] are abandoned in favor of the nonstandard counterparts [ʔ t d ʒ]. The standard diphthongal pronunciations of /aw/ and /ay/ are abandoned for the nonstandard (and in some cases supralocal) monophthongal pronunciations /o:/ and /e:/ in Tunisia (Jabeur 1987). At the morphosyntactic level, speakers of dialects that, similarly to the standard, maintain gender distinction in the second- and third-person pronouns, pronoun suffixes, pronominal suffixes, verbal inflections, and nominal endings abandon this system in favor of a system that neutralizes gender in these forms and paradigms.[25]

Standard Arabic clearly has a function in Arabic-speaking societies, as the norm used in formal written and spoken domains; it undoubtedly also has a psychological claim on native speakers of Arabic. But it does not play a role, nor does it have a normative effect on the structure of variation in the core domains of phonology, morphology, and syntax, as explained in the next point.

10.4.3 The Trajectory of Linguistic Change Is in the Direction of the Standard Features

A corollary to approaching variation in Arabic as an opposition between standard and nonstandard features is that in cases of variation where one of the variants happens to be identical to a standard feature and linguistic change is in progress, the trajectory of the change is anticipated to be in the direction of the standard feature. Numerous

[25] Anecdotal evidence points in the same direction: pupils generally dislike Arabic lessons; upward social mobility is not attained by speaking standard Arabic but by adhering to the most prestigious local dialects or by using a foreign language.

examples from empirical research can be cited to refute this prediction. For example, many of the traditional dialects in the Gulf region have a glide [y] as a realization of Arabic *Jim*. The most recent investigation of this feature in Bahrain is by Muna Al-Qouz (2009). This is a particularly good example because in this case we have data in real time from various sources, most importantly from the research by Clive Holes in the 1970s (Holes 1987). Al-Qouz's investigation thus presents data from Manama 30 years later. In Bahrain, linguistic variation and change is in the first place constrained by the speakers' sectarian affiliation. There are two major dialects: the more influential Arab dialect, which is numerically in the minority and which has the glide variant [y]; and the less influential Baharna dialect, which has the affricate palatal [dʒ] variant as in Standard Arabic. Holes reports that the Arab group largely does not show variation in the use of *Jim* (especially in the core dialectal lexical items), but the Baharna speakers replace their traditional (and standard) palatal variant by the glide variant. And 30 years later, one no longer finds segregated towns or neighborhoods; rather, the two groups can be found to reside in all parts of the city, and their children go to the same schools. Importantly, too, in the same period, illiteracy has decreased sharply, and the overall level of education has increased. In other words, there are no social barriers to prevent the two groups from interacting freely, and exposure to the standard variety has extended to larger sectors of the populations of both communities. Al-Qouz finds that the use of the glide variant has become the norm in the speech of the younger Baharna group and that the palatal variant occurs only occasionally, most often fossilized in a few lexical items. The development in Bahrain with respect to this feature is not isolated but seems to be a Gulf-wide development (Holes 1990). In Kuwait, Taqi (2010) shows an identical development among the young speakers from the Ajam group who were found to use the glide variant in place of their heritage feature [dʒ]. The determining factors of the geographical and social diffusion of the glide variant have to do with the social power of the Arab group in the case of Bahrain, and in the case of Kuwait, by the size of demographic representation as well as the social dominance of the dialects which have the glide The similarity or distance from the Standard feature is totally irrelevant in this domain. Many more such examples can be cited from various modern Arabic dialects.

10.4.4 Data from Arabic Contradict Generalizations

Insofar as sociolinguistics in general is concerned, the most serious outcome of analyzing variation in Arabic in a top-down fashion is that it has led sociolinguists up the garden path in searching for interpretations of gender-differentiated patterns. For instance, on the basis of the Arabic data presented in research from the 1970s and 1980s, which claimed that Arab women contradict the pattern found elsewhere by *not* using standard prestigious features as frequently as Arab men, Labov (2001: 270) writes:

> There is therefore a widespread reversal of the positions of men and women predicted by Principle 2[26] in two Muslim-dominated societies [Iran and the Arab World].

Labov also notes and seems to accept the reinterpretation offered by Haeri (1987) that the Arabic data do not in fact contradict the pattern. But he concludes:

> Principle 2 is a strong and broad generalization that must be explained by women's social role in the speech community. The cases that depart from the general pattern are from well-defined cultural areas: the Far East... and the Near East. (P. 271)

The argument that is commonly advanced to interpret Arab women's presumed divergent linguistic behavior rests on the presumption that Arab women play a less prominent role in public life, without specifying *which women* of *which Arab society*. The important point to stress here is that Arabic-speaking societies are wrongly presented as one culturally and socially invariant unit, where the roles of men and women are polarized and rigidly defined: men are the sole operators in public life and women are the homemakers. Not only does inadequate methodology yield inaccurate data (as demonstrated already), but also such data end up forming the basis of sweeping generalizations that become entrenched and difficult to correct.[27]

The interpretation of sex-differentiated patterns of variation in Arabic was revised by Mohammad H. Ibrahim (1986). Additionally, Ibrahim points out a number of problems in the interpretation of Arabic data, which stem from what he identifies as confusing the notions of "standard variety" with "prestigious variety," and suggests making a distinction between the status of the standard variety as a transnational norm and the spoken dialects that have their own hierarchy of prestige at the local level. Following Ibrahim's line of argumentation, Niloofar Haeri (1987) offers a more realistic explanation for male–female linguistic differences in Cairo Arabic, which refutes the claim made earlier that sex-differentiated patterns in spoken Arabic contradict the general pattern. I argue (Al-Wer 1997) that the involvement of standard Arabic in sociolinguistic interpretation seems to be based on ideological considerations rather than on empirical data. I suggest there that, by setting the standard variety aside, paradoxical patterns disappear and findings from Arabic regarding gender differentiation fall in line with generalizations in sociolinguistics that have been made on the basis of data from a wide range of languages and societies.

The potential for fallacy that lies behind the top-down model of analysis of variation in Arabic is demonstrated by the fact that such a model does not hold up to the empirical data, for as soon as one tries to build in the data the model simply sinks and collapses.

[26] Principle 2 states: "For stable sociolinguistic variables, women show a lower rate of stigmatized variants and a higher rate of prestige variants than men" (Labov 2001: 266).

[27] Of the mainstream sociolinguistic publications since the revision of the interpretation of sex-differentiated language variation in Arabic, only Jack Chambers (2003: 157–162) revises the case of Arabic correctly.

A sound analytical model, on the other hand, is one that begins by grounding the linguistic data in the linguistic system from which they are derived (the local dialect) and the social context with which they interact (the local community), as illustrated in the next section.

10.5 The Alternative Model: A Locally Based Analysis and Interpretation

A framework of analysis that begins with the locality and the local dialect, sampling the speakers according to independent variables that relate to the community's history and evolution, identifying linguistic variables that are meaningful and relevant, and deriving the interpretations from the local community's structure, characteristics, and the daily pursuits of its members is a model that is capable not only of accounting for language use but also of being flexible enough to accommodate, and perhaps uncover, new dimensions of variation. These are the underlying principles of sociolinguistic research in general, which have been recently incorporated in a number of insightful research studies in various localities around the Arab World. The developments seen in handling Arabic data and Arab speech communities also reflect advancements in sociolinguistic research in general.[28]

In the remainder of this chapter, I will cite four case studies that exemplify some of the new dimensions of variation in modern Arabic societies and identify new linguistic variables.

10.5.1 A New Linguistic Variable in An Old City: (r) in Damascus

The first case is an investigation of variation and change in Damascus, completed in 2008 by Hanadi Ismail.[29] Ismail's analysis of the community's history in relation to the socioeconomic changes in Damascus shows that, as a result of the physical expansion of the city that began in the early 1970s, new dimensions of linguistic variation emerged that related to two aspects of life in the city: residence in a traditional inner-city district (Shaghoor); and residence in a new satellite suburb (Dummar). These in turn broadly correlate with two different "life modes," self-employed and professional, respectively.

[28] We no longer see, for instance, large-scale surveys of the sort conducted by Labov in New York in 1968, but now investigations are smaller and more focused.

[29] Full details of this research are in Ismail (2008); see also Ismail (2007, 2009).

Table 10.2 Innovative (= non-trill) "r" variants in two Damascus neighborhoods (all correlations statistically significant)

	Male	Female
Shaghoor		
Y	29% (406)	23% (407)
M	4% (294)	5% (449)
O	1% (380)	3% (393)
Dummar		
Y	19% (422)	27% (499)
M	21% (414)	10% (393)
O	4% (379)	20% (427)

Note: Y = young; M = middle age; O = old age.
Source: Based on Ismail 2007: 207, fig. 9.8.

Ismael uses the construct of life mode (Højrup 2003) to explain observed linguistic differences.

One of the new variables identified in Damascus is /r/, which is undergoing a process of lenition. Four types of variants were identified. Besides the inherited trill, there are three innovative values: retroflex approximate [ɻ], fricative [ɣ], and aveolar approximant [ɹ]. In all, 47,603 tokens were coded for five phonetic environments. The results of the GoldVarb analysis, adapted for presentation here, are given in Table 10.2.

Table 10.2 shows correlations of the use of the most advanced /r/ variant with age, gender, and neighborhood. Statistically, all correlations were found to be significant and the variable of age was found to have the most significant effect, thus indicating a change in progress toward an approximant type of /r/. The table also shows that the locus of the change is the suburb, where the new pronunciation appears in significant proportions in the speech of the middle- and old-age groups as well. The gender effect is particularly interesting: here we notice that, while in the suburb the female speakers have a clear lead, in the inner-city locality of Shaghoor it is the young male speakers that lead the change over all other groups. This particular finding is explained by Ismail in relation to the employment situation; at the time of research, all except one of the women were unemployed, and all of the men were employed in the retail business, which brought them in direct and regular contact with customers from all walks of life and all parts of the city.

In addition to identifying a new linguistic variable, the example from Damascus shows how research that is designed to incorporate the social and economic dynamics of the local community is capable of correlating the variables in a meaningful way. These data also provide a well-analyzed example of a male-led linguistic change.[30]

[30] Male-led changes are rather hard to come by in the sociolinguistic literature; for a summary, see Labov (1990).

10.5.2 New Dimensions of Variation: Style and Dialect Leveling in Casablanca

The second example comes from Atiqa Hachimi's research in Casablanca (2005).[31] In this case, Hachimi shows how growth and increasing heterogeneity in the city's population have disrupted the old rural–urban dichotomy, the once dominant characteristic of Moroccan city dialects and identities.[32] In Casablanca, mass migration has created a new linguistic urban model, represented by the newly formed koines: Fessi (from Fez) and Casablancan. The research investigated the linguistic and social outcomes of the Fessi–Casablancan contact in Casablanca. Hachimi's research employs the "communities of practice" method for the first time in Arabic research.[33] Three linguistic variables were investigated: two phonological, (r) and (q); and one morphosyntactic 2FSG (-i) (which concerns gender neutralization versus the maintenance of gender distinction in the second-person feminine subject clitic). These variables distinguish between the Casablancan and Fessi (Fez) dialects. The results overall show that the speakers use the linguistic forms as a resource in the construction of identities and different styles that are directly related to their lives and daily pursuits in the city. In addition to the old identities, such as "pure Fessi" and their linguistic correlates (maintenance of the heritage variants), the speakers construct hybrid identities that correlate with hybrid linguistic behavior. For instance, for a Fessi to become Casablancan, the heritage variants [ʔ] and [q] are selectively filtered in favor of [g] in [ga:l], and Casablancan trilled /r/ is adopted instead of the Fessi approximant [ɹ]. The overall conclusions show very clearly that in a complex social structure the linguistic variables can be interpreted as stylistic variation reflecting different identities created through combining resources from different linguistic stock. The stylistic shifts in the informant's speech are dictated not by the diglossic situation or by a shift of task or topic but by a dynamic that is directly related to the everyday realities that inhabitants of the heterogeneous city have to negotiate on daily basis in an attempt to maximize gain and minimize loss in social interactions.

10.5.3 Migrant Groups, New Social Variable, and Linguistic Constraints: (k) in Jeddah

The phenomenon of migrant groups in large cities is commonly found all over the Arab World, which provides an exciting area of research on variation, dialect acquisition, and contact-induced linguistic change.[34] The research reviewed in this section is by Aziza

[31] Also see Hachimi (2007).

[32] Also see Miller (2005: 904–906).

[33] In her study in Detroit, Penelope Eckert (2000) introduces this method into sociolinguistic research; it employs an ethnographic approach and investigates speakers' behavior closely in their communities of practice (Eckert 2000).

[34] A particularly interesting research in this field is Catherine Miller's (2005) study of Upper Egyptian migrants in Cairo, which investigated phonological, morphological, and morphosyntactic adaptations.

Al-Essa (2009), which investigated the linguistic developments in the speech of Najdi migrants in the Hijazi city of Jeddah.[35]

The investigation included nine phonological and morphophonemic variables. I will focus on the variable (k), which concerns the affrication of [k] in the environment of front vowels and close back vowels (Cantineau 1960, Johnston 1963). Al-Essa's analysis of this feature in the context of a dialect contact situation shows that the variation that results from the contact situation in Jeddah is quite complex. First, her analysis reveals that the process of affrication of [k] to [ts] differs depending on whether the consonant occurs in the stem, as in *mika:n* > *mitsa:n* "a place," or in the suffix as in *ʔumm-ik* > *ʔumm-its* "your (f) mother." The second variable concerns [k] in the second-person feminine suffix; therefore, it was analyzed as a morphophonemic feature, while affrication of [k] in the stem was analyzed as a phonological feature. Furthermore, while affrication occurs in the phonological variable only in the environment of front vowels, variation in the morphophonemic variable is also present in the environment of close back vowels, such as *ʔubu:-ts* "your (f) father." With respect to the phonological variable, that is, [k] in the stem, the results show that affrication is disappearing very fast, with an overall usage of only 6% of a total of 668 tokens.

On the other hand, in the case of [-k] in the suffix, the data show much more complex patterns. First, the affricated (heritage) variant shows a considerably higher rate of maintenance, 22%, or nearly four times the frequency of occurrence of the phonological variable. Second, interdialectal forms are used. Al-Essa explains the results for the morphophonemic variable as relating to (a) the complexity of the distribution of the feminine suffix in the target dialect (Jeddah) vis-à-vis the Najdi dialect, and (b) the fact that [ts] versus [k] carries gender information; that is, it has a morphosyntactic function in the Najdi dialect. The complexity of the suffix in the target dialect can be seen in the following schema, which outlines the forms found in both the Najdi and Hijazi dialects:

	Najdi	*Hijazi*	
Masc.	-ik	-ak	
Fem	-its	ik\C-,	ki\V-

Notice that the Hijazi feminine form *–ik* is identical to the Najdi masculine form; thus, *ʔummik* is "your (m) mother" in Najdi but is "your (f) mother" in Hijazi. The Najdi dialect relies on the change in consonant to signal gender distinction while the vowels in both forms are identical (phonetically [ə] or thereabouts), whereas the Hijazi dialect relies on vowel change to signal gender, and in the case of the feminine ending the form varies morphophonologically according to the preceding sound, *-ik* before a consonant and *-ki* before a vowel, thus *ʔumm-ik*, but *ʔabu:-ki*. Thus, for the Najdi speakers to accommodate to the Hijazi forms correctly, they would have to (a) deaffricate / ts/, (b) acquire the vowel distinction, and (c) observe the phonological conditioning of the choice between *–ik* and *-ki*. These linguistic constraints seem to explain the finding that deaffrication in the suffix lags behind deaffrication in the stem by a wide margin.

[35] Also see Al-Essa 2008.

Additionally, Al-Essa finds instances of both hypercorrection in the target data, for instance *-ki* used by the Najdi speakers not only postvocalically (as in the target dialect) but also after a consonant, such as *maʕki* "with you (f)," and neutralization of contrasts, such as *ʔubu:k* "your (f) father" (Al-Essa 2009: 155–173). With respect to contact, the results showed positive and systematic correlation between amount of contact (quantified according to the index) and use of the target variants. Al-Essa's research thus provides invaluable innovative methodological and analytical insights for future research.

10.5.4 Koineisation and the Formation of New Dialects: The Phonology of the Feminine Ending in Amman

In some cases, the linguistic developments represent not continuation of change in a dialect but the formation of a new dialect from scratch. A case in point is the capital city of Jordan, Amman. As an Arabic-speaking community, its history started only in 1921 when it was declared the capital city of Jordan. From then on, the city's population grew steadily and at points abruptly, especially between 1950 and 1990. Currently it is home to 1.6 million. The two major groups that constitute the city's population are the Jordanians and the Palestinians. With such a recent history and no truly native population, Amman naturally does not have a traditional dialect, but a new dialect is in the process of forming. The ingredients that went into the formation of the new dialect are a range of Jordanian and Palestinian dialects.[36]

In 1998, I launched a project to investigate the process of the formation of the new dialect. So far, 13 linguistic features have been analyzed and shown to be at an advanced stage of focusing. This section cites the data concerning the feminine ending /ah/.

This feature concerns the raising of the feminine ending /a/ to /e/. Urban Palestinian dialects and Jordanian dialects differ in the phonology and phonetics of the suffix. Jordanian dialects (central and northern dialects) use /a/ in all environments except after coronal sounds, in which case the ending is raised to a half-open vowel. [ɛ] (i.e., /a/ is the default variant)

/*ħilwa*/ "pretty," /*ʃara:ka*/ "partnership," /*biʃʕa*/ "ugly" vs. /*madanijjɛ*/ "modern or urban," /*fattɛ*/ "Fatte, a traditional dish," /*mdʒawwazɛ*/ "married," /*sanɛ*/ "a year,"

On the other hand, in urban Palestinian the feminine ending is realized as /e/ except after velarized, emphatic, and pharyngeal sounds where /a/ is used (i.e., /e/ is the default variant). The raised variant is [e] (cardinal vowel 2 or closer).

/*ħilwe*/ "pretty," /*saʕbe*/ "difficult," /*mixtilfe*/ "different" vs. /*manṭiqa*/ "area/region," /*ruxṣa*/ "a licence," /*sulṭa*/ "authority," /*ʒa:mʕa*/ "university," /*mari:ḍa*/ "ill."

[36] See Al-Wer (2003, 2007) for details about the process of the formation of the new dialect.

In Amman, the contact between speakers of the two types of dialects has resulted in the emergence of a *fudged* form, which combines Palestinian phonology and Jordanian phonetics, that is, /a/ is raised everywhere except after velarized, pharyngeal, and emphatic sounds, and the raised variant is phonetically half-open [ɛ] (cardinal vowel 3). Regional koineization in this case also exerts an influence on the course of developments in Amman, seeing as the urban Palestinian system is identical to the system found in all of the major city dialects in the Levant (identical in phonology but not in phonetics).

The previously cited examples represent the diversity of situations that influence linguistic variation and change in modern Arabic. In none of these situations do we see the standard variety play any role in the structure of variation or in the dynamics of the change.

References

Abdel-Jawad, Hassan. 1981. *Lexical and phonological variation in spoken Arabic of Amman*. PhD diss., University of Pennsylvania.

Abdel-Jawad, Hassan and Mohammad Awwad. 1989. Reflexes of Classical Arabic interdentals: A study in historical Sociolinguistics. *Linguistische Berichte* 122: 259–282.

Abdel-Jawad, Hassan and Saleh Suleiman 1990. Lexical conditioning of phonological variation. *Language Sciences* 12: 291–330.

Al-Amadidhi, Darwish. 1985. *Lexical and sociolinguistic variation in Qatari Arabic*. PhD diss., University of Edinburgh.

Al-Essa, Aziza 2008. *Najdi speakers in Hijaz: A sociolinguistic investigation of dialect contact in Jeddah*. PhD diss., University of Essex.

——. 2009. When Najd meets Hijaz: Dialect contact in Jeddah. In *Arabic dialectology*, ed. Enam Al-Wer and Rudolf de Jong, 203–222. Amsterdam: Brill.

Al-Jehani, Nasir M. 1985. *Sociostylistic stratification of Arabic in Makkah*. PhD diss., University of Michigan.

Al-Khatib Mahmoud. 1988. *Sociolinguistic change in an expanding urban context*. Ph.D. diss., University of Durham.

Al-Wer Enam. 1991. *Phonological variation in the speech of women from three urban areas in Jordan*. PhD diss., University of Essex.

1997.Arabic between reality and ideology, *International Journal of Applied Linguistics* 7:2, 251–265.

——. 2002. Jordanian and Palestinian dialects in contact: Vowel raising in Amman. In *Language change: The interplay of internal, external and extra-linguistic factors*, ed. Mari Jones and Edith Esch, 63–79. Berlin: Mouton de Gruyter.

——. 2003. New dialect formation: The focusing of -kum in Amman. In *Social dialectology: In honour of Peter Trudgill*, ed. David Britain and Jenny Cheshire, 59–67. Amsterdam: Benjamins.

——. 2007. The formation of the dialect of Amman. In *Arabic in the city: Issues in dialect contact and language variation*, ed. Catherine Miller, Enam Al-Wer, Dominique Caubet, and Janet Watson, 55–76. New York: Routledge.

Al-Qouz, Muna. 2009. *Dialect contact, acquisition and change among Mananma youth, Bahrain*. PhD diss., University of Essex.

Bergsträsser, Gotthelf. 1915. Sprachatlas von Syrien und Palästina. *Zeitschrift des Deutschen Palästina-Vereins* 38: 169–222.
Blanc, Haim. 1969. The fronting of the Semitic G and the qāl-gāl dialect split in Arabic. In *Proceedings of the International Conference on Semitic Studies, Jerusalem, 7–37.*
Cantineau, Jean. 1936/1937. Etudes sur quelques parlers nomades arabe d'Orient. *Annales de l'Institut d'Etudes Orientales (Université d'Alger)*, II, 1–118; III, 119–227.
——. (1940). *Les parlers arabes du Ḥōrān. Atlas.* Paris: Klincksieck.
——. 1960. *Cours de phonétique arabe: Suivi de notions générales de phonétique et de phonologie.* Paris: Klincksieck.
Chambers, Jack K. 2003. *Sociolinguistic theory.* Oxford: Blackwell.
Eckert, Penelope. 2000. *Linguistic variation as social practice.* Oxford: Blackwell.
Eckert, Penelope and John Rickford. 2001. *Style and sociolinguistic variation.* Cambridge, UK: Cambridge University Press.
Fisher, John. 1958. Social influences on the choice of a linguistic variant. *Word* 14: 47–56.
Gordon, Elizabeth and Tony Deverson. 1998. *New Zealand English and English in New-Zealand.* Auckland: New House Publishers.
Gordon, Elizabeth, Lyle Campbell, Jennifer Hay, Margaret Maclagan, Andrea Sudbury, and Peter Trudgill. 2004. *New Zealand English: Its origins and evolution.* Cambridge, UK: Cambridge University Press.
Hachimi, Atiqa. 2005. *Dialect leveling, maintenance and urban identity in Morocco.* PhD diss., University of Hawaii.
——. 2007. Becoming Casablancan: Fessis in Casablanca as a case study. In *Arabic in the city: Issues in language variation and change*, ed. Catherine Miller, Enam Al-Wer, Dominique Caubet, and Janet Watson, 97–122. London: Routledge.
Haeri, Niloofar. 1987. Male/Female Differences in Speech: an Alternative Interpretation. *In Variation in Language: NWAV-XV at Stanford: Proceedings of the Fifteenth Annual Conference on New Ways of Analyzing Variation*, edited by Denning, Keith M., Sharon Inkelas, John R. Rickford, and Faye McNair-Knox, 173–183. Stanford, CA: Stanford University.
——. 1996. *The Sociolinguistic market in Cairo: Gender, class, and education.* London: Kegan Paul International.
Hary, Benjamin. 1996. The Ǧīm/Gīm in colloquial urban Egyptian Arabic. In *Israel Oriental studies XVI, studies in modern Semitic languages*, ed. Shlomo Izre'el and Shlomo Raz, 154–168.
Højrup, Thomas. 2003. *State, culture and life-modes.* Ashgate, UK: Aldershot.
Holes, Clive. 1987. *Language in a modernising Arab state: The case of Bahrain.* London: Kegan Paul International.
——. 1990. *Gulf Arabic.* London: RoutledgeCurzon.
Horvath, Barbara. 1985. *Variation in Australian English: The sociolects of Sydney.* Cambridge, UK: Cambridge University Press.
Ibrahim, Muhammad H. 1986. Standard and prestige language: A problem in Arabic sociolinguistics. *Anthropological Linguistics* 28: 115–126.
Ismail, Hanadi. 2007. The urban and suburban modes: Patterns of linguistic variation and change in Damascus. In *Arabic in the city: Issues in dialect contact and language variation*, ed. Catherine Miller, Enam Al-Wer, Dominique Caubet, and Janet Watson, 188–213. London: Routledge.
——. 2008. *Suburbia and the inner-city: Patterns of linguistic variation and change in Damascus.* PhD diss., University of Essex.

——. 2009. The Variable (h) in Damascus: Analysis of a stable variable. In *Arabic dialectology*, ed. Enam Al-Wer and Rudolf de Jong, 249–272. Amsterdam: Brill.

Jabeur, Mohamed (1987). *A Sociolinguistic study in Rades: Tunisia*. PhD diss., University of Reading.

Johnstone, T. M. 1963. The affrication of "kaf" and "gaf" in the Arabic dialects of the Arabian Peninsula. *Journal of Semitic Studies* 8: 210–226.

Kurath, Hans, et al. 1941 *Linguistic atlas of New England*. Providence RI: American Council of Learned Societies.

Labov, William. 1963. The social motivation of a sound change. *Word* 19: 273–309.

——. 1970. The study of language in its social context. *Studium Generale* 23: 66–84.

——. 1972. *Sociolinguistic patterns*. Philadelphia: University of Pennsylvania Press.

——. 1990. The intersection of sex and social class in the course of linguistic change. *Language Variation and Change* 2: 205–254.

——. 2001. *Principles of linguistic change: Social factors*. Oxford: Wiley-Blackwell.

Miller, Catherine. 2005. Between accommodation and resistance: Upper Egyptian migrants in Cairo. *Linguistics* 43: 903–956.

Milroy, James, Lesley Milroy, Sue Hartley, and David Walshaw. 1994. Glottal stops and Tyneside glottalization: Competing patterns of variation and change in British English. *Language Variation and Change* 6: 327–357.

Milroy, Lesley. 1987. *Language and social networks*. Oxford: Blackwell.

Milroy, Lesley and Matthew Gordon. 2003. *Sociolinguistics: Method and interpretation*. Oxford: Blackwell.

Owens, Jonathan. 1998. *Neighborhood and ancestry: Variation in the spoken Arabic of Maiduguri (Nigeria)*. Impact: Studies in Language and Society 4. Amsterdam: John Benjamins.

——. [2006] 2009². *A Linguistic history of Arabic*. Oxford: Oxford University Press.

Schilling-Estes, Natalie. 2002. Investigating stylistic variation. In *The handbook of language variation and change*, ed. Jack Chambers, Peter Trudgill, and Natalie Schilling-Estes, 375–401. Oxford: Blackwell.

Schmidt, Richard. 1974. *Sociolinguistic variation on spoken Egyptian Arabic: A re-examination of the concept of diglossia*. PhD diss., Brown University.

Shorab, Ghazi. 1982. *Models of socially significant linguistic variation: The case of Palestinian Arabic*. PhD diss., State University of New York at Buffalo.

Taqi, Hanan. 2010. *Two ethnicities, three generations: Phonological variation and change in Kuwait*. PhD diss., University of Newcastle.

Trudgill, Peter. 1974. *The Social differentiation of English in Norwich*. Cambridge, UK: Cambridge University Press.

——. 2004. *New-dialect formation: The inevitability of colonial Englishes*. Edinburgh: Edinburgh University Press.

Woidich, Manfred 1993. *Bilbliographie zum Agyptisch-Arabischen*. Ms. Amsterdam, I.M.N.O.

Woidich, Manfred and Elisabeth Zach. 2009. The g/ğ question in Egyptian Arabic revisited. In *Arabic dialectology: In honour of Clive Holes on the occasion of his sixtieth birthday*, ed. Enam Al-Wer and Rudolf de Jong, 41–60. Leiden: Brill.

Wolfram, Walt. 1969. *A sociolinguistic description of Detroit Negro speech*. Washington, DC: Center for Applied Linguistics.

CHAPTER 11

ARABIC FOLK LINGUISTICS

between mother tongue and native language

YASIR SULEIMAN

11.1 Arabic Diglossia: A Port of Entry into a Semiliquid World

This paper deals with some long-standing issues in Arabic sociolinguistics. Its starting point is the concept of diglossia, which has become the port of entry for any discussion of the semiliquid language situation in the Arabic-speaking world. By way of an aside, the concept of *izdiwājiyya lughawiyya* "linguistic duality" was the subject of discussion and debate in the Levant in the 19th century (Khūri 1991), well before Ferguson's seminal study of the topic in 1959 and William Marçais's first use of the term diglossia in 1930. Discussions of this topic in the 1880s were centered on literacy and modernization, but the debates that took place in the emerging press, mainly from the Levant, were inconclusive as to whether diglossia represents an insurmountable hindrance to these societal goals. The fact that we are still debating diglossia and its impact on literacy and modernization in the twenty first century testifies to its durability as a phenomenon and a conceptual tool.

Diglossia is too well-known in the literature to warrant restating here. Criticisms of diglossia are also well-known in the literature. But let me outline what I consider to be the most abiding ones and offer my thoughts on these as a prelude to what I want to say about Arabic folk linguistics. First, as expounded by Ferguson, diglossia is said to be impressionistic and fuzzy (Boussofora-Omar 2006). This is true; but this can hardly be regarded as a criticism, not least because Ferguson did not intend his paper (of some fifteen pages) on diglossia to be of an empirical kind similar to the research we are now accustomed to in the quantitative variationist paradigm with its emphasis on statistical correlations. Ferguson aimed at developing the parameters of the concept in a comparative fashion for further application and elaboration, and he has admirably succeeded in doing so judging by the impact of his research. There is a salutary lesson for us in this as Arabic linguists: we should not be afraid to conduct qualitative research, similar to Ferguson's work on diglossia, because of the ability of this kind of research to tap domains of inquiry which the quantitative method may not be able to delve into owing to the limitations of the correlationst paradigm in its logico-positivist orientation (Suleiman 2011). Ethnographies of language such as Haeri's (2003) study of Egypt, with which I will deal later, is an example of what I have in mind.

Second, it is often said that Ferguson's discussion of diglossia created a dichotomy or a binary opposition between what he termed the high and low varieties of the language, the *fuṣḥā* "standard" and the range of *ʿāmmiyyas* "dialects" in the Arabic speaking world respectively. The "di-" in diglossia may have created this impression of bi-polarity, aided in this regard by Ferguson's attempt at clarity in conceptualizing the two outer ends of the linguistic situation he was describing at the expense of attending to the liquidity of the middle ground, which has been described as "slippery" and "messy" in the literature (Boussofara-Omar 2006: 630). The truth, however, is rather different. Ferguson was aware of intermediate forms of Arabic, including what Mitchell (1986) over two decades later called Educated Spoken Arabic. This is how Ferguson describes this intermediate form of the language (1959: 10):

> A kind of spoken Arabic much used in certain semi-formal or cross-dialectal situations [which] has a highly classical vocabulary with few or no inflectional endings, with certain features of classical syntax, but with a fundamentally colloquial base in morphology and syntax, and a generous admixture of colloquial vocabulary.

Ferguson's view of diglossia is, therefore, more nuanced than the "di-" in the term suggests. He is in fact aware that the spectrum between the end points of diglossia is a continuum of some sort that defies strict categorization. Criticisms that Ferguson's conceptualization of diglossia posited a rigid "categorical" [a better term is categorial] divide between the high and low varieties of the language is, therefore, unwarranted (Mahmoud 1986). In spite of this, the search for the middle ground between the end points of diglossia was driven to some extent by this perceived dissatisfaction with the impression of bipolarity in Ferguson's treatment of this phenomenon. Badawī's well-known five "levels" (*mustawayāt*) of Arabic in Egypt is an attempt at creating a taxonomy that covers the full range of variation between (and involving) the high and low varieties (1973). In a similar vein, Meiseles (1980) recognizes four categories on the diglossic spectrum to overcome the same problem of ill definition. However, the fact that Arabic sociolinguists have not been able to agree on the number of Arabic levels or categories on the diglossic continuum, or on their ontology (whether they are levels/registers/styles or categories of self-contained classification) reflects the semi-liquidity or viscosity of the Arabic language situation at its outer ends and its liquidity in the middle. It further reminds us of the difficulties Ferguson had in drawing up his definition of diglossia.

The third criticism is that Ferguson assigned prestige to the high variety only. It is, I believe, this allocation of prestige that underlies the semi-metaphorical description of the *fuṣḥā* as "high" and the *ʿāmmiyya*s as "low." Ibrahim (1986) argued that this assignment of social value to the outer points of diglossia fails to take account of the prestige of some dialectal forms in the *ʿāmmiyya* domain. While this is true, it is still possible in my view to rescue Ferguson's notion of prestige from this criticism. It is not difficult to argue in this regard that the prestige of an *ʿāmmiyya* form "dialect" is normally pitched in relation to other less prestigious *ʿāmmiyya*s in the orality domain, but hardly ever in my experience to the *fuṣḥā* as the written and standard form of the language. The weakness in Ferguson's position is that he treated prestige as a unitary concept that applies to the full gamut of forms in the language indiscriminately, although it is very clear that he was primarily interested in the allocation of prestige across the written/standard versus oral/dialectal divide.

11.2 Arabic Folk Linguistics

In spite of these criticisms I want to argue that Ferguson's concept of diglossia is, to a large degree, still valid in the way he set it out. My argument is based on folk linguistics (Nieldzielski and Preston 2000), by which I mean the range of views and attitudes people have about their language, including its origin and the myths surrounding it, that "allow us to come closer to the overt or covert orientations, assumptions, and hidden ideologies of the community and how these relate to its linguistic repertoire" (Suleiman 2008: 28). These views are socio-psychological in nature: they tell us something about the role language plays in society as cultural capital and as a site of identity conceptualizations that feed into how the linguistic assets of the community are deployed (or not deployed) in education, the media, law, the religious domain and other fields of societal activity and organization, as well as about the various forms of institutional and grass roots resistance to alternative ways of organizing the public sphere linguistically. In modern linguistic theory, folk linguistic views and attitudes may be found to lack the authority and "objectivity" of the findings of modern linguistics, based as it is on empirical investigation and model building. In spite of this folk linguistics is an important source of information in exploring the role of language in the life of a community. Most Arabic speakers are oblivious of the findings of modern linguistics. This is to some extent true of educationists, whether they are curriculum designers, teachers, inspectors or school administrators. What matters more to these constituencies of professionals in my experience are the socially available conceptualizations of the language, rather than those of modern linguistics, against which they frame their work as practitioners in their respective fields. Tapping these conceptualizations is,[1] therefore, important in understanding

[1] For a classic paper on the topic see Parkinson (1991) which uses the matched guise technique to investigate reactions to various forms of Arabic.

how the public sphere is configured and why it remains resistant to importations from modern linguistics.

Let me illustrate this by exploring the meaning some Arabic speakers attach to the term *al-lugha al-ʿarabiyya* ("the Arabic language"). I have asked fifty illiterate speakers in Amman, Jordan all of whom Muslim women over sixty (it is hard to find Christian women in this age range who are illiterate), what this term means. I chose illiterate women only as informants in my interviews to neutralize, to the extent possible, the effect schooling may have on their answers. A variety of formulations and illustrative examples were provided in response to my question, but these coalesced around an understanding of the term which primarily designates the *fuṣḥā*, the minority view, or refers to all forms of Arabic including the *fuṣḥā*, the majority understanding. When the latter dominant meaning is intended my informants framed their answers in terms of a duality involving what professional linguists call *fuṣḥā* and *ʿāmmiyya*, which are seen as related but different. My informants are aware of the different spoken varieties and of the different values these may have in society. And they tended to impart greater coherence to the *fuṣḥā* which they evaluated highly as the language of the Qur'an and literacy.[2] I, therefore, contend that their understanding of the term *al-lugha al-ʿarabiyya* is not so very different from Ferguson's characterization of how diglossia applies in the Arabic language situation. For these illiterate speakers, two forms of Arabic exist: *fuṣḥā* and *ʿāmmiyya*. These speakers are aware of intermediate forms of Arabic but they tend not to give them the same category recognition as the primary categories of *fuṣḥā* and *ʿāmmiyya*. These intermediate forms are described as different ways of speaking in a manner that corresponds to the notions of style and register in modern linguistics, being in some respects akin to Badawi's notion of levels above with all its ambiguity.

Ferguson's notion of diglossia does not capture the full complexity of the intermediate forms of Arabic on the *fuṣḥā* to *ʿāmmiyya* continuum as these forms are constructed in modern linguistics but, in my view, it corresponds well to the folk linguistic understanding of this continuum in which the prominence of the two ends of this continuum in their semi-liquid state are accentuated at the expense of the fuzzy middle in all its liquidity.[3] Because of this I think Ferguson's diglossia has greater folk linguistic resonance than scientific/empirical linguistic validity, and this goes for his notion of prestige above. This folk linguistic understanding of diglossia is consistent with Mushira Eid's observation that the "perceived dichotomy [between *fuṣḥā* and *ʿāmmiyya*] is deeply ingrained in the collective consciousness of Arabic speakers/writers," whether in Egypt, which is her primary field of interest, or in other Arabic-speaking countries (2002: 204). It is also consistent with some of the folk linguistic views to which Haeri (2003) refers in her ethnographic study of Arabic in Egypt. In Haeri's study *ʿāmmiyya* and *fuṣḥā* emerge as the

[2] See Hussein and El-Ali (1988) for evidence from Jordan that corroborates this view.

[3] See Kaye's discussion of diglossia (1972) for the notions of "well-defined" and "ill-defined" which are relevant in this context.

bi-polar forms of Arabic in relation to which Egyptians orient themselves ideologically and in terms of language behavior.

Folk linguistics is important in enabling us to construct an *insider* or ethnographic perspective of the language situation in the Arabic speaking countries. To begin with, in Arabic folk linguistics the *fuṣḥā* is treated as indivisible into pre-modern and modern forms, which are sometimes called in Western discussions of the topic as Classical and Modern Standard Arabic respectively. This indivisibility of the *fuṣḥā* is also an integral part of most expositions of the Arabic language among Arab linguists in the indigenous tradition. Linguists/grammarians in this tradition would not subscribe to the plethora of Arabic varieties that some Western linguists recognize, such as those that Versteegh deploys in his book *The Arabic Language* (1997): Proto-Arabic, Old Arabic, Early Arabic, Classical Arabic, Early Middle Arabic, New Arabic, Muslim Middle Arabic, Christian Middle Arabic and Judaeo-Arabic. I think most Arabs would agree that there are differences between different manifestations of the *fuṣḥā* across the ages, but they are very reluctant to treat these differences as the basis for sub-categorization in the body of the language as Versteegh has done. While Arabic speakers are aware of linguistic change, they are more struck by linguistic continuity in their conceptualizations of *fuṣḥā*. It is in my view important to acknowledge this indigenous or folk linguistic perspective if we are to develop an insider's understanding of Arabic by accessing the way Arabs construct their language. This insider perspective has its own socio-psychological validity which must be incorporated into any study of the social life of Arabic, even though it may not withstand the scrutiny of empirical linguistics.

Furthermore, folk linguistics enables us to appreciate the double commitment Arabic speakers have to *ʿāmmiyya* and *fuṣḥā* and to reconcile some of the attitudinal differences that pervade these commitments, such as the fact that native speakers do not always hold their spoken varieties with the same esteem as the *fuṣḥā*, even though *ʿāmmiyya* is their mother tongue and *fuṣḥā* is not. Even the most ardent supporters of *ʿāmmiyya* in the Western academy acknowledge this (e.g., Haeri 2003: 38). From a folk linguistic perspective the issue, therefore, is how to conceptualize the relationship Arabic speakers have with the two salient varieties of their language.

11.3 Mother Tongue and Native Language: A New Conceptualization

The term mother tongue is used to designate the *ʿāmmiyya*s in modern linguistics. The *ʿāmmiyya*s are acquired informally and are the site of personal and community intimacy. Although the *ʿāmmiyya*s are sometimes committed to writing, the cultural norm is to use them in oral communication in everyday situations [Holes, "Orality"]. The use of "tongue" in designating the *ʿāmmiyya*s captures the orality of this form of Arabic well. In folk linguistics, the *ʿāmmiyya*s are not regarded as languages but as dialects. They are also thought to be devoid of grammar (a mistaken view in scientific terms) owing to their being perceived as corrupt forms of *fuṣḥā* [Retsö, "Arabic?"], [Owens, "History"]. Haeri's (2003) use of vernacular to refer to the *ʿāmmiyya*s is, therefore, not completely consistent with this folk linguistic understanding of the Arabic language situation. The term vernacular evokes an emerging language on apar with the rise of the European languages as competitors of Latin in the print, ethnic or national identity domain in post medieval times. In other words, when applied to Arabic the term vernacular ascribes to the *ʿāmmiyya*s a status that they do not or may not have in comparison with *fuṣḥā* or in the eyes of those who speak them as mother tongues. It is true that there have been attempts at establishing the dialects as national languages, but to this day none of these attempts has succeeded to either establish these *ʿāmmiyya*s as widely recognized print or school languages, or even to dent the authority of *fuṣḥā* in the print or educational domain to any significant degree (Suleiman 2003). Whether a spoken form or variety of Arabic is a language or not is not, therefore, an issue which can be decided by modern linguistics on behalf of those whose medium of communication it is. As Davies rightly reminds us "on sociolinguistic grounds... dialects are dialects of the same language because their speakers claim them to be so, and they are distinguished from languages in terms of power" (2003: 58). So, if *ʿāmmiyya*s are the mother tongues of Arabic speakers what is *fuṣḥā* to them?

Clearly *fuṣḥā* cannot be their mother tongue because it is acquired formally through education over a long period of time. Acquisition of *fuṣḥā* in this way is a rite of passage to literacy; one cannot achieve the status of being literate without schooling in *fuṣḥā*. In addition, *fuṣḥā* is a normative code whose inculcation is deliberate. The use of *ʿāmmiyya* in everyday speech is the default position in Arabic speaking countries; in comparison the use of *fuṣḥā* in the same domain is marked practice in the same way that the use of *ʿāmmiyya* in writing is. Clearly Arabs relate to the two ends of their linguistic repertoire differently. To capture this I have elsewhere designated *fuṣḥā* as the Arabs' native language to set it apart from *ʿāmmiyya* as their mother tongue. The distinction between mother tongue and native language needs some theorization that I hope to provide following.

In doing so I will follow Blommaert (2006: 243) who makes an important distinction between what he calls (following Silverstein 1996, 1998) *linguistic* communities on the one hand, and *speech* communities on the other where "the former are groups professing adherence to the normatively constructed, ideologically articulated 'standard' language... and the latter are groups characterized by the actual use of a specific speech form." Blommaert glosses this distinction by saying that its two partners are not "isomorphic, and the distance between the sociolinguistically definable community and the linguistic-ideologically definable community reveals the degree of hegemony of language ideologies, often resulting in blind spots for sociolinguistic phenomena" (ibid.). Blommaert's comment on this distinction draws attention to the ideological impregnation of folk linguistics. If we understand language ideology to be the "cultural system of ideas about social and linguistic relations, together with their loadings of moral and political interests" (Irvine 1989: 255), folk linguistics cannot but be an ideological hub in which the beliefs and attitudes of the community must be taken into consideration in any treatment of the social life of language. It would in fact be impossible to produce an ethnography of a language without tapping its language ideology no matter how mundane, obvious or politically problematic this ideology is. Thus, whereas modern linguistics establishes as an article of faith that all languages are equal in the way they fulfill the instrumental needs of their communities, folk linguistics, being ideologically impregnated, does not heed this principle of equality. From a folk linguistic perspective languages are often linked to myths of election which ascribe greater worth to them than their competitors whether in terms of beauty, lexical richness, logicality and so on. For the modern linguist all languages are structurally and instrumentally equal; in folk linguistics some languages are more equal than others.[4] Each view operates within its own domain from which it derives its validity.

Treating *fuṣḥā* as native language and *ʿāmmiyya* as mother tongue, and linking these two dualities to the concepts of linguistic and speech community respectively, allows us to construct two triadic chains that are not mutually exclusive in describing the Arabic language situation from a folk linguistic perspective.[5] The first chain consists of *fuṣḥā*, *native language* and *linguistic community* and corresponds to the high end of Ferguson's diglossia. The second consists of *ʿāmmiyya*, *mother tongue* and *speech community* and corresponds to the low end of the diglossia spectrum. I am aware that ideology is not exclusively linked with *fuṣḥā* as native language. *ʿĀmmiyya* as mother tongue has its own ideological associations in cultural and political terms. However, I have chosen to highlight the ideological in the *fuṣḥā* in constructing the above categorical distinction because the ideology in this unit of analysis, more than the ideology of *ʿāmmiyya*, is the subject of hegemonic formulations in folk linguistics insofar as national identity construction is concerned.

The above separation of mother tongue and native language may be problematic in modern linguistics because, ordinarily, the two terms are used interchangeably in the literature (Bonfiglio 2010). The overlap between the two is reflected in talk about the native speaker as the native speaker of his mother tongue and of his native language in instrumental terms. However, in the process of conceptualizing these two notions as notational variants of each other differences between them are also acknowledged, the most important of which is the overwhelming orality of the mother tongue in comparison with the written nature of the native language that links it to standardization and schooling. In some cases the empirical distance between mother tongue and native language is not very great; in others it is. It is the fact that empirical distance does exist

[4] Sociolinguistics accepts this principle of inequality, often expressed in the different prestige/status values attributed to different languages and to different varieties within a language.

[5] This characterization of native language and linguistic community would imply that, for some speakers in Lebanon and North Africa, French may qualify as a native language, albeit the case that French lacks the cultural depth of Arabic and its wider meanings in religious and political terms in the MENA region (see footnote 6 below for further elaboration of this point). See Davies (2003) for the linkage among politics, symbolism and instrumentality in framing the concept of native speaker.

between the two notions in modern linguistics that allows me to deploy them differently in dealing with the Arabic language situation and, furthermore, to link them to the two notions of speech community and linguistic community. These two communities overlap but they are sufficiently different in category terms to be configured differently in folk linguistic terms. Arabic speakers, according to this, belong to overlapping but different communities that are defined in terms of speech and language, and that correspond to the low and high forms of the language in Ferguson's diglossia. Consistent with the autonomy of the triadic chains I have established above and their folk linguistic orientation, I propose to designate the mother tongue in Arabic as *al-lisān al-umm* and the native language as *al-lugha al-umm*.

Furthermore, I am of the view that most theories of language in the social world cannot totally escape the empirical fields that inform their construction, in spite of the claims of universality that may be attributed to them. Most theories of language are in fact *restricted* theories with aspirational aims to universality. Matthews (1972) made a similar point over three decades ago in developing his views on word and paradigm morphology and the close fit this model has with inflectional languages, using Latin as an example. For this reason the conflation of mother tongue with native language cannot be extended to all language situations without doing some of those situations injustice. Applying to the Arabic language situation theoretical frameworks of restricted nature that do not sufficiently differentiate between mother tongue and native speaker is, in my view, a form of Procrustean and epistemic violence that is similar, in many respects, to enforcing a separation of these two categories on those language situations that do not need it or are best described without it. Whereas in the one situation we would have a case of under categorization: in the other we would commit the error of over-categorization. What we need, therefore, is a different solution that deploys different conceptual horses for different sociolinguistic courses that are in tune with the particularities of their folk linguistic terrain. A native speaker of a language does not, in sociolinguistic terms, have to have full fluency in it as a spoken or written language to qualify as native speaker. As Davies perceptively comments the "politicisation of native speakerness with particular reference to language" enables individuals to "regard themselves (and others) as native speakers for symbolic rather than [instrumental] purposes" (2003: 76).

Native speakerness, I wish to argue, does not have to be yoked to the performance-bound notions of authenticity, reliability and representativeness which cognitive and applied linguistics demand of the native speaker to a high level (Coulmas 1981). In folk linguistic terms one can operate with lower levels of performance across these three criteria as long as these levels are linked to a structure of "attitudes and feelings of identity" that define a sense of belonging to a national community in symbolic terms (Davies 2003: 76). An Arabic speaker does not have to have the same facility in *fuṣḥā* as he has in his *ʿāmmiyya* for him to be recognized in folk linguistic terms as a native speaker of the former in the same way he is recognized as a native speaker of the latter. This is a deviation from cognitive linguistics which may in fact claim that *fuṣḥā* and *ʿāmmiyya* are wired differently in the brain—suggesting that they may in fact behave as different languages—but it reflects a societal attitude which sociolinguistics must capture if it is to come to grips with the social life of a language, and how this language resonates with those who think they belong to it and it belongs to them [Ryding, "Acquisition"].

I am, however, willing to accept that some Arabic linguists may still feel uncomfortable with my use of native language to designate *fuṣḥā*, which is often said to be no one's native language in studies of Arabic (Haeri 2003: 146), in spite of the fact that in the educational field it is referred to in Arabic as the mother language (*al-lugha al-umm*). *Fuṣḥā* can be legitimately described as an *indigenous* language in folk linguistic terms, in spite of the fact that some writers have described it as a foreign language in parts of the Arabic speaking world and have accused it of being a force of internal colonialism/imperialism in those parts, for example Egypt (Ahmed 2000). To avoid the unnecessary debate about "indigenousness," I prefer the term native language in referring to *fuṣḥā* to capture the Arabic term *al-lugha al-umm* Arab educationists consistently use to describe it. This term is also preferable to *official* language that is available to us. Some, if not most, Arab constitutions establish *fuṣḥā* as "(the) official language of the state" (*al-lugha al-rasmiyya*), but I find this term wanting in folk linguistic terms. While some of my informants in Jordan were aware that Arabic was the official language of the state, the legal meaning of this term did not resonate with them. *Fuṣḥā* is also considered as the "national" (*al-lugha al-waṭaniyya*) or "pan-national" (*al-lugha al-qawmiyya*) language in the Arabic speaking countries, but people do not use this identity inflection as their primary compass in orienting themselves towards this form of Arabic, at least in the Middle East (in some countries of North Africa the situation may be different). For many speakers *fuṣḥā* is equally, if in fact not more, connected to Islam as an extra-territorial phenomenon that cuts across nation-states. To reflect this structure of associations I prefer to stick to native language, which as a term has the ability to hover over all these conceptualizations without discrimination. As a native language *fuṣḥā* can be indigenous, official, national or pan-national separately or together without contradiction.[6]

I have also rejected the possibility of treating *fuṣḥā* as a *second* language. If we adopt this perspective we would have to designate *ʿāmmiyya* (in its capacity as mother tongue) as *first* language. But the use of the first and second language terminology would skew the relationship between *fuṣḥā* and *ʿāmmiyya* into a bilingualism framework that clashes with the folk linguistic conceptualizations of the Arabic language situation. None of my informants considered themselves to be bilingual, and I cannot imagine that many Arabs would describe themselves as such in describing their relationship with *fuṣḥā* and *ʿāmmiyya*. I have seen many applications for jobs in the Arab world where knowledge

[6] Although French may be established as "native language" in some countries of North Africa and Lebanon, it is not normally conceptualized as "indigenous," "official" or "national" in the way these epithets are applied to *fuṣḥā*. This situation varies from country to country and between different segments of the populations in the same country depending on ethnicity, education and faith.

of languages is mentioned. Only in two cases did the applicants list their *ʿāmmiyya* and *fuṣḥā*, together with English in one case and English and French in another, as part of their language repertoire. These two cases were the source of amusement by those who evaluated the applications, a very telling reaction. Furthermore, the use of the first and second language terminology favors the instrumental role of language over its symbolic function as the two classificatory principles underlying *ʿāmmiyya* and *fuṣḥā* respectively. This may be justifiable on cognitive grounds but it fails to accord with Arabic folk linguistics wherein *fuṣḥā* seems to be given greater social value than *ʿāmmiyya*, as Haeri (2003) notes in her ethnography of the language situation in Egypt. Adopting a folk linguistic perspective we might, in fact, be justified to treat *fuṣḥā* as first language and *ʿāmmiyya* as second.

To avoid the clash of instrumentality and symbolism as principles of classification on the one hand, and cognitive and folk linguistics on the other it would be preferable to drop the terms first and second language in talking about the Arabic language situation in favor of mother tongue and native language. The fact that a conceptual distance exists between mother tongue and native language in the linguistic literature creates a terminological space which allows us to reserve the latter as a designation of *fuṣḥā*. To this we may add that alternative terms are problematic; they introduce theoretical perspectives which sit uncomfortably or stray outside folk narratives of the language. Native language, while not a perfect term for *fuṣḥā* because of some of the cognitive loadings it has is, nevertheless, serviceable not least because it can allow the other terminological narratives above to operate in ethnographic accounts of the Arabic language situation.

11.4 Native Language and Mother Tongue: Custodianship versus Ownership

To reflect the difference between *fuṣḥā* and *ʿāmmiyya* in social terms and how speakers relate to them Haeri applies the concepts of custodianship to the former (which she calls Classical Arabic) and ownership to the latter (which she calls the vernacular) in her ethnographic study of Egypt. The same classificatory schema would presumably apply to other Arabic speaking countries; Haeri signals this to be the case but she does not explicitly generalize beyond Egypt. Haeri links *fuṣḥā* to sacredness and *ʿāmmiyya* to the "mundane," quotidian or "profane" (ibid. 3, 105)—hence the opposition in the title of her book between sacred language and ordinary people—and uses this distinction as the basis of her claim about custodianship and ownership. Haeri vacillates between ascribing sacredness to the language of the Quran as revelation or to *fuṣḥā* in all its totality, including the Quran as revelation, but there is a clear sense in her discussion that she favors the second more inclusive application of the term. In my fieldwork in Jordan similar vacillation existed for some informants, but all informants reserved sacredness to the language of the Qur'an only as revelation when questioned about the topic. In my experience ordinary Muslims do not distinguish sharply between Quran and *muṣḥaf* (text of the Quran as in a printed copy of it), but they do make a clear distinction between the printed word when it is a manifestation of the revelation, and when print is used in ordinary every day domains. One can test the sacredness thesis, therefore, by comparing the reaction to dropping the text of the Quran (*muṣḥaf*) on the floor and the reaction to dropping a school book, novel or newspaper. In the former case, Arab Muslims would immediately pick up the *muṣḥaf*, kiss it and ask for God's forgiveness as if they had committed a sin. I have never seen the same reaction in dealing with other manifestations of the printed word. In these situations Arab Muslims will pick up the book, novel or newspaper but without anything like the urgency or feelings of transgression against the divine they exhibit in the other case. I have in fact used this litmus test, so to speak, to help my informants decide whether *fuṣḥā* in its totality is or is not a sacred language. It is true that *fuṣḥā* is treated with veneration, especially in religious contexts, but "veneration" (*taqdīs, tabjīl*) is not the same as "sacredness" (*qudsiyya*) in the way Haeri seems to use this term.

Haeri articulates the juxtaposition between *ʿāmmiyya* and *fuṣḥā* as sacred language in "terms of ownership/custodianship, arbitrariness of the sign, translatability and human versus divine origin" (ibid.: 143). She also says that *fuṣḥā* as "the language of the Quran continues to separate the sacred from the profane, writing from speaking, and prescribed religious rituals from personal communication with God" (ibid.: 1). As an example of the profane, or "the most profane of activities" Haeri mentions "selling" (ibid.: 105). The arbitrariness of the sign and translatability are linked in Haeri's exposition. Because Muslims believe that the Quran as God's revelation is His word verbatim, Haeri argues that the relationship between form and meaning in the Quran is non-arbitrary and extends the same to *fuṣḥā* in its totality. Thus, while it is possible to translate (translation is always an act of interpretation) the meaning of the Quran into other languages, any such translation cannot be regarded as a Quran because it breaks the non-arbitrary relationship between form and meaning in the revelation.

I believe this to be fundamentally wrong. A better way of conceptualizing the relationship between form and meaning in the Quran would be *theological/doctrinal inseparability*, which is different from non-arbitrariness in the sense this term is understood in the literature following Saussure (1966, originally published in French in 1916). For Saussure the arbitrariness of the sign refers to the lack of a natural or other knowable reason for linking a particular form with a particular meaning or vice versa. According to this interpretation it would be possible to describe the link between form and meaning in the language of the Quran as arbitrary without challenging the sacredness of the revelation. This in my view would apply regardless of whether or not we ascribe to Arabic a "divine" (*tawqīf*) or "human" (*iṣṭilāḥ*) origin. Arabic grammarians have debated this issue centuries ago. The theologians have done the same in dealing with the "createdness" (*khalq*) of the Quran. The Arabic linguistic and theological traditions contain ample evidence to suggest that the arbitrariness of the sign thesis is compatible with the view of the theological inseparability of form and meaning that underlies the Quran as sacred revelation.[7]

The untranslatability of the Quran thesis is not a linguistic principle but a primarily theological one. In fact if we accept the arbitrariness thesis as a feature of all languages, including *fuṣḥā*, we would be able to say that a translation and its original are not the same, no matter which pair of languages is involved. When we translate, we translate meaning not form. And is not this similar to the untranslatability thesis of the Quran? A translation of a poem by the Palestinian poet Mahmud Darwish is not a poem by Mahmud Darwish but a rendering of it in another language, making the original poem as a duality of form and meaning untranslatable if by translation we mean sameness. Translation does not aim to produce sameness but to minimize loss (Hervey and Higgnis 1992), although in the case of such texts as the Quran that are deeply embedded in their cultures translation loss can be extreme owing, among other things, to their reception history. This is why translations of the Quran tend to veer towards foreignization rather domestication (Venuti 1995), wherein the reader is taken to the text in the former and vice versa in the latter. What distinguishes the untranslatability of the Quran from the untranslatability of a Mahmud Darwish poem, therefore, is the theological impregnation of the former and its rootedness in the intellectual history of Arabo-Islamic culture as integral features of the sacredness of revelation.

In addition to the above conceptual problems it is not clear where the sacred ends and the profane begins for Haeri. If selling, as she claims, is one of the "most profane" activities with which *fuṣḥā* would need to be reconciled (ibid.: 105) in the Arabic speaking world how would one deal with the fact that, in its long history, *fuṣḥā* was the medium of poetry and other prose compositions that dealt with such activities as homosexuality and wine drinking that unquestionably belong to the domain of profanity? Arabs may object to and deplore these activities or their depiction in poetry on doctrinal grounds, but very few people would do the same because these activities are the topics of poetic compositions in *fuṣḥā*. *Fuṣḥā* is both the language of the sacred and the profane (and all that lies between them) in spite of the fact that, attitudinally, it is linked to Islam as faith and culture. These linkages do not make Arabic sacred, contrary to what Haeri says. Furthermore, does not the fact that the vast majority of the Arabic grammarians excluded most of the Prophetic Traditions from their corpora suggest that, outside the

[7] Arbitrariness as a property of the linguistic sign is subsumed under the concept of *waḍʿ al-lugha* (the founding of language) in the Arabic linguistic tradition [Larcher, "ALT II"]. Weiss (2009: 684) characterizes this relationship as follows: "The relationship between ... utterances and ... meanings was not [considered in this tradition] as a natural or intrinsic relationship. In principle, an utterance could have any meaning. That an utterance had a particular meaning was due entirely to its being assigned to that meaning. The meaning of an utterance had to be learned; it could not automatically be known from the utterance." An utterance here covers any unit of form and meanings regardless of size.

strict confines of revelation, sacredness is an extremely tenuous notion when applied to *fuṣḥā*? If the second most important source of Islamic legal thinking (*tashrīʿ*), representing the "tradition" (*sunna*) of the Prophet, is excluded from the purview of grammatical description and model building in the early periods of Islam,[8] does not this suggest that Muslims operated with a heavily circumscribed understanding of sacredness in the linguistic domain? Expanding the sacred beyond its limits as Haeri does is not just unwarranted on various grounds, but it also leads to creating the problematic distinction between custodianship and ownership in her description of the Arabic linguistic landscape.

Haeri argues that because *fuṣḥā* is a sacred language, Arabs cannot be its owners because they do not have the right over it (*ḥaqq al-taṣarruf*, p. 146). She explains this as follows: "if language is considered to be the Word of God then its users are its custodians, not its owners. If so, the right to change it, mould it, translate it, negotiate its boundaries and so on is always contested" (ibid.: 69–70). If we accept this description of the meaning of custodianship, then the speakers of most languages, especially those with a long written tradition, are closer to being their custodians than their owners. Attempts to change a language of this pedigree, mould it and negotiate its boundaries will always be contested. The linguistic literature is full of examples that testify to this. Furthermore, producing new translations of sacred texts, even when these texts are not regarded as the Word of God verbatim, is always the subject of controversy and contestation because of the history of reception of established translations which the new translations seek to replace or supplement. Producing new translations of the Bible in English in the twentieth century has not been free of controversy and contestation on linguistic, theological and aesthetic grounds. The fact that contestation in the case of Quran translations tends to be accentuated because of its status as revelation in form and meaning in doctrinal terms makes this contestation special in terms of degree, not kind.

Furthermore, *fuṣḥā* has undergone considerable changes over time and, as Haeri rightly points out, some Arabs believe that a modern inflection of *fuṣḥā* has developed that "stands on its own, independent of the *fuṣḥā* of religion" (ibid.: 21). In most cases, linguistic change takes place surreptitiously with little deliberate interference from the users of the language. The idea of deliberate and directed change in language is the exception not the rule, as the work of language academies testifies (see Cooper 1989). This is true of *fuṣḥā* and Egypt as it is true of standard French and France.

Haeri links the presumed sacredness of *fuṣḥā* with the long-standing issue of the checkered history of modernization in Arab societies. In doing this, she argues that modernization in the full sense cannot be achieved without replacing

[8] The lateness of the texts of the *ḥadīths* is an important factor in their exclusion from the empirical data of most grammarians. The fact that they were considered as the second source in *fiqh* wasn't sufficient to redeem them in the eyes of the grammarian.

fuṣḥā with *ʿāmmiyya* in all fields in society, including translating the Quran into *ʿāmmiyya* (ibid.: 148). The following quotation sets some of Haeri's view on the topic (ibid.: 146):

> A sacred language cannot become a fully living language unless it loses that status. Since modernisation efforts [in Egypt] began, renovated forms of the language have carried with them at every turn, all the contradictions, accusations, uncertainties and struggles that are inherent in attempts to make a sacred language contemporary. Whether one calls changes to the language "modernisation," or "simplification" the point is that change necessarily goes against purity and sacredness. Put simply, [*fuṣḥā*] is not the mother tongue of Egyptians or other Arabs and, not being its "owners," their rights to the language will remain precarious. The dilemma is that were they to take steps to own it, the language would cease to be sacred. Few if any of these problems would have arisen had *fuṣḥā* remained simply the language of religion, while other spheres of life would be served by writing in Egyptian Arabic.

Furthermore, Haeri links the dominance of *fuṣḥā* with a "certain denial of the contemporary self" in Egypt, leading to "an uneasy relation with self" (ibid.: 148). She also argues that the "status of being a citizen is put in doubt [in Egypt] in the absence of any acknowledgement of that citizen's mother tongue" (ibid.: 151). In the same vein, *fuṣḥā* as official language is said to act as an "obstacle to participation in the political realm" and as one reason for the "absence of democracy in Egypt" (ibid.).[9] It is true that language, Self, citizenship and democracy are linked in the social sphere, but ascribing some of the tensions and deficits in these domains to the sacredness of *fuṣḥā* is a step too far, not least because this sacredness is very much in doubt as a property of *fuṣḥā* in its totality. As we have seen above, the sacredness of *fuṣḥā* is an exception not the rule of Arabic folk linguistics. We must, therefore, be careful before we inject linguistic sacredness into the analysis of modernization in Egypt by linking it with various ills in society.

Calls to replace *fuṣḥā* by *ʿāmmiyya* are not new in Egypt. They go back to the nineteenth century when Willcocks (1893) argued that the Egyptians cannot regain their "power of invention" (*quwwat al-iḫtirāʿ*) until they use their spoken language as the medium of education and modernization.[10] Willcocks, who was ignored and reviled in Egypt, did not talk about the sacredness of Arabic (Suleiman 2004: 62–72). Haeri acts more boldly but it is unlikely that her analysis would resonate with most Egyptians simply because it clashes with the folk linguistic conceptualization of the Arabic language situation. I have dealt with this topic obliquely in my discussion of al-Shūbāshī's book (2004) on reforming Arabic grammar, with its provocative title *li-taḥyā al-lugha al-ʿarabiyya: Yasquṭ Sībawayhi*: "Long Live the Arabic Language! Down with Sibawayhi" (Suleiman 2006). Haeri (ibid.: 119, 121), however, is right when she talks about the perilous state of Arabic

[9] It would be interesting to reflect on this view in the context of the Arab Spring and Egypt's place and role in it, but this would take us outside the scope of this study.

[10] The Egyptian Salāma Mūsā championed this solution in the twentieth century. For a discussion of his views see Suleiman (2003: 180–90).

language teaching in schools and the poor image of Arabic teachers who, she tells us, are referred to disparagingly as the "Grammar Brothers" (*al-iḫwān al-nahwiyyīn*) by analogy with the well-known party of the Muslim Brothers (*al-iḫwān al-muslimīn*).

11.5 Conclusion

I have argued in this paper for incorporating a folk linguistic perspective in studying Arabic in the social world. This perspective is important in developing an insider understanding of the language which, it must be acknowledged, may be at odds with the findings of modern linguistics. To aid the process of developing this perspective we will need to adopt the terminology and conceptual frameworks Arabic speakers use in describing their language situation wherever possible; hence my choice of *fuṣḥā* and *ʿāmmiyya* instead of any of their translations into English, including Classical Arabic and vernacular which Haeri (2003) uses. Being approximations of the Arabic originals, foreign terms skew the meanings of their Arabic equivalents by injecting into them target language attitudes, ideologies and reception histories that may be absent from the original counterparts. The term vernacular, as I have argued herein, is a case in point.

The insider perspective in folk linguistics is important in two important ways. On the one hand, it enables us to understand the deployment of language as a cultural asset in society, together with the structure of feelings and attitudes that inform and accompany this deployment. On the other hand, we can use folk linguistic views to understand the limits of language modernization or, even, to predict the obstacles that may face this modernization in the educational sphere, how to negotiate these obstacles and the ways and means that may be adopted to soften up societal resistance to educational reform.

I have also argued in this paper that in spite of the criticisms of Ferguson's diglossia in modern linguistics, this concept has a great deal of validity in folk linguistic terms. I have, therefore, used this concept in its folk linguistic incarnation to argue for a description of the Arabic language situation in which two conceptual chains operate: (1) *fuṣḥā*, linguistic community and native language (*lugha umm*), and (2) *ʿāmmiyya*, speech community and mother tongue (*lisān umm*). I believe that these triadic chains capture how the Arabs think about their language situation. This includes the supremacy of language symbolism in the first chain and instrumentality in the second. This analytical framework provides the parameters of a new conceptualization of the Arabic language situation that, while building on Ferguson's seminal work on diglossia, aims to transcend it.

Little work has been done on Arabic from an ethnographic and qualitative perspective. Haeri's study (2003) is one of a few exceptions in this regard. For this reason it is a welcome addition to the study of Arabic in the social world. In spite of this, however, I disagree with some of Haeri's main principles and conclusions in describing the Arabic language situation in Egypt, which, in some respects, intersect with the views expressed by writers such as Ahmed (2000), ʿAwaḍ (1947, 1965), Mūsā (1947), Safouan (2007), and Willcocks (1893). These writers share a vernacularizing perspective whose aim is to establish the *ʿāmmiyya* of Egypt as its national language. It is not my aim here to deal with the pros and cons of this perspective, but I will highlight three issues with which any future move in the direction of vernacularization will have to contend.

First, some Arabic speakers will read vernacularization sociopolitically as an attempt to weaken the cultural and political ties among the Arabic speaking countries. Vernacularization will, more importantly, be further read as a sinister attack whose aim is to undermine the ties which Arab Muslims have with the text of the Quran and the cultural edifice it has given rise to and continues to underpin. These readings will, in turn, raise the issue, at a heightened level in society, as to whether the benefits that may accrue from vernacularization would justify the social and political upheaval it is bound to create. Second, vernacularization will raise extremely divisive issues in status and corpus planning terms (Cooper 1989). These will include the selection of the base variety or varieties for constructing the new vernaculars in Arabic speaking countries; the choice of scripts for rendering the vernaculars in writing; the authoring of new grammars, lexica, style manuals and spelling rules; the production of new curricula for schools and institutions of higher education; and teacher training programs to equip the teachers with the skills of teaching the new languages to students. Finally, the corpus planning consequences of vernacularization will not be cost free: they will require substantial investment in time and effort that may not be justified by the benefits promised by the vernacularizers.

REFERENCES

Ahmed, Leila. 2000. *Border passage*. New York: Penguin Books.

ʿAwaḍ, Luwīs. 1947. *Plutoland*. Cairo: Matb'aṭ al-Karnak.

——. 1965. *Mudhakkarāt ṭālib baʿtha*. Cairo: al-Kitāb al-Dhahabī.

Badawī, El-Saʿīd. 1973. *Mustawayāt al-ʿarabiyya al-muʿāṣira fī Miṣr*. Cairo: Dār al-Maʿārif.

Blommaert, Jan. 2006. Language policy: and national identity. In *An introduction to language policy—Theory and method*, ed. Thomas Ricento, 238–254. Oxford: Blackwell Publishing.

Bonfiglio, Thomas Paul. 2010. *Mother tongues and nations: The invention of the native speaker*. New York: Walter de Gruyter.

Boussofara-Omar, Naima. 2006. Diglossia. In *EALL I*, ed. Kees Versteegh et al., 610–637.

Cooper, Robert. 1989. *Language planning and social change*. Cambridge: Cambridge University Press.

Coulmas, Florian. 1981. The concept of native speaker. In *A festschrift for native speaker*, ed. Florian Coulmas, 1–25. The Hague: Mouton.

Davies, Alan. 2003. *The native speaker: Myth and reality*. Clevedon: Multilingual Matters.

Eid, Mushira. 2002. Language as choice—Variation in Egyptian women's written discourse. In *Language contact and language conflict in Arabic variations on a sociolinguistic theme*, ed. Aleya Rouchdy, 203–232. London: Routledge Curzon.

Ferguson, Charles. A. 1959. Diglossia. *Word* 15: 325–340.

Haeri, Niloofar. 2003. *Sacred language, ordinary people*. New York: Palgrave Macmillan.

Hervey, Sàndor and Ian Higgns.1992. *Thinking translation: A course in translation method*. London: Routledge.

Hussein, Riad F. and Nasir El-Ali.1988. Subjective reactions towards different varieties of Arabic. *al-Lisān al-ʿarabī* 30: 7–17.

Ibrahim, Muhammad. 1986. Standard and prestige language: A problem in Arabic sociolinguistics. *Anthropological Linguistics* 28: 115–126.

Irvine, Judith. 1989. When talk isn't cheap: Language and political economy. *American Ethnologist* 16: 248–267.

Kaye, Alan. 1972. Remarks on diglossia in Arabic: Well-defined vs. ill-defined. *Linguistics:* 81: 32–48.

Khūri, Yūsuf Qazmā, ed. 1991. *Najāḥ al-umma al-ʿarabiyya fi lughatihā al-aṣliyya*. Beirut: Dar al-Ḥamrāʾ.

Mahmoud, Youssef. 1986. Arabic after diglossia. In *The Fergusonian impact: In honour of Charles A. Ferguson on the occasion of his 65th Birthday*, ed. Joshua Fishman, Andree Tabouret-Keller, Michael Clyne, Bh. Krishnamurti and Mohamed Abdulaziz, 239–251. Berlin: Mouton de Gruyter.

Matthews, Peter. 1972. *Inflectional morphology: A theoretical study based on aspects of Latin verb conjugation*. Cambridge: Cambridge University Press.

Meiseles, Gustav. 1980. Educated spoken Arabic and the Arabic language continuum. *Archivum Linguisticum* 2: 118–148.

Mitchell, T. F. 1986. What is educated spoken Arabic? *International Journal of the Sociology of Language* 61: 7–32.

Mūsā, Salāma. 1947. *al-Balāgha al-ʿaṣriyya wa l-lugha al-ʿarabiyya*. Salāma Mūsā li-l-Nashr wa-l-Tawzīʿ. (First published in 1945.)

Nieldzielski, Nancy A. and Preston, Dennis R. 2000. *Folk linguistics*. Berlin/New York: Mouton de Gruyter.

Parkinson, Dilworth. 1991. Searching for modern Fuṣḥā: Real life formal Arabic. *Al-ʾArabiyya* 24: 31–64.

Safouan, Moustapha. 2007. *Why are the Arabs not free—The politics of writing*. Oxford: Blackwell.

de Saussure, Ferdinand. [1959] 1966. *Course in general linguistics*, ed. C. Bally and A. Sechehaye. New York: McGraw-Hill Company.

Silverstein, M. 1996. Encountering languages and languages of encounter in North American ethnohistory. *Journal of Linguistic Anthropology* 6: 126–144.

——.1998. Contemporary transformations of local linguistic communities. *Annual Review of Anthropology*, 401–426.

Suleiman, Yasir. 2003. *The Arabic language and national identity: A study in ideology*. Georgetown: Georgetown University Press.

——. 2004. *War of words: language and conflict in the Middle East*. Cambridge: CUP.

——. 2006. Arabic language reforms, language ideology and the criminalisation of Sibawayhi. In *Grammar as a window onto Arabic humanism: A collection of articles in honour of Michael Carter*, ed. Lutz Edzard and Janet Watson, 66–83. Wiesbaden: Harrassowitz Verlag.

——. 2008. Egypt: From Egyptian to pan-Arab nationalism. In *Language and National Identity in Africa*, ed. Andrew Simpson, 26–43. Oxford: Oxford University Press.

——. 2011. *Arabic, Self and identity: A study in conflict and displacement*. New York: Oxford University Press.

Al-Shūbāshī, Sharīf. 2004. *Li-taḥyā al-lugha al-ʿarabiyya: Yasquṭ Sībawayhi*. Cairo: Madbūlī (third printing).

Venuti, Laurence. 1995. *The translator's invisibility: A history of translation*. London: Routledge.

Versteegh, Kees. 1997. *The Arabic language*, Edinburgh: Edinburgh University Press.

Weiss, Bernard. 2009. Waḍʿ al-lugha, In *EALL IV*, ed. Kees Versteegh et al., 684–687.

Willcocks, William. 1893. Lima lam tūjad quwwat al-ikhtirāʿ ladā al-miṣriyyīn al-ʾān?. *Al-Azhar* 6: 1–10.

CHAPTER 12

ORALITY, CULTURE, AND LANGUAGE

CLIVE HOLES

12.1 Speech

12.1.1 Conversation

NATURAL, unmonitored talk in Arabic is almost always in a dialectal variety of the language. Arabic dialects are defined primarily by geography, but there are also distinctions based on social variables within the geographical boundaries of any dialect area and some variables that cross-cut geography. Religion or sect is associated with dialect difference in some places, notably Baghdad and other parts of Iraq ("Muslim" vs. "Christian" dialects and, prior to the early 1950s, "Jewish" dialects; Blanc 1964) and Bahrain ("Sunni" vs. "Shiʿite" dialects[1]; Holes 1983a, 1983b; [Behnstedt and Woidich, "Dialectology"]). Historical lifestyle is also an important dialect variable and essentially opposes Bedouin-descended dialects to sedentary ones, so that Bedouin dialects of different countries (e.g., Syria, Jordan, Egypt) may have as much or more in common with each other than they do with dialects of sedentary origin in the same country, which are geographically nearer. (Rosenhouse 1984 provides a general characterization of Bedouin dialects.) And, increasingly, a speaker's response to exposure to nonlocal varieties of the language, whether Modern Standard Arabic (SA or MSA)[2]

[1] Strictly speaking, this distinction is only coincidentally sectarian—the basic difference is originally one of geography and genealogy, between groups descended from Bedouin stock who have tribal links with central Arabia (the so-called ʿArab), who are all Sunni, and those descended from a sedentary coastal, largely farming population (the so-called Baḥārna), who are all Shiʿite.

[2] Grammatically and morphologically virtually identical with Classical Arabic (CA) but with a massively changed vocabulary that reflects the modern world.

or other dialects, may be reflected in his speech production, though this phenomenon differs from one Arab country to another[3] and is also often related to gender.[4] Generally speaking, in cross-dialectal situations, local features tend to be leveled and replaced by those of a regionally dominant dialect, often that of a capital city or of some other variety associated with a socially prestigious group. But the extent to which "dialectal leveling" actually occurs is related not just to the speaker's degree of exposure to external influences but also to contingent pragmatic factors in the speech context, such as who he is talking to, what is being talked about, the roles of the participants, and the setting and the purpose of the interaction. In more educated speakers' styles, in addition to vernacular–SA mixing,[5] there is often a great deal of hybridization, whereby elements from the dialect are combined with elements from SA. This is noticeable in major sentence constituents such as the verb phrase, where saliently SA lexical elements (e.g., verb stems) are combined with dialectal morphemes expressing categories like tense, number, and negation, and the noun phrase, where, again, saliently SA lexical items may be combined with dialectal morphemes expressing, for example, deixis. As an Egyptian example, compare the following ways of saying "he isn't accepted":

(1) SA: lā yuqbalu
Cairene: ma byit'abalš
hybrid: ma byuqbalš

It can be seen from this that the dialectal discontinuous negative morpheme, ma...š and b- tense/mood prefix are combined with a saliently SA passive verb stem to form the hybrid form. Examples of the converse process—for example, the combination of vernacular lexical items with SA function morphemes for tense, voice, negation, number, and deixis—do not occur except in the humorous mimicking of the speech of foreigners or of the illiterate's attempts to speak SA.

The kind of mixed and hybridized language illustrated is typical of unscripted conversation in media chat shows and programs involving interviews with politicians, journalists and educated people generally and occurs across the Arabic-speaking world. As noted, the hybridizing of the SA and dialectal systems is by no means random, even if there is a certain degree of fluidity in what occurs, and it appears that the asymmetrical nature of the combinatorial relationships between the lexical and functional morphemes of SA and the dialects previously noted holds good for all Arabic-speaking speech communities. However, the exact nature of the constraints on how the two systems may be combined has yet to be worked out in detail.[6]

[3] Egyptian speakers, in particular, show great loyalty to their dialect in dialect contact situations.

[4] Female speakers, as in other societies, have been shown by several studies to lead the way in switches to "prestige" local varieties compared with men (Abd-el-Jawad 1986: 57–61 for Jordanian urban centers) and to propagate a kind of variability that targets non-CA/SA forms (Haeri 1996: 231–232 for Cairo).

[5] For many educated North African speakers of Arabic, French replaces SA as the code with which they mix and to which they switch (see Section 12.1.3 on computer-mediated communication, or CMC).

[6] An attempt for Cairene can be found in Mejdell (2006).

Code switching between Arabic and English has become something of a fashion among the Western-educated youth of several Arab countries. This kind of speech is known as ʿArabīzī, a portmanteau word coined from *ʿarabī* ("Arabic") and *inglīzī* ("English"), which gave its name to a 52-minute film on the subject made in 2006. ʿArabīzī involves a constant to and fro between sentences or phrases in the speaker's dialect and in English (often American accented). Many of those who use this speech style had an English-medium education and work in fields in which English is becoming the global "default" language—international banking, commerce, law, journalism. They often admit to a poor mastery of SA. An example of ʿArabīzī, taken from the film of the same name, is as follows:

> ismi ʿayša xālidī, mawlūda bil-kwēt, and I also lived in Egypt when I was younger, u ʿišt arbaʿ snīn fi amrīka fil-jāmʿa... I'm the sports editor of the *Daily Star*. I love that job; it's amazing. I was a journalism major so it worked out for me. ʿumrī arbaʿ u ʿišrīn sana u ana atḥačča ʿArabīzī.
>
> [My name is Aysha Khalidi, born in Kuwait, and I also lived in Egypt when I was younger, and I lived for four years in America at university... I'm the sports editor of the *Daily Star*. I love that job; it's amazing. I was a journalism major so it worked out for me. I am 24 years old, and I speak ʿArabīzī.]

Conversational code switching between Arabic and French is a phenomenon of much longer standing in North Africa (Bentahila 1983; Heath 1989) and occurs with other European languages among émigré groups (see Nortier 1990 for Dutch–Moroccan Arabic). See also Section 12.1.3 on computer-mediated communication (CMC) for examples from Internet chat rooms [Davies et al., "Code Switching"].

12.1.2 Monologue

Where the speech is scripted, as in many types of formal monologue (political speeches, sermons in a mosque or church, lectures, media news bulletins), the language variety used is usually SA, but always with some degree of phonological influence from the speaker's underlying vernacular. However, this statement needs qualification. The purpose of a political speech is often to convince an audience of nonpoliticians, who will have varying degrees of competence in SA. Both these considerations can lead speakers to resort to the vernacular at certain points, either to make themselves clearly understood or to use as a tactic of persuasion (see Mazraani 1997 for evidence from Egypt, Libya, and Iraq). Recounting personal experiences or telling humorous anecdotes to underline a point, for example, or simply showing sympathy with their audience's concerns, are rhetorical moves that take the speaker off script and into affective and interpersonal domains in which the dialect is strongly favored. Dialect is also often resorted to when some political axiom, couched in SA "officialese," needs to be explained. The late president of Egypt, Gamāl ʿAbdul-Nāṣir, was a master of this kind of code switching, which he often used quite deliberately to manipulate the emotions of his audience (Holes 1993). Sermons are another type of monologue in which code switching commonly occurs, when, for example, the imam needs to explain or "translate" into the vernacular religious material in the Classical language that the audience may otherwise not fully understand (Bassiouney 2006). However, this is a matter of choice, and some extremely popular religious orators, such as the fiery Egyptian critic of Anwar Sadat, 'Abdul-Ḥamīd Kišk (d. 1987), derived part of their popularity from their ability to deliver their messages in flawless Classical Arabic, however little some of their audiences may have understood what they were saying. Similarly, public figures who cultivate an image of regal dignity as part of their public persona, such as Sultan Qaboos of Oman or the late King Hussein of Jordan, avoid the use of dialect in public speaking. This is also typical of groups of speakers for whom dialect avoidance is an element in a cultural agenda. The Egyptian literary poet and literary critic Fārūq Šūša, who appears frequently on popular Egyptian radio and TV shows, is one such, and his radio program "Our Beautiful Language" has been running continuously since 1967. In his case, it is part of a personal campaign to persuade the wider public to actively use and engage with Classical Arabic language and literature. Islamic radicals in the public eye, such as spokesmen for the Palestinian group Hamas and the Lebanon-based, Iran-backed Hezbollah, always use SA in their speeches but also even in impromptu media conversations and interviews. Here the reasons seem to be the dogma that CA, the language of the Quran, is the only true form of Arabic and the only one fit to carry their religiously inspired political message.

Media news bulletins are overwhelmingly the preserve of SA, but, as al-Batal (2002) shows, dialectal Arabic has made inroads here: the local news on the Christian-owned LBCI channel of Lebanese TV has recently begun to use a form of "vernacularized" SA for its local news bulletins. This, and the increased use of French and English in the channel's general programming, is seen as an assertion of Christian identity in post–civil war (1975–1990) Lebanon.

12.1.3 Computer-Mediated Communication

According to a recent report by Etling et al. (2009), the Arabic blogosphere is organized primarily around countries, with Egypt by far the biggest cluster, followed by Saudi Arabia and Kuwait. There are Levantine–English "bridge" blogs in the eastern Arab World and Maghreb–French ones in North Africa, in which bloggers frequently use the European language alongside Arabic. The bloggers are predominantly young and male, and the most important issues for most of them relate to their personal life and local issues, with religion and human rights featuring strongly. An offshoot of CMC (as in the West) has been the commercially published blog, which has generated at least one best seller. This is Ghāda 'Abdul-'Āl's *'Ayza Atgawwiz*[7] (I Want to Get Married), written entirely in Egyptian colloquial Arabic and published as a book in 2008. The author is a

[7] http://www.wanna-b-a-bride.blogspot.com.

29-year-old Egyptian pharmacist, who claims to be speaking on behalf of the 15 million unmarried Egyptian women aged between 25 and 35 who are being pressured by society to marry, "even though it's not their fault they are on the shelf." The book is a selection of the author's often witty and satirical Internet posts on the subject of marriage and contains apparently personal anecdotes. This blog book was turned into an Egyptian TV serial in 2010 and has even been translated into English.[8]

The Arabic "speech" of CMC (email, Internet chat rooms, message boards, blogs, social networking sites), insofar as can be judged from the wide variety of orthographic conventions that have arisen, presents a similar picture of variation related to extralinguistic factors. Normally, the Arabic spelling reflects the grammatical structures and vocabulary of the contributor's vernacular (pronunciation is less easy to tell), though in "conversations" on certain topics, especially Islam, the variety used is usually SA, or the contributor's best effort to write it. But there are local peculiarities. In Egypt, the use of dialectal Arabic in CMC is particularly prevalent; there is even an "Egyptian Wikipedia," parallel to the pan-Arab Wikipedia, whose rules forbid the use of any Arabic variety other than Egyptian (effectively, this means Cairene). In particular, some Copts (Christian Egyptians) write only in Egyptian vernacular, thereby foregrounding their "Egyptian identity" and eschewing the use of SA, which they see as part of a "pan-Arab identity" they do not share.[9]

When, for technical reasons, the Arabic alphabet is not available to the Internet user or in cell-phone text messaging, a romanized "Arabic chat alphabet" is sometimes used. This uses digits and other symbols for certain Arabic letters whose sounds do not occur in Western languages (though there is some variation in the correspondences).[10] A typical example is:

(2) alsalam 3alikom wa ra7mato Allah wa barakatoh

which would appear in the normal Arabic script as:

(3) السلام عليكم ورحمة الله وبركاته

and would be phonetically transcribed as:

(4) as-salāmu ʿalaykum wa raḥmatu llāh wa barakātuh
"Peace be with you and God's mercy be upon you."

On websites frequented by speakers of North African dialects, there is a great deal of code switching and code mixing (as there is in ordinary speech) between the dialect and

[8] By the University of Texas's Department of Middle Eastern Studies under the title "I want to get married."

[9] I am indebted to Ivan Panovic for this observation.

[10] See http://en.wikipedia.org/wiki/Arabic_chat_alphabet.

French, all elements of which are expressed in romanized script. For example (Arabic elements written here in italic):[11]

(5) Je n'ai pu me retenir *7ta yfout* le tribunal
"I was unable to hold myself back *until he entered* the court."
rani ndirha f wa7ed l'institut privée
"*I am doing it in a* private institute."

12.1.4 Arabic Pidgins

An Arabic-based Pidgin is widely used in the Arabian Gulf States and Saudi Arabia as a consequence of the large-scale immigration of construction workers, laborers, shop assistants, nannies, maids, and other predominantly unskilled workers from the Indian subcontinent and southeast Asia, beginning in the mid-1960s (Smart 1990; Næss 2008; al-Azraqi 2010). A similar phenomenon has been noted in Lebanon for Sri Lankan maids (Bizri 2005). By 2006, over 80% of the population of the United Arab Emirates (UAE) was non-Arab, the vast majority of whom were from India, Pakistan, Bangladesh, and Sri Lanka (Naess 2008: 21). Many of the men live in construction site work camps, and both the amount and type of linguistic contact these migrant workers have with the native Arabic-speaking population is severely limited. The Gulf Pidgin that has developed has all the classic features of Pidgin languages: compared with the superstrate language, Gulf Arabic, it shows a lack of inflectional morphology, preference for analytical structures, reduced verbal, nominal and pronominal paradigms, commonly a single preposition, and a tendency toward subject–verb–object (SVO) word order (Romaine 1988: 25–31). It is typically used in formulaic and usually fleeting encounters with native Arabic speakers in the workplace and marketplace and, though now seemingly stable, shows no signs of Creolization or of being replaced by Arabic learned as a foreign language, given the legal impossibility of the migrants gaining citizenship, however long they stay, and the social distance between them and the indigenous population [Tosco and Manfredi, "Creoles"].

12.2 Poetry and Song

12.2.1 Poetry

Poetry is the paramount verbal art form in all Arab societies and has been so over the course of their recorded history. The earliest poetry that has come down to us (from

[11] In this orthography, "7" stands for the Arabic pharyngeal voiceless fricative (ḥ), "3" for its voiced counterpart (ʿ), and "9" for the voiceless uvular stop (q). I am grateful to my former student Mary Montgomery for permission to quote these examples.

the 6th and 7th centuries AH) was, as far as we can tell, memorized oral recitation that had to conform to strict schemata of scansion and rhyme to qualify for the designation shiʿr ("poetry"; the basic meaning is "knowledge or perception by means of the senses"). Its social functions in preliterate Arabia were many: as a repository of tribal history; as a vehicle for satire, elegy, praise, and the giving of advice; for describing nature; for expressing love; for celebrating the hunt. The original audience for this poetry was the poet's fellow tribesmen. After the Islamic conquests, as literacy slowly began to take hold in the towns, the old poetic genres were developed and embellished as new literary influences from conquered territories exerted themselves. Traditional oral poetry continued in the Bedouin milieu but went almost completely unrecorded, except as a reservoir of Bedouin (= "pure") language for medieval philologists and dictionary makers; serious poetry was a literate and literary art of the city and the court. And, in contrast to the oral tradition that continued to reflect the evolving language of speech, the language of poetry and writing more generally adhered to the fixed rules of CA, which, certainly by no later than two centuries after the Islamic conquests, (i.e., by no later than c. 235/850) was no one's mother tongue (if it had ever been anyone's).

Occasionally in the medieval period we catch glimpses of this continuing but now subaltern oral tradition. Ibn Xaldūn (1332–1382), the North African philosopher of history, quotes several examples of the oral Bedouin odes of his time, using them to expatiate on the difference between "eloquence" (balāġa) and "grammatical correctness" (ʾiʿrāb) and condemning the literary critics who confounded the two and who dismissed this poetry's claims to eloquence on the grounds that its language did not conform to the inflectional system of CA (Rosenthal 1958: vol. 3, 414–415; [Larcher, "ALT II"]). These odes are, like pre-Islamic ones, monorhymed and nonstrophic. Slightly before Ibn Xaldūn, the Iraqi Ṣafiyaddīn al-Ḥillī (1278–1348), presents a treatise (Hoenerbach 1956) on the poetics of the "seven arts" of the dialectal poetry of his era. These poems are different from the Bedouin odes cited by Ibn Xaldūn in that they are strophic and have different rhyme schemes. Some of them were based on models imported from Andalusia; others were developed in Iraq. The modern practice of colloquial poetry continues to reflect these ancient differences: the contemporary so-called nabaṭī Bedouin poetry of Arabia is structurally similar to the Bedouin material quoted by Ibn Xaldūn and to that of the pre-Islamic period. On the other hand, many modern types of dialectal poetry from the urban and rural milieus of Egypt, Lebanon, Syria, and Iraq seem to have developed from the types described by Ṣafiyaddīn al-Ḥillī. Occasional early modern examples have survived: one such is a celebrated 17th-century spoof poem by an imaginary Egyptian named Abū Šādūf (lit. "the man who operates the counterpoise," a device used for raising irrigation water from the Nile, used for centuries by Egyptian peasant farmers) to which a "learned commentary" by one Yūsuf al-Širbīnī is appended. The poem describes in mock-heroic terms the wretchedness, squalor, and ignorance of Egyptian peasant life, adding further ridicule via the device of the fake commentary.[12]

[12] Davies (2008) provides an English translation.

Today, dialect poetry is composed in every Arab country and is a popular art form in the true sense, being composed by people at very top and at the very bottom of the social pyramid and all points in between. Although originally a purely oral art form and often practiced by the illiterate, composing poetry in dialect is today often also the choice of the educated. The spoken dialects evoke a set of cultural resonances different from those of SA. Because they are the natural way for hundreds of millions of Arabs to articulate their feelings about the ups and downs of everyday life, often in vividly concrete and personal ways, they are the natural poetic idiom for ridicule, satire, and vituperation and, in a region in which a tight rein is kept on the media, hence for expressing dissenting political opinion. This applies to poetry composed in the Bedouin tradition just as much as it does to the urban one.

In Egypt, the educated dialect poet Maḥmūd Bayram al-Tūnisī (1893–1961) composed much colloquial verse that was critical of the Egyptian establishment and the British colonial powers of the early 20th century and suffered decades of enforced exile for his pains. His compatriot of the next generation, Aḥmad Fu'ād Nigm (1929–), who was at the height of his fame in the 1970s at the time of Anwar Sadat's presidency and darling of the student movement of that time, produced a torrent of linguistically inventive satirical verse on social inequality and political corruption in Egypt. This landed him and his partner, al-Šayx Imām (d. 1995) who put many of his barbs to music, more than once in prison. Their work circulated clandestinely on cassette tapes and faxes, and for a number of years it was illegal in Egypt to own such material.[13] Similarly, the Iraqi ʿAbbūd al-Karxī (1861–1946) provides a running poetic commentary in Iraqi Arabic on all aspects of the politics of the Iraq of his time. Like Maḥmūd Bayram al-Tūnisī in Egypt, he was hounded for it by the authorities of the British mandate and afterwards. His successor and cultural heir was ʿAzīz ʿAlī (c. 1911–1995), who wrote amusing barbed monologues in Baghdadi Arabic on many aspects of social and political life that he set to music and performed on Baghdad radio and television. Today, the exiled Iraqi dialect poet ʿAbbās Jījān is a well-known figure on Arabic satellite television channels, and some of his most memorable compositions, critical of Saddam Hussein's regime and of the American invasion of Iraq that brought it down, have attained global celebrity by being posted as video clips on YouTube.

In a similar vein, the modern Bedouin colloquial poetry of Jordan and Sinai has reinvented itself as a means for making critical comment on a host of social and political issues: where once the focus was on intertribal conflict, nowadays it is more likely to be anti-Bedouin discrimination, police brutality, high taxes, government corruption, the weak leadership of the Arab countries, and the political situation in the Middle East (Holes and Abu Athera 2009). In a lighter vein, in the Gulf tradition there are poems that treat issues such as the pros and cons of marrying a non-Arab woman, the lax morals of the young, and the "keeping up with the Joneses" mind-set of some Gulf Arabs (Holes and Abu Athera 2011). Individual poets' work circulates by a variety of means: word

[13] Abdel-Malek (1990).

of mouth, on cheap cassettes, even by text messaging, and, in the case of better-known poets, in locally printed books and occasionally the newspapers. But colloquial poetry is finding new audiences well beyond its traditional ones. In the emirate of Abu Dhabi, one of the seven that makes up the UAE, a satellite TV colloquial poetry competition began in December 2006 called šāʿir il-milyūn ("Poet of the Million")[14] and is now in its fifth season. It has become a huge hit not just with UAE viewers but also more widely in the Gulf and the neighboring areas of the Arab World. Poets aged between 18 and 45, and not just from Arabia and the Gulf but from countries as far away as Syria, Jordan, and Iraq, recite a colloquial poem before a theater audience, which is commented on by a judging panel of experts and voted via text messaging from the viewers of the program, similar to "X Factor," the UK (and now global) singing competition. The program proceeds on a "knock-out" basis, and the winner receives a banner and a large cash prize. The poems can be on any subject, including politics, but they must be in the colloquial. In the most recent season of the program, a fully veiled Saudi housewife won third prize for a poem criticizing some of the extreme fatwas issued by the religious authorities in her home country, causing much adverse comment and even death threats. The program now has its own dedicated TV channel, as does a parallel one, Amīr aš-Šuʿarāʾ (The Prince of Poets), in which poets of the Classical language compete with one another. These televised public displays of poetic talent play to the age-old self-image of the Arabs (and the Gulf Arabs in particular) as a nation of poets. It is one element in the creation of an identity in which the past is being reclaimed and rebranded for the post-oil generations—generations whose adoption of Western lifestyles, cultural preferences, and even "the loss of Arabic" is beginning to alarm Gulf governments.

12.2.2 Song

The relationship between song and poetry in Arabic-speaking communities has always been close. Traditional Bedouin oral poetry was often, and occasionally continues to be, sung to the accompaniment of the one-stringed rabāba ("rebec") and, in rural Egypt, a variety of simple string and woodwind instruments: the simsimiyya (similar to a lyre), the mizmār, and arġūl (types of reed pipe) are still in use. From the earliest times, poems or parts of poems in the Classical language were also put to music.[15] This tradition has continued to the present day, and some of the most famous songs of the greatest modern singers are in this category. Most notable is Umm Kulthūm (c. 1900–1975) of Egypt, whose lyrics include many poems in the Classical language by the Egyptian neoclassical poet Aḥmad Šawqī and the Syrian Nizār Qabbānī as well in the colloquial by Egyptian poets such as Maḥmūd Bayram al-Tūnisī (q.v.) and Ṣalāḥ

[14] The title seems to be a double entendre: the winner originally got a million UAE dirhams (now it's more) as a prize, but it can also be understood as "poet in a million."

[15] The greatest early compilation is the *Kitāb al-Aġānī* (Book of Songs) of the poet and musicologist Abū l-Faraj al-Iṣfahānī (897–972).

Jāhīn. Her lifelong lyricist Aḥmad Rāmī also wrote for her largely in the colloquial. It is important to note that what we are terming *colloquial* language in song, as in poetry, is not the same as ordinary speech. In love songs in particular,[16] many stock figures (e.g., "the backbiter," "the criticizer," "the liar") are drawn from a poetic repertoire shared for centuries by Classical and colloquial poetry as well as many shared similes and figures of speech. Apart from these features, the main formal difference between the colloquial of song/poetry and ordinary speech is in a somewhat more classicized pronunciation and morphology. The repertoire of the feted Lebanese singer Fayrūz was also partly in SA, partly in the colloquial, but with a strong bias toward the colloquial end of the range, as defined here. It is instructive to examine the types of song in which she used different registers of the language. By and large, songs whose sentiments are personal or love oriented or which describe the concrete details of the real, physical world are in the colloquial; songs that address bigger, grander, and more abstract themes are in the Classical language. A good example of the contrast is provided by two famous songs about Palestine, both of which date from 1971, four years after the end of 6-Day War with Israel. In the first, titled on the album sleeve *al-Quds al-ʿAtīqa* (though pronounced in the song in the colloquial fashion *al-ʾids il-ʿatīʾa*) "Old Jerusalem," Fayrūz leads the listener through the streets of the ancient eastern (Arab) part of the city and talks to the shopkeepers about recent shocking events. She receives the gift of a flower vase from them, "the people who wait" (sc. for deliverance) and imagines the nameless Palestinian families who worked for centuries "under the sun, in the wind" to build the city, only to see their houses torn town by "the black hands" that battered down their doors and erected barbed wire fences. All of this domestic, physical description is delivered in succinct Lebanese colloquial in a song lasting three minutes. But in another song titled *Zahrat al-Madāʾin* (Flower of Cities), from the same album, *al-Quds fī l-Bāl* (Jerusalem on My Mind), the mood and language are quite different. In this song, Fayrūz starts by declaring that she is praying for the sake of Jerusalem, the "city of prayer," and meditates on the connections of the three monotheistic faiths with it: "our eyes," she sings, apparently speaking on behalf of all Palestinians, "wander through the colonnades of the temples, embrace the ancient churches, and wipe away the sorrow from the mosques." This yearning reverie continues with a lilting evocation of "the child in the grotto, whose mother is Mary" and "two faces weeping" (those of Mary and Joseph—Fayrūz is a Christian) but is eventually interrupted by the urgent, martial call of trumpets and painful memories of Jerusalem's fall at the hands of (Israeli) troops, in which "peace was martyred in the city of peace," followed by defiant predictions of its reconquest by warriors who will ride atop "terrifying steeds." The song's mood then shifts back once more to contemplative reverie and ends with the singer's fervent hope that peace will once more be restored to the ancient city. The emotional and musical canvas is on the grand scale—the song lasts for eight and a half minutes, with full orchestra and choir—and the words are delivered, as befits the elevated sentiments and religious and nationalist symbolism, in flawless Classical Arabic. The

[16] Though renowned for her love songs, Umm Kulthūm also sang many with a political message.

linguistic contrast with the intimacy and domesticity of "Old Jerusalem" could hardly be starker. For a period in the 1970s and 1980s, such was its popularity that "Flower of Cities" became a virtual Palestinian national anthem, a point that underlines that "popular" in the linguistic culture of Arab speech communities does not always equate to "colloquial."

The commercial popular music of the present day, whether Egyptian, Levantine, or Gulf love songs, or songs that carry a social or political "message" in genres such as Algerian *rāy* (lit. "opinion") and Tunisian *mizwid* normally uses the local form of the colloquial. In the case of *rāy*, this often involves, as in ordinary North African speech, a mix of French and Arabic. A novel feature of the music scene in the Arab world today is the way local musical traditions have become popular outside their original areas, largely as a result of satellite television and the Internet. Gulf popular music, for example, in a style known as *xalījī* ("Gulf"), has a following in countries as far afield as Tunisia, despite the difficulty listeners must initially have had in understanding the dialect of the lyrics. But the general homogenization of speech caused by increased contact with and exposure to nonlocal forms of Arabic has had an effect here too. Furthermore, with the passing of a generation of Egyptian superstars like Umm Kulthūm (d. 1975), Abdul-Ḥalīm Ḥāfiḍ (d.1977), Farīd al-Aṭraš (d.1974), and Muḥammad ʿAbdul-Wahhāb (d. 1991), the foursome that dominated Arab popular music for most of the 20th century, has come a new and more diverse linguistic and musical era that coincides with the weakening of Egyptian political and cultural domination over the rest of the Arab World. It was the superstar of Algerian *rāy*, Chebb Khalid (though now, at the age of 50, he has dropped "Chebb" ["youth"] from his stage name) who was invited to sing one of his (nonpolitical) songs at the opening of the 2010 football World Cup in South Africa—which he duly did in Algerian Arabic.

12.3 Cinema, Theater, and Television Drama

Drama in the western sense is not an indigenous art form in the Arabic-speaking world. It first appeared in the 19th century as a result of cultural contact with Europe (Sadgrove 1996) and posed an immediate linguistic problem. The impact of any play relies in part on the language of its dialogue: it should be "speakable" and based on an observable or (in the case of historical dramas) imagined social reality. This means that the language should normally have been the colloquial. But for many Arab playwrights, drama was seen first and foremost as a form of "high" art and therefore the natural preserve of CA/SA, which is not the natively spoken form of the language for any Arab. This issue was perceived to be less acute in dramas set in the Arab past, in which the common (though historically false) folk-belief that normal speech back then was indeed in CA could be exploited. An example is Maḥmūd Taymūr's play *Ibn Jalā* (A Man of Celebrity), which portrays the career and character of the famous

8th-century Umayyad governor of Iraq, al-Ḥajjāj ibn Yūsuf, in which the dialogue is in high-flown CA throughout. But what to do about the dialogue in plays set in the present-day and in a specific geographical location? Dialect, and geographically specific dialect at that, seemed to be required for any semblance of sociolinguistic reality. Yet there was hesitation here. In the play "Parents and Children," a contemporary social drama set in a small Lebanese town written in 1917 by the Lebanese Christian author Mixā'īl Nu'ayma, the educated characters speak SA (even when drunk) and the uneducated speak dialect, even when talking to each other. The result is artificial and stilted, even comical and absurd (Badawi 1988: 137). A contemporary of Taymūr's, Tawfīq al-Ḥakīm, tried to come to grips with the conundrum in another way, in a play he wrote in the mid-1950s, *al-Ṣafqa* ("The Deal"). In it he wrote the dialogue in what he termed "the third language," a form of Arabic that conformed as far as possible to the syntactic rules of CA/SA on the printed page, avoiding lexical choices that were either saliently local or standard. Because normal Arabic orthography underspecifies the phonological realization of words, this meant that the text could be performed in something akin to the dialect of any group of actors who shared this vocabulary (roughly, that of the eastern Arab World) via the omission of most (unmarked) grammatical inflections and the performing of the short vowels (always unmarked in normal Arabic script) according to their own local dialect. But the result of this experiment was unnatural, an artificial form of Arabic that was neither fish nor fowl, and unlike the real "third language" that educated Arabs speak on a daily basis (see Section 12.1.1). Tawfīq al-Ḥakīm's idea was quickly abandoned, and writers simply adopted their normal spoken language as the default choice for drama set in the contemporary world. In fact, the "foreignness" of CA/SA as a means of spoken communication has sometimes been exploited for comic effect. In the Egyptian writer Yūsuf Idrīs's play *Gumhūriyyat Faraḥāt* ("Faraḥāt's Republic"), the following farcical exchange takes place between Faraḥāt, a beaten-down suburban policeman, and an equally miserable peasant woman. The exchange occurs when Faraḥāt is taking a statement from her, and she completely fails to understand the SA "officialese" (in bold in the quotation) required of a representative of the state, which he then "translates" for her into Egyptian colloquial Arabic (Idrīs 1981:101):

(6) Policeman: yā bitt... **hal ladayki 'aqwālun 'uxrā** ?
Woman: **'uxrā** ēh yā sīdi?
Policeman: 'ayza t'ūli ḥāga tānya, ya'ni?!
Policeman: Now then, girlie... **Do you have any further statements to make**?
Woman: "**Further**" is what, sir?
Policeman: I mean, got anythin' else you wanna say?!

Idrīs made more extended dramatic use of spoken SA in his play *al-Laḥẓa al-Ḥariga* (The Critical Moment), set in Egypt at the time of the Suez Crisis of 1956. The dialogue is in Egyptian spoken Arabic, except for the words of the British soldiers. In reality, of course, they would have spoken English (perhaps punctuated with some Egyptian "kitchen Arabic" of the "šufti bint" type common among the troops), but Idrīs makes them speak SA, presumably to create a similarly foreign and alienating effect. The actual effect, however, is merely jarring and unnatural. Historical subjects, on the other hand, especially religious ones, have continued to be scripted in SA/CA, as have, in the main, the Arabic translations of the works of classic western playwrights like Shakespeare.[17]

The same principles apply, a fortiori, to the dialogue of drama in cinema and television, both of which have a much broader popular appeal than the theater. From the 1930s until roughly the 1980s, Arab cinema, and the ever popular TV *musalsal*, or "drama serial," often in 13 but sometimes many more parts, were dominated by the Egyptian film and television industries. The setting for the hundreds of films and serials made in this period was almost invariably Egypt—usually Cairo or Alexandria—with Egyptian actors and Egyptian dialogue. This had the side effect of accustoming generations of non-Egyptian Arab moviegoers and television audiences to the rhythms and vocabulary of Egyptian speech at a time when many of them had hardly traveled outside their own town or village.[18] The exception has again been historical costume drama, particularly if it has a religious content. The blockbuster film *al-Risāla* (The Message), an account of the rise of Islam, made in separate Arabic and English versions in 1976 and funded by Libya, used only CA/SA for the Arabic dialogue. Although many of those who saw it would have struggled to understand the dialogue, that did not prevent it being a huge international hit around the Arab (and indeed non-Arabic-speaking parts of the Muslim) world.

Since the 1980s, however, the Egyptian film industry has been in relative decline. Although Egyptian films and serials remain popular, there are now many rival sources of production, particularly for the TV market—Syria, Lebanon, Jordan, and the Gulf States—with plots, scenarios, and dialects to match. But where the aim is seen as educative rather than merely entertaining, as in much children's programming, a simplified form of SA/CA is often used, which can come quite close to the "third language" Tawfīq al-Ḥakīm experimented with in the 1950s. A good example of this is *Iftaḥ yā Simsim!* (Open, Sesame!), an Arabic version of the U.S.-produced "Sesame Street" that became enormously popular throughout the Arab world in the 1980s and that employed a simplified form of SA for dialogue between the puppet characters.

12.4 Writing

Although this chapter is concerned with language and orality, a few remarks will be made here about language levels in prose writing in the modern Arabic-speaking world since in certain text types orality is bound to be an issue.

[17] However, the Egyptian author Muḥammad 'Uthmān Galāl (1829–1898) experimented with translating French playwrights of the 17th century, such as Molière and Racine, into Egyptian colloquial Arabic.

[18] Recorded Egyptian popular music, as we have noted, was also hugely popular and had a similar effect.

Any Arab creative writer with pretensions to having his work considered as "serious" literature has traditionally composed it in SA. That was axiomatic until perhaps 30 years ago. While it still remains the case that SA is overwhelmingly the vehicle of choice for serious creative prose writing, in recent times, and particularly in Egypt, there has been some experimentation with writing in the vernacular. This had long existed as a marginal and not very respectable phenomenon. In the early 20th century, we find sometimes lurid accounts of "edgy" aspects of urban life, rather like the "penny dreadfuls" of Victorian England. A whole series with the title "Diary of a...," mostly running to 60 or 70 pages and purporting to be autobiographical, was published in the 1930s, selling for a few pennies on the streets of Cairo. A good example is *Muḏakkirāt Naššāl* (Diary of a Pickpocket) by one ʿAbdul-ʿAzīz al-Nuṣṣ (probably a pseudonym), which supposedly gives the respectable reader an autobiographical insight into the tricks of the petty thief's trade and is written in a broad Cairene argot. Other vernacular prose works published around the same time sought to amuse: an example is Maḥmūd Bayram al-Tūnisī's (q.v.) *Is-Sayyid wi Marātu fi Bārīs* (The Master and His Wife in Paris), which satirizes, largely through their own conversation, the pretensions of middle-class Egyptians traveling to Europe for the first time. But perhaps the most eye-catching example is a recent (1994) novel written entirely in colloquial Egyptian Arabic by the major Egyptian writer Yūsuf al-Qaʿīd, titled "Sparrows' Milk" (a proverbial expression for anything of great rarity, similar to "hens' teeth" in English), in which the story is a first-person narration by an illiterate peasant woman speaking directly to the reader. She tells what happens when a member of her family finds a million Egyptian pounds in the street and the trials and tribulations that follow from this at first sight extraordinary piece of good luck. The author has denied that he was motivated to write in Egyptian colloquial by any ideological considerations, describing the work as a literary "experiment" and observing that to make the narrator speak SA would have been absurd, given that she and her family are drawn from the ranks of Egypt's illiterate poor. Rather different considerations motivated the writing of the vernacular novel *Nuzūla wa Khayṭ aš-Šayṭān* (Tenants and Cobwebs) (1986) by the Iraqi Jewish author Samīr Naqqāsh. The story focuses on a Baghdadi apartment house of the old style during the late 1940s, in which the tenants are a mixture of Muslims, Christians, and Jews—a setup that would have been quite normal in the years before the foundation of Israel in 1948. All the characters tell their story in their distinctive Baghdadi dialect: Muslim, Christian, or Jewish. By the end of the book, the house is in semiruin, and all the tenants have left, save a lone madwoman. The work seems to be an allegory for the 20th-century fragmentation of civil society in Iraq, symbolized by the author's extraordinary ability to write dialogue in the three dialects of the communities[19]

[19] Naqqāsh left Iraq in his teens but seems to have had an ear for and memory of the Baghdadi vernaculars of his boyhood. The work is heavily footnoted since few Arabs—even Iraqis of the present generations—would now understand these communal dialects, which have now largely disappeared from the public arena (disappeared completely in the Jewish case after the emigration en masse of the Jewish population to Israel in the early 1950s). Blanc (1964) provides a detailed linguistic description of the three

that constituted it. The complex orality of Iraqi society, the passing of which the book seems to mourn, has been one of the casualties of international politics, it seems.

As noted already, some categories of written Arabic are produced in a quasi "real-time" interactional context, where it is difficult to draw a line demarcating them formally from speech. But these are not the only contexts in which a non-standard form of the language is used in writing. Diaries, private messages, notes, personal letters, the captions to newspaper cartoons, and caricatures are all "speech-like" in one sense or another; this tends to be reflected in the non-SA forms used in them. However, it seems that written texts in which *different levels of Arabic alternate* are becoming commonplace even in commercially published work. As ever, the epicenter of this new development is Egypt. Rosenbaum (2000) dubs this "alternating style" "fuṣḥāmmiyya," a portmanteau term formed from fuṣḥā, the Arabic term for CA/SA and ʿāmmiyya, the term for colloquial, non-standard Arabic. This style has characteristics that differentiate it from the mixed, "hybridized" speech style exemplified at the beginning of this chapter: first, the fact that SA and the colloquial *alternate* at the level of phrases and whole sentences in an apparently random fashion (and this has seemingly nothing to do with rhetorical function) and do not form hybrids at word level; second, the frequency of *hendiadys*—that is, the repetition of a meaning element, often a lengthy phrase, in both codes, one after the other; third, the *commutative* nature of the alternations—that is, that readers will readily accept fuṣḥāmmiyya texts in which the original SA and colloquial sections have been "translated" into the other code so that the text they are presented with for comment is like a photographic negative of the original.[20] This style has been shown to occur in a variety of written text types: magazine articles on fashion or sport but also with current affairs of the day as they impact on the individual reader as well as in humorous and anecdotal stories.[21] As Rosenbaum points out, none of these texts involve the transcription of actual speech, whether face to face or computer mediated, but planned and edited *written* texts that are the result of conscious choice. That is, the code alternation seems to be meaningful *in itself* and serve a number of purposes, all of which can be seen as examples, in Gumperz's terms, of "metaphorical" rather than "situational" code switching: expressing emotional commitment to a point of view; emphasizing a statement; being sarcastic, ironic, or flippant, depending on the context. A recent study of the language of three Egyptian newspapers (Ibrahim 2010) shows a similar pattern of code switching in two of them, even in headlines.

dialects, but it is not nearly as rich in the detailing of their individual idioms and vocabulary as this work of fiction.

[20] Shown by an experiment in which Rosenbaum (2000: 78) sought readers' reactions to a fuṣḥāmmiyya text he had "reversed."

[21] Rosenbaum (2000: 74) notes plentiful examples in a book of reminiscences titled "Memoirs of a Young Egyptian Washing Dishes in London."

The Egyptian Revolution of January 25–February 11, 2011, was particularly interesting from the standpoint of how the protesters conveyed their message to the media of the Arab and the wider world. Though the history of how the revolution was organized has yet to be written, it is clear that the "social media"—Facebook, Twitter, and Internet blogs—were a major tool in the early stages. This fact has already given rise to at least one joke—Egyptians are famed throughout the Arab World for their sense of humor—that is widely circulating on the Internet (in the colloquial, inevitably, as are virtually all jokes):

> بعدما مات، مبارك قابل عبد الناصر و السادات. قالوا له: "هاه، سم ولا منصة؟" قال لهم بحرقة: "لا... ده الفيسبوك"
>
> After he died, Mubarak met Nasser and Sadat. "So," they said to him, "was it poison or a podium?" "No," he answered bitterly, "it was Facebook."[22]

However, once Mubarak's regime closed down the Internet and the mobile phone networks, as it did about four days into the uprising, Egyptians started appearing in Tahrir Square carrying homemade placards of all shapes and sizes to convey to the world their verdict on their president and government. Some were in rudimentary English, with messages like "Go to Hell," "Game Over," and "Get Out." But many were written in spoken Egyptian Arabic and often inventive and funny. Some examples follow.

A photograph of Obama shaking hands with Mubarak has the following speech bubbles:

> Obama: In my opinion you should write a letter of farewell to the Egyptian people.
> Mubarak: Why? Where are they going?

A placard written in felt tip reads: "The Union of Egyptian Carpenters asks Master Carpenter Mubarak—what kind of glue do you use?"

> Another: "The woman wants to give birth, but the baby doesn't want to see you."

Inevitably also, colloquial poetry came to the fore. Egyptian past master Aḥmad Fu'ād Nigm, now in his 80s, led the charge with anti-Mubarak compositions such as *Ka'annak mā fīš* ("It's as if you don't exist") and *'Ayzīn nugarrab khil'a tanya* ("We'd like to try a different face"). A performance of the first poem on YouTube is given by someone who is described as *miṣrī ṭāli' 'ēnuh*, roughly "an Egyptian fed up to the back teeth."[23] What the Egyptians displayed in their use of such orate weapons was what Nigm himself invented a word for in one of his poems: *nikta-lūgia*, roughly "joke-ology": the ability to beat an enemy by joking and mockery, but always with a light heart (*khiffat id-dam*).

[22] The reference here is to the way the two previous Presidents of Egypt met their deaths. It has long been rumoured, though never proven, that Nasser (president 1954–70) died as a result of drinking poisoned coffee. Sadat (president 1970–81) was assassinated by Islamists as he sat on a podium, watching a march past of Egyptian forces. The "bitterness" of Mubarak is because his presidency ended so relatively ingloriously.

[23] http://www.youtube.com/watch?v=jGJ1nlJyFtM.

12.5 Concluding Remarks

As this chapter has sought to show, the relationship between orality and language in Arabic is complex. The layman's mental landscape is of a "high," literary, codified variety of the language strongly identified with a unifying religion (Islam) and a "golden age" of past imperial and literary glories, carrying great cultural prestige; and a "low," chaotic (often regarded as grammarless), but homely variety associated with domesticity, intimacy, and the daily round. The emotional resonances of the two varieties are and always have been different, and as a consequence they have, down the ages, occupied separate functional niches in all linguistically mediated communication, be it speech, writing, song, poetry, cinema, or theatre. It is undeniable that the 21st century is bringing about a narrowing of this gap, both formally and functionally. This is partly as a result of new technologies, and some new forms of identity are crystallizing to which novel forms of language use are central. But some conservative currents are also going against this tide, a major one being the deliberate public oral use of CA/SA by religious leaders who thereby seek to use it as a symbol that marks them out and harks back to an imagined past that they (and the many who follow them) would like to see return. It should never be forgotten that the call to prayer is precisely a *call* or that the Quran, Islam's holy book, was originally an entirely *oral* recitation of the prophet Muḥammad. Its daily cantillation, amplified through the streets by a thousand mosque loudspeakers, blaring from radios and television sets in every home and at every street corner, and sung or spoken as the preamble to any public event, is still perhaps the most pervasive public expression of Arab orality and the one that immediately impresses itself on the consciousness of any visitor to the region.

References

'Abdul-'Āl, Ghāda. 2008. *'Ayza atgawwiz* ("I want to get married"). Cairo: Dār al-šurūq.

——. 2011. *'Ayza atgawwiz* ("I want to get married"). Available at http://www.wanna-b-a-bride.blogspot.com/.

Abd-el-Jawad, Hasan. 1986. The emergence of an urban dialect in the Jordanian urban centers. *International Journal of the Sociology of Language* 61: 53–63.

Abdel-Malek, Kamal. 1990. *A study of the vernacular poetry of Aḥmad Fu'ād Nigm*. Leiden: Brill.

Al-Azraqi, Munira. 2010. Pidginisation in the eastern region of Saudi Arabia: Media presentation. In *Arabic and the media*, ed. Reem Bassiouney, 159–179. Leiden: Brill.

Badawi, Mustafa. 1988. *Early Arabic drama*. Cambridge, UK: Cambridge University Press.

Bassiouney, Reem. 2006. *Functions of code-switching in Egypt: Evidence from monologues*. Leiden: Brill.

Al-Batal, Mahmoud. 2002. Identity and tension in Lebanon: The Arabic of local news at LBCI. In *Language contact and language conflict in Arabic: Variations on a sociolinguistic theme*, ed. Aleya Rouchdy, 91–115. London: RoutledgeCurzon.

Bentahila, Abdelâli. 1983. *Language attitudes among Arabic–French bilinguals in Morocco*. Clevedon: Multilingual Matters.

Bizri, Fida. 2005. Le Pidgin Madam, Un nouveau pidgin arabe. *La Linguistique* 41: 53–66.

Blanc, Haim.1964. *Communal dialects in Baghdad*. Cambridge, MA: Harvard University Press.

Davies, Humphrey. 2008. *Yusuf al-Shirbini's brains confounded by the ode of Abu Shaduf expounded (Kitāb hazz al-quḥūf bi-Šarḥ qaṣīd Abī Šādūf)*, vol. 2. English translation and notes. Louvain: Peeters.

Etling, Bruce, John Kelly, Robert Faris, and John Palfrey. 2009. *Mapping the Arabic blogosphere: Politics, culture, and dissent*. Cambridge, MA: Berkman Center for the Internet & Society, Harvard University.

Haeri, Niloofar. 1996. *The sociolinguistic market of Cairo*. London: KPI.

Heath, Jeffrey. 1989. *From code-switching to borrowing: a case study of Moroccan Arabic*. London: KPI.

Hoenerbach, Wilhelm. 1956. *Die vulgärarabische Poetik al-Kitāb al-ʿāṭil al-ḥālī wa l-muraxxaṣ al-ġālī des Ṣafīyaddīn Ḥillī*. Wiesbaden: Franz Steiner Verlag.

Holes, Clive. 1983a. Patterns of communal language variation in Bahrain. *Language in Society* 12: 433–457.

——. 1983b. Bahraini dialects: Sectarian dialects and the sedentary/nomadic split. *Zeitschrift fuer arabische Linguistik* 10: 7–37.

——. 1993. The uses of variation: A study of the political speeches of Gamāl ʿAbdul-Nāṣir. In *Perspectives on Arabic linguistics V*, ed. Mushira Eid and Clive Holes, 13–45. Amsterdam: John Benjamins.

Holes, Clive and Said Salma Abu Athera. 2009. *Poetry and politics in contemporary Bedouin society*. Ithaca, NY: Reading.

——. 2011. *Nabati poetry of the United Arab Emirates*. Ithaca, NY: Reading.

Ibrahim, Zeinab. 2010. Cases of written code-switching in Egyptian opposition newspapers. In *Arabic and the media*, ed. Reem Bassiouney, 23–45. Leiden: Brill.

Idrīs, Yūsuf. 1981. *Malik al-Quṭn, Gumhūriyyat Faraḥāt* (The cotton king and Faraḥāt's republic). Cairo: Dār Miṣr li l-ṭibāʿa.

Mazraani, Nathalie. 1997. *Aspects of language variation in Arabic political speech-making*. London: Curzon.

Mejdell, Gunvor. 2006. *Mixed styles in spoken Arabic in Egypt: Somewhere between order and chaos*. Leiden: Brill.

Naqqāš, Samīr. 1986. *Nuzūla wa khayṭ aš-Šayṭān* (Tenants and cobwebs). Jerusalem: Association for Jewish Academics from Iraq.

Næss, Unn Gyda. 2008. Gulf Pidgin Arabic: Individual strategies or structured variety? MA thesis, Department of Culture Studies and Oriental Languages, University of Oslo.

Nortier, Jacomine. 1990. *Dutch–Moroccan Arabic code-switching*. Dordrecht: Foris.

Al-Nuṣṣ, ʿAbdul-ʿAzīz. 1930. *Muđakkirāt naššāl* (Diary of a pickpocket). Cairo: al-Yūsufiyya Press and Bookshop.

Al-Qaʿīd, Yūsuf. 1994. *Laban al-ʿaṣfūr* (Sparrows' milk). Cairo: Dār al-Hilāl.

Romaine, Suzanne. 1988. *Pidgin and Creole languages*. London: Longman.

Rosenbaum, Gabriel. 2000. Fuṣḥāmmiyya: Alternating style in Egyptian prose. *Zeitschrift für arabische Linguistik* 38: 68–87.

Rosenhouse, Judith. 1984. *Bedouin Arabic*. Wiesbaden: Harrassowitz.

Rosenthal, Franz (trans.). 1958. *Ibn Khaldûn: The Muqaddima, An introduction to history*. 3 vols. London: Routledge & Kegan Paul.

Sadgrove, Philip. 1996. *The Egyptian theatre in the nineteenth century, 1799–1882*. Ithaca, NY: Reading.

Smart, Jack. 1990. Pidginization in Gulf Arabic: A first report. *Anthropological Linguistics* 32: 83–118.

Al-Tūnisī, Maḥmūd Bayram. N.d. (first published 1923). *Is-sayyid wi Marātu fi Bārīs* (The master and his wife in Paris). Cairo: Dār Miṣr li l-ṭibāʿa.

Wikipedia. 2013. *Arabic chat alphabet.* Available at http://en.wikipedia.org/wiki/Arabic_chat_alphabet

http://www.youtube.com/watch?v=jGJ1nlJyFtM

CHAPTER 13

DIALECTOLOGY

PETER BEHNSTEDT AND MANFRED WOIDICH

13.1 Introduction

Geographically, Arabic is one of the most widespread languages of the world, and Arabic dialects are spoken in an unbroken expanse from western Iran to Mauritania and Morocco and from Oman to northeastern Nigeria, albeit with vast uninhabited or scarcely inhabited areas and deserts in between. It is not easy to give the exact number of speakers; estimates from 1999 count 206 million L1 speakers, a figure that today seems too low rather than too high.[1] This geographical range is marked by extreme dialectal differences in all fields of phonology, grammar, and lexicon, at times to the extent that different varieties are mutually unintelligible.

Arabic dialects[2] may have millions of speakers, and in some Arab countries the dialect of a politically or economically prominent city plays the de facto role of a Standard language, at least with respect to oral communication; Cairo Arabic in Egypt and Casablanca Arabic in Morocco (Aguadé 2008: 288a; Caubet 2008: 273b) are relevant cases. Although they have their principal domain in oral communication, dialects are also used for writing and even in some forms of literature (see Aguadé 2006 for Morocco and Rosenbaum **2004**; Woidich 2010 for Egypt; see also [Holes, "Orality"]).

Arabic dialectology is closely connected with a number of other disciplines of Arabic linguistics such as historical linguistics [Owens, "History"] and sociolinguistics including urban linguistics [Al-Wer, "Sociolinguistics"]. In fact, it constitutes an indispensable prerequisite as it provides these with the necessary data.

[1] Ethnologue: http://www.ethnologue.com/show_language.asp?code=arb. Egypt alone counts more than 84 million inhabitants now, nearly all of them speakers of a variety of Arabic.

[2] If we consider any variety of a language a dialect, Modern Written Arabic and Classical Arabic are dialects of Arabic as well and should be treated as such. Nevertheless, Arabic dialectology is concerned only with dialects of Arabic that have native speakers.

This article limits itself to what may be called traditional Arabic dialectology (TAD). The subject matter of traditional dialectology is the collection of linguistic features in a given geographic area and the study of these features with regard to their distribution in this area to establish dialectal borders lines, transitional areas, core areas, and dialectal continua. All this can be best made visible as a linguistic landscape by reproducing these features on maps. For more detail, see Behnstedt and Woidich (**2005**).

13.2 A Glance at History

The interest in the regional varieties of spoken Arabic has a relatively long history. In the course of the 19th century, a considerable number of word lists, smaller or larger dictionaries, and practical guides and textbooks appeared as the result of increased possibilities of tourism and scientific research in the Arabic-speaking world. A few more comprehensive treatises on the colloquial had appeared before this time (Alcalá 1505; Dombay 1800; Caussin de Perceval 1833; Ṭanṭāvy 1848). Wallin (1851, 1852) and Wetzstein (1868) provide samples of folk poetry and stories furnished with phonological and factual annotations, which give valuable insights into the Bedouin Arabic of Syria.

A real linguistic interest in Arabic dialects, however, and the creation of a discipline "Arabic dialectology" as part of academic Oriental and Semitic studies did not develop until the final quarter of the 19th century, when the first systematic grammars and elaborate dictionaries appeared, which went far beyond previously published works. These were often accompanied by text collections provided with glossaries (e.g., Spitta 1880), which at the same time were of great value for ethnographic and folkloristic studies. The early days of Arabic dialectological studies thus ran parallel to the time when the great enterprises in dialectology, that is, the national projects of the French and German dialect atlases, started. Beside the professional scholars in Arabic and Semitic studies, a considerable number of valuable data of linguistic and ethnographic interest were collected also by archeologists working in Egypt or Iraq, such as Maspéro (1914) and Weissbach (1908–1930). The first attempts at dialect atlases for the Arab world—today historical documents because of the political developments, creation of new states, and movement of populations—were made as early as in 1915 by Gotthelf Bergsträßer (Palestine) and 1940 by Jean Cantineau (Ḥawrān).

The first half of the 20th century saw many more publications in the field, and, as early as in 1961, Anton Spitaler could observe that a huge amount of material on Arabic dialects was available, so that it was difficult to maintain an overview over the material [135/226]: "Insgesamt verfügen wir heute absolut genommen über ein gewaltiges, nur mehr schwer übersehbares Tatsachenmaterial, das sich über weite Gebiete des arabischen Sprachraums von Marokko bis Buchara erstreckt" "Altogether we have at our disposal a huge amount of primary material extending over a large area of the Arabic-speaking region from Morocco to Bukara, so that an overview of it is difficult" (Spitaler

1961: 133). This amount of data was despite its patchiness sufficient and detailed enough to enable the first comparative overviews by Hans R. Singer (1958) on interrogatives and by Wolfdietrich Fischer on demonstratives (1959), both students of Hans Wehr.

Nevertheless, Arabic dialectology was at this point not really an academic profession. Despite the fact that its importance for Arabic linguistic history can hardly be overestimated, it had remained a field to which serious scholars would devote only their Sunday afternoons, as Spitaler used to tell his students. David Cohen, in his "Préface" to *Actes des premières journées de dialectologie arabe de Paris* (Caubet and Vanhove 1994), states something similar: "Les arabophones méprisaient leurs dialectes, les arabisants la dialectologie.", "Arabic speakers despised their dialects, Arabicists dialectology." Arabic studies at that time, following their historical origin, more or less resembled the study of the classical languages Greek, Latin, and Hebrew. Making an academic career in dialectology only was next to impossible for Arabists, as chairs for Arabic and Semitic studies were designed with a far wider profile including Arabic literature, history of the Near East, and Islamic studies. Several developments in the 1960s and 1970s changed this state of affairs to some extent.

First of all, the growing political and economic importance of the Arab countries together with the expanded possibilities for traveling, visiting, and researching these countries led to an increased interest in "real Arabic," that is, the spoken language of daily life or the modern Arabic dialects. Many students would no longer limit themselves to Classical or Modern Standard Arabic for second-language learning but chose to acquaint themselves with the colloquial as a language of daily life as well. Certainly, as a consequence of this, more academic interest for the field was stimulated.

Second, the unimagined advances in the technology of speech recording that had begun in the 1950s was not without impact on Arabic dialectology: recording living speech allowed a far more systematic and scientific approach to fieldwork and was less prone to the predilections and deficiencies of the individual researcher. While in earlier times texts could be recorded only by means of dictation—a rather unnatural form of speech—it was now possible to record speech without too much technical effort and cost. Haim Blanc and Wehr were the first dialectologists of Arabic to use a tape recorder in the field (Jastrow 2002: 350). These recordings, as well as the recordings of entire elicitation sessions, when necessary, could be repeated and checked by the researcher or by others for verification in nearly the same way as they had been recorded. This made it possible to embark on projects covering larger areas more systematically and with better scientific methods than ever before. It is beyond any doubt that these technical improvements led to a far higher reliability of the recorded data.

Third, descriptive structural linguistics, in particular taxonomic phonology and morphology, which had already been developed in other philologies in the 1930s and 1940s, were gradually adapted by Arabic dialectologists and applied in their works. In particular, Cantineau's (**1960**) adaptation of the Prague phonology in several articles from the early 1950s proved to be seminal. His remark that "la dialectologie arabe n'est guère progressiste; les nouvelles techniques de recherche ont du mal à s'y acclimater," "Arabic dialectology is not at all progressive; new research methods have difficulty becoming established in it" (ibid., 277) proved incorrect for the years to follow, which saw a fruitful adaptation of modern methods of descriptive linguistics. Phonology, in particular, played an important role here. Good examples of strictly taxonomy-oriented grammars including phonology and morphology are provided in the following: for Egyptian, see Harrell (1957); for Moroccan, see Harrell (**1962**); for Damascus, see Grotzfeld's (1964) monographs and Ambros (1977); for Mḧallami/ Anatolia, see Sasse (1971); for Daragözü, see Jastrow (1973); on Maltese, see Schabert (1976). Although formerly a rather intricate phonetic notation with dozens of diacritic marks prevailed in transcription, projecting only an apparent phonetic accuracy, the analysis of the sounds based on phonological principles now led to a limited set of phonemes that were used for transcribing the data and thus allowed for better writability and readablility. To see the difference, one may compare the transcriptions used, for instance, by French dialectologists working on North African dialects, such as W. Marçais and Ph. Marçais, with more recent ones, for instance, R. S. Harrell, D. Caubet, and J. Aguadé.

Fourth, up until the 1950s, research concentrated with few exceptions on easily accessible places and areas, a fact deplored by Cantineau (**1955**). For Egypt, to give an example, only the great cities of Cairo and Alexandria had attracted major scholarly attention, but not the Nile Delta, let alone Upper Egypt or the Oases in the Western Desert. Cairo Arabic was seen as Egyptian Arabic par excellence. Supported by the technical and methodological improvements previously mentioned, fieldworkers endeavored from the 1960s onward to uncover the treasures hidden in many places that had heretofore remained either hardly accessible or neglected for some (other) reason. Very important regional overviews were published that colored in a number of white spots on the map (Iraq, Anatolia, Egypt, Yemen, Syria, Arabian Peninsula, Oman, Sudan, Sahel) and offered a wealth of data both for the dialect geographer and the historical linguist.

Already in the 1960s Arabic dialectologists were aware of the fact the existence of many dialects was being threatened. Spitaler (1961: 136/227) quotes Henri Fleisch (Orbis VIII 1959: 386) on the situation in Lebanon justifying his research in rural Lebanon: "L'évolution des parlers se précipite actuellement, elle pénètre partout et tend à un nivellement des parlers qui leur enlève leur originalité. L'urgence de l'enquête était très grande.", "The evolution of varieties is currently accelerating. It penetrates everywhere and tends towards a leveling of varieties which effaces their originality. The urgency of research is large." Replacing older, outdated, and sometimes unreliable sources by new ones that meet modern standards and covering the vast areas that have underresearched or not researched at all still belongs to the urgent desiderata of TAD.

As a result of political developments and subsequent migrations, many varieties spoken by minorities, above all the religious ones, are in acute danger. In particular, the Jewish dialects are threatened by extinction. The long established tradition of Jewish Arabic studies (Cohen 1912; Brunot-Malka 1940; Cohen 1964) became of prime importance for the recording of these dialects bound for extinction and was taken up again by Blanc (1974), Cohen (1975), Stillman (1988), Jastrow (1990), Mansour (1991), Heath (**2002**), Rosenbaum (2003), and Yoda (2005).

The global phenomenon that local dialects are disappearing in favor of more regionally expanded varieties of a language, as a matter of course, applies to the Arab world too. On one hand, recording these dwindling specimens of speech has become more urgent than anybody could imagine at Fleisch's time, while, on the other hand, the new media offered by the Internet (blogs, Facebook, Twitter) facilitate the use of the colloquial, albeit further developed in written and supraregional forms.

These developments, together with the ever increasing migrations of the population from rural areas to the cities, and from country to country, offer other possibilities for scientific study that go far beyond traditional dialectology and have in the meantime supplanted the latter to some extent: urban dialectology, all types of contact linguistics including diglossia studies, youth language, Pidgin and Creole studies, and other sociolinguistically oriented matters.

No wonder that, starting in the 1980s and 1990s with the emergence of sociolinguistics and variational linguistics, many Arabic language researchers such as Jonathan Owens, Gunvor Mejdell, Nilofaar Haeri, Catherine Miller, and Enam Al-Wer directed their interests to these branches of studies of linguistic varieties and developed them into more or less separate fields of activity ([Davies et al., "Code Switching"; Al-Wer, "Sociolinguistics"]). Despite that, the traditional descriptive approach has not been abandoned but has been falling behind somewhat over the last few years (Jastrow 2002, 2008).

For all these reasons, the last 50 years saw an unprecedented expansion and increase in fieldwork and in the amount of data accessible to the researchers. Data collections such as monographs, atlases, grammatical sketches, text collections, textbooks, dictionaries, and other linguistic descriptions keep flowing continuously. The mass of data increased again far beyond what had been imagined only some years earlier.

This expansion called for a more formal organization. Since both older and younger researchers such as Wolfgang Fischer, Hans Singer, Otto Jastrow, Hartmut Bobzin, Peter Behnstedt, and Manfred Woidich felt an urgent need for a regular forum for publication and discussion dedicated to Arabic dialectology and linguistics, Jastrow and Bobzin founded the journal *Zeitschrift für Arabische Linguistik* (*ZAL*). Its purpose was to make new findings and recent studies accessible to the public as swiftly as possible. The *ZAL*, the first issue of which appeared in 1978, developed into an important specialized forum for presentation of research and discussion; more than 50 volumes have been published to date. In 1983, the French journal *Matériaux Arabiques et Sudarabiques-GELLAS* followed. Jastrow started the series *Semitica viva* in 1987, which in the years to follow hosted many of the most important publications in the field. In 1993, French dialectologists from the renowned INALCO (above all Caubet and Vanhove) took the initiative and convened all colleagues in the field to Paris at a Colloque International, the first conference dedicated to Arabic dialectology. The conference was concluded with the foundation of the Association Internationale de la dialectologie Arabe (AIDA) and thus marked the beginning of a series of nine highly successful conferences to date. The proceedings of these conferences very aptly mirror the most recent developments in the field, both with respect to traditional approaches as well as to other types of Arabic dialectology.[3] To conclude, the particular situation in Spain with its Andalusian

[3] See http://www.aida.or.at.

background and its focus on the Maghreb led to the foundation of another journal with the programmatic title *Estudios de dialectologia norteafricana y andalusí* (*EDNA*) in 1996, which since then has also developed into an important forum for documentation and discussion.

Maltese, with its rich indigenous linguistic academic landscape, split off from general TAD and formed its own association, L-Għaqda Internazzjonali tal-Lingwistika Maltija (GĦILM) in 2007, which convenes regular conferences.[4]

13.3 The State of the Art

As Owens (2006: 8) rightly puts it, "The modern dialects have an indispensable role in an account of Arabic language history."[5] We would even say that the modern Arabic dialects, their development, and their relation to Classical Arabic (or Old Arabic, whatever one may call it) are the central object of research for Arabic historical linguistics. This gives TAD fundamental importance for any research in Arabic historical linguistics. TAD, therefore, is heavily and primarily fieldwork oriented, not theory driven. In more detail, it aims at the following:

1. Recording contemporary Arabic speech as much as possible from a number of representative community members, all over the Arab world and beyond, wherever a variety of Arabic is spoken
2. Documenting these data and making them accessible for the researcher in various forms of publication: monographs such as atlases, grammars, (Ortsgrammatiken), bidirectional dictionaries, handbooks, collections of texts (of ethnographic, folkloristic interest), and textbooks
3. Describing the variation and differences between one local dialect and another by providing regional and overall comparative descriptions in monographs and articles
4. Classifying the dialects according to synchronic and diachronic criteria: grouping the dialects, clustering, establishing core areas and transitional areas, detecting dialect continua, and showing the linguistic relations between various regions in the Arab world
5. Collecting the older evidence of Arabic dialects as documented in historical records such as historiography, literary works, historical lexical studies, and travel accounts.

TAD overlaps here with the study of Middle Arabic; see, for instance, Davies (1981), Lentin (2008), and Zack (2009).

[4] See http://www.fb10.uni-bremen.de/ghilm/about.aspx.

[5] It goes without saying that in this short article not all important publications can be quoted.

13.4 Presentation of the Data

13.4.1 Atlases and Maps

The main goal of traditional dialectology is to document its findings in atlases (see Chambers-Trudgill 1998).[6] Very early, before World War I, Bergsträßer (**1915**) made the first attempt at this type of documentation for what was then Palestine, and Cantineau (1940) followed somewhat later with the adjacent region of Ḥawrān, now southern Syria. Both constitute important documents for historical comparison today. It was not until 1961 that Abul-Fadl followed with geographical research on the distribution of phonological and morphological features in the Egyptian province of Šarqiyya in the Nile Delta. Behnstedt and Woidich's (1983) map on Arabic dialects in Egypt was the first of its kind and was followed by the five volumes of Egyptian dialect atlas (**1985–1999**); Behnstedt published his atlas on North Yemen in **1985**. Arnold-Behnstedt (**1993**) covers the Qalamūn Mountains in Syria, with a focus on Arabic–Aramaic contacts. Behnstedt's (**1997**) Syria atlas is the most comprehensive one so far in terms of number of maps and data.

The first two volumes (of a planned total of four) of the *Wortatlas der arabischen Dialekte* (**WAD**) by Behnstedt and Woidich appeared in **2011** and **2012**, respectively, with 311 full-color onomasiological maps on "Mensch, Natur, Fauna, Flora" and "Materielle Kultur," each map accompanied by a commentary. The WAD is the first atlas to cover the entire Arab world and provides a survey of the lexical richness and diversity of the Arabic language and its semantic developments.

Some regional monographs contain a rather extensive series of maps in their appendices: Arnold (1998) on the province of Hatay (Antiochia, Turkey); and de Jong (**2000**, 2011) on Sinai. A collection of maps on the terms for animal and body parts resulting from an unfinished survey on Northern Morocco is published in Behnstedt (2005, 2007). Other maps for illustrative purposes can be found in Procházka (1993) on prepositions, Mörth (1997) on numbers, Jastrow (1978–1981) on *qəltu*-dialects in Mesopotamia and Anatolia, and Johnstone (**1967**) on the Gulf area. Heath (**2002**) gives an appendix with a series of rather abstract maps on Muslim and Jewish varieties spoken in Morocco. Six simplified maps in Abboud-Haggar (2011) serve as a quick first overview on the geographic distribution of the Arabic dialects; another can be found in Corriente and Vicente (2008).

Quite a few publications use maps for illustration: for example, Cantineau (1940a) on Algeria; Fleisch (**1974**) on Lebanon; Ingham (1973) on southern Iraq and Khuzistan; and Owens (1985) on the Sahel. Vanhove (2009) contains a dialect map of Yemen, and Taine-Cheikh (1998–1999) published seven maps on the distribution of certain "macrodiscriminants" (*q and the interdentals) in the Arabic-speaking world.

[6] For more details, see the chapter "Die arabischen Sprachatlanten" in Behnstedt-Woidich (2005: 4–7).

Projects on dialect surveys have been announced for Northern Israel (Talmon 2002) and Tunisia (Mejri 2002; Sandly 2002)[7] but have not materialized so far.

Behnstedt and Woidich (**2005**) give a general introduction to Arabic dialect geography and incorporates a chapter on dialectometry.

13.4.2 Regional Studies

The second edition of the Encyclopedia of Islam (1986) offers concise information in the article "ʕArabīya" on "Arabian and North Arabian dialects" (Fleisch) and on the "Western Dialects" (Colin). Marçais (1977) provides a comprehensive survey on the phonological and morphological features of the Western Arabic dialects. To date, there is no equivalent study for the Eastern part of the Arab world. Blanc (1971) gives a concise report on sub-Saharan Arabic. Fleisch (1974) sketches a number of villages all over Lebanon together with text samples and arrives at a preliminary description of dialect areas. Kaye (1976) deals with Chadian and Sudanese Arabic in light of comparative Arabic dialectology. Jastrow's (1978) work on the *qəltu*-dialects in northern Iraq and Anatolia had a great impact on the further development of the field. Prochazka (**1988**) gives the first systematic phonological and morphological survey on the Arabic dialects spoken on Saudi Arabian territory. Arnold (1998) covers the Arabic-speaking regions of Antiochia in Turkey, and Owens (1985, 1993b) reports on Chad and Nigeria. Ingham (**1982**, 1997) deals with the dialects of northeast Arabia. Palva (1984) classifies the Palestinian and Transjordanian dialects, and Woidich (1996) gives a concise account on the distribution of 41 features in the rural dialects of Egypt. The Arabian Peninsula and Iraq are very competently dealt with in Holes (2006); Al-Wer (2006) tackles the Arabic-speaking Middle East, and Walters (2006) addresses north Africa.

Among these regional studies, several should be further listed: Blanc (1953) on North Palestinian Arabic; Blanc (**1964**), the seminal study on Bagdad and Iraq; Johnstone (**1967**) on the Gulf area; Grand'Henry (1972, 1976) on Algeria; Diem (1973) and Behnstedt (**1985**) on Yemen; Ingham (1976) on southern Iraq and Khuzistan; Behnstedt and Woidich (1982) on the Egyptian oases; Doss (1981) on Middle Egypt; Ingham (1982, 1997) on Bedouin Arabic in the Najd and elsewhere on the Arabian Peninsula; Holes (1983) on Baḥrayn; Owens (1984) on Libya; Rosenhouse (1984a, 1984b) on the Bedouin in northern Israel; Holes (1989) on Oman; Arnold and Behnstedt (**1993**) on Qalamūn in Syria; Arnold (1998) on Antiochia; Behnstedt (1998–1999) on Djerba; Heath (**2002**) on Morocco; Procházka (**2002**) on Çukurova; Heath (2004) on Ḥassāniyya; Henkin (2010) and Shawarbah (**2011**) on Negev; and de Jong (2000, 2011) on Sinai.

Regarding the Arabic "Sprachinseln" of Uzbekistan, Vinnikow (1962), Tsereteli (1954, 1956), Fischer (**1961**), Axvlediani (1985), Chikovani (2008, 2009), and Zimmermann (2009) give us valuable information. On Cyprus we have Borg (2004) and Roth-Laly

[7] See further a number of articles in the procedings of AIDA 6 (Mejri 2006).

(2006) and, on Afghanistan, Kieffer (1981, 1985, 2000) as well as Ingham (1994a, 2002). On the newly discovered Arabic dialects in Iran, see Seeger (2002). For the situation in border areas where Arabic is a minority language such as Anatolia, Afghanistan, Eritrea/Djibouti, and Central Asia, one may consult the publications by Owens (2000), Simeone-Senelle (2002), and Csató et al. (2005). Heine's (1982) book on Ki-Nubi introduced Creole studies to the field of Arabic dialectology, followed by Wellens (**2005**) and Luffin (2005) [Tosco and Manfredi, "Creoles"]. Corriente, in numerous publications, provided for the systematic analysis and description of the extinct dialect of Andalusia; see Corriente (**1977**, 1997), and for a short account on its evolution see Vicente (2011).

13.4.3 General and Comparative Studies

The first state-of-the-art-reports appeared in the 1950s from the pens of Brockelmann (1954) and Cantineau (**1955**) and also give a good overview of the available literature. A rather complete bibliography can be found in Fischer (1959), later followed by those in Sobelman (1962), Bakalla (1983), and Eisele (1987).

The work of Caussin de Perceval (1833), which is today only of historical interest, can be seen as a first attempt to give a comparative overview of the grammar of Arabic dialects for pedagogical purposes. Nöldeke (**1904**) analyzes the relationship of the dialects with Classical Arabic and arrives at the conclusion that the former developed from the latter, a view that for good reasons has been abandoned today. Bergsträßer (1928) gives a short historical sketch and some texts within the framework of a handbook of Semitic languages. In his opinion, the dialects did not develop directly from Classical Arabic: "Die neuarabischen Dialekte gehen im großen ganzen auf eine einheitliche Grundform zurück, die im allgemeinen der klassischen Sprache nahestand, in Einzelheiten von ihr abwich" (ibid., 156). In the years to come, and in fact until this day, this has been the scenario many historical linguists accepted, in particular those with a German background, even if Nöldeke's view has continued to be taken as a starting point for historical discussion.[8] Fischer-Jastrow (1980), which incorporates regional sketches and text samples, followed as a comprehensive general account of the situation at the end of the 1970s, but in view of the rapid increase of available data and new insights over the past 30 years it needs to be updated.

More recently collected data, but without fundamentally new insights, are offered in Kaye and Rosenhouse (**1997**), which treats Maltese independently from other Arabic dialects; in Durand (2009); and in Abboud-Haggar (2009). Corriente and Vicente (2008) offer a comprehensive discussion of genesis and classification of Vicente's modern dialects. Other shorter overview articles, some directed at a more general public, are Jastrow (2002, 2008), Versteegh (2011a, 2011b), and in particular Watson (2011), with a critical discussion of some of the features used to discriminate between Old Arabic and

[8] For a sharp refutation see Sima (2006: 98) and Owens (2006: 9).

modern dialects. Naturally, general introductions to Arabic linguistics and language history such as Schippers and Versteeegh (1987), Versteegh (1997), Ferrando (2001), and Holes (2004) deal with Arabic dialectology and use its data in the relevant chapters.

Other comparative studies focus on particular grammatical topics, describe these, and sketch their historical development. The first ones—Singer (1958) on interrogatives and Fischer (1959) on demonstratives—we owe to the school of Hans Wehr. Blanc (1970) deals with dual and pseudo-dual; Janssens (1972) studies stress and word structure; Czapkiewicz (1975) examines the morphology of the verb; and Diem (1979) looks at the substrate question. Eksell Harning (1980) on the genitive exponent and Retsö (1983) on the passive voice discuss their topics both with respect to morphology and to syntax. Mörth (1992) deals with cardinal numbers from 1 to 10, Procházka (1993) with the prepositions, and Dahlgren (1998) with word order. Isaksson (1998) offers a comparative survey of the pronouns. Brustad (**2000**) analyzes syntactic structures comparing four dialects under modern criteria independent from traditional Arabic syntax. Watson (**2002**) compares phonology and morphology of two rather different types of Arabic: Cairene and Ṣanʕāni. Diem (2002) describes the syntax of translocative verbs of some dialects and their historical changes, and Taine-Cheikh (2004, 2009) looks at the expression of future. Versteegh (2004) deals with the interrogatives again, and Procházka (2004) wrestles with unmarked feminine nouns. Vanhove et al. (2009) give an account with grammaticalization of modal auxiliaries in Maltese and Arabic, placing them in a larger theoretical framework with European languages. Aguadé (2011) presents in a concise survey the vowels systems of Moroccan dialects.

A different type of resource is represented in the Encyclopedia of Arabic Language and Linguistics (EALL), which could serve as a TAD handbook. It contains 37 grammatical sketches of Arabic dialects and 26 linguistic profiles of Arab countries easily accessible to the scholar, in addition to a number of articles on general issues concerning Arabic dialectology, such as "Creole" (Owens), "Gypsy" (Matras), "Dialect Geography" (Behnstedt), and "Dialects: Classification" (Palva).

13.4.4 Grammatical Descriptions of Individual Varieties

Today, we have at our disposal several dozens of systematic descriptions of local dialects in the form of monographs and, above all, hundreds of sketches describing the most important phonological and morphological features of the dialects spoken in various places of the Arab world ranging from major cities to the most remote areas, both for rural and Bedouin Arabic. Astonishingly enough, there is no comprehensive grammar in the form of a monograph on one of the major Bedouin dialects of Saudi Arabia, Ingham (**1994b**) on Najdi Arabic being the laudable exception. Due to lack of space, only some major monographs published in the recent years will be mentioned here:[9]

[9] For further titles, we refer here to the relevant articles in EALL.

Palva (**1976**) on al-Balqāʾ/Jordan; Cowell (1964), Grotzfeld (1964), and Ambros (1977) on Damascus; Abu-Haidar (1979) on Baskinta/Lebanon; Reichmuth (1983) on the Shukriyya tribe in Sudan; Owens (**1984**) on Benghazi; Singer (**1984**) on Tunis; Owens (1993) on Nigeria; Seeger (2009) on Ramallah,; Julien de Pommerol (1999) on Chad; Talay (1999) on the Khawētna/Syria; Werbeck (**2001**) on Manāxa/Yemen; Wittrich (2003) on Āzəx/Anatolia; Borg and Azzopardi (2005) for Maltese; Woidich (2006) on Cairo; Gralla (**2006**) on Nabk/Syria; Pereira (2010) on Tripoli; Manfredi (2010) on the Baggāra in Kordofan. The century-old interest of the Maltese in their spoken language produced very early grammatical descriptions and dictionaries, making it to one of the best described and researched varieties of Arabic; see Borg and Azzopardi (2005). In addition to that, there are quite a few PhD and MA theses on Arabic dialects written by native speakers at European and American universities, but many of these are difficult to come by.

The degree of comprehensiveness of these grammars differs, as their interest generally is limited to the basic facts of phonology and morphology, while syntax is treated rather marginally. Some exceptions to this point deal with many important syntactic issues: Spitta (1880) on Cairo; Harrell (**1962**) on Rabat; Cowell (1964) on Syrian; Jullien de Pommerol (**1992**) on Chad; Caubet (**1993**) on Fes; Woidich (**2006**) on Cairo; Naïm (2009) on Ṣanʕāʾ.

A classical structuralistic study of the phonology of Egyptian Arabic is Harrell (1957); a thorough study with a high level of abstractness is Dickins (2007) on the phonology of Sudanese (Khartoum) Arabic.

Studies on the syntax of individual dialects include Feghali (1928) on Lebanese, Abboud (1964) on Ḥiğāzi, Bloch (1965) on Damascene, Piamenta (1966) on Palestinian, Denz (1971) on Kwayriš/Iraq, Sieny (1978) on Urban Ḥiğāzi, Watson (1993) on Ṣanʕāni, Vanhove on Maltese (1994), and Eisele (**1999**) on Cairene. Most important in this respect is Brustad (**2000**), as it is the only monograph to treat syntactic issues from a comparative perspective and in the light of a fresh modern syntactic approach while not relying on traditional Arabic grammar or a particular modern linguistic school. The latter is an important issue, since in recent years, quite a few articles and monographs on Arabic syntax appeared, but, unfortunately enough, many of these use a particular linguistic framework and are aimed more at serving the further development of syntactic theories than at adding to the knowledge of Arabic.[10]

Owens and Elgibali (**2010**) provide a series of articles on structural and pragmatic sources and offer an introduction to information structure as used in spoken Arabic.

Of particular linguistic interest are "Sprachinseln" in Uzbekistan, Afghanistan, Turkey, and Iran, which on one hand preserve many old features due to an early split from mainstream Arabic, thus shedding light on earlier linguistic situations in Mesopotamia (Jastrow 2011), and on the other hand show peculiar developments due to their isolation from the core area of Arabic and their contact with other languages.

[10] Cf. the introduction to Brustad (2000: 2–4).

The Creolized versions spoken in Africa (Ki-Nubi/, Juba Arabic/Sudan) are a particularly interesting case for general Creole studies, as they are not based on one of the European languages; see Miller (1983), Prokosch (1986), and Owens (2006) in the *Encyclopedia of Arabic Language and Linguistics* and also Tosco and Manfredi ["Creoles"].

13.4.5 Dictionaries

Arabic dialectologists have a number of dictionaries at their disposal, although many of them are rudimentary and are better classified under the categories "vocabulary" or "glossary" than dictionary. Some are outdated today but have nevertheless been republished without any adaptations (Belkassem 2001), the Georgetown series (see following), and Spiro (1980). The 12 volumes of de Premare (1993–1999) provide a rather comprehensive dictionary for Moroccan. For Maltese, the dictionary by Aquilina in six volumes (2000) (a shorter version is Aquilina 1987–1990) forms an indispensable source for Maltese studies, providing even etymological and comparative information. Others are Landberg (1909) for South Arabia, Spiro (1925) and Hinds and Badawi (**1986**) for Egypt, Barthélémy (1936) for Syria and the Levant, Taine-Cheikh (**1988–1998**, 1990) for Ḥassāniyya/Mauretania, Piamenta (1990) and Behnstedt (1992–2007) for Yemen, Qafīšeh (1997) for the Gulf area, Jullien de Pommerol (1999) for Chad, Holes (2001) for Baḥrayn, Qāsim (2002) for Sudan, Elihay (2004) for Palestinian, Kurpershoek (2005) for Saudi Arabia/Dawāsir, Beaussier et al. (2006) for Algeria, and Chaker and Milelli (2010) for Lebanese. The older dictionaries should be seen as valuable historical documents rather than as reflections of modern language. Still useful, though somewhat outdated today, are the dictionaries of the Georgetown series: Stowasser and Ani (1964) for Syria; Woodhead and Beene (1967) for Iraq; and Harrell (1966) for Morocco. Lentin and Salamé carried out a major project, a comprehensive documentation of Syrian Arabic vocabulary, the [B] having recently appeared as a first letter.[11] More in the category "word list," see Vocke and Waldner (1982) on Anatolia and Jastrow (2005) on Kinderib/Anatolia.

Many text editions, in particular those on Maghrebi dialects, were followed by glossaries with very useful comparative and etymological annotations. Particularly noteworthy examples are, for instance, the monumental Takroûna/Tunisia glossary by Marçais and Guîga (1958–1961) with nearly 4000 pages, Marçais (1911) on Tanger, Brunot (1952) on Rabat/Morocco, and Boris (1958) on Marāzīg/Tunis, which all contain a host of comparative lexical notes as well. For the southern part of the Arabian Peninsula, Landberg's monumental documentations on Ḥaḍramawt (1901) and Daṯīna (**1905–1913**) are still indispensable, more than 100 years after their publication.

[11] See http://halshs.archives-ouvertes.fr/halshs-00504180/fr/.

There are only few dictionaries or glossaries with Arabic as target language. Among these are the bidirectional ones: Sobelman and Harrell (1963) for Moroccan; Clarity et al. (**1964/2003**) for Iraqi; and Stowasser and Ani (1964) for Syrian. As part of the Georgetown series, these have the advantage of providing rather systematically example sentences illustrating the use of the item listed. Others, mainly intended for practical usage, are Stevens and Salib (2004) and Jomier (1976) for Cairo, Bauer (1957) and Elihai (1985) for Palestinian Arabic, Hillelson (1925) for Sudan, Cohen (**1963**) and Taine-Cheikh (1990) for Ḥassāniyya, and Aguadé and Benyahya (2005) for Morocco. For Maltese see Moser (2005), a rather comprehensive Maltese–German and German–Maltese dictionary.

13.4.6 Lexical Studies

The study of etymology and the foreign vocabulary in the dialects has always been a favorite topic for dialectologists and Arab philologists alike. From earlier times we may adduce Vollers' (1896, 1897) still very useful studies on Egyptian, Almkvist (1891, 1925) on Levantine, and to a certain extent Landberg (1901, 1905–1913), all of which contain rich comparative annotations to other dialects that were already described at that time. Borg (2004) offers an important analysis of the lexicon of the Arabic of Kormakiti/Cyprus with copious references to other Arabic dialects. See further Prokosch (1983) for Turkish loans in Egyptian and Reinkowski (1998) in Baghdad. Kotb (2002) gives a detailed account on Egyptian somatisms, that is, idioms formed with the names of body parts.

Special mention should be made of quite a few works of this kind authored by Arab scholars, such as Taymūr (1978–2001) on Egyptian, Frayḥa (1947) and Abu Saʕd (1987) on Lebanese, and ʕAbd ar-Raḥīm (2003) on Syrian Arabic.

Since the existence of the Internet, one may also try one's dialectological luck in this medium. Many sites, from Saudi Arabia, Ḥaḍramawt, Libya, Jordan, and elsewhere, proudly announce lexical peculiarities of remote regions. The researcher is faced with some problems here: (1) the use of the Arabic script, normally not or insufficiently voweled, makes it difficult to discern the correct pronunciation; (2) uncertain origin, copying original sources without references is not uncommon; (3) as these notes are directed from insiders to insiders, the semantic content is often insufficiently described by just giving a MSA equivalent. Checking the validity of this kind of information is thus difficult, and it should thus be handled with prudence.

13.4.7 Text Collections

It is a well-established tradition of Arabic dialectologists to document their research not only by means of grammars and dictionaries but also by samples of transcribed texts. Text collecting plays a prominent role in their activities from the very beginning, to the extent that Cantineau (**1960**: 277) wrote in the conclusion to his article: "on est frappé par la disproportion des résultats: trop de textes, pas assez de grammaires et de dictionnaires." "In the text, which is rarely spontaneous, there is as much of the one who transcribes as there is of the one who speaks." "One is struck by the disproportionality of results: too many texts, not enough grammars and dictionaries." His remark is quite to the point, and even more so after speech recording became possible from the 1960s onward. Most grammars, regional overviews, and atlases are furnished with texts or accompanied by text volumes; see, for instance, Peter Behnstedt's (**1997–2000**) works on Syria and Otto Jastrow's (**1978–1981**) on *qəltu*-dialects. They not only serve a documentary purpose but also are meant to serve studying the dialect and practicing it. Initially, the interest focused on folklore and popular culture (fairy tales, folk poetry) and paremiology (proverbs), maybe due to the fact that recording speech was not possible yet. The texts had to be noted down by dictation, which means that they had to be present in the memory of the informants so that they could be repeated if necessary. And as story telling played an important role in rural life of that time, this was a relatively simple way to get people to speak. To avoid the highly formulaic language associated with fairy tales and folk poetry, this focus turned to ethnographical issues and oral history in the course of time. Today, these collections offer a wealth of information on urban and rural life in earlier times and are therefore of prime importance not only for the dialectologist but also for the ethnographer and folklorist. For the dialectologist, the problem with these records is that speakers tend to use here an acrolectal type of speech that remains rather descriptive and often features stereotype phrases and does not reflect everyday unmonitored speech, or as Cantineau (1960: 277) puts it: "dans le texte, rarement spontané, il y a autant de celui qui le recueille que de celui qui le dicte." Therefore, despite the fact that they offer much useful lexical information, texts of this sort are of less value with respect to syntax, phraseology, and pragmatics. Well aware of these deficiencies, dialectologists today prefer to record more personal accounts, life stories, jokes, and similar texts or in any case a good mix of various types of text to provide more space to the speaker for elaborate syntactic constructions, everyday phraseology, rhetorical devices, as is described exemplarily in the introduction to Holes (**2005:** xviii–xxi). Of course, the observer's paradox "to monitor unmonitored speech" can never be avoided totally. For linguistic purposes, recorded texts should never be "edited" or "improved" by the transcriber but should be presented with all the deficiencies of natural speech, for example, the Algerian texts given in Bergman (2006), which consciously display the characteristic interferences from French.

Large collections of texts are available, both from earlier and modern times: see, for example, Marçais (1911) in Tanger; Rhodokanakis (1911) in Ḏofār; Schmidt and Kahle (1918–1930) for Bīr Zēt in Palestine; Marçais and Guîga (1925) Takroûna in Tunisia; Hillelson (1935) in Sudan; Destaing (1937) Šluḥ's of the Sous (Morocco); Jastrow (**1978–1981**) in Anatolia and north Iraq; Behnstedt and Woidich (**1985–1999**) in Egypt; Stewart (1988–1990) in Sinai; Mansour (1991) in Jewish Baghdadi; Palva (1991) in al-Balqā'/Jordan; Behnstedt (**1997–2000**) in Syria; Jastrow (2003) Kinderib in Anatolia; Luffin (2004) Kinubi in Mombasa; and Bettini (2006) in Syrian Ǧazīra. Text publications as articles in journals and Festschriften run into the hundreds, and for many localities our data come from publications of this kind. Arab scholars, too, are interested in folkloristic issues and published quite a number of collections of folk songs and suchlike.

Paremiology is represented in copious collections of proverbs such as the classical ones by Frayha (1938) on Lebanon, Westermarck (1930) on Morocco, Burckhardt (1830) and Taymūr (1970) on Egypt, Goitein (1970) on Yemen, Mahgoub (1968) on Egypt with a linguistic analysis, Nataf and Graille (2002) on Libya, and El Attar (1992) and Lemghūrī (2008) on Morocco. Again, following classical tradition, collecting colloquial proverbs was an activity that attracted Arab scholars as well. In addition, numerous amateur collections are available on the market. Unfortunately, in many of these collections the proverbs are not given in transliteration but in Arabic script, a fact that together with their syntactical and lexical peculiarities makes them unsuitable for many linguistic purposes.

As for audio texts, the "Semitisches Tonarchiv" [SemArch] at the University of Heidelberg[12] offers a number of recordings together with their transcriptions, which unfortunately cover only a small part of the Arab world. It is hoped that the new Project "EALL on-line" (Leiden: Brill) will be able to undertake similar activities in nearby future.

13.4.8 Textbooks

Arabic dialectologists have always displayed a pedagogical interest, which is evident from quite a number of text books and language handbooks designed for tourists, business people, administrative or military staff, and the like. In fact, writing colloquial grammars started this way with Dombay (1800), Savary (1813), and Caussin de Perceval (1833). Both well-known scholars such as Vollers, Nallino, Ferguson, Mitchell, and interested laymen published to serve this purpose. This tradition has continued, and in recent years Otto Jastrow's series "Semitica Viva" opened a specialized branch titled "Series Didactica" with Watson (1996) as a first textbook for Ṣanʕāni Arabic. Despite the fact that didactical publications are not recognized by the academic administrations as real "scientific" work, quite a few contemporary scholars developed activities in this field (cf. Holes 1984; Woidich 2000; Bergman 2002). The reason for this pedagogical interest lies in the particular linguistic situation of the Arab world, which creates a specific need for this kind of resources. It was, and still is, quite useful for a non-Arab traveler or resident to learn the local dialect or "real Arabic" of a country he wants to visit or stay in, a language that would be useful in daily life, more so than Standard Arabic, which Arabs themselves have to learn at school and which can be handled properly only by a limited number of well-educated, highly motivated, and trained persons. By speaking a dialect of one of the major cities of the Levant (Beirut, Jerusalem, Damascus), for instance, one can make oneself understood in the whole region: Iraqi (Baghdad) will be

[12] [http://www.semarch.uni-hd.de/index.php43?lang=en]

helpful in Gulf area and Saudi Arabia; due to the omnipresence of Egyptians, Egyptian Arabic (Cairo) is well understood all over the Arab world, certainly in the East but also to some extent in the West. Since serious dialectological studies begin at the university, textbooks on an appropriate level should be written; examples are Ambros (1998) for Maltese, Woidich and Heinen-Nasr (2006) for Cairene, and Watson (1996) for Ṣanʕāni.

13.4.9 Historical Evidence

For the now long extinct dialects of Andalusia we can rely on the comprehensive works of Corriente (**1977**, 1997); on Sicily, see Agius (1996) and Lentin (2007). In general, historical evidence for a deliberate use of the colloquial in writing, which would allow more insight into earlier stages of the dialects, is scarce. Nevertheless, there are some texts, mostly poetry; see, for instance, Kallas (2007) for Aleppo. Davies (1981, 2005) and Zack (2008) publish and linguistically analyze two important texts on Egyptian Arabic of the 17th century: aš-Širbīnī and al-Maghribī, respectively [Holes, "Orality"].

Vrolijk (1998) on Ibn Sūdūn goes back even further to the middle of the 15th century, while Drozdík (1972) and Woidich (1995) deal with sources from the middle of the 19th century. Significant features of modern Egyptian Arabic are present in the 15th and 17th century; see Woidich and Zack (2008). On Levantine Arabic in the 17th century see Zwartjes and Woidich (2011).

13.5 Interpretation of the Data

Collecting, describing, and editing the data of individual dialects for the use of the historical linguist is one side of the coin; the other one is to bring order into the apparent diversity and to cluster the dialects into groups and determine their interrelations. This has to be done by forming either a linguistic hierarchy based on linguistic variables or other ones based on extralinguistic facts.

13.5.1 Linguistic Classification and Dialect Geography

As to the linguistic classification, we have to realize here that no generally accepted linguistic variables are available to serve for a linguistic classification of the Arabic dialects as a whole and to say something meaningful when projected onto a map showing their distribution.[13] For geographic reasons with deserts and large uninhabited areas and,

[13] This is common for dialects of European languages, like in German, where the variables maken–machen, ik–ich, dat–dass, appel–Apfel, that is, the stops developing to affricates, separate Northern and Southern varieties rather neatly. Within the German context these variables correspond to continuous isoglosses on the map and form the famous "Rhenish fan" (Niebaum and Macha 2006: 107, Map 30).

above all, for a history of continuous movement and settlement of the populations and their mutual influence by contacts, single macrodiscriminants such as the reflexes of *q or the existence of interdentals present themselves in a rather scattered way when projected on the dialectological map of the Arab world, as a glance at the maps in Taine-Cheikh (**1998–1999**) shows. Nevertheless, using linguistic variables in this way as discriminants is possible, it seems, on a lower level for smaller regions, for instance, when we talk about *bukṛa*- versus *bukaṛa*-dialects[14] in Middle Egypt (Behnstedt 1979) or about *k*- versus *t*-dialects[15] in Jemen (Behnstedt **1985**: 226, Map 169).[16] The macrodiscriminants q/ʔ and g/ǧ in the Egyptian context of the Nile Delta give a rather clear figure on the map, the Cairo-Damiette corridor; see Behnstedt and Woidich (**2005**, Maps 69 and 70).

Linguistic variables thus are adopted in traditional dialect geography by projecting a number of selected features on maps by means of symbols and the subsequent drawing of isoglosses to delineate the areas where these features prevail. When all isoglosses are compiled on one map, these—ideally—form bundles, which are then interpreted as borderlines between different dialect areas, each of them with a core area and a more or less extended transitional area in between depending on the nature of the bundles; see Behnstedt and Woidich (**1985**, Maps 554–559) for Egypt. The problem of whether some isoglosses or variables should be given more weight than others in this procedure is still unsolved in theory, and the researchers follow their own intuitions. Similar methods have been applied in the regional atlases mentioned already, as aptly described in Palva's (2006) introduction. The features represented in the bundles of isoglosses can be used for the classification of the dialects and be combined with appropriate extralinguistic features; see Woidich (1996) for Egypt.

The "step-method" may be seen as a further methodological development in the classification of dialects that introduces a statistical approach. Neighboring dialects are compared with a set number of variables, all of them considered of the same weight. The number of differences between the two dialects compared is then expressed as a percentage of the total number of the variables. If the percentage is (relatively) low, the dialects belong to the same typological group; conversely, if it is (relatively) high, they

[14] That is, insertion of a vowel preceding /r/ in a cluster -vCr(v).

[15] According to the initial consonant of the morphemes of the first and second perfect, such as *katab-t* ~ *katab-k* "I wrote."

[16] Bailey (1980) uses implicational scales for a classification of Ancient Greek dialects. This has not been done for Arabic dialects yet. One possible implication would be, for instance, *q > g ⊃ *g > ǧ/ž, that is, dialects with a voiced reflex of *q will have an affricated/sibilant reflex of *g. To the best of our knowledge, no dialect has yet been found that falsifies this implication. The Alexandria example found in the texts published in Behnstedt (1980) seems more a case of dialect mixing and a fact of "parole," not of "langue." The reverse of this implication *g > ǧ/ž ⊃ *q > g can easily be falsified, since there are several dialects with /ǧ/ž/ and /q/, for instance, the oasis Farafra in Egypt. Taine-Cheikh (1998: 15) points out another implication: dialects with /ʔ/ (glottal stop) for *q will have replaced the interdentals with dentals, that is, *q > ʔ/ ⊃ ṯ > t in, for instance, /*ṯalāṯa/ "three." There has been no systematic research done so far on implications of this type. Holes (1987) uses, in fact, implicational scales for sociolinguistic variables in his study on Baḥrayn.

belong to different groups. The method was successfully applied to illustrate the continuum of dialects spoken on the northern Sinai littoral, that is, from a Northwestern Bedouin Arabic dialect type to a largely sedentary (rural) dialect type spoken in the eastern Šarqiyya province of the Nile Delta in Egypt (or vice versa); see de Jong (**2000**, 2011).

Another recent and promising way to establish and visualize the subgroups and their interrelations (distance, closeness) is provided by dialectometry, which compares all the data recorded for an area, not only an arbitrary choice according to the predilections of the researcher, by means of more refined statistical methods. As a purely quantitative approach, dialectometry gives all variables the same weight and importance, which makes it more independent on the intuitions of the researcher. It has not yet been applied to Arabic dialects on a larger scale except for a small region, the oases in the Western desert of Egyptian; see Behnstedt and Woidich (**2005**, Chapter 11).[17] This first attempt corroborates the findings of the isogloss method, showing that the dialects of the two oases at the extremes (Baħariyya, Kharga) share more variables with standard Cairene than the two others (Farafra, Dakhla) situated farther away from the Nile valley in terms of traveling distance.

For a more detailed discussion of these approaches, see Behnstedt and Woidich (2005, 2006: 586).

13.5.2 Traditional Classifications

There is no traditional classification of the Arabic dialects based only on linguistic features, as all rely heavily on extralinguistic (i.e., geographical, social, sectarian, and historical) facts, which are then related to certain linguistic features.

13.5.2.1 *Geography*

All surveys and state-of-the-art reports in their classifications of present-day Arabic dialects rely on geography. This means that the dialects are listed and described mainly within the framework of larger geographical entities such as the Levant, Mesopotamia, and Gulf area, Arab Peninsula with Yemen and Oman, Egypt with Sudan and sub-Sahara, North Africa, and Mauretania (e.g., Fischer and Jastrow **1980**; Taine-Cheikh 1998; Corriente and Vicentes 2008; Watson 2011; Versteegh 2011), to which the "islands" Uzbekistan, Afghanistan, Iran, Anatolia, and Cyprus are added. Maltese, as a fully "ausgebaute" written language, is sometimes considered an independent language (Kaye and Rosenhouse **1997**).

More or less uncontroversial is the subdivision in Western/North African and Eastern dialects with the border running between Egypt and Libya (but see Owens 2003). The linguistic variable most commonly adduced with respect to this dichotomy concerns

[17] Whether dialectrometry can ever be applied to the entire of Arab world is doubtful in view of the density of data and the proximity of the research points it needs.

the paradigmatic leveling that occurred in the imperfect: eastern a-ktib/n-iktib versus western n-iktib/n-iktib-u "I write"—"we write." But this single feature is far from being conclusive if we want to assign a given dialect to one of these two groups, since there are dialects in Egypt at the Western part of the Delta and in Upper Egypt that have this Western conjugation but that in other respects (stress, syllable structure) clearly belong to the Egyptian, that is, Eastern phylum.[18] The Sudanic area, too, is problematic here since the Western type is the norm in Chad, but not in Nigeria or in most of the Sudan. The question as to whether the oases of the Egyptian Western desert should be seen as Western or Eastern (Egyptian) Arabic was answered differently in Woidich (1993a) and Behnstedt (1998), the first being in favor of Egypt and the second in favor of the Maghreb.[19]

13.5.2.2 *History*

As a variant of the geographic approach but involving a historical fact as well (i.e., the Arabic expansion starting in the 7th century), the subdivision of the Arab linguistic world can be seen in three zones, as introduced by Jastrow (2002: 348). The Arab Peninsula, from where the Arabic expansion started, is considered Zone I, all the territories (Levant, Irak, Egypt, North Africa, parts of Iran) Arabicized due to this expansion are Zone II, and the remaining "Sprachinseln" (Anatolia, Iran, Afghanistan, Uzbekistan, Cyprus, Malta, sub-Saharan Africa) surrounded today by other languages as Zone III. Watson (2011) adopts this view but excludes the southern regions of the peninsula from Zone I, once the stronghold of South Arabic tongues. It is Zone I where we find, according to Jastrow (ibid.), the most archaic dialects today. The question remains: what does "archaic" exactly mean, and how is it defined? See the discussion of allegedly archaic features in Edzard (1998: 142) and Retsö (2003: 116). Zone II "could be called colonial Arabic" with dialects characterized by their innovative features. This is against all experience with other languages forming colonial areas such as English and Spanish. The dialects spoken in the former colonies North America and, respectively, South America are quite homogeneous compared with the respective homelands, a generally recognized fact in dialect geography. Why then the apparent diversity in Arabic "colonial" regions? Can it be attributed only to population movement and contact (Watson 2011),

[18] This division does not mean, as Owens (2003) apparently assumes, that dialectologists suggest that this paradigmatic leveling developed in North Africa. What is said is that this feature was reimported to Egypt by tribes migrating back to the East. It developed much earlier, maybe not even in Egypt, but on the Arabian Peninsula in "pre-diaspora" times; see next footnote.

[19] A paradigm of the present tense with the same synchronic structure, that is, one single morpheme for the first person (I, we) and one for the plural, can be found farther to the East in the contemporary northwest Aramaic language of Maʕlūla in Syria (Arnold 1990: 74). There it is the natural outcome of the development of a new paradigm from participles, not a case of paradigmatic leveling as in Arabic. As to the older variety of Galilean Aramaic (Lipiński 2001: 382), only the 1st sg. receives a *n*-prefix, and Dalman (1905: 213) considers this as a "Plural der Selbstermunterung." Similar paradigms, though due to different provenance, are thus attested for other Semitic languages. For the discussion of this historical development in Arabic, see Owens (2003), who places its origin in Egypt, and Corriente (2011), who argues for its origin in Yemen.

or did it exist before the expansion (Retsö 2000; Owens 2006; [Retsö, "Arabic?"])? The criterion "history" no longer works for Zone III, the language islands; the reason for their being lumped together in a group is the fact that they are surrounded by other languages and separated from zones II and III.

In a similar vein, Owens (2006) discusses what he calls pre-diaspora Arabic, that is, Arabic before the conquests "at a time and a place when the ancestral populations were still together" (Owens 2006: 3; [Owens, "History"]), which in one interpretation would correspond to Zone I of Jastrow's approach. As a "convenient fiction," he takes Sībawayhi's approximate date of death (790 CE) as the endpoint of "pre-diaspora" Arabic, thus taking roughly the first 150 years of "diaspora" as "pre-diaspora." Relating linguistic features reconstructed by means of comparative methods from the modern dialects to this pre-diaspora Arabic, which ended around 790, seems as arbitrary to us as attributing features to the neo-Arabic language type or not.

Neither of these two approaches is convincing for the linguistic subgrouping, because they cannot be related to linguistic variables that would justify them.

13.5.2.3 *Social/Lifestyle: Sedentary versus Nomadic, Urban versus Rural*

The division of Arabic dialects into sedentary ones and Bedouin was referred to in Marçais (1938) to explain the Arabization of North Africa. Because of their nomadic lifestyle, Bedouin are considered a group distinct from sedentary people, and since many of their dialects show certain features such as a /g/-reflex of *q, interdental consonants, and feminine forms in the plural, these are considered Bedouin features. This may have been true in the past—the distinction between sedentary and Bedouin speakers with a voiced /g/-reflex of *q is already described by Ibn Sīna in the 11th and Ibn Xaldūn in the 14th centuries (Blanc **1964**: 29)—but it would be erroneous to reverse the argument and consider all /g/-speakers Bedouin, let alone nomads.[20] Nor can these "Bedouin" features be found with all Bedouin, as in the Sahel region, for instance, interdental consonants have been replaced by dentals (Blanc 1971; Taine-Cheikh 1998; Rosenhouse 2011). So "Bedouin" today is more of a convenient label for a bundle of features and tells us nothing about the present-day lifestyle of the speakers.

The same is true for the distinction urban versus rural, which often is related to certain variables, the unvoiced pronunciation of the reflexes of *q, for instance, is considered urban in certain regions (Levant, Morocco). Nevertheless, many villagers today speak urban dialects with a glottal stop, due to the spread of urban speech around the urban centers (Cairo, Damascus) and along trade routes, like in North Africa (Marçais 1938; Singer 1994) between the larger cities and the harbors associated with them. On

[20] H. Blanc's (1964: 28, emphasis added) statement (based on Cantineau 1939): "The *present-day* distribution of reflexes of OA /q/ throughout the Arabic-speaking world presents a striking dichotomy: most sedentary populations have a voiceless reflex and all non-sedentary populations a voiced reflex" can today be considered true only for its second part. There are numerous regions in the present-day Arab world, for example, the whole of Upper Egypt, large parts of the Nile Delta, Sudan with a sedentary population speaking voiced /g/, and not a voiceless reflex of *q, due to the settlement of and mixing with Bedouin over the course of history.

the other hand, there are numerous cities, the dialects of which show so-called Bedouin features such as the voiced pronunciation of reflexes of *q (Baghdad, Tripoli/Libya, Khartoum, Mecca). The distinction thus says nothing about the whole Arab world and is applicable for smaller regions, Syria for instance, only. On a synchronic level, there is no "urban dialect" delineable by discrete features, each city or town having its own characteristics. It all depends on the history of settlement and migration; the Muslims of Baghdad, for instance, speak their "Bedouin" dialect because they originate from the countryside, which repopulated Baghdad in the Ottoman era (Blanc **1964**; Holes 2008; [Retsö, "Arabic?"]).

13.5.2.4 *Sectarian: Muslim–Christian–Jewish, Sunnī–Šīʕī, Muslim–Christian, Muslim–Jewish*

The linguistic situation in Baghdad is a relevant and often cited example of sectarian differentiation, or "communal dialects," although the situation today no longer exists: the three different religious communities—Muslims, Jews, and Christians—used to speak different dialects. Again, this differentiation harks back to the history of settlement: Muslims originate from the Bedouin population in southern Iraq (from the 17th century CE), whereas Christians have their origins in different cities in northern Iraq (Blanc 1964; Abu-Haidar **1991**; Mansour 1991). Due to migration to Israel, the number of communal dialects has been reduced to two.

Another well-documented situation (Holes 1983, **1987**) exists in Baḥrayn where the Šīʕī community speaks a dialect different from their Sunnī compatriots. The Šīʕī dialect is related to sedentary or seminomadic dialects spoken "in an area which extends around the periphery of Arabia proper from Yemen to Oman to lower Mesopotamia" (Holes 1983: 8), whereas the Sunnī dialect corresponds the nomadic type common in the Najd. Again this situation goes back to population movement as the Bedouin tribes arrived there from the Najd in 1782–1783 only (Holes 2001: xxvvii).

For the city of Aleppo, see Behnstedt (1989), where Christians use other dialects than the Muslims (cf. Behnstedt and Woidich **2005**). Behnstedt (1998–1999) reports on the rather complicated situation on the island of Djerba/Tunisia with at least three different communal dialects, Muslim, Ibadi, and Jewish, and even Berber in some villages.

In general, Jewish communities used and still use Arabic dialects deviating from the Muslim varieties. This is in particular so in the Maghrib; see Stillman (1988) and Heath (**2002**) for Morocco; Cohen (1912) for Algiers; Cohen (1975) for Tunis; and Yoda (2005) for Tripoli/Libya. For Cairo, see Blanc (1981) and Rosenbaum (2003); for Iraq, see Jastrow (1990a, 1990b) and Mansour (1991).

13.6 Future Prospects

Despite a great deal of progress that has been made and a constant flow of new data over the last 50 years, the coverage of the Arabic-speaking area is still thin compared with what we are accustomed to in the dialectological studies of European countries. Talking about "a relative surfeit of information... on modern dialects" (Owens 2005: 274) is far from reality. Egypt, for instance, a country that has been, compared with others, researched quite well over the last decades, still needs closer study in such key areas as Upper Egypt and the Western oases. On the core of the Arab world, the Arabian Peninsula, in particular its northwestern area Ḥiǧāz, its southern parts ʕAsīr, Ḥaḍramawt, and ʕUmān, we have only very limited knowledge. And the same is true for the Sudan and the sub-Saharan areas and for Libya, parts of Algeria, let alone the "Sprachinseln," such as those in Uzbekistan, Afghanistan, and Iran. All these areas still need much fieldwork.

Another important point here concerns the validity of data we find in publications from earlier times, often the only ones we have, before dialectology became a more professionalized discipline. A considerable number of these we owe to the efforts of single individuals only, sometimes not even a trained linguist or Arabisant. We cannot be sure that these are free from errors. Redoing fieldwork in places from where we have some older information is not a superfluous task for the future.

Systematic research is best done in the framework of projects aiming at drawing linguistic atlases. These should not be limited to Arabic-speaking regions but should also include other languages spoken in the areas under study. To give an example, in Morocco it is highly advisable to extend the research to Berber-speaking areas because of the mutual interferences of the two languages [Kossmann, "Borrowing"]. There are some activities concerning atlases (Israel/Palestine, Tunisia, Morocco), but many more areas have until this day remained unresearched or underresearched (Algeria, Tunisia, Libya, Jordan, Iraq, Saudi Arabia, Sudan). The reasons for this may be seen in facts such as geographical conditions, security problems, and the negative attitude and lack of understanding toward dialect studies prevailing in most Arab countries, which prevents many native Arab scholars from pursuing academic activities in this field. In this respect, much more explanatory work could be done to involve these academics in serious fieldwork in their home countries. Otherwise, it is to be feared that atlases for such countries as Algeria, Libya, Sudan, Saudi Arabia, and Jordan, comparable to Behnstedt and Woidich (**1985**) and Behnstedt (1999), will never see the light of day. Moreover, atlases should not be confined to regions or states but should cover the Arabic-speaking world as a whole and collect all the data gathered so far to provide us with a means to detect and visualize the migratory processes so important for the understanding of "the history of the linguistic contacts of speakers of varieties of Arabic" (Versteegh 2011b: 549). The recent "Wortatlas der arabischen Dialekte" (Behnstedt and Woidich **2011, 2012**) can be seen only as first step in this direction. Regional atlases should, besides the linguistic data, collect and document as much information as possible about the histories of movement and settlement of the population. To a much larger extent than in the European situation, linguistic features were transported by the speakers themselves through physical migration, to mention only the second Arabization of North Africa by

[21] For some conspicuous examples, see Behnstedt and Woidich (2005, Chapter 5.2).

the migration of the Banī Hilāl, in addition to diffusion through contact.[21] The distributions of many features, therefore, show highly irregular geographical patterns.

A prerequisite for future fieldwork is a generally acknowledged but also regularly updated questionnaire to avoid the idiosyncrasies and predilections of the individual fieldworker to make the incoming data better comparable and to ensure an evenly distributed set of data without surprising and unwanted lacunae.[22] This questionnaire should not only reflect the traditionally recognized variables of phonology, morphology, syntax, and lexicon but also—at least to some extent—take account of issues relevant in the current linguistic discourse. As a methodological step forward, newer quantitative approaches such as those developed in dialectometry should be applied to the data given in these atlases to arrive at more objective classifications and should be less dependent on the personal views of the individual researchers.

As to comprehensive descriptive grammars, there are major cities in the Arab world—Beirut, Mosul, Omdurman, Aden, Masqat, Oran, and Constantine may serve as examples—of which the dialects have not been sufficiently described so far, let alone those of rural areas and of many Bedouin tribes that are still partially or entirely undocumented. What we have at our disposal is very sketchy in most cases, as only the basic facts of phonology and morphology are described. Although syntax is still being treated like an orphan in many a grammar, interesting projects are now being carried out; see, for instance, Isaksson (2009) on circumstantial qualifiers.

The same can be said about lexical documentation. There are lots of word lists and glossaries, some of them quite voluminous, which are limited to listing a number of lexemes, in some manner deviating in form or content from mainstream Arabic and that more or less by chance appear in a text or were recorded by the researcher. Here much systematic work is waiting for engaged lexicographers who should try to cover the entire lexicon of a dialect, combining this with in-depth semantic analysis that includes phraseology and pragmatics.[23] For regions such as Tunisia, Libya, Oman, and the Arabian Peninsula in general, no substantial dictionaries are available. In other cases, such as the Levant, Iraq, and Algeria, we have reasonable dictionaries, but these are sometimes outdated and need to be replaced or updated. An important point here is the desperate lack of bidirectional dictionaries, which can make the search for an appropriate expression for a given concept a tedious task. With the possibilities of modern databases and the computer, developing glossaries and dictionaries in both directions does not seem an unreasonable request [Buckwalter and Parkinson, "Modern Lexicography"]. These modern facilities make us think of a step further: as there is already a large amount of vocabulary available in the literature, all this could

[22] An example for Maghrebi dialects is Caubet (2002).

[23] It is strange that old dictionaries, grammars, and textbooks, some of them dating back to the 19th century, are recycled by publishing houses instead of producing up-to date publications based on fresh and recent research. Only recently (June 2011), Vollers and Burkitt (1895), which is based on the German version by Vollers (1890), was reedited and offered as a textbook for Egyptian Arabic. No doubt, this was an excellent short book in its time, but we are 120 years later; both life and research have progressed.

be collected in one large database. Such a resource not only would be very helpful for dialectology itself but also could serve a general philological interest as already stated by Spitaler (1961: 135/226): a "Sammelwörterbuch würde ... der weiteren Erforschung des Mittelarabischen die größten Dienste leisten." "a collective dictionary would be a great service to the the study of Middle Arabic".

As was pointed out already, documentation for Arabic dialects abounds in publications of text collections, which could be used far more efficiently if presented in digitalized form. This means not only that they should be accessible by means of a computer but also that they should be prepared in the necessary way according to a standard tagging protocol to make them fully operable for statistical approaches as developed in corpus linguistics. Such a corpus containing all relevant texts from all regions covered so far would be an invaluable resource for detailed syntactic and phraseological studies, two underdeveloped fields in Arabic dialectology, and particularly helpful for comparison and classification.[24] There are individual dialectologists who apply these research methods already (Isaksson 2004; Persson 2008, 2009). More generally speaking, syntactic and semantic research should take the typological and functional frameworks as developed in general linguistics more into account to take part in the contemporary linguistic discussion. The Arabic language in general and Arabic dialects in particular have much to contribute here, but they have remained rather underrepresented so far in the scientific discourse.

These last points, if realized, would contradict Jean Cantineaus's dictum "la dialectologie arabe n'est guère progressiste; les nouvelles techniques de recherche ont du mal à s'y acclimater." "Arabic dialectology is not at all progressive; new research methods have difficulty becoming established in it" (1960: 277). No doubt, this would be a tremendous task that can be fulfilled only within the framework of full-fledged international cooperation, together with the *aṣḥāb al-luġa* themselves.

References[25]

Abu-Haidar, Farida. 1991. *Christian Arabic of Baghdad*. Wiesbaden: Harrassowitz.

Arnold, Werner and Peter Behnstedt. 1993. *Arabisch–Aramäische Sprachbeziehungen im Qalamūn (Syrien). Eine dialektgeographische Untersuchung*. Wiesbaden: Harrassowitz.

Behnstedt, Peter. 1985. *Die nordjemenitischen Dialekte. Teil 1: Atlas*. Wiesbaden: Harrassowitz.

——. 1997–2000. *Sprachatlas von Syrien. I. Beiheft, Kartenteil. II. Volkskundliche Texte*. Wiesbaden: Harrassowitz.

Behnstedt, Peter and Manfred Woidich. 1985–1999. *Die ägyptisch-arabischen Dialekte*. 5 vols. Dialektatlas von Ägypten. Beihefte zum Tübinger Atlas des Vorderen Orients Reihe B (Geisteswissenschaften) 50/1–5. Wiesbaden: Reichert.

——. 2005. *Einführung in die arabische Dialektgeographie*. Leiden: Brill.

——. 2011. *Wortatlas der arabischen Dialekte. Band I: Mensch, Natur, Fauna, Flora*. Leiden: Brill.

[24] A first step in this direction will be taken within the framework of a project titled "Idiomaticity, Lexical Realignment, and Semantic Change in Spoken Arabic," which Jonathan Owens and Manfred Woidich started recently at the University of Bayreuth.

[25] References refer to boldfaced entries in the chapter.

——. 2012. *Wortatlas der arabischen Dialekte. Band II: Materielle Kultur*. Leiden: Brill.
Bergsträßer, Gotthelf. 1915. Sprachatlas von Syrien und Palästina. *Zeitschrift des Deutschen Palästina-Vereins* 38: 169–222.
Blanc, Haim. 1964. *Communal dialects in Baghdad*. Cambridge, MA: Center for Middle Eastern Studies.
Brustad, Kirsten E. 2000. *The syntax of spoken Arabic: A comprehensive study of Moroccan, Egyptian, Syrian, and Kuwaiti dialects*. Washington, DC: Georgetown University Press.
Cantineau, Jean. [1955] 1960. La dialectologie arabe. In *Études de linguistique arabe. Mémorial Jean Cantineau*, 25–278. Paris: Klincksieck.
Caubet, Dominique. 1993. *L'Arabe marocain. Tome I Phonologie et Morphosyntaxe. Tome II Syntaxe et Catégories Grammaticales, Textes*. Paris: Éditions Peeters.
Clarity, Beverley E., Karl Stowasser, and Ronald G. Wolfe. 1964. *A dictionary of Iraqi Arabic. English–Arabic*. Washington, DC: Georgetown University Press.
Cohen, David. 1963. *Le dialecte arabe ḥassānīya de Mauritanie (parler de la Gəbla)*. Paris: Klincksieck.
Corriente, Federico C. 1977. *A grammatical sketch of the Spanish Arabic dialect bundle*. Madrid: Instituto Hispano-Árabe de Cultura.
Cowell, Mark W. 1964. *A reference grammar of Syrian Arabic: Based on the dialect of Damascus*. Washington, DC: University of Georgetown.
de Jong, Rudolf E. 2000. *A grammar of the Bedouin dialects of the Northern Sinai littoral: Bridging the linguistic gap between the Eastern & Western Arab world*. Leiden: Brill.
Eisele, John C. 1999. *Arabic verbs in time: Tense and aspect in Cairene Arabic*. Wiesbaden: Harrassowitz.
Fischer, Wolfdietrich. 1961. Die Sprache der arabischen Sprachinsel in Uzbekistan. *Der Islam* 36: 232–263.
Fleisch, Henri. 1974. *Études d'arabe dialectal*. Beirut: Dar El-Machreq.
Harrell, Richard S. 1962. *A short reference grammar of Moroccan Arabic*. Washington, DC: Georgetown University Press.
Heath, Jeffrey. 2002. *Jewish and Muslim dialects of Moroccan Arabic*. London: RoutledgeCurzon.
Hinds, Martin and Elsaid Badawi. 1986. *A dictionary of Egyptian Arabic: Arabic–English*. Beirut: Librairie du Liban.
Holes, Clive. 1987. *Language variation and change in a modernising Arab state*. London: Kegan Paul International.
——. 2005. *Dialect, culture, and society in Eastern Arabia*. Vol. 2, Ethnographic texts. Leiden: Brill.
Ingham, Bruce. 1982. *North east Arabian dialects*. London: Kegan Paul International.
——. 1994. *Najdi Arabic: Central Arabian*. Amsterdam: Benjamins.
Jastrow, Otto. 1978–1981. *Die mesopotamisch-arabischen qəltu-Dialekte*. 2 vols. Wiesbaden: Harrassowitz.
Jastrow, Otto and Wolfdietrich Fischer (eds.). 1980. *Handbuch der arabischen Dialekte*. Wiesbaden: Harrassowitz.
Johnstone, Thomas Muir. 1967. *Eastern Arabian dialect studies*. London: Oxford University Press.
Jullien de Pommerol, Patrice. 1992. *Grammaire pratique de l'arabe Chadien*. Paris: Karthala.
Kaye, Alan S. and Judith Rosenhouse. 1997. Arabic dialects and Maltese. In *The Semitic languages*, ed. Robert Hetzron, 263–311. New York: Routledge.

Landberg, Carlo de. 1905–1913. *Études sur les dialectes de l'Arabie Méridionale. Glossaire daṯînois*, vol. 2. *Daṯînah*, vol. 1–3. Leiden: Brill.

Nöldeke, Theodor. [1904] 1982. Das Klassische Arabisch und die arabischen Dialecte. In *Beiträge zur semitischen Sprachwissenschaft*, 1–14. Amsterdam: APA-Philo Press.

Owens, Jonathan. 1984. *A short reference grammar of Eastern Libyan Arabic*. Wiesbaden: Harrassowitz.

Owens, Jonathan and Alaa Elgibali (eds.). 2010. *Information structure in spoken Arabic*. London: Routledge.

Palva, Heikki. 1976. *Studies in the Arabic dialect of the Semi-Nomadic əl-ʕAǧārma Tribe (al-Balqāʔ District, Jordan)*. Göteborg: Acta Universitatis Gothoburgensis.

Prochazka, Theodore, Jr. 1988. *Saudi Arabian dialects*. London: Kegan Paul International.

Procházka, Stephan. 2002. *Die arabischen Dialekte der Çukurova (Südtürkei)*. Wiesbaden: Harrassowitz.

Rosenbaum, Gabriel. 2004. Egyptian Arabic as a written language. *Jerusalem Studies in Arabic and Islam* 29: 281–340.

Singer, Hans-Rudolf. 1984. *Grammatik des Arabischen von Tunis*. Berlin: de Gruyter.

Shawarbah, Musa. 2012. *A grammar of Negev Arabic: Comparative studies, texts and glossary in the Bedouin dialect of the ʿAzāzmih tribe*. Wiesbaden: Harrassowitz.

Taine-Cheikh, Cathérine. 1988–1998. *Dictionnaire Hassaniyya-Français*. 8 vols. Paris: Geuthner.

Vanhove, Martine. 1994. *La langue Maltaise*. Wiesbaden: Harrassowitz.

Versteegh, Kees, et al. (eds.). 2006–2009. *EALL*. 4 vols. Leiden: Brill.

Watson, Janet C. E. 2002. *The phonology and morphology of Arabic*. Oxford: Oxford University Press.

Wellens, Ineke. 2005. *The Nubi language of Uganda*. Leiden: Brill.

Werbeck, Wolfgang. 2001. *Laut- und Formenlehre des nordjemenitisch-arabischen Dialekts von Manāḫa*. Münster: RHEMA.

Woidich, Manfred. 2006. *Das Kairenisch-Arabische. Eine Grammatik*. Wiesbaden: Harrassowitz.

CHAPTER 14

CODESWITCHING AND RELATED ISSUES INVOLVING ARABIC

EIRLYS DAVIES, ABDELALI BENTAHILA, AND JONATHAN OWENS

14.1 Introduction

Bilingual speech involving Arabic has been an important source of linguistic research on the language. The greater part of this research has involved Arabic in contact with other languages; in recent years greater systematic attention has been given to Arabic diglossic speech as well. This article examines Arabic in contact with other languages and with diglossic speech.[1] In addition, we briefly summarize the use of secret languages, which has close structural parallels to codeswitching.

14.2 Issues in Codeswitching Research

The systematic study of codeswitching, defined roughly as the use of more than one language within a single piece of discourse or interaction, began to attract the serious attention of linguists in the 1970s and early 1980s. Since then, the lion's share of research has been concerned with identifying permissible switch points. Early analyses offered highly specific syntactic constraints but were followed by attempts to state purportedly universal constraints, first ones formulated in terms of surface structure (Poplack

[1] Sections 14.2–14.4 and 14.6 are mainly the work of Bentahila and Davies; Section 14.5 is mainly from Owens.

1980), later ones evoking underlying syntactic relations (Di Sciullio, Muysken, and Singh 1986, Sankoff 1998), and more recently attempts to account for all possibilities in terms of principles already motivated for the grammars of the two languages, such as MacSwan's (1999) minimalist approach [Benmamoun and Choueri, "Syntax"]. Once it was noted that there were often clear asymmetries between the roles of the two languages in codeswitching discourse, many models identified one of them as the "base," "host," or "matrix" language into which elements of the other language were "embedded" (Joshi 1985; Myers-Scotton 1993a, 2002). At the same time many researchers felt the need to draw distinctions between codeswitching and other phenomena, both the old-established category of borrowing (Heath 1989) and new ones used in the elaboration of their models.

Codeswitching has also been approached from other angles. Its discourse and communicative functions were explored by Gumperz (1982) and Bentahila (1983a) and later became the subject of more systematic models like that of Myers-Scotton (1993b). Many studies noted the impact on switching patterns of sociolinguistic variables such as language dominance, proficiency, and prestige. A conversational framework is used in Auer (1998), and the use of codeswitching as a literary device has also been examined (Keller 1979; Tessier 1996).

Looking back over these developments, we can draw a distinction between two general approaches to codeswitching. On one hand, we have the strictly formalistic models, focusing largely on structure, formulating absolute generalizations, and claiming to identify universal principles; on the other, there are more holistic, interdisciplinary approaches that take a wider view, acknowledging the relevance of many other variables and drawing on insights from fields such as sociolinguistics, psycholinguistics, pragmatics, discourse, and conversation analysis.

14.3 Studies of Codeswitching Involving Arabic

The absence of any comprehensive survey of published studies on codeswitching involving Arabic may relate to a number of facts. First, the considerable syntactic, phonological, and lexical differences between the colloquial Arabic varieties used across the Arabic-speaking world [Behnstedt and Woidich, "Dialectology"] may make it difficult for scholars to interpret and compare and data from different communities. Second, the published works report on a diverse range of configurations, covering switching between Arabic and a number of other languages, including French, English, Dutch, Spanish, Hausa, with some studies looking at tri- or even quadrilingual switching (Owens 2005a, 2005b; Edwards and Dewaele 2007), as well as switching between colloquial and standard Arabic (see Section 14.4). Third, the bodies of work published in different languages have tended to remain separate; for instance, discussions of

Arabic–French switching published in French frequently ignore similar studies written in English and vice versa.

Yet the very diversity of existing studies of codeswitching involving Arabic can be seen as a valuable opportunity for those seeking new and deeper insights into the phenomenon. The availability of detailed studies on different language pairs offers the possibility of comparative studies to explore the impact of the nature of a language on the patterns observed. Moreover, the data available also illustrate a variety of sociolinguistic contexts, from the ex-French colonies of North Africa, where Arabic is the official and majority language, to large immigrant communities in Europe, where it is a minority language but an important community in-group marker, and other cases of more isolated immigrants with no such community support. There is also the possibility of exploring the functions of codeswitching between colloquial and standard Arabic, varieties generally described as being in a diglossic relationship. And the many Arabic-speaking communities that are undergoing sociolinguistic transformations, such as changes in immigration patterns, education systems, ideology, or attitudes, offer the chance to investigate the consequences of such variation on the codeswitching behavior of a community. The wealth of material available for investigation is thus a complicating factor for research on codeswitching involving Arabic but also a stimulating one.

Studies where Arabic is one of the languages in a codeswitching configuration are of course of intrinsic interest for what they may reveal about these specific instances of language contact. However, in what follows we will try in particular to assess what these studies have contributed to the theory of codeswitching in general.

14.4 Contributions of Codeswitching Studies Involving Arabic

In the extensive debate on syntactic constraints on codeswitching, studies of data involving Arabic have played a number of important roles. First, there are the proposals directly inspired by the analysis of corpora involving Arabic. The earliest studies, in keeping with contemporaneous studies of other language pairs, merely stated ad hoc constraints identifying specific syntactic configurations where switches were or were not observed (Stevens 1974; Abbassi 1977). Bentahila and Davies (1983) attempt to account for nonoccurring switches in terms of subcategorization restrictions. Belazi, Rubin, and Toribio (1994) propose a Functional Head constraint prohibiting switching between a functional head (e.g., a numeral, quantifier, negative particle or modal) and its complement NP or VP, while allowing switching between a lexical head and its complement, such as between a verb or preposition and its object. All these studies were based on data from Arabic–French codeswitching. Boumans (1998), on the other hand, studies Moroccan Arabic–Dutch codeswitching and postulates the monolingual structure approach, a modification of Myers-Scotton's MLF model, to describe it in terms of insertions of elements from an embedded language into structures provided by a matrix language. Aabi (1999) claims that the possibilities for Moroccan Arabic–French and Moroccan Arabic–Classical Arabic switching can be accounted for in terms of his functional parameter constraint, which evokes selectional restrictions to predict possible switch configurations. More recently, Owens (2005a, 2005b) adopts a processing-based account to explain certain patterns in Nigerian Arabic–English and Hausa–English switching, and Ziamari (2009) also looks at the implications of processing factors for Arabic–French switching.

However, it must be admitted that none of the models based initially on the examination of codeswitching involving Arabic has been widely tested on other language pairs. On the other hand, evidence from data including Arabic has frequently been evoked in attempts to evaluate models originally based on other data, with significant results, as will be shown.

Poplack (1980) is among the first to postulate purportedly universal constraints, with her equivalence constraint, prohibiting switching at points where the two languages do not exhibit similar syntactic structure, and free morpheme constraint, prohibiting switching between root and bound morphemes. However, among the counterexamples to these generalizations offered by other researchers were the very common strings of the type Arabic determiner + French determiner + noun described by Bentahila and Davies (1983) and also attested by many other studies on North African codeswitching. Strings like (1) and (2), which are typical of the discourse of Moroccan bilinguals, respect Moroccan Arabic syntax, where the demonstratives *dak*, *ħad* and the indefinite marker *waħed* require a following definite article but do not conform to French rules. (In the following examples from Bentahila and Davies 1983: 317, French is in italics.)

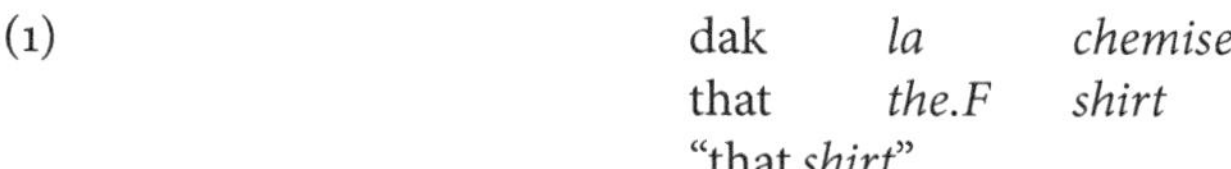

(1) dak *la* *chemise*
that *the.F* *shirt*
"that *shirt*"

(2) waħed *le* *liquide*
one *the.M* *liquid*
"a *liquid*"

This problem led some of Poplack's colleagues to look at Arabic–French data for themselves, and Nait M'Barek and Sankoff (1988) sought to preserve the equivalence constraint by arguing that these examples should not be classified as code switches at all but as instances of a separate phenomenon termed constituent insertion. In a similar way, faced with the counterexamples to her free morpheme constraint observed in many language pairs, including Arabic–French examples like (3), where a French verb is accompanied by Arabic inflections, Poplack, Sankoff and Miller (1988) sought to deal with them by postulating another category distinct from codeswitching, that of nonce-borrowings:

(3) ma-bqa-š *y-fonctionner*
not-remain.NEG 3-function
"It stopped working" (Bentahila and Davies 1983: 315)

However, these attempts to protect the supposed universal constraints by simply relabeling problematic examples as something other than codeswitching leave Poplack's account open to accusations of circularity and of course reduce the generality of its earliest formulation, based on Spanish–English switching.

Data involving Arabic have posed still greater problems for Myers-Scotton's long battle to defend her matrix language frame model as a universal theory of codeswitching. The basis for the earliest versions of this model, which was heavily based on Levelt's (1989) model of speech production, was the assumption that codeswitching involves the insertion, into a syntactic frame provided by a matrix language (ML), of elements from an embedded language (EL), and that in mixed ML and EL constituents syntactic structures and system morphemes must be provided by the ML (Myers-Scotton 1993a). Over the years, material from language pairs including Arabic has played a significant part in pushing Myers-Scotton to modify all the basic components of her theory: the identification of the matrix language, the definition of system morphemes, and the rules constraining embedded language elements. For instance, she originally identified the matrix language in very concrete terms, as the language contributing the largest number of morphemes to a piece of discourse (Myers-Scotton 1993a). Reactions to this included Bentahila's (1995) review objecting to her own identification (Myers-Scotton 1993a: 89, 151) of Arabic as the matrix language in isolated Arabic–French fragments like (1) and (4), (taken from Bentahila and Davies 1983: 319)

(4) naaḍ-u *les* *privés*
arise-3PL *the.PL* *private*
"*The private practitioners* rose up (in protest)"

This is depite the fact that she had no access to the conversations from which these fragments are taken and therefore no way of performing a morpheme count. Like Poplack, Myers-Scotton was pushed to take Arabic data into account to improve her model (Myers-Scotton, Jake, and Okasha 1996). Significantly, in a later version the ML is defined only at the level of a complement phrase (CP) and ultimately becomes not a language at all but merely "an abstract frame for the morphosyntax of the bilingual CP" (Myers-Scotton 2002: 66). Moreover, while the original version made the strong generalization that mixed language constituents must respect ML word order and use ML system morphemes, problematic examples including common Arabic–French configurations like those previously cited led Myers-Scotton to weaken these claims. First, she relaxed the rule to allow for examples like (5):

(5) kan-t dak *la* *semaine* dyal ta-y-zuwl-u *les* *permis*
was-F that *the.F* *week* of IMPF-3-take-PL *the.PL* *permits*

"It was that-(*the*) *week* where they take away *the driving licences*" (Bentahila and Davies 1992: 449, cited by Myers-Scotton and Jake 1995: 1012)

She did this by acknowledging the possibility of an EL island internal to a larger ML + EL constituent. Later she weakened her claim still further by admitting that such EL system morphemes as determiners, demonstratives, and possessive markers are permitted in mixed constituents, thus solving the problem posed by examples like (6):

(6) *Ça depend de quel degré de connaissance* dyal *la personne*
"*That depends on the degree of knowledge* of *the person*" (Bentahila and Davies 1998: 38; also cited by Myers-Scotton 2002: 91)

But she was then forced to find another explanation for the scarcity of switches for determiners in her own data by introducing both a further constraint, the uniform structure principle, requiring that all constituents satisfy the well-formedness requirements of their language, and a notion of "specific congruence" that offers a loophole: EL system morphemes may occur in mixed constituents if the structures of the two languages are sufficiently similar, even if not identical. In a move reminiscent of Poplack's argumentation, she also (2002: 8) drew a distinction between what she termed classic codeswitching, that used by speakers proficient in the ML, and composite codeswitching, the latter becoming a convenient dumping ground for problematic data.

Nevertheless, even after all these modifications, there remain recurrent patterns in Arabic–French switching that no version of the MLF model seems able to account for. For instance, in the speech of highly proficient Moroccan bilinguals (who presumably use classic codeswitching), we commonly find isolated grammatical items from Arabic within otherwise entirely French strings, as illustrated in (7):

(7) *tu ne vas pas t'amuser chaque fois à former des pelotons à traduire chaque fois* dak l *matériel*
"*You are not going to bother every time training squads to translate every time* that (the) *material*" (Bentahila and Davies 1998: 38)[2]

(8) *ils contredisent* ħad *la théorie de Darwin pour trois raisons*
"*they contradict* this-*the theory of Darwin for three reasons*" (Bentahila and Davies 2007: 458)

If the MLF model's constraints are weakened yet again to allow even an isolated EL demonstrative (8) or demonstrative + determiner string (7) to occur within an

[2] Myers-Scotton (2000: 57) even resorts to suggesting that examples like (7) are merely "performance errors," the only basis for this suggestion apparently being the problem such examples pose for her model.

otherwise entirely ML clause/sequence of clauses, then its remaining predictive power seems negligible.

Data on codeswitching involving Arabic can thus be seen to have served a useful corrective function, exposing overgeneralizations in purportedly universal models and showing the astonishing lengths to which some researchers will go in defending these models.[3] The quest for syntactic universals has clearly led some to quite desperate measures, where data get reinterpreted, reclassified, or oversimplified merely to shore up theoretical claims. However, Owens's (2005a) material illustrating the complex multilingual discourse of Maiduguri, Nigeria, where switching involves Nigerian Arabic, Standard Arabic, Hausa, and English, suggests that other approaches should also be pursued. Far from seeking to describe this material within some further modification of the MLF, Owens argues that we must recognize that certain types of codeswitching cannot be subsumed under this model; the concept of a matrix language is a very useful one, but seeking to make it a universal model of all codeswitching behavior will only reduce its effectiveness.

Still more controversies have come from comparisons of switching patterns between different language pairs involving Arabic. Arabic–Dutch, and Arabic–French data have been compared by Nortier (1990, 1995) and Boumans and Caubet (2000). Interestingly, in contrast to the typical Arabic–French patterns illustrated in (1)–(2), in Arabic–Dutch switching there is instead a strong tendency to use bare Dutch nouns, as in (9), which contrasts with (2):

(9) waḥed *Ø-bejaardencentrum*
one *Ø—old people's home*
"an *old people's home*" (Nortier 1990: 199)

Nortier (1995: 89) talks of a "suspension of syntax" in such configurations, Boumans and Caubet (2000: 131) suggest that the second determiner is omitted because it is redundant, and others have suggested various linguistic explanations for the contrast between French and Dutch (the more clitic-like nature of French determiners; Muysken 2000: 83; Versteegh 2001: 223), phonological similarities between French and Arabic determiners (Heath 1989: 35), and the lack of structural congruity between Arabic and Dutch (Myers-Scotton 2002: 126).

However, there is a need for caution in seeking to attribute such differences directly to formal features of the languages involved. There are after all significant sociolinguistic contrasts between the North African and Dutch communities concerned (e.g., duration

[3] We may also note here that those embroiled in theoretical controversies have sometimes been careless in citing or interpreting others' data. Apart from the comments by Myers-Scotton, there are many others. For instance, Jake (1994) is apparently happy to invent her own hypothetical example of Arabic–French switching and then to declare that such examples do not occur in Bentahila and Davies's (1983) Arabic–French data, while Alby and Migge (2007: 55), commenting yet again on the much cited string (1), wrongly claim that a French article is obligatory in this string (perhaps because they attribute both examples and observation to Nortier [1990] rather than its original source Bentahila and Davies 1983).

of language contact, stability of the bilingual community, status of the languages and their users). Owens (2005b) argues that factors such as language proficiency and the differing social statuses of the languages involved may explain whether bilinguals opt for the bare noun or the integrated noun patterns, and after exploring the way the two possibilities appear in switching among Hausa, Nigerian Arabic, and English he offers a processing-based explanation, suggesting that uninflected forms are more rapidly processed.

In fact, the studies of different corpora involving Arabic may serve to remind us of the importance of looking beyond syntax when seeking to account for the types of switch that occur. For instance, the pragmatic distinction between old and new information is evoked by Owens (2005a), who observes that in Hausa–Nigerian Arabic switching Arabic (L1) tends to be used for the topic and Hausa (L2) for the comment. Ziamari (2009), on the other hand, observes that in her Arabic–French data French (L2) is often used even for topics and suggests that this pattern is characteristic of situations of stable, long-established bilingualism. Carrying this point further, it has been shown that social variables even within a single overall community may be reflected in distinctive switching patterns. Bentahila and Davies (1991, 1992, 1995, 1998) compared switching patterns across two generations of Moroccan bilinguals and noted that the distribution of switch types varied according to their language background and proficiency. Three different switching styles were identified: one used mostly by balanced bilinguals, where there is frequent alternation between clauses in one language and those in the other; a second favored by the younger group who are not as fluent in French, dominated by insertion of French lexis into an Arabic matrix; and a third described as the "leak" style and used by those extremely fluent in French, where discourse almost entirely in French is dotted with occasional fillers and grammatical items from Arabic. Since then similar distinctions have been drawn using different data sets: Jacobson (2000a) endorses the distinction between alternation and insertion with data from other language pairs, and Muysken (2000) adopts a similar distinction between alternation and insertion switching. The "leak" switching style is comparable to patterns described by Lipski (2005) in Spanish–English switching.

Another point that has emerged clearly from studies of switching involving Arabic is that, in a stable bilingual community, codeswitching can become a highly norm-governed variety, following conventions specific to the community and fulfilling an important function as an identity marker. Whatever explanation is offered for some of the controversial switches noted already, it is clear that certain patterns have become emblematic markers of a particular group. The NP pattern illustrated in (1), (2), (5), and (8) is a good example. Theoreticians may struggle with what they consider the exceptional nature of such switches, but the fact remains that they are so deeply entrenched in the everyday speech patterns of Arabic–French bilinguals in Morocco that even 4-year-old children are already regularly using them (Bentahila and Davies 1994).

On the other hand, members of another community using the same language pair may favor quite different patterns. Sefiani (2003) reports on the Arabic–French codeswitching of 12- to 25-year-olds from the third generation of North African immigrant families settled in Besançon, France. Some of these subjects use only French at home, with their bilingual parents, because they are conscious of their limited proficiency in Arabic, but between themselves they use a codeswitching variety to mark their in-group status. Sefiani notes many examples where a speaker inserts, into a French structure where a past participle would be required, the 3PL masculine singular imperfect form of an Arabic verb, this being the form generally used to cite a verb, in the way an infinitive form is used in French or English:

(10)	*elle a*	ħlef	
	she has	swear.PST.3M[4]	
	"*She has*	sworn"	

(11)	*il a*	xṭob	*la fille mais ça a pas marché*
	he has	ask-to-marry.PST.3M	*the girl but it did not work*
	"*He has*	asked the hand of *the girl but it didn't work.*" (Sefiani 2003: 57)	

Melliani (2005) reports very similar patterns in the speech of young people of Moroccan origin in the Rouen area. Such examples seem outlandish and amusing to Moroccan bilinguals living in Morocco, who instead are very comfortable inserting French verb roots, complete with Arabic inflections, into Arabic strings, as in (3). Clearly, different configurations can become particularly idiomatic in-group markers in different communities using the same language combinations.

A particularly interesting case is that described by Nortier and Dorleijn (2008), who report on what they call Moroccan-flavored Dutch (MLD), an in-group variety that has emerged only in the last few years and that is used in Dutch cities by youths of varied origins (Turkish, Moroccan, Surinamese, and even native Dutch). Apart from a Moroccan accent and certain nonstandard grammatical features, Nortier and Dorleijn report that this variety is also marked by the insertion of Arabic fillers, interjections, and certain grammatical morphemes such as *dak*, *waħed*, and the interrogative particle *waš*, which may remind us of the leak style of Arabic–French switching mentioned already. This adoption of features of Arabic codeswitching style by non-Arabic speakers can be seen as an instance of language crossing (Rampton 1995) and again highlights the symbolic value that codeswitching patterns may acquire: the originally Moroccan features have now become symbolic of a wider group of streetwise urban youths.

The role of switching patterns as identity markers may be particularly obvious in public discourse and may be accessible to a wider audience, not merely to in-group members. Interesting examples of this situation may be seen in the use of codeswitching in the lyrics of North African popular songs, both the local genre of rai and that of rap as performed by North African hip-hop artists. This is examined in Bentahila and Davies

[4] If indeed speakers perceive the bare insertional form as morphologically marked.

(2002) and Davies and Bentahila (2006, 2008a, 2008b), where it is argued that incorporating both Arabic and French into the lyrics of a single song may serve to manipulate the audience targeted [Holes, "Orality"]. Codeswitching using the local style may be a strong identity marker and make the lyrics unintelligible to anyone outside the group, achieving an effect of localization and exclusion of the Other. On the other hand, including some French in an otherwise Arabic text may open the song up to a wider audience of outsiders, thereby helping to globalize the message. Williams (2009) makes similar observations about the codeswitching between Arabic and English used by Egyptian hip-hop groups. Jablonka (2009) argues that codeswitching in rai lyrics is used to create a social communicative style, and he also notes the symbolic use of English by some performers, this being another case of language crossing. In fact, the symbolic value of codeswitching involving Arabic in rap lyrics can be set beside similar strategies observed in many different countries and language combinations (Androutsopoulos and Scholz 2002; Sarkar and Winer 2006), and there would seem to be much more to investigate in this constantly evolving genre.

Finally, a significant phenomenon can be noted, which in one of its two realizations can be regarded as the most extreme form of in-group codeswitching. Secret languages are closely linked socially and structurally to codeswitching. Socially, a secret language can be thought of as an even more restricted in-group variety than is a code-switched variety, used by a closed social group, such as a professional caste, student organization, or marginal occupational groups such as thieves. Structurally, rather than taking the content vocabulary from a language of the wider environment, as happens with codeswitching, speakers of secret language make up the forms to be inserted themselves.

Arabic is rich in documented secret languages, as a recent comprehensive overview of the phenomenon (Wolfer 2011) shows. Following a well-defined dichotomy, Arabic secret languages can be divided into argots and ludlings. The former consist of a secret vocabulary, while the latter are purely phonologically manipulations (see Berjaoui 1996 for extensive documentation of the latter).

How words are formed in an argot is multifarious and ingenious, but they always reflect in one way or another the immediate environment of their existence and hence are semantically semitransparent; that is, if one knows the local culture well enough, the basis of the secret meaning can often be deduced. For instance, in the "market language" (liɣa suuʔiiye) of Damascus a *mihbir* is a "rich customer," a stem IV verb (CA, not Damascene), which is derived from Damascene *habra* "good red meat." Hebrew was and still is a favorite source of secret vocabulary among Judeo-Arabic speakers (Wolfer 2011: 29, 34). In the secret language of Koranic school students in northeast Nigeria (termed *waris*), the local pronunciation of the Koranic word *ka-ṣaahibi*, lit. "like the friend of" means "fish," the word taken from the Quran 68:48, *ka ṣaaħibi l-ħuut* "like the companion of the fish." In Nigerian Arabic *huut* is the word for "fish," here converted to a secret designation via syntagmatic displacement to the adjacent *ka ṣaaħibi*, *ṣaahib* itself being one NA word for "friend." Obviously the association would be transparent only to those who have studied the Quran extensively (Owens and Hassan 2000: 229).

Once created, the secret words function in an analogous way to single word insertions in codeswitching. For instance, to say that one has eaten fish today, one inserts the secret word in the appropriate matrix sentence that is provided by Nigerian Arabic:

(12) akal-na ka-ṣaahibi aloom
ate-we like-friend today
"We ate fish today."

One could equally have substituted English /fiš/ or Hausa /kifi/ here.

Ludlings are purely phonological secret languages and hence have no direct analogy in CS. Extraneous material is added by a rule that has no effect at all on the meaning of the base words on which they operate. For instance, the ʕaṣfuuri secret language in Damascus adds a -CV after each syllable of the base word, -V being harmonious with the vowel of the preceding syllable. Thus, to say *haati šaay* "bring.F" tea one has the following, with the ludling syllables in bold (Wolfer 2011: 10).

(13) ha-zaa-ti-zi ša-zaa-y

Besides their cultural and anthropological value, Arabic ludlings are interesting as evidence in the debate about the minimal unit of morphological analysis in Arabic, consonantal root or voweled stem ([Ratcliffe, "Morphology"]; [Boudelaa, "Psycholinguistics"]). From a quantitative perspective, the vast majority of Arabic ludlings are formed by the addition of either syllables, as in (13), or fixed segments of arbitrary length (e.g., women's talk in Algiers inserting *-anga-* within each word; Wolfer 2011: 17). Thirty of Wolfer's documented ludlings fall into this category, as opposed to only three that operate only on the root consonants (e.g., transposing R1 and R3 with no change in the vowel). Certainly this evidence speaks strongly in favor of a key role for a voweled stem in word processing.[5]

14.5 Diglossic Switching, Diglossic Mixing

A prominent aspect of Arabic is that it is in contact not only with other languages, the situation underlying codeswitching, but also, as it were, with itself. With marginal exceptions, for instance, Arabic in southern Turkey, Khorasan and in Nigeria, Cameroon and Chad, Standard Arabic is an ever-present variety in the everyday life of Arabs. The

[5] There are interesting hybrid secret languages as well. Al-Agbari (2010) reports on a naming practice in Omani Arabic in which a new derogatory secret name is formed on the same pattern as the real personal name, whereby the new word has a derogatory (and deliberately insulting) meaning. For instance, the personal name *gamiil-ah* "pretty" becomes *qamiil-ah* "lice." Like a ludling, the secret word is constrained phonologically, having to be of a similar morphological pattern as the basic word; however, like an argot, the secret word itself has its own meaning.

well-known linguistic term for this is diglossia ([Suleiman, "Folk Linguistics"]; [Al-Wer, "Sociolinguistics"]).

While Arabic diglossia as a concept has an intellectual pedigree as old as that of studies on codeswitching itself, the relation between the two remains to be specified. In an earlier characterization (Owens and Bani Yasin 1987; Owens 2001: 451), diglossic Arabic was conceptualized in terms of borrowing. A different approach has been to apply models of CS to the variety of speech in which SA and CollA are mixed in some fashion. Eid (1982, 1988, 1992) is an earlier example of this approach. Recent studies of so-called diglossic switching have shown that the situation extends beyond borrowing (Bassiouney 2006; Mejdell 2006), though it is equally not clear that classic codeswitching models can be readily applied to it. In this section, a neutral term, *mixed Arabic,* will be used to describe this variety of Arabic, with elements from both SA and CollA.

14.5.1 Contextual Clues

There are two factors to be treated here. One is the linguistic structure of the CS, which will be discussed in Section 14.5.2. A second, broadly speaking, is what Gumperz (1982; see also Auer 1998) terms contextual clues. These concern nonlinguistic aspects of the speech situation that impinge on code choice: the social relationships of the speakers, their social roles, conversation type, type of interactional exchange, audience design and occasion, and (problematically it must be said) topic.

In a typical multilingual codeswitching situation, CS is associated with the following set of contextual features:

(14) Contextual clues: multilingual CS
- Social relationship: among equals
- Social role: friends, unofficial[6]
- Conversation type: dialogue
- Interactional exchange: two-way· Topic: open
- Audience design: flexible according to situation but also often irrelevant (Myers-Scotton, CS as the unmarked choice)
- Occasion: spontaneous, unplanned

To these background factors we would add that the languages involved in the switching are all part of the normal oral communicative repertoire of the community that engages in the codeswitching. There will be many occasions for speakers to use the languages in a monolingual mode.

Turning to diglossic switching or mixing, one may ask whether the contextual factors governing it differ from those when different languages are involved. There are clear examples indicating the answer is "no." A good illustration of this is Alfonzetti's (1998)

[6] Whereas one might codeswitch with an individual as a friend, if the same individual is also your director, CS may be less likely (see Myers-Scotton 1976, Bentahila 1983b, Chebchoub 1985).

study of Sicilian–Italian switching, in which the contextual factors are essentially the same as those set out in (14).

As far as Arabic goes, recent corpora studies (Bassiouney 2006, 2010a; Mejdell 2006) suggest that the background factors are often special. These show Arabic mixing unfolding either in largely monologic contexts or in what can be termed moderated dialogues, media discussions involving two or more individuals. These are two formats where there can be a high degree of interaction between SA and colloquial.

Bassiouney (2006) and Mejdell (2006) exemplify the monologic style in detail. In one, for instance, a political speech by then president Housni Mubarak (Bassiouney 2006: 245–246) is divided into three parts. Part 1 of the speech is characterized as EgA, part 2 as SA, and part 3 as mixed SA/EgA. The political speech provides clear exemplification of a style of mixing SA/colloquial, whereby one and the same speaker, with input from no one else, is in total control of choosing the different style at his disposal to convey his message.

Linguistic studies of the ever-growing domain of moderated dialogues are just emerging (Bassiouney 2010b), even if this genre is perhaps the premier forum where spontaneous SA/colloquial contact can be observed.

(15) Contextual clues: Arabic mixing

- Social relationship: either unequal (president, preacher to audience) or professionally defined coevals
- Social role: strangers, colleagues in official function
- Conversation type: monologue; moderated dialogues
- Interactional exchange: often, none; moderated dialogues
- Topic: circumscribed (politics, current events, religion, academic, social issues)
- Audience design: use of SA/CA often a staged event; speakers choose variety to effect an outcome on audience rather than in response to a developing interactional situation (Holes 1993; Mazraani 1997; Bassiouney 2006: 173). CS as unmarked choice rarely an option. In moderated dialogues, same panel of speakers may display marked individual differences in SA/colloquial usage (Mejdell 2006: 376), suggesting that mixing is dependent on individual choice and style more than on group-based norm.
- Occasion: planned, staged or for public performance

Finally, as Holes ["Orality"] points out, SA is itself a variety that never serves as the basis of spontaneous informal speech, so there is an inherent bias toward a higher dialectal functionality (see also Mejdell 2006: 390).

A first point then that emerges in a comparison of (14) and (15) is that Arabic mixing has unique properties requiring typologization to contrast the salient properties of Arabic with diglossic switching situations.[7]

[7] In fact, Alfonzetti, following Trumper (1989: 40), characterizes the Sicilian situation as macro-codeswitching. The contextual contexts of the codes in the opposed microdiglossic category are characterized as being largely complementary, a characterization that seems more appropriate to the Arabic situation.

14.5.2 Linguistic Properties

Turning to the linguistic properties of mixed Arabic, two basic observations are as follows. First, the varieties involved are linguistically very close to one another. All varieties of Arabic have a shared phonemic inventory, a verb system based on perfect–imperfect with inflectional number–gender suffixes or prefixes; they all have broken plurals, common NP structures such as the idaafa, and so on [Owens, "History"]. The starting point in terms of a switching analysis therefore lies in what Muysken (2000) terms congruent systems. His example is Frisian–Dutch. Muysken emphasizes that where there are high degrees of congruency, teasing out clear linguistic borders between the varieties is not easy. Basic structural contrasts between congruent switching as opposed to interlanguage switching are found within one speech community in the quadrad Nigerian Arabic–SA–English–Hausa (Owens 2007). Here insertions from SA into Nigerian Arabic follow a very different pattern from insertions from Hausa and English. SA noun insertions, for instance, use the idaafa possessor, whereas insertions from Hausa and English are effected via an analytic possessive construction. In general, SA insertions mimic basic Nigerian Arabic structures to a far higher degree than do insertions from the noncongruent Hausa and English.

Second, given the bias toward the colloquial, grammatical morphemes and phonology from the colloquial will be the norm. This will be reflected in the wider distribution of colloquial morphemes: they will co-occur with both colloquial and SA morphemes, whereas SA grammatical morphemes will tend to be restricted to SA items (see Section 14.5.2.3). This reflects a basic markedness principle, namely, that the form of wider distribution is the unmarked one.

Major linguistic reflexes of this situation will be discussed in the following.

14.5.2.1 *Borrowing*

Extensive lexical borrowing from SA into colloquial has been noted in nearly every sociolinguistic study carried out on spoken discourse (Abdel Jawad 1981: 367–378; Holes, 1987: 54; Haeri 1996; [Newman, "Nahda"]; [Kossman, "Borrowing"]). The phonological realization may vary from pure SA to highly dialect-adapted patterns. In the standard sociolinguistic studies, these borrowings occur in texts that otherwise are devoid of SA structural borrowings. In the monologic and mediated dialogues described in (15), extended passages may be dominated by SA vocabulary, even while only limited grammatical morphemes intrude from it. In (16), for instance, *yi-qawmu* is lexically SA, but its morphological envelope is EgA: preformative *i-*, object suffix *–u* (not *–hu*) as well as having the EgA phonological shortening of [aa] (< qaawim]) and deletion of short [i] in an open syllable (cf. SA yu-qaawim-u-hu; in the following, colloquial is in italics, and SA is in normal font):

(16) *fi* aṭfaal *mumkin bi-yi-staħmil-u, wi yi-*qawm*-u,* ila aaxiru
"*There are* children *who can bear it and* struggle *against it,* and so on." (Bassiouney 2010b: 110)

14.5.2.2 *Lexically Correlated Phonological Variation*

Often SA and colloquial words differ only phonologically. In Bassiouney (2010b: 110), a passage is exemplified in which "poverty" plays an important role. The SA form of the word *faqr* occurs four times versus the colloquial *faʔr* twice. The tokens occur side by side and by no means correlate with EgA/SA environments. One token of *faʔr*, for instance, occurs in a largely SA environment:

(17) istiɣlaal haaẓa *il-faʔr* *il*-mawguwd
exploitation this.M DEF-*poverty* DEF-present
"the exploitation of this *poverty*..."

On the other hand, a token of SA faqr occurs in a clause begun in pure colloquial:

(18) *ma fi-š* *ħaaga* *ʔisma-ha* al-faqr faqat
not exist-NEG *thing* *name-its*.F DEF-poverty only
"*There is no such thing as* 'poverty' only."
(Bassiouney 2010b: 111)

In some cases, even if the lexemes are of SA provenance, the phonological realization will vary between SA and colloquial values, for instance, in terms of vowel and syllable structure in the following active participle–verb pairs (from Bassiouney 2010b: 110; see Sallam 1980 for correlations between word class and vowel quality):

(19) SA-colored colloquial-colored
munqiđ *yi*nqiđ-ha "saving/he saves her" (AP/verb)
mutafakkika *tit*fakkak "get unhinged from" (AP/verb)

It is not unusual for the SA origin of a word to be symbolized by a single SA phonological trait. In (16), *yi*-qawm-*u* betrays its SA origin primarily in the [q].

14.5.2.3 *Implicational Relations and Grammatical Morphemes*

Two patterns showing the dominance of the colloquial in mixed Arabic are very striking implicational patterns, and the intrusion of colloquial inflections onto SA stems. Regarding the first, a limited number of implications have held up under different studies, all involving the directional implication: if a certain SA grammatical morpheme is used, then it must be accompanied by an SA form. A SA negative morpheme such as lam or lan is always followed by a SA verb form:

(20) lam y-a-kun
not 3-PRE-be
"He was not"
(Mejdell 2006: 254; also Eid 1988)

In (20) the apocopated (jussive) form of the weak medial for kaan is used, while the SA preformative [a] marks the verbs as SA. Until now, *lam yakun-š has not been reported (mixed SA–EgA negative).

The direction of the implication reflects the dominant role of the colloquial. The SA negative grammatical morphemes are distributionally restricted to SA verbal complements, even if it is not possible to claim that SA system morphemes never occur with colloquial morphemes or stems. For instance, Mejdell (2006: 426) reports sa-*ti-šrab* "she will drink" with an SA future prefix before an EgA imperfect stem and person prefix.

Still, it can be noted, the rarity of such hard and fast implications (Mejdell 2006: 391) underscores the congruence of SA and the colloquial noted previously, and the vast majority of structures allow for a mixture of SA and colloquial elements. Colloquial grammatical morphemes, in particular, intrude relatively easily onto SA stems. Bassiouney (2010b: 111) contains the following sentence:

(21)	ʕaadatan	*il*-ṭifl	la	*bi*-yu-qbal	*hina*...
	usually	*DEF*-child	not	*HAB*-3.M-accept.PSV	*here*

"Usually *the* child *won*'t be accepted... "

Here and elsewhere in published corpora, SA stems, in this case the highly characteristic internal passive, do not, inversely to the previously described situation, implicate SA grammatical morphemes.

The combination of colloquial grammatical morphemes with SA stems can have a semantic logic. In the present example, the clause is largely, though not entirely, in SA. The internal passive verb sets it off as SA, as well as the [q] and negative la. The verb prefix *bi*- is clearly from colloquial Egyptian, as is *hina* "here." The assertion in (21) describes a habitual state of affairs. In SA the habitual statement would simply be laa yuqbal-u (the indicative -u plays no differentiating role here), so in theory an SA frame has no need for the inserted *bi*-. Clearly, however, the habituality of the statement is guaranteed by the Egyptian *bi*-. EgA, unlike CA, does distinguish habitual from other modal and tense values, with the use of *bi*- (see Eisele 1999; Mejdell 2006: 391).

14.5.2.4 *Accounting for the Data*

From a linguistic perspective, the mixed Arabic described here was originally described in Mitchell's (1986) educated spoken Arabic model within statistically characterized parameters. This approach continues to be used, for instance, in Mejdell (2006). She shows that grammatical classes exhibit differing degrees of SA–colloquial usage; for instance, attributive demonstrative pronouns show a higher percentage of SA forms than certain other classes, like complementizers or suffixed object pronouns. Detailed linguistic studies will continue to rely on statistically based descriptive models in this domain for two reasons. First, given the close structural similarity among varieties of Arabic, hard and fast barriers to mixing will be the exception. Second, given that SA itself is not a variety normally used for spontaneous conversation, speakers who do use it do so selectively.

Given the various complexities involved, it may be suggested that applying "off-the-shelf" codeswitching models to mixed Arabic should proceed with great caution. Regarding (21), for instance, to say (as Myers-Scotton 2010: 94 might) that this exemplifies a composite frame is to beg the question of how the frame is to be set in the first place (see Section 14.4). On one hand, it is not for instance obvious in what sense the EgA *b*- is being inserted into an SA frame; on the other, if the variety is composite, there are no discrete codes to effect the switching (see Auer 1998: 16 on mixed codes).

The formal linguistic description of the phenomenon serves as a backdrop to integrating discourse functional interpretations of the use of mixing. In some instances it is not particularly problematic to discern why a mixed form of Arabic is used or why more SA or colloquial is used at a given point. In the monologic varieties, in particular, degree of mixing can be directly correlated with the content of the message, as has been often pointed out. In Mubarak's speech, for instance, more colloquial signals solidarity with the audience, a common touch, whereas more SA creates distance, authority, abstractness, and affairs of state. A more challenging discourse context is that of media dialogue. Without the benefit of longer-term preparation and with having to respond quickly to interlocutee, shifts and demishifts between the varieties occur throughout a dialogue. Examples (16), (17), and (21) are typical in this respect.

In some cases speech-act interpretations for these shifts can be plausibly developed. In (18), for instance, the main point of the message, and the new information, is introduced in the relative clause. The SA rendition al-faqr (note SA al-, not colloquial *il*-) lends the argument the weight and authority of SA. Explaining (21), Bassiouney (2010b) suggests that the use of the SA internal passive is again a demonstration of weight and authority. However, the clause itself is mixed SA–colloquial, so it is clear that the speaker is not "appropriating" SA as a holistic syntactic entity but is rather choosing symbolic facets of it to advance her argument.

It can be assumed that up and down the scalar choice of SA–colloquial variants, individual elements have a differentiated symbolic value. [q], for instance, is a powerful phonological element signaling SA; short vowel values, on the other hand, are less so. The internal passive is a serious SA weapon; the choice of SA complementizer is less so. Furthermore, choice of where in a clause or larger discourse context to deploy SA–colloquial elements is significant. The emblematic value of SA references linguistic properties from the phonological to the discourse level.

14.6 Avenues for Further Research

Systematic empirical research related to diglossic mixing in educated spoken Arabic, despite going back over 25 years, is still in its early stages. Two salient characteristics have emerged from this research. First, it represents a linguistic challenge to describe the structural and pragmatic aspects of the usage. Second, related to the first, it can be expected that theoretical models elucidating the Arabic phenomena will need to be developed with the emerging descriptive material itself. Integrating diglossic mixing with interlanguage codeswitching follows as a further challenge.

Turning to the larger domain of interlanguage switching, there are other approaches to codeswitching where relatively little work has been done on Arabic-speaking communities. For instance, studies based on discourse analysis or conversational analysis seem scarce. Some exceptions are Sayahi (2004), who examines the use of switching between Spanish and Arabic in conversational transactions; Bentahila (1983a), who identifies some discourse functions of switching by Moroccans; and Taha (2008), who reports on the use of switching between English and Arabic in classroom interactions in Sudan. Bentahila and Davies (2002) and Davies and Bentahila (2006, 2008a, 2008b) look at the role of codeswitching as a literary and aesthetic device, showing that in popular song lyrics Arabic–French switching can be exploited for poetic effects relating to rhyme and line divisions and for rhetorical effects such as emphasis, contrast, or repetition. Analyses using a psycholinguistic approach are also rare, but Owens (2005a, 2005b) relates switching patterns to processing needs. All these areas offer interesting avenues for further investigation.

There are also many bilingual Arabic-speaking communities whose codeswitching behavior has not yet been examined in any depth. These may yield valuable comparisons both between different language pairs and between users with different sociolinguistic profiles. For instance, while most studies seem to have focused on speakers for whom Arabic is a native language, it would be interesting to look at the use of codeswitching by, say, foreigners living in Arabic-speaking communities, or non-Arab minorities in Arab countries. Studies of switching by young children would also be of interest.

Finally, an area that has been relatively neglected is the occurrence of codeswitching involving Arabic in written discourse. Given the diglossic situation in Arabic-speaking societies, Standard or Classical Arabic has, of course, traditionally been seen as the appropriate variety for written discourse, but in recent years there has been a noticeable tendency for the colloquial varieties to appear in writing. Studies of written texts including both colloquial and standard Arabic include Belnap and Bishop (2003) and Ibrahim (2010). This trend has been fueled by the arrival of the Internet and mobile phone messaging, whose technologies have also pushed users to write Arabic using the Latin alphabet. Young people in many parts of the Arab world now find it perfectly normal to use a variety featuring frequent codeswitching between their own variety of colloquial Arabic and French or English in computer-mediated communication. Warschauer, Said, and Zohry (2002) note this trend in Egyptians' use of English and Arabic in online communications, and Al Khatib and Sabbah (2008) report Jordanians' codeswitching in text messages. The same trend is becoming obvious in printed materials; for instance, in Morocco, advertisements composed in a mixture of Arabic and French are now becoming commonplace. The situation is developing rapidly and definitely deserves a closer look [Holes, "Orality"].

Returning to the distinction between the formalistic and the more holistic approaches to codeswitching mentioned at the beginning of this paper, we may venture to suggest that the work done so far on codeswitching involving Arabic has served to demonstrate the more promising avenues offered by the second of these approaches. The constant refinements of purely structural models to account for apparent counterexamples or to exclude them as irrelevant often seem marked by circularity, ad hoc distinctions, and rather sterile debate. In contrast, exploration of the functional and social variables affecting this communicative phenomenon seems a fruitful source of further insights. This, surely, is the path for future research to follow.

References

Aabi, Mustapha. 1999. *The syntax of Moroccan Arabic/French and Moroccan Arabic/Standard Arabic codeswitching*. PhD diss., University of Sheffield.

Abbassi, Ahmed. 1977. *A sociolinguistic analysis of multilingualism in Morocco*. PhD diss., University of Texas, Austin.

Abdel Jawad, Hassan. 1981. *Lexical and phonological variation in spoken Arabic in Amman*. PhD diss., University of Pennsylvania.

Al-Agbari, Khalsa. 2010. Derogatory forms of personal names in Omani Arabic. *Anthropological Linguistics* 52: 344–357.

Alby, Sylvie and Bettina Migge. 2007. Alternances codiques en Guyane française: Les cas du kali'na et du nenge. In *Pratiques et représentations linguistiques en Guyane: regards croisés*, ed. I. Léglise and Bettina Migge, 49–72. Paris: IRD Editions.

Alfonzetti, Giovanna. 1998. The conversational dimension in codeswitching between Italian and dialect in Sicily. In *Codeswitching in conversation: Language, interaction and identity*, ed. P. Auer, 180–210. London: Routledge, 180–210.

Al Khatib, Mahmoud A. and Enaq H. Sabbah. 2008. Language choice in mobile text messages among Jordanian university students. *SKY Journal of Linguistics* 21: 37–65.

Androutsopoulos, Jannis and Arno Scholz. 2002. On the recontextualization of hip-hop in European speech communities: A contrastive analysis of rap lyrics. *PhiN* 19: 1. Available at http://web.fu-berlin.de/phin/phin19/p19t1.htm.

Auer, Peter (ed.). 1998. *Codeswitching in conversation: Language, interaction and identity*. London: Routledge.

Bassiouney, Reem. 2006. *Function of codeswitching in Egypt*. Leiden: Brill.

—— (ed.). 2010a. *Arabic and the media*. Leiden: Brill.

——. 2010b. Identity and code-choice in the speech of educated women and men in Egypt: Evidence from talk shows. In *Arabic and the media*, ed. R. Bassiouney, 97–122. Leiden: Brill.

Belazi, Hedi M., Edward J. Rubin, and Almeida J. Toribio. 1994. Codeswitching and X bar theory: The functional head constraint. *Linguistic Inquiry* 25: 221–237.

Belnap, R. Kirk and Brian Bishop. 2003. Arabic personal correspondence: A window on change in progress? *International Journal of the Sociology of Language* 163: 9–25.

Bentahila, Abdelali. 1983a. Motivations for codeswitching among Arabic-French bilinguals in Morocco. *Language and Communication* 3: 233–243.

——. 1983b. *Language attitudes among Arabic-French bilinguals in Morocco*. Clevedon, England: Multilingual Matters.

——. 1995. Review of *Duelling languages: Grammatical structure in codeswitching* by Carol Myers-Scotton. *Language* 71: 135–140.

Bentahila, Abdelali and Eirlys E. Davies. 1983. The syntax of Arabic-French codeswitching. *Lingua* 59: 301–330.

——. 1991. Constraints on codeswitching: A look beyond grammar. In *Papers from the Symposium on codeswitching in bilingual studies: Theory, significance and perspectives (Barcelona, March 1991)*, 369–403. Strasbourg: European Science Foundation Network on Codeswitching and Language Contact.

——. 1992. Codeswitching and language dominance. In *Cognitive processing in bilinguals*, ed. Richard J. Harris, 443–458. Amsterdam: Elsevier.

——. 1994. Two languages, three varieties: Bilingual children's codeswitching. In *The cross-linguistic study of bilingual development*, ed. Guus Extra and Ludo Verhoeven, 113–128. Publications of the Royal Netherlands Academy of Arts and Sciences. Amsterdam: North-Holland.

——. 1995a Patterns of codeswitching and patterns of language contact. *Lingua* 96: 75–93.

——. 1998. Codeswitching: An unequal partnership? In *Codeswitching worldwide*, ed. Rodolfo Jacobson, 25–49. Trends in Linguistics: Studies and Monographs 106. Berlin: Mouton de Gruyter.

——. 2002. Language mixing in rai music: Localisation or globalisation? *Language and Communication* 22: 187–207.

——. 2007. Review of *Contact linguistics: Bilingual encounters and grammatical outcomes* by Carol Myers-Scotton. *Language and Society* 36: 455–459.

Berjaoui, Naser. 1996. Parlers secrets d'El-Jadida: Notes préliminaires. *Estudios de Dialectologia Norteafricana y Andalusi* 2: 147–158.

Boumans, Louis. 1998. *The syntax of codeswitching: Analysing Moroccan Arabic/Dutch conversations*. Tilburg: Tilburg University Press.

Boumans, Louis and Dominique Caubet. 2000. Modelling intrasentential codeswitching: A comparative study of Algerian/French in Algeria and Moroccan/Dutch in the Netherlands. In *Arabic as a minority language*, ed. Jonathan Owens, 113–180. Berlin: Mouton de Gruyter.

Chebchoub, Farida. 1985. *A sociolinguistic study of the use of Arabic and French in Algiers*. PhD diss., Edinburgh University.

Davies, Eirlys E. and Abdelali Bentahila. 2006. Codeswitching and the globalisation of popular music: The case of North African rai and rap. *Multilingua* 25: 367–392.

——. 2008a. Codeswitching as a poetic device: Examples from rai lyrics. *Language and Communication* 28: 1–20.

——. 2008b. Translation and codeswitching in the lyrics of bilingual popular songs. *Translator* 14: 247–272.

Di Sciullo, Anne Marie, Pieter Muysken, and Rajendra Singh. 1986. Code mixing and government. *Journal of Linguistics* 22: 1–24.

Edwards, Malcolm and Jean-Marc Dewaele. 2007. Trilingual conversations: A window into multicompetence. *International Journal of Bilingualism* 11: 221–242.

Eid, Mushira. 1982. The non-randomness of diglossic variation in Arabic. *Glossa* 16: 54–84.

——. 1988. Principles of codeswitching between Standard and Egyptian Arabic. *Al-Arabiyya* 21: 51–79.

——. 1992. Directionality in Arabic-English codeswitching. In *The Arabic language in America*, ed. Aleya Rouchdy, 50–57. Detroit, MI: Wayne State University Press.

Eisele, John. 1999. *Arabic verbs in time: Tense and aspect in Cairene Arabic*. Wiesbaden: Harrassowitz.

Gumperz, John J. 1982. Conversational codeswitching. In *Discourse strategies*, ed. John J Gumperz, 59–99. Cambridge, UK: Cambridge University Press.

Haeri, Niloofar. 1996. *The sociolinguistic market in Cairo: Gender, class, and education*. London: Kegan Paul International.

Heath, Jeffrey. 1989. *From codeswitching to borrowing: A case study of Moroccan Arabic*. London: Kegan Paul International.

Holes, Clive. 1987. *Language in a modernising Arab state: The case of Bahrain*. London: Kegan Paul International.

——. 1993. The uses of variation: A study of the political speeches of Gamal Abd al-Nasir. In *Perspectives on Arabic linguistics*, vol. 5, ed. Mushira Eid and Clive Holes, 13–45. Amsterdam: John Benjamins.

Ibrahim, Zainab. 2010. Cases of written codeswitching in Egyptian opposition newspapers. In *Arabic and the media*, ed. R. Bassiouney, 23–46. Leiden: Brill.

Jablonka, Frank. 2009. Styles sociaux communicatifs et alternance de langue dans le rai: Passages transculturels. *PhiN* 50: 4. Available at http://web.fu-berlin.de/phin/phin50/p50t1.htm#zbib23.

Jacobson, Rodolfo. 2000a. Language alternation: The third kind of codeswitching mechanism. In *Codeswitching worldwide,* vol. 2, ed. R. Jacobson, 59–72. Berlin: Mouton de Gruyter.

—— (ed.). 2000b. *Codeswitching worldwide,* vol. 2. Berlin: Mouton de Gruyter.

Jake, Janice L. 1994. Intrasentential codeswitching and pronouns: On the categorical status of functional elements. *Linguistics* 32: 271–298.

Joshi, Aravind K. 1985. Processing of sentences with intrasentential codeswitching. In *Natural language parsing*, ed. David Dowty, Lauri Karttunen, and Arnold D. Zwicky, 190–205. Cambridge, UK: Cambridge University Press.

Keller, Gary. 1979. The literary strategems available to the bilingual Chicano writer. In *The identification and analysis of Chicano literature*, ed. F Jiménez, 263–316. New York: Bilingual Press.

Levelt, William. 1989. *Speaking: From intention to articulation*. Cambridge, MA: MIT Press.

Lipski, John M. 2005. Codeswitching or borrowing? No sé *so* no puedo decir, *you know.* In *Selected proceedings of the second workshop on Spanish sociolinguistics*, ed. Lotfi Sayahi and Maurice Westmoreland, 1–15. Somerville, MA: Cascadilla Proceedings Project.

MacSwan, Jeff. 1999. *A minimalist approach to intrasentential codeswitching*. New York: Garland.

Mazraani, Nathalie. 1997. *Aspects of language variation in Arabic political speech-making*. Richmond, England: Curzon.

Mejdell, Gunvor. 2006. *Mixed styles in spoken Arabic in Egypt*. Leiden: Brill.

Melliani, Fabienne. 2005. Le métissage langagier en questions: De quelques aspects morphosyntaxiques. In *Comment les langues se mélangent: Codeswitching en Francophonie*, ed. Cécil Canut and Dominique Caubet, 59–72. Paris: Harmattan.

Mitchell, Terence. 1986. What is educated spoken Arabic? *International Journal of the Sociology of Language* 61: 7–32.

Muysken, Pieter. 2000. *Bilingual speech: A typology of code-mixing*. Cambridge, UK: Cambridge University Press.

Myers-Scotton, Carol. 1976. "Strategies of Neutrality: Language choice in uncertain situations." *Language* 52: 919–941.

——. 1993a. *Dueling languages: Grammatical structure in codeswitching.* Oxford: Clarendon Press.

——. 1993b. *Social motivations for codeswitching: Evidence from Africa*. Oxford: Clarendon Press.

——. 2000. The matrix language frame model: Development and responses. In *Codeswitching worldwide,* vol. 2, *ed. R.* Jacobson, 23–58. Berlin: Mouton de Gruyter.

——. 2002. *Contact linguistics: Bilingual encounters and grammatical outcomes*. Oxford: Oxford University Press.

——. 2010. Patterns and predictions for codeswitching with Arabic. In *Arabic and the media*, ed. R. Bassiouney, 81–96. Leiden: Brill.

Myers-Scotton, Carol and Janice L. Jake. 1995. Matching lemmas in a bilingual competence and production model: Evidence from intrasentential codeswitching. *Linguistics* 33: 981–1024.

Myers-Scotton, Carol, Janice L. Jakeand M. Okasha,1996. Arabic and constraints on codeswitching. In *Perspectives on Arabic linguistics, vol. 9*, ed. Mushira Eid and Dilworth Parkinson, 9–43. Amsterdam: John Benjamins.

Nait M'Barek, M. and David Sankoff. 1988. Le discours mixte arabe/français: emprunts ou alternances de langue? *Canadian Journal of Linguistics* 33: 143–154.

Nortier, Jacomine. 1990. *Dutch and Moroccan Arabic in contact: Codeswitching among Moroccans in the Netherlands*. Dordrecht: Foris.

——. 1995. Codeswitching in Moroccan Arabic/Dutch versus Moroccan Arabic/French language contact. *International Journal of the Sociology of Language* 112: 81–95.

Nortier, Jacomine and Margreet Dorleijn. 2008. A Moroccan accent in Dutch: A sociocultural style restricted to the Moroccan community? *International Journal of Bilingualism* 12: 125–142.

Owens, Jonathan. 2001. Arabic sociolinguistics. *Arabica* 48: 419–469.

——. 2005a. Hierarchicalized matrices: Codeswitching among urban Nigerian Arabs. *Linguistics* 43: 957–993.

——. 2005b. Bare forms and lexical insertions in codeswitching: A processing-based account. *Bilingualism: Language and Cognition* 8: 23–38.

——. 2007. Close encounters of a different kind: Two types of insertion in Nigerian Arabic codeswitching. In *Arabic in the city*, ed. C. Miller, D. Caubet, J. Watson, and E. Al-Wer, 249–274. London: Curzon Routledge.

Owens J. and R. Bani Yasin. 1987. The lexical basis of variation in Jordanian Arabic. *Linguistics* 25: 705–738.

Owens, J. and Jidda Hassan. 2000. Making a fish of a friend. *Waris*: The secret language of Arabic Koran school students in Borno. In *Arabic as a minority language*. ed. J. Owens, 221–258. Berlin: Mouton.

Poplack, Shana. 1980. Sometimes I'll start a sentence in English y termino en español: Toward a typology of codeswitching. *Linguistics* 18: 581–618.

Poplack, Shana, David Sankoff, and Chris Miller. 1988. The social correlates and linguistic processes of lexical borrowing and assimilation. *Linguistics* 26: 47–104.

Rampton, Ben. 1995. *Crossing: Language and ethnicity among adolescents*. London: Longman.

Sallam, A. 1980. Phonological variation in educated spoken Arabic. *Bulletin of the School of Oriental and African Studies* 43: 77–100.

Sankoff, David. 1998. The production of code-mixed discourse. In *COLING-ACL '98: Proceedings of the 36th Annual Meeting of the Association for Computational Linguistics*, 8–21. Montreal: University of Montreal Press. Available at http://albuquerque.bioinformatics.uottawa.ca/Papers/PCD.pdf.

Sarkar, Mela and Lisa Winer. 2006. Multilingual codeswitching in Quebec rap: Poetry, pragmatics and performativity. *International Journal of Multilingualism* 3(3): 173–192.

Sayahi, Lotfi. 2004. Bargaining in two languages: Conversational functions of transactional codeswitching. *Proceedings from the annual meeting of the Chicago Linguistics Society* 40(1): 335–347.

Sefiani, Kheira. 2003. Pratiques langagières des jeunes français issus de l'immigration maghrébine: Phénomène de bilinguisme, d'alternance codique à travers l'usage du franco-arabe-maghrébin. *SudLangues*. Available at http://www.sudlangues.sn/spip.php?article51.

Stevens, Paul B. 1974. *French and Arabic bilingualism in North Africa with special reference to Tunisia*. PhD diss., Georgetown University.

Taha, T. A. 2008. Language alternation in university classrooms. *Journal of Instructional Psychology* 35: 336–346.

Tessier, Jules. 1996. Quand la déterritorialisation déschixophrénise, ou de l'inclusion de l'anglais dans la littérature d'expression française hors Québec. *TTC* 9: 177–207.

Trumper, John. 1989. Observations on sociolinguistic behavior in two Italian regions. *International Journal of the Sociology of Language* 76: 7–30.

Versteegh, Kees. [1997] 2001[2]. *The Arabic language*. Edinburgh: Edinburgh University Press.

Warschauer, Mark, Ghada R. El Said, and Ayman Zohry. 2002. Language choice online: Globalization and identity in Egypt. *Journal of Computer Mediated Communication* 7(4). Available at http://jcmc.indiana.edu/vol7/issue4/warschauer.html.

Williams, Angela Selina. 2009. *"We ain't terrorists, but we droppin' bombs": Language use and localization of hiphop in Egypt*. MA thesis, University of Illinois at Urbana Champaign.

Wolfer, Claudia. 2011. Arabic secret languages. *Folia Orientalia* 47: 8–49.

Ziamari, Karima. 2009: Moroccan Arabic-French codeswitching and information structure. In *Information structure in spoken Arabic*, ed. J. Owens and A. Elgibali, 243–259. London: Routledge.

CHAPTER 15

BORROWING

MAARTEN KOSSMANN

15.1 Introduction

This chapter describes borrowing—mainly lexical borrowing—in relation to Arabic. It consists of three parts. First, a short introduction is provided to early loans in Arabic; then borrowing in written Arabic is treated. The major part of the chapter deals with borrowing in spoken Arabic. The literature on this subject is vast, corresponding to the large geographical area and many languages involved in contact with Arabic. This chapter will therefore offer typologies of the linguistic processes by which borrowing out of and into Arabic can be understood, without claiming comprehensiveness.

15.2 Early Loanwords in Arabic

The existence of loanwords in pre-Classical and early Classical Arabic has been recognized by the Arab exegetes, lexicographers, and grammarians at an early stage (Siddiqi 1930; Kopf 1976 [1961]; Versteegh 1997a: 14; Fischer 2003). Sībawayhi [Baalbaki, "ALT I"] dedicates two paragraphs to the question of Arabicization (and lack thereof) of foreign words (*al-Kitāb*, par. 524 and 525), especially loans from Persian, his native language. Many others followed, culminating in the book *Al-muʿarrab min al-kalām al-ʾaʿǧamī ʿalā ḥurūf al-muʿǧam*, a dictionary of foreign terms by Abū Manṣūr al-Ǧawālīqī (539/1144). The presence of foreign terms in the Quran was (and remains) a major issue of debate in Islamic theology, mainly because of the apparent contradiction with the Quranic characterization of its language as Arabic. (For a recent overview of this question, see Rippin 2002.)

Because of the location of pre-Islamic Arabic in the space roughly delimited by Aramaic (and, to a lesser extent, Greek) in the west, by Persian in the north, and by

South Arabian languages in the south, it is little wonder that these languages contributed most to the loanwords in early Arabic texts, such as pre-Islamic poetry, the Quran (Jeffery 1938; Margoliouth 1939), and Ibn Hishām's biography of the Prophet (Hebbo 1984).

Among these, Aramaic is by far the most prolific contributor, including domestic terminology (housing, clothing) as well as terminology connected to economic, political, and religious concepts (Fraenkel 1886). Aramaic loanwords are not always easy to keep apart from common Semitic heritage, but in many cases phonetic arguments can be given, such as with Arabic *tilmīḏ* "apprentice." In this word, *ḏ* does not constitute the regular counterpart of *d (cf. the Semitic root LMD) but reflects the lenited allophone of /d/ in Aramaic (Fraenkel 1886: 46). There are many different layers of Aramaic loans in early Arabic, reflecting both the long duration of the contact and, possibly, the dialectal differentiation inside Aramaic. Some of these are characterized by different phonetic reflexes of some phonemes, for example, the interpretation of Aramaic /š/, which is /s/ or /š/ according to the chronology of the borrowing (Schall 1982: 149–150; McDonald 1974: 41). Aramaic has been the mediator of words of different origins, such as Ar. *faḫḫār* "potter" < Aramaic *paḫḫārā* < Akkadian *paḫḫāru* < Sumerian *baḫar* (cf. Salonen 1952: 11). Prominent among these are the Greek loans in early Arabic, which mainly came in via Aramaic (Gutas 2007), for example, *ṣirāṭ* "way" < Aramaic *ʿsṭrṭ* < Greek *στράτα* < Latin *strata* (Ciancaglini 2008: 7).

Iranian languages also contributed a large number of items to the early Arabic lexicon (cf. Asatrian 2006 for a critical overview; Siddiqi 1919; Eilers 1962; Eilers 1971; Tafażżolī 1987). Phonetic developments in Iranian often allow us to date the borrowing. Thus, many Arabic loans from Persian contain a reflex of *g* or *k* in positions where it was lost in New Persian (clearly already in Sībawayhi's times, as he takes great pains to explain the anomaly, *Kitāb*, chapter 525). This implies that they date back to the Middle Iranian period or earlier, for example Ar. *šawbaq* ~ *šawbak* "rolling pin" from a Middle Iranian form *čōpaɣ* rather than from New Persian *čūba* (Eilers 1971: 590). Eilers (1971) (cf. also Asatrian 2006) distinguishes many chronological strata on this basis. The basic problem with this analysis is that it neglects the role of Aramaic as a mediator. If Nöldeke is right that Persian words "zum größten, ich möchte sagen zum allergrößten Teil, erst durchs Aramäische vermittelt waren" ("(Persian words) were to the greatest degree, indeed to the very greatest degree, transmitted via Aramaic") (Nöldeke 1921: 267; cf. Siddiqi 1919: 75), the form of the Iranian loan would reflect the date of their introduction into Aramaic rather than Arabic. Thus, for example, if Arabic *ward* "rose" is considered to be mediated by Aramaic *wardā* (Salonen 1952: 2), there is no reason to consider it an Achaemenidian loan in Arabic (Eilers 1971: 583), in spite of its Iranian archaic form.

The contribution of Ancient South Arabian and Ethiopian languages to the Arabic lexicon may very well be considerable (cf. Weninger 2007; Zammit 2009) and includes such salient terms as *muṣḥaf* "copy of the Quran" and *minbar* "pulpit." The extent of this influence is difficult to assess, however, especially for Ancient South Arabian, because of its close relationship with Arabic and the limited knowledge that we have of its lexicon.

15.3 Later Loanwords in Classical and Standard Arabic

Loanwords from non-Arabic sources found their way into the classical language and its offshoot Standard Arabic, especially from Persian, Turkish, and Greek (Schall 1982) and, in the modern period, from Italian, French, and English. This happened through two channels. In the first place, some words were deliberately introduced to provide the written language with the terminology it needed. This is certainly the case with much of scientific terminology, ranging from the introduction of Greek terms in classical times to that of modern Western science in more recent periods. In both cases, there exists an important countercurrent, which aims at using only "genuine" Arabic words; there is at this point little difference between the classical translators' development of an Arabic terminology for philosophy (cf. Versteegh 1997a: 85) and the endeavors of the Arab language academies today. In both cases, some of the Arabicized terms came across, while others are in fierce competition with loanwords.

The second type of foreign terms in the written language has been mediated by the spoken language. This is doubtlessly the case of much of the modern-world terminology found in today's Standard Arabic; like in the former type, there is strong competition from Arabic terms, which are favored by official language boards but do not always meet with success.

The vast majority of foreign terms that have entered written Arabic—at whatever period—concern "new" concepts, that is, concepts for which there was no need to express them in Arabic at an earlier stage. Such concepts include natural phenomena irrelevant to the Arab Peninsula, such as *timsāḥ* "crocodile" (< Coptic); cultural artifacts that were introduced in the Arab world, such as the pre-Islamic loan *'istabraq* "silk brocade" (< Persian) and modern *tilfāz* "television set"; cultural concepts that were introduced in the Arab world, such as *faylasūf* "philosopher" and *narfazah* "nervousness."

While in absolute numbers loanwords are certainly not rare, their rate of usage is rather low outside the technical sphere (cf. Issawi 1967 studying a number of text types), The reason behind this rarity of foreign loans in modern Arabic prose is both ideological and sociolinguistic. On one hand, as in many other language communities, there is the explicit wish to keep the language free from foreign influences, as, for example stated in the 1932 initial manifesto of the Cairo language academy: "the Academy has to substitute the *ʿāmiyya* as well as the non-arabicized foreign words by *fuṣḥā* words" (text cited from Shraybom-Shivtiel 1993: 196). However, the success of this endeavor is linked to the diglossic situation, and one may assume that word usage is much more strongly monitored by both professional and occasional writers of standard Arabic than by writers of—for example—standard German or even standard French [Newman, "Nahḍa"].

Morphologically, loanwords are integrated into Arabic patterns; typically, basic nouns retain their original shape, while verbs derived from them are adjusted to Arabic patterns, such as *'uksīd* "oxide"–*(ta)'aksada* "oxidize"; *fusfāt* "phosphate"–*fasfata* "phosphatize"; *'ayūn* "ion"–*(ta)'ayyana* "ionize"; *yūd* "iodine"–*yawwada* "iodinate" (exx. from Al-Khatib 1981).

Modern Arabic phraseology has undergone strong influence from European languages, especially French and English (Blau 1981 and many other studies), for example, *la*ᶜ*iba dawran* "he played a role" (Versteegh 1997b: 181).

Written Arabic, as the language of the Islamic scriptures, has had enormous impact on the languages of the Islamic world, often without mediation by spoken varieties. In many cases the central concepts, which constitute necessary knowledge for new converts, show different strategies of insertion from other borrowed vocabulary. In some languages, the new concepts are expressed not by loans but by neologisms or by old terms acquiring new meanings. Thus Songhay uses the new formation *mee-haw* "fast, Ramadan," lit. "mouth-tie" and the month Rabīᶜ al-'awwal (the month of the Mawlid celebrations) is known as *gaani*, lit. "dancing." In other languages, the names of the central concepts reflect the language of the first missionaries rather than Arabic. Thus, for example, Wolof uses Berber terms such as *tabaski* "ᶜīd al-kabīr," and Yoruba has a great number of Islamic terms from Songhay (Reichmuth 1988). Finally, loans stemming ultimately from Arabic may have been transformed through a mediating language, such as Hausa *azùmii* "fast" (< Berber *aẓum* < Arabic *ṣawm*; cf. van den Boogert and Kossmann 1997; Kossmann 2005: 76). Such intermediation is often difficult to prove, as shown by van Dam's (2010) convincing refutal of Campbell (1996), who assumed Persian mediation for Arabic loanwords in Indonesian.

Apart from these central concepts, all Islamic cultures borrowed extensively from Arabic, especially, one may assume, through the effect of learned local elites (see, e.g., Baldi 1988, 2008 for various west African languages and Swahili; Drewes 2007 for Amharic; Leslau 1990 for Ethio-Semitic in general; Stachowski 1975–1986 for Ottoman Turkish; van Dam 2010 for Indonesian; and relevant entries in Versteegh 2006–2009). The effect of this borrowing can be very strong; thus in everyday literary vocabulary of Persian about 40% of the types are from Arabic (Perry 2008: 575). The borrowing also involves functional markers, such as coordinating conjunctions, such as Swahili *au* "or" and *lakini* "but" (Matras 1998: 303).

The association of these loanwords with Islamic culture and Arab nationality have lead to an important countercurrent in some of these language communities, which wants to get rid of all (or most) Arabic vocabulary and replace it by native idioms or neologisms. The best-known endeavor of this kind is the Turkish language reform under Kemal Atatürk in the 1920s (cf. Lewis 1999 for a critical evaluation), but similar efforts have been undertaken for languages as different in sociolinguistic status as Persian (Perry 1985) and Berber (Taifi 1997).

15.4 Loanwords in Spoken Arabic

Linguistic borrowing in Spoken Arabic (dialectal Arabic) for the most part has a different dynamics from the one found in written Arabic. Four principal sociolinguistic contact situations relevant to spoken Arabic will be distinguished. They will be called by the traditional terms substratum, adstratum, and superstratum, which convey the ordering of my presentation. In addition to this, gradual convergence is considered a contact situation on its own. These terms are used in a historical sense; that is, they refer to the situation at the moment that a foreign element was inserted into the language and became an integral part of it. To maintain coherence in the presentation, examples will be drawn, where possible, from contact situations in Morocco and Algeria. This region is interesting as it affords ample examples of both borrowing from and borrowing into Arabic. The focus of the presentation will be on lexical, phonological, and morphological influence rather than on syntax and phraseology and calques (on which see Drewes 1994 for Maltese; Owens 1996b for Nigerian Arabic), that is, rather on the takeover of linguistic "matter" than on that of linguistic "patterns" (Sakel 2007).

15.4.1 Substratum

In the early Islamic period, the Arabic language acquired many new adult speakers, who had different languages as their native tongue. It is therefore no wonder that features of these languages surface in the different Arabic vernaculars [Behnstedt and Woidich, "Dialectology"]. In the Arab world, three major complexes of substratum have been studied: the Aramaic substratum in Iraq, Anatolia, and the Levant (e.g., Féghali 1918; Arnold and Behnstedt 1993); the Coptic substratum in Egypt (e.g., Behnstedt 2006); and the Berber substratum in the Maghrib (cf. outside Morocco and Algeria; Taine-Cheikh 1997, 2008, 2010 on Mauritania; Souag 2009, 2010 on Siwa); other substrata are much less studied, for example, the influence of Nilo-Saharan and Cushitic languages on mainstream Sudanese Arabic and the influence of non-Arabic Semitic languages on Gulf Arabic (Holes 2002). As an example, in the following the Berber substratum in northern Africa will be discussed in some detail.

In northern African Arabic, Berber substratum features have been identified especially in phonology and in the lexicon. Many of the proposed features are problematic, however. Among the alleged substratum features in Maghribinian Arabic, the development of its syllable structure is the most well-known (e.g., Diem 1979; Chtatou 1997; Elmedlaoui 2000). Different from most other Arabic varieties, Moroccan and Algerian Arabic have deleted all short vowels in an open syllable. This development is accompanied by a strong reduction in the short vowel system: in most dialects, *i* and *a* have collapsed into *ə*, while *u* is found only in a subset of etymological **u*, mainly in surroundings with a velar or uvular consonant. For many dialects, this could be analyzed as consonantal labialization rather than as a vowel phoneme (cf. Heath 2002: 192; Voigt 1996; and the discussion in Behnstedt and Benabbou 2002: 62, n. 30).

The situation in Berber is to a large degree similar. In all Moroccan and Algerian varieties (except Tuareg), short vowels are disallowed in open syllables. Moreover, the large majority of Berber languages have only one single short vowel, schwa, which is to a large degree predictable from word structure (cf. for an overview of the question Kossmann

1995; Dell and Elmedlaoui 2002). In a number of Moroccan and Algerian Berber languages, there are phonemic labialized velar and uvular consonants.

The standard account of Maghribinian Arabic takes Berber as the model for the Arabic developments: Maghribinian Arabic would have copied Berber syllable patterns, vowel systems, and labialization (e.g., Chtatou 1997; Elmedlaoui 2000). Unfortunately, accounts of this type present an ahistoric view of Berber: structures as attested in modern languages are taken for granted without questioning the historical development in Berber. In fact, Tuareg, Ghadames (Libya), and Zenaga (Mauritania) evidence shows that in earlier stages of Berber, short vowels also occurred in open syllables. Medieval Tashelhiyt texts suggest that this was also the case in parts of Morocco up till at least the 11th century CE (van den Boogert 1997: 105). Moreover, there is plenty of evidence for an ancient contrast between at least two short vowels, *ă* and *ə* (Prasse 2003); finally, according to some analyses (e.g., Kossmann 1999), Berber labialization would be the remnant of *ŭ* adjacent to a uvular or a velar consonant.

Maghribinian Berber therefore seems to have undergone basically the same developments as Maghribinian Arabic. It cannot be excluded that this happened simultaneously in Berber and in Arabic and that the similarities are due to parallel developments rather than a substratum.

Similar problems occur in other parts of phonology. It has been suggested that the development *ḍ* > *ṭ*, typical of scattered Moroccan and Algerian Arabic dialects, is due to Berber substratum (Marçais 1956: 608; Heath 2002: 160). However, while this development is indeed attested in adjacent varieties of Berber, it is far from being general in the language family, and in most Berber varieties Arabic *ṭ* is substituted by *ḍ* in loanwords. It is difficult to decide whether the development started in Berber and spread to Arabic or the other way around. Another widespread feature of Maghribinian Arabic that has been related to substratum (e.g., Fischer 1917: 21–22, n. 1; Heath 2002: 135) is the affricate pronunciation of /t/ as [tˢ]. This pronunciation is also found in many Berber varieties; there is, however, no argument that would establish the language of origin of this innovation.

On the local level, a convincing case of substratum influence on phonology is the phonetically conditioned lenition of alveolar and velar stops to interdental and palatal fricatives found in Arabic dialects of northwestern Morocco (Moscoso 2003: 37; Behnstedt and Woidich 2005: 177). The process of lenition is typical of the entire northern part of the Berber territory in Morocco and Algeria and is certainly not due to Arabic influence. An interesting complication is that the exact conditions of lenition are different between Arabic and most Berber varieties; while the lenition is almost general in Berber, it mainly targets intervocalic and other postvocalic consonants in Arabic. Only the small Berber enclave of Ghomara (northwestern Morocco) has very similar conditioning, but in this case secondary influence from the surrounding Arabic varieties cannot be excluded.

Borrowing of morphology is found in Algerian and Moroccan varieties of Arabic in the case of the circumfix *taa-*… *-t*, which derives abstracta from nouns of any etymological background, such as Jijel *taakəbbuurt* "the fact of boosting" and *taawəḥḥuunt* "the fact of having labor pains (woman)" (Marçais 1956: 232, 319). In Moroccan Arabic, this is the regular formation for nouns of professions and characteristic traits, such as Moroccan Arabic *taanəžžaaṛt* "carpentry" and Moroccan Judeo-Arabic *taadaayyaant* "the profession of rabbinical judge" (Chetrit 2007: 468; cf. Marçais 1977: 111). This formation copies the Berber feminine marker *ta-... -t*.[1] It is not entirely clear how it came to mark professions and characteristic traits in Arabic, however. Certainly, the use of *ta-... -t* to mark professions and characteristic traits is also found in Berber languages. However, in the semantic field of professions Moroccan and Algerian Berber almost exclusively use Arabic loanwords, and one wonders to what extent this Berber usage is a calque on the Arabic construction rather than its origin.

One interesting case of takeover of an independent grammatical morpheme on the local level is found in Jijel and its surroundings. In these Algerian dialects, the Berber predicative particle *ḏ* has been taken over as a focus marker—in the first place in nonverbal sentences, where it closely follows Berber patterns, but also in verbal sentences, where it sometimes deviates from the original (Marçais 1956: 465). As shown in Kossmann (forthcoming), Diem's (1979: 51) Arabic derivation of *d* cannot be maintained, and the element seems to be genuinely Berber—for a scenario of its introduction and functional change, see Kossmann (ibid.).

Berber influence on Arabic syntax is difficult to pin down, as the direction of influence is mostly unclear. Thus, Brugnatelli (1986) proposes that the double negation in Maghribinian Arabic is due to a Berber substratum, while Lucas (2007) argues for an Arabic (and ultimately Coptic; Lucas and Lash 2010) origin of the phenomenon in Berber.

Substratum influence is most visible in lexicon. One may distinguish three types of substratum lexicon (cf. also Féghali 1918: 87–95; Behnstedt 2006: 503), the first two of which are easily understood functionally:

1) Substratum words for concepts that were unknown to the speakers of Arabic when they arrived in their new environment. This includes flora and fauna, as well as specific types of agricultural implements.

2) Items denoting concepts of daily life that are so much restricted to the intimacy of the household that a second-language speaker may not learn them. This includes terms for small insects, such as Eastern Moroccan Arabic *səlluuf* "tick" (< Berber *tasəlluft*) and *taarẓəẓẓi* "wasp" (< Berber *aṛẓəẓẓi*). It includes numerous other animal terms, such as Moroccan Arabic *fəkṛuun* (< Berber *ifkər*) and *žṛaana* "frog" (< Berber *ižṛan*, pl. of *ažṛu* "frog"). See also northwest Moroccan Arabic *aawərz* "heel" (< Berber *awrəz*) (Behnstedt and Benabbou 2002).

3) Items denoting concepts that presumably were present to all speakers of the language, for example, Moroccan Arabic *ṣiifəṭ* "to send" (< Berber *sifəḍ*; Heath 2000) and *saaruut* "key" (< Berber *tasarut*).

[1] Note that phonetically the vowels /aa/, /ii/, /uu/, transcribed as long vowels in Maghribinian Arabic, have similar quantity to the so-called plain vowels /a/, /i/, /u/ of Maghribinian Berber.

For much substratum material there exist various regional forms. Thus, in Moroccan Arabic, both *žṛaana* and *gṛaana* "frog" are attested, which, at least partly, corresponds to the local pronunciation of the word in Berber (*ižran* and *ig*^{w}*ran*, respectively). Logical as this may seem, it is not unproblematic. The core of substratum words in Morocco seems to be relatively stable and to some degree arbitrary (e.g., "frog," "send," "key," "tick"; but not "mouse," "bring," "lock," "louse")—apparently, they were not borrowed only locally but are part of a larger complex. The similarity to local Berber pronunciations therefore suggests that even after the introduction of a certain substratum term into Arabic it may undergo adaptation to local varieties of Berber.

The introduction of substratum vocabulary implied questions of integration. In particular, the situation with nouns is often complicated because of the Arabic definiteness system. The situation with Berber loans into Arabic is highly interesting. Berber has a nominal prefix (mostly M:SG *a-*, F:SG *ta-*, M:PL *i-*, F:PL *ti-*), which is an obligatory part of the noun and which does not express definiteness. However, by virtue of its pre-stem position and its regularity, it is apparently sometimes put on a par with the Arabic article. This can be shown in Arabic loans in Berber, but it also appears in Berber loans in Arabic, which are often taken over without the prefix, for example, Moroccan Arabic *žṛaan* "frogs" < Berber *i-žṛ-an* "frogs."

Other words are taken over together with the Berber prefix. Such loanwords show abnormal behavior regarding definiteness, as they cannot be combined with the article. This looks like copying of syntactic behavior: because in Berber forms like *awtul* "hare" are neutral to definiteness—a category not expressed in the language—the same remains true once they are taken over into Arabic, even though definiteness is a highly salient category there. As a result, words with the Berber prefix are incompatible with the Arabic article, such as Jijel *aawtuul* "the, a hare" (Marçais 1956: 313) and Tangier *taamaara* "the, a physical pain" (Marçais 1911: 223).

In the plural of borrowings with the prefix, sometimes the prefix is omitted, such as Jijel *aawtuul*, pl. *uutaayəl* "hare"; such plurals allow for the use of the Arabic article. In other cases, the prefix is kept in the plural, and a suffix *-ən* (Jijel) or *-aan* (Tangier) is added, which resembles Berber external plural formation, such as Jijel *aasrəf*, pl. *aasərfən* "bush" (Marçais 1956: 313) and Tangier *aamdaar*, pl. *aamdraan* "branch" (Marçais 1911: 223). These plurals do not represent genuine Berber forms, as in Berber the prefix is *i* in the plural—one would have expected *iisərfən* and *iimdraan* from a Berber perspective.

15.4.2 Adstratum

I shall use the term adstratum for borrowings that enter the language as a result of widespread bilingualism in another spoken language. It is different from substratum in that the latter does not involve second language speakers; adstratum borrowings enter the language because the native speakers of that language also use another language. At times, the difference between the two types of influence is difficult to make, and in some circumstances the difference may be arbitrary, especially in mixed-speech communities. For Arabic, large-scale adstratum influence on all levels of the language is especially found in varieties spoken outside the great dialect continuum, such as Central Asian Arabic (e.g., Jastrow 2005; Ratcliffe 2005), Maltese (e.g., Krier 1976; Mifsud 1995), Cypriot Arabic (Newton 1964; Borg 1985), and Nigerian Arabic (e.g., Owens 1996a, 1996b, 2000). Strong adstratum influence by spoken Arabic is found in a number of languages, a.o. Sorani Kurdish, Kumzari (an Iranian language in Oman), and northern Berber. One also remarks the influences of Andalusian Arabic on the Romance languages of the Iberian peninsula (e.g., Corriente 2003, 2008).

Influence on phonology involves in the first place the introduction of new phonemes, for example, of *p* and *č* in Maltese and many other Arabic varieties and of the Arabic pharyngeals ᶜ and *ḥ* in Kurdish and Berber. In northern Berber, the pharyngeals, as well as other loan phonemes from Arabic, frequently appear in native words, where they seem to add to the expressive value of the word. For example, in a number of varieties ᶜ has been added to terms relating to the human trunk, such as Riffian *aᶜəddis* "belly" (cf. *adis* elsewhere), *ṯaᶜəbbuṭṭ* "navel" (cf. *tabuṭṭ* elsewhere), and *aᶜrur* "back" (cf. *aruru* elsewhere). Looking at the influence in the other direction, Cypriot Arabic has undergone a major restructuring of its consonant system inspired by Greek, especially where voicing is concerned. Some of these changes are similar in outcome but different in derivation from what is found in Greek (as argued in Borg 1997); others simply copy the Greek pattern. For example, in Cyprus, both in local Greek and in Arabic clusters of two stops are dissimilated into a fricative-stop cluster, such as **qtilt* > *xtilt* "you killed"; **baquum* > *fkum* "I get up," cf. Cypriot Greek *oxtò* < ὀκτω "eight"; and *ftoxòs* < πτωχός "poor" (Borg 1997: 224).

Morphological borrowing comes in two types: borrowing of isolated morphemes and borrowing of morphological patterns together with lexicon. In the realm of Arabic, the first type concerns only derivational morphology. Cypriot Arabic, for example, has substituted the Arabic diminutive formation by the Greek diminutive suffix, including Greek gender–number inflection, such as masculine *payt–payt-ui–payt-ukkya* "house—little house–little houses," feminine *žežže–žežž-ua–žežž-ues* "hen–little hen–little hens" (Borg 1985: 126). In the opposite direction, Ghomara Berber has transposed Arabic patterns of diminutive formation to Berber nouns in a fairly regular way, such as *ayyul*, dim. *aywəyyəl* "donkey" and *taqəmmumt*, dim. *taqmiməmt* "mouth" (Mourigh forthcoming).

When inflectional morphology is taken over, it is always in conjunction with specific lexical items. In the case that a lexical item is borrowed in several different forms, the effect is the presence of (part of) a foreign morphological system in the language. In contexts with a strong adstratum, such parallel systems are well attested in the world's languages (Kossmann 2010). In the realm of Arabic, they seem to be common with Greek lexicon in Cypriot Arabic (Kossmann 2008) and—in the opposite direction—with Arabic lexicon in northern Berber.

In the following, the processes of borrowing and their effects on inflection will be illustrated on the basis of Arabic influence on northern Berber.

As shown already, Berber nouns have an obligatory prefix and the possibility of a suffix. The prefix expresses gender, number, and what is called "state" in Berber linguistics; the suffix expresses gender and number. Arabic loans can be integrated into this morphology, such as Riffian *aᶜəkkaz* "walking stick"; pl. *iᶜəkkazən* < Ar. *ᶜukkaaz*; *ṯaməqyasṯ* "bracelet"; and pl. *ṯiməqyasin* < Ar. *məqyaas*. Other Arabic loans have not been integrated into Berber morphology and have their own patterns instead. This pattern is in most nouns as follows:

- The Arabic article has become a fixed part of the word, which cannot be omitted.
- The Arabic plural form is taken over without modification.
- The feminine suffix *-a* ~ *-ət* (status constructus) is taken over as *-ət* (note that this is not the case in Kabyle and in Ghomara Berber, which have *-a*).

These three phenomena are illustrated by the Riffian Berber noun *zzənqəṯ* "street," pl. *zznaqi* < Moroccan Arabic *z-zənqa*, pl. *z-znaaqi*.

The fixedness of the Arabic article shows its identification with the Berber prefix; in Arabic words with Berber morphology (i.e., with the Berber prefix) it is normally not found (cf. *ṯaməqyasṯ* instead of **ṯařməqyasṯ* as listed previously). The origin of the feminine suffix *-ət* in non-Berberized Arabic loans is not clear. There are several possibilities, none of which are entirely satisfactory. In the first place, *-ət* is similar to the Berber feminine suffix *-t*. It has different syllable structure, however, as shown by the difference between non-Berberized *zzənq-əṯ* "street" < Ar. *z-zənqa* and Berberized *ṯa-šᶜəf-ṯ* "ankle" < Ar. *kəᶜb*. Therefore, this solution cannot be maintained (Kossmann 1995). Another possibility is to consider *-ət* the reflex of the Arabic status constructus form. This is highly problematic, as in Arabic the status constructus cannot co-occur with the article. One would have to admit a highly original blend of two Arabic forms (Kossmann 2009). A third solution would be to consider the Berber form a loan from an Arabic variety that uses the suffix **-at* in all definite contexts, including in combination with the article. Such varieties are nowadays restricted to some regions in Yemen (Behnstedt 1987: 54) but may have had a larger extension in the early Islamic period. As there is an undeniable Yemeni element in Maghribinian Arabic (cf. Retsö 2000; [Retsö, "Arabic?"]), this option is not entirely impossible. However, there is no further indication that this form has ever been used in the Maghrib. If the last solution is correct, the pattern must have evolved at an early moment in Arabic–Berber contacts. Its occurrence in Medieval Berber texts, where it is written as a *tā' marbūṭah* with a *sukūn*, attests to at least some ancientness of the phenomenon.

In pronominal systems, one sometimes finds full Arabic paradigms being taken over together with Arabic particles, such as in Figuig Berber forms such as *ᶜəmmṛ-u* "he never." In this variety, using a Berber pronominal element with *ᶜəmməṛ-* and a number of other particles is forbidden (Kossmann 1997: 186). Maghribinian Arabic and Berber often have similar shapes of verb stems (compare the formal identity of the Moroccan Arabic verb *təfṛəḍ* "she imagined" with the native Figuig Berber verb *təfṛəḍ* "she swept"). This has simplified the task of inserting Arabic verbs into Berber inflectional patterns.

This includes the application of Berber apophonic patterns and morphophonological alternations to Arabic verbs, such as the Arabic verb *šwa* "grill" in Figuig Berber *i-šwa* "he grilled," *ul i-šwi* "he did not grill," *i-šəkk^{w}a* "he always grills," *šəkku* "the fact of grilling." The large-scale merger of the short vowels typical of most of Maghribinian Arabic means that the difference between perfect and imperfect is visible only in the stem form of a restricted number of verb types. When verbs belonging to such types are taken over in Berber, either the perfect or the imperfect form is chosen without any clear conditioning, for example, Arabic *faat/fuut* "to pass" has been taken over as *fat* in Figuig Berber, while *faaḥ/fuuḥ* "to diffuse a smell" has been taken over as *fuḥ*.

Ghomara Berber is the odd one out, as it takes over Arabic verbs together with their full Arabic morphology. Compare the inflection of the 1SG in the verbs *ẓẓu* "to plant" (< Berber) and *ṣṣaḏ* "to fish" (< Arabic) in this language: perfective *ẓẓa-x/ṣṣaḏi-ṯ*; imperfective *təẓẓa-x/ka-nə-ṣṣaḏ;* and future *š-a-ẓẓu-x/š-n-əṣṣaḏ*. The inflectional endings in the verb *ṣṣaḏ* as well as the prefix *ka-* stem entirely from Moroccan Arabic (Mourigh forthcoming). This cannot be analyzed as code switching, as basic verbs such as *ṣṣaḏ* constitute the only way of expressing the concept, and there is no Berber alternative; the verbs with Arabic morphology constitute a morphological class inside the Ghomara Berber language, and it is not allowed to use Berber inflections with verbs of this class.

The lexical influence of Arabic on northern Berber is enormous and also involves basic lexicon. Thus, for example, in the Swadesh-100 word list, several Berber languages have between 15 and 20% of borrowings; in Ghomara Berber this figure rises to about 35% (Mourigh forthcoming; compare English, which has only about 5%). In the much larger LoanWord Typology database (Haspelmath and Tadmor 2009), Riffian Berber was shown to have over 50% of loanwords, which puts it among the languages most open to lexical borrowing in the 40-language sample studied in the project. Borrowings include domains that are often assumed to be resistant to borrowing, such as basic verbs (e.g., Figuig Berber *ṛaḥ* "to go," *žbəd* "to pull") and body parts (e.g., Ghomara Berber *xnafəṛ* "nose," *ḍḍmaġ* "head"). Even terms that in other contexts would be considered typical substratum residues have been borrowed, for example, small insects such as Beni Snous Berber *lbəqq* "bug," *nnamus* "mosquito."

15.4.3 Convergence

If a language is strongly influenced by a closely related language, it may gradually adjust its forms and structures into those of this other language. In such a situation, the end effect may be the loss of most defining salient features of the earlier language. While its effects may be similar to that of substratum, the sociolinguistic history is entirely different. In the substratum case we are dealing with people who switch from one language to another, in the convergence case the language gradually becomes more and more similar to its neighbor. Convergence is paramount in contact between dialects, and Arabic dialectology is full of examples of it. Convergence of two languages seems to be attested in Yemen. Formerly, several languages belonging to the South Arabian family were spoken in Yemen. However, already before the advent of Islam, a language called Himyarite became the most important tongue. According to Hamdani, writing in the 10th century CE, Himyarite was still spoken in parts of the Yemeni highland (Robin 1991a). The little evidence we have on Himyarite suggests that it was closely related to Arabic, and most sources indicate that it was largely understandable to speakers of Arabic. Modern Yemeni dialects contain elements that were identified as Himyarite in medieval sources (Robin 1991b). Such elements include the use of suffixes with the consonant *k* instead of *t* in the perfect, such as *katabku* "I wrote" and *katabka* "you (m.) wrote" (ᶜIgz, Behnstedt 1985: 117); the negative marker *daw'* (Behnstedt 1985: 170); and the relative marker *ḏii* (Behnstedt 1985: 65; also attested in the Maghrib). The Yemeni article *am* seems to correspond to Himyarite *an* (cf. Behnstedt 1985: 64; *am* is more generally West Arabian; cf. Rabin 1951: 35, 205). Certain modern Yemeni Arabic dialects seem to be the result of a slow process of convergence toward Arabic rather than the result of language shift (Rabin 1951: 52); put otherwise, they represent direct descendents of Himyarite, which have undergone such a strong restructuring that they now constitute exotic varieties of Arabic rather than a different language. One remarks that the most salient survivals of Himyarite—*k*-Perfects, *daw'*, and the *am*- article—do not appear in the same modern dialects; *k*-perfects are typical of the central Highlands, *daw'* belongs to the southern tip of the peninsula, while the article *am*- is typical of the coastal plains. Apparently, the convergence targeted different elements in different regions, thereby scattering the attestations of ancient Himyarite materials (see [Owens, "History"] for different interpretation).

15.4.4 Superstratum

The term superstratum will be used here for influence from languages that are considered of higher status than the normal spoken language, at least by some speakers. There are two types of superstratum in the Arab world. In the first place, superstratum influence may come from foreign elites, who impose their language (or elements of it) on indigenous populations. This is the case of Persian in Iraq, of Turkish in the Ottoman empire (cf. Prokosch 1983), and of various Western languages during the colonial period. The other type of superstratum influence may be called diglossic superstratum. This concerns the influence of languages present in a society, which mainly fulfill communicative roles that are considered of high status. This is, of course, the case of Standard Arabic, but the way French and English function nowadays in many independent Arab countries is of the same type. In the following, the contribution of Standard Arabic to spoken varieties will not be dwelled upon [Newman, "Nahḍa"].

There are important differences between the process and the results of superstratum influence depending on the degree of knowledge of the superstratum language in a speech community. As a rule of thumb, one may say that less familiarity leads to less predictability in the outcome of the borrowing. In a speech community where an important part of the population has reasonable knowledge of the superstratum language, one expects relative faithfulness in dealing with semantics and conventionalized ways of integrating (or not) the word in phonology and morphology. In a speech community where there is little knowledge of the superstratum language available, there are less clear-cut models for integration, leading to less conventionalization, and the original semantics of the word may be blurred by the local interpretation of the term. In the context of rural Moroccan Arabic, which, at an early stage, had little contact with French, there are instances of unexpected changes in phonology, such as *bəqšliiṭa* < French *biciclette* "bicycle." One also remarks the tendency to lose unstressed initial syllables, such as Algerian Arabic *zaṛṭa* "to desert" (< *déserter*), *gaṛṣiiṣ* "exercise" (< *exercice*), and *biisrii* "grocery" (< *épicerie*) (Hadj-Sadok 1955). Important semantic shifts are observed in the same varieties in the denomination of cars. In rural Moroccan Arabic, *taaksi* refers to a normal passenger car, while *piižu* refers to a pickup truck. This is a considerable shift from French *taxi* "taxi" and *Peugeot* "a mark of cars" and reflects an interpretation of terminology at a time that the only passenger cars available to the rural population were taxis, while Peugeot was the main brand for pickup trucks.

When important parts of the community are bilingual, changes are expected to be less pervasive. This does not mean that the forms are not adapted to the recipient language. However, it is expected that these adaptations follow certain patterns, such as French [y] (< u >) always being integrated as /i/ or French verbs being always inserted into the class of *a*-final verbs (Talmoudi 1986). On the other hand, as the original form is available to (many) speakers, one may encounter numerous doublets: one with original(-like) pronunciation and the other in a more adapted form. Thus, Sadiqi (2007: 295) points to the difference between (educated Moroccan) male speakers, who tend to use phonologically and morphologically integrated form of French loanwords, and (educated) female speakers, who use more French-like forms, such as male *t-traan* "the train" and female *lə-tʁɛ̃* "train" (transcription adapted).

In bilingual communities it is often difficult to draw a line between code switching and borrowing (see, e.g., Heath 1989; [Davies et al., "Code Switching"]), This is very strongly so the case in superstratum influence. While there are many cases of clear-cut borrowings (e.g., Moroccan Arabic *ṭuumuubiil* "car") and others that are clearly code switched (e.g., *tous* in the phrase *l'éducation dyaal tous* "the education of everybody," heard in Morocco), there is an important grey zone in the lexical domain. Certain words may constitute the preferred (or only) expression of a concept, which makes them borrowing like, but on the other hand speakers may be highly aware of their foreignness. In such cases, there may even be a difference between the use of the same item by highly bilingual speakers—for whom it would be a codeswitch—and for speakers with less knowledge of the superstratum language, for whom it would be a borrowing, a dynamic analysis proposed for Hebrew–Aramaic influence on Moroccan Judeo-Arabic in Chetrit (2007).

Superstratum influence mainly concerns lexicon; together with lexicon, however, phonological features may be taken over, as witnessed by the introduction of the phoneme *p* in many Arabic varieties. Morphological influence from superstratum languages seems to be very restricted; one remarks, however, the spread of the Turkish suffix *-ci* in the realm of the Ottoman empire, which forms occupational nouns, such as Tunis *ṣawwaar-ži* "photographer" and *balġaa-ži* "slipper maker" (Singer 1984: 560–562); Iraq *saaᶜa-či* "watch dealer, repairman" and *čaay-či* "tea vendor" (Erwin 1963: 170).

Superstratum influence is paramount in the introduction of vocabulary for new concepts or for concepts that have undergone changes in meaning and associations due to political and cultural innovations. Thus, in the late colonial period, Hadj-Sadok (1955) lists 1665 borrowings from French in a rural Algerian dialect. Among these borrowings over 90% are new concepts or concepts intimately linked to the colonial sphere (cf. also Brunot 1949 for Morocco).

In addition to borrowings of this type, which fill a lexical gap in the language, another important sphere of influence lies in terms of address. Egyptian Arabic, which has a very rich system in this respect, provides numerous instances of loans in terms of address, such as from Turkish *afandi* "sir" and *baaša* "sir" and from French *madaam* "Mrs." and *misyu* "mister." Turkish as well as European languages also provided kinship terms; their introduction may have been strengthened by their use as terms of address, such as from Turkish *ʔabeeh* "older brother" and *ʔaḅla* "older sister" and from French *ṭanṭ* "aunt" (Parkinson 1985). The introduction of superstratum terms of address is functionally well-founded. Knowledge of the superstratum language is highly valued, and terms of address are both highly salient and frequent in language use. Moreover, such terms being mostly extrasyntactic, they are easily inserted in discourse, even by people with little further knowledge of the superstratum language and therefore may spread quickly in a speech community.

Superstratum loans sometimes show interesting layering. Thus, in large parts of northern Africa, including Egypt, there is an important role for Italian and Spanish, which is not linked to direct political domination. One may note Italian terms in Egyptian and Tunisian Arabic, such as Egyptian *banziin* "petrol" (< Italian *benzina*), Tunisian *frišk* "fresh" (< It. *fresco*), and *žiilaaṭ* "ice cream" (< It. *gelati*) (Cifoletti 2009), or Spanish loans in Moroccan Arabic, many of which go back to the precolonial period, such as *faalṭa* "error, offense" (< Spanish *falta*) (Fischer 1917: 25).

15.5 Afterword

Arabic is a highly interesting language complex as regards contact phenomena. Its wide distribution places it in contact with many different languages, in a whole range of different sociolinguistic situations. It functions as a majority language (e.g., in relation to modern Aramaic and Berber) and as a minority language (e.g., in Uzbekistan or Nigeria), or simply as the neighbor; it exercises and undergoes influence both through the written and the spoken medium. The present article provides a tantalizing glimpse of the many interesting and relevant issues in this realm.

References

Arnold, Werner and Peter Behnstedt. 1993. *Arabisch-aramäische Sprachbeziehungen in Qalamūn (Syrien). Eine dialektgeographische Untersuchung.* Wiesbaden: Harrassowitz.

Arnold, Werner and Hartmut Bobzin (eds.). 2002 *"Sprich doch mit deinen Knechten aramäisch, wir verstehen es!" Festschrift für Otto Jastrow zum 60. Geburtstag.* Wiesbaden: Harrassowitz.

Asatrian, Mushegh. 2006. Iranian elements in Arabic: The state of research. *Iran and the Caucasus* 10: 87–106.

Baldi, Sergio. 1988. *A first ethnolinguistic comparison of Arabic loanwords common to Hausa and Swahili.* Napoli: Istituto Universitario Orientale.

——. 2008. *Dictionnaire des emprunts arabes dans les langues de l'Afrique de l'Ouest et en swahili.* Paris: Karthala.

Behnstedt, Peter. 1985. *Die nordjemenitischen Dialekte. Teil 1: Atlas.* Wiesbaden: Ludwig Reichert.

——. 1987. *Die Dialekte der Gegend von Ṣaʿdah (Nord-Jemen).* Wiesbaden: Harrassowitz.

——. 2006. Coptic loanwords. In *Encyclopedia of Arabic Language and Linguistics* I, ed. Kees Versteegh. Associate Editors: Mushira Eid, Alaa Elgibali, Manfred Woidich, Andrzej Zaborski, 501–505. Leiden: Brill.

Behnstedt, Peter and Mostafa Benabbou. 2002. Zu den arabischen Dialekten der Gegend von Taza (Nordmarokko). In *"Sprich doch mit deinen Knechten aramäisch, wir verstehen es!" Festschrift für Otto Jastrow zum 60. Geburtstag.* ed. Werner Arnold and Hartmut Bobzin, 53–72. Wiesbaden: Harrassowitz.

Behnstedt, Peter and Manfred Woidich. 2005. *Arabische Dialektgeographie, Eine Einführung.* Leiden: Brill.

Blau, Joshua. 1981. *The renaissance of Modern Hebrew and Modern Standard Arabic. Parallels and differences in the revival of two Semitic languages.* Berkeley: University of California Press.

Boogert, Nico van den. 1997. *The Berber literary tradition of the Sous. With an edition of "The Ocean of Tears" by Muḥammad Awzal (d. 1749).* Leiden: Nederlands Instituut voor het Nabije Oosten.

Boogert, Nico van den and Maarten Kossmann. 1997. Les premiers emprunts arabes en berbère. *Arabica* 44: 317–322

Borg, Alexander. 1985. *Cypriot Arabic: A historical and comparative investigation into the phonology and morphology of the Arabic vernacular spoken by the Maronites of Kormakiti village in the Kyrenia district of North-Western Cyprus.* Stuttgart: Franz Steiner Wiesbaden.

——. 1997. Cypriot Arabic phonology. In *Phonologies of Asia and Africa (including the Caucasus) I*, ed. Alan Kaye and Peter Daniels, 219–244. Winona Lake, IN: Eisenbrauns.

Brugnatelli, Vermondo. 1986. La negazione discontinua in berbero e in arabomagrebino. In *Atti della 4a Giornata di Studi Camito-semitici ed Indoeuropei*, ed. Giuliano Bernini and Vermondo Brugnatelli, 53–62. Milano: Unicopli.

Brunot, Louis. 1949. Emprunts dialectaux arabes à la langue française. *Hespéris* 36: 347–430.

Campbell, Stuart. 1996. The distribution of -at and -ah endings in Malay loanwords from Arabic. *Bijdragen tot de Taal-, Land- en Volkenkunde* 152: 23–44.

Chaker, Salem and Andrzej Zaborski (eds.). 2000. *Études berbères et chamito-sémitiques. Mélanges offerts à Karl-G. Prasse.* Paris: Peeters.

Chetrit, Joseph. 2007. *Diglossie, hybridisation et diversité intra-linguistique. Études sociopragmatiques sur les langues juives, le judéo-arabe et le judéo-berbère*. Paris: Peeters.

Chtatou, Mohamed. 1997. The influence of the Berber language on Moroccan Arabic. *Journal of the Sociology of Language* 123: 101–118.

Ciancaglini, Claudia A. 2008. *Iranian loanwords in Syriac*. Wiesbaden: Ludwig Reichert.

Cifoletti, Guido. 2009. Italianismes dans les dialectes arabes. In *Romanisierung in Afrika: Einfluss des Französischen, Italienischen, Portugiesischen und Spanischen auf die indigenen Sprachen Afrikas*, ed.Thomas Stolz, Dik Bakker, and Rosa Salas Palomo, 31–40. Bochum, Germany: N. Brockmeyer.

Corriente, Federico. 2003. *Diccionario de arabismos y voces afines en iberorromance*. Madrid: Gredos.

——. 2008. *Dictionary of Arabic and allied loanwords: Spanish, Portuguese, Catalan, Galician and kindred dialects*. Leiden: Brill.

Csató, Éva Ágnes, Bo Isaksson, and Carina Jahani (eds.). 2005. *Linguistic convergence and areal diffusion: Case studies from Iranian, Semitic, and Turkic*. London: RoutledgeCurzon.

Dam, Nikolaos van. 2010. Arabic loanwords in Indonesian revisited. *Bijdragen tot de Taal-, Land- en Volkenkunde* 166: 218–243.

Dell, François and Mohamed Elmedlaoui. 2002. *Syllables in Tashlhiyt Berber and in Moroccan Arabic*. Dordrecht: Kluwer Academic Publishers.

Diem, Werner. 1979. Studien zur Frage des Substrats im Arabischen. *Der Islam* 56: 12–80.

Drewes, Abraham J. 1994. Borrowing in Maltese. In *Mixed languages: 15 case studies in language intertwining*, ed. Peter Bakker and Maarten Mous, 83–111. Amsterdam: IFOTT.

——. 2007. Amharic as a language of Islam. *BSOAS* 70: 1–62.

Eilers, Wilhelm. 1962. Iranisches Lehngut im arabischen Lexicon: Über einige Berufsnamen und Titel. *Indo-Iranian Journal* 5: 203–232.

——. 1971. Iranisches Lehngut im Arabischen. In *Actas do IV Congresso de Estudos Árabes e Islâmicos, Coimbra-Lisboa, 1 a 8 de setembro de 1968*, 581–660. Leiden: Brill.

Elmedlaoui, Mohamed. 2000. L'arabe marocain, un lexique sémitique inséré sur un fond grammatical berbère. In *Études berbères et chamito-sémitiques. Mélanges offerts à Karl-G. Prasse*. ed. Chaker, Salem and Andrzej Zaborski, 155–88. Paris: Peeters.

Erwin, Wallace M. 1963. *A short reference grammar of Iraqi Arabic*. Washington, DC: Georgetown University Press.

Féghali, Michel T. 1918. *Étude sur les emprunts syriaques dans les parlers arabes du Liban*. Paris: Champion.

Fischer, August. 1917. *Zur Lautlehre des Marokkanisch-Arabischen*. Leipzig: J.C. Hinrichs.

Fischer, Wolfdietrich. 2003. Muᶜarrab. In *Encyclopaedia of the Qur'ān*. ed. J. MacAuliffe Vol. 3, 261. Leiden: Brill.

Fraenkel, Siegmund. 1886. *Die aramäischen Fremdwörter im Arabischen*. Leiden: Brill.

Al-Ğawālīqī, Abū Manṣūr. 1361 AH [1942]. *Al-muᶜarrab min al-kalām al-'aᶜğamī ᶜalā ḥurūf al-muᶜğam*, ed. Aḥmad Muḥammad Shākir. Al-Qāhira: Dār al-Kutub al-Miṣriyya.

Gutas, Dimitri. 2007. Greek loanwords. In *Encyclopedia of Arabic Language and Linguistics* II, ed. Kees Versteegh. Associate Editors: Mushira Eid, Alaa Elgibali, Manfred Woidich, Andrzej Zaborski, 198–292. Leiden: Brill.

Hadj-Sadok, Mahammed. 1955. Dialectes arabes et francisation linguistique de l'Algérie. *Annales de l'Institut d'Études Orientales (Université d'Alger)* 13: 61–97.

Haspelmath, Martin and Uri Tadmor (eds.). 2009. *Loanwords in the world's languages: A comparative handbook*. Berlin: De Gruyter Mouton.

Heath, Jeffrey. 1989. *From code-switching to borrowing: A case study of Moroccan Arabic*. London: Kegan Paul.

——. 2000. SIFT-ing the evidence. Adaptation of a Berber loan for "send" in Moroccan Arabic. In *Études berbères et chamito-sémitiques. Mélanges offerts à Karl-G. Prasse*. ed. Chaker, Salem and Andrzej Zaborski, 223–32. Paris: Peeters.

——. 2002. *Jewish and Muslim dialects of Moroccan Arabic*. New York: Routledge Curzon.

Hebbo, Ahmed. 1984. *Die Fremdwörter in der arabischen Prophetenbiographie des Ibn Hischām (gest. 218/834)*. Frankfurt a.M.: Peter Lang.

Holes, Clive. 2002. Non-Arabic Semitic elements in the Arabic dialects of eastern Arabia. In ed. Werner Arnold and Hartmut Bobzin, 269–279.

Issawi, Charles. 1967. Loan-words in contemporary Arabic writing: A case study in modernization. *Middle Eastern Studies* 3: 110–133.

Jastrow, Otto. 2005. Uzbekistan Arabic: A language created by Semitic-Iranian-Turkic convergence. In ed. Csató, Isaksson and Jahani, 131–139.

Jeffery, Arthur. 1938. *The foreign vocabulary of the Qur'ān*. Baroda: Oriental Institute.

Al-Khatib, Ahmed Sh. [5]1981. *A new dictionary of scientific and technical terms: English-Arabic*. Beirut: Librairie du Liban.

Kopf, Lothar. 1976. The treatment of foreign words in mediaeval Arabic lexicography. In *Studies in Arabic and Hebrew lexicography*, ed. M. H. Goshen-Gottstein, 247–261. Jerusalem: Magnes Press and Hebrew University.

Kossmann, Maarten. 1995. Schwa en berbère. *Journal of African Languages and Linguistics* 16: 71–82.

——. 1997. *Grammaire du parler berbère de Figuig (Maroc oriental)*. Paris: Peeters.

——. 1999. *Essai sur la phonologie historique du berbère*. Cologne: Rüdiger Köppe.

——. 2005. *Berber loanwords in Hausa*. Cologne: Rüdiger Köppe.

——. 2008. On the nature of borrowing in Cypriot Arabic. *ZAL* 49: 5–24.

——. 2009. Loanwords in Tarifiyt, a Berber language from Morocco. In ed. Haspelmath and Tadmor, 191–214.

——. 2010. Parallel system borrowing: Parallel morphological systems due to the borrowing of paradigms. *Diachronica* 27: 459–487.

——. Forthcoming. On substratum: The history of the focus marker *d* in Jijel Arabic (Algeria). In *Hommage à Robert Nicolaï*, ed. Carole de Féral.

Krier, Fernande. 1976. *Le maltais au contacte de l'italien*. Hamburg: Buske.

Leslau, Wolf. 1990. *Arabic loanwords in Ethiopian Semitic*. Wiesbaden: Harrassowitz.

Lewis, Geoffrey. 1999. *The Turkish language reform: A catastrophic success*. Oxford: Oxford University Press.

Lucas, Christopher. 2007. Jespersen's cycle in Arabic and Berber. *Transactions of the Philological Society* 105: 398–431.

Lucas, Christopher and Elliott Lash. 2010. Contact as catalyst: The case for Coptic influence in the development of Arabic negation. *Journal of Linguistics* 46: 379–413.

MacAuliffe, Jane Dammen (ed.). 2001–2006. *Encyclopaedia of the Qur'ān*. 6 vols. Leiden: Brill.

Marçais, Philippe. 1956. *Le parler arabe de Djidjelli (Nord constantinois, Algérie)*. Paris: Maisonneuve.

——. 1977. *Esquisse grammaticale de l'arabe maghrébin*. Paris: Maisonneuve.

Marçais, William. 1911. *Textes arabes de Tanger*. Paris: Leroux.

Margoliouth, D. S. 1939. Some additions to Professor Jeffery's "Foreign Vocabulary of the Qur'an." *Journal of the Royal Asiatic Society of Great Britain and Ireland* 1: 53–61.

Matras, Yaron. 1998. Utterance modifiers and universals of grammatical borrowing. *Linguistics* 36: 281–332.

McDonald, M.V. 1974. The order and phonetic value of Arabic sibilants in the "abjad." *Journal of Semitic Studies* 19: 36–36.

Mifsud, Manwel. 1995. *Loan verbs in Maltese: A descriptive and comparative study*. Leiden: Brill.

Moscoso García, Francisco. 2003. *El dialecto árabe de Chaouen (N. de Marruecos). Estudio lingüístico y textos*. PhD diss., Universidad de Cádiz.

Mourigh, Khalid. Forthcoming. *A grammar of Ghomara Berber*. PhD diss., Universiteit Leiden.

Newton, Brian. 1964. An Arabic-Greek dialect. In *Papers in memory of George C. Pappageotes*, ed. R. Austerliz (Supplement to *Word* 20), 43–52.

Nöldeke, Theodor. 1921. Review of Siddiqi (1919). *Der Islam* 11: 267–270.

Owens, Jonathan. 1996a. Grammatisierung, Semantisierung und Sprachkontakt: Arabisch im Tschad-See-Gebiet. *Sprachtypologie und Universalienforschung* 49: 79–85.

——. 1996b. Idiomatic structure and the theory of genetic relationship. *Diachronica* 13: 283–318.

——. 2000. Loanwords in Nigerian Arabic: A quantitative approach. In *Arabic as a minority language*, ed. Jonathan Owens, 259–346. Berlin: Mouton de Gruyter.

Parkinson, Dilworth B. 1985. *Constructing the social context of communication: Terms of address in Egyptian Arabic*. Berlin: Mouton de Gruyter.

Perry, John R. 1985. Language reform in Turkey and Iran. *International Journal of Middle Eastern Studies* 17: 295–311.

——. 2008. Persian. In *Encyclopedia of Arabic Language and Linguistics* III, ed. Kees Versteegh. Associate Editors: Mushira Eid, Alaa Elgibali, Manfred Woidich, Andrzej Zaborski, 573–580. Leiden: Brill.

Prasse, Karl G. 2003. La vocalisation du protoberbère. In *Afrasian: Selected comparative-historical linguistic studies in memory of Igor M. Diakonoff*, ed. M. Lionel Bender, David Appleyard, and Gábor Takács, 41–54. Munich: Lincom Europe.

Prokosch, Erich. 1983. *Osmanisches Wortgut im Ägyptisch-Arabischen*. Berlin: Klaus Schwarz.

Rabin, Chaim. 1951. *Ancient West-Arabian*. London: Taylor's Foreign Press.

Ratcliffe, Robert R. 2005. Bukhara Arabic: A metatypized dialect of Arabic in Central Asia. In ed. Csató, Isaksson, and Jahani, 141–160.

Reichmuth, Stefan. 1988. Songhay-Lehnwörter im Yoruba und ihr historischer Kontext. *Sprache und Geschichte in Afrika* 9: 269–299.

Retsö, Jan. 2000. *Kaškaša*, t-passives and the ancient dialects in Arabia. *Oriente Moderno* New Series 19(80): 111–118.

Rippin, Andrew. 2002. Foreign vocabulary. In *Encyclopaedia of the Qur'ān*. ed. J. MacAuliffe Vol. 2, 226–37. Leiden: Brill.

Robin, Christian (ed.). 1991. *L'Arabie antique de Karib'īl à Mahomet*, special issue of *Revue du Monde Musulman et de la Méditerranée* (61). Aix-en-Provence: Édisud.

——. 1991a. La pénétration des Arabes nomades au Yémen. In *L'Arabie antique de Karib'īl à Mahomet*, ed. C. Robin, 71–88. Aix-en-Provence: Édisud.

——. 1991b. Les langues de la péninsule Arabique. In *L'Arabie antique de Karib'īl à Mahomet*, ed. C. Robin, 89–112. Aix-en-Provence: Édisud.

Sadiqi, Fatima. 2007. The gendered use of Arabic in Morocco. In *Perspectives on Arabic linguistics XIX. Papers from the nineteenth Annual Symposium on Arabic Linguistics, Urbana, Illinois, April 2005*, ed. Elabbas Benmamoun, 277–300. Amsterdam: John Benjamins.

Sakel, Jeanette. 2007. Types of loan: Matter and pattern. In *Grammatical borrowing in cross-linguistic perspective*, ed. Yaron Matras and Jeanette Sakel, 15–30. Berlin: Mouton de Gruyter.

Salonen, Armas. 1952. *Alte Substrat- und Kulturwörter im Arabischen*. Helsinki: Societas Orientalis Fennica.

Schall, Anton. 1982. Geschichte des arabischen Wortschatzes. Lehn- und Fremdwörter im Klassischen Arabisch. In *Grundriß der arabischen Philologie, Band I: Sprachwissenschaft*, ed. Wolfdietrich Fischer, 142–153. Wiesbaden: Ludwig Reichert.

Shraybom-Shivtiel, Shlomit. 1993. Methods of terminological innovation used by the Cairo language academy. In *The Arabist: Budapest Studies in Arabic 6–7 = Proceedings of the colloquium on Arabic lexicology and lexicography (C.A.L.L.)*, ed. K. Dévényi, T. Iványi, and A. Shivtiel, 195–202. Budapest: Eötvös Loránd University,

Siddiqi, Abdussattar. 1919. *Studien über die persischen Fremdwörter im klassischen Arabisch*. Göttingen: Vandenhoeck and Ruprecht.

——. 1930. *Ibn Duraid and his treatment of loan-words*. Allahabad: Indian Press.

Singer, Hans-Rudolf. 1984. *Grammatik der arabischen Mundart der Medina von Tunis*. Berlin: De Gruyter.

Souag, Lameen. 2009. Siwa and its significance for Arabic dialectology. *ZAL* 51: 51–75.

——. 2010. *Grammatical contact in the Sahara: Arabic, Berber, and Songhay in Tabelbala and Siwa*. PhD diss., School of Oriental and African Studies, London.

Stachowski, Stanisław. 1975–1986. *Studien über die arabischen Lehnwörter im Osmanisch-Türkischen*. 4 vols. Wrocław: Zakład Narodowy im. Ossolińskich/Polska Akademia Nauk.

Tafażżolī, Aḥmad. 1987. Arabic language II: Iranian loanwords in Arabic. In *Encyclopaedia Iranica*, vol. 2, ed. Ehsan Yarshater, 231–233. New York: Center for Iranian Studies.

Taifi, Miloud. 1997. Le lexique berbère: entre l'emprunt massif et la néologie sauvage. *Journal of the Sociology of Language* 123: 61–80.

Taine-Cheikh, Catherine. 1997. Les emprunts au berbère zénaga. Un sous-système vocalique du ḥassāniyya. *Matériaux Arabes et Sudarabiques (MAS-GELLAS)* 8: 93–142.

——. 2008. Arabe(s) et berbère en contact: le cas mauritanien. In *Berber in contact. Linguistic and sociolinguistic perspectives*, ed. Mena Lafkioui and Vermondo Brugnatelli, 113–139. Cologne: Rüdiger Köppe.

——. 2010. Aux origines de la culture matérielle des nomades de Mauritanie. Réflexions à partir des lexiques arabes et berbères. *Maghreb Review* 35: 64–88.

Talmoudi, Fathi. 1986: *A morphosemantic study of Romance verbs in the Arabic dialects of Tunis, Sūsa and Sfax. I. Derived themes II, III, V, VI and X*. Göteborg: Acta Universitatis Gothoburgensis.

Versteegh, Kees. 1997a. *The Arabic linguistic tradition*. London: Routledge.

——. 1997b. *The Arabic language*. Edinburgh: Edinburgh University Press.

Versteegh, Kees, et al. (eds.). 2006–2009. *Encyclopedia of Arabic language and linguistics*. 5 vols. Leiden: Brill.

Voigt, Rainer. 1996. Die Labiovelare im Marokkanisch-Arabischen. In *Romania Arabica. Festschrift für Reinhold Kontzi zum 70. Geburtstag*, ed. Jens Lüdtke, 21–29. Tübingen: Gunter Narr.

Weninger, Stefan. 2007. Ethiopic loanwords. In *Encyclopedia of Arabic language and linguistics*, vol. 2, ed. Kees Versteegh. Associate Editors: Mushira Eid, Alaa Elgibali, Manfred Woidich, Andrzej Zaborski, 57–58. Leiden: Brill.

Zammit, Martin R. 2009. South Arabian loanwords. In *Encyclopedia of Arabic language and linguistics*, vol. 4, ed. Kees Versteegh. Associate Editors: Mushira Eid, Alaa Elgibali, Manfred Woidich, Andrzej Zaborski, 295–297. Leiden: Brill.

CHAPTER 16

PSYCHOLINGUISTICS*

SAMI BOUDELAA

16.1 Introduction

Interest in our faculty of language is a long-standing one going back to the ancient Egyptians, the Greek philosophers, and the Romans (Altman 2006; Garnham, Garrod, and Sanford, 2006). However, the history of *psycholinguistics*, the scientific study of the mental processes underpinning our ability to acquire, produce, and comprehend language, is relatively a recent one, although the philosophical seeds of this discipline might be traced back to various points in time.

Being Arab myself, I tend to intuitively search for precursors of scientific disciplines in the rich Arabic–Islamic intellectual legacy. A cursory examination of this legacy reveals that several ancient Muslim scholars such as Sibawaih (180/796), Ibn Jinni (392/1002 CE), and Ibn Khaldūn (808/1406) had elaborate views on issues currently at the heart of pycholinguistics such as language *acquisition*, language *learning*, and the interaction between *language production* and *language perception*. For instance, Ibn Khaldūn in his famous *Muqaddimah* formulated very detailed claims about what is known in modern generative linguistics as the distinction between *competence* and *performance*, the language acquisition device, and he had detailed views about the *critical period hypothesis*, that is, the neurobiological maturation of the language system (Ibrahim 1987). For Ibn Khaldūn language is a *skill*, a "malakah" as he puts it, consisting in the acquisition not so much of individual words but of a syntax that governs the way words are strung together to build utterances. More significant perhaps is Ibn Khaldūn's explicit view that language is too creative and complicated a skill to be acquirable by imitation. For him the mechanism underlying language acquisition—or indeed the acquisition

* This research was supported in part by a United Arab Emirates University grant to Sami Boudelaa (FHSS22201) and by a European Research Council Neurolex Advanced Grant to William Marslen-Wilson. The author is indebted to Jonathan Owens and Dimitrios Ntelitheos for helpful comments on earlier versions of this manuscript.

of any other high-level behavior—is the unique ability of the human being to abstract a system of rules and laws that govern all observable phenomena (Bencheikh 1979; Ibrahim 1987). Similarly penetrating analyses of phonological and phonetic processes are offered in Sibawaih's *Kitāb,* rightly considered by Carter (1973) as the spiritual forerunner of contemporary structural linguistics and by Edzard (2001) as the predecessor of modern-day *optimality theory* (OT). In particular, Edzard maintains that Sibawaih's descriptive approach meshes well with OT as he often lists several forms—candidates—(e.g., [watid], [watd], [tida], and [wadd] *peg*), which he then tags, or ranks, as "good," "better," or "Arabic" based on certain parameters, or constraints. Another example of Sibwaih's analyses that prefigured linguistic theory is his treatment of *imala*, the process by which the phonemes [a] and [aa] are fronted and raised to be produced as [e] and [ie], respectively (Owens, 2006). In his treatment of linguistic phenomena, Sibawaih often times invokes the perceptual and articulatory constraints weighing on the language speaker and hearer. For instance, the fact that the possessive singular feminine suffix "-ki" is realized as "-ši" is attributed to the perceptual salience of the "-ši" compared with "~ki," an explanation that has an unmistakable psycholinguistic feel to it.[1]

For European scholars, in contrast, the tendency is to trace scientific origins to Ancient Greece (Altman 2006; Garnham et al. 2006). Accordingly, Plato in his *Republic* is credited with developing an explicit *theory of concepts* where he tackles questions such as *what a word means* and *whether the referent of a word is external to the user*, which are important issues in modern psycholinguistics. In more recent history, Wilhelm M. Wundt (1832–1920), a German physician and psychologist, is claimed to have kicked off psycholinguistics with the establishment of a psychology lab in Leipzig in 1879, where he explored mental disorders, abnormal behavior, and empirical and philosophical issues pertaining to language (Blumenthal 1970).

For North American scholars, the landmark event that established psycholinguistics was a 1951 conference organized by the Social Science Research Council at Cornell University. This was concluded by forming a committee on linguistics and psychology with psychologist Charles E. Osgood as chairman. The conference was followed by two catalytic events: a seminar held at Indiana University under the auspices of the Linguistics Institute in 1953; and the release of a book based on that seminar with "psycholinguistics" in its title for the first time: *Psycholinguistics: A Survey of Theory and Research Problems* (Osgood Sebeok 1954).

As its name suggests, psycholinguistics is a blend of psychology and linguistics. It was particularly heavily influenced by generative linguistics as developed by Chomsky (1957, 1959, 1986). The primary data used by generative linguists are intuitions about what counts as a grammatical or nongrammatical utterance. This emphasis on internal knowledge was accompanied by an emphasis on what humans can do with language and how they acquire and store it in their long-term memories. This marked a departure from the emphasis of the *structuralist* school on the analysis and description of linguistic

[1] This particular example was brought to my attention by Jonathan Owens.

units (Harris 1951). The influence of generative linguistics on psycholinguistics contrasted with that of psychology. Indeed, at the inception of psycholinguistics, there were at least two ambient psychological paradigms. The first was *Information Theory* (Shannon and Weaver 1949), which emphasized probability and redundancy in linguistic communication and viewed the language processor as a device that could generate and understand sentences by moving from one state to another. The second research paradigm, and by far the more dominant until the late 1950s, was *behaviorism*. Here all things that a living organism does like acting, thinking, and feeling are viewed as *behaviors* (Skinner 1957). Behaviorists contend that such behaviors can be studied and understood as a relationship between an input (*stimulus*) and an output (*response*). There is no need to invoke either internal physiological events or hypothetical constructs such as the mind. There are no differences between publicly observable concrete processes such as *eating an apple* or *drinking a cup of tea* and abstract unobservable processes like *thinking* and *feeling*. Hence, language is merely a behavior like any other, and its acquisition and use are amenable to be studied and understood with the standard behaviorist toolkit using *conditioning* and *reinforcement*.

Behaviorism was infelicitous to the emergence of a new discipline disposed to focus on the mind–brain as the seat of language. If psycholinguistics were to flourish, somehow the dominance of behaviorism had to be harnessed. This was soon achieved partly through the criticism leveled by Chomsky (1959) against Skinner's book *Verbal Behavior* and partly through the emergence of a new kind of psychology known as *cognitive psychology*.[2] Chomsky (1959) argues that unlike behaviorism, his *transformational grammar* provided not only an account of the underlying structure of language but also of people's knowledge of their native language. For its part, cognitive psychology viewed people as dynamic information processing systems whose mental operations might be described in computational terms (Neisser 1967). The synergistic interplay of generative linguistics and cognitive psychology laid the groundwork for psycholinguistics, and this soon became a thriving discipline testing and falsifying the psychological implications of linguistic theory using the experimental tools of cognitive psychology.

16.2 State of the Art

Any attempt to strictly delineate the research questions addressed by current-day psycholinguistics is bound to be exclusionary at best and misleading at worst. This is because the discipline has ramified almost beyond recognition compared with what it was during the 1950s and the 1960s (Gaskell 2007). Contemporary psycholinguists use research tools borrowed from other disciplines such as machine learning techniques

[2] For a different evaluation of the behaviorism, its legacy, and interaction with generative linguistics, see Roediger (2004).

developed within the field of artificial intelligence, brain imaging techniques such as functional magnetic resonance imaging (fMRI), transcranial magnetic stimulation (TMS), electroencephalography (EEG), and magnetoencephalography (MEG) developed within medical sciences and a host of new behavioral tasks developed by psychologists. With this caveat in mind, I will restrict the current exposition to two general strands of research that will give a rough idea about the present-day psycholinguistic enterprise:[3] language comprehension and language production. In what follows, I firstly give a brief presentation of each of these. Second, I present the research techniques used in psycholinguistics and follow it by a presentation of the major issues driving research in the field. Third, I give a summary of the specific questions that Arabic raises for psycholinguistic research and conclude with some remarks about the future of psycholinguistics.

16.2.1 Language Comprehension

Language comprehension is an umbrella term that covers the comprehension of spoken, written, and signed language. Understanding any of these three forms of linguistic communication requires much more than knowing the meaning of individual words. It requires understanding what is intended when words are strung together in a sentence. Importantly, it brings into synergistic play a host of skills and dispositions, including *communicative awareness* and *linguistic knowledge*, without which language understanding and communication fail. Communicative awareness refers to the fact that the language user knows that (1) language has meaning, (2) contextual factors should be taken into consideration in interpreting the message, (3) misinterpreting another's communication is likely, and (4) correct interpretation of a message often requires an effort. What we know about it comes from research with patient populations suffering in particular from autism and Asperger's syndrome. Such patients are characterized by a striking inability to use and comprehend language in context because they fail to properly develop communicative awareness (White et al. 2006).

Linguistic knowledge, on the other hand, refers to knowledge of various linguistic domains namely, phonology, morphology, semantics, syntax, and orthography in the case of written language comprehension. There is now a wealthy research tradition dating back to the early days of psycholinguistics where pioneering researchers in the field frenetically sought to explore and validate the *psychological reality* of syntactic processing by showing, for instance, that perceptual complexity as measured by reaction time was related to linguistic complexity as described by generative grammar (Miller and McKean 1964). Today, in the area of syntactic processing the focus is on the psychological, not the linguistic, mechanisms by which syntactic structure and syntactic dependencies are determined (Brennan and Pylkkänen 2012). Sentence comprehension is

[3] Many other equally interesting research aspects like bilingualism, second-language learning, and sign language cannot be covered here for lack of space.

thought to involve not the kind of transformations that formed part of the formalism of generative grammar, but many interrelated processes, including syntactic parsing, semantic composition, and pragmatic inference.

The other domains of linguistic knowledge have also attracted a huge research effort. For instance, earlier research in the field of morphological processing sought to determine whether morphological structure plays a role that can be distinguished from that of orthography, phonology, and semantics (Taft and Forster 1975; Marslen-Wilson et al. 1994). Subsequently, the emphasis shifted toward determining the time course of morphemic processing as opposed to phonological, orthographic, and semantic processing on one hand, and establishing the neural substrates supporting morphological parsing and representation on the other. The goal was to build a cognitive neuroscience account that embeds a computationally specific cognitive claim about the functional properties of morphological processing within a specific analysis of the neural system supporting it (Feldman and Soltano 1999; Rastle et al. 2000; Pylkkänen and Marantz 2003; Boudelaa and Marslen-Wilson 2004a, 2004b, 2005).

In the area of semantic representation, the questions of interest—at least in the literature on single word representation—relate to how the meaning of each word is represented in the brain–mind, whether the meanings of words are related to one another, and whether the same organizing principle holds for concrete and abstract words (Rogers and McClelland 2004; Vigliocco and Vinson 2007). These have been answered in various ways, and different models have been suggested, such as *featural theories* where word meaning combines a set of conceptual features and *holistic theories* where lexical concepts correspond to the meanings of the words. A considerable amount of behavioral, brain imaging, and modeling research has been conducted to adjudicate between the two main contending theories of semantic representations or various versions of them (Hinton and Shallice 1991; Hauk, Johnsrude, and Pulvermüller 2004; Taylor et al. 2012). Most of this research has focused, however, on the representation and processing of words referring to objects, contrasting man-made objects (e.g., *scissors, car, table*) with natural categories (e.g., *banana, tiger, fire*). Only a few studies have focused on the semantics of words from other content domains like events or properties.

Regarding the final two domains of linguistic description, (i.e., phonology and orthography), it is important to note that they are typically investigated in parallel since orthography is designed to represent spoken language and its underlying phonological structure in particular phonemes and syllables (Grainger and Jacobs 1996; Rastle 2007). Different research strands are being pursued in this respect, and one of the driving research questions relates to whether phonology is systematically involved in reading: when reading a word like "cat", for instance, do we access the meaning of *a small four-legged fury animal with a tail and claws usually kept as a pet* directly from print, or do we use the phonological representation /kæt/ to access that meaning? A second equally important question is whether access to word meaning is affected by the forward consistency of the mapping from orthography to phonology as when orthographic 'oo' is pronounced differently in *blood* and *moot*, or by the feedback consistency from phonology to orthography when a phonological pattern can be orthographically rendered in various ways like the English sound /u/, which is spelled in different ways (Ziegler,

Stone, and Jacobs 1997). A third question in this area relates to phonological awareness, that is, the ability to detect and manipulate units like phonemes and syllables and the impact that such a skill can have on orthographic processing and learning to read in general (Perfetti et al. 1987).

These various research questions have given rise to different models of visual word recognition, ranging from models that acknowledge routine involvement of phonology in reading to those that posit direct access to meaning from script, with dual route models postulating parallel access to meaning from phonology and orthography (Rastle 2007). Other research strands have developed more recently that focus more exclusively either on the orthographic or the phonological domain. A case in point is the surge of interest in what is known as *the orthographic input coding scheme* within which researchers aim at developing detailed models of how the order of the letters in a word is represented and how the identity of those letters is computed (Norris 2009; Davis 2010; Kinoshita and Norris 2010). Echoing the burgeoning interest in new methodologies used to study syntactic, morphological, and semantic processing, there is now a growing body of imaging research using hemodynamic and electrophysiological methodologies to look at the neural substrates underpinning orthographic and phonological processing. The espousal of such techniques reveals an ambition to move from purely cognitive models of orthographic and phonological processing to a new generation of models that are neurally grounded and computationally constrained (Carreiras et al. 2007; Graves et al. 2010).

16.2.2 Language Production

Language production refers to a varied set of research interests connected, if loosely, by an emphasis on understanding the mechanisms underlying the way we communicate using spoken, written, or signed language. Research into language production lags relatively behind that in the language comprehension field, arguably because the investigation of language production lends itself less readily to experimental control (Alario et al. 2006). We now have reasonably detailed accounts of spoken and written language comprehension. In what follows I will briefly describe the process of speech production and written language production.

The process of speech production consists of three broad stages: *conceptualization*, *formulation*, and *execution* (Levelt 1989). During the stage of conceptualization the speaker decides on the message they intend to convey. The product of this stage is a message that does not have as yet a linguistic form. The conversion of this preverbal message into a linguistic form defines the *formulation stage*, which involves specific semantic, lexical, syntactic, and phonological planning. The completion of the encoding stage paves the way for the *execution stage* during which detailed phonetic and motor planning is capped by the *articulation* of the message. Although there is a large degree of agreement on the previous stages of speech production, vigorous debate continues over (1) whether the different stages are executed serially or in parallel, (2) how many levels of representations are needed to account for the dynamics of speech production, and (3) the kind of data that theorists should bring to bear on the issues of spoken language production (Dell 1986; Caramazza 1997).

Turning to written language production, it is important to note that the processes involved in this domain are more integrated and syntactically complex than their counterparts in spoken language. Although some cognitive processes apply across the two modalities (Perret and Laganoro 2012), it is clear that producing written language takes more time, that the output can be edited and planned, and that little interaction with other people is involved during this process. Roughly three processing stages subserve the production of written language (Hayes and Flower 1986): the *planning stage* when information is retrieved from memory and organized into a plan, followed by the *translation stage* during which written language is produced and finally the *reviewing stage* when the writer proofreads what has been written. What we now know about the psycholinguistic mechanisms that convert thought into written language comes essentially from neuropsychological data showing various types of dissociations such as dysgraphia where patients can spell familiar words but fail to generate spelling for nonwords (Shallice 1981), or where they manage to spell nonwords at the expense of producing significant overregularization errors (Beauvois and Derouesné 1981).

16.3 The Psycholinguist's Research Kit

As an empirical science, psycholinguistics relies heavily on experimental tasks to tap into mental processes that support linguistic behavior. The following is a nonexhaustive presentation of some of the tasks and techniques used in the field.

16.3.1 Behavioral Tasks

A behavioral task is generally one in which a participant is presented with a stimulus and asked to generated a response. If the response is timed—that is, if the subject is for instance given no more than 2 seconds to output his or her response and if the reaction time is measured—the task is said to be an *online* task. If there is no time limit as to when the participant should produce a response, the task is *offline*. There is a considerable number of behavioral tasks used nowadays. A 1996 special issue of the journal *Language & Cognitive Processes* featured a detailed analysis of 18 experimental tasks used in spoken word recognition. Sixteen years on, the number of tasks has increased as experimentalists developed new tasks or adapted old ones to the specific requirements of the emerging neuroimaging research.

The difference underlying the tasks pertains to the kind of *independent variables* that they manipulate and the *dependent variables* that they measure. Consider *the lexical decision task* and the *phoneme monitoring task* to illustrate this point. The lexical decision task, perhaps the most frequently used task in language studies, entails speeded classification of written or spoken stimuli into existing or nonexisting words in the language of the participant. The dependent variables obtained in this task are *response latencies* and *classification accuracies*. The independent variables obviously vary depending on the experimental questions at hand. Some of the extensively studied variables in this task include lexical characteristics such as length of the stimuli, frequency, and neighborhood size (Luce et al. 2000). In contrast, the phoneme monitoring task requires the participant to make a response as soon as he or she hears a stimulus with a predefined target sound. Here the dependent variables are *phoneme detection latencies, detection accuracy,* and *false alarms*. The independent variables in this task can be the frequency of the carrier word, its lexical status, and the position of the target phoneme in the carrier word (Connine and Titone 1996).

The lexical decision task and the phoneme monitoring task are instances of online tasks used in the study of language comprehension and speech processing. Other areas of psycholinguistics like language acquisition have developed tasks like the *nonnutritive sucking task* and the *head-turning task* used in language acquisition research or the *picture-naming task* used in language production research.

16.3.2 Computational Modeling

A computational model is an executable computer program that simulates an abstract model of a particular behavior. To build a computational model of a particular linguistic phenomenon, the modeler needs to develop explicit mathematical descriptions of the processes that go on in the brain when that phenomenon is dealt with. An explicit mathematical description forces the researcher to develop explicit theoretical claims and helps generate testable predictions, hence the value of modeling.

Linguistic behavior has been modeled in various ways, but perhaps the most popular approach in this respect is the connectionist modeling approach where processing occurs through the interaction of many simple interconnected units. Connectionist models have been very influential and have, according to some, led to a paradigm shift in psycholinguistics by emphasizing, for instance, that we learn language not by internalizing a set of symbolic rules, but by building connections among overlapping representations that emerge through continued exposure to the environment (Chater and Manning 2006). The connectionist modeling efforts provided important insights in all areas of psycholinguistics such as reading, language production, language acquisition, and comprehension. For instance, Seidenberg and McClelland (1989) developed a model of reading that accounted for how readers recognize letter strings as words and read them. Patterson, Seidenberg, and McClelland (1989) used a connectionist network to model surface dyslexia. By lesioning the model, that is, probabilistically resetting a portion of the units or the connections among them to zero, Patterson et al. (1989) were able to simulate the behavior of surface dyslexic patients. One of the commonly used dependent variables in this kind of modeling research is the ability of the model to generalize to novel items on which they were not trained.

16.3.3 Imaging Techniques

Imaging is a general term covering a range of techniques that allow the psycholinguist, or more precisely the cognitive neuroscientist, to study how the brain functions without invasive neurosurgery (Saur and Hartwigsen 2012; Gernsbacher and Kaschak 2003). A number of safe techniques are used in the study of language functions nowadays. These can be broadly divided into *hemodynamic* techniques, which rely on the measurement of the dynamic regulation of the blood flow in the brain, and *neurophysiological* responses, which gauge electrical or magnetic activity in the brain. In both cases the response measured is related to the presentation of linguistic stimuli either visually or auditorily; hence, the two classes of techniques are said to be *event related* methods.

Among the hemodynamic methods commonly used in language studies, fMRI and positron emission tomography (PET) rank high. FMRI works by detecting the changes in blood oxygenation and flow triggered, if indirectly, by neural activity. When a brain area is more active, it consumes more oxygen. To meet this increased demand, blood flow increases to the active area, and fMRI serves to produce activation maps showing which parts of the brain are involved in a particular mental process. PET traces amounts of short-lived radioactive material to map functional processes in the brain. When the material undergoes radioactive decay, a positron is emitted, and this is picked up by the detector. Areas of high radioactivity are associated with brain activity.

Regarding neurophysiological techniques, two of the heavily used techniques are EEG and MEG. EEG works by measuring the electrical activity of the brain by recording from electrodes placed on the scalp. The resulting traces are known as an electroencephalogram and represent an electrical signal from a large number of neurons. MEG, on the other hand, measures the magnetic fields produced by electrical activity in the brain via extremely sensitive devices known as SQUIDs (superconducting quantum inference device).

The use of imaging techniques has ushered in a number of methodological issues concerning experimental design and statistical analyses. It has also highlighted the need for the psycholinguist to learn and integrate information from neurophysiology, neurobiology, and physics. Interestingly, the use of such techniques is promoting the building of neurocognitive accounts of language (Marslen-Wilson and Tyler, 1997).

16.4 Major Issues in Psycholinguistics

Being concerned with the nature of the mental computations and processes supporting linguistic behavior, psycholinguistics features a number of theoretical–epistemological issues that permeate all areas of psycholinguistic analyses and extend well into a host of allied fields. The following is a brief exposition of the three major issues, which, it must be stressed, are intimately linked to each other and to other issues not covered here (Pinker and Ullman 2002).

16.4.1 To What Extent Is the Language System Modular?

Modularity refers to the decomposability of cognition into components that can be considered in relative independence of each other. Fodor (1983) defines a module as a coalition of processing properties that are domain specific, encapsulated, fast to deliver an output, neurally hard-wired, autonomous, and not assembled. One of the attractive characteristics of modularity is that it saves low-level systems from consulting all an organism's knowledge to do its work. Besides, from a developmental perspective, it is arguably true that a restricted domain of operation simplifies learning.

Modular psycholinguistic models contending that processing in one level is not influenced by processing in higher levels are called *autonomous* models. Examples of such models have been developed to account for processing in different areas like visual word recognition (e.g., *serial search model;* Forster 1976) and spoken word recognition (*merge;* Norris, Cutler, and McQueen 2000).

This class of models contrasts with a competing view on which processing is not modular but *interactive* with various levels of representation affecting each other. Depending on whether the various stages of processing are thought to be overlapping or not, the interactive model is either *discrete* or *cascaded.* In a discrete model processing one level can begin only once the preceding level has completed its work, while a cascaded model allows information to flow from one level to the next before processing is fully completed (Marslen-Wilson 1975; McClelland and Rumelhart 1981).

With the existing experimental data it is not possible to adjudicate in favor of either modular autonomous models or interactive models. Consequently, questions about whether the whole language system is a self-contained special module for interfacing between social processes and cognition, or whether it is simply a window into wider cognitive process are still open questions and continue to elicit interest across a variety of domains (Meunier, Lambiotte, and Bullmore 2010).

16.4.2 Is Any Part of Language Innate?

The question of language innateness is intimately linked to the issue of modularity. Exponents committed to the claim that language processes are modular vehemently argue that a significant part of our language capacity is also innate (Fodor 1983). This line of thought is often referred to as *nativism* and contrasts with *nonnativism* or *empiricism.* Although one might use the label nativism to loosely describe the general claim that our innate psychological endowment is rich enough to allow the acquisition of linguistic knowledge, and in particular syntax, this label certainly does not refer to a single well-defined position but instead characterizes a number of contemporary views (Samuels 2002). Some nativist claims are said to be *local* pertaining to relatively specific psychological traits, while others are considered to be *general* claims that aspire to be a theory about the overall composition of the mind (ibid.).

In psycholinguistics, the focus is on the local claims of nativism, and the questions addressed are the extent to which the acquisition of syntax depends on generally applicable human cognitive capacities. Proponents of nativism have put forward different mechanisms by which language (i.e., syntax) is acquired. An example of such mechanisms is the *principles and parameters* formulated by Chomsky. The nonnativist camp, on the other hand, suggests that general properties of the learning system can and do play the role of what appears to be innate, language-specific knowledge. Nonnativists further suggest that linguistic behavior, and arguably cognitive behavior in general, emerges from the interaction of nature and nurture (Elman et al. 1996). They level two general criticisms at nativism. The first is that it fails to provide a clear account of exactly how the allegedly innate information might actually be genetically coded for (ibid.). The second is that contemporary nativist theory makes little or no testable predictions (Sampson 1997).

16.4.3 Does Language Processing Use Rules?

The fundamental issue here is whether mental computations involve the use of rule-based manipulation of strings of symbols with a syntax, or whether they rely on distributed systems operating without syntax (Rumelhart and McClelland 1986; Pinker and Prince 1988; Marslen-Wilson and Tyler 1997). Two competing views have been offered in this respect.

According to the first, generally held by researchers committed to modularity and nativism, much of our linguistic knowledge is encapsulated in the form of linguistic rules and the essence of language processing consists in symbol manipulation (Pinker and Prince 1988; Marcus and Fisher 2003). A symbol, or variable, is an abstract placeholder. For example, the category *noun* is a symbol in the sense that it enumerates a large number of tokens including familiar ones (e.g., *car, room*) and novel ones (e.g., *blish, flonx*). Symbols treat all tokens in the same way, abstracting away from their specific idiosyncrasies at the level of form or meaning. For example, most English verbs take a regular past tense suffix (*walk–walked*), which is applied to new verbs (e.g., *blogged, wugged*), suggesting the application of a mental rule *add -ed to a verb* (Marcus et al. 1995). Exceptional linguistic materials for which a symbolic rule of some sort cannot be invoked (e.g., the alternation *ring–rang, bring–brought*) are argued to be stored in memory.

According to the contending view, developed within the general framework of connectionism, mental computation is *subsymbolic*, graded, probabilistic, interactive, context sensitive, and importantly does not require the use of symbols (Rumelhart and McClelland 1987 Elman et al. 1996; Plunkett 1998). Thus, the processing of regular and irregular linguistic phenomena does not invoke different processing mechanisms (McClelland 2010). Rather, processing takes place in the interaction of many simple massively interconnected units. Different generations of connectionist models have been developed over the past 25 years to vindicate that the general claim that a unitary processing mechanism subserves linguistic computations holds for various domains. Some of these models were successfully used to simulate language acquisition (Marchman, Plunkett, and Goodman 1997) and language production by patients (Joanisse and Seidenberg 1999).

Like the divide over all major psycholinguistic issues, the one over the nature of mental computations is certain to continue to fuel research. An important way of shedding new light on this question is by focusing on understudied languages that may offer novel insights.

16.5 Psycholinguistics and Arabic

I have deliberately avoided entitling this section *Arabic Psycholinguistics*, or indeed even *The Psycholinguistics of Arabic*. This is because psycholinguistic investigation into Arabic is scant, and the little we know in this respect is due to research conducted in Western or Israeli universities. Although this is an expected situation considering that no Arab university today features a department of psycholinguistics, it is nonetheless a dispiriting one because Arabic is undeniably a real treasure trove for the psycholinguist to gain novel insights about questions that could not be asked, let alone answered if research were confined to Indo-European languages (Marslen-Wilson 1999; Share 2008). Some of the psycholinguistically most significant features of Arabic are (1) the orthographic system, (2) the morphological system, (3) the phonological system, (4) the syntactic system, and the (5) the diglossic situation. Each one of these domains contrasts sharply with what is afforded by Indo-European languages, and those of them that have been psycholinguistically studied so far have shed new light on ongoing debates in the field and have helped constrain existing views. In what follows, I will summarize the main findings of the available psycholinguistic research on various aspects of Arabic.

16.5.1 Arabic Orthography and Reading

The Arabic orthographic system operates with a dominantly consonantal orthography with short vowels experienced only in instructional and religious texts, leading to a significant number of *heterophonic homographs*, that is, words with one spelling, different pronunciations, and different meanings, such as the form سحب, which can be read as *saħab* "drew/pulled," *saħb* "drawing/pulling," *suħub* "clouds" [Buckwalter and Parkinson, "Modern Lexicography"]. Second, Arabic is written from right to left in a cursive manner, with most letters connecting to each other and appearing as different allographs depending on their position within the word [Daniels, "Writing"]. A third relevant peculiarity of Arabic pertains to the situation of *diglossia* where one linguistic variety, Modern Standard Arabic, needs to be acquired against the backdrop of a regional variety typically used for and associated with mundane daily linguistic needs. These characteristics of Arabic have motivated a number of empirical studies over the past few years (Roman and Pavard 1987; Farid and Grainger 1996; Saiegh-Haddad 2003; Abu-Rabia and Taha 2004; Mughazy 2006; Ibrahim, Eivatar, and Aharon-Peretz 2007; Most, Levin, and Sarsour 2007; [Suleiman, "Folk Linguistics"]; [Al-Wer, "Sociolinguistics"]).

Focal among the questions addressed in this respect is whether the use of the diacritical marks to signal the short vowels has beneficial effects on reading. Early work by Roman and Pavard (1987) and Bentin and Ibrahim (1996) suggests that lexical decision is slowed down for isolated voweled Arabic words (i.e., words with the diacritical marks) compared with unvoweled ones. This is an interesting finding. It belies the intuitive expectation that orthographically ambiguous forms would take more time to process than unambiguous words and aligns with the general phenomenon of the *ambiguity advantage* found in Indo-European languages and where ambiguous words like *belt* seem to be faster to respond to and less error-prone (Lupker 2006). In contrast to lexical decision with single words, sentence reading suggests that voweling is conducive to faster and more accurate performance (Roman, Pavard, and Asselah 1985). More recent research, however, tones down the gain engendered by voweling in sentence context and instead emphasizes the benefit of factors such as context, lexical frequency, and morphological structure, thus suggesting that, unlike reading in Indo-European language, Arabic reading processes are more significantly influenced by top-down lexical information than by bottom-up information (Mughazy 2006).

Another example vindicating the novel insights offered by Arabic and Semitic languages in general is the recent discovery that items with transposed letters (e.g., مستمع "listening" written as ممستع) fail to be treated as instances of the same percept in Arabic, while they are treated as such in Indo-European languages (Perea, Abu Mallouh, and Carreiras 2010). Letter transposition often triggers a change in the allograph used and apparently these allographs are treated as different percepts during the task of lexical decision resulting in the disappearance of priming between a target word and its transposed letter prime. The absence of transposed letter effects is in keeping with findings from research into letter position dyslexia, a form of dyslexia characterized by a disproportionate number of reading errors typically involving word-internal letter transpositions (e.g., reading *slat* as *salt*; Friedmann and Haddad-Hanna 2012).

The final dimension of interest with respect to Arabic orthography and reading pertains to diglossia. Here the focus is on ways language background affects early school achievement, and in particular learning to read. Arab children speak a local dialect of some sort, whereas the language in the school is Modern Standard Arabic. It has been suggested that this dialect mismatch has many effects on the child's school experience making tasks such as learning to read literally more difficult. For instance, kindergarteners show a much better performance monitoring phonemes that occur in both Standard Arabic and dialectal (e.g., /b/), than phonemes that exist only in Standard Arabic (e.g., /q/; Saiegh-Haddad 2007). This situation has prompted many to focus on young children's knowledge of the alternative dialects, and ways that negative effects of the mismatch can be ameliorated in the hope of providing supplementary language experiences early on in life when the child's neural plasticity for language is still high. One of the venues that has not been explored so far is the use of computational models of reading to predict where dialect differences will interfere with progress and how experience can be structured to improve performance.

16.5.2 Arabic Morphology

Morphology is perhaps the domain of linguistic knowledge that provides the sharpest contrast between Arabic and the psycholinguistically better-studied Indo-European languages. Arabic is standardly described as a non-concatenative morphology language where morphemes—a root and a word pattern—are interleaved within each other rather than appended linearly one after the other (Versteegh, 1997; [Hellmuth, "Phonology"]; [Ratcliffe, "Morphology"]).

The special morphological characteristics of Arabic have motivated a number of psycholinguistic studies focusing on the cognitive and neurocognitive processing and representation of morphology (Boudelaa and Marslen-Wilson 2001, 2004a, 2004b, 2005, 2009, 2011). One of the critical questions in this respect is whether roots and word patterns as bound morpheme have independent lexical representations. In a series of priming experiments Boudelaa & Marslen-Wilson (2004a, 2004b, 2005) sought to establish whether root priming[4] in Arabic exists and whether it can be distinguished from meaning-based and form-based effects. Table 16.1 depicts a typical design used to answer these questions.

Condition 1, labeled +R+S, would consist of prime and target pairs that share a root and a strong semantic relationship like *kitaabah–maktab* "writing–office." The strength of the semantic relation between a prime and a given target is usually established on the basis of pretests where at least 15 judges are asked to rate words as semantically strongly related or unrelated at all on a scale from 1 to 9, with 1 being semantically unrelated and 9 strongly related. The average rating is 7 for semantically related words and 2 for semantically unrelated words. Condition 2, would consist of words pairs sharing a root but a weak semantic relationship as exemplified by [*katiibah*]–[*maktab*] "squadron–office". Condition 3 would consist of words that are semantically related without sharing a root like [*ʔidaarah]-[maktab]* "administration–office", while Condition 4 would be comprised of word pairs that share some phonological overlap without sharing a root

[4] The prime is a stimulus (e.g., word, picture) that precedes the word to be identified. A priming effect occurs if the prime facilitates the identification of the word as measured by a faster response and a lower error rate.

Table 16.1 Typical experimental design used to establish root priming in MSA as a purely morphological phenomenon

Condition	Prime	Target
1. +Root + Semantics	كتابة kitaabah "writing"	مكتب maktab "office"
2. +Root -Semantics	كتيبة katiibah "squadron"	مكتب maktab "office"
3. -Root + Semantics	إدارة ʔidaarah "office"	مكتب maktab "office"
4. +Form	مكتئب muktaʔib "sad"	مكتب maktab "office"
5. Baseline	نحافة naħaafah "leanness"	مكتب maktab "office"

or a semantic relationship as exemplified by the pair *[muktaʔib]-[maktab]* "sad–office". Both Conditions 3 and 4 would be control conditions. Finally, Condition 5 would be a baseline condition consisting of unrelated word pairs like [*naħaafah*]-[*maktab*] "leanness–office".

Participants in experiments with a design such as the above are asked to make a lexical decision to the target word. Typically strong priming is observed in conditions 1 and 2 with no effects or much weaker effects in Condition 3 and a tendency for a nonsignificant inhibition in Condition 4 as illustrated in Figure 16.1.

This pattern of results is usually interpreted as strong evidence that the root plays a critical role in lexical processing and representation in Arabic. Figure 16.1 clearly shows that relationships based only on semantics (i.e., Condition 3) or on form (i.e., Condition 4) fail to generate any facilitation. Conversely, the root exerts a facilitatory effect even when it has different interpretations in the prime and target word, as is illustrated in Condition 2. Importantly, this facilitation has been documented not only in covert priming (i.e., masked) but also in overt priming (i.e., cross-modal and auditory–auditory). Furthermore, root priming is observed even in cases of allomorphic variation where the root in the prime word surfaces with a consonant assimilated to the environing consonant of the word pattern as in the pair *ʔittijaah–wijhah* "direction – direction", where the first consonant of the root {wjh} surfaces as a /t/ in the context of the word pattern {ʔiftiʕaal} (Boudelaa and Marslen-Wilson 2004b). Note that this is not the case in English where functionally equivalent pairs like "department–depart" facilitate each other only in covert tasks.

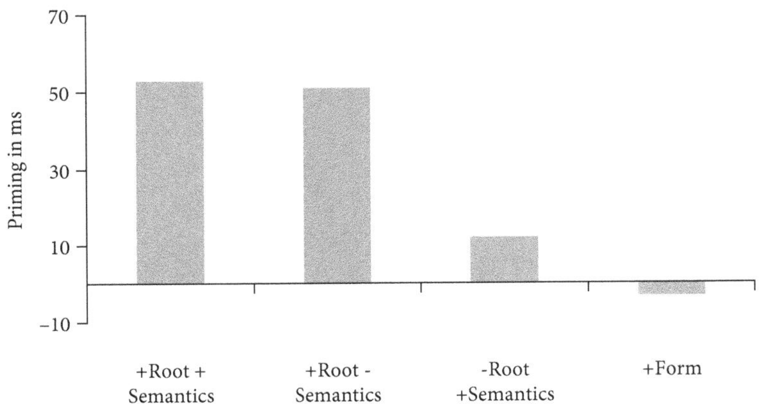

FIGURE 16.1 Typical outcome of a priming experiment assessing root priming in Arabic.

Table 16.2 Example of stimuli used to probe for word pattern effects in Arabic

	Prime	Target
1. +Word Pattern +Meaning	حسود ħasuud "covetous"	عجول ʕajuul "rush"
2. +Form	معول miʕwal "pickaxe"	عجول ʕajuul "rush"
3. Baseline	تمساح timsaaħ "alligator"	عجول ʕajuul "rush"

Turning to word patterns, a similar approach is taken as illustrated in Table 16.2, and lexical decision is used with various priming formats (i.e., masked, cross-modal, and auditory–auditory).

Condition 1 in Table 16.2 features a prime–target pair sharing the word pattern {faʕuul}. The question of interest here is whether words related by a word pattern morpheme show evidence of facilitation that is different from word pairs in Condition 2 that share some phonological overlap. Figure 16.2 illustrates priming results that have been consistently obtained using different priming formats.

Figure 16.2 clearly shows a strong facilitatory priming effect for words sharing a word pattern compared with words sharing some phonological or orthographic overlap. The effects of the word pattern are consistently found with both Arabic nouns and verbs. However, two factors modulate word pattern priming in nouns. First, the shared word pattern has to co-occur with a productive root, that is, one that participates in the creation of many surface forms such that, for instance, *šaamit* "malicious" with the

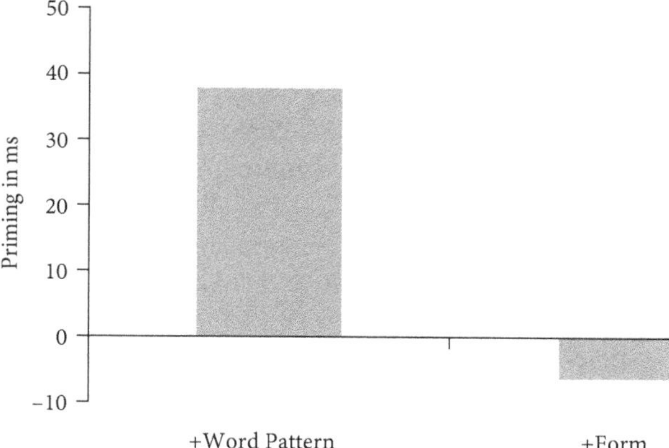

FIGURE 16.2 Priming for words sharing a word pattern and words sharing form overlap.

nonproductive root {šmt} does not prime the target *kaatib* "writer" but *laaʕib*[5] "player" with the productive root {lʕb} does. Second, the shared word pattern has to convey the same morphosyntactic interpretation; thus, the prime word *duxuul* "entering" facilitates *nuzuul* going down by virtue of sharing the pattern {fuʕuul} and morphosyntactic interpretation "singular deverbal noun", whereas the prime *quruud* "monkeys" where the pattern {fuʕuul} has a plural interpretation fails to do so (Boudelaa and Marslen-Wilson 2011, 2012). These two constraints on word pattern priming in nouns reflect the processing dependency of the word pattern as a morphemic unit whose extraction from the full form is contingent on the prior extraction of a root morpheme and whose subsequent integration into the interpretative stage of the lexical access process depends on the identification of the correct root.

Overall, the presence of root and word pattern priming demonstrates the importance of morphological structure in lexical access processes. This is in keeping with almost all approaches to morphology that assume a level of conceptual semantic representation distinct from processes of morphological decomposition and morphological representation (Zwitserlood, Bolwiender, and Drews 2005), such that upon the processing of a form like *katiibah* "squadron" and a form like *maktab* "office"[6] the same underlying root is accessed although this root has different interpretations in the two words. The fact that this happens across the board in Arabic, but only in covert tasks in Indo-European languages reflects perhaps the properties of nonconcatenative productive morphology interacting with the different demands of the priming tasks.

[5] The root {ʃmt} occurs in 6 forms; therefore, it is less productive than the root lʕb, which occurs in 22 forms (Boudelaa and Marslen-Wilson 2010b).

[6] The finding of facilitation among word pairs such as [katiibah]–[maktab] in overt priming tasks contrasts with the absence of such facilitation among word pairs like "department"–"depart" in English and other Indo-European languages like it (Marslen-Wilson 2007).

Evidence from neurophysiology, using event-related potentials that measure the electrical activity of the brain time-locked to a certain stimuli, suggests that roots and word patterns elicit neural activation with different time courses and different topographies. Specifically, word pairs differing by a consonant belonging to the root (e.g., *ʕariis–ʕariif* "bridegroom–corporal") generate a bihemispheric fronto-central activity 160 ms after the divergence point, that is, after the final consonant in this case. In contrast, word pairs differing by a vowel belonging to the word pattern (e.g., *ʕariis–ʕaruus* "bridegroom–bride") give rise to a left lateralized brain activation at 250 ms after the divergence point. This suggests that abstract bound morphemes have independent neurocognitive representations and that these morphemes are extracted during online processing (Boudelaa et al. 2009). This decompositional account of Arabic is further consolidated by recent fMRI findings suggesting that even function words elicit an increased activation of the left lateralized inferior frontal gyrus typically involved in morphological parsing processes, provided they are analyzable into a root and a pattern (Boudelaa et al. 2010a; Bozic et al. 2010).

The findings from research into Arabic morphology are interesting and clearly have far-reaching theoretical consequences stirring up debates between symbolic and subsymbolic models of morphological processing (Boudelaa and Gaskell 2002) and dual route models and connectionist models of reading (Boudelaa and Marslen-Wilson 2005). Thus, it is important not to delay any further the investigation of all other domains of linguistic description in the context of Arabic. This will benefit the field of psycholinguistics in general and will have translational benefits for Arabic language learning and language rehabilitation.

16.6 Future Trends

It is probably fair to roughly describe the evolution of psycholinguistics in terms of at least two periods. The first goes from the inception of the field in the mid-1950s to the mid-1980s when the discipline had to launch by sloughing off the fetters of behaviorism, establishing itself, and defining a research agenda. The second period started in the early 1990s and continues until today. During the current period the field has expanded at an amazing pace, has clad itself as a pivotal player in the cognitive science revolution, and has invested in the use of new imaging and computational modeling techniques—and that is essentially where the field is now.

A number of forces are likely to have a prolonged and pervasive impact on the discipline. Central among these is the revolution in brain sciences and biology that has made available a host of imaging techniques that, when combined, provide invaluable insights into the neural substrates of language processing. A second equally important force is the emergence of a growing body of research at the interface of language and other domains such as vision and memory, suggesting that the boundaries between the study of language and other aspects of cognition is narrowing. A third force is the emergence of cross-linguistic research into languages that were psycholinguistically terra incognita during the first 30 years of the discipline. Studies of such languages as Arabic, Chinese, Finnish, and Polish is certain to continue to grow and should in due course be conducive to building more universal psycholinguistic theories.

References

Abu-Rabia, S. and Taha, H. 2004. Reading and spelling error analysis of native Arabic dyslexic readers. *Reading and Writing* 17: 651–690.

Alario, F.-X., A. Costa, V. S. Ferreira, and M. J. Pickering. 2006. Architectures, representations and processes of language production. *Language & Cognitive Processes* 21: 777–789.

Altman, G. 2006. History of psycholinguistics. In *Encyclopaedia of language and linguistics*, ed. Keith Brown, 1–9. Amsterdam: Elsevier.

Beauvois, M.-F. and J. Derouesné. 1981. Lexical or orthographic agraphia. *Brain* 104: 21–49.

Bencheikh, J. E. 1979. From language molds to poetic styles: Ibn Khaldūn the definition of poetry. *Théories Analyses* 1: 13–22.

Blumenthal, A. L. 1970. *Language and psychology: Historical aspects of psycholinguistics*. New York: Wiley.

Boudelaa, S. and G. M. Gaskell. 2002. A re-examination of the default system for Arabic plurals. *Language and Cognitive Processes* 17: 321–343.

Boudelaa, S. and W. D. Marslen-Wilson. 2004a. Abstract morphemes and lexical representation: The CV-Skeleton in Arabic. *Cognition* 92: 271–303.

Boudelaa, S. and W. D. Marslen-Wilson. 2004b. Allomorphic variation in Arabic: Implications for lexical processing and representation. *Brain and Language* 90: 106–116.

Boudelaa, S. and W. D. Marslen-Wilson. 2005. Discontinuous morphology in time: Incremental masked priming in Arabic. *Language and Cognitive Processes* 20: 207–260.

Boudelaa, S. and W. D. Marslen-Wilson. 2010b. ARALEX: A lexical database for Modern Standard Arabic. *Behavior Research Methods* 42: 481–487.

Boudelaa, S. and W. D. Marslen-Wilson. 2011. Productivity and decomposability: Roots and nominal word patterns in Arabic. *Language and Cognitive Processes* 26: 624–652.

Boudelaa, S., F. Pulvermüller, O. Hauk, Y. Shtyrov, and W. D. Marslen-Wilson. 2010a. Arabic Morphology in the neural language system: A mismatch negativity study. *Journal of Cognitive Neuroscience* 22: 998–1010.

Bozic, M., Tyler, L. K., Ives, D. T., Randall, B., & Marslen-Wilson, W. D. (2010). Bi-hemispheric foundations for human speech comprehension. *Proceedings of the National Academy of Sciences, U.S.A.*, 107, 17439–17444.

Brennan, J. and L. Pylkkänen. 2012. The time-course and spatial distribution of brain activity associated with sentence processing. *Neuroimage*. 60: 1139–48.

Caramazza, A. 1997. How many levels of processing are there in lexical access? *Cognitive Neuropsychology* 14: 177–208.

Carreiras, M., A. Mechelli, A. Estevez, and C. J. Price. 2007. Brain activation for lexical decision and reading aloud: Two sides of the same coin? *Journal of Cognitive Neuroscience* 19: 433–444.

Carter, M. 1973. An Arab grammarian of the eighth century A.D. *Journal of the American Oriental Society* 93: 146–157.

Chater, N. and C. D. Manning. 2006. Probabilistic models of language processing and acquisition. *Trends in Cognitive Sciences* 10: 335–344.

Chomsky, N. 1957. *Syntactic structures*. The Hague: Mouton.

——. 1959. Review of "Verbal behavior" by B. F. Skinner. *Language* 35: 26–58.

——. 1986. *Knowledge of language*. New York: Praeger Special Studies.

Connine, C. and D. Titone. 1996. Phoneme monitoring. *Language and Cognitive Processes* 11: 635–645.

Davis, C. J. 2010. The spatial coding model of visual word identification. *Psychological Review* 117: 713–758.

Dell, G. S. 1986. A spreading activation theory of retrieval in sentence production. *Psychological Review* 93: 283–321.

Edzard, L. 2001. Sibawayhi's observations on assimilatory processes and re-syllabification in the light of optimality theory. *Journal of Arabic and Islamic Studies* 3: 48–65.

Elman, J. L., E. A. Bates, M. H. Johnson, A. Karmiloff-Smith, D. Parisi, and K. Plunkett. 1996. *Rethinking innateness: A connectionist perspective on development*. Cambridge, MA: MIT Press.

Farid, M. and J. Grainger. 1996. How initial fixation position influences visual word recognition: A comparison of French and Arabic. *Brain & Language* 53: 351–368.

Feldman, L. B. and E. G. Soltano. 1999. Morphological priming: The role of prime duration, semantic transparency, and affix position. *Brain and Language* 68: 33–39.

Fodor, J. A. 1983. *The modularity of mind*. Cambridge, MA: MIT Press.

Forster, K. I. 1976. Accessing the mental lexicon. In *New approaches to language mechanisms*, ed. R. J. Wales and E. C. T. Walker, 257–287. Amsterdam: North Holland.

Friedmann, N. and M. Haddad-Hanna. 2012. Letter position dyslexia in Arabic: From form to position. *Behavioural Neurology*.

Garnham, A., S. Garrod, and A. Sanford. 2006. Observations on the past and present of psycholinguistics. In *Handbook of psycholinguistics*, ed. M. J. Traxler and M. A. Gernsbacher, 1–18. London: Elsevier Ltd.

Gaskell, M. G. 2007. *The Oxford handbook of psycholinguistics*. Oxford: Oxford University Press.

Gernsbacher, M. A. and M. P. Kaschak. 2003. Neuroimaging studies of language production and comprehension. *Annual Review of Psychology* 54: 91–114.

Grainger, J. and A. M. Jacobs. 1996. Orthographic processing in visual word recognition: A multiple read-out model. *Psychological Review* 103: 518–565.

Graves, W. W., R. Desai, C. Humphries, M. S. Seidenberg, and J. R. Binder. 2010. Neural systems for reading aloud: A multiparametric approach. *Cerebral Cortex* 20: 1799–1815.

Harris, Z. S. 1951. *Methods in structural linguistics*. Chicago: University of Chicago Press.

Hauk, O., I. Johnsrude, and F. Pulvermüller. 2004. Somatotopic representation of action words in human motor and premotor cortex. *Neuron* 41: 301–307.

Hayes, J. R. and L. S. Flower. 1986. Writing research and the writer. *American Psychologist* 41: 1106–1113.

Hinton, G. E. and T. Shallice. 1991. Lesioning an attractor network: Investigation of acquired dyslexia. *Psychological Review* 98: 74–95.

Ibrahim, H, M. 1987. A medieval Arabic theory of language acquisition. In *Papers in the history of linguistics: Proceedings of the Third International Conference on the History of the Language Sciences (ICHoLS III)*, ed. H. Aarsleff, L. G. Kelly, and H.-J. Niederehe, 97–104. Amsterdam: Benjamins.

Ibrahim, R., Z. Eivatar, and J. Aharon-Peretz. 2007. Metalinguistic awareness and reading performance: A cross language comparison. *Journal of Psycholinguistic Research* 36: 297–317.

Joanisse, M. F. and M. S. Seidenberg. 1999. Impairments in verb morphology following brain injury: A connectionist model. *Proceedings of the National Academy of Sciences, USA* 96: 7592–7597.

Kinoshita, S. and D. Norris. 2010. Masked priming effect reflects evidence accumulated by the prime. *Quarterly Journal of Experimental Psychology* 63: 194–204.

Levelt, W. J. M. 1989. *Speaking: From intention to articulation*. Cambridge, MA: MIT Press.

Luce, P. A., S. D. Goldinger, E. Auer, and M. Vitevitch. 2000. Phonetic priming, neighbourhood activation, and PARSYN. *Perception & Psychophysics* 62: 615–625.

Lupker, S. (2007). Representation and processiong of lexically ambiguous words. In ed. M. G. Gaskell, *The Oxford Handbook of Psycholinguistics*, 159–174. Oxford University Press.

Marchman, V., K. Plunkett, and J. Goodman, J. 1997. Overregularization in English plural and past tense inflectional morphology. *Journal of Child Language* 24: 767–779.

Marcus, G. F. and S. E. Fisher, S. E. 2003. FOXP2 in focus: What can genes tell us about speech and language? *Trends in Cognitive Sciences* 7: 257–262.

Marcus, G. F., U. Brinkmann, H. Clahsen, R. Wiese, and S. Pinker. 1995. German inflection: The exception that proves the rule. *Cognitive Psychology* 29: 189–256.

Marslen-Wilson, W. D. 1975. Sentence perception as an interactive parallel process. *Science* 189: 226–228.

Marslen-Wilson, W. D. 1999. Morphological processes in language comprehension. In *Language processing*, ed. S. Garrod and M. Pickering, 101–119. Hove, UK: Psychology Press.

Marslen-Wilson, W. D. 2007. Abstractness and combination: The morphemic lexicon. In ed. M. G. Gaskell, *The Oxford handbook of psycholinguistics*, 175–93. Oxford: Oxford University Press.

Marslen-Wilson, W. D., L. K. Tyler, R. Waksler, and L. Older. 1994. Morphology and meaning in the English mental lexicon. *Psychological Review* 101: 3–33.

Marslen-Wilson, W.D. and L. K. Tyler, L.K. 1997. Dissociating types of mental computation. *Nature* 387: 592–594.

McClelland, J. L. 2010. Emergence in cognitive science. *Topics in Cognitive Science* 2: 751–770.

McClelland, J. L. and D. E. Rumelhart. 1981. An interactive activation model of context effects in letter perception: Part 1. An account of basic findings. *Psychological Review* 88: 375–407.

Meunier, D., R. Lambiotte, and E. T. Bullmore. 2010. Modular and hierarchically modular organization of brain networks. *Frontiers in Neurosciences* 4: 200.

Miller, G. A. and K. E. McKean. 1964. A chronometric study of some relations between sentences. *Quarterly Journal of Experimental Psychology* 16: 297–308.

Most, T., I. Levin, and M. Sarsour. 2007. The effect of Modern Standard Arabic orthography on speech production by Arab children with hearing loss. *Journal of Deaf Studies and Deaf Education* 13: 417–431.

Mughazy, M. 2006. Reading despite ambiguity: The role of metacognitive strategies in reading Arabic Authentic texts. *Journal of the American Association for teachers of Arabic* 39: 57–74.

Neisser, U. 1967. *Cognitive psychology*. New York: Appleton, Century, Crofts.

Norris, D. .2009. Putting it all together: A unified account of word recognition and reaction-time distributions. *Psychological Review*. 116: 207–219.

Norris, D., J. M. McQueen, and A. Cutler. 2000. Merging information in speech recognition: Feedback is never necessary. *Behavioral and Brain Sciences* 23: 299–370.

Osgood, C. E. and T. A. Seboek (eds.). 1954. *Psycholinguistics: A survey of theory and research problems*. Bloomington: Indiana University Press.

Owens, J. 2009[2] [2006]. *A linguistic history of Arabic*. Oxford: Oxford University Press.

Patterson, K. E., M. S. Seidenberg, and J. L. McClelland. 1989. Connections and disconnections: Acquired dyslexis in a computational model of reading processes. In *Parallel distributed processing: Implications for psychology and neurobiology*, ed. R. G. M. Morris, 131–181. Oxford: Clarendon Press.

Perea, M., R. Abu Mallouh, and M. Carreiras. 2010. The search of an input coding scheme: Transposed-letter priming in Arabic. *Psychonomic Bulletin and Review* 17: 375–380.

Perfetti, C. A., Beck, I., Bell, L., & Hughes, C. (1987). Phonemic knowledge and learning to read are reciprocal: A longitudinal study of first grade children. *Merrill- Palmer Quarterly, 33*, 283–319.

Perret, C. and M. Laganaro. 2012. Comparison of electrophysiological correlates of writing and speaking: A topographic ERP analysis. *Brain Topography* 25: 64–72.

Pinker, S. and A. Prince. 1988. On language and connectionism: Analysis of a parallel distributed processing of language acquisition. *Cognition* 28: 73–193.

Pinker, S. and M. Ullman. 2002. The past and future of the past tense. *Trends in Cognitive Science* 6: 456–463.

Plunkett, K. 1998. Language acquisition and connectionism. *Language and Cognitive Processes* 13: 97–104.

Pylkkänen, L. and A. Marantz. 2003. Tracking the time course of word recognition with MEG. *Trends in Cognitive Sciences* 7: 187–189.

Rastle, K. 2007. Visual word recognition. In *The Oxford handbook of psycholinguistics*, ed. M. G. Gaskell *The Oxford handbook of psycholinguistics*, 71–88. Oxford: Oxford University Press.Rastle, K., Davis, M. H., Marslen-Wilson, W., & Tyler, L. K. 2000. Morphological and semantic eVects in visual word recognition: A time course study. *Language and Cognitive Processes*, 15: 507–538.

Roediger, R. 2004. What happened to behaviorism? Available at http://www.psychologicalscience.org/observer/getArticle.cfm?id=1540.

Rogers, T. T. and J. L. McClelland. 2004. *Semantic cognition: A parallel distributed processing approach*. Cambridge, MA: MIT Press.

Roman, G. and B. Pavard. 1987. *A comparative study: How we read Arabic and French*. Amsterdam: Elsevier.

Roman, G., B. Pavard & B. Asselah, 1985. Traitement perceptive des phrases ambigues en Arabe. Cahiers de psychologie cognitive 5: 5–22.

Rumelhart, D. E. and J. L. McClelland. 1987. Learning the past tenses of English verbs: Implicit rules or parallel distributed processing. In *Mechanisms of language acquisition*, ed. B. MacWhinney, 194–248. Mahwah, NJ: Erlbaum.

Saiegh-Haddad, E. 2003. Linguistic distance and initial reading acquisition: The case of Arabic diglossia. *Applied Psycholinguistics* 24: 431–451.

Saiegh-Haddad, E. 2007. Linguistic constraints on children's ability to isolate phonemes in Arabic. *Applied Psycholinguistics* 28: 605–627.

Sampson, G. 1997. *The "language instinct" debate*. London: Continuum International Publishing Group.

Samuels, R. 2002. Nativism in cognitive science. *Mind and Language* 17: 233–265.

Saur, D. and G. Hartwigsen. 2012. Neurobiology of language recovery after stroke: Lessons from imaging studies. *Archives of Physical Medicine and Rehabilitation* 93: S15–S25.

Seidenberg, M. S. and J. L. McClelland. 1989. A distributed developmental model of word recognition and naming. *Psychological Review* 96: 523–568.

Shallice, T. 1981. Phonological agraphia and the lexical route in writing. *Brain* 104: 413–429.

Shannon, C. E. and W. Weaver. 1949. *The mathematical theory of communication*. Urbana: University of Illinois Press.

Share, D. L. 2008. On the Anglocentricities of current reading research and practice: The perils of over reliance on an "outlier" orthography. *Psychological Bulletin* 134: 584–615.

Skinner, B. F. 1957. *Verbal behaviour*. New York: Appleton-Century-Crofts.

Taft, M. and K. I. Forster. 1975. Lexical storage and retrieval of prefixed words. *Journal of Verbal Behaviour Behavior* 14: 638–647.

Taylor, K. I., B. J. Devereux, K. Acres, B. Randall, and L. K. Tyler. 2012. Contrasting effects of feature-based statistics on the categorisation and basic-level identification of visual objects. *Cognition* 122: 363–374.

Vigliocco, G. and D. P. Vinson. 2007. Semantic representation. In ed. M. G. Gaskell. *The Oxford handbook of psycholinguistics*, 196–215. Oxford: Oxford University Press.

White, S., E. Hill, J. Winston, and U. Frith. 2006. An islet of social ability in Asperger Syndrome: judging social attributes from faces. *Brain & Cognition* 61: 69–77.

Ziegler, J. C., G. O. Stone, and A. M. Jacobs. 1997. What's the pronunciation for _OUGH and the spelling for /u/? A database for computing feed forward and feedback inconsistency in English. *Behavior Research Methods, Instruments, & Computers* 29: 600–618.

Zwitserlood, P., A. Bolwiender, and E. Drews. 2005. Priming morphologically complex verbs by sentence context: effects of semantic transparency and ambiguity. *Language and Cognitive Processes* 20: 395–415.

CHAPTER 17

SECOND-LANGUAGE ACQUISITION

KARIN CHRISTINA RYDING

17.1 Overview of Arabic Second-Language Acquisition Research

The field of second-language (L2) acquisition (SLA) studies has emerged to a great extent in response to progress made in understanding the patterned and predictable nature of first-language (L1) acquisition and cognitive development. As models developed for testing and assessing the cognitive growth of human language systems, including phonology, morphology, syntax, semantics, and pragmatics, researchers in foreign language learning turned to some of these questions and models to probe the nature of second- or foreign-language learning.[1] Second-language acquisition studies since the 1980s have focused primarily on learners' internal representation of the target language (TL) and its development measured by the state of TL performance at various stages (interlanguage). It is "the study of how learners create a new language system with only limited exposure to a second language" (Gass and Selinker 2001: 1). Doughty and Long (2003: 3) define the scope of SLA as broad, encompassing "basic and applied work on the acquisition and loss of second (third, etc.) languages and dialects by children and adults, learning naturalistically and/or with the aid of formal instruction, as individuals

[1] A distinction made between "foreign"-language learning and "second"-language learning is that foreign language learning takes place in foreign-language classrooms in the L1 environment (e.g., studying Arabic in the United States), whereas second-language learning takes place in the L2 environment (e.g., studying Arabic in an Arab country), both in and outside the classroom. That said, "foreign"- and "second"-language learning are often used synonymously in both public and informal discourse about language learning.

or in groups, in foreign, second language, and lingua franca settings." SLA is driven by questions about learner success and failure, about the cognitive challenges facing adult learners of foreign languages and the fact that, once the critical period has passed, "ultimate attainment" or full acquisition of a foreign language becomes more difficult, more lengthy, and less likely to occur.[2] SLA research is also driven by pedagogical concerns about learners and how learning happens, with the ultimate goal of enhanced teaching capabilities.[3]

17.1.1 Some SLA Theories

The field of SLA explores the cognitive processes of language acquisition based on theoretical premises. As yet, no one theory has emerged that accounts for the full range of SLA research findings, but it is understood that "a theory ought to account for and explain observed phenomena and also make predictions about what is possible and what is not" (VanPatten and Williams 2007: 4). One of the problems in determining valid theoretical constructs for SLA is that each theory deals with limited aspects or components of language development and may be proved wrong in some respects but right in others. For example, behaviorism's reliance on external stimuli to account for learning has been proven inadequate for language learning but not totally wrong. The monitor model proposed and developed by Stephen Krashen in the 1970s and 1980s provided five useful hypotheses for experimentation and research design: the acquisition–learning distinction; the monitor theory; the natural-order hypothesis; the input hypothesis; and the affective filter hypothesis.[4] These hypotheses have led to substantial amounts of SLA research, some validating and some refuting particular claims of these hypotheses. In particular, research on the input hypothesis has led to significantly more emphasis on L2 "input" (from listening and reading), less tolerance of L1 use, and reduced emphasis on explanation of technical points of the grammatical system in the L2 classroom. This type of theory is referred to as "interactionist SLA" (Norris and Ortega 2003: 723).

Theory generation also resulted from Chomsky's concept of universal grammar (UG), applied originally to the study of first-language acquisition and subsequently extended to the examination of second-language acquisition, to determine whether universal principles and parameters are factors in SLA.[5] Other recent approaches

[2] The "critical period" of cognitive development refers to a point in brain maturation (variously estimated at 5–16 years of age), after which it becomes considerably more difficult to acquire a foreign or second language, especially to reach the level of "ultimate attainment." Gass (2001: 452) goes so far as to define the critical period as "A time after which successful language learning cannot take place." See Ioup et al. (1994) for analysis of this concept as it applies to an Arabic learner.

[3] "The field of SLA grew out of concerns of pedagogy so much so that in the past and to some extent, today, the fields are erroneously seen as one" (Gass 2006: 21).

[4] For an overview of these theories see VanPatten and Williams (2007: 17–35); for more detail see Krashen (1981, 1985).

[5] See Bolotin (1996) for a study of parameter resetting in Arabic language learners.

include DeKeyser's skill acquisition theory, Schmidt's noticing hypothesis, and Manfred Pienemann's processability theory.[6]

17.1.2 SLA as Distinct from Pedagogy

A key factor in the SLA research paradigm has been the deliberate distancing of SLA research and theory from the traditional applied linguistics fields of methodology and teacher training. On this topic, Alhawary (2009: 21) observes:

> Whereas foreign language pedagogy is concerned with the various approaches, methods, and techniques of how a foreign or second language should be taught, the field of second language acquisition is concerned with how a language is learned. In other words, while foreign language pedagogy reflects the teacher's perspective, SLA instead focuses on the learner, including the nature of the learner's developing language or what is referred to as the 'Interlanguage' (IL) system.

Thus, the examination of stages of learning, their characteristics, strengths, and weaknesses at various points lies at the heart of SLA studies as well as the exploration of the underlying competence that learners gradually develop as they learn the L2. The characterization of Arabic interlanguage stages in the learner, however, has been problematized by the nature of curricular decisions as to the degree of formality expected in performance of language tasks. For example, students may be taught about the Arabic case and mood systems, but are they expected to use them in oral performance? Since most native speakers do not speak *fuṣḥā*, let alone *fuṣḥā* with full case and mood inflection, how is oral performance taught and measured? How is such learner interlanguage to be analyzed?

A parallel question can be raised about the impact of learning spoken Arabic vernaculars and how testing and measurement of them fits in with assessments of more global Arabic tasks and skill levels. Different educational programs make different choices in this regard, and widely varying levels of expertise may be expected in the various modalities of speaking, listening, reading, and writing. The substantive distinctions in vernacular Arabic and its complex allotropic subsystems receive little attention in Arabic language teaching; alternative curricular models are few, and theory development has been limited.[7] That the vernacular-SA relationship is deeply contested is borne out by the fact that the American Council on the Teaching of Foreign Languages (ACTFL) proficiency assessment guidelines for Arabic, originally drafted in 1989, have only recently been revised and updated. For the most recent version see <http://actfl-proficiencyguidelines2012.org/arabic/>."[8]

[6] These theories are elaborated in DeKeyser (2007a, b), Schmidt (1995b), and Pienemann (1989, 2007).

[7] See Ryding (1991, 1995) for further discussion of this topic.

[8] For the original guidelines and their history see Allen (1985, 1987, 1989, 1990).

17.1.3 Research Issues

Major issues in current Arabic SLA research center on the development of skills in both primary and secondary discourses and on the efforts to balance these in formal and informal learning environments. Primary discourse is the language of home, family, friends, and informal relations, whereas secondary discourse is the language of formal, public, and academic situations.[9] Key constructs such as "educated native speaker" and native speaker perceptions of *fuṣḥā* use and performance have not been well defined and have underlain difficulties in research efforts. In fact, some research projects have been directed specifically to examining these constructs because of their cognitive slipperiness.[10]

Despite the spotlight on Arabic learning since the events of 9/11, the total number of Arabic-specific second-language acquisition studies is still low compared with equivalent published data and research in other foreign language fields. There are a number of reasons for this, among which are the following.

First of all, the number of Arabic SLA researchers remains small, despite substantially increased enrollments in Arabic classes and programs over the past 10 years. At most U.S. universities, the steady increase in undergraduate enrollments has not been met with increased funding for long-term SLA research or for graduate linguistics programs to expand fellowship opportunities. The nature of contemporary second-language acquisition research requires training in applied linguistics methodologies including statistical analysis, and few PhD students in Arabic language, literature, or culture have the background to pursue this research.

Second, few PhDs in applied linguistics have the necessary Arabic language skills or interest in Arabic-based research. Third, the pressure to produce teaching faculty to deal with greatly expanded Arabic undergraduate student enrollments has strongly outweighed the need to produce researchers in Arabic language acquisition. Fourth, language teaching faculty—even those with research backgrounds—are often pressured to engage in intensive and extensive language teaching that leaves little time for research and publication.

Fifth, and perhaps most importantly, if the focus of SLA research is normally on spoken interlanguage, how is this to be measured in formal Arabic classrooms? Most Modern Standard Arabic (SA)-based Arabic classes focus on narratives in SA, on reading, and on writing. Interactive discourse is difficult to practice in SA because it is artificial; moreover, it cannot lead to the development of authentic cross-cultural pragmatics because actual use depends on situation and context and often (in the real world)

[9] Whereas most European language teaching at the beginning-to-intermediate levels privileges primary or everyday discourse, Arabic language teaching does the reverse. This approach has been labeled "reverse privileging" (Ryding 2006b: 16).

[10] See Parkinson (1991, 1993, 1996, 2003) for case studies of variation in Arabic native speaker perceptions of *fuṣḥā*.

involves delicately calibrated code shifting or code mixing of registers, levels, and styles on the part of native Arabic speakers.[11]

A number of academic linguists have studied the structure and usage of spontaneous hybrid forms of spoken Arabic, going back to the Leeds Project on educated spoken Arabic, directed by T. F. Mitchell, "based on a corpus of spoken Arabic collected in different parts of the Arab world in the late 1970's" (Mitchell 1994: xiii). This project resulted in a number of articles by Mitchell (1980, 1985, 1986, 1990) and others (e.g., El-Hassan 1978; Sallam 1979; Meiseles 1980; Ibrahim 1986; Agius 1990) and one book (Mitchell and al-Hassan 1994). Several dissertations also appeared on the topic of educated spoken Arabic (Schmidt 1974; Schultz 1981; Wilmsen 1995; Mehall 1999). Gunvor Mejdell's (2006) seminal volume on mixed styles of spoken Arabic in Egypt is built around a corpus of what she terms *spoken academic discourse,* but it also includes a thorough review of previous efforts to deal with mixed forms of spoken Arabic. Ryding's entry on Educated Arabic appeared in the *Encyclopedia of Arabic Language and Linguistics* (*EALL*) in 2006. Sociolinguist Reem Bassiouney (2010) examines mixed styles in Arabic media, and Mushira Eid (2008, 2010) conceptualizes the nature of "core" and "peripheral" features of educated spoken Arabic through analysis of spoken corpora taken from broadcast interviews in Egypt. It is clear, then, that the pervasive nature of hybridity is an important factor in accurately accounting for spoken forms of Arabic [Davies et al., "Code Switching"].

17.2 State of the Art: Arabic Acquisition Studies

A limited number of published studies exist in Arabic SLA, primarily in the form of articles rather than books. The only single-author book explicitly using data-driven SLA methodology for Arabic up to now is Alhawary's (2009a) publication, *Arabic Second Language Acquisition of Morphosyntax*. In this useful book Alhawary, aside from introducing his own data and research findings, includes a chapter summarizing Arabic as a second-language research, acknowledging that such published research is until recently very "sporadic" and sparse (ibid., 48). He includes the following topics in his review of published research: contrastive and error analysis studies; performance studies; developmental interlanguage studies; and studies on SLA and UG. Topics that Alhawary does not deal with include word recognition, language learning strategies, listening

[11] As Schmidt (1996: 156–157) notes, sociopragmatic knowledge is necessary for learners to make contextually appropriate choices of strategies and linguistic forms in interpersonal discourse, and in most assessments of interlanguage development and progress non-native speakers (NNS) subjects' performance is measured against a native speaker norm. Standard practice for other foreign language performance contrasts with standard Arabic practice. In this regard, Badawi (2006: xiii) comments that "there still seems to be a barrier separating the learner from intimate internalization of Arabic in a degree similar to that achievable by serious foreign learners of say English or other commonly taught languages."

comprehension, and interlanguage pragmatics. Three of these topics have received some attention in other published works (see Khalil 2003; Keatley et al. 2004; Elkhafaifi 2005a, 2005b; Hansen 2010).

17.2.1 Hybrid Studies

In addition to the limited amount of pure SLA Arabic research, there are articles and edited books on the teaching of Arabic as a foreign language (TAFL) from the perspective of experienced scholars (see especially Agius 1990; Al-Batal 1995/2008; Wahba 2006a). Arabic pedagogy and methodology have received attention from a number of theoretical viewpoints, but as has been pointed out this kind of analysis is not necessarily identical with SLA research. One of the most salient features of Arabic language-related publications is that they are largely pragmatic and directed toward the teaching of Arabic as a foreign language based on experiential knowledge, surveys, and introspection about teaching methods and effectiveness. Many publications on teaching Arabic as a foreign language incorporate applied linguistics terminology, theories, and methods, placing them somewhere between pure SLA research and more traditional pedagogical approaches. These can be called "hybrid" studies (see, e.g., Alosh 1997).

As mentioned earlier, in addition to the relatively standard SLA and applied linguistics topics, a central issue applies particularly to Arabic and underlies analysis and evaluation of learner interlanguage: the theoretical construct of "educated native speaker" (ENS) and how it affects Arabic learner goals, approaches, strategies, and outcomes. This term has been borrowed into Arabic proficiency assessment procedures from its more general use in the U.S. Interagency Language Roundtable (ILR) proficiency skill-level descriptions, but crucial characteristics of the Arabic speech community are not normally taken into consideration when using the ENS term, such as the functional separation and variation between written and spoken language, code mixing between the two, and the different norms needed for each.[12]

17.2.2 The "Educated Native Speaker" Construct

17.2.2.1 *Badawi's Contention*

In a 2002 article, Elsaid Badawi addressed the challenge of developing level-4 ("distinguished") performance in Arabic for nonnative speakers. Among other things, he observed that the ACTFL guidelines requiring that a "superior speaker of Arabic should have superior-level competence in both Modern Standard Arabic (SA) and a spoken dialect and be able to switch between them on appropriate occasions." He stated that "to

[12] The ILR website is at http://www.govtilr.org.

the best of my knowledge, no native speaker of Arabic has superior-level speaking ability in both" (Badawi 2002: 159).

That is, Badawi disputed the defining characteristics of an educated native speaker upon which the ACTFL proficiency guidelines currently rest. In particular, he found the idea of speaking skills in SA at the superior level inappropriate for most educated Arabic speakers because these are what he termed "dormant" or receptive skills used primarily for reading and listening, and thus when "called upon [for oral use] on special and rare situations… the required skill is used haltingly and in deviation from prescriptive linguistic rules" (Badawi 2002: 160).

For Badawi, therefore, oral skills for spontaneous expression in SA are *not* part of educated everyday native Arabic ability. Then, is oral fluency in SA an appropriate or logical goal for nonnative learners? This question remains at the heart of curricular debates in the field and complicates SLA research.

17.2.2.2 *Wahba on the "Educated Language User"*

Wahba (2006b) focuses on developing a "descriptive framework" for what he terms "a realistic model of Arabic language use," a communicative model that includes vernacular Arabic that the native speaker of Arabic uses "in his or her daily life situations." This is necessary, he states, because the "communicative approach" to Arabic teaching using only SA produces "a disabled learner who cannot communicate adequately" (ibid., 141). In line with Badawi, Wahba points out that the "ideal native speaker, who is competent on equal bases in [SA and the regional vernacular] is an unusual occurrence" (ibid., 146). He suggests that a realistic approach to curriculum design would incorporate "pragmatic functional variables that account for… code mixing" based on learner needs for particular situations, shifting the "communicative" aspect of Arabic onto firm functional ground, rather than based on SA only.[13]

17.3 Current Research

Five strands of research distinguish themselves in the analysis of Arabic second-language acquisition: studies on reading comprehension and word recognition; listening comprehension; learning strategies; attitude and motivation; and acquisition order of morphosyntactic features. Since the first two fall together under comprehension studies, I will treat them first. Both reading comprehension and listening comprehension are enhanced by learners' schemata (previous knowledge of a topic area), contextual clues, familiarity with a situation, and knowing key vocabulary.

[13] Note also Schmidt's (1986: 57) observation that "the important thing to note… [in Arabic code switching] is that such switching and mixing are orderly rather than random, and variation is not really free." See also Bassiouney (2004) and Hassan (2004).

17.3.1 Reading Comprehension and Word Recognition

This area of research has yielded some of the most important findings about learning Arabic as a foreign language. Hansen's (2010: 567) carefully researched article on word recognition investigates "whether the missing [short] vowels inhibit reading speed and comprehension and whether learners are able to apply the system of root and pattern in Semitic morphology to compensate for the lack of vowel information." Her findings indicate that Arabic script constitutes a serious obstacle to comprehension at all levels. Even after vowels are added into a text, "for beginning and intermediate learners of Arabic, the additional graphical information that vowels represent adds a heavy cognitive burden on the already heavily charged decoding system" (ibid., 578). She calls the impact of the "unfamiliar graphemes" of Arabic "remarkable" in its effect on reading speed and decoding and also notes that any improvement made during the first two years of study "seems to stagnate" thereafter. These are key findings with extensive implications for teaching materials and approaches. She closes with the observation that "a fundamental principle in reading instruction" for children is to expose learners "to a multitude of easily read text material without new vocabulary and unfamiliar grammatical structures" (2010: 579). She advises building reading skills with adult foreign language learners in much the same way: "texts should be understood so easily that learners' cognitive capacity can be directed toward word recognition alone—instead of an analytical process" (ibid., 579). Certainly this contrasts with the common practice of presenting new texts loaded with unfamiliar vocabulary and requiring students constantly to decipher words as well as grasp the text's meaning.

Along these lines, Ryan's (1997/2009) research on native Arabic speakers learning to read English provides complementary data. Noting that "Arabic speaking learners of English seem to have difficulty in distinguishing English words with a similar consonant structure... and are seriously confused by the excessive amount of information present in English [orthography]" (ibid., 186). She labels this problem "vowel blindness" (ibid., 189) and proposes that "this may be due to a lack of awareness of the function which vowels perform in English. The problem seems to take the form of ignoring the presence of vowels when storing vocabulary and also an almost indiscriminate choice as to which vowel to use when one is needed" (ibid.). Ryan's conclusions are echoed by Mughazy (2005–2006: 57), where he affirms that native Arabic speakers "do not make significant use of vowel marking" but employ top-down strategies that rely "on their knowledge of content, morpho-phonemic patterns, and intuitions about the statistical probabilities of word order."

These findings, taken together with those of Khaldieh (1996, 2001), yield solid confirmation of what many professionals already know intuitively from both teaching and learning experiences. The authors' research methodologies provide empirical, data-driven results leading to the firm conclusion that considerably more attention must be paid to the cognitive processes involved in learning to read Arabic as a foreign language to improve learners' grasp of orthography and meaning.

17.3.2 Listening Comprehension

Few published works on Arabic listening comprehension have been done with the exception of the substantial work of Elkhafaifi. Khaldieh's (1993) article is a survey of listening comprehension tasks and how they could be constructed for possible use in Arabic instruction. He reviews the literature on comprehensible input, test types, and particularly recall protocol for assessing Arabic listening comprehension and gives an example of an Arabic text divided into "pausal units," which are defined as "any group of words that are syntactically related" (ibid., 213). He then describes how such a text can be used in "immediate recall protocols" to assess levels of comprehension (ibid., 215).

More recently, Elkhafaifi (2001, 2005a, 2005b) examines key aspects of listening in Arabic. In his 2001 article he surveys 56 Arabic faculty as to their academic backgrounds, awareness of methodologies, and inclusion of listening comprehension activities as classroom exercises. Among other findings, almost 99% (55 of 56) of the teachers surveyed said that they "use prelistening activities," which Elkhafaifi (2001: 63) defines as "any kind of advance organizer that prepares students for the listening comprehension passage or exercise." Just over half the respondents used authentic materials for listening exercises, with various forms of modification for lower-level learners, either in the text itself or in the task required of the students. Elkhafaifi (2001: 73) refers to this article as a "preliminary investigation" (2001: 73), admitting limitations of size and "lack of correlational analysis." It is, however, the only survey article on this topic, and the author followed up on listening comprehension in subsequent articles.

In his two 2005 articles Elkhafaifi dealt with the effects of prelistening activities and anxieties for Arabic learners. Elkhafaifi's (2005a: 2009) study on anxiety addresses "how foreign language learning anxiety and listening anxiety are related, and how, in turn, they affect student achievement and listening comprehension performance in Arabic." He surveyed over 200 students at various U.S. institutions and found that there were "significant negative correlations among listening and foreign language learning anxiety, students' listening comprehension scores, and final grades as a measure of overall achievement" (ibid., 214). Students in third-year Arabic had the lowest levels of anxiety, whereas second-year Arabic learners showed the highest levels. Elkhafaifi (2005a) speculates that the second year is often a "watershed" experience, wherein materials often become significantly more complex and challenging and performance expectations of both students and teachers rise considerably. He advises much more comprehensible listening input, the teaching of listening strategies, and conscious efforts by instructors to control stress and attend to learner anxieties at this level in particular.

According to Elkhafaifi (2005b: 509), prelistening activities that presented and previewed vocabulary words, as well as prelistening activities that previewed questions on the listening passage, "significantly improved students' overall scores." Moreover, multiple exposures to the listening passage also increased listening comprehension, regardless of the prelistening activity. Elkhafaifi (2005b: 510) concludes that "the single most useful technique the instructor can employ is to provide multiple exposures to the listening passage."

A noticeable omission in the writings on listening comprehension is any mention or discussion of comprehension of everyday spoken language, the vernacular. Attention is paid only to understanding passages in SA. This is not surprising given that almost all tertiary-level study is of SA only. However, it also points up the conceptual gap in Arabic studies between real-world Arabic skills and academic Arabic skills.

17.3.3 Learning Strategies

Research on foreign language learning strategies has expanded greatly since the 1980s, but very little has been done to analyze strategies used by Arabic learners. As Elkhafaifi (2007–2008: 73) notes, "Studies of Arabic learners in general are scarce; research on listening strategy use in particular is virtually nonexistent." Four research projects will be mentioned here: Khalil (2003), Elkhafaifi (2007–8), VanPee (2010), and Keatley et al. (2004). In general, strategies refer to conscious, explicit actions taken by learners to improve their skills. These actions can be classified as cognitive, metacognitive, compensatory, affective, social, and memory strategies. Cognitive strategies involve activities such as concept formation, analysis, reasoning, and formal practice. Metacognitive strategies include organizing, planning, and evaluating one's learning. Compensatory strategies have to do with overcoming limitations, that is, knowing how to guess, how to use context for clues to meaning, and how to manage when faced with difficult situations. Affective strategies include positive self-talk and lowering one's anxiety. Social strategies involve working with others to study, to talk, to ask questions. Memory strategies are activities that focus on retention, such as regular reviewing of material and using word lists or flash cards to memorize vocabulary.

Khalil (2003) uses Oxford's Strategy Inventory for Language Learning (SILL) to analyze strategies of 162 students of Arabic in U.S. tertiary institutions.[14] He tested for differences in strategy use by level of proficiency and gender. Results indicate that proficiency level was not a factor in strategy use but that female students "used compensatory, metacognitive and social strategies significantly more often than males" (ibid., 34).[15] Elkhafaifi's (2007–2008) study of listening strategies for 30 Arabic students confirms that gender was a factor in strategy use, stating that "overall, females reported more strategy use than males" (ibid., 80). His results also show that "cognitive strategy use predominates at each course level" and that "as the course level increased, so did reports of metacognitive strategy use" (ibid., 81).

VanPee's (2010) study of vocabulary-learning strategies among 39 students at Georgetown University confirms Elkhafaifi's (2007–8) finding about differences in strategy use by gender but found that the concept of more diverse strategy use among successful students was not valid. The most successful students found a limited number

[14] See Oxford (1990, 1994).

[15] Khalil references previous studies on strategies for Arabic learning including Aweiss (1993) and Alosh (1997).

of strategies that worked for them and stuck with them rather than experimenting with others. Lower-performing students tried many different strategies but had less success overall.

Keatley et al. (2004) focuses on a group of nine intermediate level students and the differences in learning strategies between heritage and nonheritage learners. For vocabulary, a range of memorization strategies (kinesthetic, auditory, visual) took first place over find–apply morphological patterning. In reading, vocabulary study took precedence over contextualized cues or root–pattern cues. Learners who had studied Latin or German found it easier to understand the system of desinential inflection. Interestingly, handwriting turned out to be a problem for many at the intermediate level because learners had not hitherto been required to write clearly and quickly, and a number of them had to strategize to improve their writing, mainly by painstaking practice and special attention to detail. For speaking SA (the only option for these students), many reported needing to "find opportunities to practice" as a strategy, but heritage learners devised different strategies, needing to convert their vernacular skills into SA through keeping separate language tracks in their minds and consciously monitoring their performance.

17.3.4 Affect: Attitudes, Motivations, Beliefs, Myths

Issues surrounding affect and anxiety are key ones for Arabic and have received some well-designed attention in published SLA research. Standard attitude problems such as Westerners' unfamiliarity or discomfort with regard to Arabic language and culture have been intensified in recent years by Western media spotlighting and highlighting adversarial aspects of Arab society and politics (particularly Islamist movements), so that even when students are seriously interested in learning Arabic many nonetheless have reservations and even fears about Arab culture and behavior or about visiting an Arab country. This is to say that myths about Arabic (pace Ferguson 1959) still survive and have sometimes morphed into powerful negative stereotypes. Learner affect and anxiety are therefore issues that need to be explored and understood because they impact learner progress, potential, and proficiency.[16] Studies carried out in Israel as well as the United States and Europe have dealt with affective issues in Arabic learning. Key topics include reactions to study abroad experiences as well as L1 culture-based and classroom-based motivations, beliefs, and anxieties.

One of the earliest articles on this topic was Suleiman's (1991) longitudinal study of five graduate students of Arabic at the University of St. Andrews in Scotland. It focuses on two sets of learner variables, affective issues and personality factors, and finds that, among other things, "none of the learners betray the slightest hint of being interested in the TL from an integrative motivation perspective" (ibid., 100). It also finds that learners'

[16] Regarding myths about Arabic, see also Ryding (1995).

primary motivation was "neither instrumental nor integrative, but rather intellectual and personal" (100), with several of them stating that they originally chose to study Arabic because it presented a learning challenge. A more recent article (Husseinali 2006) investigates 120 students in first- and second-year AFL classes in the United States. The findings of Husseinali focused on differences in motivation between heritage and non-heritage learners, suggesting that heritage learners need special coursework "with literary content as their mainstay" and that nonheritage learners might be "better-served if focus is placed on the linguistic message within a general and contemporary frame of Arabic culture" (ibid., 409).

Kuntz and Belnap (2001), Palmer (2008), and Ishmael (2010) all examine attitudes and beliefs of Arabic study-abroad students. Their findings are interesting for several reasons, indicating that students need and want to study vernacular Arabic before their study-abroad experience (Palmer 2008), that women have significantly more difficulty meeting and interacting with native Arabic speakers than men (Ishmael 2010), and that the academic quality of study abroad programs "is key to most students' successful attainment of higher levels of proficiency" (Kuntz and Belnap 2001: 108). Although some of these findings may seem self-evident, their impact on most university curricula has been minimal.

Israeli scholars have investigated Arabic learning from a social–political status point of view (Brosh 1993) as well as in terms of the teaching of SA in comparison with vernacular (Brosh and Olshtain 1995; Donitsa-Schmidt, Inbar, and Shohamy 2004). "The Israeli context presents an unusual and conflicted interethnic setting in which Arabic, the second official language, is acquired by Hebrew speakers," state Brosh and Olshtain (1995: 250), who measured achievement in SA based on previous exposure to vernacular Arabic in middle school. They find that students without previous exposure to spoken Arabic "gained significantly higher scores" (ibid., 257) than those who had previously studied Palestinian vernacular. They analyze this unusual result carefully, advising further research. Donitsa-Schmidt et al., on the other hand, in a later article conclude that it is "vital to include the spoken variety as a major component of the curricula" (ibid., 227) and that "young learners who study spoken Arabic, as opposed to those who do not, report holding more positive attitudes towards the Arabic language and its culture" (ibid., 226). Given the dominant, founding Israeli cultural narrative, the study of Arabic in this context is deeply problematic in many respects, in terms of cultural values, attitudes, motivations, and myths—with respect not only to students but also to their parents and even to their teachers.

17.3.5 Acquisition of Arabic Word Order and Morphosyntactic Features

The two major contributors to this field are Alhawary (2009a, 2009b, 2009c) and Nielsen (1994, 1996, 19971, 1997b, 2009). Both of these researchers undertake analyses testing Pienemann's (2007) processability theory (PT) for its validity when applied to Arabic learners, and both use spoken SA as their research medium. PT theory posits a "processability hierarchy" (ibid., 151) wherein "L2 learners can produce only those linguistic forms for which they have acquired the necessary processing procedures" (ibid., 152) and that "given the hierarchical nature of the processability hierarchy none of the processing procedure constraints in the hierarchy can be skipped because every lower procedure constitutes a prerequisite for the next higher one. Therefore frequency cannot override the constraints of the hierarchy" (ibid.). In other words, this hierarchy represents a fixed linear structure for the L2 learner wherein no developmental stages can be skipped or omitted. Two implications of Pienemann's theory are that (1) frequency of input is irrelevant, and (2) formal instruction will have little or no effect on learners unless or until they have progressed through the hierarchy to a point where they are cognitively ready to notice the instruction, assimilate it, and incorporate it in their interlanguage. In his 1989 article, Pienemann asserts that "the influence of teaching is restricted to the learning of items for which the learner is 'ready'... teaching can only promote acquisition by presenting what is learnable at a given point in time. To put this another way, items in a syllabus need to be taught in the order in which they are learnable" (63). Pienemann refers to this as the "teachability hypothesis."

The role of L1 transfer is a key issue here, determining to some extent just where learners are located on the processability hierarchy prior to their exposure to the L2. (French learners of Arabic, for example, apparently have fewer problems acquiring gender agreement in noun–adjective structures.)[17]

Working with Danish learners of Arabic, Nielsen (1997b: 63) examines acquisition order for the use of the definite article "*al-* in noun-phrase initial position...; agreement procedures in noun phrase structures of noun-adjective, idafa constructions, and demonstrative noun phrases, and...agreement procedures between noun or noun-phrase subjects and verbs." Her findings both confirm and question processability theory. The findings include her observation that "the transfer of gender from a noun to an adjective is a process that starts when the learner acquires a certain adjective" (ibid., 76) with learners using one "universal form" (masculine, feminine, or plural) of the adjective in all situations until they learn the rules for modification of form. Nielsen also investigates the acquisition of the demonstrative noun phrase and the idafa structure, "neither of which was acquired by the learners" (ibid., 79) during her study.[18] Her analysis of these results, both of which require "regressive transfer" (i.e., transfer of information from a noun to an item that precedes it), relies on transfer from the learners' L1, Danish "to circumvent regressive transfer of morphological information" (ibid.,

[17] Inasmuch as Arabic is often taught as an L3 or even L4, features of the foreign language hierarchy—such as gender agreement—learned for previously studied languages (often French, German, or Spanish for Americans) may be retained for validation as processing requirements in Arabic, thereby accelerating the acquisition process.

[18] Acquisition of language structures is seen by Pienemann as a process "the most interesting point of which is the first systematic use of the structure" rather than full mastery of the structure (Nielsen 1997b: 58).

83). That is, they fail to apply regressive transfer and instead use a structure more similar to Danish, that is, **hādhā ijtimā‘* instead of *hādhā l-ijtimā‘* for the definite demonstrative phrase (Danish: *dette möte*), or **al-madīna tūnis* (Danish: *byen Tunis*) instead of *madīnat tūnis*.

Alhawary (2009a) deals with gender agreement, tense/aspect and verbal agreement, acquisition of null subjects, and acquisition of negation, mood, and case, dedicating a chapter of his book to each one. In accord with Nielsen's findings, he notes that learners found demonstrative gender agreement difficult; much more difficult than verbal agreement (between subject and verb; 70). Alhawary's study of the emergence of negative constructions shows that *laa* was acquired early, *maa* was acquired in few participants, *lam* was produced only once in one participant, but the negative future marker *lan* emerged in all participants by the end of the study (ibid., 145). Use of the accusative case on the predicate of *kaana* or *laysa* does not emerge at all in his study. Alhawary's studies include a wide range of participants (L1 English, Spanish, French, or Japanese) and comes to the conclusion that processability theory "does not provide an adequate account of the data" (ibid., 170) but that "the role of L1 transfer... seems to have a significant role" (ibid., 171). In his chapter on application of findings, he advises that basic forms be "recycled continuously in the input for a considerable amount of time" (ibid., 178).

As instances of pure SLA research into Arabic, both these authors provide excellent models for further research into Arabic target language forms and their acquisition patterns over time.

17.4 Major Issues, Future Trends in Arabic SLA

Materials and methods of teaching need to take SLA research findings into account, and the amount of SLA research needs to expand greatly. Major issues that face the field of Arabic language learning today include clarification of teaching and learning goals, incorporation of vernacular Arabic into academic programs, and revision of proficiency skill-level descriptions.[19] A key aspect of research is problematization: developing key questions whose answers provide a theoretical framework for further research and application. A second major aspect is prioritization: which are the central topics and themes that require applied linguistics research in the immediate and long-term

[19] A major issue that relates to Arabic pedagogy is the expansion, upgrading, and professionalization of teacher training, including exposure to the Arabic grammatical tradition. Although this topic is not within the parameters of this study of second-language acquisition, it is an essential parallel component of progress in Arabic language learning. See Owens 2005: 116; Al-Batal 2006: 42–43; Al-Batal and Belnap 2006: 393–394.

future? Gass (2006: 22) lists interlanguage, errors, the role of the native language (L1), and developmental sequences as key topics for future SLA research for Arabic. Some other key areas of investigation include the following topics:

1) How exactly does the vernacular–literary split affect the acquisition of ultimate attainment in Arabic as a foreign language? Is there a way to accelerate the accurate development of interpersonal discourse as well as the acquisition of interlanguage pragmatics?
2) What classroom approaches and materials would be most effective for developing proficiency in all four skills: reading, writing, listening, speaking?
3) What forms of Arabic have maximal generality or projection value for use throughout the Arab world?
4) What templates of study abroad programs yield the best results?
5) In proficiency testing, what is the most effective approach to identifying and analyzing problem areas, including sample ratability, tester training, interrater reliability, compatibility of different systems, and issues regarding the validity and appropriateness of Arabic register shifting and code mixing?
6) What are best practices for Arabic heritage learners? How can their linguistic and cultural backgrounds be most effectively developed into professional-level skills?

Research design; data analysis; concepts such as input, intake, and interaction; the natural order hypothesis, skill acquisition theory; processability theory; sociocultural theory; error correction and feedback; and other topics need to be further investigated and redefined for Arabic-specific purposes. Little is known about Arabic learner cognition, memory, or ultimate attainment. If significant research into acquisition of Arabic as a foreign language does not happen, key decisions on how to build fluency, accuracy, and authentic interactive discourse skills will continue to be based not on Arabic-grounded findings but solely on research within Western language paradigms.

References

Agius, Dionisius (ed.). 1990. *Diglossic tension: Teaching Arabic for communication*. Leeds: Folia Scholastica.

Aweiss, S. 1993. Cognitive processes in foreign language reading: Reasoning operations, comprehension monitoring, strategy use, and knowledge sources. *Al-Arabiyya* 26: 1–17.

Alhawary, Mohammad T. 2009a. *Arabic second language acquisition of morphosyntax*. New Haven, CT: Yale University Press.

——. 2009b. Second language acquisition. In *Encyclopedia of Arabic language and linguistics*, Vol. 4, ed. Kees Versteegh, Associate Editors: Mushira Eid, Alaa Elgibali, Manfred Woidich, Andrzej Zaborski, 138–146. Leiden: Brill.

——. 2009c. Speech processing prerequisites or L1 transfer? Evidence from English and French L2 learners of Arabic. *Foreign Language Annals* 42: 367–390.

Allen, Roger. 1985. Arabic proficiency guidelines. *Al-Arabiyya* 18: 45–70.
——. 1987. The ACTFL guidelines and Arabic. *Al-Arabiyya* 20: 43–49.
——. 1989. The ACTFL Arabic proficiency guidelines. *Foreign Language Annals* 22: 373–392.
——. 1990. Proficiency and the teacher of Arabic: Curriculum, course, and classroom. *Al-Arabiyya* 23:1–30.
Alosh, Mahdi. 1997. *Learner, text and context: in foreign language acquisition: An Arabic perspective.* Columbus: Ohio State University National Foreign Language Resource Center.
Badawi, Elsaid M. 1985. Educated spoken Arabic: A problem in teaching Arabic as a foreign language. In *Scientific and humanistic dimensions of language: Festschrift for Robert Lado*, ed. Kurt R. Jankowsky, 15–22. Amsterdam: John Benjamins.
——. 2002. In the quest for the level 4+ in Arabic: Training level 2–3 learners in independent reading. In *Developing professional-level language proficiency*, ed. Betty Lou Leaver and Boris Shekhtman, 156–176. Cambridge, UK: Cambridge University Press.
——. 2006. Arabic for non-native speakers in the 21st century: A shopping list. In *A handbook for Arabic language teaching professionals in the 21st century*, ed. Kassem Wahba, Zeinab Taha, and Liz England, ix–xiv. Mahwah, NJ: Lawrence Erlbaum Associates.
Bassiouney, Reem. 2004. Diglossic switching in the Egyptian speech community: Implications for teaching spoken Egyptian Arabic. In *Contrastive rhetoric: Issues, insights and pedagogy*, ed. Nagwa Kassabgy, Zeinab Ibrahim, and Sabiha Aydelott, 95–114. Cairo: American University in Cairo Press.
—— (ed.). 2010. *Arabic and the media*. Leiden: Brill.
Al-Batal, Mahmoud (ed.). [1995] 2008. *The teaching of Arabic as a foreign language.* Provo, UT: American Association of Teachers of Arabic. Reprint, Georgetown University Press.
——. 2006. Facing the crisis: teaching and learning Arabic in the United States in the post-September 11 era. *ADFL Bulletin* 37: 39–46.
Al-Batal, Mahmoud and Kirk Belnap. 2006. The teaching of Arabic in the United States: Realities, needs, future directions. In *A handbook for Arabic language teaching professionals in the 21st century*, ed. Kassem Wahba et al., 389–400.
Bolotin, Naomi. 1996. Resetting parameters in acquiring Arabic. In *PAL*, vol. 9, ed. Mushira Eid and Dilworth Parkinson, 167–178. Amsterdam: John Benjamins.
Brosh, Hezi. 1993. The influence of language status on language acquisition: Arabic in the Israeli setting. *Foreign Language Annals* 26: 347–358.
Brosh, Hezi and Elite Olshtain. 1995. Language skills and the curriculum of a diglossic language. *Foreign Language Annals* 28: 247–260.
DeKeyser, Robert. (ed.). 2007a. *Practice in a second language: Perspectives from applied linguistics and cognitive psychology*. Cambridge, UK: Cambridge University Press.
——. 2007b. Skill acquisition theory. In *Theories in second language acquisition*, ed. Bill VanPatten and Jessica Williams, 97–114. London: Routledge.
Donitsa-Schmidt, Smadar, Ofra Inbar, and Elana Shohamy. 2004. The effects of teaching spoken Arabic on students' attitudes and motivation in Israel. *Modern Language Journal* 88: 217–228.
Doughty, Catherine J. and Michael H. Long. 2003. *The handbook of second language acquisition.* Oxford: Blackwell.
Eid, Mushira. 2008. Arabic or Arabics: The core and the variable. Paper presented at the Arabic Linguistics Symposium 22, March, College Park, Md..
——. 2010. Hybridity and the crossing of linguistic borders. Paper presented at the Georgetown University Round Table on Language and Linguistics, March.

Elgibali, Alaa (ed.). 1996. *Understanding Arabic: Essays in contemporary linguistics in honor of El-Said Badawi*. Cairo: American University in Cairo Press.

—— (ed.). 2005. *Investigating Arabic: Current parameters in analysis and learning*. Leiden: Brill.

Ferguson, Charles A. 1959. Myths about Arabic. In *Readings in the sociology of language*, ed. Joshua Fishman, 375–381. The Hague: Mouton.

Gass, Susan. 2006. Models of second language acquisition. In *A Handbook for Arabic language teaching professionals in the 21st century*, ed. Kassem Wahba et al., 21–33. Mahwah, NJ: Lawrence Erlbaum Associates.

Gass, Susan M. and Larry Selinker. 2001. *Second language acquisition: An introductory course*. Mahwah, NJ: Lawrence Erlbaum Associates.

Hansen, Gunna Funder. 2010. Word recognition in Arabic as a foreign language. *Modern Language Journal* 94: 567–581.

El-Hassan, S. A. 1978. Educated spoken Arabic in Egypt and the Levant: A critical review of diglossia and related concepts. *Archivum Linguisticum* 8: 112–132.

El-Khafaifi, Hussein. 2001. Teaching listening in the Arabic classroom: A survey of current practice. *Al-Arabiyya* 34: 55–90.

Hassan, Mona Kamel. 2004. Classical and colloquial Arabic: Are they used appropriately by non-native speakers? In *Contrastive rhetoric: Issues, insights and pedagogy*, ed. Nagwa Kassabgy, Zeinab Ibrahim, and Sabiha Aydelott, 83–94. Cairo: American University in Cairo Press.

Husseinali, Ghassan. 2006. Who is studying Arabic and why? A survey of Arabic students' orientations at a major university. *Foreign Language Annals* 39: 397–414.

Ibrahim, Muhammad. 1986. Standard and prestige language: A problem in Arabic sociolinguistics. *Anthropological Linguistics* 28: 115–126.

Ioup, Georgette, Elizabeth Boustagui, Manal El Tigi, and Martha Moselle. 1994. Reexamining the critical period hypothesis: A case study of successful SLA in a naturalistic environment. *Studies in Second Language Acquisition* 16: 73–98.

Ishmael, Aja. 2010. Studying abroad in the Arabic-speaking world: Gender perspectives. Paper presented at the Georgetown University Round Table on Languages and Linguistics (GURT), March.

Kassabgy, Nagwa, Zeinab Ibrahim, and Sabiha Aydelott (eds.). 2004. *Contrastive rhetoric: Issues, insights and pedagogy*. Cairo: American University in Cairo Press.

Keatley, Catharine, Anna Chamot, Shawn Greeenstreet, and Abbe Spokane. 2004. *Learning strategies of students of Arabic*. Washington, DC: National Capital Language Resource Center. Available at http://www.nclrc.org.

——. 2005a. Listening comprehension and anxiety in the Arabic language classroom. *Modern Language Journal* 89: 206–220.

——. 2005b. The effect of prelistening activities on listening comprehension in Arabic learners. *Foreign Language Annals* 38: 505–513.

——. 2007–2008. An exploration of listening strategies: A descriptive study of Arabic learners. *Al-Arabiyya* 40–41: 71–86.

Khaldieh, Salim. 1993. Listening comprehension: Construct, tasks and tests. In *Investigating Arabic: Linguistic, pedagogical and literary studies in honor of Ernest N. McCarus*, ed. Raji Rammuny and Dilworth Parkinson, 207–218. Columbus, OH: Greyden Press.

——. 1996. Word recognition of Arabic as a foreign language by American learners: The role of phonology and script. *Al-Arabiyya* 29: 129–152.

——. 2001. The relationship between knowledge of iʿraab, lexical knowledge, and reading comprehension of nonnative readers of Arabic. *Modern Language Journal* 85: 416–431.

Khalil, Aziz. 2003. Assessment of the use of language learning strategies of American learners of Arabic as a foreign language. *Al-Arabiyya* 36: 27–47.

Krashen, Stephen. 1981. *Second language acquisition and second language learning.* Oxford: Pergamon Press.

——. 1985. *The input hypothesis: Issues and implications.* London: Longman.

Kuntz, Patricia and R. Kirk Belnap. 2001. Beliefs about learning held by teachers and their students at two Arabic programs abroad. *Al-Arabiyya* 34: 91–113.

Mehall, David John. 1999. *The verb morphology of unscripted media Arabic.* PhD diss., Georgetown University.

Meiseles, Gustav. 1980. Educated spoken Arabic and the Arabic language continuum. *Archivum Linguisticum* 11: 118–143.

Mitchell, T.F. 1980. Dimensions of style in a grammar of educated spoken Arabic. *Archivum Linguisticum* 11: 89–106.

——. 1985. Sociolinguistic and stylistic dimensions of the educated spoken Arabic of Egypt and the Levant. In *Language standards and their codification*, ed. Douglas J. Woods, 42–57. Exeter: Exeter University Press.

——. 1986. What is educated spoken Arabic? *International Journal of the Sociology of Language* 61: 7–32.

Mitchell, T. F. and Shahir el-Hassan. 1994. *Modality, mood and aspect in spoken Arabic.* London: Kegan Paul International.

Mejdell, Gunvor. 2006. *Mixed styles in spoken Arabic in Egypt.* Leiden: Brill.

Mughazy, Mustafa. 2005–2006. Reading despite ambiguity: The role of metacognitive strategies in reading Arabic authentic texts. *Al-Arabiyya* 38–39: 57–74.

Nielsen, Helle Lykke. 1994. How to teach Arabic communicatively: A preliminary evaluation of aims, achievements and problems at the Odense TAFL program. *Al-Arabiyya* 27: 27–50.

——. 1996. How to teach Arabic communicatively: Toward a theoretical framework for TAFL. In *Understanding Arabic*, ed. Alaa. Elgibali, 211–239. Cairo: American University in Cairo Press.

——. 1997a. Acquisition order in Arabic as a foreign language: A cognitive approach. In *Ethnic Encounter and Culture Change*, ed. M'hammed Sabour and Knut S. Vikør, 250–270. Bergen: Nordic Society for Middle Eastern Studies.

——. 1997b. On acquisition order of agreement procedures in Arabic learner language. *Al-Arabiyya* 30: 49–93.

——. 2009. Second language teaching. In *Encyclopedia of Arabic language and linguistics*, Vol. 4, ed. Kees Versteegh, Associate Editors: Mushira Eid, Alaa Elgibali, Manfred Woidich, Andrzej Zaborski, 146–158. Leiden: Brill.

Norris, John and Lourdes Ortega. 2003. Defining and measuring SLA. In *The handbook of second language acquisition*, ed. Catherine J. Doughty and Michael H. Long, 717–761. Oxford: Blackwell.

Owens, Jonathan. 2005. The grammatical tradition and Arabic language teaching: A view from here. In *Investigating Arabic: Current parameters in analysis and learning*, ed. Alaa Elgibali, 103–116. Leiden: Brill.

Oxford, Rebecca. 1990. *Language learning strategies: What every teacher should know.* New York: Newbury House.

——. 1994. Teaching learning strategies and cross-culturalism in the language classroom. Paper presented at the Georgetown University Roundtable on Languages and Linguistics, Georgetown University.

Palmer, Jeremy. 2008. Arabic diglossia: Student perceptions of spoken Arabic after living in the Arabic-speaking world. *Arizona working papers in SLA & Teaching* 15: 81–95. Available at http://w3.coh.arizona.edu/awp/AWP15/AWP15%5BPalmer%5D.pdf.

Parkinson, Dilworth. 1991. Searching for modern *fusha*: Real-life formal Arabic. *Al-Arabiyya* 24: 31–64.

——. 1993. Testing native speakers: Implications for teaching Arabic to non-native speakers. In *Investigating Arabic: Linguistic, pedagogical and literary studies in honor of Ernest N. McCarus*, ed. Raji Rammuny and Dilworth Parkinson, 191–206. Columbus, OH: Greyden Press.

——. 1996. Variability in standard Arabic grammar skills, In *Understanding Arabic*, ed. Alaa. Elgibali, 91–101. Cairo: American University in Cairo Press.

——. 2003. Verbal features in oral *fusha* performances in Cairo. *International Journal of the Sociology of Language* 163: 27–41.

Pienemann, Manfred. 1989. Is language teachable? Psycholinguistic experiments and hypotheses. *Applied Linguistics* 10: 52–79.

——. 2007. Processability theory. In *Theories in second language acquisition*, ed. Bill VanPatten and Jessica Williams, 137–154. London: Routledge.

Rouchdy, Aleya (ed.). 1992. *The Arabic language in America*. Detroit, MI: Wayne State University Press.

Ryan, Ann. [1997] 2009[10]. Learning the orthographical form of L2 vocabulary—A receptive and a productive process. In *Vocabulary: Description, acquisition and pedagogy*, ed. Norbert Schmitt and Michael McCarthy, 181–198. Cambridge, UK: Cambridge University Press.

Ryding, Karin.1991. Proficiency despite diglossia: A new approach for Arabic. *Modern Language Journal* 75: 212–218.

——. 1995. Discourse competence in TAFL: Skill levels and choice of language variety in the Arabic classroom. In *Teaching of Arabic as a foreign language: Issues and directions*, ed. Mahmoud Al-Batal, 223–231. Provo, UT: American Association of Teachers of Arabic.

——. 2006a. Teaching Arabic in the United States. In ed. Kassem Wahba et al., 13–20.

——. 2006b. Educated Arabic. *Encyclopedia of Arabic language and linguistics*, Vol. 1, ed. Kees Versteegh, Associate Editors: Mushira Eid, Alaa Elgibali, Manfred Woidich, Andrzej Zaborski, 666–671. Leiden: Brill.

Saleh, M.S. 1999. *Cognitive and metacognitive learning strategies used by adult learners of Arabic as a foreign language*. DEd. diss., Virginia Tech, Blacksburg.

Sallam, A. M. 1979. Concordial relations within the noun phrase in educated spoken Arabic. *Archivum Linguisticum* 10: 20–56.

Schmidt, Richard W. 1974. *Sociolinguistic variation in spoken Egyptian Arabic: A re-examination of the concept of diglossia*. PhD diss., Brown University, Providence RI.

——. 1986. Applied sociolinguistics: The case of Arabic as a second language. *Anthropological Linguistics* 28: 55–72.

—— (ed.). 1995a. *Attention and awareness in foreign language learning*. Manoa: University of Hawaii Second Language Teaching and Curriculum Center.

——. 1995b. Consciousness and foreign language learning: A tutorial on the role of attention and awareness in learning. In *Attention and awareness in foreign language learning*, ed. Richard

Schmidt, 1–64. Manoa: University of Hawaii Second Language Teaching and Curriculum Center.

——. 1996. Developmental issues in interlanguage pragmatics. *Studies in Second Language Acquisition* 18: 149–169.

Schultz, David. 1981. *Diglossia and variation in formal spoken Arabic in Egypt*. PhD diss., University of Wisconsin, Madison.

Suleiman, Yasir. 1991. Affective and personality factors in learning Arabic as a foreign language: A case study. *Al-Arabiyya* 24: 83–110.

VanPatten, Bill and Jessica Williams (eds.). 2007. *Theories in second language acquisition*. London: Routledge.

VanPee, Katrien. 2010. Vocabulary learning strategies of university learners of Arabic. Paper presented at the Georgetown University Round Table on Languages and Linguistics (GURT), March.

Wahba, Kassem. 2006. Arabic language use and the educated language user. In ed. Kassem Wahba et al., 139–155. Mahwah, NJ: Lawrence Erlbaum Associates.

Wahba, Kassem, Zeinab Taha, and Elizabeth England (eds.). 2006. *A handbook for Arabic language teaching professionals in the 21st century*. Mahwah, NJ: Lawrence Erlbaum Associates.

Wilmsen, David. 1995. *The word play's the thing: Educated spoken Arabic in a theatrical community in Cairo*. PhD diss., University of Michigan.

CHAPTER 18

THE ARABIC WRITING SYSTEM*

PETER T. DANIELS

18.1 Introduction

THE Arabic language has been written with essentially the same script since the Quran first took written shape, and indeed sporadically even before. A few commercial papyri have also survived from the first decades AH (640s–650s CE). The script and orthography of the Quran have been normative for written Arabic of all kinds since the fixing of a canonical, vocalized text by the 5th/11th century.[1]

This chapter begins with a linguistic description of the components of Classical/Modern Standard Arabic writing, followed by accounts of their use to represent the language and of the use of the script as art and in technology. The chapter is completed by summaries of both the past and prospects of the script.

18.2 What It Is

As in all the ancestral scripts of the West Semitic family, the basic symbols denote only consonants, and they are written in horizontal lines from right to left, the linear skeleton

* My thanks to Woodford A. Beach, Tim Buckwalter, Beatrice Gruendler, Elinor Saiegh-Haddad, Clive Holes, Larry Hyman, and Dorit Ravid for valuable assistance and especially to Jonathan Owens for his careful reading and penetrating suggestions.

[1] The authoritative summary from the previous generation is Endress (1982) (and subsequent chapters in the volume), containing even bibliographies for topics not treated in the text. See also Sourdel-Thomine (1978) and especially Moritz (1918).

(*rasm*)[2] of most words being written as a unit, without lifting the pen. Largely optional symbols are available for vowels and certain morphophonemic features of the language.

18.2.1 Consonants

The Arabic script has 28 consonant letters and one obligatory ligature that has sometimes been counted as a 29th letter. Presentations of Arabic script customarily show (Table 18.1) that each letter appears in four forms (initial, medial, final, and independent), but this is misleading: the different "forms" of the letters are simply shapes conditioned by their surroundings, and most need not be learned separately. The shapes traditionally called "initial" can be taken as the bases (Table 18.2).

Most of the letters within a word can be written without lifting the pen except to add the dots and the strokes (of ك, ط, and ظ) that complete some of the letters. The shape of a few letters changes to accommodate the stroke connecting it from the preceding letter to the right, most noticeably the two letters ﻋ, ﻏ (or better, this one shape) > ـﻌ, and ﻫ unwinds to ﻬ or sometimes the alternative form ـہـ. Exceptions to joining are ا, د, ذ, ر, ز, and و; these six letters (or better, these four shapes) do not connect with any letter that follows them on the left. The succeeding letter within the word then appears in the base shape. At the end of the word, several of the shapes receive decorative flourishes: ﺑ ﺗ ﺛ ﻓ become a shallow bowl (the dots move off the tooth [sometimes called a minim] but not off the loop): ب ت ث ف; ﻗ ﻧ become a deeper bowl: ق ن; and ﻳ takes an "oil lamp" shape: ي. The [3]ح, ص, س, and ع shapes

Table 18.1 Excerpt from traditional presentation of the Arabic script

Independent	Final	Medial	Initial	Transliteration
ب	ـب	ـبـ	بـ	b
ح	ـح	ـحـ	حـ	ḥ
—	ـد	—	د	d
ص	ـص	ـصـ	صـ	ṣ

Table 18.2 The letters of Arabic (read right to left)

ﻳ	ﻭ	ﻫ	ﻧ	ﻣ	ﻟ	ﻛ	ﻗ[a]	ﻓ[a]	ﻏ	ﻋ	ﻇ	ﻃ	ﺿ	ﺻ	ﺷ	ﺳ	ﺯ	ﺭ	ﺫ	ﺩ	ﺧ	ﺣ	ﺟ	ﺛ	ﺗ	ﺑ	ا
y	w	h	n	m	l	k	q	f	ġ	ʿ	ẓ	ṭ	ḍ	ṣ	š	s	z	r	ḏ	d	x	ḥ	ğ	ṯ	t	b	ā

a. In Maghribi (northwest African) writing, *f* is ڢ and *q* is ڧ.

[2] Traditional Arabic terminology is added where useful.

[3] But not ط; note that ﺻ has a minim following the loop and ﻃ does not.

acquire a graceful curve (clockwise following a minim, counterclockwise otherwise): ع ح س ص. The ک adds a miniature of itself: ك. The letters ل and م reach below the baseline: م ل. Final ه has the distinctive shape ـه, and when it is unconnected to the right or left, ه. These ten shapes (amounting to 20 or 21 [ة; 18.2.3] letters; the rest are the six nonconnectors plus ط and ظ) account for most word-ending characters, so there is little need for extra space between words in Arabic-script texts.

Because the letter that originally denoted the glottal stop /ʔ/ is no longer used for that purpose (see 18.4.3.1), a character not counted as a letter—but not omissible—has been introduced: ء (*hamza*; see 18.3.1.3).

In handwriting and in careful typography (a standard that has only recently been approached in computer Arabic typesetting; 18.3.3), numerous ligatures (distinctive combinations of adjacent shapes—in which the separate letters can sometimes be hard to distinguish) have developed, but only one is obligatory: the sequence ل then ا appears as لا. The name *Allāh* is condensed to الله.

18.2.2 Vowels

The three vowel phonemes of Classical and Modern Standard Arabic are notated optionally with َ *a* (*fatḥa*), ِ *i* (*kasra*), and ُ *u* (*ḍamma*). The marks are placed above or below the letter for the consonant that precedes. A further mark, ْ (*sukūn*), is placed above the letter for a consonant followed by no vowel.

18.2.3 Other Points

A number of other points can be considered morphophonemic. A triplet of signs that indicate the pronunciation of a consonant *n* not written with a letter is ً ٍ ٌ (*tanwīn*), effectively doubling the vowel signs, to mark indefiniteness with each of the case endings *-an*, *-in*, and *-un*, respectively. Consonant length ("doubling") is marked with ّ (*šadda*);[4] in generally unpointed text, this is the mark that is most likely not to be omitted. Where *kasra* is used with *šadda*, it can appear below it rather than below the consonant: قَتِّلَ *qattila*, as if the *šadda* itself were a second consonant. The feminine ending *-t* that is pronounced in context but omitted in pause combines the letter ه *h* with the dots of ت *t*: ة (*tāʾ marbūṭah*).

18.2.4 Excursus on Terminology

The writing system under discussion is traditionally called the Arabic **alphabet**. However, considerations based in the historical typology of writing (Daniels 1992)

[4] Including the assimilation of the ل of the definite article to the "sun letters": اَلشَّدَّةُ *aš-šaddatu* "the šadda"; no *sukūn* on the ل.

suggest that the term *alphabet* should be restricted to writing systems in which consonants and vowels are represented on an equal footing (like the Greek or Latin alphabets), with the term **abjad**[5] used for systems in which only consonants are represented.[6]

The dots that distinguish consonants are often called **diacritics** (e.g., Revell 1975). But since the dots are (now) integral parts of the letters, as much so as the dot on ⟨i⟩, they should not be given that label in synchronic description. (The term could perhaps be used of the vocalic and morphophonemic pointing, but it seems unnecessary because of the term *pointing*.)

A term that has found new life in phonological theory is **mora**, used to account for "heavy" and "light" syllables. It was first used in modern linguistics to label the units of the Japanese writing system (McCawley 1968), where each symbol denotes either a CV syllable, vowel length, or consonant length [Hellmuth, "Phonology"]. In an influential but unpublished paper, Poser (1992) is said to have claimed that virtually all "syllabographies" are actually "moraographies," but elsewhere[7] we learn that, for him, "a syllabic writing system is one in which each syllable is represented by a distinct graph"—that is, the speech stream is fully analyzed and represented; whereas in traditional usage, in a syllabary each *graph* represents a distinct *syllable*, even if some segments go unrepresented. Poser's definition is also at odds with phonological theory, where the initial C of any syllable is not included in any mora at all (cf. Watson 2002).[8] If, however, we revert to the original Japanese-style sense, then Standard Arabic orthography—unpointed except for *šadda*—is a pure moraography (even in Poser's sense), with a symbol for each CV syllable, each added V, and each added C. For fuller discussion, see Daniels in press a.

The term **grapheme** has been used in a variety of senses in writing-systems studies, perhaps most often to refer to a unit of correlation between sound and spelling (thus English ⟨ee⟩, ⟨ea⟩, and ⟨e–e⟩ for [ij] would be three different graphemes), though the extension of "emic" analysis to properties of the consciously devised phenomenon of writing is problematic (Daniels 1991b, 2018: 164–173).[9] However, it has recently been found among nonlinguists as the label for the 18 different linear shapes of the Arabic script (Massey 2003: 472b; Blair 2006: 8; Gacek 2009: 130a). This should be discouraged.

The traditional account of the tri*literal* Semitic **root** is just that: an account by lexicographers based *in the writing system*. It is doubtful that grammarians of any tradition, including the Arabic, would have come up with the notion of a CCC unit of language (as opposed to a pronounceable CCVC unit, say, as in Gray 1934), if it were not exactly what they saw written in virtually every word. Significantly, when the existing Syriac

[5] This word is borrowed from Arabic, where *ʾabjad* denotes the ancestral order of the letters (Table 18.3), still reflected in their rare function as numerals.

[6] In practice, only Phoenician was written with a pure abjad (see 18.3.1.2).

[7] From the detailed handout accompanying a presentation under the same title three weeks later.

[8] Saiegh-Haddad (2003: 444) found incidental evidence from Arabic-speaking children that the English-based C-V(C(C)) analysis of syllables embodied in modern phonological theory is not universally optimal and that a CV-C analysis better fits the facts.

[9] *Grapheme* is also often seen used as nothing more than a synonym for "letter" or other unit of a script, with no theoretical content at all.

grammatical tradition began to be influenced by the nascent Arabic grammatical tradition, a notion that was not imported was the triliteral root (Bohas 2003, 2004; Daniels 2012 [Ratcliffe, "Morphology"]).[10]

18.3 How It Is Used

18.3.1 Orthography

Classical/Standard Arabic orthography is quite straightforward. Each consonant (short/'single' or long/'double') and long vowel (18.3.1.2) is written with one letter, right to left in sequence. In addition there are various conventions associated with particular signs.[11]

18.3.1.1 *Alif*

An *alif* is added after the *wāw* of the 3PL verb suffix: كَتَبُوا *katabū* "they wrote", رَمَوْا *ramaw* "they threw" (*alif al-wiqāya*). It is also added to support the ـً (except after ة and ء): رَجُلٌ *rağulun* رَجُلاً *rağulan* "a man (nom., acc.)"; مَدِينَةً *madīnatan* "a town"; سَمَاءً *samāʾan* "(a) heaven." Final *ā* is usually written with *alif* curling below the line, resembling a *yāʾ* without the dots: رَمَى *ramā* "he threw" (*alif maqṣūra*). The exception is III*w* roots: دَعَا *daʿā* "he summoned" (and after يـ). It does not change for ـً: هُدًى *hudan* "right guidance."

18.3.1.2 *Matres Lectionis*

The use of certain consonant letters to indicate the presence of vowels is characteristic of Aramaic orthography. Such letters are called *matres lectionis* "mothers of reading" (Lat.; sg. *mater lectionis*). In Arabic, every long vowel is marked with the letters ا for *ā*, ي for *ī*, and و for *ū*. There are a few lexically determined exceptions, common words like هٰذا *hāḏa* "this" and ذٰلِكَ *ḏālika* "that"—and اللّٰه *Allāh*—in which when the text is pointed, the *dagger alif* is used for *ā*. In pointed texts, the appropriate vowel point for a long vowel or a diphthong appears on the consonant preceding the vowel, and when the text is very carefully pointed, the vowellessness mark is added to the following *mater* or diphthong-closing letter.

18.3.1.3 *Hamza*

The glottal stop marker usually appears in conjunction with a "seat of the hamza." If *ʔ* is preceded or followed by *ĭ*, then it appears on ى (without dots): بِئْرٌ *biʾrun* "a well"; قَائِمٌ *qāʾimun* "rising." If it is preceded or followed by *ŭ* but not *ĭ*, then it appears on و: رَؤُفَ *raʾufa* "he showed mercy." If it is preceded and/or followed by *ă*, then it appears on ا: رَأْسٌ *raʾsun* "a head"; أَرْأَسُ *ʾarʾasu* "most important"; سَأَلَ *saʾala* "he asked"; قَرَأَ *qaraʾa* "he read." After a long vowel or a consonant, it appears with no seat: سَمَاءٌ *samāʾun* "(a) heaven";

[10] The psycholinguistics of "roots" is explored in Shimron (2003).

[11] Wright (1896–1898, vol. 1: 10–26) seems not to have contemplated that his students might ever have occasion to *write* Arabic, as he gives instructions only for *reading* these and other phenomena. Fischer (2002, 7–13) is followed here.

بَرِيءٌ *barīʾun* "innocent"; سُوءٌ *sūʾun* "a misfortune"; سَاءَلَ *sāʾala* "he questioned"; مَسْأَلَةٌ *masʾalatun* "a question."[12] The sequence *ʔā* is spelled آ (*alif madda*) rather than أا: اَلْقُرْآنُ *al-qurʾānu* "the Quran." Initially, if *ʔ* is followed by *a* or *u*, then it appears above *alif*: أَمْرٌ *ʾamrun* "a command"; أُخْتٌ *ʾuxtun* "a sister," and if it is followed by *i*, then it appears below *alif*: إِبِلٌ *ʾibilun* "camels."

When the glottal stop is not a "real" consonant but introduces a phrase-initial prothetic vowel (*a* in the definite article: اَلْكِتَابُ *al-kitābu* "the book"; *u* in Form I imperatives اُقْتُلْ *uqtul*; *i* in nonimperfect CC derived forms and a few short words: اِنْقَتَلَ, اِبْنٌ *inqatala*, *ibnu* "son"; but excluding the Form IV prefix *ʾa* أَقْتَلَ *ʾaqtala*), it is not written; phrase internally, where the prothetic vowel is replaced by the final vowel of the preceding word, in pointed text the *alif* is "elided" with *waṣl* ٱ: عَبْدُ ٱلْمَلِكِ *ʿabdu l-maliki* "the king's servant."

18.3.2 Calligraphy

Calligraphy is "beautiful writing." In this era when print rather than handwriting represents the norm, the term can refer to just about any neatly written manuscript; it is this sense that enables Healey (1990–1991) to mention in this connection that early Arab scribes were exposed to carefully written manuscripts in both Syriac and Nabataean[13] (though Déroche 2003: 258a points out that even the earliest Quran fragments are written in long lines while other Near Eastern manuscript traditions used columns). But the more pertinent distinction is brought out by Blair (1998: 8): "The inscriptions ... were designed for clarity and immediate comprehension, the [calligraphy] was designed for aesthetic impact"; "The symbolic importance of many inscriptions is underscored by the fact that some are nearly unreadable and were meant to affirm symbolically the presence of the ruler" (ibid., 42).

Why should calligraphy have become the principal means of artistic expression in Islamic civilization? The facile answer is the prohibition in some circles of representational art, but similar strictures operated in Judaism and no similar efflorescence of calligraphic art involving Hebrew script ensued. Hoyland (2002: 25) mentions the precedent in Mesopotamian and Classical civilizations of using inscription as a major part of the decorative program of public buildings, but again this did not result in calligraphic freedom in cuneiform, Greek, or Latin scripts. Blair's (2006: 6–16) observation that the many tall verticals of *alif* and *lam* which lent themselves to decoration and intertwining might have sowed the seed is valid.[14] But what explains the move to ludic use, to visual play, to favoring "aesthetic impact" over legibility? Volov (1966), in an apparently

[12] Word internally, the Classical situation; in more modern texts, the *hamza* may take a ئ or أ seat.

[13] Even in Neo-Punic, concern is evidenced for the beauty of inscribed writing (Daniels in press b [1996]).

[14] She also points to the presence of spaces within words as inviting decorative treatment, contrasting them with roman-script words written without a lift of the pen—but surely this contrast is valid only for Western handwriting of recent centuries and not for the formal bookhands of the manuscript era, where not only space-saving ligatures but even individual letters normally required more than one pen stroke.

little-known article given prominence by Blair (2006: 12f.), finds at least an impetus to it in the aniconic coinage of the Caliphate (late 1st/early 8th century),[15] but art historians seem not to have asked this question.

Traditionally (e.g., Coulmas 1996: 20), Arabic bookhands have been divided into two classes: the angular *kufic* of the earliest Quranic manuscripts; and the rounded *nasx* (everything else). But in an extended series of publications beginning with Déroche (1980), the concept of "kufic" has been deconstructed (but in part recuperated by Blair 2007);[16] terminology in general is dealt with by Gacek (2009).[17] Ory (2001) focuses on the characteristics of the traditional scripts found in Quran manuscripts—though we have the names of the "six scripts" accepted by the calligraphic masters, how they were assigned to the scripts actually used is not always clear. The definitive work is Blair (2006).

18.3.3 Typography

As early as 1485, Sultan Bayazid II forbade printing in Arabic characters by Muslims throughout the Ottoman Empire (Bloom 2001: 214–26); several authors suggest this was the result of lobbying by the scribes' and copyists' guilds.[18] Arabic was first printed from movable type[19] in 1514 and 1516 in Venice and Genoa, in volumes intended for Arab Christians—though a 1537–1538 Venice Quran printing probably intended for export to Turkey contained errors and the entire edition was destroyed (but for one copy). Thereafter, Arabic was not printed again until 1566 in Rome: these fonts could not be considered aesthetic successes. Not until 1580 was there another attempt at an Arabic font, this time done well—by the distinguished typographer Robert Granjon, whose fonts and fonts modeled on them remained in use through the 20th century (Glass and Roper 2002)—and it was first used in 1584–1585, for "the first printed book to consist entirely of a text from a secular Muslim, rather than a Christian source" (Roper 2002: 138). The printing of Arabic from movable type lagged behind the printing of other "exotic" scripts: "No printer or punch-cutter was likely to invest time and money in perfecting type-faces and composing techniques, unless there was a prospect of continuing

[15] The far-reaching scope of Volov's article is belied by its title. Volov in turn borrows a sort of componential analysis of Arabic letters from Flury (1920: 237, n. 2), created about the same time as but independently of Edward Johnston's calligraphic analysis that I hoped to introduce to paleographers in Daniels (1984).

[16] It is odd to find Blair (2006: 105–16) claiming a conflict between what she calls the "paleographic" and the "art history" approaches to dating manuscripts. The latter, as she shows, incorporates the former.

[17] And in Gacek's other articles in this work: "Maġribī," "Muḥaqqaq," "Nastaʿlīq," "Nasx," "Ruqʿa," "Ṯuluṯ," with references. Abbott (1941) attempts to sort out the names of scripts in the traditional literature.

[18] Importation of printed Arabic (etc.) books was allowed a century later, and an Arabic printing-house was licensed in 1727. The relevant firmans are translated by Christopher M. Murphy in Atiyeh 1995, 283–85.

[19] Whole texts had been carved on and printed from woodblocks in earlier times (Schaefer 2002); the first Arabic printed in Europe was in one of seven woodcuts accompanying Bernhard von Breydenbach's *Peregrinatio in Terram Sanctam* (1486), also the source of the first European view (before any manuscripts had been imported) of the Ethiopic script (Daniels 1991a). Ross (2014) discusses Breydenbach's illustrations in great detail but barely mentions the alphabets (p. 68b), albeit incidentally reproducing the Arabic (p. 64 fig. 26).

demand for books which made use of them...; and the demand for Arabic texts among European scholars was minimal until the Renaissance revival of classical and Hebrew philology eventually extended to Arabic and other oriental languages, and the practical value of studying Arabic scientific texts in the original began to be appreciated" (Roper 2002: 141f.).[20]

Christians in Ottoman lands introduced printing in Quzḥayya, Lebanon, in 1610, and nearly a century later in Aleppo, Syria, the equipment imported from Europe. Napoleon brought a French printing-house to Alexandria in 1798, but it was not until Muḥammad 'Ali's post-Napoleonic modernization attempts in Egypt that Muslims began sacred printing;[21] newspapers and books soon followed. Publishing thrived in Beirut, again in Christian Arab hands. Almost as soon as there was printing of Arabic, there were suggestions of how to reform Arabic to make it more convenient to print. Glass (2004) is a comprehensive survey of the contents of one newspaper over decades, and (2004, vol. 2: 479–95) presents the discussion from the 1850s to the 1920s of a variety of reform proposals [Newman, "Nahḍa"]. Smitshuijzen AbiFares (2001: 73–78)[22] shows examples from the 20th century, including a system for simplification that underlay the IBM Selectric typewriter's Arabic element that was used surprisingly successfully for American pedagogical materials for many years. Blair (2006: 604–11) adds still more examples. Hunziker (1985: 18–20) discusses one in detail but concludes that compromise is unwise. Nemeth (2006) presents the difficulties involved in biscriptal printing and notes that a not unsuccessful approach is to extend the ascenders and descenders of the roman letters (rather than to force Arabic letters to conform to the irrelevant concept of x-height) as is done in John Hudson and Mamoun Sakkal's (2002) font "Arabic Typesetting" supplied with Microsoft products. Recent developments in electronic font technology allow the machine to substitute ligatures (some quite elaborate) for letter sequences, but satisfactory results remain elusive.

The Quran could not be printed in Muslim lands; after the Venetian failure of 1537–1538, brief excerpts appeared in Europe across the 17th century, in either grammatical or (hostile) theological contexts, capped by complete editions in 1694 (Hamburg; text only) and 1698 (Padua; with translation, commentary, and refutation). Complete Qurans were first printed for Muslim use in St. Petersburg under Catherine the Great after Russia had taken considerable Turkish territory; by 1803, the enterprise had moved to Kazan. The invention of lithography paved the way for printed Qurans from Persia and India and, finally, Istanbul (1850) and Cairo (1864).[23] What became the standard

[20] No comprehensive history of Arabic printing has yet been published; the extensive bibliographies in the volume cited here suggest that the time may be ripe for such a survey.

[21] Secular Turkish printing had begun in the 18th century in Istanbul.

[22] Despite the title, this volume is both a survey of Arabic script and an introduction to printing technology. Its timeline of developments in printing Arabic is convenient (Smitshuijzen AbiFares 2001: 44–85), but the author views the question of the parentage of Arabic writing (Nabataean vs. Syriac, see 18.4.2) as no more than a quarrel of British versus French and Arab scholars and opts to follow the latter (ibid., 26)!

[23] Nothing but contemporary mentions of an 1833 printing ordered by Muḥammad 'Ali has survived: it is not known whether it was a complete text or excerpts, or whether it was typeset or lithographed (Albin 2004, 269–71).

European edition of the Quran first appeared in Leipzig in 1834 (typeset); the standard Muslim edition was published in 1924 by al-Azhar in Cairo (lithographed) (Bobzin 2002; Albin 2004).

18.4 Where It Came From

18.4.1 West Semitic Writing

The oldest known direct ancestor of the Arabic abjad is the "Proto-Sinaitic" of Twelfth-Dynasty Egypt (ca. 1800 BCE), which exemplifies the accidental nature of much script innovation (Daniels 2013: 58–60; 2018: 141–44). The letter shapes, borrowed from Egyptian hieroglyphs, depict the objects whose names (Table 18.3) begin with each identified sound of the deviser's language (words did not begin with vowels, so there are no symbols for vowels; Harris 1932;[24] Hamilton 2006), confirming the *acrophonic principle* of the creation of the abjad.[25] This system was used throughout the Levant, changing over the centuries to lose its pictographic character, for Canaanite languages (Phoenician, Hebrew) and then, in more rounded forms, for Aramaic languages, which came to spread throughout the Fertile Crescent and beyond. A signal characteristic of Aramaic orthography is the gradual introduction of *matres lectionis* (Cross and Freedman 1952); in Middle Aramaic (of the turn of the Common Era), virtually every *ī* and *ū* was spelled with ⟨y⟩ and ⟨w⟩ (Cantineau 1930–1932, vol. 1: 67).

18.4.1.1 *Old North Arabic*

Tens of thousands of graffiti from almost everywhere in Arabia (Macdonald 2000) in languages closely related to Arabic (Macdonald 2004) are preserved in a South Semitic script notating the 29 consonants that does not use *matres lectionis* (except word-finally in one language). The script is clearly related to the monumental script of South Arabian, though it cannot be said with certainty whether the former is a cursivization of the latter or the latter a formalization of the former.

18.4.2 Nabataean Aramaic

The Middle Aramaic abjad had developed dozens of identifiable local varieties, some of them used by Arabic-speaking peoples who nonetheless kept their records in Aramaic; yet a consistent orthography of Arabic names was in use throughout their territory by the 5th century BCE (Diem 1976: 253). One such people was the Nabataeans, who

[24] Summarized in Harris 1936: 11–17.

[25] The objections of Gelb (1952) to the notion of acrophony seem to be based in the absence of evidence at the time he was writing (late 1930s) of intermediate forms between Proto-Sinaitic and Phoenician. See now Naveh 1987, Sass 1988, Cross 2003.

Table 18.3 Numerical values and names of Arabic letters

Numerical value	Arabic letter[a]	Reconstructed letter name (Hamilton 2006)		Arabic letter name
1	ا	**ʾalp*	"ox"	*ʾalif*
2	ب	**bēt*	"house"	*bāʾ*
3	ج	**gaml*	"throwstick"	*ǧīm*
4	د	**dalt*	"door"	*dāl*
5	ه	**hī*	"lo!"	*hāʾ*
6	و	**waw*	"mace"[b]	*wāw*
7	ز	**zayn*	"weapon"	*zāʾ*
8	ح	**ḥēṭ*	"fence"	*ḥāʾ*
9	ط	**ṭēt*	"spindle"??[c]	*ṭāʾ*
10	ي	**yōd*	"hand"	*yāʾ*
20	ك	**kapp*	"palm of hand"	*kāf*
30	ل	**lamd*	"coil of rope"[d]	*lām*
40	م	**mēm*	"water"	*mīm*
50	ن	**nūn*	"fish"	*nūn*
60	س	**samk*	"pillar"[e]	*sīn*
70	ع	**ʿayn*	"eye"	*ʿayn*
80	ف	**pi*	"edge"[f]	*fāʾ*
90	ص	**ṣadē*	"papyrus"[g]	*ṣād*
100	ق	**qop*	"monkey"	*qāf*
200	ر	**riʾš*	"head"	*rāʾ*
300	ش	**šin*	"bow"[h]	*šīn*
400	ت	**taw*	"mark"	*tāʾ*
500[i]	ث	–		*ṯāʾ*
600	خ	–		*xāʾ*
700	ذ	–		*ḏāl*
800	ض	–		*ḍād*
900	ظ	–		*ẓāʾ*
1000	غ	–		*ġayn*

a. "Independent" form. b. Or: "peg." c. Suggestion of W. F. Albright (1966). d. Or: "oxgoad." e. Or: "fish." f. Or: "mouth." g. Or: "cricket." h. Or: "tooth." i. These "added letters" are known as *rawādif*; sg. perh. *ridf* (Lane 3:1068b lines 6–7) "what follows."

occupied the rock-cut city of Petra (in southern present-day Jordan) and dominated the Sinai peninsula to the west, up to Damascus in the north, and the northwest of Arabia to the south and east; but they controlled the caravan routes throughout Arabia. Thousands of Nabataean inscriptions are known, from the Jordanian, Syrian, and Sinai deserts (and a few from Petra), dating between the 1st century BCE and the early 4th century CE [Retsö, "Arabic?"]. Cantineau (1930–1932) shows the increasing influence of Arabic on the language of the inscriptions, and eventually (with political developments) writing in Nabataean was abandoned. Healey (1990–1991) and Gruendler (1993) exhibit the changes in Nabataean letter shapes leading to early Arabic; Nehmé (2010) identifies a "transitional Nabataean" script in inscriptions, some previously known but most discovered in a 2004 survey of a northwest Saudi Arabian ancient caravan route, dating between the 3rd and 5th centuries CE.

Before the discovery of Nabataean inscriptions, it was assumed that the Arabic script developed from the Syriac (Gesenius 1815: 140). But as soon as the inscriptions were deciphered (Beer 1840), they were recognized as the antecedents of Arabic writing (Lewis and Macdonald 2003: 47). This became the standard account (Taylor 1883, vol. 1: 326–32; Giles 1903: 900b = 1910: 730a;[26] though Wright 1890: 40 clung to the earlier view); Taylor already anticipated Healey's suggestion (18.3.2) of Syriac influence: "the resemblance ... may be explained partly by the derivation of both alphabets from a common source, and partly by an assimilation to Syriac forms which seems to have taken place after the Arabs had established themselves in Syria" (ibid., 320 n. 2).[27] In 1964, however, Starcky (1966) devotes just a few columns (962–964) to reviving the older notion, expanded on by Sourdel-Thomine (1966). The definitive refutation is provided by Grohmann (1971, vol. 2: 12–21) even without benefit of the discovery of "transitional Nabataean."[28]

18.4.3 Paleography

The discussions in Arabic sources of the history of Arabic writing are treated (but not quoted or translated) by Nabia Abbott (1972: 3–17).[29] Arabic paleography has long been subsumed in and subordinated to Arabic calligraphy (18.3.2);[30] more recently, the traditional paleographic tasks of isolating characteristics useful in dating undated manuscripts and drawing up stemmata of the different bookhands has been pursued

[26] For Giles, see Daniels (2005: 508–511, 513).

[27] Abbott (1939: 19–21) specifies this influence dating to the centuries immediately around the Hijra, noting that the earliest surviving Christian Arabic manuscripts (to the 3rd century AH) bear a resemblance to Estrangelo Syriac, with later ones looking more ordinary.

[28] It is odd to find Blair (2006: 79) opting for the Syriac connection on the basis of general *Gestalt* and of mistaken claims by other authors, such as that Nabataean, unlike Arabic and Syriac, suspends letters from a roofline rather than supporting them on a baseline, or that Nabataean, unlike Arabic but like Syriac, merges ⟨d⟩ and ⟨r⟩. The *lām-alif* ligature is identical in Nabataean and early Arabic; Syriac ⟨b⟩, ⟨y⟩, ⟨n⟩, and ⟨t⟩; ⟨g⟩ and ⟨ḥ⟩; ⟨r⟩ and ⟨z⟩ show no resemblance.

[29] Semaan (1967) offers a user-friendly integration of tradition and description.

[30] This practice may have been encouraged by Arabists' habit of dividing the textual material into "manuscripts" (the Quran; literature sacred and secular) and "documents" (everything else) and until recently ignoring the latter (cf. Sijpesteijn 2008: 513).

by Grohmann (1966,[31] 1967, 1971),[32] Gruendler (1993), and especially F. Déroche; see the detailed bibliographies in Gruendler (2006) and particularly Gruendler (2001) and Déroche (2003) and the modern treatment by Sijpesteijn (2008). The paleography of "documents" is explored—using photographs of details—by Khan (1992, 27–46).

18.4.3.1 *Consonants, Dotting, Pointing*

Diem (1979–1983) describes the development of Arabic consonantal orthography out of Nabataean. By the time of the fixing of Arabic orthography, an intricate interplay of dialect difference (the *rasm* was recorded in Hijazi, a dialect that had lost /ʔ/ entirely) and analogy had resulted in adding the sign ء (*hamza*) to the system and using ا for *ā* (Diem 1976).

The oldest known Arabic "document" (a sheep delivery receipt from 22/644) already shows sporadic use of the dots that were to become parts of the letters, in the standard positions; thus, the system already existed but was optional. Dots are used not only to distinguish letters whose shapes happen to have grown uncomfortably similar in Nabataean (such as *b*/*n*, *f*/*q*), for which there was precedent both there and in Syriac (*d*/*r*), but also to separate phonemes that had merged in Aramaic but not in Arabic (such as *t*/*ṯ*, ʻ/*ġ*)—in preference to phonetic similarity, which would presumably have led *ṯ* to be written as a differentiation from *f*—showing etymological awareness on the part of the deviser of dotting (Daniels 2013: 64).[33]

Tradition ascribes the invention of vowel points to Abū l-Aswad al-Du'alī (d. 69/688). Acceptance was slow: "Ibn 'Abī Dā'ūd al-Sijistānī (d. 316) states that vowel signs were to be used only where strictly necessary whereas Al-Dānī (d. 444), writing over a century later, prescribes complete vocalization" (Khan 1990–1991: 57b). The earliest forms were a (red)[34] dot above for *a*, below for *i*, and on the line for *u*—it is difficult not to draw the connection with the contemporary Syriac vowel pointing, where "fuller" vowels were marked with a dot above, "slighter" vowels with a dot below[35] (Segal 1953: Appendix line II). The modern forms appear in the 3rd/9th century. In that century also, miniature letters, abbreviating suitable words, which became the *šadda*, *madda*, *waṣl*, and so on, began to be used (Gruendler 2001: 141a = 2006: 152b).[36]

[31] Grohmann includes all manner of "documents" under "Papyruskunde."

[32] Grohmann's (d. 1974) 1967 volume treats the history of the subject, and writing materials; the 1971 volume devotes most of its 300+ large pages and 66 plates to inscriptions only.

[33] Diem's (1980: 75–82) "etymological" explanation for the absence of a reflex of Aramaic ס (*semkaṯ*) in the Arabic abjad, and its replacement with س (corresponding to ש [*šīn*]), is vigorously disputed by Macdonald (1986: 149–51 n. 123), who observes that *semkaṯ* is all but nonexistent in later Nabataean inscriptions anyway; but, his argument relies in part on unlikely assumptions about the phonetic nature of Arabic sibilants (Daniels 2010), a question not to be gone into here.

[34] Dutton (1999–2000) finds that other colors are used systematically in early manuscripts, albeit with differing functions in different manuscripts.

[35] Syriac *u* has a dot below the letter *waw*, *o* a dot above.

[36] In particular, *sukūn* is a *mīm* for *ǧazm* and not, as has been suggested, the numeral 0, which had probably not yet been imported from India. For a recent history of Arabic numerals, see Kunitzsch (2005).

18.4.3.2 *Letter Order and Names*

The ancestral Northwest Semitic letter order is known from 12th-century BCE abecedaries excavated at Ugarit on the Syrian coast, and it survives to the present in Hebrew and Syriac.[37] It is this order that provides the still occasionally used numerical values of the letters ("*'abjad*" order; Table 18.3), and it is the basis for the standard Arabic order (Table 18.2), in which letters sharing the same shape have been brought together in the ordinal place of the first one for each shape.

A totally different order was used for South Semitic scripts—it is attested for both South Arabian and Old North Arabic—of which a variant survives as the Ethiopic order.[38]

The Arabic letter names (Table 18.3) reflect the reconstructed West Semitic names, with alterations resulting from regular change and from the pattern pressure of reciting as a list; they generally have no meaning in Arabic.

18.5 Where It Has Gone

18.5.1 The Perso-Arabic Sphere

Wherever Islam has gone, Arabic script has gone, too. Sometimes, as in Iranian lands, it replaced indigenous scripts; sometimes, vernaculars are written for the first time with adaptations of Arabic script. These adaptations have been facilitated by the structure of the consonantary: the regularities of differentiation by dotting (18.4.3.1) accommodate fairly well the consonantal inventories of languages with considerably different phonological structure. A complication ensues because (except in the Turkic language Uyghur) the many vocabulary items borrowed from Arabic retain the Arabic spellings, even when characteristically Arabic consonants like *ṯ ḏ ṭ ḍ ṣ ẓ ʻ ġ* assimilate to native phonology, so that their simple dottings are not available for different sounds in the borrowing language (Daniels 1997).

Vowel notation is a different matter, and languages have devised divergent ways of notating their inventories of more than three vowels, short and long. Some add new

[37] There have been numerous attempts to account for the ancestral letter order. Driver (1976, 179–85, 268–73) discusses and refutes many of them. A proposal by W. C. Watt (*JNES* 46 [1987]: 1–14) that the Phoenician order resulted from arranging the consonants in phonetically determined columns (more sophisticated than those used by the Sanskrit grammarians a millennium later!) and reading them in arbitrarily assigned rows (with arbitrary gaps in the grid to make them come out right) falls because he was apparently unaware of the preexisting Ugaritic order—and his attempt to repair this (*Semiotica* 74 [1989]: 61–108) involves the incorporation of even more gaps. Most likely, the letters were simply set down as they came to the mind of the deviser (which could account for associative sequences like **yōd* "hand" and **kapp* "palm of hand").

[38] A fascinating, though not entirely persuasive, reconstruction of an Ancient Egyptian letter order from which both the Northwest Semitic and the South Semitic orders can be derived is offered by Kammerzell (2001). The fullest discussion of Arabic letter orders is provided by Macdonald (1986).

points, some devise new consonant shapes to serve as *matres*, and some do both. Vowel pointing is generally optional, as in Arabic.[39]

The list of languages for which an Arabic script has been adapted over the centuries is long (compiled from several sources and doubtless incomplete):[40] Adyghe (West Circassian), Afar, Afrikaans, Albanian, Amharic, Argobba, Asante, Avar, Azerbaijani, Bambara, Bashkir, Beja, Belarusian, Chechen, Chimwiini, Crimean Tatar, Dagbani, Dargi, Djoula, Dunganese (Hui), English, Fulani, Gbanyito, Gonja, Harari, Hausa, Ingush, Kabardian (East Circassian), Kabyle, Kanuri, Karachay-Balkar, Karakalpak, Kashmiri, Kazakh, Kirghiz, Kotokoli, Kumyk, Kurdish, Lak, Lezgian, Maba, Makua, Malagasy, Malay, Malayalam, Mamprule, Mande, Mogofin, Nafusi, Nogay, Nubian, Nupe, Oromo, Pashto, Persian, Portuguese, Serbo-Croatian, Serer, Silt'e, Sindhi, Siwi, Somali, Songhay, Soninke, Spanish, Susa, Swahili, Tajik, Tamasheq, Tamazight, Tamil, Tarifit, Tashelhit, Tatar (Volga Tatar, Kazan Tatar), Tigrinya, Turkish, Turkmen, Urdu, Uyghur, Uzbek, Wolof, Yoruba, Zanaga, Zerma (Cohen 1958; Diringer 1968; Comrie 1996; Coulmas 1996; Mumin 2009).

18.5.2 The Modern Linguistic Sphere

While vernacular Arabics may have been written for centuries (and even institutionalized in the form of Judeo-Arabic, which used Hebrew script and thus is outside our purview),[41] and while colloquial language has begun to creep into published literature, attention is rarely paid to how the orthography accounts for features, primarily phonological, that differ between Colloquial and Standard written Arabic.[42] Somekh (1991: 26) observes, "Dialects in the Arab world never developed writing systems of their own, and AM [*ʿāmmiyya*] is normally reduced to the uncongenial orthography of FU [*fuṣḥā*]. Thus the reader, especially one who is not a native speaker of the dialect in question, faces many difficulties in deciphering them. Moreover, as there is no stable tradition for committing the dialects to writing, texts that employ AM are very often inconsistent in the use of Arabic characters for this purpose." Holes (1995: 304) notes that the celebrated Egyptian playwright Tawfiq al-Hakim attempted a "third language" in *al-Ṣafqa* (The Deal) (1956), "avoiding lexical and syntactic choices which are markedly dialectal on the one hand, and 'high-flown' on the other. However, because

[39] In modern African orthographies, however, vowel-point notation is often obligatory (Mumin 2009).

[40] The attribution of a list of "the twelve languages for which the Arabic script has at one time been used" (Macdonald 2010: 22 n. 47) to Daniels (1997) is ludicrous.

[41] Maltese is often called a separate language from Arabic not only because of heavy Italian influence but precisely because it is written with an expansion of the roman alphabet (e.g., Kaye and Rosenhouse 1997: 263).

[42] Thus, Rosenbaum (2000) presents seven passages with the code switching between *fuṣḥā* ("eloquent") and *ʿāmmiyya* ("popular") but does not disclose the criteria for distinguishing the two registers; the promised publication of the dissertation in which they may have been set forth has apparently not occurred. Davies (2006) says not a word on the topic.

M[odern]S[tandard]A[rabic] orthography underspecifies the morphophonological realization of words, the text can be performed in something akin to the dialect of any group of actors" [Holes, "Orality"].

In his pioneering study of informal written Arabic, Meiseles (1979: 278–89) describes a number of orthographic deviations[43] from Standard Arabic in a rather ill-specified corpus ("from Egypt and the East-Mediterranean area"). These include the occasional use of vowel points to clarify nonstandard verb forms, *plene* writing (i.e., with *matres lectionis*) even of all short vowels in foreign loans[44] and sometimes in pronominal suffixes (the latter confirmed by Belnap and Bishop 2003: 15), numerous inconsistencies in *hamza* use, and frequent substitutions like ز *z* for ذ *ḏ* and ک *k* for ق *q*; particularly interesting is ج *ǧ* ([g] in Egyptian) for French *ž*. Van den Boogert (1989: 33f.) lists ڭ, ڨ, and چ for Maghribi Arabic /g/ (without noting whether they are used etymologically) and ڢ or ڥ for [v] in borrowed French words. Surface-phonological substitutions for morphophonemic spellings include replacement of *tanwīn* with ن *n* (Holes 1995: 77 [for Bahraini dialect]) and of ة *tāʾ marbūṭah* with ت *t* (Holes 1995: 76, probably; Meiseles 1979: 286).

18.6 Research Needs

As noted above (18.4), investigation of the prehistory of Arabic script continues, and continues to make exciting discoveries, while the tens of thousands of surviving "documents" from the early Islamic centuries are only beginning to be studied seriously, particularly concerning their evidence for the history of Arabic script. It may become possible to learn something of the development of Quranic orthography from the trove of pre-standardization manuscript fragments discovered in Sanʿa, Yemen, decades ago (Puin 2011).

A much more pressing need is the investigation of the acquisition of Arabic literacy by young native speakers, a field that has barely been touched. Older surveys like Altomah (1970) and Biesterfeldt (1996) discuss only institutions and materials for teaching reading, not the learning process itself; for a newer summary see Taouk and Coltheart (2004: 33–41). As Share (2008) details, the vast preponderance of English in the study of literacy acquisition is likely to be highly misleading, especially for languages that are not alphabetically written. The English-oriented attention to "phonological awareness" (to the exclusion of attention to other levels of linguistic analysis)[45] led the first investigators

[43] Meiseles's article is marred by the use of such terms as "substandard" and "mere vulgarism."

[44] The spelling of English loanwords in Arabic has been investigated by Odisho (1992) and Weninger (2001).

[45] But Sandra (2011) shows that many studies ostensibly of the relationship of "phonological awareness" to literacy acquisition also showed the relevance of the morphological and other linguistic levels as well.

of Arabic children learning to read to focus on that question, as well as on the specifically Arabic question of diglossia (e.g., Abu-Rabia 2000; Saiegh-Haddad 2003).[46] Even in numerous studies of shallow ("vowelized") verus deep orthography (summarized in Abu-Rabia and Taha 2006: 323–25), Abu-Rabia attributes the greater success afforded by the former to the phonological and not the morphological cues provided. Not yet published work is beginning to turn in these new directions (see now Saiegh-Haddad 2017).

References

Abbott, Nabia. 1939. *The rise of the North Arabic script and its Ḳurʾānic development, with a full description of the Ḳurʾān manuscripts in the Oriental Institute*. Oriental Institute Publications 50. Chicago: University of Chicago Press.

—— 1941. Arabic paleography. *Ars Islamica* 8: 65–104.

—— 1972. *Studies in Arabic literary papyri III: Language and literature*. Oriental Institute Publications 77. Chicago: University of Chicago Press.

Abu-Rabia, Salim. 2000. Effects of exposure to literary Arabic on reading comprehension in a diglossic situation. *Reading and Writing* 13: 147–157.

Abu-Rabia, Salim and Haitham Taha. 2006. Reading in Arabic orthography: Characteristics, research findings, and assessment. In *Handbook of orthography and literacy*, ed. R. Malatesha Joshi and P. G. Aaron, 321–338. Mahwah, NJ: Erlbaum.

Albin, Michael W. 2004. Printing of the Qurʾān. In *Encyclopaedia of the Qurʾān*, vol. 4, ed. Jane Dammen McAuliffe, 264–276. Leiden: Brill.

Albright, William Foxwell. 1966. *The Proto-Sinaitic inscriptions and their decipherment*. Harvard Theological Studies 22. Cambridge, MA: Harvard University Press.

Altomah, Salih J. 1970. Language education in Arab countries and the role of the academies. In *Current trends in Linguistics*, vol. 6: *Linguistics in South West Asia and North Africa*, ed. Thomas A. Sebeok, 690–720. The Hague: Mouton.

Atiyeh, George N. (ed.). 1995. *The book in the Islamic world: The written word in the Middle East*. Albany: State University of New York Press.

Beer, E. F. F. 1840. *Studia Asiatica III: Inscriptiones veteris litteris et lingua hucusque incognitis ad Montem Sinai in magno numero servatae*. Leipzig: Barth.

Belnap, R. Kirk and Brian Bishop. 2003. Arabic personal correspondence: A window on change in progress? *International Journal of the Sociology of Language* 163: 9–25.

Biesterfeldt, A. A. 1996. Lese- und Schreibunterricht im arabischen Sprachraum. In *Schrift und Schriftlichkeit*, vol. 2, ed. Hartmut Günther and Otto Ludwig, 1299–1309. Handbücher zur Sprach- und Kommunikationswissenschaft 10. Berlin: de Gruyter.

Blair, Sheila S. 1998. *Islamic inscriptions*. Edinburgh: Edinburgh University Press.

——. 2006. *Islamic calligraphy*. Edinburgh: Edinburgh University Press.

——. 2007. Kufic. In *Encyclopedia of Arabic Language and Linguistics*, vol. 2, ed. Kees Versteegh, Associate Editors: Mushira Eid, Alaa Elgibali, Manfred Woidich, Andrzej Zaborski, 597–604. Leiden: Brill.

Bloom, Jonathan M. 2001. *Paper before print: The history and impact of paper in the Islamic world*. New Haven, CT: Yale University Press.

[46] There is apparently a universal belief that *fuṣḥā* is "too difficult" for young children, so that their first encounter with writing is also their first encounter with the standard language.

Bobzin, Hartmut. 2002. From Venice to Cairo: On the history of Arabic editions of the Koran (16th–early 20th century). In *Middle Eastern languages and the print revolution: A cross-cultural encounter*, ed. Eva Hanebutt-Benz, Dagmar Glass, and Geoffrey Roper, 151–176, 529–530. Mainz: Gutenberg Museum.

Bohas, Georges. 2003. Radical ou racine/schème? L'organisation de la conjugaison syriaque, avant l'adoption de la racine. *Le Muséon* 116: 343–376.

Bohas, Georges. 2004. Sur l'hypothèse de la racine triconsonantique en syriaque. *Langues et Littératures du Monde Arabe* 5: 135–158.

Cantineau, Jean. 1930–1932. *Le nabatéen*. 2 vols. Paris: Leroux.

Cohen, Marcel. 1958. *La grande invention de l'écriture et son évolution*. 3 vols. Paris: Imprimerie Nationale.

Comrie, Bernard. 1996. Script reform in and after the Soviet Union. In *The world's writing systems*, ed. Peter T. Daniels and William Bright, 781–784. New York: Oxford University Press.

Coulmas, Florian. 1996. *The Blackwell encyclopedia of writing systems*. Oxford: Blackwell.

Cross, Frank Moore. 2003. *Leaves from an epigrapher's notebook: Collected papers in Hebrew and West Semitic palaeography and epigraphy*. Harvard Semitic Studies 51. Winona Lake, IN: Eisenbrauns.

Cross, Frank Moore and David Noel Freedman. 1952. *Early Hebrew orthography: A study of the epigraphic evidence*. American Oriental Series 36. New Haven, CT: American Oriental Society.

Daniels, Peter T. 1984. A calligraphic approach to Aramaic paleography. *Journal of Near Eastern Studies* 43: 55–68.

——. 1991a. Ha, La, Ḥa or Hōi, Lawe, Ḥawt? The Ethiopic letter names. In *Semitic Studies in honor of Wolf Leslau on the occasion of his eighty-fifth birthday*, ed. Alan S. Kaye, 275–288. Wiesbaden: Harrassowitz.

——. 1991b. Is a structural graphemics possible? In *18th LACUS Forum* (Ann Arbor), 528–537.

——. 1992. The syllabic origin of writing and the segmental origin of the alphabet. In *The linguistics of literacy*, ed. Pamela Downing, Susan D. Lima, and Michael Noonan, 83–110. Amsterdam: John Benjamins.

——. 1997. The protean Arabic abjad. In *Humanism, culture, and language in the Near East: Studies in honor of Georg Krotkoff*, ed. Asma Afsaruddin and A. H. Mathias Zahniser, 83–110. Winona Lake, IN: Eisenbrauns.

——. 2005. Language and languages in the eleventh *Britannica*. In *Polymorphous linguistics: Jim McCawley's legacy*, ed. Salikoko S. Mufwene, Elaine J. Francis, and Rebecca S. Wheeler, 505–529. Cambridge, MA: MIT Press.

——. 2010. Arabian sibilants again. Paper presented at the annual meeting of the American Oriental Society, St. Louis, MO, March.

——. 2013. The history of writing as a history of linguistics. In *Oxford handbook of the history of linguistics*, ed. Keith Allan, 53–69. Oxford: Oxford University Press.

——. in press a. Moraic writing systems versus syllabic writing systems. In *"May You Favor the Work of His Hands": Essays in Memory of M. O'Connor*, ed. Peter T. Daniels, Edward L. Greenstein, John Huehnergard, Mark S. Leson, and Philip C. Schmitz. Winona Lake, IN: Eisenbrauns.

——. 2018. *An Exploration of Writing*. Sheffield: Equinox.

——. in press b. Writing is not language: The possibility of calligraphy. In *Inscriptions as art in the world of Islam*, ed. Habibeh Rahim. Brooklyn, NY: AMS Press [proceedings of a conference at Hofstra University, April 1996].

Davies, Humphrey. 2006. Dialect literature. In *EALL*, vol. 1, ed. Kees Versteegh, Associate Editors: Mushira Eid, Alaa Elgibali, Manfred Woidich, Andrzej Zaborski, 597–604. Leiden: Brill.

Déroche, François. 1980. Les écritures coraniques anciennes: Bilan et perspectives. *Revue des Etudes Islamiques* 48: 207–224.

——. 2003. Manuscripts of the Qurʾān. In *Encyclopaedia of the Qurʾān*, vol. 3, ed. Jane Dammen McAuliffe, 254–275. Leiden: Brill.

Diem, Werner. 1976. Some glimpses of the rise and early development of the Arabic orthography. *Orientalia* N.S. 45: 251–261.

——. 1979–1983. Untersuchungen zur frühen Geschichte der arabischen Orthographie. *Orientalia* N.S. 48: 207–257; 49: 67–106; 50: 332–383; 52: 357–404.

Diringer, David. 1968. *The alphabet: A key to the history of mankind*, 3d ed. Reinhold Regensburger. 2 vols. New York: Funk & Wagnall's.

Driver, G. R. 1976. *Semitic writing* Schweich Lectures, 1944. 3rd ed., ed. S. A. Hopkins. London: Oxford University Press for the British Academy.

Dutton, Yasin. 1999–2000. Red dots, green dots, yellow dots and blue: Some reflections on the vocalisation of early Qurʾanic manuscripts. *Journal of Qurʾanic Studies* 1: 115–140; 2: 1–24.

Endress, Gerhard. 1982. Herkunft und Entwicklung der arabischen Schrift. In *Grundriss der arabischen Philologie, I: Sprachwissenchaft*, ed. Wolfdietrich Fischer, 165–197. Wiesbaden: Reichert.

Fischer, Wolfdietrich. 2002. *A grammar of Classical Arabic*. Trans. Jonathan Rodgers. New Haven, CT: Yale University Press. (Original German 1972.)

Flury, S. 1920. Bandeaux ornamentés à inscriptions arabes. *Syria* 1: 234–249, 318–328.

Gacek, Adam. 2009. Script and art. In *EALL*, vol. 4, ed. Kees Versteegh, Associate Editors: Mushira Eid, Alaa Elgibali, Manfred Woidich, Andrzej Zaborski, 130–138. Leiden: Brill.

Gelb, I. J. 1952. *A study of writing*. Chicago: University of Chicago Press.

Gesenius, Wilhelm. 1815. *Geschichte der hebräischen Sprache und Schrift: Eine philologisch-historische Einleitung in die Sprachlehren und Wörterbücher der hebräischen Sprache*. Leipzig: Vogel.

Giles, Peter. 1903. Writing. In *Encyclopædia Britannica*, 10th ed., vol. 33, 888–903. London: The Times.

——. 1910. Alphabet. In *Encyclopædia Britannica*, 11th ed., vol. 1, 723–732. Cambridge: Cambridge University Press.

Glass, Dagmar. 2004. *Der* Muqtaṭaf *und seine Öffentlichkeit: Aufklärung, Räsonnement und Meinungsstreit in der frühen arabischen Zeitschriftenkommunikation*. 2 vols. Würzburg: Ergon Verlag.

Glass, Dagmar and Geoffrey Roper. 2002. Arabic book and newspaper printing in the Arab world. In *Middle Eastern languages and the print revolution: A cross-cultural encounter*, ed. Eva Hanebutt-Benz, Dagmar Glass, and Geoffrey Roper, 177–216, 221–226, 531–534. Mainz: Gutenberg Museum.

Gray, Louis H. 1934. *Introduction to Semitic comparative linguistics*. New York: Columbia University Press.

Grohmann, Adolf. 1966. *Arabische Chronologie; Arabische Papyruskunde*. Handbuch der Orientalistik, I, Supplement 2, part 1. Leiden: Brill.

——. 1967, 1971. *Arabische Paläographie*. Österreichische Akademie der Wissenschaften, phil.-hist. Klasse, Denkschriften 94. 2 vols. Vienna: Böhlau.

Gruendler, Beatrice. 1993. *The development of the Arabic scripts: From the Nabataean era to the first Islamic century according to dated texts.* Harvard Semitic Studies 43. Atlanta: Scholars Press.

——. 2001. Arabic script. In *Encyclopaedia of the Qur'ān*, vol. 1, ed. Jane Dammen McAuliffe, 135–144. Leiden: Brill.

——. 2006. Arabic alphabet: Origin. In *EALL*, vol. 1, ed. Kees Versteegh, Associate Editors: Mushira Eid, Alaa Elgibali, Manfred Woidich, Andrzej Zaborski, 148–165. Leiden: Brill.

Hamilton, Gordon J. 2006. *The origins of the West Semitic alphabet in the Egyptian scripts. Catholic Biblical Quarterly* Monograph 40. Washington, DC: Catholic Biblical Association of America.

Harris, Zellig S. 1932. *The origin of the alphabet.* [cf. Mumin 2009 below] M.A. thesis, University of Pennsylvania, Philadelphia.

——. 1936. *A grammar of the Phoenician language.* American Oriental Series 8. New Haven, CT: American Oriental Society.

Healey, John F. 1990–1991. Nabataean to Arabic: Calligraphy and script development among the Pre-Islamic Arabs. *Manuscripts of the Middle East* 5: 41–52.

Holes, Clive. 1995. *Modern Arabic: Structures, functions, and varieties.* London: Longman.

Hoyland, Robert. 2002. Epigraphy. In *Encyclopaedia of the Qur'ān*, vol. 2, ed. Jane Dammen McAuliffe, 25–43. Leiden: Brill.

Hunziker, Hans Jürg. 1985. Aspects of Arabic script reform. *TM/Swiss Typographic Monthly Magazine (Typographische Monatsblätter)* 104(4): 1–36.

Kammerzell, Frank. 2001. Die Entstehung der Alphabetreihe: Zum ägyptischen Ursprung der semitischen und westlichen Schriften. In *Hieroglyphen Alphabete Schriftreformen: Studien zu Multiliteralismus, Schriftwechsel und Orthographieneuregelungen*, ed. Dörte Borchers, Frank Kammerzell, and Stefan Weninger, 117–158. *Lingua Aegyptia* Studia monographica 3. Göttingen: Seminar für Ägyptologie und Koptologie.

Kaye, Alan S. and Judith Rosenhouse. 1997. Arabic dialects and Maltese. In *The Semitic languages*, ed. Robert Hetzron, 263–311. London: Routledge.

Khan, Geoffrey. 1990–1991. Standardisation and variation in the orthography of Hebrew Bible and Arabic Qur'ān manuscripts. *Manuscripts of the Middle East* 5: 53–58.

Khan, Geoffrey. 1992. *Selected Arabic papyri.* Studies in the Khalili Collection 1. Oxford: Oxford University Press for the Nour Foundation.

Kunitzsch, Paul. 2005. *Zur Geschichte der "arabischen" Ziffern.* Munich: Bayerische Akademie der Wissenschaften, phil.-hist. Classe, Sitzungsberichte, no. 3.

Lewis, N. N. and M. C. A. Macdonald. 2003. W. J. Bankes and the identification of the Nabataean script. *Syria* 80: 41–110.

Macdonald, M. C. A. 1986. ABC's and letter order in ancient North Arabian. *Proceedings of the Seminar for Arabian Studies* 16: 101–153.

——. 2000. Reflections on the linguistic map of Pre-Islamic Arabia. *Arabian Archaeology and Epigraphy* 11: 28–79. (Repr. with addenda in *Literacy and identity in pre-Islamic Arabia*, Farnham: Ashgate, 2009.)

——. 2004. Ancient North Arabian. In *The Cambridge encyclopedia of the world's ancient languages*, ed. Roger D. Woodard, 488–533. Cambridge, UK: Cambridge University Press.

——. 2010. Ancient Arabia and the written word. In *The Development of Arabic as a written language*, ed. M. C. A. Macdonald, 5–27. Oxford: Archaeopress for the Seminar for Arabian Studies.

Massey, Keith. 2003. Mysterious letters. In *Encyclopaedia of the Qur'ān*, vol. 3, ed. Jane Dammen McAuliffe, 471–476. Leiden: Brill.

McCawley, James D. 1968. *The phonological component of a grammar of Japanese*. The Hague: Mouton.

Meiseles, Gustav. 1979. Informal written Arabic: A preliminary evaluation of data. *Israel Oriental Studies* 9: 272–314.

Moritz, Bernhard. 1918. Arabia. d. Arabic writing. In *The encyclopaedia of Islam*, vol. 1, 381–393. Leiden: Brill.

Mumin, Meikal. 2009. *The Arabic script in Africa*. M.A. thesis, Institut für Afrikanistik, Universität zu Köln, Cologne.

Naveh, Joseph. 1987. *Early history of the alphabet*, 2d ed. Jerusalem: Magnes.

Nehmé, Laïla. 2010. A glimpse of the development of the Nabataean script into Arabic based on old and new epigraphic material. In *The development of Arabic as a written language*, ed. M. C. A. Macdonald, 47–88. Oxford: Archaeopress for the Seminar for Arabian Studies.

Nemeth, Titus. 2006. *Harmonization of Arabic and Latin script: Possibilities and obstacles*. Master's essay, Department of Typography and Graphic Communication, University of Reading. Available at http://www.tntypography.com/publications.html.

Odisho, Edward Y. 1992. Transliterating English in Arabic. *Zeitschrift für arabische Linguistik* 24: 21–34.

Ory, Solange. 2001. Calligraphy. In *Encyclopaedia of the Qurʾān*, vol. 1, ed. Jane Dammen McAuliffe, 278–286. Leiden: Brill.

Poser, William J. 1992. The structural typology of phonological writing. Paper presented at the annual meeting of the Linguistic Society of America, Philadelphia, January 12.

Puin, Gerd-R. 2011. Vowel letters and ortho-epic writing in the Qur'ān. In *New perspectives on the Qur'an: The Qur'an in its historical context* 2, ed. Gabriel Reynolds, 147–190. London: Routledge.

Revell, E. J. 1975. The diacritical dots and the development of the Arabic alphabet. *Journal of Semitic Studies* 20: 178–190.

Roper, Geoffrey. 2002. Early Arabic printing in Europe. In *Middle Eastern languages and the print revolution*, ed. Eva Hanebutt-Benz, Dagmar Glass, and Geoffrey Roper, 129–150, 526–529. Mainz: Gutenberg Museum.

Rosenbaum, Gabriel, M. 2000. "Fuṣḥāmmiyya": Alternating style in Egyptian prose. *Zeitschrift für arabische Linguistik* 38: 68–87.

Ross, Elizabeth. 2014. *Picturing Experience in the Early Printed Book: Breydenbach's Peregrinatio from Venice to Jerusalem*. University Park: Penn State University Press.

Saiegh-Haddad. 2017. Learning to read Arabic. In *Learning to Read across Languages and Writing Systems*. ed. By Ludo Verhoeven and Charles Perfetti, 127–154. Cambridge: Cambridge University Press.

Saiegh-Haddad, Elinor. 2003. Linguistic distance and initial reading acquisition: The case of Arabic diglossia. *Applied Psycholinguistics* 24: 431–451.

Sandra, Dominiek. 2011. Spelling strategies in alphabetic scripts: Insights gained and challenges ahead. *The Mental Lexicon* 6: 110–140.

Sass, Benjamin. 1988. *The genesis of the alphabet and its development in the second millenium B.C.* Wiesbaden: Harrassowitz.

Schaefer, Karl. 2002. Arabic printing before Gutenberg: Block-printed Arabic amulets. In *Middle Eastern languages and the print revolution: A cross-cultural encounter*, ed. Eva Hanebutt-Benz, Dagmar Glass, and Geoffrey Roper, 123–128, 525–526. Mainz: Gutenberg Museum.

Segal, J. B. 1953. *The diacritical point and accents in Syriac*. London Oriental Series 2. London: Oxford University Press.

Semaan, Khalil I. H. 1967. A linguistic view of the development of the Arabic writing system. *Wiener Zeitschrift für die Kunde des Morgenlandes* 61: 22–40.

Share, David. 2008. On the anglocentricities of current reading research and practice: The perils of overreliance on an "outlier" orthography. *Psychological Bulletin* 134: 584–615.

Shimron, Joseph (ed.). 2003. *Language processing and acquisition in languages of Semitic, root-based, morphology*. Amsterdam: John Benjamins.

Sijpesteijn, Petra M. 2008. Palaeography. In *EALL*, vol. 3, ed. Kees Versteegh, Associate Editors: Mushira Eid, Alaa Elgibali, Manfred Woidich, Andrzej Zaborski, 513–524. Leiden: Brill.

Smitshuijzen AbiFares, Huda. 2001. *Arabic typography: A comprehensive sourcebook*. London: Saqi.

Somekh, Sasson. 1991. *Genre and language in modern Arabic literature*. Wiesbaden: Harrassowitz.

Sourdel-Thomine, Janine. 1966. Les origines de l'écriture arabe: À propos d'une hypothèse récente. *Revue des Etudes Islamiques* 34: 151–157.

Sourdel-Thomine, Janine. 1978. Khaṭṭ. In *Encyclopaedia of Islam*, 2d ed., vol. 4, 1112–1122. Leiden: Brill.

Starcky, Jean. 1966. Pétra et la Nabatène. In *Dictionnaire de la Bible: Supplément*, ed. Henri Cazelles and André Feuillet, vol. 7, cols. 886–1017. Paris: Letouzey & Ané.

Taouk, Miriam, and Max Coltheart. 2004. The cognitive processes involved in learning to read Arabic. *Reading and Writing* 17: 27–57.

Taylor, Isaac. 1883. *The alphabet: An account of the origin and development of letters*. London: Kegan Paul, Trench.

van den Boogert, N. 1989. Some notes on Maghribi script. *Manuscripts of the Middle East* 4: 30–43.

Volov, Lisa. 1966. Plaited Kufic on Samanid epigraphic pottery. *Ars Orientalis* 6: 107–134.

Watt, W. 1987. The Byblos matrix. *Journal of Near Eastern Studies* 46: 1–14.

Watson, Janet C. E. 2002. *The phonology and morphology of Arabic*. Oxford: Oxford University Press.

Weninger, Stefan. 2001. Zur Wiedergabe englischen Sprachmaterials in modernen Hocharabisch. In *Hieroglyphen Alphabete Schriftreformen: Studien zu Multiliteralismus, Schriftwechsel und Orthographieneuregelungen*, ed. Dörte Borchers, Frank Kammerzell, and Stefan Weninger, 175–191. *Lingua Aegyptia* Studia monographica 3. Göttingen: Seminar für Ägyptologie und Koptologie.

Wright, William. 1890. *Lectures on the comparative grammar of the Semitic languages*. Ed. W. Roberstson Smith. Cambridge, UK: Cambridge University Press.

Wright, William. 1896–1898. *A grammar of the Arabic language*. Ed. W. Robertson Smith and M. J. de Goeje. 2 vols. Cambridge, UK: Cambridge University Press.

CHAPTER 19

WHAT IS ARABIC?

JAN RETSÖ

19.1 Introduction

These sentences from Jastrow (2007: 7) all mean the same: "What do you want now?"

1) wiš taba ḏaḥḥīn
2) šū bəddak hallaʔ
3) š-ítrīd hassa
4) ʕāwiz ēh dilwaʔti
5) āš bġēt^s dāba
6) māḏā turīdu l-ʔān

At first glance they do not seem to have much in common except one thing: they are said to be Arabic. They represent different varieties within the Arabic linguistic complex: (1) Riyadh; (2) Damascus; (3) Baghdad; (4) Cairo; (5) Rabat. Even if the elements making up the words and sentences often can be found in most varieties of Arabic, idiomacy and pragmatics create a wide difference between many varieties that make them more or less mutually incomprehensible. At the same time, the existence of many of the elements (morphemes, words) in most varieties makes it possible that linguistically conscious speakers often can make their way and understand each other in spite of the differences.

To this is added the role of the language represented by the last example (6), the *fuṣḥā* or the Arabiyya, a variety that has not been spoken as a first language for centuries or even millennia but that is the official language of all the Arab countries and is taught in schools from the first day of the first grade in its modernized variant Modern Standard Arabic [Suleiman, "Folk Linguistics"; Al-Wer, "Sociolinguistics"]. Some regional varieties, such as Cairene and, nowadays probably also Syro-Lebanese, are at least passively understood by a large audience in the entire Arab world, listening to songs and watching films and TV soap operas produced in Egypt and the Levant [Holes, "Orality"]. But the fact remains that the linguistic differentiation in the Arab world is considerable. If we then take the epigraphically documented languages of Central and North Arabia from the pre-Islamic period into account, which traditionally is included in the Arabic complex, the Arabic language appears as an extremely variegated phenomenon (Lipiński 1997: 70–77). The Arabiyya has a special position, not only by being a second language for everyone but also because of its typlogical features, many of which set it apart not only from all the modern spoken varieties but also from the epigraphic languages.

The word Arabic itself as a linguistic term originates primarily from the Quran. In 11 passages in the Holy Book, an ʕarabī-language is mentioned (Retsö 2010). All passages are found in texts that, according to traditional opinion, were revealed before the year 622 CE. The Quranic word "ʕarabī" undoubtedly refers to the language of the Holy Book. In that text we also encounter another linguistic term: *ʔaʕǧamī*, as it seems opposed to the word *ʕarabī* (Q 26:195, 198; 41:44). The traditional opinion is that this word means "non Arabic-speaker," that is, speakers of Persian or perhaps Greek. This is undoubtedly the meaning it acquired during the Islamic Middle Ages. There is, however, clear evidence that the word originally designates a kind of Arabic, a variety that deviates from some kind of norm. In the *Lisān al-ʕarab* it is said that an *ʔaʕǧamī* is someone who does not speak correctly even if he is an Arab, a remark that is found already in al-Khalīl's *Kitāb al-ʕayn*. The *Lisān* opposes *ʔaʕǧam(ī)* to *faṣīḥ* and the *ʕuǧm* are those whose language is not *faṣīḥ* (Retsö 2002: 139–140). A similar use of the root ʕGM is found in a non-Arabic, pre-Islamic source. In the Jewish midrash *Ba-Midbar Rabbah* (Chapter 10) it is said about a drunken person that his tongue is *ʕagum* so that he cannot speak clearly. The root obviously means "crooked."

It thus seems that Arabic in the Quran has a quite narrow linguistic definition, and, consequently, there were many dialects and languages in Arabia at the time of the Prophet that we today probably would call Arabic but that are referred to in the contemporary sources as *ʔaʕǧamī*, that is, "non-ʕarabī."

It is worthwhile to take a look at the earliest use of the adjective "Arabic" as a linguistic term (Retsö 2002: 140–141). The earliest attestation is in a text by Agatharchides of Cnidus, written ca. 140 BCE, in which the word *arabistí* characterizes the name of a plant growing in the Red Sea area. In Acts 2:11 the meaning is that people from Arabia (i.e., Nabataea) heard the Christian message in their own language. In the *Periplus Maris Erythraei*, written more or less at the same time as Acts, we read about holy men on the island of Sarapis off the coast of Oman who use *hē arabikē glōssa*. In a fragment of Uranius' *Arabiká*, probably written shortly after 300 CE, we read that the place-name Motho, a site in the Provincia Arabia (i.e., Nabataea), in *hē arábōn phonē* means "death." In the same century Epiphanius writes that a festival was celebrated in Elousa in the Negev in *arabikē diálektos* in which the local goddess was called by an Arabic (*arabistí*) name. The Bible translator Hieronymus refers to *Arabicus sermo* or *Arabica lingua* when discussing linguistic peculiarities in the Biblical texts. Hieronymus lived in Judaea, and his possible knowledge of an "Arabic" language is likely to have come from the (then former) Provincia Arabia.

To this evidence from Greek and Latin sources are added the remarks on Arabic language in the rabbinical literature. We find around 35 words that are characterized as "Arabic" or coming from Arabia by which most likely is meant the region of Nabataea or *Provincia Arabia* (Krauss 1916: 338–349; Cohen 1912–1913). This corpus is as close as we can get to what could be called "Arabic" in Late Antiquity. It should be underlined that we are dealing with linguistic material that in contemporary sources are explicitly characterized as "Arabic," not what in our modern handbooks is classified as Arabic.

From this evidence it is possible to draw some preliminary conclusions:

1) The concrete linguistic material characterized as Arabic in the ancient sources does not exhibit any immediate identity with the *lisān ʕarabī* of the Quran. The list of words found in the rabbinical sources contains a few specimens that might be called Arabic even today; rather, most of them look more like Aramaic or general Semitic. Most of the evidence seems to come from Nabataea. In the Nabataean kingdom Aramaic was the language used at least for writing, probably also widely spoken, even if there is interference from something that looks more Arabic than Aramaic. But the possible "Arabic language" that we catch a glimpse of in the Nabataean inscriptions may not be identical with the Arabiyya of the Quran either (feminine suffix always *-t*, case suffixes *-ū*, *-ī*, and *-ā* in a different distribution, no trace of *tanwīn*; cf. Cantineau 1931: 171–172; Müller 1982b; O'Connor 1986; Healey 1993: 59–63).
2) "Arabic language" does not seem to have been a general designation of the language(s) of the Peninsula. The majority of data comes from northwestern Arabia. Only one instance refers to a completely different part of the peninsula. The Isle of Sarapis in the Periplus most probably refers to the island of Masīra off the coast of Oman. The statement about Arabic there is remarkable. The impression is that Arabic was in use by these "holy men" on that island and nowhere else.
3) Many of the notices about an Arabic language refer to religious contexts. The Periplus and Epiphanius are quite explicit, but also the notice in Acts could belong to this category. One could in this connection refer to the passage in Herodotus (3.8) where he mentions two gods of Arabia, Alilat and Orotalt, both of which seem to have good Arabic names. The first one is the earliest certain documentation of the definite article (a)l: *al-ʔilāt*. The other one is probably identical with the god whose name is written *Ru-ul-da-a-ú* in cuneiform text from the 7th century BCE, representing the Arabic word *ruḍā*^{n}. The two deities mentioned by Herodotus were worshipped more or less in the same area where Epiphanius mentions the Arabophone cult in the 4th century CE.
4) Taking the purely linguistic evidence into account one could conclude that the concept "Arabic language" from the beginning does not refer to any linguistically definable phenomenon. It seems rather to be a functional designation. The Quranic evidence indicates that the concept of *lisān ʕarabī* in the Holy Book is of a similar kind. It has been suggested that the mentioning of a *ʕarabī* language in

> the Quran is part of the argumentation about its authenticity as divine speech or at least speech sanctioned by a nonhuman authority. The fact that the Quran is in *lisān ʕarabī* is adduced as proof that it has a nonhuman origin. Its language is the language used by the divine world. The consequence would be that it is not a language spoken in the everyday life of humans (Retsö 2010). The term *ʔaʕǧamī* most likely refers to a language or languages we would today call Arabic and, probably, the languages actually spoken in Arabia in the days of the Prophet.

This raises the question of what we today mean by the term Arabic. Our definition of the term is obviously much wider than the one we find in the Quran and also more extensive than the use of the concept in antiquity. We use the term Arabic as a designation for the whole complex of spoken languages from Oman to Morocco, from southern Turkey to Chad, including almost the entire Arabian peninsula. Which are the purely linguistic criteria upon which our modern use of the term is based? Which are the isoglosses that set the vast complex labeled Arabic apart from the other Semitic languages?

The use of the word Arabic as a linguistic term in the Middle Ages demands a special investigation that will not be undertaken here. In this essay "Arabic" will be used in its modern sense when nothing else is indicated. It seems that an immediate underlying argument for the present-day usage is the historical fact that the spoken varieties, just like the Arabiyya with its variants, "Classical" Arabic and Modern Standard Arabic, have their origins on the Arabian Peninsula. Languages and dialects from the peninsula were spread outside the area by successive waves of conquest and migration that established them as mother tongues of people who otherwise had no connection with Arabia. The overwhelming majority of present-day speakers of Arabic have no historical links with the peninsula, just as very few of the speakers of Indo-European languages in India have any genealogical links to the Arian invaders of the subcontinent more than 3000 years ago.

19.2 Can linguistic criteria define Arabic?

But which are the linguistic criteria for defining Arabic as a language? The textbooks are full of descriptions of grammatical features of the Arabiyya as well as the vernaculars, but none of them takes the comparative aspect into consideration except en passant (Hecker 1982; Fischer 1997; Holes 1995: 7; Kaye and Rosenhouse 1997; Versteegh 1997: 9–22). In fact, a linguistic definition of Arabic is never given. To give a linguistically tenable characterization of Arabic according to the present-day use of the term, one must also define the borders between this language/language complex and the other Semitic languages.

It is not possible to make an exhaustive investigation of the problem here. Suffice it to take a handful of phenomena from phonology and morphology, sketch their structure within the Arabic complex as a whole, and compare them to Semitic in general. A good start is the list of 10 features given by Mascitelli (2006: 19) that are claimed to distinguish Arabic from other Semitic languages. Of these, seven are worth discussing here: the preservation of initial *w*; the reflex of the sibilants s^1, s^2, and s^3; the existence of emphatics and interdentals; the broken plurals; the definite article [']*al* (should actually be [*ʔa*]*l*-); the causative verbs with the *ʔv*-prefix; and the particles *fī*, *fa*-, and *ʔinna*. To this list will be added a few more cases.

The preservation of initial *w* distinguishes all forms of Arabic from Northwest Semitic. But this feature is also found in Akkadian and in all the other languages on the peninsula as well as in Ethio-Semitic. It is thus not functional as a specific characteristic of Arabic.

In Arabic the Semitic phoneme s^1 appears as [s] and is thus identical to the appearance of s^3 whereas s^2 appears as [š]. This sets Arabic apart from North Semitic (Ugaritic, Hebrew, Aramaic, Akkadian) and at least partially Modern South Arabian where we find s^1 as [š] and s^2 appears as [š] or [s] (Simeone-Senelle 1997: 382). But it seems that the other ancient languages on the peninsula as well as Geez treated the sibilants in the same manner as Arabic since s^1 in the south Semitic alphabet (used for Ancient South Arabian and Geez) is written with a sign derived from the original sign for s^3, whereas s^2 is written by the sign <š>. Most remarkable is, of course, that the Quranic orthography uses one sign only, <š> "shīn," for all three sibilants. The documentation of sibilants in the epigraphic languages of ancient Arabia is complicated (Knauf 2010: 207–208, 212), but the evidence from the languages mentioned seems clear enough. Consequently, the treatment of sibilants in Arabic is not specific but is a feature shared with non-Arabic languages originating on the Peninsula.

The so-called emphatic consonants in most spoken varieties of Arabic in reality indicate backing of consonants and vowels ([Embarki, "Phonetics"]; [Hellmuth, "Phonology"]) a feature that as a rule extends across several segments and syllables in a word: synharmony (Reichmuth 1983: 63–67; Mitchell 1990: 30; Kaye 1997: 193–219; cf. Watson 2002: 267–286). In other Semitic languages (Ethio-Semitic, partly Modern South Arabian), these phonemes have at least ample traces of an ejective articulation (Johnstone 1975: 6–7; Lonnet and Simeone-Senelle 1997: 348–349; Watson 2009: 5–10; but cf. Watson and Bellem forthcoming). This was most likely the pronunciation in Ancient Hebrew or Canaanite in general as well as in Akkadian (Steiner 1982). The (basically Aramaic) orthography of the Arabiyya reflects ejective articulation, not synharmony. Whether this was also the actual articulation of the "Arabic" language first written with this orthography or if it was just orthographic convention taken over from the Aramaic script cannot be substantiated. It is also uncertain when, if Aramaic originally had ejectives (which is indicated by the orthography), these phonemes disappeared, and the system of synharmony arose that is found in the Neo-Aramaic languages today. If one accepts the description of emphasis given here, that is, that "emphasis" is a case of phonetic synharmony, it can be observed that similar systems are found not only in spoken Arabic but also in the Neo-Aramaic languages (Younansardaroud 2001: 19–63; Kaye 1997; Kästner 1981: 33–36; Watson 2002: 267; Davis 2009). Ejective articulation is found also in some Yemeni Arabic in a similar distribution as in some variants of Mehri

(Prochazka 1987: 58–59; Watson and Bellem 2011). There are also indications of ejective articulation of the "emphatics" in early medieval Arabic (Steiner 1982: 75–81). But in the end it has to be stated that "emphasis," or synharmony, is not a specific feature for the Arabic complex.

The presence of phonemic interdentals, basically /ṯ/ and /ḏ/, is not limited to Arabic but was also found at least in Ugaritic and Ancient South Arabian as well as in Modern South Arabian (Johnstone 1975: 4; Lonnet and Simeone-Senelle 1997: 346; Watson 2009: 4). At the same time interdentals are absent in many modern varieties of Arabic, which means that neither from a synchronic nor a diachronic viewpoint can the interdentals be said to be a distinctive feature of Arabic.

The so-called broken plurals, that is, the lexicalization of plurals of nouns and adjectives, is a feature common to the Arabiyya and the dialects and is often presented as one of the most characteristic phenomena of Arabic in general. We still miss, however, a systematic comparison between the plural morphology of the Arabiyya and the modern vernaculars to see to which degree the different variants use the same patterns and which kind of local variation there. This is, in fact, one of the most interesting tasks for young scholars in the field today that would shed much light on the relationship between the vernaculars and the Arabiyya. At the same time it should be pointed out that this phenomenon is not an Arabic specialty either (Ratcliffe 1998). It exists in Geez as well as in Ancient South Arabian (Tropper 2002: 71–75; Stein 2010). It is found in modern northern Ethio-Semitic (Tigrinya and Tigre; Leslau 1941: 32–33; Palmer 1962: 16–34) and in the Modern South Arabian languages (Johnstone 1975: 21).

The prefixed *l-* as a definite article is often seen as a very distinctive feature of Arabic that is not found in other Semitic languages. This might be true, but the fact is that not all varieties within the Arabic complex have it either. In some parts of South Arabia we find a prefixed *m-* or *n-* in this function (Vanhove 2009: 753, 756), which is also documented for the pre-Islamic dialects in Western Arabia and that of Ṭayyiʔ (Rabin 1951: 34–37, 50, 205; al-Sharkawi 2009: 692), and in the dialects in Central Asia it is absent altogether (Zimmermann 2009: 616). Unless one is prepared to exclude these varieties from the Arabic complex and call them something else (what?) one has to admit that the *l-* is not a pan-Arabic feature and does not constitute an isogloss distinguishing Arabic in its modern sense from everything else.

The formation of causative verbs with a *ʔv-* prefix to the perfect (but absent in the imperfect) is a feature that is found not only in the Arabiyya and some modern spoken forms of Arabic but also in Middle Aramaic and Ethio-Semitic. On the other hand, it is absent in many modern Arabic dialects. It can even be argued that it never existed in some of them (Retsö 1989: 95–138). But even skeptics about this issue must agree that this causative formation is not a characteristic of Arabic setting it apart from other Semitic languages.

Some particles, like *fī*, *fa-*, and *ʔinna*, are characteristic of the Arabiyya, and traces of them can be found in most dialects. On the other hand, it is evident that at least *fa-* and *ʔinna* are not limited to Arabic but appear in other languages as well like Hebrew *hinne* or Sabaean *f* (Nebes 1995) or Ugaritic *p* (Tropper 2000: 788).

To this list some more features could be added as potential candidates for a modern linguistic definition of Arabic.

The so-called stem IX of the verb, *ifʕall-*, is a morphological element that seems to be found only within the Arabic complex. This form, however, is not found everywhere there. In large parts of the Maghrib we instead find *fʕāl*. Some scholars have been inclined to believe that the latter is a secondary formation derived from *ifʕall-* or *ifʕāll-* (Cohen 1912: 237; Marçais 1956: 200–201; Cohen 1975: 122; Marçais 1977: 64; Singer 1984: 392). As so often is the case with suggestions like this one it is difficult or even impossible to prove, and it has a taste of an explanation ad hoc: one has already made up one's mind how things must have been ("we all know that spoken Arabic comes from the Arabiyya"), which then becomes the explanation. To make this allegation acceptable one would have to come up with some kind of rule that documents the change -*v*CC > -v̄C/-*v*ll > v̄l-, showing that this is a regular change in Maghribi. The verbs and elatives from roots III geminatae would be a good example. Unfortunately, these words do not show any traces of this change (Marçais 1977: 43). Unless one is hypnotized by the idea that everything must derive from "Classical Arabic" or at least from the Arabiyya, there are other explanations that are at least as likely and even more likely. It has been suggested that the Maghribi *fʕāl* in fact goes back to a form *fuʕāl*, well-known from the Arabiyya but also found in Aramaic with meanings similar to those in Maghribi. We would here have one of several features connecting Maghribi Arabic with Aramaic (Retsö 2000).

The dual in the Arabiyya is a well-developed morphological category with marked dual forms not only with nouns but also with adjectives, pronouns (personal, deictic), and finite verbs (second and third person). A similar dual system is found in Ancient South Arabian but not in any known Arabic dialect (Stein 2003: 71, 92–94, 134, 169–172, 177–178, 181). In the latter the system looks quite different with markings of dual only with nouns. At the same time the "dual" suffix also serves as a plural marker with certain classes of nouns. The closest parallel to this is found in biblical Hebrew (Blanc 1970; Retsö 1997). This is one of the cases where there indeed is a wide gap between the Arabiyya and the modern vernaculars that cannot be bridged except by drastic and unlikely ad hoc explanations. Both share isoglosses with other Semitic languages, but the Arabiyya goes with the southern neighbors whereas the vernaculars follow the languages in the northwest.

A traditional designation of Arabic is *luġat ḍād*, "the *ḍād*-language". It refers to the sound represented by the 15th letter of the Arabic alphabet that, according to the early medieval grammatical tradition, had some kind of lateral articulation that was apprehended as peculiar (Steiner 1977: 57–101; Versteegh 2006). Traces of such an articulation are found in some modern dialects in the southern peninsula (Vanhove 2009: 754; Watson et al. 2010; Watson and Al-Azraqi 2011), but in almost all variants of Arabic that are documentable we find an interdental or a apicodental pharyngealized realization. The traditional term thus has no relevance for present-day Arabic, either the vernaculars or the Arabiyya.

Some traces of the lateral articulation are found far back in pre-Islamic times (see the previous example of Ruḍā) as well as from the Islamic Middle Ages. A well-known example is the Spanish *alcalde* "mayor," which is the Arabic *al-qāḍī* "judge." If we look at the cognate roots in other Semitic languages containing this phoneme we find contradictory evidence not always easy to analyze. In Old Aramaic the phoneme is written with a <q> and in later Aramaic it is articulated as a laryngeal voiced fricative [ʕ] and written by the letter ʕayn. The Ancient South Arabian alphabet has a distinctive sign for it, but the phonetic reality behind it escapes us. In the Modern South Arabian languages we find a lateralized and glottalized apico-alveolar consonant that etymologically corresponds to Arabic /ḍ/ (Steiner 1977: 12–56; Lonnet and Simeone-Senelle 1997: 348; Simeone-Senelle 1997: 382; Watson and Al-Azraqi 2011). There seem to be traces of a similar articulation in other ancient Semitic languages as well (Steiner 1977).

It is thus clear that (1) the lateral articulation is not limited to the language complex called Arabic and (2) the lateral articulation is in fact not a specific characteristic of the Arabic complex—if by that we include what we usually call Arabic. On the contrary, it is extremely rare. In fact, there is no real evidence that the present-day realization of the *ḍād* is secondary and that in all spoken varieties as well as in the Quranic recitation it originates from the lateral variant.

The voiced uvular fricative, *ġayn*, is a pan-Arabic phoneme shared by the Arabiyya as well as most Arabic dialects although in some areas we find *q* or *g* instead (Jastrow 1980: 143; Singer 1980: 252; Owens 1985: 46; Behnstedt 1997 map 7). It is found also in Modern South Arabian (Johnstone 1975: 4; Lonnet and Simeone-Senelle 1997: 346; Watson 2009: 4). It also most likely existed in Ugaritic although with a somewhat different distribution (Tropper 2000: 125–127). Likewise, the South Arabian alphabet has a sign that most likely represents the same phoneme (Stein 2003: 19). It is thus not a characteristic feature of Arabic.

The few examples adduced show the problem clearly. In an overview of the Arabic complex it is very difficult to find linguistic elements that allow us to draw a distinctive line between the Arabic complex and the rest of the Semitic languages. One could, for example, argue that the elative *ʔafʕal-* pattern, which seems to be found in nearly all documented dialects, is a uniting feature between the Arabiyya and the dialects. But the fact remains that such phenomena are quite few and often uncertain due to the still missing information on many spoken Arabic dialects. A more principal question is whether the existence of a few isoglosses uniting all forms of spoken Arabic with the Arabiyya and, at the same time, distinguishing the two from other Semitic languages, would make it meaningful to proclaim this immense complex as being one language. What would give, for example, the *ʔafʕal-* form the status that decides and defines an enormous linguistic complex as one language, in spite of the fact that an overwhelming amount of phenomena, on the contrary, do not support such a definition? It seems that a quite arbitrary process of thinking lies behind this. First one decides which languages should be called Arabic, and then one begins to look for linguistic criteria supporting the idea.

The traditionalist argument against this would be that the modern spoken forms after all are historically derived from an Arabiyya-like language. Even if the distinctive features are not preserved in the modern dialects they still form a unity with the Arabiyya since they are developed from it or at least from a close relative.

There are several objections against this statement. The first is, of course, that it confuses synchronic analysis with diachrony. Such a confusion tends to blur distinctions and clear thinking even when the diachronic background for synchronic phenomena is well documented. With this kind of argument we will end up considering, for example, French or Italian, as a variety of Latin. Most diachronic statements about the relationship between the Arabiyya and the modern dialects, however, are just assumptions, not documented processes. When it is claimed that the interdentals have disappeared in many modern madani dialects, that the syllable structure of many dialects deviating from that of the Arabiyya represents a development from that of the Arabiyya, that the "internal" passive conjugation of the verb has disappeared due to phonological developments, that the case and mood distinctions of the Arabiyya have been reduced or disappeared, or that short final vowels have been lost, all these claims are in fact descriptions of existing differences between the dialects and the Arabiyya, nothing more. Why these differences exist is another matter altogether. The attempts that have been made to reconstruct an assumed diachronic process, establishing the line of development from the Arabiyya to modern vernaculars (Birkeland 1952; Garbell 1958) are highly speculative and, as it seems, not in harmony with evidence. The evidence shows that the distinction between "Classical Arabic" and languages of the modern vernacular type has been around at least since the 7th century CE, that is, during the entire period from which we have extensive documents. The evidence from before this period about languages in most parts of Arabia is much more fragmentary. It is most likely that the Arabiyya documented by the poetic tradition once upon a time also existed as a spoken idiom. It is quite likely that varieties of the modern vernacular type also existed in the pre-Islamic period although the documentation is almost nonexistent. But this means that the assumed process of transition from an Arabiyya-type of language to an early variant of the modern vernaculars cannot be verified. Further, a comparative perspective shows that, for example, the passive conjugations of the dialects as a rule are identical to the ones found in Aramaic, Geez, and Hebrew, the syllable structure in many dialects is similar to the ones found in Aramaic and Hebrew and so on. The many similarities between the vernaculars and the other Semitic languages, contrasting them to the Arabiyya, put a question mark at the derivation of the modern vernacular type from an Arabiyya-like forebear.

A traditionalist argument explaining the latter point would be that Arabic shows an internal development parallel to the one in Semitic in general. The "simplification" of the phonology and morphology is the result of "drift," a common tendency present in the entire Semitic (cf. Blau 1969) or even Afro-Asiatic (cf. Diakonoff 1988) complex. But all these allegations are built upon presumptions that are highly uncertain and in many cases demonstrably wrong. It is without further consideration assumed that (1) there existed a Proto-Semitic language and (2) this language was practically identical with the Arabiyya, at least as far as phonology and morphology are concerned. But this remains a hypothetical assumption since no such Proto-Semitic is documented and on closer inspection its existence turns out to be unlikely. If there ever existed something deserving the name Proto-Semitic, we should assume that it was a heterogeneous phenomenon from the beginning. The variation was there already. From an unprejudiced comparative

Semitic viewpoint, the passive conjugation, the formation of causative verbs, the dual marking, as well as at least substantial parts of the case- and mood-marking system in the Arabiyya are most likely to be innovations or later systematizations, which means that the dialects, together with biblical Hebrew, Aramaic, Geez, and Akkadian represent an earlier stage of case, number, and diathesis marking (Retsö 1989, 1994, 1995, 1997; cf. Petráček 1981; Denz 1982: 58–59; [Owens, "History"]). The similarities between many phenomena in the modern dialects and other Semitic languages are due to common heritage, not parallel development from an assumed more or less unified proto-Semitic, being suspiciously similar to "Classical" Arabic, which in Semitic–Arabic studies has tended to be seen as a kind of Semitic Sanskrit (Denz 1982).

19.3 Stammbaum vs. Continuum of Isoglosses

The view of the history and identity of Arabic and the Semitic languages in general has until this day been formed by the traditional *Stammbaum* model of linguistic development launched by Schleicher in 1861. The application of this model to linguistic history has often led to the view of each language as a closed world on its own, living an inner life of developments only occasionally affected by external "influences." J. Schmidt's counterattack in 1872, launching the wave model, seems not really to have caught on among Arabists until now. It might be that the *Stammbaum* model is a plausible model for the Afro-Asiatic phylum as a whole, but its routine application to the Semitic linguistic world leads to serious misunderstandings. It is obvious that the Semitic languages, being as closely related as they are, constitute a continuum of isoglossses rather than a tree with distinct branches (Rabin 1963: 114–115). Careful use must also be made of documentary material. The written evidence, which is crucial for the diachrony of Semitic, does not necessarily represent distinct languages. It is not certain that the language of the Hebrew Bible represents a language that was spoken in Palestine with a distinct border against surrounding Aramaic, Phoenician, or Arabic. If we imagine a traveler going from oasis to oasis, from village to village from the Northern Hijaz to the upper Euphrates let us say in the time of Alexander the Great, he would most likely never be aware of passing from "Arabic"-speaking areas into "Hebrew"-speaking ones, then passing the border to the people speaking "Aramaic." He would instead notice continuous small differences in the speech of the locals on his way. Today, a similar picture would be created by a similar journey from Mauritania to Oman through the Arabophone areas. Within the branches of a linguistic phylum like Semitic in Afro-Asiatic, or Germanic, Romance, or Slavonic in Indo-European, distinct dialectal borders are exceptions, gradual change the rule. Our traveling linguist would get the same picture today making the same journey from Sicily to Vallonia or from the villages around the Vierwaldstättersee to Finnmark. The current model still used by most Arabists describing the linguistic realities is outdated. Notably, the work by the Arabic dialectologists during the 20th century has made this completely clear (Behnstedt and Woidich 2005: 83; [Behnstedt and Woidich, "Dialectology"]). The picture of a language consisting of a mosaic of distinct dialects with clearly discernible borders corresponds to reality only in some special cases. When encountering sharp dialectal borders in the Arabophone area today, like the one between *badawī* and *ḥaḍarī* dialects, this is the result of migrations, not diverging linguistic developments in the area (Rabin 1963: 105–106).

Considering the fact that "Arabic," defined as the Arabiyya and the modern dialects, has its origin in the Arabian Peninsula one should consider the fact that the documentation clearly shows that there was a considerable linguistic variation in that area from the beginning of the period documented by texts, that is, roughly from 800 BCE until the Islamic conquest. The original view that the languages on the peninsula were dialects of the same language, reflected in the terms South and North Arabic, however, turned out not to be tenable. The southern languages were then called South Arabian, the term (North) Arabic being reserved for the rest. North Arabic thus indicated all pre-Islamic languages documented between Yemen and the Syrian Desert and were considered early stages of Arabic. A development was assumed from Proto-Arabic, that is, the epigraphically documented languages such as Thamudic, Lihyanitic, and Safaitic, to Old or Early Arabic, which in its turn was the basis for "Classical" Arabic and the modern vernaculars (Rabin 1960). This view is still adhered to by many scholars (cf. Knauf 2010). Recent research, however, has clearly shown that most of the languages documented epigraphically are not direct predecessors to what we today call Arabic, and the latest suggestion is that we should distinguish between Ancient South Arabian (ASA), Ancient North Arabian (ANA), and Old Arabic (Müller 1982a; Macdonald 2000, 2004, 2008; Knauf 2008, 2010). These entities are represented by the epigraphic documents from at least the 8th century BCE onward. If one takes the entire peninsula into consideration, one should also presume the existence of a complex that is the forebear to the modern South Arabian languages and somewhere also possibly a complex from which Ethio-Semitic ultimately derives. We should not see these labels as representing distinct languages. They are at best continua of linguistic varieties that can be shown to share a few isoglosses, such as different forms of the definite article and the appearance of verbs IIIw/y. It is also worth pointing out that the ASA languages share some important isoglosses with the northern languages, including those of Syria, for example, the tense system opposed to the one found in Modern South Arabian and Ethio-Semitic (and Akkadian).

It thus looks as if even the epigraphically documented "Proto-Arabic" died out without leaving any descendants. The forebears of the Arabiyya as well as the modern vernaculars are to be looked for in the Old Arabic group that was independent from the ANA. Unfortunately, documentation of this Old Arabic is fairly limited, but it should not be assumed without any further consideration that Old Arabic was a more or less unitary phenomenon (cf. Mascitelli 2006). Still, most scholars adhere to the idea that the modern vernaculars are the descendants of a more or less Arabiyya-like language (ibid., 49–87). As already mentioned, Retsö (2010) indicates, however, that the chasm between the Arabiyya and the forebears of the vernaculars was much wider than usually assumed and that they are not directly diachronically related (cf. Diem 1978). Perhaps the concept Old Arabic should be discarded and replaced by at least two terms, one for the Arabiyya type and one for the modern vernacular type, the *ʔaʕǧamī* of the Quran. Among the latter we should look for the forebears of the modern dialects. There are large parts of the peninsula where we have no documentation of local languages but where one could assume that these dialects thrived. The Arabiyya undoubtedly goes back to a spoken language; however, rather than being the grandfather of modern spoken Arabic, that language seems to have died out without leaving any descendants, like Ugaritic and Akkadian to which it has many resemblances. Instead, other, undocumented languages became dominant in Arabia replacing the ANA languages and, later on, even the ASA (Diem 1978: 138). It has been remarked that the linguistic type represented by the modern Arabic vernaculars shows many similarities to Aramaic (Fischer 1982b: 83).

We should not assume that these replacing languages constituted a unitary linguistic complex either. Judging from their modern descendants, one must assume considerable variation even here from the beginning (Fischer 1995). Many isoglosses connected different local varieties with other Semitic languages both in the south and in the north. The Arabic complex in general shares several features with other "South Semitic" languages such as the transition $p > f$ or $s^1 > s$ but also others with the languages in the northwest such as the "perfect–imperfect," *qatvl-/yaqtvl-* opposition.

There has been a long debate about the position of Arabic within Semitic as a whole. The traditional view that Arabic as a whole belongs to the Southwestern branch of Semitic, thus drawing a distinct border between the languages of Arabia and those of Syria was challenged already in the 1930s by J. Cantineau (1932) and was followed by scholars like G. Garbini (1984), R. Hetzron (1976, 1977: 9–15), W. Diem (1980), and R. Voigt (1987). These scholars pointed out features that Ethio-Semitic and modern South Arabian have in common with Akkadian, thus splitting the South Semitic group in two, of which the northern one, which includes Arabic, has several basic features in common with the languages of Syria. The old Northwestern Semitic group was subsumed together with Arabic by the term Central Semitic [Owens, "Introduction"].

The discussion whether Arabic should be classified as Central Semitic or South Semitic is not very meaningful. We can map isoglosses that show that Arabic has features in common with languages in Syria, Mesopotamia, and South Arabia/Ethiopia. The question of classification is dependent on which phenomena are considered important enough or crucial for the "identity" of a language. Considering the immense variation within the complex called Arabic, it is doubtful if it is possible to make an evaluation of the phenomena. Is the formation of plurals of nouns a more important feature than the morphology of the verbal tenses? Or is the change $p > f$ more important than the treatment of interdentals? Whichever answer is given, none of these distinguishes Arabic in its modern sense from the other languages.

When looking at the linguistic map of pre-Islamic Arabia, one should assume that linguistic variation was there from the beginning. That is the picture that emerges from the evidence we have from the pre-Islamic period. Considerable linguistic variation is found there even today, even within the complex that we label "Arabic" (Holes 2010), and we have no reason whatsoever to assume that at the time of the Prophet everybody in Arabia spoke something like the Arabiyya (Versteegh 1997: 38). That would have been a completely unique situation unparalleled before or after. That the Arabiyya was understood in many areas when heard in poetry or even formal speech (*xuṭba*) is another matter. This is the situation even today, and not only in Arabia but in the entire Arab world.

The Semitic languages, like Germanic, Romance, or Slavonic, are from the beginning a continuum of isoglosses with no definite borders between dialects or languages. It remains unlikely that these branches, including Romance, have developed from a unified proto-language. A Proto-Semitic language did not emerge in full armor like Athena from the head of Zeus. It was from the beginning a variegated complex of dialects or languages ultimately originating in the northeastern part of the African continent. What it inherited from there we do not know yet. The comparative study of Afro-Asiatic is still in its beginnings and is beset with many difficulties. Many of the features usually ascribed to Proto-Semitic are probably innovations that occurred in the linguistic continuum and spread to different degrees. One could, for example, assume that a case system marked by vocalic suffixes, perhaps only in the pronominal system, was present in some parts of the continuum and developed into a more comprehensive declination system in nouns in some areas. In others it did not catch on and the original marking of case even disappeared. The Arabiyya and perhaps Ugaritic would have been a final stage in such a development, whereas Akkadian still represents an earlier stage. The rudimentary case system of Geez could represent an even earlier stage. In other parts on the Semitic continuum, the development did not occur at all. From this part of Semitic arose Hebrew, Aramaic, and most of the forebears of the modern Arabic dialects.

We need not assume that the gap between "proto-Arabiyya" and the forebears of the modern dialects was as wide as it seems from the documentation from the 7th century and onward. It has been suggested, supported by evidence, that there might have been a continuum even between these languages, which actually is what we should expect (Owens 2006). The Arabiyya has been subject to normative cultivation that has cemented its characteristics vis-à-vis the dialects. It is, in fact, possible to define the Arabiyya by using morphological criteria that sets it apart from other Semitic languages, including the dialects. As far as we can see the case system (the full three-case marking even in the construct state, the diptosy), the *tanwīn*, the mood system of the verb, and the pausal system are all features specific to the Arabiyya and not found in other Semitic languages. Some of these elements are traceable in other languages as well, but the system in the Arabiyya is unique for that language. The traditional view among Arabs about the *ʔiʕrāb* as the basic characteristic of the Arabiyya is thus not completely off the track (cf. Diem 1991: 298).

But the modern concept of Arabic as encompassing both the Arabiyya and the modern vernaculars is not meaningful as a pure linguistic concept. Searching through the phonology and morphology of the complex we call Arabic today, it seems impossible to find anything which delimits the group from other Semitic languages in a meaningful way. The modern concept "Arabic" is a cultural and political concept, important as such but not a linguistic entity, even if the majority of the inhabitants in the "Arab world" see themselves as speakers of Arabic, albeit a corrupted or even "wrong" variant of it. We should make a clear distinction between the Arabic complex as a cultural–political phenomenon and the linguistic realities (Suleiman 2003; [Suleiman, "Folk Linguistics"]). From a purely linguistic viewpoint the Arabic complex is dissolved into a large variety of languages that in varying degrees have elements in common with each other as well as with other Semitic languages.

References

Behnstedt, P. 1997. *Sprachatlas von Syrien. Kartenband*. Wiesbaden: Harrassowitz.

Behnstedt, P. and M. Woidich. 2005. *Arabische Dialektgeographie. Eine Einführung*. Handbuch der Orientalistik I:78. London: Brill.

Birkeland, H. 1952. *Growth and structure of the Egyptian Arabic dialect*. Avhandlinger utgitt av Det Norske Vitenskaps-Akademi i Oslo. Hist.-filos. Klasse Nr. 2. Oslo.

Blanc, H. 1970. Dual and pseudo-dual in the Arabic dialects. *Language* 46: 42–56.

Blau, J. 1969. Some problems of the formation of the old Semitic languages in the light of Arabic dialects. In *Proceedings of the International Conference on Semitic Studies Held in Jerusalem 19–23 July 1965*, 38–44. Jerusalem: The Israel Academy of Sciences and Humanities.

Cantineau, J. 1931. *Le nabatéen II: Choix de textes—Lexique*. Paris: Librairie Ernest Leroux.

—— 1932. Accadien et sudarabique. *Bulletin de la Société Linguistique* 33: 175–204.

Cohen, A. 1912–1913. Arabisms in Rabbinical literature. *Jewish Quarterly Review* 1912–1913: 221–233.

Cohen, M. 1912. *Le parler arabe des juifs d'Alger*. Paris: La Société Linguistique de Paris.

Cohen, D. 1975. *Le parler arabe des juifs de Tunis. II: etude linguistique*. Janua linguarum Series Practica 161. The Hague: Mouton.

Davis, S. 2009. Velarisation. In *Encyclopedia of Arabic language and linguistics*, Vol. 4, ed. Kees Versteegh, Associate Editors: Mushira Eid, Alaa Elgibali, Manfred Woidich, Andrzej Zaborski, 636–638. Leiden: Brill.

Denz, A. 1982. Die Struktur des klassischen Arabisch. *Grundriss der arabischen Philologie Bd. I: Sprachwissenschaft* ed. W. Fischer 58–82. Wiesbaden: L. Reichert Verlag.

Diakonoff, I. M. 1988. *Afrasian languages*. Moscow: Nauka.

Diem, W. 1978. Divergenz und Konvergenz im Arabischen. *Arabica* 25: 128–147.

—— 1980. Die genealogische Stellung des Arabischen in den semitischen Sprache. Ein ungelöstes Problem der Semitistik. *Studien aus Arabistik und Semitistik Anton Spitaler zum siebzigsten Geburtstag von seinen Schülern überreicht*. ed. W. Diem and S. Wild, 64–85. Wiesbaden: Harrassowitz.

—— 1991. Vom Altarabischen zum Neuarabischen. Ein neuer Ansatz. *Semitic Studies in Honor of Wolf Leslau on the Occasion of his Eighty-fifth Birthday Nov. 14h 1991*, vol. 1, ed. A. S. Kaye, 297–308. Wiesbaden: Harrassowitz.

Fischer, Wolfdietrich (ed.). 1982a. *Grundriss der arabischen Philologie Bd. I: Sprachwissenschaft*. Wiesbaden: L. Reichert Verlag.

—— 1982b. Das Neuarabische und seine Dialekte. In *Grundriss der arabischen Philologie Bd. I: Sprachwissenschaft*, ed. W. Fischer, 83–141. Wiesbaden: L. Reichert Verlag.

—— 1995. Zum Verhältnis der neuarabischen Dialekte zum Klassisch-Arabischen. In *Dialectologia Arabica: A collection of articles in honour of the sixtieth birthday of Professor Hekki Palva*, 75–86. Studia Orientalia 75. Helsinki: The Finnish Oriental Society.

—— 1997. Classical Arabic. *The Semitic languages*, ed. Robert Hetzron, 187–219. London: Routledge.

Garbell, I. 1958. Remarks on the historical phonology of an East Mediterranean Arabic dialect. *Word* 14: 303–337.

Garbini, G. 1984. *Le lingue semitiche: Studi di storia linguistica*, 2d ed. Napoli: Istituto Orientale di Napoli.

Healey, J. F. 1993. *The Nabataean tomb inscriptions of Mada'in Salih. Edited with introduction, translation and commentary* (Journal of Semitic Studies Supplement 1). Oxford: Oxford University Press.

Hecker, K. 1982. Das Arabische im Rahmen der semitischen Sprachen. In *Grundriss der arabischen Philologie Bd. I: Sprachwissenschaft*, ed. W. Fischer, 83–141. Wiesbaden: L. Reichert Verlag.

Hetzron, R. 1976. Two principles of genetic reconstruction. *Lingua* 38: 89–108.

—— 1977. *The Gunnän-Gurage languages*. Napoli: Istituto Orientale di Napoli.

Holes, C. 1995. *Modern Arabic: Structures, functions and varieties*. London: Longmans.

—— 2010. The Arabic dialects of Arabia. *Proceedings of the Seminar for Arabian Studies* 36: 25–34.

Jastrow, O. 1980. Das mesopotamische Arabisch. *Handbuch der arabischen Dialekte*.ed. W. Fischer and O. Jastrow, 140–173. Wiesbaden: Harrasowitz.

—— 2007. Das Spannungsfeld von Hochsprache und Dialekt im arabischen Raum. *Sterben die Dialekte aus? Vorträge am interdisziplinären Zentrum für Dialektforschung an der Friedrich-Alexander-Universität Erlangen-Nürnberg 22.10.-10.12.2007*, ed. H. H. Munske. <http://www.dialektforschung.phil.uni-erlangen.de/sterbendialekte>.

Johnstone, T. M. 1975. *The modern South Arabian languages* (Afroasiatic Linguistics 1/5). Malibu.

Kästner, H. 1981. *Phonetik und Phonologie des modernen Hocharabisch*. Leipzig: VEB Verlag Enzyklopädie.

Kaye, A. S. 1997. Arabic Phonology. *Phonologies of Asia and Africa* vol. 1, ed. Alan Kaye, 187–204. Winona Lake: Eisenbrauns.

Kaye, A. S. and J. Rosenhouse. 1997. Arabic dialects and Maltese. R. Hetzron (ed.): *The Semitic languages*, ed. R. Hetzron 263–311. London: Routledge.

Knauf, E. A. Thamudic. 2008. *Encyclopedia of Arabic language and linguistics*, Vol. 4, ed. Kees Versteegh, Associate Editors: Mushira Eid, Alaa Elgibali, Manfred Woidich, Andrzej Zaborski, 477–483. Leiden: Brill.

—— 2010. From ancient Arabic to early Standard Arabic. *The Qur'ān in Context. Historical and Literary Investigations into the Qur'ānic Milieu*, ed. A. Neuwirth, N. Sinai, M. Marx, 197–254. Leiden: Brill.

Krauss, S. 1916. Talmudische Nachrichten über Arabien. *ZDMG* 70: 321–353.

Leslau, W. 1941. *Documents tigrigna (éthiopien septentrional). Grammaire et textes*. Paris: Klincksieck.

Lipiński, E. 1997. *Semitic languages. Outline of a comparative grammar* (Orientalia Lovaniensia Analecta 80). Leuven: Peeters.

Lonnet, A. and M.-C. and M.-C. Simeone-Senelle. 1997. La phonologie des langues sudarabiques modernes. In *Phonologies of Asia and Africa*, Vol. 1, ed. A. S. Kaye 337–372. Winona Lake: Eisenbrauns.

Macdonald M. C. A. 2000. Reflections on the linguistic map of Pre-Islamic Arabia. *Arabian Archaeology and Epigraphy* 2: 28–79.

—— 2004. Ancient North Arabian. *The Cambridge Encyclopedia of the world's ancient languages*, ed. R. Woodard, 488–533. Cambridge: CUP.

—— 2008. Old Arabic (Epigraphic). *Encyclopedia of Arabic language and linguistics*, Vol. 3, ed. Kees Versteegh, Associate Editors: Mushira Eid, Alaa Elgibali, Manfred Woidich, Andrzej Zaborski, 464–477. Leiden: Brill.

Marçais, Ph. 1956. *Le parler arabe de Djidjelli (Nord constantinois, Algérie)*. Paris: Adrien Maisonneuve.

—— 1977. *Esquisse grammaticale de l'arabe maghrébin*. Paris: Maisonneuve.

Mascitelli, D. 2006. *L'arabo in epoca preislamica. Formazione di una lingua* (Arabia antica 4). Roma: L'Erma di Bretschneider.

Mitchell, T. M. 1990. *Pronouncing Arabic 1*. Oxford: OUP.

Müller, W. W. 1982a. Das Altarabische und das klassische Arabisch, In *Grundriss der arabischen Philologie Bd. I: Sprachwissenschaft*, ed. W. Fischer, 17–29. Wiesbaden: L. Reichert Verlag.

—— 1982b. Das Altarabische der Inschriften aus vorislamischer Zeit, In *Grundriss der arabischen Philologie Bd. I: Sprachwissenschaft*, ed. W. Fischer, 30–36. Wiesbaden: L. Reichert Verlag.

Nebes, N. 1995. *Die Konstruktionen mit fa- im Altsüdarabischen. Syntaktische und epigraphische Untersuchungen*. Wiesbaden: Harrassowitz.

O'Connor, M. 1986. The Arabic loanwords in Nabatean Aramaic. *Journal of Near Eastern Studies* 45: 213–229.

Owens, J. 1985. Arabic dialects of Chad and Nigeria. *ZAL* 14:45–61.

—— 2006. *A linguistic history of Arabic*. Oxford: OUP.

Palmer, F. R. 1962. *The morphology of the Tigre noun* (London Oriental Series 13). Oxford: OUP.

Petráček, K. 1981. Le système de l'arabe dans une perspective diachronique. *Arabica* 28:162–177.

Prochazka, Th. 1987. The spoken Arabic of Zabīd. *ZAL* 17:58–69.

Rabin, C. *Ancient West Arabian*. London: Taylor's Foreign Press.

—— 1960. ᶜArabiyya. *Encyclopaedia of Islam* 2nd ed. I: 561–567.

—— 1963. The origin of the subdivisions of Semitic. *Hebrew and Semitic studies presented to G. R. Driver* 104–115. Oxford: OUP.

Ratcliffe, R. 1998. *The "Broken" plural problem in Arabic and comparative Semitic*. Amsterdam: John Benjamins.

Reichmuth, Stefan. 1983. *Der arabische Dialekt der Šukriyya im Ostsudan*. Hildesheim: Olms.

Retsö, J. 1989. *Diathesis in the Semitic languages: A comparative morphological study*. Leiden: Brill.

—— 1994. *'iᶜrāb* in the forebears of modern Arabic dialects. *Actes des premières journées internationales de dialectologie arabe de Paris. Colloque tenu à Paris du 27 au 30 janvier 1993*, ed. D. Caubet and M. Vanhove 333–342. Paris: Publications Langues'O.

—— 1995. Pronominal state in colloquial Arabic. A diachronic attempt. *Dialectologia arabica. A collection of Articles in honour of the sixtieth birthday of professor Hekki Palva*, 183–192. Helsinki: The Finnish Oriental Society.

—— 1997. State and plural marking in Semitic. *Built on solid rock. Studies in Honour of Professor Ebbe Egede Knudsen on the occasion of his 65th birthday April 11th 1997*, ed. E. Wardini, 268–282. Oslo: Novus Forlag.

—— 2000. Kaškaša, t-passives and the dialect geography of ancient Arabia. *Oriente Moderno* 19/80 N.S. 111–118.

—— 2002. Das Arabische der vorislamischen Zeit bei klassischen und orientalischen Autoren. *Neue Beiträge zur Semitistik. Erstes Arbeitstreffen der Arbeitsgemeinschaft Semitistik*

in der Deutschen Morgenländischen Gesellschaft vom 11. Bis 13. September 2000 an der Friedrich-Schiller-Universität Jena, ed. N. Nebes. 138–146. Wiesbaden: Harrassowitz.
—— 2010. Arabs and Arabic in the time of the Prophet. *The Qur'ān in context. historical and literary investigations into the Qur'ānic milieu*, ed. A. Neuwirth, N. Sinai, M. Marx 281–192. Leiden: Brill.
al-Sharkawi, M. 2009. Pre-Islamic Arabic. *Encyclopedia of Arabic language and linguistics*, Vol. 3, ed. Kees Versteegh, Associate Editors: Mushira Eid, Alaa Elgibali, Manfred Woidich, Andrzej Zaborski, 689–699. Leiden: Brill.
Simeone-Senelle, M.-C. 1997. The modern south Arabian languages. In *The Semitic Languages*, ed. R. Hetzron, 378–423. London: Routledge.
Singer, H.-R. 1980. Das Westarabische oder Maghribinische. In *Handbuch der arabischen Dialekte* ed. W. Fischer and O. Jastrow, 249–285. Wiesbaden: Harrasowitz.
—— 1984. *Grammatik der arabischen Mundart der Medina von Tunis*. Berlin/New York: Walter de Gruyter.
Stein, P. 2003. *Untersuchungen zur Phonologie und Morphologie des Sabäischen* (Epigraphische Forschungen auf der arabischen Halbinsel Bd 3). Rahden: Verlag Marie Leidorf.
—— 2010. *Die altsüdarabischen Minuskelinschriften auf Holzstäbchen aus der Bayerischen Staatsbibliothek in München 1: Die Inschriften der mittel- und spätsabäischen Periode (Epigraphische Forschungen auf der Arabischen Halbinsel 5)*. Tübingen: Wasmuth.
Steiner, R. C. 1977. *The case for fricative-laterals in Proto-Semitic* (American Oriental Series 59). New Haven.
—— 1982. *Affricated Ṣade in the Semitic languages*. New York: The American Academy for Jewish Research Monograph Series no. 5.
Suleiman, Y. 2003. *The Arabic language and national identity. A study of ideology*. Edinburgh: Edinburgh University Press.
Tropper, J. 2000. *Ugaritische Grammatik* (Altes Orient und Altes Testament Bd. 273). Münster: Ugarit-Verlag.
—— 2002. *Altäthiopisch. Grammatik des Ge'ez mit Übungstexten und Glossar* (Elementa Linguarum Orientis 2). Münster: Ugarit-Verlag.
Vanhove, M. 2009. Yemen. *Encyclopedia of Arabic language and linguistics*, Vol. 4, ed. Kees Versteegh, Associate Editors: Mushira Eid, Alaa Elgibali, Manfred Woidich, Andrzej Zaborski, 750–758. Leiden: Brill.
—— 1997. *The Arabic language*. Edinburgh: Edinburgh University Press.
—— 2006. Ḍād. *Encyclopedia of Arabic language and linguistics*, Vol. 1, ed. Kees Versteegh, Associate Editors: Mushira Eid, Alaa Elgibali, Manfred Woidich, Andrzej Zaborski, 544–545. Leiden: Brill.
Voigt, R. M. 1987. The classification of Central Semitic. *Journal of Semitic Studies* 32:1–21.
Watson, J. C. E. 2002. *The phonology and morphology of Arabic*. Oxford: OUP.
—— 2009. Introduction. Sima, A. *Mehri-Texte aus der jemenitischen Šarqīyah*, transkribiert unter Mitwirkung von ᶜAskari Ḥugayrān Sacd, bearbeitet und herausgegeben von Janet C. E. Watson und Werner Arnold (Semitica Viva Bd. 47) 1–28. Wiebaden: Harrassowitz.
Watson, J. C. E., B. Glover-Stalls, Kh. al-Razihi, Sh. Weir. 2010. The Language of Jabal Rāziḥ: Arabic or something else?. *Proceedings of the seminar for Arabian studies* 36:35–41.
Watson, J. C. E. and M. Al-Azraqi. 2011. Lateral fricatives and lateral emphatics in southern Saudia Arabia and Mehri. *Proceedings of the Seminar for Arabian Studies* 41: 425–432.

Watson, J. C. E. and A. Bellem. 2011. Glottalisation and neutralisation in Yemeni Arabic and Mehri. In *Arabic Instrumental Phonetics*, ed. B. Heselwood and Z. Hassan, 235–256 Amsterdam: Benjamins.

Younansardaroud, H. 2001. *Der neuostaramäische Dialekt von Särdär:ïd* (Semitica Viva Bd. 26). Wiesbaden: Harrassowitz.

Zimmermann G. 2009. Uzbekistan Arabic. *Encyclopedia of Arabic language and linguistics*, Vol. 4, ed. Kees Versteegh, Associate Editors: Mushira Eid, Alaa Elgibali, Manfred Woidich, Andrzej Zaborski, 612–623. Leiden: Brill.

CHAPTER 20

HISTORY

JONATHAN OWENS

20.1 Introduction

In surveying conceptions of history of the Arabic language, one finds not so much a history as histories, with different intellectual traditions often having rather different interpretations. Common motifs include the following:

Linearity: The dominant one, linearity, will be discussed in greater detail in a future section. In it, Arabic language history falls into easily divisible units, one linearly following another. This motif has various subreflexes. In one, Arabic has a history akin to English, with Old, Middle, and Modern periods as in Blau (1988, Corriente 1971), following what was at the point of his writing, still a dominant conception of Arabic language history.

Life cycle: A different approach sees periods of development, growth, and decline. This is Chejne's (1969) characterization. Chejne, however, applies his organic metaphor only to the literary language. Furthermore, development and decline are restricted entirely to vocabulary, the ability to express modern concepts, technical terms, and differentiated lexical domains [Newman, "Nahda"]. This represents what I will call the "first metonymic fallacy," Classical/Standard Arabic stands in for the entire Arabic language, a widespread fallacy both in the Arabic world and among western scholars (see criticisms in Ryding 2006). The metonymy, moreover, extends beyond discrete lexical domains. The decline in the Arabic language becomes a stand-in for the perceived decline of Arabic culture in general after 1258 (sack of Baghdad by the Mongols). Both the life cycle and the linear conceptualization are very attractive to a wider population of learned individuals. They are simple, easily graspable metaphors. In one, the language is a living organism; in the other, it goes from one stage to another, mirroring historical chronology itself. Simplicity is hardly a negative attribute; to the contrary, other things being equal, it is good. However, as will be argued, other things are not equal.

"Language" as asynchronic, polyphonous, polygenetic: Few systematic alternatives to these two models exist. There are individual works and authors who clearly contradict them. Notable here is Vollers (1892, 1906), who argued that the modern dialects represent a phonologically older variety of Arabic than Classical Arabic. In a slightly different vein, Rabin (1951: 2) suggests that what he called "ancient West Arabian," the area of Yemen and the Hijaz, was "a language which, while closely related to Classical Arabic, has from very early times developed along different lines... in fact a different language" (see also [Retsö, "Arabic?"]). In these conceptions, languages can have, as it were, multiple histories. Neither Vollers nor Rabin, however, developed coherent models as to what their "Arabic," or "Arabics," looked like as a whole, their understanding of "language" remained undefined, and Rabin himself elsewhere points out the paucity of old textual material for defining dialects. It is the task of the historical linguist to provide such a model. A further exception in this respect is Edzard (1998), who uses the metaphors of "polygenesis, convergence and entropy" and goes so far as to speak of a "non-reconstructionist" approach to understanding Semitic language history, Arabic included (32), arguing that it is difficult to reconstruct a deterministic Semitic proto-language (47). The view taken in this article is that proper comparative linguistics has hardly been applied to an understanding of Arabic language history. Once this is done in a broad, consistent and detailed fashion, Edzard's position may prove a fruitful one. However, it is methodologically premature to adopt it at this point.

20.1.1 Arabic among the Semitic Languages

While not often represented as such, the very classification of Arabic within Semitic is indicative of the problems in a purely linear approach to language history. There are excellent linguistic criteria to classify Arabic in two ways: either among the South Semitic languages or as Central/Northwest Semitic (Faber 1997 for summary; see [Owens, "Introduction"]). For linearity to work, there must be traits (innovations) that distinguish all daughter varieties from the mother. Within West Semitic itself, however, identifying the traits that justify linearity is problematic in the case of Arabic. More will be said about this in following sections.

20.1.2 The Different Mediums of Arabic

While Chejne's notion of Arabic language history is far too narrow, it does illustrate the reality that there is not really one history but rather two, a history of the literary language and a history of the spoken. The difference, however, is based on the medium of expression rather than on common historical linguistic categories. *Diglossia* is a key concept in this context ([Suleiman, "Folk Linguistics"]; [Al-Wer, "Sociolinguistics"]). Some scholars see an Arabic diglossia going back to the pre-Islamic era (Bellamy 1985).

I think the split did not take place until the mid-2nd/8th century (Larcher 2010), though the dating is not at this point crucial. What emerged was a literary language on one hand and an uncodified spoken language[1] on the other. The literary language was codified in the great grammatical works; it served and in many ways still serves today as the basis of the erudite and scholarly writing of Arabic–Islamic culture. It is the learned, official Arabic of modern Arab states. Its remarkable trait, from a linguistic perspective, is that it is in its fundamental grammatical structure, unchangeable. The grammar of Ibn Al-Sarraj's 4th/10th century Al-*Uṣuwl fiy l-Naħw* is essentially the same as what one reads on al-Jazeera net or *Al-'Ahram* (see [Newman, "Nahḍa"] for changes in the standard language).

The spoken language, on the other hand, is the native language. To date explanations for the split have been largely phrased in myth-like motifs—the language was corrupted by nonnative speakers or by urban life, for instance (see Nöldeke in 20.2.1 below). There are, however, no comprehensive studies that detail the subtle ways observations of the very variegated nature of Arabic by the early scholars Sibawaih (173/798) or Farra' (214/822) became integrated into the standardized grammar of Sarraj or how, for instance, Farra's observations on Bedouin variation in Koranic verses (I: 3–6) came to be either rejected (al-Zajjaj I: 7–8) or reinterpreted (al-Naħħas I: 169–170) by later interpreters. In this context, it should be noted that one remarkable aspect of the Arabic linguistic tradition in its entirety is that it on the whole preserved the observations of the earliest grammarians, using one integrative scheme or another.

To summarize the situation, at this point we know that a standardization of a single variety, the Classical language, took place by the early 4th/10th century. The intellectual apparatus behind this standardization—descriptive, prescriptive, theoretical, attitudinal—in short, the early historical sociolinguistics of Arabic, is a topic awaiting more detailed research.

20.2 Arabic and the Comparative Method: Linearity Versus Minority Viewpoints

I now turn in the rest of this chapter to one approach to interpreting Arabic language history that has received little attention in the Arabicist tradition, even if it is the method that defines historical linguistics as an independent subdiscipline.

While Arabic historical linguistics began in the 19th century, the era when historical linguistics itself developed as a methodologically independent discipline, it was neither informed by its premises, nor did its practitioners partake in the theoretical

[1] A significant exception is Maltese, the one "dialect" that became a national, standard language (Owens 2010).

development of the discipline as a whole. What may be considered a milestone in Arabic historical linguistics was an article published in 1854 by the Orientalist Fleischer in a review of an edited edition of Tha'alabi's *Fiqh al-Luɣa* in which he suggested that Arabic could be divided into three historical periods: Old Arabic (Altarabisch), Middle Arabic (Mittelarabisch), and Neo-Arabic (Neuarabisch). Fleischer gives no comparative linguistic justification for this development, and it is clear that his criterion is simply chronological: the oldest attested varieties are Old Arabic; the youngest (i.e., the modern dialects) are Neo-Arabic. The linearization of Arabic language history is hereby established. It will be seen, however, that historical chronology has nothing inherently at all to do with linguistic history as the product of the application of the comparative method. Nonetheless, the Old–Middle–New typology has been taken over by most scholars working on Arabic, up to and including the present day. A brief survey follows.

Without going into linguistic details, Nöldeke (1899: 61) speaks of the Classical language restructuring and deteriorating into dialects ("… sich umzubilden und in Dialecte zu zerfallen", "… restructuring and breaking down into dialects."). Brockelmann (1908: 45, 50) assumes the Old–New dichotomy as historical linguistic stages, without justifying them linguistically. In general, however, Brockelmann takes a distanced view of historical reconstructions (ibid., 4–5), viewing them as purely abstract entities, which were difficult to decipher among the closely related Semitic languages. Equally, however, he shows no interest in language contact or other explanatory constructs for understanding similarities among Semitic languages and hence on the whole stands outside the interesting theoretical debate that existed in his era about historical linguistics and language contact (see [Retsö, "Arabic"] for similar criticisms).

One of the relatively few Semiticists–Arabicists to justify the Old–New dichotomy was Bergsträßer (1928: 156) in his assessment that "die neuarabischen Dialekte gehen im großen und ganzen auf eine einheitliche Grundform zurück" ("on the whole the neo-Arabic dialects derive from a unitary basis"). Were this assessment correct, the condition for linearity would indeed be met, namely, that the reputed transition from Old (Classical) to New was marked by a set of across-the-board linguistic innovations (however, see Section 20.4.2; [Behnstedt and Woidich, "Dialectology"]).

Fück (1950) and, following him, Ferguson (1959) attempted to give historical plausibility to the Old–New differentiation by defining the sociohistorical context of the differentiation: Classical Arabic (Fück) developed in the new urban Islamic centers, but, by the same token, massive influxes of nonnative speakers led to the simplification of the language and development of the modern dialects. Ferguson roughly turns Fück on his head: the new urban areas are where Arabs met and developed a simplified koine, while a purer classical Arabic remained among the rural Bedouins. Fück had little of linguistic substance in his summary. Ferguson argues that the emerging koine, the ancestor of the modern dialects, is marked by 14 features that differentiated all of them from Classical Arabic. Ferguson probably comes closer than anyone else to actual application of the comparative method. However, he does not systematically compare Arabic dialects one with another, does not attempt to define proto-forms, and essentially looks for features by which many dialects differ from Classical Arabic and assumed that this was evidence enough for an historical development encompassing all of them. Most recently, Fischer and Jastrow (1980), Blau (1988), and Versteegh (1997: 99–102) develop Ferguson's perspective.

A major problem in this approach can be termed the second metonymic fallacy: a difference between Classical Arabic and one single dialect, or certain dialects, justifies the whole dichotomy between Old (Classical) and Neo (dialect) Arabic. Versteegh (1997: 99) explicitly admits to the fallacy, even while trying to justify the Old–New dichotomy. He notes, for instance, to illustrate the difference between Old and Neo-Arabic, that interdental fricatives have shifted to stops in what he terms sedentary dialects. At the same time he notes that most "bedouin" dialects have them, as does Classical Arabic. It is hard to discern what historical linguistic model underlies this observation of partial merger.

There have been other approaches to defining historical stages of Arabic as well. Ferrando (2007: 262) speaks of "Early Arabic (or Proto-Arabic)," which he identifies with the attested North Arabian varieties Thamudic, Liḫyanic, Safaitic, and Hasaitic. Here it appears that Proto-Arabic is a mnemonic device to label a group of early varieties. The larger Semiticist tradition is basically that of Brockelmann, discussed already. Semitic language history is concerned essentially with the Classical languages, and the "neo-" varieties, such as the modern dialects, have no role to play in the interpretation of earlier Semitic stages.

Other things being equal, the convenience of this approach is unquestionable. A stereotypicalized Classical Arabic can be viewed as the proto-language from which the contemporary dialects derive. An example of this is Yoda (2005), an excellent descriptive account of Tripolitanian Jewish Arabic (TJA) in Libya. In one section he summarizes the historical sources of TJA, stating that they derive from Classical Arabic. TJA /ž/, for instance, is said to derive from Classical /ǧ/ (= /dž/; ibid., 56). Yet in what is undoubtedly the best eyewitness account of early Arabic phonemes and phones, Sibawaih (II: 452) describes a sanctioned alternative which he describes as "the shiyn like a jiym." This is very likely an alternative pronunciation of the jiym (= [ž]), which is common in many parts of the Arabic world today (Levant, North Africa in particular).[2] However, if this alternative pronunciation of "jiym" existed in the Arabic described by Sibawaih, then it is hardly legitimate to represent the TJA as deriving from (innovating from) a different Classical Arabic variant. Yoda does not discuss this perspective at all. Of course, it is a matter of ongoing debate as to what the *proto*-value of "jiym" might have been ([dž], [g], [ɟ], perhaps more than one of these), and one could attempt to relate the TJA variant to one of these. Yoda, however, does not do this, because he is in fact not describing a historical development but rather is merely making a typological comparison: the sound that conventionally in contemporary Standard Arabic is pronounced [dž] corresponds

[2] In general, Sibawaih's description of nonstandard sounds, X ka-Y, uses "X" to represent place and manner, "Y" voicing, hence, the baaʔ like a faaʔ = [p], place, manner of [b], voicing of [f], the shiyn like a jiym = [ž], place and manner of [š], and voicing of jiym, see Owens (2013a).

to TJA [ž]. Examples of this type abound. What is often taken to represent a historical development from Classical Arabic to the dialects is in fact an illustrative statement of typological equivalence.

What all these approaches have in common is the aprioristic assumption that we know the history of Arabic before we actually try to ascertain it by comparative linguistic means.[3] The basis of this assumption, though not always explicitly stated, is various: what is chronologically attested earlier (i.e., Classical Arabic) must be an earlier linguistic stage than what is attested later historically (the modern dialects); another subtext is that Classical Arabic as one of the bases of Islamic culture must be historically prior to the modern dialects.

There are, however, counterpositions. Vollers, Rabin, and Edzard have been mentioned already. Kahle (1948), in discussing the status of case endings in Arabic, suggests that a caseless form of Arabic was at least contemporaneous with a variety with cases, that is, with Classical Arabic. Both Diem (1973) and Larcher (2010) point in the same direction. The contemporary dialects, caseless, can thus be seen as having as old a pedigree as Classical Arabic. Zaborski (2000) rather briefly admonishes us to apply a more rigorous comparative linguistic approach to Arabic linguistic history, while in separate articles Holes (1991, 2011) uses the comparative method as applied to purely dialectal material to establish the age of certain phonological and morphological changes. Owens (2009) advocates a systematic application of the comparative method to Arabic, which is the approach that will be summarized in the rest of this article.

20.3 State of the Art: Two Basic Issues

There are two important issues, both relating to the fortunate reality that there are a plethora of resources both old and new for interpreting Arabic language history.

20.3.1 Old Arabic Sources

Interpreting Arabic language history is, paradoxically, exacerbated by the richness of the sources that it has at its disposal. First and foremost is the rich array of sources from the Classical era itself. Quranic Arabic is one, often (circularly) defined as that early form of Arabic that is Classical Arabic, minus the features that deviate from what later became codified in Classical Arabic. Thereafter, beginning in the late 2nd/8th century are the

[3] This, unfortunately, is a position taken over all too easily by non-Arabicists like McWhorter (2007: Chapter 7), who apply Fleischer's 19th-century model of Arabic language stages to argue for their own model of language change. In this tradition, the rigors of 19th-century historical linguistics, as exemplified by the neo-grammarians and Schuchardt, never come into play.

Classical sources proper, the defining work of the linguist Sibawaih, the collections of pre-Islamic poetry, the first works of Quranic exegesis, and Islamic law. At some point between this date and the early part of the 4th/10th century Classical Arabic as we know it today became established. This form of Arabic became an independent entity unto itself, lacking native speakers, timeless in its phonological, morphological, and syntactic structure. At the risk of compounding terminological ambiguity, the practice is adopted here of terming the corpus of early-attested Arabic, "Old Arabic." In this sense, it refers to the physical *documents* or copies thereof attested in the Classical era.

It is clear from the earliest sources that Arabic had a fairly high degree of linguistic diversity, a point reflected in early observers of the linguistic situation, such as the 4th/10th century scholar Ibn al-Nadiym (*Fihrist*: 7). Here it is relevant to mention how representative early sources described it.

The most important, Sibawaih's *Kitaab*, is equally one of the most sophisticated grammars ever written (see Baalbaki 2008; [Baalbaki, "ALT I"]). Sibawaih appreciated the large amount of variation found in 2nd-/8th-century Arabic, and he had various parameters by which he differentiated the variation. Some variants were related to individual tribes or areas, some were forms he heard and accepted as legitimate Arabic but that by some theoretical consideration were less preferable than others; occasionally he actually condemned a variant as bad (e.g., the "jiym like a kaaf," II: 452), though these instances were a small minority of the total variation he noted. In some cases, as Carter (1972) acutely observes, he used an ethically derived metaphor, *mustaqiym* "correct," *jayyid* "good," *qabiyħ* "ugly," *radiyʔ* "bad," to differentiate the linguistic legitimacy of constructions. Still, against the large corpus of variants that Sibawaih describes, the largest category are those he evaluates on his own linguistic terms, without recourse to a specific, fixed vocabulary. As a case in point, chapter 504 (II: 322–323) deals with variation in the second person singular bound pronouns. In all, a total of nine different variants are mentioned. The 2FSG (second person feminine singular) object suffix, for instance, has *-ki*, *-ši*, *-kis* and *-kiš* (see (5) below). None of these are proscribed in any way; none are described in terms of ethical vocabulary. All, however, are given a linguistic legitimacy. *-ši*, for instance, is considered to be a very logical form, as it maintains a contrast to M *-ka* even in pause, in contrast to the FSG *-ki*. It was one aspect of Sibawaih's genius that he always looked for the linguistic legitimacy of a given variant. Legitimacy as part of the ʕarabiyya did not come, for Sibawaih, from a fixed vocabulary or from a pregiven standard variety of Arabic but rather from his own inimitable way of judging legitimacy, using reasoning, methods, and argumentation from across the many domains of language he worked on.

Early exegetical Quranic literature, particularly al-Farra's (204/822) *Maʕaaniy al-Quran* discusses many alternatives to given constructions and passages from the *Quran* and from the language of the Bedouins (ʻArab). The *Quran* itself was not definitively codified into seven variant readings until Ibn Mujahid in the early 4th/10th century, and his work shows that in countless points of detail the *Quran* itself is a variable document. The linguistic variation is compounded in the early *Koranic* manuscripts, many of which are only partly analyzed (see, e.g., Puin 2011). An important source of information comes from the so-called Middle Arabic texts. While Blau (1966) in his original formulation saw these texts as a missing link between Classical Arabic and the modern dialects, the current consensus is that they are texts with a basically Classical Arabic literary base but are influenced to a greater or lesser degree by nonstandard dialect influences. They are thus essentially a stylistic genre (Larcher 2001; Blau 2002; Versteegh 2005; Lentin 2008). These are interesting because they show that even from the earliest era, what today are regarded as dialectal elements were attested, for instance in a text from 22/643 (Larcher 2010: 107) *ibn Abuw Qiyr* where Classical Arabic would require the genitive *ibn Abiy Qiyr*).

All of these written sources are crucial for understanding the history of Arabic. It is equally important, however, to appreciate that they do not exhaust our understanding of the earlier stages of Arabic, as will become clear in the following discussion.

20.3.2 Retroprojection: Viewing the Past through the Present

A second issue pertains to how, from the vantage point of the 21st century, observations from the early Islamic era can be interpreted. The idea of "dialect" is a case in point. It is not uncommon for a correlation to be drawn between modern dialects and old Arabic dialects, such as pre-Islamic or early Islamic, such that modern dialects will be seen as direct descendants of the old dialects but will have no direct genealogical relationship with Classical Arabic. There are, however, two problems with this position.

First, it proceeds on the potentially problematic assumption that the observed varieties in the Old Arabic texts have a one to one correspondence with an intellectual endeavor that was first defined in Europe in the 19th century. Rabin (1951: 9), for instance, notes that a term like *luɣa*, a potential candidate for "dialect" in Old Arabic, has no less than eight different meanings, depending on context.[4]

Second, even if this assumption were correct, it assumes that old dialects are a well-defined entity. In fact, in what remains the most detailed treatment of the material until today, Rabin (1951: 13) notes:

> It would be difficult, if not impossible, to discover why the [Arabic j.o.] philologists recorded just those dialect features they did.... The net result is that we have a great deal of information on minor points of dialect usage, but get only occasional glimpses of the basic forms. We cannot reconstruct the complete paradigm of any tense in any dialect; we can hardly say with certainty what a complete word may have sounded like.

This summary is remarkably faithful to the detailed presentation and analysis of his data. There is nowhere near enough data to create an old Arabic dialectology approaching

[4] Note the very different status of grammar, naħw, where the West had to wait until the 20th century to replicate the sophistication of the Arabic tradition.

the detail of modern dialectology [Behnstedt and Woidich, "Dialectology"]. The idea that we have direct access to old Arabic dialectology is wishful thinking of the 21st-century mind.

20.4 Reconstruction

At this point it is time to turn to an interpretation of Arabic language history from the perspective of historical linguistics itself. The basis of modern historical linguistics rests on the comparative method, which was one of the great analytical developments in linguistics itself in the 19th century. Its basis is simple. Variants can be compared one against another, and divergences among them can be "explained" as resulting from (1) innovation in one variant, vis-à-vis a postulated older form, or (2) retention of the postulated older variant. Innovation, in turn, can be due to internal change, or change via contact:

- innovation
  - internal change
  - contact
- retention

Innovations are defined in linguistic terms: linguistic elements can be lost completely, lost in certain contexts only, changed into something else, changed into something else in certain contexts only, and so on. Changes can be simplifying, and they can be complicating. The sum total of the results of the comparative method yields a reconstructed proto-language. This is a hypothetical ancestral language that provides an analytical starting point against which the changes are postulated.

Two very brief examples can be given before returning to more general issues and problems.

In many North African littoral dialects beginning in northern Tunisia, as well as Maltese second person singular merges M and F, *ktib-it* = "you wrote" (unmarked for gender). Clearly this is an innovation in these dialects. In this case, looking at all dialects outside of this region the distinction in gender is maintained, so it would be highly unlikely to assume the North African situation to be the original one, all varieties outside of this area innovating to the gender distinction.

This can be represented as follows:

(1) Maltese, North African Arabic innovation

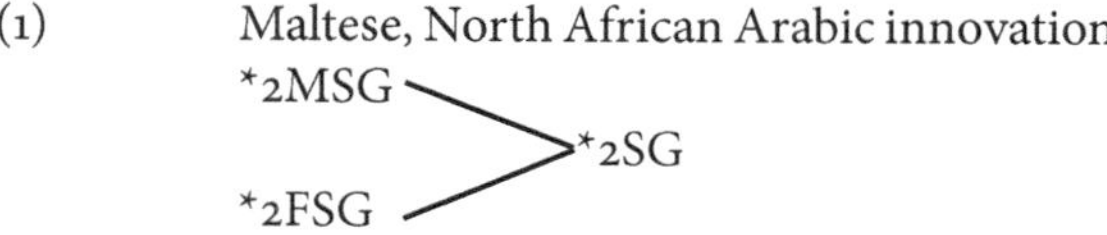

The categories of 2M/F are said to have merged in these dialects.

An opposite, more complicated change, which will be illustrated in simplified form here, concerns the development of complex morphophonemic variation in Western Sudanic Arabic. The current example comes from Nigerian Arabic, though the same change is found in Chadian and the Arabic of the western part of the Sudan.

In the 1/2M perfect, the suffix *-t* is lost in the following contexts

(2) Nigerian Arabic, 1/2MSG perfect verb
t > Ø/C_# (word final)

The suffix *-t* is lost after a consonant, if word final. This produces a split paradigm that includes, inter alia, the following forms:

(3) *katáb* "I wrote" deletion as per (2)
katáb-t-a "I wrote it": no deletion because before -V (not word final)
ramee-t "I threw": no deletion because after V-

In comparative linguistic terms, a morphophonemically conditioned split has occurred. Again, as the change is attested only the WSA area, is must be assumed that the change is a WSA innovation.

In each case, a daughter variety is marked by an innovation.

The exemplification of the basic methodology is easy. Behind the single examples lurk a range of interesting methodological and interpretive issues deriving both from the nature of Arabic and the nature of inquiry in historical linguistics.

20.4.1 What Entities Are To Be Reconstructed?

A basic question is how one knows what the comparative method is to be applied to, to which languages, varieties. This was a point often emphasized by Greenberg (2005): one needs a hypothesis about what is to be shown to be related before one can reasonably begin to apply the method. In the case of Arabic, it has been the practice to apply the comparative method not internally to Arabic but rather to Arabic compared with other Semitic languages.

What can be termed *naïve nominalism* will tell us "Arabic" is a language. However, the comparative method must be applied between languages, hence, one needs to look beyond "Arabic" to apply it.

Such a perspective begs the question of how much variation is needed before it is worthwhile applying the comparative method. As already discussed, the very idea of "Arabic" has a sociolinguistic background, and one would add a political and cultural one. For instance, from the cultural perspective, European comparative studies in particular have largely limited comparative work in the Semitic languages to the Classical language. This by definition excludes the application of the comparative method to an entity that, as it were, does not exist, namely, an internally variegated object, which is also called "Arabic."

However, as is well-known in many linguistic circles, the idea of a language is only partly, in some cases only marginally, defined in linguistic terms. For many, Maltese is Maltese, an independent language. Yet in *comparative* linguistic terms, it clearly derives from the littoral North African dialects described in (1) (Owens 2010). Thus, rather than a prioristically restricting the application of the comparative method to entities that tradition defines as "languages," a linguistic interpretation of what is to be compared can have only a linguistic answer. Criteria include:

- Degree of variation among the varieties to be compared
- Degree of mutual intelligibility between them
- Historical background

20.4.2 Degree of Variation, Mutual Intelligibility, Historical Background

In fact, contrary to Bergsträßer, there is a great deal of variation among varieties of Arabic. Two examples can illustrate this. The first two serve to answer, as it were, a Semiticist perspective that the history of Arabic starts with Classical Arabic.

The 2FSG has four variants in Arabic, two of which are found in other Semitic languages (data from articles in Hetzron 1997, Behnstedt 1985).

(4) 2FSG object suffix

Arabic	Soqotri	Amharic	Ge'ez	Ma'lula Aramaic	Biblical Aramaic
-ki, -č, -ts, -iš	*-š*	*-əš*	*-ki*	*-iš*	*-ek*

Of the Arabic forms, *-ki* and *-iš* are found in Sibawaih and hence are part of Old Arabic in the chronological sense of the term used here, while *-č* certainly and perhaps *-ts* as well also go back to Sibawaih (Johnstone 1963; Owens 2013a.). The interesting point is that two of these variants are found in different language subfamilies. *-š* is attested in the modern South Arabian languages such as Soqotri, in Amharic, in Gurage, and in other southern Ethiopian Semitic languages and in present-day Ma'lula Aramaic. *-ki*, the Classical Arabic form, is equally attested across a range of Semitic languages. Both *-ki* and *-š* are thus distributed across the South Semitic family, and the Central or Northwest Semitic, and within the single language, Arabic, however it be classified. Similarly, Arabic has two variants of the first and second person perfect verb, variants otherwise defining different Semitic sub-families.

(5) 1, 2F perfect verb

Arabic	Ge'ez	Biblical Aramaic
-t ~ -tu, -t/-ku, -ki	*-ku, -ki*	*-it, -ti*

Here again, with Arabic itself is recapitulated much of the variation found in the entire Semitic language family (Rabin 1951: 51).

Examples such as this could be compounded (e.g., syllable structure, reflexes of various sounds). Where they all point is to a situation in which Arabic has maintained in one variety or another what often are cited as fundamental isoglosses *separating* and serving as classificatory criteria of the Semitic language family. If Arabic contains elements distinctive enough to serve a language distinctors, it allows application of the comparative method internally as well.

While there are few studies actually testing mutually intelligibility among varieties of Arabic, it may be very difficult for speakers to understand speakers of another region, or of Classical Arabic for that matter, which they have no experience in. Arabs of Jordan will not readily understand Moroccans, and vice versa, unless a general koine is used.

While there are many gaps in many aspects of the history of Arabs, still a considerable amount is known, for instance, that Arabic spread out of the Arabian peninsula and surrounding regions into Central Asia, North Africa, Spain, the Sudanic region of Africa between 620 and 1500. Beyond this, as noted, there are a very few attestations going back as far as 323 CE. The period beginning 300 CE up to the present is comparable to the period between the attestation of early West Germanic and its modern reflexes, modern English, German, Frisian, Dutch, and Plattdeutsch. Given the age of separation, and the great geographical expanse of the Arabic diaspora, its stands to reason that one can consider, if only on a prima facie basis, a comparative Arabic, just as one has a comparative West Germanic.

All in all, the bulk of evidence argues for applying the comparative method to Arabic. Ultimately, the justification for this is to be seen in the results of the application of the method itself.

20.5 General Issues of Historical Linguistics

There are standard problems in historical linguistics that impinge in their unique way on Arabic language history as well.

20.5.1 Parallel Independent Development

An important confound to be considered in the application of the comparative method is parallel independent development. For instance, both Sudanic Arabic and Uzbekistan Arabic invariably have the 2SFG suffix *-ki* (as in Classical Arabic). Most dialects have an innovative form, such as *-ič*, *-its*, and *-ik* (see (4)). Given the unlikelihood that an assumed proto-Arabic *-*ki* switched to –*ik* or some other intermediate form, then back to *-ki* in these two dialects, in two independent steps, one assumes that an original **ki* was retained in these two very widely separated areas.

Some cases are not so easy as this, particularly certain phonological innovations, as when [θ] changes to [s], for instance in Uzbekistan Arabic and in Bagirmi Arabic in WSA. A change from [θ] to [s] is a natural one, and in general Arabic interdentals often shift to something else so it is possible in this case that the common reflex developed in two independent steps.

In general parallel independent development, by Occam's razor, is a disfavored explanation for shared, observed innovations. However, different domains of grammar change in different ways, and different rates, so it cannot be ruled out in principle.

20.5.2 Relative, Not Absolute Chronology

The language history that emerges from historical reconstruction is a relative one, not one that automatically correlates with a dated chronology. Linkages to dated chronology need to be made by inference. For instance, the 2M/F merger that occurred in littoral North African certainly occurred after the population had moved into North Africa. As we know that Malta was settled by Arabic speakers at the latest by 1090 CE and that Maltese shares in the merger, the change must have taken place by that time. Given its fairly wide distribution all the way into Morocco, it probably occurred considerably before then, but after the ancestral population moved into North Africa, that is, between circa 80/700 CE and 482/1090 CE.

One point is to be emphasized in this context: merely being attested in the written historical record first does not automatically mean that the forms so attested are older than those that emerge by other means, as by the comparative method. This follows from what can be termed the principle of incompleteness. What is attested in old, historical documents will always be incomplete to one degree or another, while other methods can fill in for this inherent incompleteness.

20.5.3 Type of Change, Why Change?

(1)–(3) are examples of innovation. There is nothing inherent in them that tells whether they are due to change via contact or change for internal reasons. As far as the WSA example goes, all evidence points to internal change (see Owens 2009: Chapter 6). Regarding the loss of the 2FSG in North African Arabic, the distribution of the change in what was part of the diasporic, post-Islamic domain of Arabic, with strong Berber contact, Berber, lacking a distinctive masculine-feminine contrast in the second-person singular, suggests that simplification via contact is a distinct possibility.

One of the great challenges to linguistics in general is to answer the question of why languages change at all. If contact was indeed the cause of the merger in North African Arabic, why hasn't an analogous change occurred in Anatolian Arabic, where Arabic is in contact with two languages, Kurdish and Turkish, which have no M/F distinction in the second person? Language internal explanations do often have a plausible linguistic basis. The loss of the *-t* of the 1SG and 2MSG in NA cited in (2), for instance, can be assumed to have occurred because NA, unlike many other dialects, lacked a rule of epenthesis to "protect" the final, nonsonorant *–t* (cf. Baghdadi *msak-it̲* "I grabbed"). Such explanations themselves, however, demand further questions: for instance, why did rules of epenthesis develop in one way in one area and in another in another?

20.5.4 Contact

One of the great confounds in historical linguistics is distinguishing change due to contact from internally caused change. A possible exemplification of these two effects was suggested in (1) versus (2). If nothing will be said about contact in this chapter, it is not because contact is irrelevant to understanding Arabic language history but rather simply from a methodological perspective, deducing change via contact is adventitious upon internal genetic change. To simplify the issue, the comparative method assumes that change is language-family internal. At the same time, it recognizes that some changes cannot be accommodated within this explanatory framework. In this case, other factors are adduced, change via contact being an important one. Evaluating change via contact thus goes hand in hand with having an effective comparative historical framework, which, it is argued in this chapter, is only minimally in place in the case of Arabic ([Kossmann, "Borrowing"]; [Retsö, "Arabic?"]).

20.6 Arabic Language History and Comparative Method: A Basic Typology

At this point it is relevant to present a basic typology of the major results that emerge from an application of the comparative method to varieties of Arabic. In particular, rather than contrast the Old Arabic sources with evidence from the contemporary dialects, as has been a standard practice in interpretations of Arabic language history, this summary emphasizes commonalities between them. Such commonalities emerge from a reasoned application of the comparative method.

Before beginning, a question that can be raised is how the comparison between a reconstruction based on contemporary sources and Old Arabic sources should be conceived of. The following approach is followed here. The results of the reconstruction run parallel to the Old Arabic sources, as it were, with the latter serving as a filter against which the results are judged. The Old Arabic sources themselves cannot be brought into the reconstruction, since they are actual attestations and therefore on a different conceptual level as the reconstruction, which is an object that is the result of a method.

The filter acts as follows. It will let pass identical results (i.e., reconstruction = Old Arabic), but it will block nonidentical results. To begin with, modern and Old sources

Table 20.1 Potential outcomes of reconstruction

	Modern sources	Reconstruction	Old source	Result
1	+	+	+	part of proto-language
2	-	-	+	blocked
3	+	+	-	blocked
4	-	-	-	not part of proto language

can be set one against the other, and a reconstruction is undertaken based on the modern sources alone. If the reconstruction based on the modern sources yields a proto-reconstruction that is at variance with the Old source, the interpretation is provisionally blocked (Table 20.1).

The blocked results then need to be subjected to further procedures of the comparative method to decide which, the OA or the reconstruction, if either or both, are candidates for proto-Arabic status. Section 20.6.1 gives examples of identical results, and Sections 20.6.2 and 20.6.3 give blocked cases.

The latter two cases lead to a methodological impasse of sorts. Discrepancies between reconstruction and the Old Arabic filter themselves need to be resolved comparatively, so it is at this point that the Old Arabic sources themselves are integrated into Proto-Arabic. These are discussed in Sections 20.6.2 and 20.6.3. Finally, there are cases where reconstruction does not argue for proto-status, and where these are not attested in the old literature (Section 20.6.4).

20.6.1 Perfect Isomorphism

Often unappreciated is how similar many basic structures are between the Old Arabic and the contemporary dialects. One fundamental example serves to illustrate this point.

Certainly the verb is a key element in Arabic grammar. A survey of a 30,000-word corpus of spoken Arabian peninsular Arabic, for instance, gives an estimate that 18.75% of all words in the corpus are verbs.

The following gives a sample of imperfect paradigms in the singular, without the tense/modal prefixes (e.g. *b-*, *k-*, *t-*), which often occur in many (not all) dialects.

(6) Imperfect verb

Uzbekistan Ar	Baghdadi	Cairene	Moroccan	Nigerian	Classical
1 *a-ktib*	*a-ktub*	*a-ktib*	*nə-ktəb*	*a-ktub*	*a-ktub-u*
2M *ti-ktib*	*ti-ktib*	*ti-ktib*	*tə-ktəb*	*ta-ktub*	*ta-ktub-u*
2F *ti-ktib-iin*	*ti-kitb-iin*	*ti-ktib-i*	*tə-kətb-i*	*ta-ktub-i*	*ta-ktub-iin*
3M *yi-ktib*	*yi-ktib*	*yi-ktib*	*yə-ktəb*	*i-ktub*	*ya-ktub-u*
3F *ti-ktib*	*ti-ktib*	*ti-ktib*	*tə-ktəb*	*ta-ktub*	*ta-ktub-u*

The structural commonalities are striking. The morphological categories are identical, allowing for the 2M/F merger noted for North African littoral Arabic (1); the order of their realization is identical, and their phonological form is either identical or very similar. Furthermore, as the reader can fill in for themselves, the perfect verb is equally homogeneous across the different varieties.

An important comparative point is that while there are differences between any given dialect and Classical Arabic, the differences between any two dialects can be equally great. For example, without quantifying the differences, it is clear that Uzbekistan is equally or more similar to Classical Arabic than it is to Moroccan Arabic. Furthermore, as will be seen, a number of differences with Classical Arabic disappear as soon as the wider Old Arabic literature is taken into consideration.

These commonalities can be explained as deriving from a common origin. In the comparative method, common origin is stated in terms of derivation from a reconstructed proto-form, indicated by an asterisk. The major proto-elements that emerge from this brief comparison are the following:

(7) Reconstructed elements of imperfect verb
* prefixes in imperfect conjugation
* perfect/imperfect related in terms of ablaut changes
*a- 1SG
*t- 2 and 3F
*y- 3M
*-ii 2F
*a/i preformative vowel

Note that some elements, for instance, the preformative vowel, have more than one proto-form. Proto-reconstruction does not necessarily yield unique solutions.

With marginal exceptions, what is reconstructible from the dialects yields a product that is isomorphic with Classical Arabic. This finding alone is enough to cast doubt on the long-held traditional view that distinguishes Old and Neo-Arabic in structural terms. It shows that contemporary Arabic is linguistically conservative in many respects having maintained structures that are attested in the Old Arabic literature.

The verb is hardly the only element that shows such broad consistency across all varieties of Arabic. A comparative account of the following items would equally reveal a reconstructed proto-variety that has uniform reflexes in the daughter varieties:

> Broken plurals and sound plural suffixes, pronouns, demonstratives, definite article, iḍaafa, relative clauses and topic-comment construction, agreement categories in the noun phrase and sentence, phoneme inventory, syllable structure,...

In this context it is relevant to note a subclass of this first category. There are elements that are attested only in some modern varieties and in some old varieties. A case in point is the 2FSG -š mentioned already. Another instance is the preformative vowel, which was tentatively reconstructed as having two proto-values, either *a or *i (standing for a short high vowel). In the Old Arabic literature a number of morphemes were noted to have variation between /a/ and /i/ = a high vowel (the so-called *taltala* of later grammarians). In this case, the reconstructed variation is mirrored in an identical attested variation in Old Arabic. Other examples that fall into this subclass include the *imaala* and deletion of short vowels in open syllables (Owens 2009: Chapters 6, 7).

20.6.2 Reconstructions in which Proto-Forms and Old Arabic Diverge

There are instances in which reconstructions based on modern dialects do not replicate structures found in the Old Arabic literature. The most prominent category here is the case and mode endings, in the Arabic linguistic tradition very central, in the dialects entirely absent.

This absence creates an interesting interpretive problem. On one hand, this divergence has been taken as *the* prime innovation for distinguishing Old and Neo-Arabic. On the other, it is not clear that the absence of case in the dialects represents loss of an original category or maintenance of an original caseless variety. The issue involves a number of elements that cannot be summarized in detail here (Owens 2009: Chapter 3), though two are worthy of mention. First, the fact that there are *no* traces of case endings in the dialects can, in comparative linguistic terms, constitute evidence against their ever having been there in the first place. Typically loss is accompanied by the formation of relic material that derives from the lost category. Such case traces are not found in the modern dialects.[5] Second, case otherwise is unambiguously attested only in Akkadian among the Semitic languages. The situation that suggests itself in Arabic is that sketched previously, where Arabic has maintained both case and caseless varieties for much of its history.

Other elements that fall into the category of case are the cross-categorical dual marking of pronouns, relative pronouns, demonstratives, nouns, adjectives and verbs, the inflected relative pronoun, and the jussive and apocopate form of verbs.

Briefly, from the perspective of considering these examples as candidates for proto-Arabic status, most of these categories are even more problematic than case. For instance, reconstruction clearly does not yield anything like the shortened jussive forms of Classical Arabic, that is, nothing like (*lam*) *yakil*. However, this is equally not a well-profiled verb class in other Semitic languages, hence, in proto-Semitic either. As far as the cross-categorical dual goes, it has been pointed out (Fischer 1996; Retsö 1995) that Classical Arabic stands nearly alone among the Semitic languages in spreading the dual throughout verbal and nominal categories.[6]

[5] Case traces have been suggested by Blau (1981) and Birkeland (1952). Other interpretations are possible, however (see Owens 2009: 102–106).

[6] Interestingly, contemporary South Arabian languages have a cross-categorical dual, suggesting a possible areal locus of the feature.

All in all, once one gives up the notion that Classical Arabic is identical to proto-Arabic, then the linguistic door is opened to argue for Classical Arabic itself as having been innovative in various ways. Minimally, those who do argue for the proto-status of Classical Arabic need to do so from a comparative linguistic position (including evidence from both proto-Semitic and proto-Arabic) rather than via fiat based on a Semiticist tradition.

Compared with the previous category, from a purely typological perspective, that is, disregarding questions of proto-status of the features, instances of isomorphy between the reconstructions and comparison with Old Arabic sources, instances of divergence constitute a less homogeneous set of linguistic phenomena.

20.6.3 Retentions, Archaisms Not Attested in Old Arabic at All

A third set of cases are those that are not attested in the OA literature at all yet for which there are strong arguments for inclusion in proto-Arabic. The most obvious example here is the 1/2 person perfect suffix -*k* (see (5)), for example, *katab-ku*, *katab-ki*, and *katab-ku*, which is found in highland Yemeni Arabic. These are not reported in Sibawaih or in other Old Arabic literature, qua forms of Arabic, yet in this case identical forms in Ethiopic Semitic and in Akkadian argue in one interpretation for an original Semitic retention.

A second interesting case involves an intrusive -in-, which is inserted in active participles before an object suffix, in a very few dialects—Nigerian Arabic, Oman, and Emirates and, in a slightly different context, in Uzbekistan Arabic, such as *kaatb-in-ha* "I have written it" instead of the more common, *kaatib-ha*, as discussed in Holes (2011) and Owens (2013b); see also Owens (2009: 104–105) on linker-*n* in noun phrase.

20.6.4 No Proto-Reconstruction

Finally there are cases like (1) and (3). Comparison of the changes observed in these two dialects, North African and WSA, with other contemporary varieties indicated that the two changes are localized innovations that occurred after the migration (diaspora) of Arabs to North Africa and the WSA area, respectively.

20.6.5 Summary

The results of the discussion in this section can be summarized in the following table. Two key points are, first, that the reconstruction can lead to contrasting features being brought into the proto-Arabic, such as both case and caseless varieties. One can think of the proto-language being indeterminate in this respect, or, equally, simply allow that the proto-language itself is heterogeneous [Retsö, "Arabic?"]. Second, lack of attestation in Old Arabic does not imply absence in the proto-language (case 3); see Table 20.2.

Table 20.2 Decision outcomes

	Reconstruction	Old source	Part of proto-language: yes/no
1	+	+	yes (structure of imperfect verb conjugation, etc.)
2	-	+	yes/yes (caseless and case varieties both in proto-language)
3	+	-	yes (-k in 1/2 perfect verb, intrusive -in in AP)
4	-	-	no (loss of 2M/F in North Africa,1/2 -t variation in WSA)

To come back to a problem that has plagued the interpretation of Arabic language history, it can be seen that the fact that not every feature in every dialect can be reconstructed into proto-Arabic—case 4 in Table 20.2—does not imply that those dialects should therefore be termed "Neo-Arabic" or in any other way opposed, as a group, against Classical Arabic. It simply means that these dialects have some *features* that are innovations. To say that the dialect as a whole is innovative is to commit a variant of the second metonymic fallacy. It would be equally misguided to say that since the intrusive *-in* is not attested in Classical Arabic, a feature found in some modern dialects, that Classical Arabic therefore must be included among Neo-Arabic varieties, having failed to preserve this feature.

20.7 Conclusion

Arabic should have a privileged place within historical linguistics. It is one of the few languages in the world for which a wealth of data exists both in the far-flung contemporary Arabic-speaking world and in a rich Classical tradition attested beginning 1400 years ago. Issues of maintenance and change, central concepts in historical linguistics, can be interpreted against a rich set of data. That they have not resides in the view of this article in the fact that basic concepts of historical linguistics have rarely been systematically applied to the language. Doing so will not only open new vistas to understanding the rich linguistic history of the language but also promises to contribute to the general study of historical linguistics.

References

Baalbaki, Ramzi. 2008. *The legacy of the Kitaab*. Leiden: Brill.

Behnstedt, Peter. 1985. *Die nordjemenitischen Dialekte. Teil 1: Atlas*. Wiesbaden: Reichert.

Bellamy, James. 1985. A new reading of the Namaarah inscription. *Journal of the American Oriental Society* 105: 31–51.

Bergsträßer, Gotthelf. [1928] 1977. *Einführung in die semitischen Sprachen*. Reprint, Darmstadt. Wissenschaftliche Buchgesellschaft Darmstadt.

Blau, Joshua. 1966. *A grammar of Christian Arabic.* Louvain: Secrétariat du Corpus.

——. 1981. The emergence and linguistic background of Judaeo Arabic. Jerusalem: Ben Zvi Institute.

——. 1988. *Studies in Middle Arabic.* Jerusalem: Magnes Press.

——. 2002. *A handbook of Early Middle Arabic.* Jerusalem: Max Schloessinger Memorial Foundation.

Birkeland, H. 1952. Growth and structure of the Egyptian Arabic dialect. *Avhandlinger utgitt av det Norske Videnskaps-Akademi* 1: 1–57.

Brockelmann, Carl. [1908, 1913] 1982. *Grundriss der vergleichenden Grammatik der semitischen Sprachen.* 2 vols. Reprint, Hildesheim: Olms.

Carter, Michael. 1972. Les origines de la grammaire arabe. *Revue des Etudes Islamiques* 40: 69–97.

Chejne, Anwar. 1969. *The Arabic language: Its role in history.* Minneapolis: University of Minnesota Press.

Corriente, Federico. 1971. On the yield of some synthetic devices in Arabic and Semitic morphology. *Jewish Quarterly Review* 62: 20–50.

Diem, Werner. 1973. Die nabatäischen Inschriften und die Frage der Kasusflexion im Altarabischen. *ZDMG* 123: 227–237.

Edzard, Lutz. 1998. *Polygenesis, convergence and entropy: An alternative model of linguistic evolution applied to Semitic linguistics.* Wiesbaden: Harrassowitz.

Faber, Alice. 1997. Genetic subgroupings of the Semitic languages. In *The Semitic languages*, ed. R. Hetzron, 3–15. London: Routledge.

Ferguson, Charles. 1959. The Arabic koine. *Language* 35: 616–630.

Ferrando, Ignacio. 2007. History of Arabic. In *Encyclopedia of Arabic language and linguistics*, Vol. 2, ed. Kees Versteegh, Associate Editors: Mushira Eid, Alaa Elgibali, Manfred Woidich, Andrzej Zaborski, 261–268. Leiden: Brill.

Fischer, Wolfdietrich. 1995. Zum Verhältnis der neuarabischen Dialekte zum Klassisch-Arabischen. *Dialectologia arabica. A Collection of Articles in Honour of the Sixtieth Birthday of Professor Hekki Palva* 75–86. Helsinki: The Finnish Oriental Society. Studia Orientalia 75.

Fischer, Wolfdietrich and Otto Jastrow (eds.). 1980. *Handbuch der arabischen Dialekte.* Wiesbaden: Harrassowitz.

Fleischer, A. [1854] 1968. *Kleinere Schriften*, vol. 3. Osnabrück: Biblio Verlag.

Fück, Johann. 1950. *Arabiya.* Berlin: Akademie Verlag.

Greenberg, Joseph (ed.). 2005. *Genetic linguistics: Essays on theory and method.* Intro. and bib. by William Croft. Oxford: Oxford University Press.

Hetzron, Robert (ed.). 1997. *The Semitic languages.* London: Routledge.

Holes, Clive. 1991. Kashkasha with fronting and affrication of the velar stops revisited: A contribution to the historical phonology of the Peninsular Arabic dialects. In *Semitic studies in honor of Wolf Leslau*, ed. Alan Kaye, 652–678. Wiesbaden: Harrassowitz.

——. 2011. A participial infix construction of Eastern Arabic—An ancient prediasporic feature? *Jerusalem Studies in Arabic and Islam* 37: 75–98.

Johnstone, T. M. 1963. "The Affrication of 'kaaf' and 'gaaf' in the Arabic dialects of the Arabian peninsula." *Journal of Semitic Studies* 8: 210–226.

Kahle, Paul. 1948. The Qur'an and the 'Arabiyya. In *Ignace Goldziher Memorial*, vol. 1, ed. S. Löwinger and Joseph Samogyi, 163–182. Budapest.

Larcher, Pierre. 2001. Moyen arabe et Arabe moyen. *Arabica* 48: 578–609.

——. 2010. In search of a standard: Dialect variation and new Arabic features in the oldest Arabic written documents. In *The development of Arabic as a written language*, ed. M. Macdonald, 103–112. Oxford: Archaeopress.
Lentin, Jerome. 2008. Middle Arabic. In *EALL*, vol. 3, 215–224.
McWhorter, John. 2007. *Language interrupted*. Oxford: Oxford University Press.
Nöldeke, Theodor. 1899. *Die semitischen Sprachen: Eine Skizze*. Leipzig: Tauchnitz.
Owens, Jonathan. [2006] 2009². *A linguistic history of Arabic*. Oxford: Oxford University Press.
——. 2010. What is a language? Review of *Maltese linguistics*. *Journal of Contact Linguistics* 3: 103–118.
——. 2013a. Chapter 504 and modern Arabic dialectology: What are kaškaša and kaskasa, really? In *Ingham of Arabia*, Rudolph de Jong and Clive Holes (eds.), 173–202. Leiden: Brill.
——. 2013b. The intrusive *-n in Arabic and West Semitic. *Journal of the American Oriental Society* 133.
Puin, Gerd-R. 2011. Vowel letters and ortho-epic writing in the Qur'ān. In *New perspectives on the Qur'an: The Qur'an in its historical context*, vol. 2, ed. Gabriel Reynolds, 147–190. London: Routledge.
Rabin, Chaim. 1951. *Ancient West Arabian*. London: Taylor's Foreign Press.
Retsö, Jan. 1995. Pronominal state in Colloquial Arabic: A diachronic attempt. In *Dialectologia arabica. A Collection of Articles in Honour of the Sixtieth Birthday of Professor Hekki Palva* 183–92. Helsinki: The Finnish Oriental Society. Studia Orientalia 75.
Ryding, Karin. 2006. Teaching Arabic in the United States. In *Handbook for Arabic language teaching professionals in the 21st century*, ed. K. Wahba, Z. Taha, and L. England, 13–20. Mahwah, NJ: Lawrence Erlbaum.
Versteegh, Kees. 1997. *The Arabic language*. Edinburgh: Edinburgh University Press.
——. 2005. Breaking the rules without wanting to: Hypercorrection in Middle Arabic texts. In *Investigating Arabic: Current parameters in analysis and learning*, ed. Alaa Elgibali, 3–18. Leiden: Brill.
Vollers, Karl. [1892] 1968. The system of Arabic sounds, As based upon Sibaweih and Ibn Ya'ish. In *Transactions of the Ninth International Congress of Orientalists*, vol. 2, ed. Edward Morgan, 130–154. Nendeln: Kraus.
——. [1906] 1981. *Volkssprache und Schriftsprache im alten Arabien*. Amsterdam: Oriental Press.
Zaborski, Andrzej. 2000. Inflected article in Proto-Arabic and some other West-Semitic languages. *Asian and African Studies* 9: 24–36.

Old Arabic Literature

al-Farra', Abu Zakariyya. n.d. *Maʕaaniy al-Qurʔaan*, ed. Mohammad Al-Najjar and Aħmad Najatiy. Beirut: 'Alam al-Kutub.
Ibn Mujahid, Abu Bakr. 1972. *Al-Sabʕ fiy al-Qiraaʔaat*,ed. Shawqi Đayf. Cairo: Dar al-Ma'arif.
Ibn Al-Nadiym. *Al-Fihrist*. Beirut: Dar al-Ma'rifa.
Al-Naħħaas, Abu Ja'far. *ʔIʕraab al-Qurʔaan*, ed. Zuhayr Rahid. 'Alam al-Kutub.
Ibn al-Sarraj. *Al-ʔUṣuwl fiy l-Naħw*, ed. Abd al-Husayn al-Fatli. Beirut: Mu'assasat al-Risala.
Sibawaih, Uthman. 1970. *Al-Kitaab*. Ed. H. Derenbourg. Hildesheim: Olms.

CHAPTER 21

THE ARABIC LITERARY LANGUAGE

the Nahḍa (and beyond)

DANIEL L. NEWMAN

21.1 Introduction*

The current chapter will discuss the developments in formal written Arabic in the early Modern period, which started with Napoleon's invasion and occupation of Egypt (1798–1802), when the Arab Muslim world first came into direct contact with the West. This event triggered increased links with European powers and, in turn, brought about momentous changes—social, political, technological, and cultural—not only in Egypt but also all over the Arab Muslim world. In more ways than one, it marked a rebirth of sorts, and the 19th century became known as that of the Arab Renaissance (*Nahḍa*). The Arabic language went through a revival of its own, emerging in a form that would eventually develop into present-day Modern Standard Arabic (SA).

21.2 The Emergence and Development of SA

Shortly after landing on Egyptian soil on that fateful July 1, 1798, Bonaparte issued an official proclamation that had previously been translated (badly) into Arabic and printed on one of the presses that accompanied the expedition. In addition to a foreign Christian military force and technology, Egyptians were introduced to alien terms

* The author gratefully acknowledges financial support from the Leverhulme Trust (Research Fellowship RF/3/RFG/2010/0389).

denoting even stranger concepts that had posed quite a challenge to Napoleon's interpreters like *ḥurriyya* in the sense of "political freedom" (rather than as the opposite of enslavement) and *jumhūr* for "republic" (Boustany 1971, vol. 9: 61; al-Turk 1998: 87).

At the time of the French invasion, Arabic—like its speakers—was suffering under the Turkish yoke and had long since ceased to be the language of government or, indeed, high culture, retaining importance only as the language of religion. Starting with the fall of Baghdad in 1258 to the Mongols, this period of Arabic decline is known as the *ʿaṣr al-inḥiṭāṭ* ("Period of Decadence").

By the end of the 18th century, the formal literary language, Classical Arabic (CA), was being written by a small elite, whose output was limited to the traditional Muslim sciences. It was far removed from the general population, the overwhelming majority of whom were illiterate and spoke only the colloquial, which was as distant from the literary language as present-day dialects are. Though CA was the norm, it is clear from the earliest literary sources of the century that very few authors possessed the required skills as there were many deviations from the norm—either plain errors or colloquialisms.[1] As a result, the literary language (apart from that used in the Islamic sciences) at that time may be qualified as "Middle Arabic" in the broad sense of the term (Versteegh 2001: 114), though a word of caution is due, not least because knowledge of the linguistic development of Arabic in the preceding centuries is still quite sketchy. Furthermore, even in the classical (i.e., pre-*inḥiṭāṭ*) period, deviations from the "pure" *ʿarabiyya* can often be encountered in the most formal writings (Fück 1955).

The rebirth of Arabic in the 19th century was driven by the serendipitous confluence of a number of factors, both external and internal.

Among the Ottoman troops sent by the Sublime Porte to assist his Egyptian vassals in their struggle against Napoleon's invasion force was a young Albanian officer by the name of Muḥammad ʿAlī (1769–1849), who would soon become the absolute ruler of his adoptive country. He had witnessed European technological and military advances firsthand and was quick to realize that his ambition to build a regional superpower relied on his acquiring the modern sciences. To this end, he sent students to Italy (1809) and France (1826–1831) at first but then also to other countries like Britain and Austria. At home, the viceroy set up European-style schools—initially for various types of military training—factories, arsenals, a printing press (1821), and a newspaper, *al-Waqāʾiʿ al-Miṣriyya* ("Egyptian Gazette," 1828) (Heyworth-Dunne 1938). In addition, foreign (predominantly French) military advisors and teachers were invited to provide instruction on the spot. In the latter half of the century, various missionary orders set up schools, which further boosted Western influence.

In Lebanon, where Arabic studies had received a fillip in the 18th century thanks to scholars such as the Maronite archbishop Germanos Farḥāt (1670–1732), Christian—both missionary and local—schools played a key role in the development of Arabic philology (Zaydān n.d., vol. 4: 8–11). The majority of the region's leading language

[1] A case in point is the chronicle by the century's first, and most famous, historian, ʿAbd al-Raḥmān al-Jabartī' (1753–1825), *ʿAjāʾib al-āthār fi l-tarājim wa l-akhbār*. Cf. Zaydān 1904a: 45.

reformers, such as Aḥmad Fāris al-Shidyāq (1804–1887) and the offspring of the al-Bustānī and al-Yāzijī dynasties, had been trained in these institutions, often by European teachers. American missionaries set up the Syrian Protestant College (1866), which would become the American University of Beirut, whereas the Jesuit college in Ghazir (1847) was the precursor to the University of St. Joseph (Tibawi 1966). Furthermore, thanks to long-standing contacts with the West, Arabic printing had been introduced into the Levant already at the start of the 18th century (Nasrallah 1958). And so the need for books coincided with the creation of a native intellectual elite and the means to distribute their output [Daniels, "Writing"]. From an ideological point of view, the preeminence of Christian scholars such as Nāṣīf al-Yāzijī (1800–1871) in Arabic studies during the *Nahḍa* constituted a significant shift toward Arabic as a secular language of Arabness rather than exclusively as the ritual language of Islam (Chejne 1969; Suleiman 2003).

In Egypt, the absence of manuals and textbooks constituted a formidable obstacle to education and modernization. The answer lay in the translation into Arabic of European originals, and for this purpose a Language School (*madrasat al-alsun*) was set up (1836), soon after added with a Translation adjunct (*qalam al-tarjama*, 1841). Both were headed by one of the alumni of the first Egyptian student mission to France (1826–1831), Rifāᶜa al-Ṭahṭāwī (1801–1873). He had already completed several translations during his stay in Paris (Newman 2004: 45) and went on to play a leading role in the ensuing translation movement, which had a significant influence on the language, both in terms of style and, especially, in the creation of modern Arabic scientific terminology (Zaytūnī 1984; al-Sawāᶜī 1999; al-Shayyāl 2000; Crozet 2008). Out of the approximately 540 books printed by the official press in Būlāq until 1850, there were no fewer than 123 Arabic translations, all from French, except one from Italian.[2]

The impact of the translators was felt first and foremost in vocabulary with the creation of a multitude of terms to denote novel concepts but also in syntax, due to source-language interference or, in some cases—like their precursors in the medieval Arabic translation movement (9th–11th centuries)—a lack of "good grounding in Arabic grammar or any aptitude for literary perfection and accomplished style" (Fück 1960–2009). Simple comprehension also played a part sometimes; for instance, Yūḥannā ᶜAnḥūrī's *Muntahā' al-aghrāḍ fī ᶜilm shifā' al-amrāḍ* (Būlāq, 1834) was based on a French original (L. C. Roches and L. J. Sanson, *Nouveaux éléments de pathologie médico-chirurgicale, ou Traité théorique et pratique de médecine et de chirurgie*, 1833), which had to be translated into Italian first by a teacher at the Medical School in Abū Zaᶜbal since he had insufficient knowledge of French in order to complete the task (Cheng-Hsiang 1985: 383–384; al-Shayyāl 2000: Appendix I).

[2] This was Francesco Vacca Berlinghieri's *Elementi di fisica del corpo umano in stato di salute* (1783), which appeared under the title of *Kitāb fī qawāᶜid al-uṣūl al-ṭibbiyya al-muḥarrara ᶜan al-tajārib li-maᶜrifat kayfiyyat ᶜilāj al-amrāḍ al-khāṣṣa bi-badan al-insān* (Būlāq, 1826).

The single biggest—and lasting—factor in both the creation and propagation of the modern language then, just as now, was the press. The latter half of the 19th century saw the rise of nongovernmental periodicals, which became the main channel for knowledge of the outside world. One of the first was *al-Jawāʾib*, which was established by al-Shidyāq in Constantinople in 1860. It is difficult to overstate the prestige this (weekly) publication enjoyed among the intellectual elite all over the Arab world as it was distributed in the major cultural centres (Beirut, Cairo, Damascus). Its style became an example for others to emulate and it has rightly been called "the father of newspaper Arabic" (Lewis et al. 1960–2009). All scholars and literati contributed to the new medium, and several even set up their own journals: for example, Jurjī Zaydān's *al-Hilāl* (1892); Buṭrus al-Bustānī's *Nafīt Sūriyā* (1860), *al-Janna* (1870) and *al-Jinān* (1870); Ibrāhīm al-Yāzijī's *al-Bayān* (1897) and *al-Ḍiyāʾ* (1898). The number of periodicals continued to increase exponentially, and by the end of the century over 100 had been founded in Egypt alone—even if most of them were ephemeral (Washington-Serruys 1897; Dī Ṭarrāzī 1913–1914). Many Arabic journals also appeared outside the Muslim world, the first one being the Paris-based bilingual (French–Arabic) *Birjīs Barīs* ("Jupiter of Paris," 1859), founded by a French missionary, François Bourgade, and a Tunisian émigré, Sulaymān al-Ḥarāʾirī (1824–1877).

The new medium was written in a new simplified language, which often betrayed a foreign influence, not least because of the high ratio of translations from European originals. Deadlines meant that authors did not always comply with the rules and at times had a creative—some might say slapdash—approach to terminology. Unsurprisingly, the press became the *bête noire* of purist grammarians who never tired of pointing out the errors that had been committed against the rules of Arabic grammar (al-Yāzijī 1901; Dāghir 1923; al-Zaᶜbalāwī 1939). Even poets joined the fray, and in his moving tribute to the Arabic language (1903), Ḥāfiẓ Ibrāhīm (1869–1932) conveyed the prevailing feeling:

> أرى كل يوم في الجرائد مزلقاً من القبر يدنيني بغير أناة!
> "Every day I see slips in the newspapers that hasten me to the grave."
> وأسمع للكتاب في مصر ضجة فأعلم أنّ الصائحين نعاتي!
> "I hear the clamour of authors in Egypt; however, know that those who cry out are announcing my death!"

21.2.1 Lexis

The most striking difference between the Classical language and SA involves vocabulary. Muḥammad ᶜAlī's translators were the first to grapple with the problem of coining new words for the new sciences (Ali 1987; al-Shihābī 1991; al-Sawāᶜī 1999; Crozet 2008) and political and cultural concepts (Rebhan 1986; Ayalon 1987, 1989). The methods they employed have, to a large extent, remained in use to this day: borrowing (*taᶜrīb*), that is, transliteration of the foreign term, paraphrase, calque (loan translation), semantic extension of existing Arabic words, derivation, and compounding.

Prior to the 19th century the main linguistic donors to Arabic were Greek, Persian, and Turkish [Kossmann, "Borrowing"], whose impact was, in fact, quite minor and restricted to a number of fields: philosophy and medicine in the case of Greek,[3] the military and government for Turkish.[4] Italian words had penetrated some of the dialects, especially those with borders on the Mediterranean, either through the *lingua franca*, in which Italian was the main substrate, or, directly, through the often sizeable Italian-speaking communities in port cities.

The 19th century for the first time saw an influx of borrowings from other European languages, especially French and, towards the end of the period, English. However, throughout the century, Italian held its own, with 53% of loanwords in Spiro's dictionary (1895) being Italian, against 33% French and a mere 10% English.[5] A cull from Wehr's (1976) dictionary yields a reversed picture, with 21% of Italian, 30% French, and 48% English borrowings.

In most cases, the origin of the borrowing can easily be determined from the form or first attestation, but sometimes appearances can be deceiving. For instance, *fābūr* ("steamship") can have a number of possible origins: *vapeur* (French), *vapor* (Spanish), or *vapore* (Italian). In cases such as these, other factors have to be taken into account, such as the fact that many of the shipping terms in Arabic (as well as Turkish) at the time were drawn from the *lingua franca*, which would make Italian the most plausible donor.

Throughout the century, the spelling of borrowings remained highly unstable, with a number of variants coexisting: for example, *urubbā, ūrubbā, ūrūbā*. In some instances, the importation of French and Italian borrowings produced doublets: for example, *bīl/baṭṭāriyya* (Fr. *pile*/It. *batteria*) and *tanbar/būl* (Fr. *timbre*/It. *pollo*).

Some loans had a history in Arabic that went back far longer, a notable example being *dīmūqrāṭiyya* ("democracy"), which first entered Arabic through Greek in the Middle Ages and was subsequently "forgotten" only to reappear as a French loanword (al-Ṭahṭāwī 1838). On occasion, Arabic even borrowed a word it had originally "loaned" to European languages: for example, *amīrāl* (< Fr. *amiral* < Ar. *amīr al-baḥr*).

In the latter half of the century, a perception—often rooted in a broader political and ideological context—grew of Arabic being invaded by foreign (European) words, a view which has survived to the present day (Monteil 1960: 306). However, this is not borne out by reality, and the figures, in fact, show a "relative paucity of foreign loanwords"

[3] The total number of Greek borrowings has been estimated at 700 (Anbūbā 1953).

[4] By way of example, al-Jabartī's history contains some 125 Turkish loanwords, about half as many from Persian (nearly all borrowed through Turkish) and a handful from Italian (*banadīra* < *bandiera*, *siqāla* < *scala*, *ṭulumba* < *tromba*, *qarābīna* < *carabina*). The first French–Arabic dictionary (Ruphy 1802), on the other hand, contained four recognizably French loans (*basājīr*, "passenger"; *basābūrṭ*, "passport"; *frank*, "franc"; *qunṣūl*, "consul"), and two from Italian (*ghāziṭa*, "newspaper"; *bilūṭa*, "pilot"). By the middle of the century, a similar picture emerges from Catafogo (1858), with 13 European borrowings, 8 from French and 5 from Italian.

[5] By comparison, Tunisian Arabic in the first quarter of the 20th century contained 30% of Italian, 27% French, 17% Turkish, and 6% Spanish loanwords (ᶜĀshūr 1992), whereas Ben Cheneb (1922) still found 239 Turkish loanwords in Algerian Arabic in the same period.

(Issawi 1967: 110). Arabic was far more reluctant to borrow than, for instance, Turkish (Barbier de Meynard 1881: III; Bosworth 1965: 60), not least because the rigid phonotactic constraints of the language make it resistant to "outright transfer" (Weinreich 1964: 61), particularly of non-Semitic elements. This also explains why a relatively low number of loanwords became inflectionally productive, and very few authors followed in the footsteps of al-Ṭahṭāwī who introduced the very first example with *kartana* ("to quarantine," < *karantīna*, "quarantine") (1834: 30).

In a study of 19 literary works dealing with Europe from between 1834 and 1900 by authors from various parts of the Arab world (Egypt, Levant, North Africa), 338 European borrowings (lexical types) were identified, 8% of which were attested previously (Newman 2002). This is a surprisingly low figure since authors' primary focus was on the unfamiliar culture and technologies they witnessed and had to convey to their home readership. The overwhelming majority of the loanwords were French (70.1%), followed by Italian (21.5%), Spanish (4.1%), which was restricted to Moroccan works, and English (3.8%). French dominance is largely due to the fact that for most of the century it was viewed as the model of modernity by Muslim nations, while most of the 19th-century accounts of visits to Europe dealt with France. In terms of regional preference, the North African works combined accounted for over 60% of all borrowings, with those by Egyptian authors contributing around 30%. Half the loanwords were related to state and the economy (26.9%) and science and technology (23.3%). As a rule, the number of borrowings steadily declined in the course of the century—particularly those denoting European political concepts—as native Arabic coinings took their place. Only 59% of the corpus made it beyond the century compared with 20% of the 60-odd loanwords found in the century's first account on Europe (al-Ṭahṭāwī 1834).

At times, the use of loanwords became a way of asserting affinity with European civilization, though carelessness cannot be excluded either, as in Khayr al-Dīn's *hublūn* (1867: 367) for "coal" (cf. Fr. *houblon*). In the early stages of the translation movement, the attitude towards borrowing was very pragmatic, as revealed by the following extract from the introduction to al-Ṭahṭāwī's first translation (1833: 2):

> As most of the terms... are foreign (*ʿajamiyya*)... we have transliterated (*ʿarrabnāhā*) them so that they can be pronounced as easily as possible, with close resemblance <to Arabic sounds> so that in the course of time they become naturalized (*dakhīla*) in our language, just like... Arabic expressions of Persian or Greek origin, provided <other> translators do likewise.

Many of the loanwords replaced by neologisms did not, however, disappear altogether and they would either continue to coexist with native alternatives (e.g., *hātif/tilifūn*) or become restricted to the dialects, which always proved to be more receptive to loanwords as the proportion of borrowings greatly exceeds that in normative written usage (Butros 1963: 35–36; Issawi 1967: 111). In 20th-century SA, European loanwords continued to represent a negligible percentage: 1.6% in Wehr's dictionary (1976) (total number of entries: ca. 40,000), which may be compared to 1.5% (of ca. 11,000) in Spiro (1895) and 1% in the Functional Linguistic Corpus (Benabdi 1986: 75). For modern literature, the (albeit very modest) sample tested by Thiry (1985: 116) revealed a figure of 0.46%. The press tended to be far less protective and the number of loanwords generally exceeded that in literature, but many of them proved to be nonce words, failing to gain currency in other genres. This trend continued in the 20th century and a study of European loanwords in the Egyptian newspaper *al-Ahrām* for the period 1956–1991 yielded a total of 5,062 items (tokens), 74% of which had a frequency of less than 1% (Araj 1993).

In terms of form, many of the phonological correspondences first adopted in 19th-century writing are still used today in the transliteration of foreign words, whereas one may observe certain regional trends, such as a higher use of "emphatic" (pharyngealized) consonants by North African authors: for example, *tiyātir* vs *tiyāṭir*, *karantīna* vs *karanṭīna* (Newman 2002).

While loanwords involve transliteration, calques are the result of a literal translation of the source item. In many cases, this was the result of misunderstanding—or negligence—on the part of the translator but some entered the language nevertheless, despite the presence of a native equivalent. Probably the oldest example is the use of *zaman* for "weather" as a translation of the French *temps* (al-Ṭahṭāwī 1834: 41), which later reappeared as *waqt* in the expression *waqt laṭīf*, "nice weather" (Mihrī 1884: 224).

The influence of European languages also made itself felt on the phraseological level (*taᶜrīb bi l-asālīb*)[6] with calques such as *taḥt al-ṭabᶜ* (Fr. *sous impression*, "in print"), *min ṭaraf* (Fr. *de la part <de>*)[7] and *laᶜiba dawran* ("to play a role") (Zaydān n.d.: IV, 244; Stetkevych 1970: 95–113; Blau 1981: 75–120). This became a very productive process, and a casual reading of any newspaper today will throw up tens of examples. Phraseological calques tend to be rapidly naturalized into the language, and their foreign origins lost in the mists of time. However, one should be careful to assume a modern European origin purely on the grounds of similarity as one cannot rule out the possibility that a particular innovation already existed previously (Monteil 1960: 6), whether as a borrowing from another language or the result of independent creation: for example, *iftaḥ 'udhnayka* ("open your ears!," "*ouvre tes oreilles!*") (al-Maghribī 1947; Blau 1981: 47–59). Crosslinguistic *correspondence* alone is not sufficient evidence for cross-linguistic *influence* or interference.

The "phraseological Europeanisms" elicited far less criticism than loanwords or intrusions from the vernacular, despite the fact that the former "go much more against the spirit of the *ᶜarabīya*" (Wehr 1943: 24–25). Calques come in a number of guises and often involve literal translations of idiomatic or proverbial expressions: for example, *ṭālamā qaraᶜat 'ādhānunā nawāqīs hātihi al-lafẓa* (*al-Ḥāḍira*, 10.08.1888: No 2), "as long as this expression rings in our ears" (cf. Fr. "*les cloches... font tinter nos oreilles*," where

[6] This term was coined by ᶜAbd al-Qādir al-Maghribī (1867–1956)—a driving force in both the Damascus and Cairo language academies—in the homonymous paper in *Majallat Majmaᶜ Fu'ād al-'Awwal li l-Lugha al-ᶜArabiyya*, I, 1934, 332–349.

[7] The first time this appeared in Arabic was in Napoleon's proclamation of July 2, 1798.

nawāqīs refers to "church bells"!); *qaddama ismahu li l-intikhābāt*, "he put his name forward for the elections" (*al-Ḥāḍira*, 03.08.1888: No. 1); *yaqbalu al-'ān ᶜaskaruhum najda li-taḥrīr Brīṭāniyya* "now, their army accepts help to liberate Britain" (*Birjīs Barīs* 1859: II, 3). Many occurrences can be found in legal texts of the century, with extensive use of phrases like *min 'ayy aḥad* ("from anyone"). Calquing also affected syntax, as we shall see later.

Translators sought inspiration from within, too, using native equivalents when they were available, and for scientific terminology they could rely on the vocabulary coined by medieval scholars. However, this avenue was not always explored fully, and new terms were invented even if an established Arabic equivalent had been available for many centuries (Crozet 2008). In some cases this was undoubtedly due to ignorance on the part of the translator, as when an early practitioner like the already mentioned ᶜAnḥūrī opted for an invention of his own, *ḥāmila*, to render "atlas verbetra," rather than using the classical *fahqa* (Braune 1933: 137). However, this cannot be considered the rule. When ᶜAlī Mubārak (1871–1873) translated "perfect number" as *ᶜadad kāmil* (instead of *ᶜadad tāmm*) and "prime number" as *ᶜadad aṣamm* (instead of *ᶜadad awwal(ī)*) it is unlikely that he did not know the accepted terms. One explanation may lie in hypercorrection, with the terminological choice being driven by a conscious desire to avoid what would be perceived as a calque, even if it was not. The use of native words also resulted in polysemy, with, for instance, *ṣināᶜa* being used for "industry," "(handi)craft," "profession," "technique," and sometimes even "art" (e.g., al-Ṭahṭāwī 1834). The pace and volume of terminological innovation meant that competition was fierce and many of the more idiosyncratic inventions, such as *muyāwama* for "newspaper" (*Birjīs Barīs* 1859–1866), quickly dwindled into oblivion.

Paraphrase, which was often used to supplement or specify the meaning of a loanword, also made a brief appearance, but, for reasons of style and economy, it never found much favour and is restricted to the early works: for example, *ᶜilm al-ᶜaqāqīr wa l-adwiya al-mufrada wa l-murakkaba* ("the science of both simple and compound medicaments and remedies"), "pharmacology" (al-Ṭahṭāwī 1834: 96).

The second technique (known as *istinbāṭ*, "extraction") consisted of reviving archaic Arabic words, coupled with semantic extension and metaphorization (*al-waḍᶜ bi l-majāz*): for example, *qiṭār*, "string of camels" → "train"; *majalla* → "written paper/ book containing science" (< *jull*, "cover of book") → "journal, magazine" (Stetkevych 1970: 29–34, 66–78). The lack of a harmonized approach meant that multiple neologisms often continued happily as synonyms: for example, *jarīda*, "palm branch stripped of leaves" → "writing scroll" → "newspaper"; *ṣaḥīfa* → "written piece of paper or skin, book, letter" → "newspaper."

Derivation (*ishtiqāq*) from Arabic roots was a very productive method (al-Maghribī 1947; Abderrahman 1981), particularly in the creation of abstract nouns from adjectives by means of the *nisba* suffix (*-iyya*), which had already proved its worth in the Greek–Arabic translation movement: for example, *intikhābiyya*, "electorability" (< *intikhāb* "election," al-Shidyāq 1871–1880, V: 247); *jumhūriyya*, "republic" (< *jumhūr* "group of people," al-Ṭahṭāwī 1833: 27); *fawḍawiyya*, "anarchy" (< *fawḍā* "mixed, without a leader," *al-Muqtaṭaf*, 1894: 18). Very early on, this was also applied to loanwords: for example, *brūtistāntiyya*, "protestantism" (< *brūtistānt* "protestant," al-Ṭahṭāwī 1833: 27), *imbaraṭūrī*, "imperial" and *imbaraṭūriyya*, "empire (system of government/territory)" (< *imbaraṭūr* "emperor," Abū Suᶜūd 1841: 200; Khalīfa 1842: 73; Khayr al-Dīn 1867: 241, 325; al-Shidyāq 1881: 228; Bayram V 1884–1893: IV, 11; al-Bustānī 1876–1900: IV, 356).

The fourth process, compounding (*naḥt*), was used very sparingly indeed, due to its inherent un-Arabicness, though there are some examples in the classical language, such as *basmala* ("to say *bi-ism Allāh*") and *ra's-māl*, "capitalism" (Ali 1987: 59–85). Towards the end of the century, compounds consisting of the negative particle *lā-* prefixed to an adjective or noun to render 'non-/un-/... became increasingly popular: for example, *lā-nihāya*, "infinity" (Zaydān 1904b: 57).

21.2.2 Grammar and Syntax

The past decades have seen descriptive studies of the syntactic features of the contemporary formal language (Monteil 1960; Stetkevych 1970; Blau 1973, 1976, 1981; Cantarino 1974; Rosenhouse 1990; Gully 1993; Holes 2004) as well as some grammars (Badawi et al. 2003; Buckley 2004; Ryding 2008), but very little attention has been paid to its immediate precursor in the early Modern period. Whether or not this is "due to the resistance of conservative... litterateurs and philologists," who regard the study of new phenomena as "a bestowal of legitimacy" (Stetkevych 1970: 97) is another matter. Nonetheless, it is telling that, to date, not a single Arabic grammar of SA exists in the Arab world, whereas it took until 2008 (ᶜUmar) for an Arabic explanatory dictionary to reflect actual current usage and include, for instance, loanwords such as *tīlīfāks* ("telefax") or *ampīr* ("ampere").

Many of the SA deviations from the CA norm found in today's language started life in the 19th century or, at least, were already present then as a continuation of Middle Arabic (Blau 1970: 173). While the foreign (especially French) influence is often apparent, it would be an oversimplification to restrict all the developments in formal Arabic as being merely reactive and thus to negate its inherent ability to change from within. Among the salient developments, one may cite:

Syntactic calques, for example:

- Speech verbs with nonpersons: for example, *rawat/qālat/akkadat al-jarīda* .. "the newspaper recounted/said/confirmed that...." (*al-Ḥāḍira*, 30.09.1888: No 8, 1)
- *bi-wāsiṭa*, as a calque of "by means of" (rather than to express an instrument): for example, *al-sirqa allatī taḥṣulu bi-wāsiṭat kasr al-akhtām*, "theft which occurs by the breaking of the seals" (Egyptian Penal code 1852, article 76)
- Exceptive *mā ᶜadā* + *dhālika* by analogy with the French *à part cela*: *mā ᶜadā dhālika fa-taḥtawī al-dā'ira ayḍan...* ("except for this/in addition, the circle also contains...") (*al-Mashriq* 1898: I, 10)

- Explication of subject pronouns without emphasis: for example, *raʾaynā naḥnu...* (Ibn Ṣiyām 1852: 18)
- Increased use of external causative with *jaʿala*: for example, *wa yajʿalūnahu yatamāwaju*, "... they cause it to break into waves" (al-Ṭahṭāwī 1834: 88)
- SVO: this is considered one of the most emblematic syntactic features of contemporary SA, especially Media Arabic (Parkinson 1981). Though not widespread, this was by no means exceptional in the 19th century and occurred quite early (al-Ṭahṭāwī 1842). Far more common in certain text types was the frequent use of the nominal sentence introduced by *ʾinna* and nonemphatic *ʾammā* ("as for"),[8] which would appear to constitute an intermediate stage from VSO to "outright" SVO: for example, *al-Ṣadā* 1878; *al-Ḥāḍira* 1888; *al-Hilāl* 1892; Washington-Serruys 1897 [Edzard, "Philology"]
- Frequent use of nonemphatic sentence-initial time and place adverbials
- *yūjad* and sentence-initial *hunāka* to render "there is/Fr. *il y a*": for example, *yūjad khārij al-madīna .... bāb...* "outside the city...there is a gate..." (*al-Hilāl* 1894–5: III, 701), *innahu yūjad rajul fī Ifransa* "there is a man in France..." (*Birjīs Barīs* 1859: IX, 3; cf., e.g., al-Ṭahṭāwī 1838: 27; al-Shidyāq 1881: 97, 102)
- Fronted sentence adverbials such as *bi l-jumla/fī l-ghālib...fa* ("generally...") (Beeston 1970: 66; e.g., al-Ṭahṭāwī 1834: 43; al-Shidyāq 1881: 39)
- Copular use of imperfect *kāna*: for example, *wa hādhihi al-khuṭūṭ takūnu...*, "These lines are... (al-Ṭahṭāwī 1842: 90) [Benmamoun and Choueri, "Syntax"]
- Extensive use of *aḥad* (f. *iḥdā*), cf. English/French "one of"/*un(e) des*";
- Nonconditional *idhā* and *ʾin* to introduce indirect questions (cf. English *whether*, French *si*) (al-Yāzijī 1901: 34; Wehr 1934: 14, 72; Monteil 1960: 245–246)
- Passive voice: the overwhelming majority of passives encountered are internal, which greatly outnumber form-VII (*muṭāwiʿ*) verbs. The common passive construction in contemporary media Arabic with *tamma* or *jarā* followed by a verbal noun (*maṣdar*) (Murgida 1993; Girod 2000) was quite rare: *ʾinna al-mufāwaḍāt bi-shaʾn al-iṣlāḥāt allatī sa-yatimmu ijrāʾuhā fī Āsiyā al-ṣughrā ...*, "the negotiations regarding the reforms which will be carried out in Asia Minor..." (*al-Ṣadā*, 28.08.1878); *tamma mubādalat ʿalāmāt bi-wāsiṭat hādha l-jihāz*, "the signals are exchanged by means of this device" (*al-Mashriq* 1898: I, 10).

"Native" features, for example:

- Widespread use of *qad* with imperfect to render possibility (cf. "might"): for example, al-Shidyāq (1881: 81, 140, 142); *al-Hilāl* (1895: III:8)
- Rare occurrences of *mā* + perfect negation, in favour of *lam* + jussive, which in contemporary SA has all but crowded out the *mā* construction (Wehr 1953; [Edzard, "Philology"]).

[8] In some cases, this is, however, a straightforward calque of the French *en ce qui concerne*.

- Deviations from CA conditional constructions:

    - o *idhā* as a conditional particle (rather than CA "when")
    - o *'in* as an equivalent of *law* to introduce hypothesis: *'in kāna al-amr kadhālika...*, "if that were/had been the case...." (*al-Mashriq* 1898: I, 66)

- Negation of *zāla* by *lā* (instead of *mā*): for example, *lā zālat al-isti*ᶜ*dādāt jāriyya bi-Ṭanja bi-qubūl al-ḥaḍra al-Sulṭāniyya*, "preparations for the reception of His Highness the Sultan are still going on in Tangiers." (*al-Ḥāḍira* 30.09.1888). (Blau 1973: 174–175)
- Compound relative pronouns *mimman* and *mimmā*: for example, *yūjad al-'ān fī Bārīs mimman ḥaḍara ilayhi li-ziyārat al-ma*ᶜ*raḍ al-*ᶜ*āmm*, "At present there are people in Paris who came here to visit the World Exhibition" (*al-Ṣadā*, 03.07.1878)
- Auxiliary function of *qāma* (+*bi*+ verbal noun), common in contemporary media Arabic (Ashtiany 2001): for example, *wa yaqūmu al-bāb al-*ᶜ*āli bi-sadād al-*ᶜ*ajz al-ḥāṣil fī l-mīzāniyyāt...*, "the Sublime Porte will settle the budget deficit..." (Washington-Serruys 1897: 19)
- Frequent use of sentence-initial *wa lladhī*, mirroring French "*et celui*"; for example, *al-Ḥāḍira* (16.06.1895)
- Increase in *sa(wfa)* + imperfect to denote future events and *kāna* + perfect for the pluperfect
- Adverbials based on adjectives used in the indefinite accusative (Wehr 1934: 16): for example, *rasmiyyan, iqtiṣādiyyan*
- The addition of a coordinated noun to an *iḍāfa*, also known as *iqḥām* (Wehr 1943: 39; Monteil 1960: 130–131; Stetkevych 1970: 93; Blau 1973: 183–184; Gully 1993: 23–30): for example, *istaqbalat kull umarā' wa amīrāt al-*ᶜ*ā'ila al-malakiyya*, "she received all the princes and princesses of the royal family" (CA: *kull umarā' al-*ᶜ*ā'ila al-malakiyya wa amīrātihā*) (Washington-Serruys 1897)
- Increased use of active participles to denote the progressive, where CA would prefer the imperfect: for example, *hum ḥā'izūna ta'thīran siyāsiyyan ladā ḥukūmāt Ūrubbā*, "they are acquiring political influence with European governments" (Washington-Serruys 1897: 13)

Dialectal influence, for example:

- Plural agreement with duals: for example, *al-sulṭān wa l-sulṭāna ahdū li-ḥaram al-brins Ḥalīm al-maṣūn wa li-banātihi al-karīmāt nayāshīn* ᶜ*uthmāniyya*, "The Sultan and Sultana presented Prince Halim's wife and his daughters with Ottoman decorations" (Abū Naẓẓāra 1880: 12)
- *wa law*: for example, *fa-lā budd 'an yadkhula fī tilka l-thalātha wa law ḍil*ᶜ*an wāḥidan* (sic), "there has to be at least one side amidst these three <parts> ...." (Abū Suᶜūd 1843: 1)

21.2.3 Script and Punctuation

The 19th century saw a number of developments in respect of script and punctuation [Daniels, "Writing"]. In terms of the former, the following may be mentioned:

- Omission of *hamza* in word-initial contexts
- Omission of *hamza* seated on *yā'* (ئ) in word-medial positions: for example,ماية ("hundred"): e.g. Ibn Ṣiyām 1852; use of *madda* in all final *ā*+hamza: for example, روسآء, فقهآء (!) (*Birjīs Barīs* 1859: I, 1, 4)
- Inconsistent "dotting" of *tā' marbūṭa*;
- Appearance of so-called three-dotted *bā'* (پ), *fā'* (ڨ) and *kāf* (ݣ) to denote /p/, /v/ and /g/, respectively, in European loanwords: for example, Ṣabbāgh 1814; Habicht 1824: 6; al-Ṭahṭāwī 1833; al-Shidyāq 1881; *Birjīs Barīs* 1859
- Inconsistent use of so-called Maghribi single-dotted *qāf* (ڧ) and *fā'* (ڢ) in Algerian publications: for example, Cherbonneau 1847; Ibn Ṣiyām 1852

Prior to the 19th century, punctuation was unknown in literary texts and for most of the period Arabic remained reluctant to import Western-style marks. For instance, in the issues of the Egyptian journal *Rawḍat al-Madāris* for 1870, the only punctuation marks found are round brackets for titles and parentheses but not for quotations, as would be the case later. Breaks between sentences tended to be marked by a line break or, occasionally, a symbol resembling an asterisk. From the 1880s onward, it was common to use round brackets to enclose proper nouns (e.g., *al-Ḥāḍira* 1888; Washington-Serruys 1897), though in some publications they were restricted to titles or parentheses (e.g., *al-Hilāl* 1892). Quotation marks appeared only towards the end of the century and came in the guise of angular French-style marks (e.g., *al-Hilāl* 1900) or English-style inverted commas to denote quotations and/or proper nouns (e.g., *al-Muqtaṭaf* 1892). The first Western-style sentence punctuation marks to appear were the full stop and colon, though their use was not widespread or consistent (e.g., *al-Mashriq* 1898).

21.2.4 Typological and Regional Variation

Naturally, the identification of a given feature does not provide any indication as to the extent to which it was employed or accepted as normative usage. A great deal more research is required on this period in the history of the Arabic language for these questions to be answered conclusively.

What is certain is that the type, number, and extent of "innovations"— or deviations from the CA norm—greatly depended on the text type, though none remained untouched. A simplistic view would be to place high literature, including religious output (Quran and *ḥadīth* exegesis), at the most conservative end of the spectrum and the press at the most "creative" or "liberal" one. In between, we find translated literature, scientific works, and new genres such as the novel and the theater that displayed specific features revealing the differences in influences. The language of the press, too, operated between widely varying fields and there are often considerable differences in the language of, for instance, literary journals and opinion newspapers or between periodicals published in Arab countries and those outside as the latter were, of course, far more exposed to foreign influences than the former. It is no coincidence, for example, that the language in a journal such as *al-Ṣadā*, published in Paris by a second-generation Egyptian (Florian Pharaon), is at times dramatically different from that used in high-brow publications like *al-Jawā'ib* or *al-Janna*, penned by leading scholars of the day.

In a category of its own was "officialspeak," that is, the language of the administration and the law, which often relied heavily on European originals (al-Harāwī 1963; Zaydān 1904b; 88–91; [Holes, "Orality"]). As the following example excerpted from the 1853 Egyptian Penal Code makes clear, this sometimes resulted in what can only be called gobbledygook: *idhā kāna man yakūnu mustakhdaman bi l-maṣāliḥ al-mīriyya…* , ("if someone employed by the tax administration…."). The *shaykh al-Azhar*, Muḥammad ᶜAbduh (1849–1905) painted a depressing picture of the decline in the literary language

> in official correspondence between government departments, in newspapers, all of which are based on, or translated from other languages, or in people's private exchanges. Written style came in two guises in Egypt, both of which were distasteful as well as counter the spirit of the Arabic language. The first was that used in government departments…, and involved putting words together in a haphazard and unintelligible fashion; it cannot be traced to any language of the world, either in form or content. Remnants may be found to this day in the writings of some Copts and those who emulate them, but thankfully it is quite rare. As for the second style, this was used by literati and al-Azhar graduates and contained hollow rhymed prose, padding and all manner of paronomasia. In addition to being in poor taste, abstruse and unpleasant to the ear, this type of writing was unable to convey the intended meaning and did not comply with the literary conventions of Arabic. Even though in form it complied with the basic rules of Arabic grammar, the style did not find favour with people. It is found to this day, especially in the writings of *shaykhs*. However, of late, another kind of strange writing has arrived from Syria, where it is used in two journals, *al-Janna* and *al-Jinān*, both of which are written by Buṭrus al-Bustānī. This style is most strange indeed, yet it is the one employed in the newspaper *al-Ahrām*. However, this influence may well be eliminated, God willing! (Riḍā 2006: I, 11–12)

Arabic in the 19th century was very much in a state of flux and changed dramatically in the course of it because of the exponential increase in output as well as the variety of the media using the formal language. Consequently, any discussion of linguistic features only provides a snapshot of a particular time and context.

Grammatical simplification and levelling, which underlay many of the features, as well as borrowing from European languages, went hand in hand with the retention of high-classical rhetorical devices such as paronomasia (*jinās*) and rhymed prose (*sajᶜ*), even in scientific works and periodicals.

The period also marks the beginning of what may be called regional *fuṣḥās* insofar as local language preferences and usage, whether or not caused by dialectal influences, manifested themselves. The differences occurred primarily at the lexical level in the latter quarter of the century, with for instance words like *kāghid* "paper," *baṭḥā'* "square," or *nahj* "street" being found almost exclusively in Tunisian writings and not in the Levant. The same applies to loanwords; while the influence of French continued in both East and West, there was a higher incidence of calquing from French in North African writings. Conversely, the early influence from English is observed only in Eastern (Egyptian and Levantine) writings. Regional SA variation has continued to the present day and is the object of a topical debate, enlightened by studies on grammar (Van Mol 2003) and, especially, lexis (Parkinson and Ibrahim 1998; Ibrahim 2009; Wilmsen and Youssef 2009).

21.3 Language Reform and Revival

The developments in Arabic in the course of the century, the increasing impact from outside (Western terminologies) and from within (dialect), led to calls for language reform, which should also be seen against a much wider ideological context fuelled by sociopolitical changes and emerging nationalisms, all of which shaped views on the position and function of the language.

The widening political and financial encroachments of Western powers all over the Muslim world only reinforced the siege perception, with Arabic being both a way of resistance and of rediscovering the Arab–Muslim cultural heritage. Yet, at the same time, increasing numbers of Arab intellectuals were being trained in Europe or were influenced by its culture and literature (especially that of France), which held great prestige.

The threat to Arabic did not come only from abroad; in more ways than one, intrusions from the dialect were considered even more dangerous to the future of the language. Up until then, dialectal presence in the formal language consisted of mere slips of the pen as the dialect was universally considered inferior to the classical language. It was standard, for instance, for debates in the Egyptian parliament, which were, of course, held in varying degrees of the colloquial, to be "translated" into the standard language (al-Harāwī 1963: 442). In the 19th century, dialectisms were increasingly found in formal writing (especially in the press), whereas the last quarter saw the birth of diglossia and the use of the colloquial as a stylistic device in literary writing (e.g., *Rawḍat al-Madāris* 1870). This is particularly associated with the Egyptian polymath Abū Naẓẓāra (James Sanua), who employed it to great effect in his multifarious media output (e.g., 1880). The "colloquialization" trend proved to be a lasting one and would in the 20th century become a two-way street, with the interpenetration of SA and vernaculars (Haeri 2003; Suleiman 2003; Holes 2004).

In addition to purist considerations, the use (or promotion) of the dialect gained much more nefarious connotations as it came to be associated with people such as

John Selden Wilmore (1856–1931) and Sir William Willcocks (1852–1932), who called for the use of the colloquial as the written language (*al-Hilāl* 1901–1902: X, 279–282; Wilmore 1905: xiii; Saᶜīd 1964: 32–42; ᶜAzīz 1968: 291–295). The argument was predicated in their belief that the standard language was an impediment to progress and the direct cause of the region's backwardness, as Willcocks attempted to prove in his article *Lima lam tūjad quwwat al-ikhtirāᶜ ladā l-Miṣriyyīn al-'ān* ("Why do contemporary Egyptians lack the power of invention?"), published in *al-Azhar* (!) journal on New Year's Day 1893. Rather than being driven by scholarly linguistic motives, Willcocks was possessed with a firebrand missionary zeal and saw the colloquial as a vital means for converting Muslims in Egypt, calling for the translation of the Bible into Egyptian Colloquial Arabic.

While most Arab scholars and literati accepted a need for language reform to forge Arabic as a tool for the modern world, it was the way this should be done that caused controversy and, at times, acerbic disputes, pitting "conservatives" like Ibrāhīm al-Yāzijī (1847–1906) and Saᶜīd al-Shartūnī (1849–1912) against the "liberal" school spearheaded by al-Shidyāq, who saw salvation in simplification (Gully 1997; Patel 2010). The participants were all Christians; for Muslims, things were more complicated inasmuch as any attempt at language reform was viewed by many as an attack on Islam itself (Waardenburg 1960–2009; [Suleiman, "Folk Linguistics"]).

21.4 Standardization

The issue of preservation was a core component within the language reform discussions and it is little surprising that as early as 1860 the suggestion was made, by the indefatigable al-Shidyāq, to have a French-style language academy as a gatekeeper to ward off foreign terms (1871–1880: I, 202). In the 1880s, the idea was relaunched in Egypt by ᶜAbd Allāh al-Nadīm (1843–1896) and, later on, ᶜAbd Allāh Fikrī (1834–1890). The 1890s saw the establishment of a number of language societies with varying life spans (Hamzaoui 1975: 41–46; Sawaie 2006). The first of these was *al-Majmaᶜ al-Lughawi al-ᶜArabi* ("Arabic Linguistic Academy"), which was essentially a *salon* held at the palatial home of Tawfīq al-Bakrī (1870–1933). It ran between May 1892 and February 1893 and counted such littérateurs as Ḥamza Fatḥ Allāh (1849–1918), Ismāᶜīl Ṣabrī (1854-1927) and Muḥammad al-Muwaylīḥī (d. 1930) among its members. The main goal was to coin Arabic terms for Western loanwords. In total, 21 (!) words were discussed, among them *misarra* "telephone," *mishjab* "clothes hook," and *quffāz* "glove," as well as *ᶜim ṣabāḥan/ masā'an* "good morning/evening" (?). Unsurprisingly, the coinings gave rise to considerable debate by those outside the association; Jurjī Zaydān and al-Yāzijī, for instance, used their periodicals to criticize various neologisms, suggesting their own creations. In some cases, history has come down on the side of the critics with, for instance, Zaydān's *muḥāmin* "lawyer" and *shurfa* "balcony" defeating the "Academy's" *midrah* "spokesman" and *ṭunuf* "ledge." Far more productive was Muḥammad Ḥifnī Nāṣif's *Nādī Dār al-ᶜUlūm* (1907), whose membership, as its name indicates, included many graduates of the Egyptian teacher training college Dār al-ᶜUlūm, It, too, focused on coining and even published a journal (*saḥīfa*). Other associations were set up, but none endured, mainly because they remained idiosyncratic efforts devoid of official imprimatur and support. That would only come in 1919, in Damascus, where King Faisal I oversaw the setting up of *al-Majmaᶜ al-ᶜIlmī al-ᶜArabī* ("Arab Science Academy") (Hamzaoui 1965; Sharaf al-Dīn 2003). It was directly patterned on the *Académie Française* (Kurd ᶜAlī 1948–1951: II, 354)—the world's first language academy (1635)—whose primary aim of rendering the language "pure, eloquent and able to deal with the arts and sciences" struck a powerful chord with Arab scholars of the day.

In the opening address of the Academy's journal, its founder and first president, Muḥammad Kurd ᶜAlī (1876–1953) stated that the institution was to be "at the service of science and the Arabic language" (*Majallat al-Majmaᶜ al-ᶜIlmī al-ᶜArabī*, I, 1921, 2). The Damascus Academy was followed by the Cairo-based *Majmaᶜ al-Lugha al-ᶜArabiyya al-Malakī*[9] (Madkūr 1964; ᶜAllām 1966; Hamzaoui 1975) in 1919, with *al-Majmaᶜ al-ᶜIlmi al-ᶜIrāqī* being established in Baghdad in 1948 (al-Alūsī 1997).[10]

Like its Syrian counterpart, the Egyptian academy, which became the most prestigious due to the central role played by the country in the Arab world, sought to emulate the *Académie française*, as its first president made clear: "As for France, it... serves as the model for other academies in the world (*qudwa li-ghayrihā min majāmiᶜ al-ᶜālam*)" (Fahmī 1934: 173).

The Iraqi academy set itself apart from the others by a broader remit, which included the advancement of science and arts, in general, and those of Arab–Muslim heritage (*turāth*), in particular. The more narrow language-centered focus and activities of the Cairo and Damascus academies were identical: simplification of grammar (e.g., *Majallat al-Majmaᶜ al-ᶜIlmī al-ᶜArabī* XXIII: 139–149; XXXII: 123–160; Hamzaoui 1975: 275–433), spelling reform (*Majallat al-Majmaᶜ al-ᶜIlmī al-ᶜArabī* V: 493–497; X: 53–59; XXIII: 141–142; Hamzaoui 1975: 211–246) and lexical expansion. As regards the last area, the academies set about replacing dialectal terms (e.g., *Majallat al-Majmaᶜ al-ᶜIlmī al-ᶜArabī*, VI, 97–104, 145–151, 193–200; Shraybom-Shivtiel 1995), coining neologisms, and attempting to unify Arabic technical and scientific terminology.

[9] In the course of its history it underwent several name changes: *Majmaᶜ Fu'ād al-Awwal li l-Lugha al-ᶜArabiyya* (1938), *Majmaᶜ al-Lugha al-ᶜArabiyya* (1954) and *Majmaᶜ al-Lugha al-ᶜArabiyya fi l-Qāhira* (1960).

[10] The second half of the 20th century witnessed the creation of a number of other academies: Jordan (*Majmaᶜ al-Lugha al ᶜArabiyya al-Urdunnī*, 1976), Algeria (*Majmaᶜ al-Lugha al-ᶜArabiyya al-Jazā'irī*, 1986), Sudan (*Majmaᶜ al-Lugha al-ᶜArabiyya al-Sudānī*, 1993), Libya (*Majmaᶜ al-Lugha al-ᶜArabiyya al-Lībī*, 1994), Palestine (*Majmaᶜ al-Lugha al-ᶜArabiyya al-Filisṭīnī*, 1994). However, except for the Jordanian academy, there is very little evidence of any activity by these organizations. In 1961 an Arabization Agency (*Bureau Permanent de l'Arabisation*) was set up in Rabat which was eventually incorporated into ALESCO (Arab League Scientific and Cultural Organization). In addition to coordination, the Bureau contributes to the modernization of the language by creating new terminology. (Sayadi 1976).

The approach tied in with the neologization devices that had already been used in the previous century by translators, authors, and the like, albeit within a more structured and strictly hierarchical framework, which prescribed the following order of preference: semantic extension of existing words (*istinbāṭ*); derivation (*ishtiqāq*); compounding (*naḥt*); and borrowing (*taʿrīb*) (al-Maghribī 1947; Monteil 1960: 162–181; Hamzaoui 1965: 27–36, 1975: 319–373, 483–522; Stetkevych 1970; El-Khafaifi 1985; El-Mouloudi 1986; Ali 1987; Shraybom-Shivtiel 1993).

Derivation proved to be the most popular neologization method, with patterns often being linked to specific semantic fields, for example:

- *faccāl*, for professions: for example, *jarrāḥ* "surgeon," *wujūdiyya* "existentialism"
- *faccāla*, particularly for nouns involving mobility, though sometimes also for instruments: for example, *sayyāra* ("car" < *sayyār* "continually moving"), *dabbāsa* "stapler"
- *fuʿāl*, for diseases: for example, *duwār* "vertigo," *judhām* "leprosy"
- *mafʿal(a), mifʿaf(a)* for nouns of place and instrument: for example, *majmaʿ* "academy," *maṣaḥḥa* "refinery," *mijhar* "microscope," *mimlaḥa* "salt cellar"

For the coining of abstract nouns, the *nisba* remains the single most productive device, and the ending "*-iyya*" (or agentive "*-ī*" to construct the adjective) is added to common and proper nouns, compounds, and even particles: e.g. *naẓarī* ("theoretical"), *wujūdiyya* ("existentialism"), *makiyāfīliyya* ("Macchiavellism"), *ghayriyya* ("altruism").

Compounding has proved to be more problematic and generally the Academies tolerate it only in scientific language, where blends such as *fawṣawṭī* (< *fawqa*, "above" + *ṣawṭ* "sound," i.e., "supersonic") have become increasingly widespread in the technical jargon (Ali 1987: 59–85). The least favored mechanism is borrowing, which is accepted only "at need" (though this was never defined), and as a last resort (al-Shihābī 1995: 71).

Just like the French academy, the Arabic institutions have been accused of conservatism and ineffectualness. The charge of conservatism is a rather spurious one since one could argue that conservatism is part and parcel of the very raison d'être of a language academy. When it comes to effectiveness, this is another matter and, to some degree, quantifiable.

Less is more when it comes to linguistic standardization, and the existence of multiple normative institutions is inherently self-defeating. Driven by political and ideological reasons, it has resulted in petty rivalries between the various organizations, each vying for authority. The formation of an umbrella institution, the Union of Language Academies (*ittiḥād al-majāmiʿ al-lughawiyya*), in 1971 brought little change, and it currently has a nominal existence only (Sawaie 2006–2009: 640–641).

On the other hand, too much emphasis has perhaps been put on the Academies' failures in, for instance, word creation: for example, *jammāz* ("swift-footed camel") for "tramway" (*trām*) or *miqwal* ("instrument for speaking") and *irzīz* ("sound of thunder") for "telephone" (*tilīfūn, hātif*). In fact, many of the academies' coinings are in current use, and the Cairo Academy alone published 20,000 new terms between 1957 and 1964

(El-Mouloudi 1986: 98). What is more, the derivational patterns endorsed by the Cairo and Damascus Academies are widely adhered to in many fields.

A more intractable obstacle is the inconsistency that has at times bedevilled neologization, leading to unnecessary (as well as confusing and unproductive) synonymy, as in the case of the Cairo Academy coining four words to render "pancreas": *miʿqad, banqirās, lawzat al-maʿida*, and *ḥulwa* (Hamzaoui 1975: 441). Unfortunately, this adds to the often bewildering inconsistency that exists in the wider speech community. Whereas English-speaking linguists have only word for "phoneme," their Arabic colleagues are spoiled for choice with 14 (!) terms that run the full gamut of neologization processes: *funīm; ṣawtam; waḥda ṣawtiyya; waḥda ṣawtiyya ṣughrā; ṣawtam lughawī; lafẓ; funīma; mutaṣwit; funīmiyya; ṣawtim; ṣawt mujarrad; ḥarf ṣawtī;* and *lafiẓ*. Even more basic terms like "consonant" and "vowel" defy consensus:

Vowel: *ḥaraka, ṣā'it, ṣā'ita, muṣawwit, ṣawt al-līn, ṣawt layyin*
Consonant: *ṣawt sākin, ṣāmit, ḥarf, ṣāmita*

It is not difficult to see how the existence of a plethora of synonymous technical terms is counterproductive and may hamper communication. Linguistics is not, however, the only field to be afflicted with this ailment, and as the problem persists the prospect of a unified terminology across the Arab world remains as remote as ever.

When it comes to grammatical simplification, the academies have also been less effective inasmuch as it has given rise to a great deal of debate but not, as yet, to a unified policy.

The lack of effective promotion and propagation of the academies' work continues to pose serious problems and the arrival of Information Age technology has had very little impact. For instance, to date not a single academy makes its creations available online, whereas most fail to update their websites. This matter is compounded by the fact that, due to their very nature, the academies are out of step with usage in view of the sheer amount of data they have to deal with. As a result, their activities remain largely unknown to the members of the speech community.

Enforcing decisions regarding language usage is a formidable challenge for any language academy, let alone competing ones; language users do not function by academy *diktat*, and the speech community remains the ultimate arbiter of usage. One may also wonder whether it is not utopian to bring about lexical uniformity across an area that straddles two continents and includes over 20 sovereign countries [Owens, "Introduction"].

Perhaps the biggest irony is that when it comes to the propagation of SA it is the medium that was most maligned (i.e., the press), which continues to exercise the biggest influence on all levels of language (Blau 1981: 60–61; Holes 2004: 46, 314–332).

That is not to say that the academies do not have an important role to play in the continued development of the modern written language as a *kā'in ḥayy* ("living being"), to use Jurjī Zaydān's expression of 1904; adaptive and dynamic, SA has succeeded where Classical Arabic never did in that it has truly penetrated all levels of society throughout the Arab world and is used in both written and spoken discourse, nationally and internationally. This is where the true renaissance of the Arabic language lies (Shraybom-Shivtiel 1995).

References

European Sources

Abderrahman, W. 1981. *The role of derivation in the process of neologisation in Modern Literary Arabic*. PhD diss., London University.

Ali, Abdul Sahib Mehdi. 1987. *A linguistic study of the development of scientific vocabulary in Standard Arabic*. London: Kegan Paul.

Araj, Samia Jabra. 1993. *Foreign words in the Arabic press: A study of the impact of Western languages on Arabic*. PhD diss., University of Texas at Austin.

Ashtiany, Julia. 2001. *Media Arabic*. Edinburgh: Edinburgh University Press.

Ayalon, Ami. 1987. *Language and change in the Arab Middle East: The evolution of modern political discourse*. New York: Oxford University Press.

——. 1989. Dimūqraṭiyya, ḥurriyya, jumhūriyya: The modernization of the Arabic political vocabulary. *Asian and African Studies* 23: 23–42.

Badawi, Elsaid, Mike G. Carter, and Adrian Gully. 2003. *Modern written Arabic: A comprehensive grammar*. Abingdon: Routledge.

Barbier de Meynard, Charles. 1881. *Dictionnaire turc-français: Supplément aux dictionnaires publiés jusqu'à ce jour*. Paris: E. Leroux.

Beeston, A. F. L. 1970. *The Arabic language today*. London: Hutchinson.

Ben Cheneb, Mohamed. 1922. *Mots turcs et persans conservés dans le parler algérien*. Algiers: Ancienne Maison Bastide-Jourdan.

Benabdi, Linda. 1986. Lexical expansion in the Maghreb: the functional linguistic corpus. *International Journal of the Sociology of Language* 61: 65–87.

Blau, Joshua. 1970. On pseudo-corrections in some Semitic languages. (Publications of the Israel Academy of Sciences and Humanities. Section of Humanities.) Jerusalem: Israel Academy of Sciences and Humanities.

——. 1973. Remarks on some syntactic trends in Modern Standard Arabic. *Israel Oriental Studies* 3: 127–231.

——. 1976. Some additional observations on syntactic trends in Modern Standard Arabic. *Israel Oriental Studies* 6: 158–190.

——. 1981. *The renaissance of Modern Hebrew and Modern Arabic: Parallels and differences in the revival of two Semitic languages*. Los Angeles: University of California Press.

Bosworth, C. E. 1965. Language reform and nationalism in modern Turkey. *Muslim World* 55: 58–65, 117–124.

Boustany, Salah el-Din. 1971. *The journals of Bonaparte in Egypt, 1798–1801*. Vol. 9: *Recueil des arrêtés et proclamation de l'autorité française en Egypte pendant l'occupation*. Cairo: Al-Arab Bookshop.

Braune, Walther. 1933. Beitrage zur Geschichte des neuarabischen Schrifttums. *Mitteilungen des Seminars fur orientalischen Sprache zu Berlin* 36: 119–123.

Buckley, Ronald. 2004. *Modern literary Arabic: A reference grammar*. Beirut: Librairie du Liban Publishers.

Butros, Albert Jamil. 1963. *English loanwords in the colloquial Arabic of Palestine (1917–1948) and Jordan (1948–1962)*. PhD diss., Columbia University.

Cantarino, Vicente. 1974. *Syntax of modern Arabic prose*. 3 vols. Bloomington: Indiana University Press.

Catafogo, Joseph. 1858. *An English and Arabic dictionary*. London: Bernard Quaritch.

Chejne, Anwar. 1969. *The Arabic language: Its role in history*. Minneapolis: University of Minnesota Press.

Cheng-Hsiang, Hsu. 1985. *The first thirty years of Arabic printing in Egypt, 1238–1267 (1822–1851)*. PhD diss., University of Edinburgh.

Cherbonneau, A. 1847. *Anecdotes musulmanes*. Paris: Librairie française et étrangère. Algiers: Dubos frères et Marest.

Crozet, Pascal. 2008. *Les sciences modernes en Egypte. Transfert et appropriation, 1805–1902*. Paris: Geuthner.

Fück, Johann. 1955. *ᶜArabīya*. Trans. Claude Denizeau. Paris: Marcel Didier.

——. 1960–2009. ᶜArabīya. In *Encyclopaedia of Islam*, vol. 1, 2d ed., ed. H. A. R. Gibb, 569–571. Leiden: Brill.

Girod, Alain. 2000. *Faits d'évolution récente en arabe moderne à travers un corpus de presse égyptien*. PhD diss., Université d'Aix-Marseille 1, Marseilles.

Gully, Adrian. 1993. The changing face of Modern Written Arabic: An update. *Al-ᶜArabiyya*, 26: 19–59.

——. 1997. Arabic linguistic issues and controversies of the late nineteenth and early twentieth centuries. *Journal of Semitic Studies* 42: 1, 75–120.

Habicht, Maximilian. 1824. *Epistolae quaedam arabicae a Mauris, Aegyptiis et Syris conscriptae*. Vratislaviae: Typis Universitatis Regiis.

Haeri, Niloofar. 2003. *Sacred language, ordinary people*. New York: Palgrave Macmillan.

Hamzaoui, M. Rachad. 1965. *L'Académie arabe de Damas et le problème de la modernisation de la langue arabe*. Leiden: Brill.

——. 1975. *L'Académie de langue arabe du Caire*. Tunis: Université de Tunis.

Heyworth-Dunne, J. 1938. *An introduction to the history of education in Modern Egypt*. London: Luzac & Co.

Holes, Clive. 2004. *Modern Arabic: Structures, functions, and varieties. Washington, DC*: Georgetown University Press.

Ibrahim, Zeinab. 2009. *Beyond lexical variation in Modern Standard Arabic: Egypt, Lebanon and Morocco*. Newcastle: Cambridge Scholars.

Issawi, Charles. 1967. European loanwords in contemporary Arabic writing: A case study in modernization. *Middle Eastern Studies* 10: 110–133.

El-Khafaifi, Hussein. 1985. *The role of the Cairo Academy in coining Arabic scientific terminology: An historical and linguistic evaluation*. PhD diss., University of Utah.

Lewis, Bernard et al. 1960–2009. Djarīda. In *Encyclopaedia of Islam*, vol. 2, 2d ed., ed. H. A. R. Gibb et al., 465–472. Leiden: Brill.

Monteil, Vincent. 1960. *L'Arabe moderne*. Paris: Klincksieck.

El-Mouloudi, Aziz Bensmaali. 1986. *Arabic language planning: The case of lexical modernisation*. Ph.D. diss., Georgetown University, Washington, DC.

Murgida, Jacqueline. 1993. *Passive and passive-like expressions in journalistic Modern Standard Arabic*. PhD diss., Georgetown University, Washington, DC.

Nasrallah, Joseph. *L'Imprimerie au Liban*. Harissa: Imprimerie de Saint Paul.

Newman, Daniel. 2002. The European influence on Arabic during the Nahda: Lexical borrowing from European languages (*taᶜrīb*) in 19th-century literature. *Arabic Language and Literature* 5: 1–32.

——. 2004. *An imam in Paris*. London: Saqi Books.

Parkinson, Dilworth. 1981. *VSO* to *SVO* in Modern Standard Arabic: A study in diglossia syntax. *Al-ᶜArabiyya* 14: 24–37.

Parkinson, D. and Ibrahim Zeinab. 1998. Testing lexical differences in regional Standard Arabics. In *PAL*, vol. 12, ed. Elabbas Benmamoun, 183–202. Amsterdam: John Benjamins.

Patel, Abdulrazzak. 2010. Language reform and controversy in the *Nahḍa*: al-Shartūnī's position as a grammarian in *sahm*. *Journal of Semitic Studies* 55: 509–538.

Rebhan, Helga. 1986. *Geschichte und Funktion einiger politischer Termini im Arabischen des 19. Jahrhunderts (1798–1882)*. Wiesbaden: Otto Harrassowitz.

Rosenhouse, Judith. 1990. Tendencies to nominalization in Modern Literary Arabic as compared with Classical Arabic. *ZAL* 22: 23–43.

Ryding, Karin. 2008. *A reference grammar of Modern Standard Arabic*. Cambridge, UK: Cambridge University Press.

Ruphy, Jean-François. 1802. *Dictionnaire abrégé français-arabe à l'usage de ceux qui se destinent au commerce du Levant*. Paris: Imprimerie de la République.

Sawaie, Mohammed. 2006. Language Academies. In *Encyclopedia of Arabic Language and Literature*, vol. 2, ed. Kees Versteegh, Associate Editors: Mushira Eid, Alaa Elgibali, Manfred Woidich, Andrzej Zaborski, 634–642. Leiden: Brill.

Sayadi, Mongi. 1976. *Le Bureau de Coordination de l'Arabisation dans le monde arabe*. PhD diss., Université de Paris III.

Shraybom-Shivtiel, Shlomit. 1993. Methods of terminological innovation used by the Cairo Language Academy. *Arabist* 6–7: 195–202.

——. 1995. The role of the Colloquial in the renaissance of Modern Standard Arabic: Language as a mirror of social change. *Israel Oriental Studies* 15: 195–202.

Spiro, Socrates. 1895. *An Arabic–English vocabulary of the colloquial Arabic of Egypt, containing the vernacular idioms and expressions, slang phrases, etc. etc., used by the native Egyptians*. Cairo: Bernard Quaritch.

Stetkevych, Jaroslav. 1970. *The modern Arabic literary language: Lexical and stylistic developments*. Chicago: University of Chicago Press.

Suleiman, Yasir. 2003. *The Arabic language and national identity: A study in ideology*. Washington, DC: Georgetown University Press.

Thiry, Jacques. 1985. Arabe moderne, arabe classique. *Rapports d'activités de l'Institut de Phonétique* 20: 95–126.

Tibawi, Charles. 1966. *American interests in Syria, 1800–1901: A study of educational, literary and religious work*. Oxford: Oxford University Press.

Van Mol, Mark. 2003. *Variation in Modern Standard Arabic in radio news broadcasts: A synchronic descriptive investigation into the use of complementary particles*. Leuven: Peeters.

Versteegh, Kees. 2001. *The Arabic language*. Edinburgh: Edinburgh University Press.

Waardenburg, J. D. J. 1960–2009. Madjmaᶜ ᶜIlmī. In *Encyclopaedia of Islam*, vol. 5, 2d ed., ed. H. A. R. Gibb et al., 1090–1101. Leiden: Brill.

Washington-Serruys. 1897. *L'arabe moderne étudié dans les journaux et les pièces officielles*. Beirut: Imprimerie Catholique.

Wehr, Hans. 1934. *Die Besonderheiten des heutigen Hocharabischen mit Berücksichtigung der Einwirkung der europäischen Sprachen*. Berlin: Reichsdruckerei.

——. 1943. Entwicklung und traditionelle Pflege der arabischen Schriftsprache in der Gegenwart. *ZDMG* 97: 16–46.

——. 1953. Zur Funktion arabischer Negationen. *ZDMG* 107: 27–39.

Wehr, Hans and J. Milton Cowan. 1976. *A dictionary of Modern Written Arabic*. Ithaca, NY: Spoken Language Services Inc.

Weinreich, Uriel. 1964. *Languages in contact: Findings and problems*. Paris: Mouton.

Wilmore, John Selden. [1901] 1905². *The Spoken Arabic of Egypt*. London: David Nutts.
Wilmsen, David and Riham Osama Youssef. 2009. Regional standards and local routes in adoption techniques for specialised terminologies in the dialects of written Arabic. *Journal of Specialised Translation* 11: 191–208.

Arabic Sources

Abū Naẓẓāra (ed.). 1880. *al-Ḥāwi*. Paris.
Abū Su^c^ūd, ^c^Abd Allāh. 1841. *Naẓm al-la'ālī' fi l-sulūk fīman ḥakama Firansā min al-mulūk*. Būlāq.
——. 1843. *Ruḍāb al-ghāniyyāt fī ḥisāb al-muthallathāt*. Būlāq.
^c^Allām, Muḥammad Mahdī. 1386/1966. *Majma^c^ al-lugha al-^c^arabiyya fī thalāthīn ^c^āman, al-majma^c^iyyūn*. Cairo: al-Hay'a al-^c^Āmma li-Shu'ūn al-Maṭābi^c^ al-Amīriyya.
al-Alūsī, Sālim. 1997. *al-Majma al-^c^ilmī fī khamsīna ^c^āman 1947–1997*. Baghdad: Maṭba^c^at al-Majma^c^ al-^c^Ilmī.
Anbūbā, ^c^Ādil. 1953. al-Muṣṭalaḥāt al-^c^ilmiyya fi l-lugha al-^c^Arabiyya. *al-Mashriq* 56: 338–351.
^c^Āshūr, Muḥammad. 1992. Jaysh al-dakhīl fi l-lisān al-Tūnisī li Muḥammad Ibn al-Khūja (1869–1942). In *Histoire et linguistique: Texte et niveau d'interprétation*, ed. Abdelahad Sebti, 89–110. Rabat: Publications de la Faculté des Lettres et des Sciences Humaines de Rabat.
Bayram V, Muḥammad. 1884–1893. *Ṣafwat al-i^c^tibār bi-mustawda^c^ al-amṣār wa l-aqṭār*. 5 vols. Cairo: Maṭba^c^at al-I^c^lām.
Bourgade, François & Rushayd al-Daḥdāḥ (eds.). *Birjīs Barīs*. 1859–1866. Paris.
Būshūsha, ^c^Alī (ed.). 1888–1889. *al-Ḥāḍira*. Tunis.
al-Bustānī, Buṭrus. 1876–1900. *Kitāb dā'irat al-ma^c^ārif wa huwa qāmūs ^c^āmm li-kull fann wa maṭlab*. 11 vols. Beirut: Maṭba^c^at al-Ma^c^ārif.
Dāghir, As^c^ad Khalīl. 1923. *Tadhkirat al-Kātib. Kitāb yatadamman al-tanbīh ^c^alā ahamm al-ghalaṭāt al-lughawiyya al-dā'ira fī alsunat al-khuṭabā' wa aqlām al-kuttāb*. Cairo: Maṭba^c^at al-Muqtaṭaf.
Ḍayf, Shawqī. 1984. *Majma^c^ al-lugha al-^c^Arabiyya fī khamsīn ^c^āman 1934–1984*. Cairo: Majma^c^ al-Lugha al-^c^Arabiyya.
Dī Ṭarrāzī, Philippe. 1913–1914. *Tārīkh al-ṣiḥāfa al-^c^Arabiyya*. 4 vols. Beirut: al-Maṭba^c^a al-Adabiyya.
Fahmī, Manṣūr. 1934. Ta'rīkh al-majāmi^c^. In *Majallat Majma^c^ al-Lugha al-^c^Arabiyya al-Malakī*, vol. 1, 170–176.
al-Harāwī, ^c^Abd al-Samī^c^ Sālim. 1963. *Lughat al-idāra al-^c^āmma fī Miṣr fi l-qarn al-tāsi^c^ ^c^ashar*. Cairo: al-Majlis al-A^c^lā li-Ri^c^āyat al-Funūn wa l-Ādāb wa l-^c^Ulūm al-^c^Āmma.
Ibn Ṣiyām, Sulaymān. 1852. *Kitāb al-Riḥla ilā bilād Faransā*. Algiers: Imprimerie du Gouvernement.
al-Jabartī, ^c^Abd al-Raḥmān. 1322/1904–1905. *^c^Ajā'ib al-āthār fi l-tarājim wa l-akhbār*. 4 vols. Cairo: Maṭba^c^at al-Ashrafiyya.
Khalīfa, Maḥmūd. 1842. *Itḥāf al-mulūk al-alibbā' bi-taqaddum al-jam^c^iyyāt fī bilād Ūrubbā, wa huwa muqaddimat tārīkh Shārl al-Khāmis*. Būlāq.
Khayr al-Din al-Tunisi. 1867. *Aqwam al-masālik fī ma^c^rifat aḥwāl al-mamālik*. Tunis: al-Maṭba^c^a al-Rasmiyya.
Madkūr, Ibrāhīm. 1964. *al-Majma^c^ fī thalāthīn ^c^āman, māḍīhu wa-ḥāḍiruhu 1932–1952*. Cairo: al-Hay'a al-^c^Āmma li-shu'ūn al-Matābi^c^ al-Amīriyya.
al-Maghribī, ^c^Abd al-Qādir. 1947. *al-Ishtiqāq wa l-ta^c^rīb*, 2d ed. Cairo: Lajnat al-Ta'līf wa l-Tarjama wa l-Nashr.
Mihrī, Muḥammad. 1884. *al-Tuḥfa al-^c^Abbāsiyya li l-madrasat al-^c^aliyya al-Tawfīqiyya*. Būlāq.

Mubārak ᶜAlī. 1871–1873. *Khawāṣṣ al-aᶜdād*. Cairo: Maṭbaᶜat al-Madāris al-Malakiyya.

Nimr, Fāris (ed.). 1876–1900. *al-Muqtaṭaf*. Beirut.

Pharaon, Florian (ed.). 1878. *al-Ṣadā*. Paris.

Riḍā, Muḥammad Rashīd. 2006. *Tārīkh al-Ustādh al-Imām Muḥammad ᶜAbduh*. 3 vols., 2d ed. Cairo: Dār al-Fāḍila.

Ṣabbāgh, Mīkhā'īl. 1814. *Nashīd tahānī li-saᶜādat al-kullī al-diyāna Luwīs al-thāmin ᶜashar malik Farānsā wa Nawārā. Cantique de félicitation à sa Majesté très chrétienne Louis le Désiré, Roi de France et de Navarre*. Paris: Imprimerie Royale.

Saᶜid, Nafūsa Zakariyyā. 1964. *Tārikh al-daᶜwā ilā l-ᶜāmmiyya wa āthāruha fī Miṣr*. Alexandria: Dār Nashr al-Thaqāfa.

al-Samarrā'ī, Ibrāhīm. 1966. *al-Taṭawwur al-lughawī al-tarīkhī*. Beirut: Maᶜhad al-Buḥūth wa l-Dirāsāt al-ᶜArabiyya.

Sawāᶜī, Muḥammad. 1999. *Azmat al-mustalaḥ al-ᶜArabī fi l-qarn al-tāsiᶜ ᶜashar: muqaddima tārīkhiyya ᶜāmma*. Damascus: Institut Français de Damas/Beirut: Dār al-Gharb al-Islāmī.

Sharaf, ᶜAbd al-ᶜAzīz. 1991. *Al-Lugha al-iᶜlāmiyya*. Beirut: Dār al-Jīl.

Sharaf al-Dīn, ᶜAbd al-Ḥusayn. 2003. *'Ilā l-majmaᶜ al-ᶜilmī al-ᶜArabī bi-Dimashq*. Beirut: Mu'assasat al-Balāgh li l-Ṭibāᶜa wa l-Nashr wa l-Tawzīᶜ.

Shaykhū, Luwīs (ed.). 1898–1905. *al-Mashriq*. Beirut.

al-Shayyāl, Jamāl al-Dīn. [1950] 2000. *Tārīkh al-tarjama wa l-ḥaraka al-thaqāfiyya fī ᶜaṣr Muḥammad ᶜAlī*. Port Said: Maktabat al-Thaqāfa al-Dīniyya.

al-Shidyāq, Aḥmad Fāris (ed.). 1861–1882. *al-Jawā'ib*. Istanbul.

al-Shihābī, Mustafā. 1991. *al-Muṣṭalahāt al-ᶜilmiyya fi l-lugha al-ᶜarabiyya fi l-qadīm wa l-ḥadīth*, 3d ed. Beirut: Dār Ṣādir.

al-Shidyāq, Aḥmad Fāris. 1871–1880. *Kanz al-Raghā'ib fī muntakhabāt al-Jawā'ib*. 7 vols. Istanbul: al-Jawā'ib.

——. 1881. *al-Wāsiṭa fī maᶜrifat aḥwāl Māliṭa/Kashf al-mukhabba' fī funūn Ūrubbā*. Istanbul: al-Jawā'ib.

al-Ṭahṭāwī, Rifāᶜa. 1833. *Qalā'id al-mafākhir fī gharā'ib ᶜawā'id al-awā'il wa l-awākhir*. Būlāq.

——. 1834. *Takhlīṣ al-ibrīz fī talkhīṣ Bārīs*. Būlāq.

——. 1838. *al-Taᶜrībāt al-shāfiyya li murīd al-jughrāfiyya*. 2nd ed. Būlāq.

——. 1842. *Mabādi' al-handasa*. Cairo: al-Maṭbaᶜa al-Amīriyya.

—— (ed.). *1870–1871*. *Rawḍat al-madāris*. Cairo.

al-Turk, Niqūlā. 1998. *Ḥamlat Būnābārt ilā l-sharq*. ed. Amal Bashshūr. Beirut: Jūrs Purs.

ᶜUmar, Aḥmad Mukhtār et al. 2008. *Muᶜjam al-lugha al-ᶜArabiyya al-muᶜāṣira*. 4 vols. Cairo: ᶜĀlam al-Kutub.

al-Yāzijī, Ibrāhīm. 1901. *Lughat al-jarā'id*. Cairo: Maṭbaᶜat al-Maᶜārif.

al-Zaᶜbalāwī, Ṣalāḥ al-Dīn Saᶜīd. 1939. *Akhṭā'unā fi l-ṣuḥuf wa l-dawāwīn*. Damascus: al-Maṭbaᶜa al-Hāshimiyya.

Zaydān, Jurjī. n.d. *Tārikh ādāb al-lugha al-ᶜArabiyya*. 4 vols. ed. Shawqī Ḍayf. Cairo: al-Hilāl.

——. 1904a. *Tārīkh al-lugha al-ᶜArabiyya*. Cairo: al-Hilāl.

——. 1904b. *al-Lugha al-ᶜArabiyya, kā'in ḥayy*. Cairo: al-Hilāl.

—— (ed.). 1892–1910. *al-Hilāl*. Cairo.

Zaytūnī, Laṭīf. 1986. *Ḥarakat al-tarjama fī ᶜaṣr al-nahḍa*. Beirut: Dār al-Nahār li l-Nashr.

CHAPTER 22

PIDGINS AND CREOLES

MAURO TOSCO AND STEFANO MANFREDI

22.1 Arabic-Based Pidgins and Creoles: What They Are and What They Are Not

The subject of this article is languages derived from the drastic restructuring of Arabic. They can be spoken either as first or second languages. Typically, pidginization results from insufficient exposure and consequent imperfect learning of a superstrate language in a highly multilingual context. When use of the variety is not discontinued, the original incipient pidgin may become extended or stabilized. Further nativization of the variety leads to its creolization, while continued exposure to the superstrate language may lead to a process of decreolization.

Many and widely different Arabic-based varieties have been called at various stages pidgins or creoles (PCs). In an attempt to classify these linguistic varieties, we distinguish two groups of PCs:[1] the Sudanic PCs and the immigrant pidgins in Arab countries. This geographical opposition turns out to be both structural and historical. A few Sudanic pidgins have developed in the course of time into stabilized pidgins and creoles, while the recent and contemporary varieties spoken by immigrant communities in a few Arab countries bear all the marks of incipient varieties. Moreover, Sudanic PCs developed and are attested out of the core of the Arab-speaking world (in present-day Chad, Southern Sudan, and East Africa), where the direct presence of speakers of the superstrate (Arabic) was minimal or indirect; they therefore adhere to the canonical conditions for the emergence of PCs (see Map 22.1).

[1] Although often inconsistent and etymologizing, we retain the authors' transcriptions throughout. On the other hand, we modify and uniformize the authors' glosses.

MAP 22.1 Geographical distribution of Arabic-based pidgins and creoles (major centers and areas of distribution)

It is important to stress the difference between Arabic-based PCs (cf. also Owens 1996 for an overview) and (1) peripheral Arabic dialects and (2) Arabic spoken as a nonfirst language as an interethnic medium.

22.1.1 Pidgins and Creoles versus Peripheral Arabic

Owens (2001) draws the parallel between peripheral Arabic and Arabic-based PCs and takes Central Asian Arabic as a representative of the former. Central Asian Arabic is spoken by at most a few thousands in various locations in Uzbekistan, Tajikistan, and Afghanistan. The first and last are particularly close, although almost nothing is known about Arabic in Tajikistan (and in many areas of Uzbekistan as well). The history of these varieties and their speakers is also shrouded with mystery and could date back to the 8th century and the Islamization of Uzbekistan or the 14th and Timur's (Tamerlane's) empire. Connections with other Arabic dialects are uncertain, apart from a certain resemblance with the varieties of Northern Mesopotamia.

Owens (2001) argues that peripheral Arabic is an "Araboid language" that has undergone so many structural changes that it can no longer be regarded as a form of Arabic—being rather a "mixed language." The mixed nature of Central Asian Arabic is disputed by, for example, Zaborski (2008), who prefers to stress the Arabic character of these varieties. Still, the profound impact of Uzbek, Tajik, and to a lesser extent Turkmen as well a, in Afghanistan, Dari, and Pashtu has been tremendous and has induced, among others:

- The change of basic sentence word order into subject–object–verb (SOV)
- The introduction of postpositions alongside the inherited Arabic prepositions
- The introduction of a present perfect based on the Arabic active participle followed, for the first and second person, by the ending *-in* and the object pronominal affixes; for example, *zorb-in-ak* "you have hit" (Zimmermann 2002: 46)
- The frequent use of "light verbs" in compounds, such as *sava* "to do" and *zarab* "to hit," on the model of Tajik and Uzbek
- The loss of the Arabic definite article and the introduction of an indefinite article *fad* (< *fard*)
- The introduction of the construction Possessor + Possessum followed by a pronominal affix, such as *duk aadami milt-u* "that man's nationality" (= that man his nationality) (Zaborski 2008: 429)

As in PCs and non-native Arabic, pharyngealization is lost (but the pharyngeal fricatives are retained).

Certainly, these "Araboid varieties" are not PCs. According to Owens (2001: 353), "creolization involves a greater degree of simplification relative to the source language(s) than does the development of a mixed language; whereas the precise source of many creole structures is opaque, that of mixed languages is relatively transparent." This is certainly true of Central Asian Arabic, where the Turkic and Iranian source is evident. Is Central Asian Arabic, then, a mixed language? Certainly not in the strong sense of a language where two grammars functionally coexist. Cases of such a "double grammar in a single language" exist, although they are exceedingly rare: Michif (Bakker 1997) and Media Lengua (Muysken 1997) are probably the best examples. It seems instead possible to use the label mixed language in a diachonic sense, as defining a language that has undergone deep structural changes and even a complete typological metathesis as a result of the impact of a second language of a radically different type. In such a weaker meaning, Central Asian Arabic (and maybe other peripheral varieties heavily restructured by contact) can certainly be considered a mixed language.

22.1.2 Pidgins and Creoles versus Non-native Arabic

A lower degree of structural simplification and alteration is attested in non-native varieties of Arabic used as interethnic lingua francas. They certainly share with Arabic-based PCs a number of features. These non-native varieties of Arabic are probably more common a phenomenon than our scanty data may suggest. The complex situation of Arabic in Chad has been described and discussed several times, most recently by Miller (2009); Ferguson (1970) reports on Ethiopia. We shall concentrate here on Eritrea, where the use of Arabic as an interethnic medium has been studied by Simeone-Senelle (2000), making in passing a few parallels with the better investigated case of Chad.

In both cases, Arabic as an interethnic lingua franca is a third variety of Arabic, distinct from both the local native dialect(s) and "official" Arabic.[2] Great differences are caused by the starkly different ethnic and linguistic picture of the two countries: in Chad, Arabic is today the major interethnic medium (spoken by maybe 60% of the total population).[3] In Eritrea, the role of Arabic, negligible as a native language, is also apparently very minor as an interethnic medium.

As a consequence, the role of the local spoken dialects is stronger in Chad than in Eritrea; in the latter, as in a typical interethnic medium, the native language of the speakers plays a bigger role in shaping Arabic: thus, in Eritrea Arabic /z/ is preserved by native speakers of Saho (which has /z/ in its inventory) and is replaced by /s/ by ʿAfars (who have no /z/ in their native language); /š/ is preserved in the Arabic as spoken by Sahos and often replaced by /s/ or palatalized by ʿAfars.

Everywhere (and, as will be seen, in the Arabic-based PCs), pharyngealization is generally lost; Simeone-Senelle (2000: 157) notes that, when preserved, "emphasis" is rather realized as pharyngealization rather than being replaced by ejective consonants, as is the case in the neighboring Semitic languages. Interdentals are either realized as alveolar stops or fricatives.

In both countries, a certain amount of morphological simplification is the rule; however—and this is a crucial difference—in contrast to PCs, verbal inflection and derivation are largely preserved. Thus, in Eritrea the first-person singular of the imperfective coalesces with the 1SG: *ánā má-nağder* "I cannot." Likewise preserved are two series of personal pronouns (independent and bound) and a certain number of Arabic plural patterns. Influence from the native languages of the speakers is somewhat stronger in syntax, where, for example, the verb tends to appear in final position, as in most Ethiopian languages.

[2] In both Eritrea and Chad Arabic is one of the two (*de jure* or *de facto*) official languages of the country (alongside Tigrinya in Eritrea and French in Chad). In both countries, therefore, official and written Arabic *is* part of the picture. Moreover, in both countries Arabic is spoken as a native language: in Eritrea by just 32,000 speakers (1% of the total population of the country) according to Simeone-Senelle (2000: 155) and by a sizable part of the population (10%) in Chad.

[3] de Pommerol (1999); Arabic surpasses French as an interethnic medium any local language as well as at least as an oral medium.

22.2 Some General Features of Arabic-Based Pidgins and Creoles

Many features that go under the general label of "simplification" are common to any restructured variety of Arabic, while others are common to most. It is of the foremost importance here that the comparison be established with the lexifying dialect and not with the Classical or Standard language (although influence from the latter may be found in the pidgin due to the well-known phenomenon of diglossia).

Pending a more detailed analysis, the following is a reasonable list.

In phonology:

- Pharyngealization is universally lost; this involves both the pharyngeal fricatives and the pharyngealized fricatives and stops. The former are usually reduced to /ʔ/ or Ø and /h/ (with further reduction to Ø possible), respectively. The pharyngealized stops and fricatives /ṭ/, /ḍ/, /ṣ/, and /ḏ̣/ are reduced to the corresponding plain sounds.
- The velar fricatives /x/ (ḫ) and /ɣ/ (ġ) usually merge with /k/ and /g/.
- The uvular stop /q/ is usually changed into /k/ or /g/.
- Gemination and vowel length are usually lost.
- Interdentals /θ/ (ṯ) and /ð/ (ḏ; both only when present in the lexifying dialect) are either changed into dental stops /t/, /d/, or into fricatives /s/, /z/.

In morphosyntax:

- The productive Semitic and Arabic root-and-pattern morphology is lost as a productive mechanism at both the inflectional and derivational level. Although inflectional morphology in general is also greatly reduced, one notes in expanded pidgins (Juba Arabic) and creoles (Kinubi) the partial retention of inflectional plural morphemes as well as the development of elaborated Tense–Mood–Aspect (TAM) marking and of the morphological use of suprasegmentals.
- The definite article *ʔal=* (and its local variants, especially *ʔil=*) is lost.
- Analytical expression of the genitival phrase is generalized, and the Arabic "construct state" (Possessum Article-Possessor) is lost as a productive device.
- Only one series of pronouns (the independent ones) is preserved, while possessive and object suffix pronouns are lost.
- Sentential word order tends to be SVO and phrasal word-order Head-Modifier, although variation is attested (especially at the phrasal level) in unstable pidgins and contact varieties.

As expected, the lexical stock is greatly reduced, and its place is taken by semantically transparent compound expressions.

22.3 Early Sources for "Pidginized" Arabic

Thomason and Elgibali (1986) are the only source on the so-called Maridi Arabic. It was found in 1982 by Alaa Elgibali in the *Kitaab al-masaalik wa-l-mamaalik* (Book of the Roads and Kingdoms) by the 11th-century Andalusian geographer Abuu 'Ubayd al-Bakrii. The book, parts of which have been lost, was written in 1068 and is based upon literature and reports from travelers and geographers from the 10th century (al-Bakrii himself never left Andalusia). The book is generally considered an important source for the history of West Africa, the trans-Saharan trade, and the Ghana Empire. In the short passage of interest here (which, it must be noted, is lacking in most editions), Al-Bakrii provides secondhand data on the Arabic spoken by "Blacks" in an unknown locality called Maridi, which Thomason and Elgibali propose to locate in central Mauritania, that is, in the westernmost part of the Sahara. It is interesting, on the other hand, that the passage is found within a description of Aswan, in Southern Egypt. Kaye (1985) suggests instead that Maridi is the homonymous town in modern Southern Sudan (in a Zande-speaking area, where Juba Arabic is nowadays the main lingua franca). This hypothesis is discussed and refused by Thomason and Elgibali, who do not think that the Arabs could have reached such a southern latitude (close to the present-day border with the Congo Democratic Republic) by the 10th–11th century.

The short specimen (just 10 sentences, but 3 of them are identical) consists of a folktale. Features typical of pidginization are the absence of an article, the uninflected verbal forms, and the presence of a preverbal aspectual particle written *dy*, which Thomason and Elgibali connect to modern-day *ge* of both Juba Arabic and Kinubi. One interesting phonological feature of the language is actually the shift of the Arabic letter *jîm* (variously realized in the Arabic dialects as /g/, /ʒ/, /ʤ/, or /ɟ/) to the letter for /d/ (the latter shift is actually attested in modern dialects of Upper Egypt and Sudan, which could be relevant for the localization of Maridi). Noteworthy is the unexpected presence of what looks like a dual personal pronoun, the lack of an existential element (like *fi* in other Arabic-based PCs) and, in syntax, the order adjective–noun. The lexical material is entirely Arabic, apart from a form written *kyk* and possibly to be interpreted as "people." Thomason and Elgibali (1986: 326) tentatively connect it with Songhay *-koi* "person who," but a much closer parallel can be found in Eastern Daju (Nilo-Saharan, Eastern Sudanic; Nuba Mountains) *kík* "man; person." The same word has entered Kordofanian Baggara Arabic as *kiik* (Manfredi 2010: 88). This is therefore a further element supporting a Sudanese location for Maridi.

Thomason and Elgibali interpret al-Bakrii's scanty data as evidence of an early Arabic-based pidgin or trade jargon spoken by Berbers. (Berbers are obviously not considered "black" by Arabs, but Thomason and Elgibali suggest that the speakers could have been Berberized "Blacks.") As a result, in Thomason and Elgibali's analysis of the text, comparison with Berber varieties features prominently. On the other hand, the authors do not take into sufficient account the fact that the text is claimed to be the reproduction of what a "dignitary from Aswan" remembered of his visit to Maridi, the black population there, and "their miserable Arabic" (*ʿarabiyyathum al-murziya*). What we have is therefore not a "language" but its caricature: the "bad Arabic" of foreigners is seen through the lens of the native speakers.

Similar cases of "broken" Arabic in literary works are of course not unknown in various European literatures. The data found in the Italian literature of the 16th century have been studied several times; Contini (1994) provides a useful summary and a few sound conclusions. Ludovico di Vartema, a traveler from Bologna who lived in the Arab world for many years, gives in his *Itinerary* (1510) a certain number of sentences in Arabic. According to Contini, these are to be interpreted as instances of the author's imperfect learning of (a Syrian dialect of) Arabic rather than as specimen of an Arabic pidgin. The case of *La Zingana*, a comedy by G. A. Giancarli (1545), whose protagonist (a gipsy woman) speaks a mixture of the Mediterranean Lingua Franca and of "Arabic," is possibly different. Contini argues that at least a part of the data can be taken to represent an incipient pidgin, possibly based upon an Egyptian variety of Arabic.

22.4 Sudanic Pidgins and Creoles

Following Tosco and Owens (1993), we adopt the definition Sudanic PCs for a linguistically homogenous group of pidgins and creoles that have a common origin in the southern Sudan. In the first half of the 19th century Arab slave traders penetrated southern Sudan from the north setting up military camps (locally known as *zaraaʔib,* SG *zariiba,* which literally means "cattle enclosure") inhabited by a heterogeneous population raided among different Nilotic groups (Mahmud 1983; Miller 1984, 2006; Owens 1985, 1990). Due to the asymmetrical linguistic intercourses between the Arabic-speaking traders and the slave population, a pidginized form of Arabic arose as a military *Lingua Franca.* This pidginized variety represented the ancestor of all the contemporary Sudanic PCs, and for that reason Tosco and Owens label it "Common Sudanic PC Arabic" (253).

The lexifier of the Common Sudanic PC Arabic was a mixture of Sudanic[4] and Egyptian dialects (with a predominance of the former dialectal subtype), while its substratum was composed of a number of Nilotic languages, such as Bari, Dinka, and Nuer. Given their common historical origin, all the Sudanic PCs share a large number of linguistic features both in domain of phonology and in that of morphosyntax, even though, due to the later geographical dispersion, Sudanic PCs also show interesting structural divergences. For the time being, the Sudanic PCs include four varieties that are, respectively, referred to as Turku, Bongor Arabic, Kinubi, and Juba Arabic. On structural grounds, these can be divided into an eastern branch including Juba Arabic and Kinubi and a western branch with Turku and Bongor Arabic.

[4] Following Owens (1993), the label "Sudanic Arabic" refers to the dialectal area stretching from Lake Chad to the west to the Red Sea to the east. It should not be confused with "Sudanese Arabic," which refers to the dialects of the Republic of Sudan.

22.4.1 Turku and Bongor Arabic

Turku[5] is the name of an Arabic pidgin once spoken in western Chad. The scanty data concerning this Arabic variety were gathered by Gaston Muraz, a French medical officer who worked in western Chad at the beginning of the 20th century. Owens and Tosco (1993) published a descriptive and comparative study of Turku on based on this account. Turku was possibly the first pidginized variety that split off from the Common Sudanic PC Arabic spoken in southern Sudan. Bongor Arabic (Luffin 2007) is instead the name generally given in Chad to a pidgin Arabic spoken in the southwestern part of the country in and around the town of Bongor, the capital of the region of Mayo-Kebbi Est. (Other Turku-like varieties could well be found in Chad but have not been reported.) Bongor Arabic should therefore not be confused with the *arabe tchadien* referred to in Section 22.1.

In 1879, following the formal abolition of slavery by the Turco-Egyptian government, a Nubian trader known as Rabeh withdrew with his slave soldiers into present-day Chad and eventually established himself in the region of Borno. According to Owens and Tosco (1993: 183), the Arabic variety that Rabeh's army brought to Chad achieved a sufficient degree of stability becoming a common means of communication for the foreign soldiers and other African populations of western Chad as well. We have no information as to whether Turku creolized, but Bongor Arabic (see 22.2.1.4) has clear structural affinities with the Arabic variety described by Muraz.

Most of the lexicon and much of the grammar of Turku derive from Sudanic Arabic. In line with the other Arabic PCs, Turku presents a reduced phonology in which secondary consonant realizations and long vowels are absent. Also Western Sudanic Arabic dialects (Owens 1993b: 86) generally lack pharyngeal sounds, but, contrary to Turku, they are far from being morphologically less complex than other Arabic dialects. Like other Sudanic PCs, Turku has only number as a morphological category. Turku verbs are uninflected forms, which derive in large part from Arabic imperatives. As in Juba Arabic and in Kinubi, verbs often present a final *-u#*. In addition, *fi* is used as an existential copula. Another important typological feature that Turku shares with the other Sudanic PCs and with Western Sudanic Arabic dialects is represented by "exceed" comparative constructions using the verb *fút(u)* "to pass," as in the following example from Tosco and Owens (1993: 211):

(1)
ínte	*awán*	*fut*	*kadábgel*
you	bad	pass	K.

"You (SG) are worse than Kedabgel."

In common with Turku, Bongor Arabic has *íntukum* as 2PL personal pronoun (which consists of the 2PL independent pronoun *intu* and the 2PL bound pronoun *-kum*), while

[5] The glossonym "Turku" finds its origin in the Arabic word *turk* ~ *turuk* for "Turkish." This term was applied by Chadian populations to the newcomers from the Sudan regardless of their different ethnic origin (Tosco and Owens 1993: 183).

in eastern Sudanic PCs we find the form *ítakum* (from the 2SG independent pronoun *i(n)ta* and the the 2PL bound pronoun *-kum*).

It is important to remark that the influence of the Western Sudanic Arabic dialects is much stronger in Turku and in Bongor Arabic than in other Sudanic PCs. For instance, differently from Kinubi and Juba, the numeral sequence of teens in Turku is 10's+1's, as in Nigerian Arabic (Tosco and Owens 1993: 250). Furthermore, the possessive marker in Turku is *ána,* which derives from the Western Sudanic form *hana.* On this account, Turku and Bongor Arabic are generally put together into the western branch of the Sudanic PCs.

Finally, it should be noted that, due to the prolonged coexistence with Chadian dialects, the structures of the pidginized variety of Bongor show instances of a steady depidginization. For example, in contrast to Turku and other Sudanic PCs, Bongor Arabic distinguishes between independent (e.g., *ána, ínti, hu*) and bound (e.g., *-(y)i, -k(i), -hú*) pronouns (Luffin 2007: 638).

22.4.2 Kinubi

The eruption of the Mahdist revolt in 1884 signaled the end of Turco-Egyptian authority in southern Sudan. In 1888, a military expedition was sent by the *Mahdi,* Muḥammad Aḥmad, in an attempt to enlarge his authority to the southern territories cut off the southernmost province, Equatoria, from the northern Sudan. The governor of the province, the German Eduard Schnitzer (better known as Emin Pasha), was forced to flee to Uganda with those slave soldiers who had remained loyal to the central government. The army first moved to Wadelai, just north of Lake Albert. Later on, the troops were co-opted into the British King's African Rifles, and they subsequently moved to Kenya and Tanzania (Heine 1982: 12; Owens 1990: 220; Luffin 2005a: 28). This series of population displacements gave rise to the current dialectal varieties of Kinubi,[6] the only Arabic creole known so far.

Unlike Turku, the dislocation of Schnitzer's army to Uganda caused a decisive break of the Common Sudanic PC Arabic from both its Arabic lexifier and its Nilotic substratum. As a consequence, the variety once used as an interethnic means of communication in the southern Sudan was rapidly nativized by the children born in Uganda. The implications of such a process concern not only the structural stabilization and the grammatical expansion of the new creolized variety but also the identity of the creole speakers. Given that Nubi communities are now surrounded by a majority of Swahili or Luganda speakers, Kinubi has become a fundamental marker of the Nubi ethnolinguistic identity. At the present time, a large amount of descriptive data is available on three Kinubi geographical

[6] The glossonym "(Ki-)nubi" derives from the Sudanese Arabic word *nuuba, nuubi,* which generally means "slave." The term was then modified by the prefix *ki-* that, among other things, marks glossonyms in Swahili (Kaye 1994: 126; Luffin 2005a: 32). (Ki-)nubi is also referred to as "Nubi" (Wellens 2005)—although we prefer to use the glossonym "(Ki-)nubi," in opposition to the ethnonym "Nubi."

varieties: (1) the Kenyan dialects of Mombasa (Luffin 2004, 2005a, 2005b, 2007, 2013) and (2) Kibera (Heine 1982; Owens 1977, 1989, 1990, 1993a, 2001; Khamis and Owens 2007) and (3) the Kinubi variety of Bombo in Uganda (Wellens 2005).

Regarding dialectal differences within Kinubi, Luffin (2005a: 75–76) proposes some possible isoglosses for the identification of the Kinubi variety of Mombasa compared with the dialects from Kibera and Bombo. These are mainly related to some conservative features (e.g., presence of the plural marker *-át*) as well as to the lower incidence of phonotactic process such as apocope and epenthesis. Wellens (2005: 179) also observes some diatopic variation among the Nubi communities of Uganda. She also notes that Kinubi speakers of Northern Uganda use the passive form of the auxiliary when the main verb is passive (e.g., *arijá sebú úo*—"he was left again," also noted for Kibera in Kenya; Owens 1977), while in the southern part of Uganda only the main verb takes the passive form (e.g., *árija futú úo* "he was passed again"). Another syntactic difference concerns the different position occupied by the negative marker *ma*; if in Uganda *ma* tends to occur sentence-finally, in Kenya it often precedes the verb (Luffin 2005a: 216–217; Wellens 2005: 250–253). Furthermore, Kinubi dialects also differ with regard to the different degree of interference from their Bantu adstratum. For example, Mombasa Kinubi has integrated from Swahili three noun markers *m-*, *wa-*, *ma-* (Luffin 2005a: 135), while in the Kinubi variety of Bombo we find only the two markers *m-* and *wa-* (Wellens 2005: 75).

Kinubi phonologies are rather similar to those of other Sudanic PCs. As in Turku and Juba Arabic, Kinubi generally lacks the Arabic pharyngealized consonants. On the other hand, it integrated secondary realizations such as *ɱ*, *ɽ*, *ŋ*, *ɲ*, from Bantu languages (Luffin 2005a: 58; Wellens 2005: 45). Kinubi presents a reduced five-vowels system (*a*, *e*, *i*, *o*, *u*); as in Turku and Juba Arabic, stress is lexically distinctive as in the opposition between *sába* "seven" and *sabá* "morning" (Owens 1985: 145). In addition, Kinubi derives an infinitive and a passive voice by means of stress shift: *ásurubu* "drink," infinitive *asurúbu*, passive *asurubú* (Owens 2001: 362). As far as Ugandan Kinubi is concerned, Wellens (2005: 54) proposes a four-way stress contrast that additionally distinguishes a gerund form: *kásulu* "wash," gerund *kasúlu*, infinitive *kásúlu*, passive *kasulú*. An alternative analysis for stress–tone distinction in Kinubi has been proposed by Gussenhoven (2006: 218), for whom Kinubi "has obligatory, culminative, metrically, bound accent, with only a single tone being inserted in the accent locations." Following this analysis, Kinubi would represent an intermediary typology between tone languages and stress-accent languages.

Kinubi and the other Sudanic PCs typically display the order Head-Modifier. The head noun is followed by either the indefinite article *wái* or a definite article *de*. Pronominal possessors, adjectives, and numerals follow (Wellens 2005: 133):

(2) *mára* *wái* *kwéisi*
woman one good
"a good woman"

One of the most discussed features of Kinubi and of other Sudanic PCs is represented by the large number of verbs ending in *-u#*. The explanation proposed by

Owens (1985) for this phonomorphological feature is that the Arabic imperative plurals ending in *-*ū* were the main morphological source for the analogical development of the pidginized verbal patterns. In Owens's diachronic reconstruction, Kinubi *-u#* subsequently generalized its morphological role to that of a verbal particle. Versteegh (1984), for his part, considers the final *-u#* as a transitivity marker derived from the Arabic 3rd SG masculine bound pronoun *-*hu*. If Luffin (2005a: 265–267) sticks to Owens's position in his description of the Kinubi of Mombasa, Wellens (2005: 138–145) chooses to share Veerstegh's hypothesis. In particular, she argues that in Ugandan Kinubi inherently transitive verbs with only one participant occur more often without *-u#* because they have a low degree of transitivity. Wellens (2005: 331–345) gives a diachronic explanation for her thesis, pointing out that Kinubi verbs mainly derived from Arabic singular imperatives (with or without an object suffix; Wellens 2005: 141):

(3)

ya	*nyerekú*	*dé*	*gi-ákul(u)*
CONJ	child	DEF	PROG-eat

"Thus the child (was) eating."

Kinubi and Juba Arabic share an innovative system of TAM marking based on the use of preverbal particles. Kinubi has three basic TAM markers:

- The preverbal particle *bi-* derives from the imperfective–indicative marker **bi-* found in Egyptian and Sudanic dialects; in Kinubi it generally expresses a future tense (Heine 1982: 53–55; Wellens 2005: 153–156).
- The particle *gi-/ge-* provides a progressive meaning to the verb since it finds its origin in the phonological reduction of the active participle **gaaʕid* (<*q-ʕ-d* "sit"), which is also used in Sudanic Arabic for expressing a progressive aspect (Luffin 2005a: 279; Wellens 2005: 148).
- The morphologically independent marker *kan* derives from the perfective 3rd singular masculine person of the verb "be" **kaan*, and in Kinubi it adds an anterior (past-before-past) meaning to both marked and unmarked verbs (Luffin 2005a: 280; Wellens 2005: 153).

According to the semantic distinction between stative and nonstative verbs, unmarked stative verbs such as *áju* "want" and *árufu* "know" express a simple present, while unmarked nonstative verbs such as *kásuru* "break" and *gum* "get up" have a perfective reference (Owens 1977: 109; Wellens 2005: 146). A few examples illustrating the most common TAM references expressed by Kinubi are as follows:

Simple present (unmarked stative verb; Heine 1982: 35):

(4)

úo	*ááju*	*júa*	*al*	*áána*	*bío*	*dé*
3SG	want	housee	REL	1SG	buy	DEF

"She likes the house I bought."

Past (unmarked nonstative verb; Luffin 2005a: 282):

(5) *núbi wósul mombása bédir*
Nubi arrive Mombasa early
"Les Nubi arrivèrent tôt à Mombasa [Nubi arrived early in Mombasa]."

Future (*bi*-marked nonstative verb; Wellens 2005: 153):

(6) *kwéis ána kamán bi-wónusu sía*
good 1SG also FT-talk little
"Good, I will also talk a little bit."

Simple/generic present (*gi*-marked nonstative verb; Luffin 2005a: 285):

(7) *mára tái gi-kélem nubi*
woman my PROG-speak Kinubi
"Ma femme parle kinubi [My wife speaks Kinubi]."

Past-before-past (*kan*-marked existential copula *fi;* Wellens 2005: 157):

(8) *kan fi rági wái fi riyagá na*
ANT EXS man one in Riyaga there
"There was a man in Riyaga there."

gi- marked passive verb; Wellens 2005: 179

(9) *gi-nyakamá anási*
PROG-capture.PSV people
"The people were captured."

Imperfect (*kan* with *gi*-marked verb; Luffin 2005a: 294):

(10) *úwo kan gi-so*
3SG ANT PROG-do
"Il faisait [He was doing]"

Counterfactual conditional (*kan* with *bi*-marked verb in the apodosis; Wellens 2005: 160)

(11) *kan kan íta árufu anás to kan ina bi-áburu so sunú*
if ANT 2SG know people his ANT 1PL IRR-try do what
"If you had known his people, what could we have tried to do?"

Finally, it is important to remark that, as in many other creole languages, Kinubi expresses a future progressive through the combination of the future/irrealis and progressive markers (Luffin 2005a: 281):

(12) *úwo* *bi-gi-já*
3SG FT-PROG-come
"Il sera en train de venir [He will be coming]"

22.4.3 Juba Arabic

Despite the partial regression of Arabic in the southern Sudan at the turn of the 20th century, the linguistic heterogeneity of the region contributed to the maintenance of the Common Sudanic PC Arabic as an interethnic means of communication. At the same time, the previously pidginized variety of Arabic started to be nativized by children born of interethnic couples. This situation gave rise over time to an "expanded pidgin"[7] or, in other words, an intermediary variety between pidgins and creoles that has become the native language for only a few of its speakers (Bakker 2008: 139). This variety is commonly known as Juba Arabic and, even if it still represents the second or third language of many southern Sudanese groups, it also became the majority native language of the Juba urban center and is a "national" language according to the Sudanese People Liberation Movement's language policy (although English is the only official language of South Sudan).

Moreover, the prolonged coexistence of Juba Arabic with Sudanese (Standard) Arabic caused this expanded pidgin to be consistently influenced by its lexifier. This situation is described as a post-creole continuum, and it generally results in increased structural affinity between creole languages and their lexifiers (Versteegh 1993: 65–68; Kaye and Tosco 2001: 94–97). Similar to diglossic situations in modern Arabic dialects, the degree of structural interference from Sudanese (Standard) Arabic to Juba Arabic varies a great deal according to sociolinguistic variables such as the speakers' residence and their type and degree of education. As a consequence, Juba Arabic is marked by a higher degree of individual variation than the more stable Kinubi. From a sociolinguistic point of view, it is also important to note that, unlike Kinubi, Juba Arabic does not represent an exclusive marker of ethnic identity. On the contrary, it furnishes an inclusive basis of identification for all southern Sudanese people regardless of their different ethnolinguistic backgrounds.

A great deal of what is known of Juba Arabic (both along the linguistic and the sociolinguistic dimensions) is due to the painstaking work of Catherine Miller (1984, 1985,

[7] The glossonym Juba Arabic (*árabi júba*) refers to Juba, the capital city of southern Sudan. Previously, Juba Arabic was as also referred to as Bimbashi Arabic, from the Turkish word *binbaşı* "major" (the military rank; Miller 1991: 179).

1989, 1993, 1994, 2001, 2002, 2003, 2006). Nhial (1975) and Yokwe (1995) attempt a comparative approach to Juba Arabic. In addition, there are at least two studies dedicated to the TMA system of Juba Arabic, Mahmud (1979) and Tosco (1995). Mahmud (1983) also provides a good sociohistorical account of the spread of Juba Arabic in southern Sudan. Bureng (1986), for his part, analyzes Juba Arabic from a substratist point of view.

Given their numerous structural affinities, and the fact that there is a high degree of mutual intelligibility between the varieties, Juba Arabic and Kinubi may be said to represent together the eastern branch of the Sudanic PCs (Tosco and Owens 1993: 250). Apart from the numerous phonological similarities, we can note that, as in Kinubi, the analytic possessive exponent of Juba Arabic is *ta/bitá* (from the Egyptian **bitaaʕ*, later introduced in Sudanese Arabic in competition with the still more common *ḥagg)*. Furthermore, as in Kinubi, transitive verbs often end with a final *-u* (Miller 1993: 152–154). As an expanded pidgin, Juba Arabic displays typical features of creole languages. For example, Juba Arabic has a prototypical passive construction. This is expressed by a transitive clause in which the patient occupies the subject position, the passive verb is marked by stress shift, and an optional agent follows the preposition *ma* "with" (Manfredi and Petrollino 2013):

(13)

john	*kutú*	*géni*	*fi*	*síjin*	*(ma*	*jés)*
J	put.PSV	stay	in	prison	(by	army)

"John was imprisoned (by the army)."

Another purely syntactic strategy for passivization involves no morphological marking on the verb and the patient in postverbal position. No agent is expressed, and the construction can be considered impersonal (cf. (9); Manfredi 2013):

(14)

áfu	*ána*	*min*	*árabi*
forgive	1SG	from	Arabic

"I was exempted from (the) Arabic (exam)."
["They exempted me from the Arabic (exam.)]"

Furthermore, in line with many creole languages, Juba Arabic uses the bare verb *gále* "say" as complementizer of verbs of speaking and knowing (Miller 2001: 470).

(15)

biníya	*de*	*ma*	*be-árufu*	*gale*	*jamá*	*de*	*gi-kábasu*	*úo*
girl	DEF	NEG	IRR-know	say	people	DEF	PROG-betray	3SG

"La fille ne sait pas qu'ils vont la tromper
[The girl doesn't know that they will fool her]."

It is also to be noted, on the other hand, that Juba Arabic and Kinubi display important grammatical divergences that may be ascribed to the prolonged contact between the Sudanese expanded pidgin and its lexifier. One of the most striking discrepancies between Kinubi and Juba Arabic concerns the use of TMA markers: Juba Arabic possesses the same TMA markers as Kinubi, but it does not allow the sequence of *bi-* and *ge-/gi-* for expressing a future progressive. That is, because the morpheme *bi-*, apart from introducing a future tense, also correlates with the habitual and the progressive aspects in Juba Arabic parallel to Sudanese (Standard) Arabic, such as *bi-mši* "he goes" (Tosco 1995: 458). In view of the fact that *bi-* also marks counterfactual conditional clauses (see (11) for counterfactual conditional in Kinubi), in Juba Arabic it generally correlates with an irrealis aspect rather than with a future tense as in Kinubi.

Second, it is a fact that both Juba Arabic and Kinubi developed innovative grammatical functions compared with their common lexifier. This notwithstanding, if the creolization of Kinubi resulted in a large, independent expansion of its grammatical structures, the influence of Sudanese Arabic on Juba Arabic halts any similar process. For instance, in Juba Arabic the particle *ya* can be used either as as a vocative marker (e.g., *ya zol* "Hey man!"; Manfredi and Tosco 2014) or as a presentative focus marker (e.g., *úo ya bíu fi yuganda de* "he buys them in Uganda", where the verb *bíu* is in focus, Manfredi and Tosco 2014). In Kinubi, on the other hand, *ya* can be used either as non-verbal copula occurring between the subject and the predicate (e.g. *áfandi marús de ya jídi téna* "Cet Efendi Marus est notre grand-père"; Luffin 2005a: 184; see also (3)) or as a contrastive focus marker (e.g. *máma táki ya ma gi-dúgu íta* "it was not your mama who beat you", where the negative operator *ma* is in focus, Wellens 2005: 172).

As a final remark, Juba Arabic and Kinubi also differ to a degree with regard to their lexicon. As other pidgin languages, Juba Arabic compensates its lexical gaps through the lexification of Arabic morphosyntactic sequences. In Kinubi, these complex lexical items have been gradually replaced with Swahili or Luganda borrowings. For example, if in Juba Arabic the relative clause *mára rágjil to mútu* (lit. "the woman whose man died") has been lexified with the meaning of "widow," in Ugandan Kinubi the same semantic reference is expressed by the Luganda loan *mamwándu* (Behnstedt and Woidich 2010: 49).

22.5 Immigrants Pidgins in Arab Countries

A number of incipient pidgins are attested among immigrant communities in the Eastern half of the Arab-speaking world [Holes, "Orality"]. Such varieties have been so far documented in the Gulf (Smart 1990; Næss 2008; Bakir 2008, 2010), Iraq (Avram 2010), and Lebanon (Bizri 2005, 2010). All share typical features of contact varieties or, to use Avram's (2010) label, "pre-pidgins."

22.5.1 Gulf Pidgin Arabic

Gulf Pidgin Arabic (GPA) is the first documented variety with Arabic as a lexifier that emerged in recent years. Following Smart's (1990) early account, GPA has received recently a good description by Næss (2008), which is based on fieldwork in the Omani town of Buraimi, on the border with the United Arab Emirates (UAE), while its verbal system has been analyzed by Bakir (2008, 2010), with data from Qatar.

The emergence of a pidginized variety of Arabic in the Gulf States (from Kuwait in the North to Oman, including Saudi Arabia) is the result of the oil boom and ensuing economic development of the area, and can be traced back to the 1970s of the past century. Næss (2008: 21) draws attention to the numerical weight of the immigrant communities in this part of the Arab world (up to over 80% of the total population in the UAE), their diverse linguistic background (although immigrants from the Indian peninsula are a clear majority), and a "politics of exclusion" (although their permanence in the country is often very long immigrants cannot ever really integrate in the host community and very rarely intermarry with locals). All these factors are conducive to the emergence of a restructured variety of the language of the host community and its possible stabilization as a structured variety.

Smart (1990) coined the term "Gulf Pidgin." In his short sketch this emergent variety is seen through Arab eyes, his data being written material of a jocular variety (mainly cartoon captions) in newspapers from the United Arab Emirates.[8] The result is probably more akin to Arabic foreigner talk than to any actual speech, but certainly the influence of foreigner talk was important in the genesis of GPA. The influence of the substratum is heavily felt in the shift of Arabic /f/ to /p/ in native speakers of Sinhala, Tagalog, Javanese, and Chavacano (who do not have /f/ in their inventories; Næss 2008: 32). Against the general trend to Head-Modifier phrasal order, many speakers produce sentences with Modifier-Head order, especially in the case of possessives *ukti binti* "sister's daughter" and *ana ukti* "my sister," an order which Næss (2008: 54) says to be quite common among Sinhala speakers. The lexicon is overwhelmingly Arabic (amounting, according to Næss 2008: 27, to more than 95% of the total). Arabic phrases are often interpreted as nouns, as in the frequent case of *šismik* (Gulf Arabic "what's your name?" from *ši-sm-ik* "what-name-your.M.SG") for "name."

The only pronominal series is made of the Arabic singular personal pronouns *ana* "I," *inte* "you (SG)," and both *huwa* (Arabic "he") and *hiya* (Arabic "she"), but without any evident gender opposition. The only plural personal pronoun is *nafarât* ("persons" in Arabic), but the use of two pronouns is also possible (such as *ana huwa* "I he" to say "we"; Næss 2008: 52).

The genitival construction employs the particle *mal* (from the Gulf Arabic possessive morpheme *maal*); a few examples of pronominal possessive affixes, such as *binti* (Arabic *bintii* "my daughter") seem lexicalized and interpreted as bare nouns. Again, the order Modifier-Head is occasionally used with genitival constructions with *mâl*, as in *mâl ana sadîg*[9] "my friend" (Næss 2008: 63). Negation is mainly expressed through *mafi*, although a

[8] See also Al-Azraqi (2010) for the media coverage of the immigrants' Arabic in eastern Saudi Arabia.

[9] Næss (2008) marks etymological (i.e., present in the Arabic lexifier) vowel length, which, of course, is not phonological in GPA.

specific negation for nonimperative verbs, *ma*, is widely used (although *mafi* tends to spread to verbal negation too). Næss (2008) does not deal with the independent negation "no."

The whole question of the verb–noun distinction in GPA is complex as well summarized by Næss (2008: 83–85). In general, only one lexeme is taken from any single Arabic root, and in principle nouns can be used as verbs; a few, such as *kalâm* "to speak," or *tâlîm* "to study, learn," are much more frequently used as verbs than as nouns. Still, only etymological nouns and adjectives are verbalized through the use of the light verb *sawwi* "to do," and only etymological nouns tend to enter into possessive constructions with *mal*. On the basis of these criteria, Næss thinks that a verb–noun distinction is possible in GPA. Arabic verbs appear to enter GPA either under the form of the (Gulf) Arabic imperative singular or of the imperfective third masculine singular, without any clear ratio: *yerid* "want" (< 3MSG IMPF) always appears in the form of the Arabic imperfective and a few others, such as *yijlis* "sit," overwhelmingly do. Still others, such as *rûh* "go," almost never appear in the Arabic imperfective form, while others, such as *šûf/šûp* or *yešûf/yešûp* "see," are strongly favored in the "imperfective." In still other cases, such as *yistagel* "to work," the preference for the imperfective form can be due to the desire to avoid an initial /st/ cluster (cf. also Bakir 2010: 208, who thinks that prefixation of y(V)- is basically phonologically determined).

The verbal system does not have real TAM markers, either in the form of affixes or discrete, dedicated morphemes; rather, the adverbs *awwal* "first" > "before" and *bâdên* "then, later," though retaining their use as adverbs, are often used in a preverbal position to mark anteriority and posteriority, respectively (Næss (2008: 85). The same function can be taken over by other adverbs too, such as *bukra* "tomorrow" and *ʔamis* "yesterday" (Bakir 2010: 211). Bakir (ibid., 212) mentions the postverbal use of *kalaas* "done, finished" as a marker of completed action:

(16) *ʔatbuk kalaas laham šilli*
cook CMPL meat take
"When the cooking is done, I raise the meat (from the pan)."

Possibility is expressed by *yimkin* or *mumkin* and necessity by *laazim* (Bakir 2010: 213). Intention may be expressed through the use of *ruuh* "to go" (Bakir 2010: 214):

(17) *ʔanaa ruuh kallim baabaa*
1SG FT speak master
"I'll talk to Master."

In contrast to Sudanic PCs, *fi* is a general copula, as in (Bakir 2010: 215, 216, respectively):

(18) *fii muškil*
COP problem
"There is a problem."

(19) *ʔinta* *fii* *majnuun*
2SG COP crazy
"Are you crazy?"

Still, *fi* is used in a much wider range of meanings; many cases point to an interpretation as a progressive marker or as a marker of factuality (Næss 2008: 89, 90, respectively):

(20) *ḫamsa* *sana* *fi* *tâlîm* *dâhil* *jâma*
five year COP education inside university
"I studied at university for five years."

(21) *alhîn* *fi* *talâk*
now COP divorce
"I'm divorced now."

As mentioned already, à propos the verb–noun distinction, the verb *sawwi* "do" is used as a light verb, as in *sawwi môt* "kill" ("make die"), *sawwi arûs* "marry" ("make bride"), *sawwi nadîf* "clean" ("make clean"), *sawwi suâl* "ask" ("make question"). GPA has not stabilized yet, and both inter- and intrapersonal variation remains huge. Following Winford (2006), Bakir (2010: 223) considers GPA to be a "stage 2" pidgin,[10] which has acquired some simple rules for predication and solutions are not idiosyncratic.

22.5.2 "Romanian Arabic Pidgin"

Avram (2010) is a short description of an Arabic-based contact variety used in Romanian-serviced oil camps in Iraq in the period between 1974 and 1990, when the outbreak of the first Gulf War marked its death. The actors in the contact situation were the Romanian workforce and both Egyptian and Iraqi Arabs. The language itself is Arabic, but there is a sizable amount of English among the approximately 150 words that, according to the author, make up the basic vocabulary of the language. They include basic nouns and verbs, such as *work*, *slip* "sleep," *spik* "speak," and *giv* "give." English-derived material may be used pronominally, as in the case of *pipol* (English *people*) employed as a personal pronoun for all persons. It is not so much the use of a common noun as a pronominal that is relevant here but rather the use of a nonprimary lexifier (English; Gulf Pidgin Arabic uses in the same context the Arabic plural

[10] A "Stage 2 pidgin" (or prototypical pidgin) is "characterized by a clear though rudimentary grammatical organization, in other words, regular though simple rules of predication.... Grammatical categories have emerged, along with basic syntactic procedures" (Winford 2006: 298).

nafarât). Equally relevant here is the use of English-derived *no* as a general negative marker.

A noteworthy feature of Romanian Arabic Pidgin is its simple two-way contact history—Romanian versus "Arabic;" the substrate is likewise limited to Romanian. Arabic-derived (either from Egyptian or Iraqi) lexicon amounts to 75% of the vocabulary, the rest being taken from English, Romanian (but the author provides no clear examples), or "international" words. Actually, this seems a surprisingly low figure, and we suspect that Arabic makes an even bigger contribution. This and other features mentioned by the author (minimal pronominal system, absence of TMA markers, absence of conjunctions and complementizers) make it clear that we are faced here with a pre-pidgin (or jargon) rather than with a prototypical pidgin.[11]

22.5.3 "Pidgin Madam"

Under the label of "Pidgin Madam," Bizri (2005, 2010) discusses the simplified Arabic used by Sri Lankan housemaids in Lebanon. Again, the contact situation is basically bilingual: Lebanese Arabic versus either Sinhalese or Tamil. The Sri Lankan languages do not contribute at all to the lexicon, which is exclusively Arabic with a sprinkling of English (again, *no* is the negative particle) and French (e.g., *bonjour* and other greetings; *merci*; *bébé*) elements, which belong to the Arabic lexifying register: for example, *bonjour and bonsoir* are part of Beirut's speech and are actually more neutral than any Arabic greeting except the informal *marḥaba* (although they are more common among Christians and the middle class; Germanos 2007). Bizri (2005: 54) rightly notes that in Pidgin Madam there is "moins d'influence du substrat que dans les pidgins traditionellement étudiés" ("less substratal influence than among the traditionally-studied pidgins".) The influence of the substrate is basically limited to the phonology (thus, vowel length is retained), but, as noted by the author, a few modifiers (adjective, determiner, demonstrative) precede their head, and this may reflect the word order of the substrate.

A striking feature of the language is the abundance of morphologically complex forms of the lexifier that enter it: verbs are not taken from imperative singular forms only but to a large extent from the imperfective. The actors in the communication event are generally the landlady (the madam that gives the variety its name) and the maid: this is therefore basically a women's language. Not surprisingly, many verbal forms have the Arabic feminine (generally, second- or third-person singular) affix: thus, *ruuhi* "go" (rather than masculine *ruuh*), *neemit* "sleep" (< "she slept"). Likewise, adjectives generally enter the language in their feminine singular form. Object pronouns and even

[11] Pre-pidgins can be identified, following Winford's (2006: 296) definition of "stage 1 pidgins," as varieties characterized by "very minimal syntactic structures, many of which lack either arguments or predicates."

modal markers are often incorporated in the verbal form: *be-t-hebbi-ni* "love, like" (< "she loves me"), *tehkii-ni* "talk" (< "that you (F) talk to me"). Reanalysis of noun phrases (NP) as bare nouns is likewise common: *s-usm-o* "name" (< "what's his name?"). Unlike Romanian Arabic Pidgin, Pidgin Madam has a copula *fi* used in a very large variety of contexts (Bizri 2005: 65):

(22)	*hayda*	*fi*	*poliis*
	this	COP	police

"ça il y a police" > "le policier qui était là-bas [the police who was here]"

(23)	*ana*	*kullu*	*fi*	*grad*
	1SG	all	COP	business

"Moi tout il y a affaires" > "Toutes les affaires qui m'appartiennent [everything that pertains to me]"

This seems to imply that, if anything, there is even more latitude for variation in Pidgin Madam than in the other varieties. Again, everything points to a pre-pidgin rather than to a prototypical or more stabilized variety.

22.5.4 Conclusions on Arabic-Based Incipient Pidgins

It is not clear to what extent these simplified varieties are used by Arab natives in their interaction with foreigners: Bizri (2005: 66) writes of "une permission d'inventer donnée par 'Madam' à la domestique," ("a leave to improvise given by the Madam to the maid.") while Avram (2010: 21) speaks of "significant inter-speaker variation, due to the influence of the speakers' first language, i.e. Romanian, Egyptian Arabic and Iraqi Arabic respectively." Still, the language he describes is consistently the one used by Romanians, and the very name he uses to define it, "Romanian Arabic Pidgin," points to the users of this variety and not to any significant role played by their native language. Rather than true contact languages, it seems we are dealing here with varieties having Arabic as their target, but with two different inputs. Pidgin Madam is based on fairly normal Lebanese Arabic in terms of morphological structure, if not in syntax, lexicon, and maybe tempo of speech. In the case of Romanian Arabic Pidgin, on the other hand, some input in terms of a restructured foreign Arabic used by natives seems more probable. According to Bizri, the basic principle at work in Pidgin Madam is mimicry, "mimétisme de la langue des maîtres." If this is so, the Pidgin is the exclusive domain of the foreigners when speaking with Arabs; in the case of Romanian Arabic Pidgin (as in Gulf Pidgin Arabic), use on the part of the natives is possible. In both cases, and different from "true" pidgins, further use on the part of a multilingual community of non-Arabs is excluded.

22.6 The Relevance of Arabic-Based Pidgins and Creoles for Arabic Linguistics and General Creolistics

Generally speaking, Arabic-based PCs have engendered very little attention among either Arabicists or creolists. On one hand, Arabic PCs were simply not considered part of Arabic studies, and, even after Versteegh's (1984) brave proposal to use pidginization as a cornerstone of Arabic historical dialectology, they have received little consideration. On the other side, general linguists working on theories of pidginization and creolization have generally limited their attention to European-based PCs. In this regard, Jonathan Owens (2001), in an attempt to draw further attention to the structural relevance of the Arabic PCs for contact linguistics, aptly calls Kinubi "the orphan of all orphans." It is also true that during the last decade our knowledge of Arabic PCs progressed a great deal thanks to new descriptions of Kinubi varieties (Luffin 2005a; Wellens 2005) and to innovative studies on immigrant pidgins in Arab countries (Bizri 2005, 2010; Bakir 2008, 2010; Næss 2008; Avram 2010). This notwithstanding, Arabic-based PCs still represent a marginal sphere of research.

Pidginization and creolization have been called on in the birth of the modern Arabic dialects (a topic not germane to the present article), most notably by Versteegh. Versteegh (1984, 2004) argues that the modern dialects arose through a stage of simplified pidginization followed by elaboration and creolization. At a later stage, the creoles came under the influence of the standardized form of the target language, thereby losing their most "deviant" features. Versteegh's hypothesis has been generally met with skepticism by Arabic scholars (e.g., Holes 1995, 2004; Fischer 2006; Owens 2009 [2006]). Catherine Miller (2002), emphasizing again the importance of Arabic-based PCs for historical Arabic linguistics, instead stresses that the analysis of the ongoing pidginization–creolization process in Southern Sudan could have a theoretical relevance for historical dialectology in respect of the fact that Arabic dialects always spread in contact environments.

As to general linguistics, the inclusion of Arabic-based PCs would greatly benefit creolists in their assumptions on pidginization and creolization, as their study may contribute to the long-standing discussion concerning the definitions of incipient pidgin, stable pidgin, expanded pidgin, creole, and post-creole. The different sociolinguistic contexts that gave rise to Arabic PCs may shed new light on the interdependence between contact situations and their linguistic outcomes and help clarify a number of questions related to pidgin and creole genesis.

Substratist accounts of creole genesis do not fare well with Arabic-based PCs: a list of words of "African" and unknown origin in Kinubi (Pasch and Thelwall 1987: 141–144) suffices to reveal how limited the impact of the substrate has been in the lexicon (most words in the list are actually recent loans from Swahili and would rather qualify as adstratal). Grammatical influence is equally limited (notwithstanding the special, but in fact limited, role played by Bari and studied by Bureng 1986). Universalist approaches have been adopted for the analysis of the verbal system of Kinubi (Owens 1993a) and Juba Arabic (Tosco 1995). Recently, it has been shown that Kinubi falls squarely into the "creole type" as defined by Bakker et al. (2011). Juba Arabic is thereby included as well.

Owens (2001: 368) proposes to analyze Kinubi in the light of the "restructuring" process that involved its Arabic lexifier. Adopting this perspective, Owens reduces the role played by substrate and universal ("no-strate") factors in creole genesis and concentrates on the innovative aspects of the Kinubi grammar compared with Sudanic Arabic. More in particular, he argues that restructuring in Kinubi allows for an expansion of the tripartite nature of the creole-origin hypotheses (i.e., superstrate, substrate, and no-strate), since the "restructuring" hypothesis is "a consequence of the inability of the other approaches to fully account for the origins of creole structures" (ibid.).

Recently, both Kinubi (Luffin 2013) and Juba Arabic (Manfredi and Petrollino 2013) have been included in the *Atlas of Pidgin and Creole Language Structure* (APiCS). APiCS gathers comparable synchronic data on the grammatical and lexical structures of a large number of PCs in an attempt to present the geographical distribution of the most relevant features for creole linguistics. Thus, the presence of two Sudanic Arabic-based PCs will give the opportunity to compare their typological proximity with non–Arabic-based PCs and to finally enlighten their superstrate–substrate against their no-strate features.

References

Al-Azraqi, Munira. 2010. Pidginisation in the Eastern region of Saudi Arabia: Media presentation. In *Arabic and the media. Linguistic analyses and applications*, ed. Reem Bassiouney, 159–174. Leiden: Brill.

Avram, Andrei. 2010. An outline of Romanian pidgin Arabic. *Journal of Language Contact* 3: 20–36.

Bakir, Murtadha. 2008. Noun and noun phrases in Gulf Pidgin Arabic. Paper presented at the 8th AIDA conference, Colchester, University of Essex, August 28–31.

——. 2010. Notes on the verbal system of Gulf Pidgin Arabic. *Journal of Pidgin and Creole Languages* 25: 201–228.

Bakker, Peter. 1997. Michif. In *Contact languages: A wider perspective*, ed. Sarah G. Thomason, 259–363. Amsterdam: Benjamins.

——. 2008. Pidgins versus creoles and pidgin creoles. In *Handbook of pidgin and creole studies*, ed. Silvia Kouwenberg and John Victor Singler, 130–157. Oxford: Wiley-Blackwell.

Bakker, Peter, Aymeric Daval-Markussen, Mikael Parkvall, and Ingo Plag. 2011. Creoles are typologically distinct from non-creoles. *Journal of Pidgin and Creole Languages* 26: 5–42.

Behnstedt, Peter and Manfred Woidich. 2010. *Wortatlas der arabischen Dialekte. Band I: Mensch, Natur, Fauna und Flora*. Leiden: Brill.

Bizri, Fida. 2005. Le Pidgin Madam, un nouveau pidgin arabe. *La Linguistique* 41: 53–66.

——. 2010. *Pidgin Madame: Une grammaire de la servitude*. Paris: Geuthner.

Bureng, G. Vincent. 1986. Juba Arabic from a Bari perspective. In *Current approaches to African linguistics*, vol. 3, ed. Gerrit J. Dimmendaal, 71–78. Foris: Dordrecht.

Contini, Riccardo. 1994. *Pidgins* arabi nella letteratura italiana del '500? *Quaderni di Studi Arabi* 12: 65–86.

de Pommerol, Patrice Jullien. 1999. *Grammaire pratique de l'arabe tchadien*. Paris: Karthala.

Ferguson, Charles A. 1970. The role of Arabic in Ethiopia: A sociolinguistic perspective. In *Languages and linguistics monograph series* 23, 355–368. Washington, DC: Georgetown University Press.

Fischer, Wolfdietrich. 2006. *Grammatik des Klassischen Arabisch*. Wiesbaden: Harrassowitz.

Germanos, Marie-Aimée. 2007. Greetings in Beirut: Social distribution and attitudes towards different formulae. In *Arabic in the city: Issues in dialect contact and language variation*, ed. Catherine Miller, Enam Al-Wer, Dominique Caubet, and Janet C. E. Watson, 147–165. London: Routledge.

Gussenhoven, Carlos. 2006. Between stress and tone in Nubi word prosody. *Phonology* 23: 193–223.

Heine, Bernd. 1982. *The Nubi language of Kibera—An Arabic creole*. Berlin: Reimer.

Holes, Clive. 1995. *Modern Arabic: Structures, functions and varieties*. London: Longman.

——. 2004. *Modern Arabic: Structures, functions and varieties*, rev. ed. Washington, DC: Georgetown University Press.

Kaye, Alan. 1985. The importance of pidgins and creoles for historical linguistics. *Diachronica* 2: 201–230.

——. 1994. Peripheral Arabic dialectology and Arabic pidgins and creoles. In *Actas del Congreso Internacional sobre interferencias linguísticas arabo-romances*, ed. Jordi Aguadé, Federico Corriente, and Marina marugàn, 125–140. Zaragoza: Navarro y Navarro.

Kaye, Alan and Mauro Tosco. 1993. Early East African pidgin Arabic. *Sprache und Geschichte in Afrika* 14: 269–305.

——. 2001. *Pidgin and creole languages: A basic introduction*. München: Lincom Europa.

Khamis, Cornelia and Jonathan Owens 2007. Nubi. In *Creole syntax: Parallel outlines of seventeen Creole grammars*, ed. John Holm and Peter Patrick, 199–216. London: Battlebridge Press.

Luffin, Xavier. 2004. Les verbes d'état, d'existence et de possession en kinubi. *Zeitschrift für Arabische Linguistik* 43: 43–66.

——. 2005a. *Un créole arabe: le Kinubi de Mombasa, Kenya*. München: Lincom.

——. 2005b. *Kinubi texts*. München: Lincom.

——. 2007. Bongor Arabic. In *Encyclopedia of Arabic Language and Linguistics*, vol. 3., ed. Kees Versteegh, Associate Editors: Mushira Eid, Alaa Elgibali, Manfred Woidich, Andrzej Zaborski, 634–639. Leiden: Brill.

——. 2013. Kinubi. In ed. Susanne Michaelis, Philippe Maurer, Martin Haspelmath, and Magnus Huber, APiCS, *Survey of pidgin and creole languages, Volume III: Pidgins, creoles and mixed languages based on languages from Africa, Asia, Australia and the Americas*, 50–53. Oxford: OUP.

Mahmud, Ushari. 1979. *Variation in the aspectual system of Juba Arabic*. PhD diss., Georgetown University, Washington, DC.

——. 1983. *Arabic in the Southern Sudan—History and spread of a pidgin-creole*. Khartoum: Khartoum University Press.

Manfredi, Stefano 2010. *A grammatical description of Kordofanian Baggara Arabic*. Unpublished Ph.D. diss., Università degli Studi di Napoli "L'Orientale."

Manfredi, Stefano. 2013. Juba Arabic corpus. Corpus recorded, transcribed and annotated by Stefano Manfredi, *ANR CorpAfroAs—A Corpus for Afro-Asiatic Languages. http://corpafroas.tge-adonis.fr/Archives/.*

Manfredi, Stefano and Mauro Tosco. 2014. The morphosyntax and prosody of topic and focus in Juba Arabic. In: Stefano Manfredi and Mauro Tosco (eds.), *Arabic-based pidgins and creoles: descriptive, comparative and socio-historical issues*. Special Issue of *Journal of Pidgin and Creole Languages* 29/2: 319–351.

Manfredi, Stefano and Sara Petrollino. 2013. Juba Arabic. In ed. Susanne Michaelis, Philippe Maurer, Martin Haspelmath, and Magnus Huber, APiCS, *Survey of pidgin and Creole languages, Volume III: Pidgins, creoles and mixed languages based on languages from Africa, Asia, Australia and the Americas*, 54–66. Oxford: OUP.

Miller, Catherine. 1984. *GLECS* 28: 295–315. Paris: Geuthner.

——. 1985. Un éxemple d'évolution linguistique: le cas de la particule "ge" en Juba-Arabic. In *Materiaux Arabes et Sudarabiques*, vol. 1, 155–166. Paris: Geuthner.

——. 1989. Bari interference in Juba-Arabic. In *Proceedings of the 4th Nilo-saharian Symposium August 30–September 2, 1989*, ed. Lionel Bender, 1–10. Tübingen: Helmut Buske.

——. 1991. De la cuisine familiale au commerce des spiritueux, Remarques sur un parler de femmes à Juba. In *Semitic studies in honor of Wolf Leslau*, vol. 2, ed. Alan S. Kaye, 1059–1084. Wiesbaden: Harrassowitz.

——. 1993. Restructuration morpho-syntaxique en Juba-arabic et Ki-nubi: À propos du débat universaux/substrat et superstrat dans les études creoles. In *Matériaux Arabes et Sudarabiques*, vol. 5, 137–174. Paris: Geuthner.

——. 1994. Créolisation et acquisition: Quelques phénomènes observés à propos de l'arabe du Soudan. In *Créolisation et acquisition de langues*, ed. Daniel Véronique and Johannes Niehoff-Pagagiotidis, 225–248. Aix-en-Provence: Publications de l'Université de Provence.

——. 2001. Grammaticalisation du verbe gale "dire" en Juba-Arabic. In *Lécons d'Afique: Filiations, ruptures et reconstitutions des langues; un hommage à Gabriel Manessy*, ed. Robert Nicolaï, 455–482. Louvain: Peeters.

——. 2002. The relevance of Arabic-based pidgin/creoles for Arabic linguistics. In *Contributions to Arabic linguistics*, ed. G. Mansour and M. Doss, 7–45. Cairo: Arab Research Centre.

——. 2003. Reduplication in Arabic-based language contact. In *Twice as meaningful: Reduplication in pidgins, creoles and other contact languages*, ed. Silvia Kouwenberg, 289–299. London: Battlebridge Publications.

——. 2006. Juba Arabic. In *Encyclopedia of Arabic Language and Linguistics*, vol. 2, ed. Kees Versteegh, Associate Editors: Mushira Eid, Alaa Elgibali, Manfred Woidich, Andrzej Zaborski, 517–525. Leiden: Brill.

——. 2009. Enjeux des dénominations de l'arabe en Afrique sub-saharienne. In *Le nom des langues. Vol. 3, Le nom des langues en Afrique sub-saharienne: pratiques, dénominations, catégorisations/Naming languages in Sub-Saharan Africa: Practices, Names, Categorisations*, ed. Carole de Féral, 233–254. Louvain-la-Neuve: Peeters.

Muysken, Pieter. 1997. Media lengua. In *Contact languages: A wider perspective*. ed. S. Thomason, 365–426. Amsterdam: Benjamins.

Næss, Unn Gyda. 2008. *"Gulf Pidgin Arabic": Individual strategies or a structured variety? A study of some features of the linguistic behaviour of Asian migrants in the Gulf countries.* Unpublished MA thesis, University of Oslo.

Nhial, Abdon. 1975. Kinubi and Juba Arabic: A comparative study. In *Directions in Sudanese linguistics and folklore*, ed. Sayyid Ḥ. Ḥurreiz and Herman Bell, 81–94. Khartoum: Institute of African and Asian Studies.

Owens, Jonathan. 1977. *Aspects of Nubi grammar*. PhD diss., London School of Oriental and African Studies, London University.
——. 1985. The origins of East African Nubi. *Anthropological Linguistics* 27: 229–271.
——. 1989. Zur Pidginisierung und Kreolisierung im Arabishen. *Afrika und Übersee* 72: 91–107.
——. 1990. East African Nubi: Bioprogam vs. inheritance. *Diachronica* 7: 217–250.
——. 1993a. Nubi, genetic linguistics, and language classification. *Anthropological Linguistics* 33: 1–30.
——. 1993b. Nigerian Arabic in a comparative perspective. *Sprache und Geschichte in Afrika* 14: 85–176.
——. 1996. Arabic-based pidgins and creole. In *Contact languages: A wider perspective*. ed. S. Thomason, 125–172. Amsterdam: Benjamins.
——. 2001. Creole Arabic: The orphan of all orphans. *Anthropological Linguistics* 43: 348–378.
Pasch, Helma and Robin Thelwall. 1987. Losses and innovations in Nubi. In *Varia Creolica*, ed. Philippe Maurer and Thomas Stolz, 94–165. Bochum: Brockmeyer.
Simeone-Senelle, Marie-Claude. 2000. L'arabe véhiculaire parlé en Erythrée sur la côte sud de la Mer Rouge de Massawa a Rahayta. *Oriente Moderno* 19(80): 153–180.
Smart, J. R. 1990. Pidginization in Gulf Arabic: A first report. *Anthropological Linguistics* 32 (1–2): 83–119.
Thomason, Sarah G. 1996. *Contact languages: A wider perspective*. Amsterdam: Benjamins.
Thomason, Sarah Grey and Alaa Elgibali. 1986. Before the lingua franca: Pidginized Arabic in the eleventh century A.D. *Lingua* 68: 317–349.
Tosco, Mauro 1995. A pidgin verbal system: The case of Juba Arabic. *Anthropological Linguistics* 37: 423–459.
——. 2007. Pidginization. In *Encyclopedia of Arabic Language and Linguistics*, vol. 3., ed. Kees Versteegh Associate Editors: Mushira Eid, Alaa Elgibali, Manfred Woidich, Andrzej Zaborski, 639–644. Leiden: Brill.
Tosco, Mauro and Jonathan Owens. 1993. Turku: A descriptive and comparative study. *Sprache und Geschichte in Afrika* 14: 177–267.
Versteegh, Kees. 1984. *Pidginization and creolization: the case of Arabic*. Amsterdam: Benjamins.
——. 1993. Levelling in the Sudan: From Arabic creole to Arabic dialect. *International Journal of the Sociology of Language* 99: 65–79.
——. 2004. Pidginization and creolization revisited. In *Approaches to Arabic dialects: A collection of articles presented to Manfred Woidich on the occasion of his sixtieth birthday*, ed. Martine Haak et al., 343–357. Leiden: Brill.
Wellens, Ineke. 2005. *The Nubi language of Uganda: An Arabic creole in Africa*. Leiden: Brill.
Winford, Donald. 2006. Reduced syntax in (prototypical) pidgins. In *The syntax of non-sententials*, ed. Ljiljana Progovac, Kate Paesani, Eugenia Casielles, and Ellen Barton, 283–307. Amsterdam: Benjamins.
Yokwe, Eluzai M. 1985. The diversity of Juba-Arabic. *Studies in African Linguistics Supplement* 9: 323–328.
Zaborski, Andrzej. 2008. Árabe de Asia Central. In *Manual de dialectología neoárabe*, ed. Federico Corriente and Ángeles Vicente, 409–437. Zaragoza: Instituto de Estudios Islámicos y del Oriente Próximo.
Zimmermann, Gerit. 2002. Das Arabische von Buchara zwischen alten Quellen und neuen Forschungsergebnissen. MA thesis, Bayreuth University.

CHAPTER 23

THE CLASSICAL ARABIC LEXICOGRAPHICAL TRADITION

SOLOMON I. SARA, S.J.

23.1 Preliminaries

The word *dictionary* is not a clearly defined term.[1] It is an all-inclusive term that may include any list, such as a third millennium BC Sumerian inventory or any full-fledged, modern dictionary such as the Oxford English Dictionary and all others in between. In place of a definition, it is more informative to illustrate the notion of a dictionary that we have in mind by taking as an example a real product that is recognized and accepted as a dictionary. For purposes of this study, Samuel Johnson's Dictionary (Lynch 2002) will serve as a model, not to show historical priority but to exemplify the notion of a dictionary. It suits the aims of this study in that it also parallels the composition of the first Arabic dictionary, over 1000 years before Johnson's. Johnson's is the first English dictionary, undertaken by a single individual and based mostly on written sources. In its preface (Lynch 2002: 25–45), Johnson carefully details the manner in which he went about collecting his data, along with his six Scot assistants, and the manner in which he integrated them into his dictionary. One might mention that the approach that Johnson followed, the use of written sources, the marking of the grammatical categories of the entries, the inclusion of etymologies, and quotations from recognized authors, has been followed ever since in subsequent dictionaries like the OED, Webster's International

[1] I wish to thank Dr. Simon Mauck for reading this chapter and for making recommendations of both style and substance. "al-Khaliil" and "al-Jawharii" is adopted as the conventional spelling of the two lexicographers. In general in proper names and titles, ج is transliterated as "j."

Dictionary (Gove 2002), the primary dictionaries of classical Greek (Liddell 1966) and Latin (William Young 1910), and almost all other Western dictionaries. Johnson designed the basic template for a comprehensive dictionary of English and of nearly all dictionaries of other languages written in English. More details are found in Clifford (1979). To be noted is that the lexicographers of English used the term dictionary from the start. That is not the case with the lexicographers of Arabic. Each one had his own notion and term for what he thought a dictionary was or what it accomplished.

23.2 Classical Arabic Lexicographical Tradition

There is evidence that tells of linguists making trips to tribal areas and collecting what vocabulary they found new among the speakers but not in a systematic fashion (Amiin 1970, vol. 2: 263). More to the point are those linguists who made efforts to collect words or lexical items that dealt with a particular topic like *Kitaab al-maṭar, The book of rain, Kitaab al-naxl wa al-karm, The book of date palms and grapevines* (Yaʕquub 1981: 28). But if linguistic activity among the Arabs began in the 8th century, then one can point to a lexicographical phenomenon, similar to Johnson's effort, when a single individual undertook the task of writing the first comprehensive dictionary of Arabic. This occurred in the burst of linguistic creativity in the 2nd/8th century, roughly a millennium before Johnson began his work in the 18th century. Though many noteworthy and comprehensive dictionaries of Arabic have appeared since that date and deserve mention and discussion on their own, each one cannot be included. A chronological listing, from al-Khaliil to al-Bustaanii, is given in Yaʕquub (1981: 29–31). This brief discussion will focus on three basic paradigmatic models that the Arabic lexicographers adopted over time. This is not to say that other groupings are not found among other chroniclers, including both the classical chroniclers like ʔAzharii (1964), Rundgren (1973), Siiraafii (1985), and ibn Nadiim (2009) as well as the contemporary ones like Yaʕquub (1981), ʕAṭṭaar (1984), Haywood (1960), Darwish (1956), Ḥurr (1994), Maʕtuuq (1999), Sezgin (1982, 1984), and Kraemer (1953). But to fully appreciate the dynamics of the Arabic lexicographic activity, we will consider the following models that encapsulate the innovative approaches that it took over the centuries. These show the maximally distinct paradigmatic models in lexicography and the paradigms behind which other lexicographers lined up. Though the three approaches are procedurally opposed, all three account for the lexical data of Arabic, and all three offer justifiable procedures of how to account for the complexity of the data and the three are maximally different from each other.

I. al-Khaliil's model in *Kitaab al-ʕayn*.
II. al-Jawharii's model in *al-Ṣiħaah*.
III. al-Bustaanii's model in *Kitaab muħiiṭ al-muħiiṭ*.

A biographical sketch of the selected lexicographers will be given, followed by a discussion of the design and composition of their dictionaries and where they fit in the historical flow of Arabic linguistic activity of their time. We intend to deal with the three basic models of Arabic lexicography in some detail, especially the first lexicographer and the final product, because, as we will note, subsequent lexicographers varied the model somewhat but did not alter it in any major sense. However, we will also touch briefly on the variations to which these first three models have been subjected. To be sure, these models were never followed slavishly by subsequent lexicographers within each model. Every lexicographer will end up having his own approach and rationale—whether to include more or less linguistic material, more or less of the *ʃawaahid* "examples of use," or other types of material, not all of which can be touched upon here.

23.3.1 al-Khaliil's Linguistic Phonetic-Anagrammatic Model

al-Khaliil, whose full name is ʕAbdu al-Rahmaan al-Khaliil ibn ʔAhmad al-Faraahiidii, (100–174/719–791), was born in ʕUmān, on the Arabian–Persian Gulf, but lived and taught in Basra in present-day Iraq. He traveled to Mecca every other year and came in contact with a variety of spoken Arabic among the peninsular tribes. By the accounts of the chroniclers (al-Siiraafii 1985: 54–56; al-Zubaydii 1973: 47–51), he was an ascetic and a creative genius who devised many ways of looking into the Arabic language and its structure. The poetic metrics of Arabic, called *al-ʕaruuḍ*, owe their formalization to him. He is also known for his other linguistic innovations. One of the most significant was the design of a comprehensive Arabic dictionary, called *Kitaab al-ʕayn* (The book of *ʕayn* [ʕ)" (al-Khaliil 1980). His aim, as he said, was "to give a comprehensive account of the speech of the Arabs, their poetry, their expressions and from which nothing was to be left out" (al-Khaliil 1980: 47). This dictionary was to include many innovations in the process of its design and composition, from the organization of the sound system to the details of the morphological system. In addition to coediting the dictionary, Maxzuumi provides further studies on the work of al-Khaliil (Maxzuumi 1960, 1986).

23.3.1.1 *Kitaab al-ʕayn*

This was the first linguistic model conceived, executed, and expressly based on a new perception of the lexical data of Arabic. al-Khaliil composed his dictionary to account for the words of Arabic in all their complexity. In the process he had to examine the writing system and the traditional organization of the letters of Arabic. Since he was going to build his dictionary on these letters, their organization was a matter of importance to him. He did not favor the traditional organization and sequencing of the letters. His introduction to the dictionary does not give the full list of the letters but only begins the treatise by saying: *this is what he composed about the letters of the alphabet,* ا, ب, ت, ث (1980: 47), which is the start of the traditional alphabetic order as we know it today. We term this order mentioned by al-Khaliil the "traditional" one. It was the one that was used by one of his contemporaries, ʔAbuu al-ʕAlaaʔ al-ʃaybaanii in his *Kitaab al-giim* (ʕAṭṭaar

Table 23.1 Traditional alphabetic order

ا - ب ت ث - ج ح خ - د ذ - ر ز - س ش - ص ض - ط ظ - ع غ - ف ق - ك ل - م ن ه و ي
A - b t θ - g ħ x - d ð - r z - s ʃ - ṣ ḍ - ṭ ẓ - ʕ ɣ - f ɢ - k l - m n h w y

1984: 74), a book composed by a member of the Kuufah school (Maxzuumi 1958). On the other hand, al-Khaliil, proceeded to re-organize them according to their manner of production, rather than following the accepted traditional organization that was based on the shape of the letters, primarily found in the work of Naṣr bin ʕAaṣim (Yaʕquub 1981: 39). He took a physiological and phonetic perspective that took into account the mode of the production of these letters and thus composed the first treatise on Arabic sound system (Sara 1991). This method had been followed by the classical Indian linguists (Law 1990). Arabic is normally written from right to left. The traditional Arabic alphabetical order that is still in use is shown above going from left to right in Table 23.1.

The traditional organization of the letters began with the *ʔalif*. This did not suit al-Khaliil because *ʔalif* is *ħarf muʕtall* "a weak letter"[2] and subject to many variations. He did not want to arbitrarily begin with the second letter. So he searched for an alternative linguistic model and came up with a novel way of conceiving the structure of Arabic words based on the articulation of the letters as follows:

[ʕ, ħ, h, x, ɣ ɢ, k g, ʃ, ḍ, ṣ, s, z, ṭ, d, t, ẓ, θ, δ, r, l, n, f, b, m w, A, y, ʔ].

His procedure is summarized in the following steps.[3]

Step 1: Group the Letters into ṣaħiiħ "Strong" and muʕtall "Weak"

Since the letters were subclassified as strong and weak, the lexical items were accordingly classified as having strong and weak roots (Table 23.2).

In the dictionary, the strong roots will come before the weak roots. The weak roots consist of the roots that include one or more weak letters. The dictionary takes note of this fact. The roots with weak radicals are prone to more radical variation in their many derivations and hence have surface forms that vary more than roots with only strong letters. The dictionary accounts for roots with strong letters first before accounting for roots with weak letters.

Step 2: Divide the Dictionary into 25 Chapters and Devoted a Chapter to Each Strong Letter

The four weak letters were grouped together as a final chapter, the 26th chapter.

[2] The "weak" letters are [w, A, y, ʔ] and are defined as such because they undergo more changes than the other letters. They are pronounced in the cavity as a whole rather than having a particular "exit."

[3] There is no reason to think that al-Khaliil followed the following steps precisely as stated here. But it is claimed that these were the elements of his design.

Table 23.2 al-Khaliil's classification of letters and sounds

ħarf "letter"	*ħayyiz* "locale" ↓	*maxrag* "exit" →
I. ṣaħiiħ "strong"	1. *ħalɢ* "throat"	1. ʕ, ħ, h, x, ɣ ع، ح، ه، خ، غ
	2. *lahāh* "uvula"	2. ɢ, k ق، ك
	3. *ʃagr* "soft palate"	3. g, ʃ, ḍ ج، ش، ض
	4. *ʔasalah* "apex"	4. ṣ, s, z ص، س، ز
	5. *niṭʕ* "palate"	5. ṭ, d, t ط، د، ت
	6. *liθθah* "gums"	6. ẓ, θ, δ ظ، ث، ذ
	7. *ðalaɢ* "laminae"	7. r, l, n ر، ل، ن
	8. *ʃafah* "lip"	8. f, b, m ف، ب، م
II. *muʕtall* "weak"	*gawf* "cavity"	ʔ, y, A, w ء، ي، ا، و

Step 3: Adopt a Phonetic Basis for the Organization of the Letters of Arabic

In his linguistic approach, al-Khaliil decided on an articulatory basis for organizing the letters by their *ʔaħyaaz* "locales" and *maxaarig* "exits" [Embarki, "Phonetics"]. That is, the speech tract will be divided into a certain number of *ʔaħyaaz* "locales" and each *ħayyiz* "locale" into a graduated list of *maxaarig* "exits." This approach provided him with a new, motivated organization of the sounds of Arabic, with their production confined to specific areas of the vocal tract, beginning at the *ħalɢ* "throat" and ending at the *ʃafatayn* "two lips."

Table 23.2 shows the inventory of the Arabic sounds divided into eight locales and each locale subdivided into a number of exits where the letters are produced, from the deepest in the *ħalɢ* "throat" to the highest, the *ʃafatayn* "two lips." The list for the strong letters begins with the [ʕ], the deepest sound produced in the throat, followed by, for example, [ħ] or [h] and ending with [m], the highest and front-most sound produced at the lips. In all this, the understanding, organization and the terminology of al-Khaliil anticipated much of current phonetic usage.

Step 4: Organize the Dictionary according to the Exits of the Letters

The organization of the lexicon followed the phonetics, according to the order of the *maxaarig* "exits" of the *ħuruuf* "letters." The place of the letters in the system was determined by the precise location of their production in the speech cavities. This new approach imposed a motivated, new ordering on the letters of the language that was radically different from the traditional sequence. The new dictionary would be organized according to this new phonetic sequencing, and the words likewise would be arranged following the same order and not the traditional order. The dictionary begins not with the letter [A] but with the letter [ʕ] and ends not with the letter [y] but with the letter [m], as in Tables 23.2 and 23.3.

In the process of sequencing, al-Khaliil had isolated the four weak letters from the strong letters without giving them specific locales or exits but considering them simply

Table 23.3 Phonetico-alphabetic order of the *Kitaab al-ʕayn*

ʕ, ħ, h, x, ɣ – ɢ, k– g, ʃ, ḍ – ṣ, s, z– ṭ, d, t – ẓ, θ, ð – r, l, n – f, b, m – w, A, y, ʔ

as cavity letters. In practice, the roots that included one or more weak letters among their radicals would be listed after the ones with strong radicals had been accounted for. For example, strong triradical roots would be treated before triradical roots including weak radicals were treated. Those consisting wholly of weak radicals would be treated at the end of the dictionary.

Step 5: List the Lexical Entries in the Dictionary in Terms of Their Radicals Only

That is, entries were listed minus the affixes and the *ħarakaat* "motions."[4] The custom of dictionaries in languages like English is to list each word in the dictionary according to its surface spelling: the word "endure" will be entered under the letter {e}, that is, after all the letters that began with the previous letter {a, b, c, d}. The word "admiration" will be entered under the letter {a}, and skipping the letters {b, c} one gets to {d}, and skipping letters {e, f, g, h} one comes to the letter {i} and so forth until one reaches the final letter, which is {n}, with no regard given to the morphological makeup of the word. al-Khaliil does not follow the obvious path by following the surface sequence of the Arabic word; rather, he looks for the common root, forgoing all the morphological additions to the root, and classifies the entries in terms of the root radicals only, that is, at a level deeper than the surface. To give an example, in English the words "class, classifier, classical, declassify, mis-classify, unclassified" cluster around the root "class," but they would not be included under the word "class" in an English dictionary, under the letter "c" of the word "class," but rather alphabetically and separately. In the Arabic dictionary of al-Khaliil, however, they would have been listed under the word "class," under the letter "c," all things being equal.

In the dictionary of al-Khaliil, an Arabic word like *ʔistaɢbalnaahum* "we met/welcomed them," a word of the Xth verb form, will not be listed under the first letter [ʔ] but under the root's first radical, which is [ɢ] of the root [ɢbl]. So one will look for this word under the letter [ɢ], overlooking all the other morphological accretions (i.e., prefixes, infixes, and suffixes). Needless to say, this is one of the challenging aspects of using al-Khaliil's dictionary or any other Arabic dictionary based on his model, especially for beginners, who must learn what needs to be stripped away from the complex word to reach the radical letters of a complex word [Buckwalter and Parkinson, "Modern Lexicography"].

Step 6: Classify the Lexical Entries in Terms of the Number of Their Radicals

Entries were classified as bi-, tri-, quadri-, and quinqueradicals. Though this is not a discussion of the analysis of the morphology of Arabic, in Arabic when one removes all

[4] The *ħarakaat* "motions" are the diacritical letters that make the word pronounceable, namely, [a, i, u].

the derivational, inflectional affixes and the *ħarakaat* "motions" from a word of the language, what remains is the root with its basic radicals. The number of radicals per stem, for native Arabic words, according to al-Khaliil, ranges from two to five radicals. By way of example, *lam* "no" has the radicals [lm], *ɢabala* "he accepted" has the three radicals [ɢbl], *ʕaɢrab* "scorpion" has the four radicals [ʕɢrb], and *safargal* "quince" has the five radicals [sfrgl]. In the dictionary, the biradical stems will come before the triradical and the triradical before the quadriradical and the quadriradical before the quinqueradicals for each word of the dictionary.

Step 7: Use the Anagrammatic Method

The anagrammatic method is a way by which all the possible permutations of a root are considered. It includes all the lexical forms in which a set of radicals occurs, irrespective of what order they occur in. We know what the possible anagrammatic permutations are in each case: for a biradical they are 2 [*lm, ml*]; for a triradical they are 6 [*ɢlb, ɢbl, bɢl, blɢ, lɢb, lbɢ*]; and similarly for quadriradicals, with 24 permutations, and for quinqueradicals, with 120 possible permutations (al-Khaliil 1980: 59). An entry in the dictionary will not simply account for that single lexical item in terms of its radicals, but in addition it will account for all the lexical roots that are the result of the anagrammatic permutations of the same radicals. For example, under the entry for the root [ɢlb] will be included the six root permutations, even though not all begin with the same radical. Lest the implications of this be missed, if one were to look up a root like [blɢ], one could not simply go to the section beginning with [b] and find this root. Since the dictionary is arranged according to the sequence of the position of the exits of the letters in the vocal tract, one must look up this root under the entry for the root [ɢlb]. That is the first of the possible permutations according to this new organization, where the postvelar [ɢ] in al-Khaliil's sequence (cf. Table 23.3) comes before [l] and [l] comes before [b]. In al-Khaliil's sequencing of proceeding from back to front, the uvular [ɢ] comes before [l], which comes before the bilabial [b]. All six roots with the same radicals, with all their internal ordering, will be under the same lexical entry. This process accounts for all the words that include the letter [ɢ] throughout the language. In this process, there is a mathematically exhaustive accounting of the occurrences of any radical because all its occurrences in all positions in all the roots are accounted for by the anagrammatic method. Hence, every time one finishes accounting for a radical the subsequent search will have one less letter to account for, with the lists growing shorter as one proceeds apace in the sequence. When one finishes accounting for [ʕ] there will be no need to account for any roots with [ʕ] under [ħ] because any root with [ʕ] would have been already encountered.

Step 8: Account only for the Roots That Are mustaʕmalah "In Use" and Leave out the muhmalah "Neglected/Unused" Roots

The dictionary sifts through the lexical items under each letter and determines which combinations *mustaʕmalah* "are used" and which combinations *muhmalah* "are unused." Those that are *mustaʕmalah* are included in the dictionary, but those that are *muhmalah* or have no known occurrence are ignored. This determination indicates that not all the possible, legitimate, and acceptable combinations are used. By way of example, in the chapter on [ʕ] with [đ], only [đ], [ʕ] are used (vol. 1: 84), and in the chapter on [ʕ] with [ɢ] and [z] only [ʕ][z][ɢ], [ɢ][z][ʕ], [z][ʕ][ɢ] and [z][ɢ][ʕ] are used (vol. 1: 132).

Step 9: Include ʃawaahid "Illustrative Examples of Usage"

Since this was the first full-fledged dictionary of Arabic, it made linguistic sense to use illustrative examples to give the dictionary a culturally authoritative status among its users. Hence, for every root and its many morphological variations there are illustrative examples from poetical sources, Quranic verses, idioms, dialectal sayings, and current use to give the contextual meaning of the term and indicate the changes in meaning of the various forms that ensue from context. One can take the lexical item [bʕd] "after" under the root [ʕbd] as an example: the opposite of a thing. The opposite of [ɢbl] "before"... [al-buʕd ḍidd al-ɢurb] "distance is the opposite of closeness." Quoting the poet al-Ṭirmaah:

تباعد منا من نحب اقترابه * وتجمع منا بين أهل الظنائن

You distance from us he whom we like near,
and bring us together those about whom we have suspicions.
al-Khaliil (1980, vol. 2: 53)

The design and execution of the dictionary was an ambitious undertaking by al-Khaliil in all its aspects. Figuring out what a lexical entry should be based on, what information to include and what to exclude, and how to make all these components come together in a final product, a dictionary, was the work of a genius. Even if it were easy to theorize, which it is not, how things should work in a dictionary, the reality of the endeavor is by no means a trivial task. Despite the coherence of the theory, one still has to implement the theory and produce a dictionary. The new order of the letters set the sequence for the dictionary that begins with the [ʕ] at the throat and ends with the [m] at the lips. Each letter forms one *kitaab* "book," like the "[ʕ] book," which includes all the roots that contain this letter no matter where they occur in the word. Each book is further organized on the basis of the number of radicals with the biradical coming before the triradical, the triradical coming before the quadriradical, and the quadriradical coming before the quinqueradical roots. A further division was made, with the roots with only strong radicals coming before the roots that included weak radicals and finally all the roots that consist only of weak radicals occur at the end of the dictionary. Examples of use from places such as the Quran and poetry were supplied to give each word its proper meaning in context. A decision needed to be made at every stage of the design as to how it would contribute to the overall shape of the dictionary. In summary, al-Khaliil's design and implementation of the dictionary became the model and inspiration for subsequent lexicographers, who copied, incorporated, modified, summarized, and found other ways of accounting for the lexical items of Arabic but never overlooked the work of al-Khaliil.[5]

23.3.2 al-Jawharii's Rhyme Model

The rhyme model of dictionary composition was created by ʔIsmaaʕiil ibn Ħammaad al-Jawharii. al-Jawharii (d. 392/1002) came from Faaraab in Turkestan, in today's southern Kazakhstan (ʕAṭṭaar 1984: 21). He was an authority on literature and language. He received his linguistic education from two prominent linguists, ʔAbuu ʕAli al-Faarisii (d. 355/966) and ʔAbuu Saʕiid al-Siiraafii (367/978) in Iraq, and he continued his studies with scholars in Hijaz. Like so many other scholars of his day, he traveled the Middle East and became familiar with some of the dialects. He polished his language skills by living with other speakers of Arabic in their proper locales. His travels included sojourns with Rabiiʕah and Muḍar tribes and a return to Khorasan for a while. He then traveled to Nishapuwr where he taught, wrote, and trained in calligraphy. It is here where he composed *Taaj al-luγah wa ṣiħaaħ al-Arabiyyah* (The crown of the language and the correct Arabic) for ʔAbi Manṣuur ʕAbd al-Raħiim al-Baykaʃii, who was a known scholar and respected by others. In his old age, al-Jawharii became afflicted with a mental illness and became delusional. It is reported that he went up to the roof of the old mosque in Nishapuwr, wrapped two door planks around his body and attempted to fly. He fell to his death in the attempt. He is reported to have said: "Folks, I have done in this life what no one had done before, and I shall do for the next life what no one before me had done."(Yaʕquub 1981: 105–112).

al-Jawharii provided the shortest introduction to his dictionary one can find. Most other lexicographers provide long and detailed introductions explaining their motives and the way they proceeded in the composition of their dictionaries. A prime example is al-Khaliil with his long and informative introduction. al-Jawharii is the exception to this trend. Here is his introduction in full:

> The Sheikh, ʔAbuu Naṣr ʔIsmaaʕiil ibn Ħammaad al-Jawharii, may God have mercy on him, said: God be praised for his gifts and prayers on Mohammad and his people. To continue: I have deposited in this book what looked correct to me of this language,

[5] al-Khaliil was also a grammarian. He included much phonological, morphological, syntactic, dialectal, and cultural material in his lexicon, although we have no systematic book on grammar attributed to him despite some claims attributing *Kitaab al-jumal fiy al-naħw* (al-Khaliil 1985) to him. His grammatical theory and insights, beyond what is found in his dictionary, have found their way into the work of his most prominent student.

Siibawayh is probably the most respected name among the grammarians of Arabic [Baalbaki, "ALT I"]. In his book, called simply *al-Kitaab* "the book," he quotes many former and contemporary linguists. The person most frequently quoted in this book is al-Khaliil. He is quoted over 600 times on various topics of grammar (Troupeau 1976: 228–230). This bespeaks not only of the close relationship between master and disciple but also of the weight that Siibawayh gave the ideas and grammatical analyses of his master.

> whose status God has honored and made the knowledge of religion and the world dependent on its knowledge, according to a system which no one has done before me nor to a level of correctness at which no one has been more successful. I have done it within 28 chapters and each chapter is in 28 sections, according to the number of the letters of the dictionary and their organization, lest there be omitted from these chapters any subsection. This was done after I had ascertained with evidence their authenticity in Iraq, mastered their meanings and communicated with native Arabic speakers in their homes in the wilderness. I did not avoid any suggestion, nor spare any effort. God has been favorable to us. Here it is for you. (ʕAṭṭaar 1984: 33)

al-Khaliil wrote the first dictionary of Arabic. He also wrote an introduction stating the motive for its construction and a detailed description of how his dictionary was to be constructed. He specified the nature of the form classes and lexical entries and how they were to be entered into the dictionary. He also specified the fundamental organization of the work. It was to have a phonetic basis and the sequencing of the lexical items was to follow this new phonetic sequence. The entries were not to follow the surface representations of the words but were to be based on the radicals of the roots and their anagrammatic permutations.

al-Jawharii provides very little guidance on what he thought his dictionary was to accomplish and how he went about constructing it except to say that he will be doing something new that no one else had done before him. There are only a few hints as to what he had in mind, and the rest of his theoretical motivation is left unstated, having to be induced from the work itself. The title is an indicator of why he wrote his dictionary. He obviously thought that there were inaccuracies in other dictionaries. So based on his experience and research this one would include only the correct and verified native words—hence the title *al-Ṣiħaaħ, Taaj al-luɣah wa ṣiħaaħ al-ʕArabiyyah* (The correct, crown of the language and the correct Arabic). To give examples of how he applied this goal in the writing of his dictionary, he specified the *ħarakaat* "motions" in the stems where confusion often occurs. For example, he writes *rahiba, bi-l-kasr, rahiba* "be afraid," with the *kasr* "break [i]"[6] (vol. 1: 140), or *al-ḍaaribu, bi-kasri al-raaʔ al-ḍaaribu* "the striker," with a *kasr* "break [i]" on the *raaʔ* [r] (vol. 1: 174).

Since al-Jawharii does not discuss his motivation for organizing words according to their last letter, their rhyme, in his dictionary, except to say that he was doing what no one else had done this before him, others have speculated about his motives. In theory, one might say there is no major obstacle in going one way or another, since languages can be written from both directions. In looking at the variations at the beginning and end of Arabic words, one might think that one or the other is the more complex. The variations at the end may be simpler than those at the beginning if one were to subtract the verbal and nominal inflections, or one might think of rhyming in language, especially in poetry where this might provide an advantage even if not a great one. But perhaps it is best to say only that the direction is arbitrary and there is no barrier to going either way.

[6] The names of the *ħarakaat* are *kasrah* "break [i]," *fatħah* "open [a]" and *ḍammah* "round [u]."

al-Jawharii was as original as al-Khaliil. al-Khaliil takes the initial radical of the root as a point of departure, while al-Jawharii takes the final radical as his point of departure. al-Khaliil's method, though logical and coherent in all its details, makes linguistic demands on its users and not many followed it, starting with Ibn Durayd (837–934), who as we will later see rearranged the dictionary into alphabetical order. al-Jawharii's method was followed by more lexicographers and ʕAṭṭaar lists 40 authors who have commented on, augmented, or corrected his rhyme scheme compared with a small number of followers of al-Khaliil's phonetic scheme (ʕAṭṭar 1984: 156).

23.3.3 Juxtaposing al-Khaliil's and al-Jawharii's models

1) al-Khaliil divides his dictionary into chapters, one for each strong letter with a chapter for the weak letters at the end. al-Jawharii divides his dictionary into 28 chapters, one for each letter of the alphabet, arranged according to the rhyme/last radical of the root instead of the initial radical, except that the chapters on [w] and [y] are combined into one chapter with a final chapter dedicated to the soft *ʔalif* [A]. Within each chapter, there are 28 sections, one for each letter of the alphabet that begins the root. Not all chapters have the full 28 sections. In a move that goes beyond what al-Khaliil did and that reflects the phonotactics and the co-occurrence of letters, al-Jawharii indicates that some chapters have less than the full number of sections, that is, not all the 28 sections, one for each letter of the alphabet. For example, the chapter on [r] is missing the section on [l] since he found no words beginning with [l] and ending in [r]. Four chapters have two sections missing: the chapter on [b] is missing the sections on [f] and [m]; the chapter on [t] is missing the sections on [ḍ] and [ẓ]; the chapter on [d] is missing the sections on [ẓ] and [y]; and the chapter on [ɢ] is missing the sections on [ẓ] and [k]. Another four chapters have three sections missing. The chapter on [ɢ] is missing the sections on [ð], [ẓ], [y]; the chapter on [ṭ] is missing the sections on [t], [d], [ẓ], and the chapter on [f] is missing sections on [b], [m], [y]. Two chapters have five sections missing. The chapter on [x] is missing the sections on [ħ], [ẓ], [ʕ], [ɣ], [y], and the chapter on [s] is missing the sections on [θ], [ð], [z], [ṣ], [ẓ]. And finally the chapter on [ẓ] is missing 12 sections, on [A], [t], [θ], [x], [ð], [z], [s], [ṣ], [ḍ], [ṭ], [ẓ], [h] (ʕAṭṭaar 1984: 127–129). This precision is possible because, while al-Khaliil approaches each root only from the direction of the initial radical, al-Jawharii approaches it from two directions, the initial and final radicals, giving rise to a much richer context. For example, [sbɢ] will occur in chapter under [ɢ] and in the section under [s]. This method gives more of the context for the co-occurrence of letters in words.
2) al-Khaliil is onset/initial based, while al-Jawharii is rhyme/final based. al-Jawharii's dictionary is a radical change in orientation. To look up a word in al-Jawharii, one must look for both the last and the first radicals, that is, the chapters and their subsections. For example, one finds *sanad* "support" in the

chapter for its rhyme, [d], then under the section [s] followed by [n] sequentially according to the position in the traditional alphabetical sequence. It approaches a root from two directions.

3) al-Khaliil arranges his dictionary according to exits where the letters are produced, from the deepest in the *ħalɢ* "throat" to the highest, the *ʃafatayn* "two lips." The organization of the strong letters begins with the [ʕ], the deepest sound produced in the throat, followed by [ħ], followed by [h], and so forth and ending with the [m], the highest and front-most sound, produced at the lips, with the weak letters following, not arranged according to exits, as seen in Table 23.3. al-Jawharii organizes his dictionary by the traditional order of the Arabic alphabet, as seen in Table 23.1.
4) Both al-Khaliil and al-Jawharii enter the words not in terms of their full morphological forms but only in terms of their root radicals, that is, stripped of their derivational and inflectional affixes.
5) al-Khaliil arranges the entries of the lexical items in terms of the number of the radicals. All the biradicals are taken up before the tri-, quadri-, and quinque-radicals. al-Jawharii does not follow this but instead mixes them under the same entry.
6) al-Khaliil and al-Jawharii account for the *mustaʕmalah* "used" roots without paying attention to the *muhmalah* "neglected" possible roots. al-Jawharii lists the used forms under each chapter with no discussion of the unused ones.
7) Both al-Khaliil and al-Jawharii include *ʃawaahid* "examples" to illustrate the use and meaning of the roots. Even if he may omit the source or the name of the quoted authority, al-Jawharii is more critical and judgmental of the quality of his *ʃawaahid*. He points out the weak and the ungrammatical in the sources.
8) Both al-Khaliil and al-Jawharii include grammatical information within their entries. But al-Jawharii is more critical in the evaluation of the examples from the sources; that is, he pointed out the degree of acceptability of the form, by saying that some uses were *gayyid* "good," others *ɢabiiħ* "ugly."
9) al-Jawharii is more consistent in providing the proper *ħarakaat* "motions" for his entries to give a more accurate rendering of the forms.
10) al-Jawharii does not use the anagrammatic method that al-Khaliil used. In al-Khaliil, entries on a root exhaust all possible combinations of that root, regardless of the order of the letters. In al-Jawharii, one accounts only for the initial occurrences and not all anagrammatic occurrences in any one root.

Due to his adoption of alphabetic order—even though it is the alphabetic order of the rhyme rather than of the onset—and dropping of the anagrammatic method, al-Jawharii's dictionary is considerably simpler to use than al-Khaliil's, particularly for beginners. Perhaps due to this, later lexicographers were more likely to follow al-Jawharii's model than al-Khaliil's. By way of example, ibn Manẓuur's *Lisaan al-ʕarab* (The Arabic language) and al-Fairuuzaabaadii's *al-Qamuus al-muħiiṭ* (A comprehensive dictionary) and Zabiidii's *Taaj al-ʕaruus* (Crown of the bride) are all major dictionaries, in print, revised, and reissued, and use al-Jawharii's model.

23.3.4 The Third Model: al-Bustaanii, The Alphabetic Dictionary

al-Bustaanii (1819–1883) was born in the Lebanese village of Dibbiye in the Chouf region. At the ʕAyn Waraqa school he learned Syriac and Latin. He spent 10 years there and learned French, Italian, and English. While working on the translation of the Bible, al-Bustaanii learned Hebrew, Aramaic, and Greek and perfected his Syriac and Latin (Maʕtuuq. 1999: 63; Yaʕquub 1981: 138).

It is sort of intriguing why the alphabetic model was not the first to be adopted and composed. While the alphabetic model would seem to be the most obvious choice for organizing a dictionary, as we have noted, it was not the one adopted in the first dictionary of Arabic, that of al-Khaliil. However, the second major dictionary of Arabic, that of Ibn Durayd in the 10th century, even though it followed al-Khaliil's model, reverted to the traditional alphabetic order of its segments. This section will discuss a later example of the alphabetic dictionary, the *Muħiiṭ al-muħiiṭ* by al-Bustaanii. al-Bustaanii considered *al-Qamuus al-muħiiṭ*, the dictionary of al-Fairuuzaabaadii *ʔAʃhar* "the most renowned" dictionary of Arabic in what it contained of the lexical items of the language, and thus it will serve as a bridge and a continuance of the lexical activity of the Arab lexicographers (al-Bustaanii 1970: 2). He added to it much that he found in other Arabic sources, as material any user would need and could not do without. The additions included the terminology used in the arts and sciences; names of important places, persons, and tribes; neologisms; colloquialisms; popular expressions; and idioms and grammatical expressions that went beyond the core of the language (al-Maʕtuuq 1999: 63). He abandoned both the phonetic and the rhyme models and followed a more thorough traditional alphabetical order in his dictionary. al-Fairuuzaabaadii himself had said that he had written his dictionary to make up for the shortcomings of al-Jawharii, so we are in a straight historical line of the development of the Arabic dictionary starting with al-Khaliil, to al-Jawharii, to al-Fairuuzaabaadii, to al-Bustaanii.

The author gives some guidance regarding the plan of the dictionary and his rationale for it. This guidance is not all in one place. It is in three sections. Section 1 is a short preface at the beginning of the dictionary on the general orientation of what the dictionary contains and how it is arranged that makes it easier for the general public rather than the specialists (2). Section 2 is inserted after the letter [r] (847–848) and is a summary of what the dictionary includes from the sciences, arts, grammar, and whatever is associated with language to make this book a sufficient source for what the seeker is in search of. It includes much that is novel and popular in expression. Section 3, at the end of the dictionary, is a brief guide on how to use the dictionary (2308).

Major features of al-Bustaanii's dictionary are as follows:

1) Abandonment of al-Khaliil's phonetic model
2) Abandonment of al-Khaliil's anagrammatical method
3) Abandonment of al-Jawharii's rhyme model
4) Adoption of the traditional alphabetical order
5) Inclusion of all *al-Muħiiṭ* by al-Fairuuzaabaadii
6) Addition to *al-Muħiiṭ* from, for example, the sciences, arts, philosophy, and novel expressions, which have added to the size of the dictionary in addition to its small print to make it unwieldy
7) Inclusion of the Hebrew and Syriac terms for the Arabic alphabetical letter (but that is the extent of its comparative venture)
8) No separation of chapters into weak and strong
9) No divisions into, for example, biradical, triradical
10) The *ʃawaahid* "examples" ranged beyond the classical period

The alphabetical has become the norm and the dominant model in Arabic dictionaries. The phonetic and rhyme models and their variations have been abandoned. The tyranny of the alphabetical, however, has overtaken even the other two basic models. For example, al-Khaliil's *Kitaab al-ʕayn* has been rearranged alphabetically by ʔAsʕad al-Ṭayyib (1993), as has *al-Ṣiħaaħ* by al-Jawharii.

23.3.5 In Between

As Haywood writes, "In the compilation of dictionaries, and other lexicographical works, the Arabs—or rather, those that wrote in Arabic—were second to none until the Renaissance" (Haywood 1965: 1). Though the basic paradigms and their authors have already been mentioned, they by no means are the only lexicographers of Arabic. Many others attempted to write a more perfect, more comprehensive, more up-to-date or more accessible lexicon of the language. We will mention some such lexicographers in two sections: from al-Khaliil to the time of al-Jawharii; and from al-Jawharii to the time of al-Bustaanii. To be noted is that while many of these dictionaries can be considered important, they are not innovative in the sense of departing from any of the models that have been discussed.

23.3.5.1 *Between al-Khaliil and al-Jawharii*

Ibn Durayd (223–321/837–933)

Though the *Kitaab al-ʕayn* was the first attempt in this effort to write a dictionary, it was followed by many equally comprehensive dictionaries that followed some, but not all of its features. The first such attempt was Ibn Durayd, whose full name is ʔAbuu Bakr Muħammad ibn Ħasan ibn Durayd. According to the editor of his dictionary *Jamharat al-luγah* (Compendium of language), he was born in Basra, the southern port of Iraq on the Arabian Gulf, in 223/838 AD. He grew up in Oman and traveled the islands on the gulf. He died in Baghdad in 321/933 AD (Ibn Durayd 1987, vol. 1: 100). He studied with the most renowned linguists of his time, 19 of them, and his disciples were also many, 45 of them, who themselves became renowned. Though his wide knowledge of the language and culture, poetry, and the Quran and traditions and many aspects of life were undoubtedly assets in this endeavor, the interest here is only in his dictionary. Ibn Durayd acknowledged the originality and fullness of al-Khaliil's dictionary, so he had to think of a way of justifying his dictionary. On this score, he claims that the phonetic sequencing was a difficult concept for the general public to grasp and implement, so he reverts to the traditional sequence without abandoning the anagrammatic method. Nevertheless, his output and arrangement of material is no easier than that of al-Khaliil. al-Khaliil follows the phonetic sequencing with each letter considered under biradical, triradical, quadriradical, and quinqueradical. Ibn Durayd, on the other hand, bases his arrangement on the patterns instead of the letters, so all the biradicals are grouped and considered before the triradicals, for example. This, though original in conception, added an extra dimension of difficulty to the dictionary.

In his introduction, Ibn Durayd discusses al-Khaliil's phonetic arrangement of the exits of the letters, and that of Siibawayh but only by way of acknowledgment, because this sequencing had no effect on the organization of his dictionary (Sara and Zawaawi 1995). In the process, he introduces new subgroupings, new terminology, dialectal variations, substitutions within the same genus of sounds, new sets of features, co-occurrence restrictions, the occurrence of the 10 derivational suffixes, and the relative frequency of occurrence of the letters. al-Khaliil's introduction prepares the reader for using his dictionary, but the introduction of Ibn Durayd and the phonetic sequencing of the letters has no influence on the arrangement of his dictionary, since he follows the traditional alphabetic sequencing. Apart from the new design of the dictionary, it supplies an abundance of new examples and lines of poetry as illustrations. Ibn Durayd says that he dictated his dictionary and that this led to some repetitions. It is a phenomenal accomplishment.

al-Qaalii (288–356/901–967)

al-Qaalii, whose full name is ʔAbuu ʕAlii ʔIsmaaʕiil ibn Qaasim al-Qaalii, in his dictionary *al-Baariʕ* was a more faithful follower of al-Khaliil's method (al-Qaalii 1975). Unfortunately we have only a defective copy of the work. What is of interest in al-Qaalii is that though he was a disciple of Ibn Durayd he did not follow his teacher, who had deviated from al-Khaliil's phonetic method and followed the alphabetical sequence for previously reasons stated, in every aspect. al-Qaalii reverted to al-Khaliil's phonetic method. Another aspect is that this dictionary was composed in faraway Spain. One did not have to be in the cradle of linguistics to be a lexicographer. It had been internationalized. His dictionary did not get the attention it deserved at the time probably due to the preeminence of his contemporary al-Zubaydii.

al-ʔAzharii (281–370/895–981)

al-ʔAzharii, whose full name is ʔAbuu Manṣuur Muħammad ibn ʔAħmad ibn Ṭalħah ibn Nuwħ ibn al-ʔAzhar al-ʔAzharii, was born in Hiraat in Khurasan, Persia (al-ʔAzharii 1864, vol. 1:5). In his youth he took a trip through Iraq on his Hag pilgrimage, and on his return he was kidnapped by Arab tribes, with whom he spent several years. While he was with them, he observed and recorded much of their Bedouin speech, which he found uncontaminated by other sources and free of obvious errors. All these data he was to incorporate in his dictionary. He finally escaped and came to Baghdad where he studied with most of its renowned linguists. al-ʔAzharii had a critical view of the linguistic scene as he saw it. He gives his opinion of the linguists he respects and those whom he does not respect in strong terms. His sojourn in Baghdad was not very long, and afterward he returned to Hiraat. He composed his dictionary after he was 70 years of age. It was the crowning achievement of his travels, studies, and reading. He died in Hiraat in 370/981.

The rationale for the dictionary was, as the title *Tahðiyb al-luγah* (Refinement of the language) indicates, to give the language its authentic forms by checking the entries against the opinions and writings of respected authorities and speakers of the language. In the background it is also understood that the Quran has to be shielded from errors of language. al-ʔAzharii provides a long list of sources, very much like an annotated bibliography, that he consulted and the value he puts on their respective merits. His dictionary has been considered as one of the more accurate due to his diligence in arriving at what was the most authentic. He eliminates foreignisms and corrects errors found in other dictionaries and includes nothing that he had not verified from dependable sources or heard from the Arabs (ibid. 16).

In the treatise on phonetics, he follows al-Khaliil and adds to it what other grammarians had said by way of clarification. He introduces new subdivisions and new groupings among the sounds, new terminology, new features, some of the substitutions among the weak letters, deletions, elisions, and some habits of pronunciation.

23.3.5.2 *Between al-Jawharii and al-Bustaanii*

Fairuuzaabaadii (898–987/1329–1415)

Fairuuzaabaadii, whose full name is Muħammad bin Yaʕquwb ʔAbuu Ṭaahir Majd al-Diin al-ʃiraazii al-Fairuuzaabaadii (Yaʕquub, 119), was born in Kaarziyn, Shiraaz. He traveled the Middle East and lived in Jerusalem, Mecca, Delhi, Baghdad, and Yemen. He wrote a huge lexicographical work, *Qaamuus al-muħiiṭ*, taking al-Jawharii's dictionary as the basis of his dictionary. While he followed al-Jawharii in adopting the rhyme model, he made some changes, among them:

1) He entered the simple forms before the complex forms.
2) He omitted many of the *ʃawaahid* "examples" to make it less bulky.

3) He added more from the more modern sources, names of tribes and cities, technical terms from the sciences, and other sources that added to the bulk of the dictionary.
4) He marked his additions to al-Jawharii's dictionary with red ink.
5) He marked the vowels for the sake of accuracy.

He is criticized for the vagueness of some of his definitions and explanations and including matters that are more appropriately material for an encylopedia, but the dictionary has become popular with just as many defenders as critics.

al-Zabiidii (1314–1374/1737–1790)

al-Zabiidii, whose full name is Muhammad Murtaḍa al-Zabiidii, was born in 1314/1732, in Balidžram, a town in India and grew up in Zabiidii in Yemen where Fairuuzaabaadii settled. He visited many Arab countries such as Saudi Arabia, Iraq, and Palestine. He traveled to Egypt and settled there, and that is where he died in 1790. He is the author of *Taaj al-ʕaruus*, an Arabic dictionary based on Fairuuzaabaadii's *Qaamuus al-muħiiṭ*. He says in his introduction that he depended on about 500 books in the composition of his book. These included all the major dictionaries of Arabic from Ibn Durayd until his time.

Lane, Edward William (1385–1462/1801–1876)

Of all the reference dictionaries of Arabic composed since the time of al-Khaliil, only one of them was translated into English. Lane's Arabic English Lexicon is the most available dictionary of its kind. It is a translation of al-Zabiidii's *Taaj al-ʕaruus*. Lane details all the steps he went through to gather the materials necessary to work on the dictionary. Even so, he did not quite finish the task but reached the letter [q], and his nephew, Stanley Lane-Poole, completed the work that his uncle had begun.

In the process of developing their lexicons, the model of al-Khaliil became the template for the future lexicographers, just as Johnson's dictionary became the template for the lexicographers of English. The fundamental components of the roots, of arranging phonetically or alphabetically, of sequencing according to the number of radicals, of explaining in terms of quotations from living sources or already authenticated oral sources—all these features have become standard and have not changed except in the sense of more or less of the same. al-Khaliil is the first and the most insightful lexicographer of Arabic. One thing we have in the case of Johnson that we lack in that of al-Khaliil is that we know more of the details in the case of Johnson, such as his work habits, the number of his associates or helpers, his written sources, and the manner of gathering and selecting the relevant entries, while the Arabic tradition is more concerned with the oral tradition and the authenticity of the information and its sources. No one makes this point more strongly than al-ʔAzharii in his introduction. The Arabs also experimented more with the format and composition of the dictionary: whether to use phonetic or orthographic orders; whether to use the initial or the final radical; whether to arrange according to number of radicals in the roots;

and how to account for the weak and strong roots. Every lexicographer is unique in the manner and extent to which he experimented with the model in his dictionary. The process began in tiny Oman in the Arabic/Persian Gulf, quickly spread to the large Arabic speaking world from Iraq, to Turkey, to Persia, to Lebanon, to Yemen, to Egypt and North Africa, and to Spain. The lexicographers come from a large area, so this was an enduring interest, a fascination, perhaps even an obsession with these authors, and they endured a great deal and went to extremes to attain their goal. Ibn Durayd dictated his dictionary; Ibn Siida was a blind linguist when he composed his *Muħkam;* and Ibn Manẓuur collated a great number of the dictionaries in the composition of the monumental *Lisaan*. al-Khaliil and the Arabic dictionary led to a good and inspiring linguistic renaissance.

References

Amiin, Ahmad. [1970?]. *Ḍuħaa al-ʔislaam*. Bayruut: Daar al-Kitaab al-ʕArabii,

ʕAṭṭaar, ʔAħmad ʕAbd al-Ghafuur. 1984. *Muqaddimat al-ṣaħaaħ*. Beyruut: Daar al-ʕIlm li-l-Malaayiin.

al-ʔAzharii, ʔAbuu Manṣuur Muħammad ibn ʔAħmad. 1964–1967. *Kitaab tahđiib al-luɣah*. Ed. ʕAbd al-Salaam Muħammad Haaruun a.o. 15 vols. Cairo: al-Muʔassasah al-Miṣriyyah al-ʕAmmah.

al-Bustaanii, Buṭrus ibn Bolus. 1970. *Kitaab muħiiṭ al-muħiiṭ, qaamuuṣ muṭawwal li-l-luɣah al-ʕarabiyyah*. Bayruut: Maktabat Lubnaan.

Clifford, James L. 1979. *Dictionary Johnson: The middle years of Samuel Johnson*. London: Heinemann.

Darwish, ʕAbdallah. 1956. *al-Maʕaajim al-ʕarabiyyah maʕa ʔiʕtinãʔ xaaṣ bi-muʕjam al-ʕayn li-l-Khaliil Ibn ʔAħmad*. Cairo: Maṭbaʕat al-Risaalah.

al-Khaliil = al-Faraahiidii al-Khaliil ʔibn ʔAħmad. 1980–1986. *Kitaab al-ʕayn*. 8 vols. Ed. Mahdii al-Maxzuumi and Ibrahim al-Saamirraaʔi. Baghdad: Daar ar-Rashid.

Fairuuzaabaadii, Majd al-Diin ʔAbuu al-Ṭaahir Muħammad ibn Yaʕquub. 1913. *al-Qaamuus al-muḥiiṭ*. 4 vols. Cairo: al-Maṭbaʕah al-Miṣriyyah.

Gove, Philip Babcock (ed.). 2002. *Webster's third new international dictionary of the English language, unabridged*. Springfield, MA: Merriam-Webster.

Haywood, John A. 1960. *Arabic lexicography: Its history, and its place in the general history of lexicography*. Leiden: E.J. Brill.

al-Ḥurr, ʕAbd al-Majiid. 1994. *al-Muʕjamaat wa al-majaamiʕ al-ʕarabiyyah: našʔatuhaa, ʔanwaaʕuhaa, nahjuhaa, taṭawwuruhaa*. Beyruut: Daar al-Fikr al-ʕal-ʕArabii.

Ibn Durayd. 1987. *Kitaab jamharat al-luɣah*. 3 vols. Ed. R. M. Baalbaki. Beirut: Daar al-ʕIlm li-l-Malaayiin.

Ibn Manẓuur. 1981. *Lisaan al-ʕarab*. 7 vols. Cairo: Daar al-Maʕaarif.

Ibn Siidah, ʔAbuu al-Ḥasan ʕAlii ibn Ismaaʕiil. *Kitaab al-muħkam wa-al-muħiiṭ al-ʔaʕẓam fii al-luɣah*. 1958–1999. 12 vols. Ed. Muṣṭafaa al-Saqqaa. Cairo: Maʕhad al-Maxṭuṭaat bi-Džaamiʕat al-Duwal al-ʕArabiyyah.

al-Jawharii, Ismaaʕiil ibn Ḥammaad, 1956. *al-Ṣiħaaħ: Taaj al-luɣah wa-ṣiħaaħ al-ʕarabiyyah*. 6 vols. Ed. ʔAħmad ʕAbd al-Ghafuur. Miṣr: Daar al-Kitaab.

Kraemer, Jörg. 1953. Studien zur altarabischen Lexikographie. *Oriens* 6: 201–238.

Law, Vivien. 1990. Indian influence on early Arab phonetics: Or coincidence? In *Studies in the history of Arab grammar*, vol. 2, ed. Michael G. Carter and Kees Versteegh, 215–227. Amsterdam: Benjamins.

Liddell, Henry George. 1996. *A Greek–English lexicon*. Compil. Henry George Liddell and Robert Scott. Oxford: Clarendon Press.

Lynch, Jack (ed.). 2002. *Samuel Johnson's Dictionary: Selections from the 1755 work that defined the English Language*. Delray Beach, FL: Levenger Press.

al-Maʕtuuq, ʔAħmad Muħammad, 1999. *al-Maʕaajim al-luɣawiyyah al-ʕarabiyya, al-maʕaajim ʔa-ʕaamah, waẓaaʔifuhaa wa ʔaθaruhaa fii tanmiyat luɣat al-naašiʔah, diraasah waṣfiyyah, taħliiliyyah, naqdiyyah*. Abuu Ẓabiy: al-Majmaʕ al-θaqaafii.

Maxzuumi, Mahdi. 1958. *Madrasat al-Kuufah wa manhajuhaa fi diraasat al-luɣah wa al-naħw*. Cairo: Muṣṭafa al-Baab al-Ḥalabii.

——. 1960. *al-Khaliil ʔIbn ʔAħmad al-Faraahiidii: ʔaʕmaaluhu wa manhajuhu*. Baghdad: Wizaarat al-Maʕaarif.

——. 1986. *ʕAbqari min al-Baṣrah*. Bayruut: Daar al-Raaʔid al-ʕArabii.

al-Nadiim, ʔAbuu al-Faraj Muħammad ibn ʔIsħaaq. 1998. *The Fihrist*. Ed. and trans. Bayard Dodge. Chicago: Kazi Publications.

al-Qaalii ʔAbuu ʕAlii ibn Qaasim al-Baɣdaadii. 1975. *al-Baariʕ fiy al-luɣah*. Ed. Hasim al-Ṭaʕʕaan. Baghdad: Maktabat al-Nahḍah.

Rundgren, Frithiof. 1973. La lexicographie arabe. *Studies on Semitic lexicography*, ed. Pelio Fronzaroli, 145–159. Florence: Istituto di Linguistica e di Lingue Orientali, Università di Firenze.

Sara, Solomon I. 1991. Al-Khalil: The first Arab phonologist. *International Journal of Islamic and Arabic Studies* 8: 1–57.

Sara, Solomon S. J. and A. O. Zawawi. 1995. The phonetics of Ibn Durayd. In *Proceedings of the XIIth International Congress of Phonetic Sciences*, vol. 3, ed. Kjell Elenius and Peter Branderud, 520–523. Stockholm: Arne Stroembergs Grafiska.

Sezgin, Fuat. 1982. *Geschichte des arabischen Schrifttums*. Vol. 8, *Lexikographie bis ca. 430 h*. Leiden: E.J. Brill.

——. 1984. *Geschichte des arabischen Schrifttums*. Vol. 9, *Grammatik bis ca. 430 h*. Leiden: E.J. Brill.

Siibawayh. 1881/1970. *Le Livre de Siibawaihi:Traité de Grammaire Arabe*. 2 vols., ed. H. Derenbourg. Hildesheim: Georg Olms Verlag.

Siiraafii, ʔAbuu Saʕiid al-Ḥasan bin ʕAbd ʔAllaah. 1985. *ʔAxbaar al-naħwiyyiin al-baṣriyyiin wa maraatibihim wa ʔaxði baʕḍihim ʕan baʕḍ*. Ed. Muħammad Ibaahiim al-Bannā. Cairo: Daar al-ʔIʕtiṣaam.

Troupeau, Gerard. 1976. *Lexique-index du "Kitab" de Sibawayhi*. Paris: Klincksieck.

Yaʕquub, Emile. 1981. *al-Maʕaajim al-luɣawiyyah al-ʕarabiyya*. Bayruut: Daar al-ʕIlm li-l-Malaayiin.

Young, William. 1910. *Young's Latin dictionary*. London: A. Wilson.

al-Zabiidii = ʔAbuu l-Fayḍ Muħammad Murtaḍaa ibn Muħammad az-Zabiidii. 1888–1890. *Taaj al-ʕaruus min jawaahir al-qaamuus*. 10 vols. Ed. ʕAbd al-Sattaar ʔAħmad Farraaj a.o. Cairo: al-Maṭbaʕah al-Xayriyyah.

al-Zubaydii ʔAbuu Bakr Muħammad bin al-Ḥasan. 1973. *Ṭabaqaat al-naħwiyyiin wa al-luɣawiyyiin*. Ed. Muħammad ʔAbuu al-Faḍl Ibraahiim. Cairo: Daar al-Maʕaarif.

CHAPTER 24

MODERN LEXICOGRAPHY

TIM BUCKWALTER AND DILWORTH B. PARKINSON

24.1 Introduction

This chapter is a critical survey of contemporary Arabic lexicography, covering a period that begins roughly with the first edition (1952) of the Hans Wehr dictionary, and extends to present-day corpus-based machine-readable dictionaries and online lexical databases. Among influential precursors to Wehr, we need to mention the Elias Arabic–English dictionary (1922), which focuses on modern usage and even includes some vocabulary from Egyptian and Iraqi dialects. According to Haywood (1991), the period from 1922 to around 1952 could be termed the "Elias era." It could be said that we still live in the "Wehr era" in terms of the influence that the last Arabic–English edition (1979) continues to hold among English-speaking researchers and students of Arabic. Researchers who are able to read Dutch will very like claim that the "Wehr era" ended in the early 2000s with the publication of the first Arabic dictionaries based primarily on extensive and systematic corpus analysis: the Arabic–Dutch learner's dictionary by Van Mol (2001) and the more extensive Arabic–Dutch lexicon by Hoogland et al. (2003).

Although we will cover both monolingual and bilingual Arabic lexicography relating both to the standard written language (commonly referred to as Modern Standard Arabic, hereafter SA) and to the dialects, we limit our discussion of bilingual publications to works in which Arabic is the *source language*. While we give equal footing to monolingual and bilingual lexicons, this review will show that the modern lexicographic description of Arabic has been dominated by bilingual lexicons. Indeed, it can be observed that these lexicons have provided a more accurate and more up-to-date description of the lexicon of contemporary Arabic than their monolingual counterparts, due primarily to the application of modern lexicographic techniques, especially corpus-based descriptive methods. Bilingual lexicons have also tended to describe what is widely attested in modern usage without regard to the normative judgments of purists, many of whom still regard dictionaries as instruments whose duty is to ratify and promote word usage rather than record actual usage.

Lexicography of the dialects has evolved alongside SA lexicography and has been equally productive. In fact, some of the finest works of Arabic lexicography are dictionaries of the dialects, as our survey will show. We will review the different solutions that both SA and dialect dictionaries have found to the issue of lemma representation (i.e., the choice of phonetic script) and the issue of lemma organization (i.e., whether to follow a root-based arrangement or one that is purely phonetic and alphabetical).

24.2 The Macrostructure of the Lexicon

24.2.1 Introduction

Dictionaries of Arabic are said to order their entries either by root or alphabetically. In this section we will outline the basic differences between these two approaches and describe the leading exponents of both systems in the modern period of Arabic lexicography, identifying some of the unresolved issues within both systems. We conclude with some remarks on how electronic and online dictionaries cast these issues in a new light, with successful dictionary lookup no longer depending on a specific arrangement of entries.

24.2.2 Root-Based and Alphabetical Dictionaries: Basic Differences

Simply stated, headword entries in root-based dictionaries are presented in groups according to their respective roots, and these roots are then presented in alphabetical order, whereas in so-called alphabetical dictionaries the headwords are presented individually in strict alphabetical order without regard to their roots (see Shivtiel 1993 for a general discussion). In root-based dictionaries words that are not based on Arabic root-and-pattern morphology (mostly function words and loanwords) are listed alphabetically. So, properly speaking, root-based dictionaries follow a hybrid approach, and the user must engage either approach according to the perceived morphology of the lookup word: when root-based lookup fails, the user must then attempt a straight alphabetical lookup. A few alphabetical dictionaries also use a hybrid approach and arrange verbal entries in root-based groups that are listed alphabetically under the base form of the verb.

Arabic dictionaries have traditionally been arranged by root [Sara, "Classical Lexicography"], [Daniels, "Writing"]; [Ratcliffe, "Morphology"]), and successful word lookup in these dictionaries requires a solid knowledge of Arabic derivational and inflectional morphology as well as some awareness of the conventions that each dictionary follows in ordering the entries under each root. Alphabetically arranged dictionaries have arisen in response to the perceived difficulty that users have in finding words in root-based dictionaries.

24.2.3 Root-Based Dictionaries: Basic Features and Areas of Variations

Dictionaries organized by root differ primarily in the internal ordering of verbal and nonverbal entries under each root. Two different trends can be observed: (1) to present verbal and nonverbal entries in separate groups; and (2) to present verbal and nonverbal entries together, in subgroups according to verb form theme.

24.2.3.1 *The Ordering of Verbal and Nonverbal Entries in Separate Groups*

The first and more common approach is to present the base form of the verb and all derived verb forms at the head of the root entry, followed by nonverbal entries, ordered according to a combination of orthographic and morphological criteria. The leading exponents of this style are Wehr (all editions) and its contemporary "successor," the Arabic–Dutch work by Hoogland et al. (2003). Whereas Western lexicographers tend to present verb forms in the order traditionally designated by the Roman numerals I through X, Arab lexicographers do not use a numbering system, and this gives them more flexibility. Indeed, the presentation order of forms II through IV often follows the order IV, III, and II, as observed in *al-Muʕjam al-wasiiṭ*, by Muṣṭafaa et al. (1960–1961), and the more recent lexicons by ʕAbd al-Masiiħ (1993-), al-Karmi (1999, 2000), and Abu Ħaaqah (2007). But overall, both Western and Arab lexicographers adhere to the same principle of presenting verbal entries in progression from simple to more complex forms. Arab lexicographers tend to present nonverbal entries in straight alphabetical order, with a few notable exceptions.

Some of the discrepancies in the internal arrangement of nonverbal entries as practiced by Western lexicographers were reviewed by Bobzin (1989), in a study that compared the order of these entries under the root *j-m-ʕ* in the Arabic–German dictionaries of Wehr (1985), Schregle (1981–1992), and Krahl and Gharieb (1984), and demonstrated how these lexicographers order nonverbal entries according to a hybrid method of morphological criteria and alphabetical sorting. To facilitate comparison with Bobzin's study (especially the table on p. 123), we believe it would be worthwhile to examine the order of nonverbal entries for the same root *j-m-ʕ* in the standard-setting Arabic–Dutch dictionary by Hoogland et al. (2003).

In this dictionary, nonverbal forms are sorted alphabetically but presented in two groups according to certain morphological criteria. The first group is headed by any nominal form (when it exists) that contains only the root letters (جمع in this example), after which are listed all words that begin with the first radical of the root, in straight alphabetical order: جامِع, جامِعة, جامِعي, جِماع, جَماعة, جَماعي, جمعة, جَمعي, جَمعية, جميع.[1] The second group contains all remaining nonverbal entries, presented in straight alphabetical sort order: اجتماع, اجتماعي, إجماع, إجماعي, أجمع, تجمُّع, تجمُّعي, تجميع, مجامعة, مجتمَع, مجتمَعي, مجمَع, مجموع, مجموعة.[2]

For sorting purposes, the various forms of *ʔalif* (with and without *hamzah*) are treated equally. All entries are fully diacritized, so words that would be homographs (without diacritics) are presented also in alphabetical sort order: for example, *mujtamaʕ* before *mujtamiʕ*, *mujammaʕ* before *mujammiʕ*.

Wehr followed a slightly different approach for ordering nonverbal entries (see 1979: xii–xiii; 1985: xvii–xviii), but it is worth noting that in practice he often deviates from his own rule by placing *nisbah* adjectives immediately after the noun they refer to, such as with *madani* "urban" after *madiinah* "city," and *qabali* "tribal" after *qabiilah* "tribe."

24.2.3.2 *The Ordering of Verbal and Nonverbal Entries in Integrated Groups*

The second and less common approach to ordering verbal and nonverbal entries under a given root is to organize entries in groups according to verb form, beginning with the base form and all its nonverbal derivatives (i.e., nouns, adjectives, and adverbs as well as active and passive participles that are either lexicalized as nouns and adjectives or whose sense cannot be obtained from the verb entry), followed by groups of derived verbs, each group with its related verbal noun and participial forms. The leading examples of this approach are the Arabic–English dictionary by Madina (1973), the dictionary of Egyptian Arabic by Hinds and Badawi (1986), the monolingual *al-Munjid* by Ħamaawi (2000), and the Bahraini glossary by Holes (2001).

In what appears to be an abridgment of the 1961 edition of Wehr, Madina (1973) rearranges the contents of each root according to the previously outlined scheme so that after the base form of the verb we find, by order of morphological increase, all nominal forms that are not related to derived verbs II through X (e.g., *jamʕ*, *jamʕi*, *jumʕ*, *jumʕa*, *jamʕiyya*, *jamiiʕ*, *'ajmaʕ*, *jamaaʕa*, *jamaaʕi*, and *majmaʕ*),[3] followed by the nominal forms related to the active and passive participles of the base form verb (e.g., *jaamiʕ*, *jaamiʕa*, *jaamiʕi*, *majmuuʕ*, and *majmuuʕa*).[4] This group of entries is then followed by each derived verb (in this example, forms II through X), and each derived verb entry is followed by nominal forms and derivatives associated with its verbal noun, and active

[1] جامِع "comprehensive, mosque," جامعة, "university,"جامعي "academic,",جِماع "sexual intercourse,", جَماعة "group,",جَماعي "collective,"جُمعة "week," جمعي "collective,",جمعية "association," جميع "all."

[2] اجتماع "meeting," اجتماعي "social," إجماع "agreement," إجماعي "collective," أجمع "entire," تجمع "gathering," تجمعي "collective," تجميع "assembly," مجامعة "sexual intercourse," مجتمَع "society," مجتمعي "societal," مجمع "academy," مجموع "collected, total," مجموعة "collection, group."

[3] *jamʕ* "gathering," *jamʕi* "collective," *jumʕ* "fist," *jumʕa* "week," *jamʕiyya* "association," *jamiiʕ* "all," *'ajmaʕ* "entire," *jamaaʕa* "group," *jamaaʕi* "collective," *majmaʕ* "academy"

[4] *jaamiʕ* "mosque," *jaamiʕa* "university," *jaamiʕi* "academic," *majmuuʕ* "collected, total," *majmuuʕa* "collection, group."

and passive participles (e.g., for form VIII we find *ijtimaaʕ*, *ijtimaaʕi*, *ijtimaaʕiyya*, *mujtamiʕ*, and *mujtamaʕa*).[5] Wehr's original arrangement listed verbal nouns and all participles (as well as their *nisbah* derivatives and the like) by order of morphological increase in two groups at the end of the root listing: verbal nouns followed by respective pairs of active–passive participles. One could argue that Madina's rearrangement facilitates the cross-checking between verbal and nonverbal entries of the same measure that Arabic dictionary users often engage in.

Hinds and Badawi's (1986) dictionary applies this same arrangement scheme to Egyptian Arabic, with adaptations for dialect-specific entries (e.g., *itgamaʕ*, passive of *gamaʕ*)[6] and slight changes in the order of derived verb groups, primarily to list active–passive pairs adjacently (e.g., *itgammaʕ* right after *gammaʕ*).[7] Nominal forms related to the active and passive participles of the base form (e.g., *gaamiʕ*, *gamʕa*, *gaamiʕi*, *magmuuʕ*, and *magmuuʕa*)[8] are listed immediately after the base form of the verb rather than at the end of that verb form group (as in Madina). In his Bahraini glossary, Holes (2001) follows the Hinds and Badawi approach but lists derived verbs in the traditional Western order.

The monolingual *al-Munjid* by Ħamaawi (2000) also follows the Western order of listing derived verbs, as did its predecessor (Maʕluuf 1908, 1956) but differs otherwise by arranging verbal and nonverbal entries in groups according to derived verb form.

24.2.4 Issues with Root-Based Dictionaries

24.2.4.1 *Phonetic Criteria in Root-Based Dictionaries of Dialect*

The leading dictionaries of Arabic dialects are noted for the attention they give to the phonetic representation of entries. In root-based dictionaries this entails a lexicographic decision concerning the root-level handling of words with dialectal phonemes. Two different approaches are worth examining.

Holes (2001) treats the /č/ and /g/ phonemes of Gulf dialects as root consonants only when they occur in foreign borrowings, such as *čakleet* "chocolate," (under *č-k-l-y-t*) and *galan* "gallon," (under *g-l-n*). However, when /č/ and /g/ occur as historical reflexes of Arabic phonemes /k/ and /q/, respectively, the word in question is entered under the relevant Arabic root: for example, *čiđb* "lie" under *k-đ-b*, and *giriib* "near" under *q-r-b*. This approach is also useful for recording variant pronunciations, such as *ʕajal* and *ʕayal*, for the word *ʔajal* "yes, of course" (listed under *ʔ-j-l*, not *ʕ-y-l*, although a cross-reference would be useful).

[5] *ijtimaaʕ* "meeting," *ijtimaaʕi* "social," *ijtimaaʕiyya* "socialism," *mujtamiʕ* "(individual) attending a meeting," *mujtamaʕ* "meeting place."

[6] *gamaʕ* "to gather, collect."

[7] *gammaʕ* "to assemble, put together."

[8] *gaamiʕ* "collector," *gamʕa*(= SA *jaamiʕa*) "university, league," *gaamiʕi* "university-related," *magmuuʕ* "sum, total," *magmuuʕa* "group."

This approach contrasts sharply with the phonetically driven approach seen in the Iraqi Arabic dictionary of Woodhead and Beene (1967: 385), where words such as *gadar* "measure," *gidir* "small cooking pot," and *mugdaar/migdaar* "amount" are entered under the root *g-d-r*, whereas *qudra* "capacity," *taqdiir* "estimate," and *miqdaar* "time period; amount" are entered under the root *q-d-r* (ibid., 367), although historically these roots are one and the same. In the Gulf Arabic dictionary by Qafisheh (1997) this approach of using the surface-phonetic representation of roots is extended to the /y/ reflex of /j/, so we find *jalsa* "session" and *jallaas* "ship cook" under *j-l-s* (ibid., 95), but *maylis* and *yaalis* "seated" under *y-l-s* (ibid., 646).

It would appear to be more useful for the dictionary user to have the entries under these root pairs (*g-d-r* / *q-d-r* and *j-l-s* / *y-l-s*) merged under a unified root where the user could also observe, for example, the distribution of /q/ and /g/ (or /j/ and /y/) over different lexical items based on historically the same root. This approach can be seen in Hinds and Badawi (1986), where words such as *talaata* "three" and *sulaasi* "triple" are entered under the same root (*t-l-t*), but with cross-references provided under the historical root *θ-l-θ* and the phonetically related root *s-l-s*.

24.2.4.2 *Polysemous Roots*

Hinds and Badawi (1986) identify numerous polysemous roots, such as *b-r-d*, *s-m-r*, and *ṭ-r-š*, each of which is given more than four separate root etymologies. Wehr (1985) also stands out in this regard, with around 100 roots marked as having three semantic divisions. The identification of polysemous roots is not an easy process, as noted by Krahl and Gharieb (1984: 8), and one lexicographic approach is to simply merge them. A good example of this practice is the Arabic–Spanish dictionary of Cortés (1996) which, for example, lists under the single root *s-w-d* essentially the same entries as *s-w-d*$^{(1)}$ and *s-w-d*$^{(2)}$ in Wehr, thereby bringing together entries related to the concept of "black, blackness" (e.g., *ʔaswad* "black," *iswadda* "to become black") and those associated with "mastery" (*sayyid* "master," *saaʔid* "prevailing"). More dramatic results can be seen with the root *ṣ-f-r*, where Cortés lists together all the entries that Wehr separates into three distinct semantic groups: (1) *ṣaffaarah* "whistle," *ṣafiir* "whistling"; (2) *ʔaṣfar* "yellow," *iṣfarra* "to become yellow"; and (3) *ṣifr* "empty, zero," *muṣfir* "empty-handed."

One could argue that the merging of polysemous roots facilitates word lookup, since all entries are now listed under one root, but this occurs at great cost to the presentation of important semantic groupings. We would argue, instead, for an increase in the identification of polysemous roots: the lexicon of SA contains many examples where the semantic connection between entries sharing a root is no longer operant, and this provides good reason for splitting such roots into new divisions.

24.2.4.3 *Geminate Roots: Their Treatment as Biliteral or Triliteral*

Geminate roots can be treated lexicographically as either biliteral or triliteral strings of characters. In the first case, words such as *ħalaal* "what is permitted" and *muħtall* "occupied" are entered under the root letters *ħ-l*, which is alphabetized before *ħ-l-b*; in the second case they are entered under *ħ-l-l*, which is alphabetized between *ħ-l-k* and *ħ-l-m*. In choosing the biliteral treatment of geminate roots, it is possible that Wehr was influenced by Lane (1863–1893; [Sara, "Classical Lexicography"]), Hava (1899), and the monolingual *al-Munjid* (Maʕluuf 1908, 1956), all of which followed this approach. Today, however, this approach is in a decided minority, with only Wehr and two Arabic–Spanish dictionaries (Cortés 1996; Corriente and Ferrando 2005) being the main practitioners. Among dialect dictionaries, only Holes (2001) alphabetizes geminate roots as biliterals, although he cites these roots as triliteral strings: for example, the root *q-ṣ* is cited as *q-ṣ-ṣ* but listed alphabetically before *q-ṣ-b*. As long as the dictionary user is aware of which system is being employed—biliteral or triliteral—it is not difficult to adjust the lookup strategy.

24.2.4.4 *True Roots versus Pseudo-Roots (Guide Words)*

In root-based dictionaries foreign borrowings with no standard or Classical Arabic antecedent (and hence no actual Semitic root) are typically listed alphabetically, under a pseudo-root or guide word that consists of the consonantal "skeleton" of the word itself (although long vowels *alif*, *waaw*, and *yaaʔ* are included). For example, the borrowing سادة *saada* "plain" is alphabetized under the pseudo-root *s-a-d-a* in Woodhead and Beene (1967) and its Arabic script equivalent سادا in Hinds and Badawi (1986). Wehr (1985) does not assign this entry a pseudo-root explicitly, but he does list it as a partial homograph of the entry سادي *saadi* "sadistic" and provides cross-references to both alphabetical entries at the end of the listings for the root *s-w-d*.

Loanwords that start out with a pseudo-root, such as سولوفان *sulufaan* "cellophane" (pseudo-root *s-w-l-w-f-aa-n*), acquire a true root when they become Arabicized as verbal nouns or participles. For example, *musalfan* "laminated; shrink-wrapped" should be lemmatized under *s-l-f-n*, perhaps bringing the entry for *sulufaan* with it (and leaving behind a cross-reference to its new location).

The placement of an entry, whether by root or alphabetically, is in effect a statement on its etymology, especially if the word's structure suggests a plausible root-and-pattern interpretation. To place the word alphabetically implies that it is a loanword, whereas to place it by root implies that it is of Semitic origin or has been Arabicized (i.e., integrated into root-and-pattern morphology).

24.2.4.5 *Cross-Referencing of Roots and Headwords*

Headword and root cross-referencing play an important role in root-based dictionaries by providing links to roots for headwords based on initially-weak roots (e.g., *ʔirθ* "inheritance" and *turaaθ* "inheritance, heritage" linked to *w-r-θ*) and for interlinking related roots, such as those with initial *hamzah*/*waaw* variation (e.g., *ʔ-ħ-d* / *w-ħ-d*, *ʔ-k-d* / *w-k-d*, *ʔ-n-s* / *w-n-s*) and some hollow roots (e.g., *q-w-m* / *q-y-m*). Triliteral–quadriliteral root pairs that differ only in the addition of *w* or *y*, such as *t-b-l* / *t-w-b-l*, *ṣ-r-f* / *ṣ-y-r-f*, *j-h-r* / *j-h-w-r*, and *n-z-k* / *n-y-z-k*, are all good candidates for cross-referencing.

Cross-referencing of roots is also useful in cases where root reconstruction has occurred, such as with SA headwords *taʔliyah* "mechanization" (*ʔ-l-y*) and *muʔallal* "mechanized" (*ʔ-l-l*), both derived ultimately from *ʔaaliyyah* "mechanism" (*ʔ-w-l*). Root reanalysis also occurs with some long-established broken plurals, such as *tawaariix* "dates, histories" (*t-r-x* <*ʔ-r-x*) and *ʔamaakin* "places" (*m-k-n* <*k-w-n*).

The Arabic–German dictionary by Krahl and Gharieb (1984) stands out for the care it gives to listing frequently used elatives and for cross-referencing them to their respective adjectival positive forms: for example, *ʔamyaz* "preferable" <*mumtaaz* "distinguished," *ʔansab* "more suitable" <*munaasib* "suitable," *ʔablaγ* "more intense; more eloquent" <*baaliγ* "extensive"/*baliiγ* "eloquent." It is surprising that this type of basic information is not offered systematically in other modern dictionaries.

24.2.5 The Alphabetical Arrangement

24.2.5.1 *A Brief History of Alphabetically Arranged Dictionaries*

The first comprehensive dictionary to be arranged by strict alphabetical order was Wahrmund's (1870–1877) Arabic–German dictionary. However, the alphabetical arrangement did not gain popularity until the 1960s and 1970s and in the form of monolingual pedagogical works aimed at simplifying word lookup for native speakers of Arabic. The first of these was *al-Marjiʕ* by ʕAbd Allaah al-ʕAlaayili (1963–), of which only the first volume was issued, ending with the entry *jaxdal* "robust." The two-volume *al-Raaʔid* by Jibraan Masʕuud (1964) is often cited as the first alphabetically arranged monolingual dictionary. It was republished as a one-volume work in 1992, and an updated and expanded version came out in 2003 under the new title *al-Raaʔid, muʕjam ʔalifbaaʔi fi al-luγah wa-al-ʔaʕlaam*. The alphabetically arranged *al-Munjid al-ʔabjadi* came out in 1967 and was followed by the *Laaruus* of Xaliil al-Jurr (1973) published in France. The pedagogical work *al-Qaamuus al-jadiid lil-ṭullaab* by Ibn al-Ħaajj Yaħyaa and several other Tunisian lexicographers came out in 1979 and was reissued in a newly typeset edition in 1997 under the title *al-Qaamuus al-jadiid al-ʔalifbaaʔi*, emphasizing the alphabetical arrangement.

Numerous alphabetically arranged bilingual works also appeared during this time period, beginning with the Arabic–German pocket dictionary by Krotkoff (1976), the comprehensive Arabic–French dictionary by ʕAbd al-Nuur (1983), the comprehensive Arabic–English work by Ruuħi Baʕlabakki (1988), the Arabic–German pocket dictionary by Kropfitsch (1993) and his comprehensive Arabic–German dictionary (1996), and the comprehensive Arabic–French dictionary by Ħajjaar (2002).

The alphabetical arrangement that was originally applied to monolingual school dictionaries has since been extended to more comprehensive and ambitious monolingual works, such as *al-Muħiiṭ* by al-Lajmi and al-Razzaaz (1993), the electronic publication *al-γani* by ʔAbu al-ʕAzm (c. 1998), and *Muʕjam al-ʕarabiyyah al-kilaasiikiyyah wal-muʕaaṣira* by Riḍaa (2006).

24.2.5.2 *Some Technical Aspects of the Alphabetical Arrangement*

The alphabetical arrangement is said to be according to the initial letters of the word (وفقاً للحروف الأولى) and is for the most part straightforward. Some issues arise with the alphabetical placement of words that have various forms of *hamzah* and words ending in *taaʔ marbuuṭah* (ة) or *ʔalif maqṣuurah* (ى). Kropfitsch (1996) adopts the sensible approach of treating word-initial *hamzah-ʔalif* (أ) and *maddah-ʔalif* (آ) combinations as equivalent to bare *ʔalif* (ا) for sorting purposes. This is also a realistic approach considering that *hamzah* and *maddah* are often missing in this word position in actual printed text. Kropfitsch also sorts words with medial or final *hamzah* according to the *hamzah* chair (i.e., ي = ئ and و = ؤ). Similarly, *taaʔ marbuuṭah* (ة) and *ʔalif maqṣuurah* (ى) are treated as variants of *haaʔ* (ه) and *yaaʔ* (ي), respectively. Under this scheme a word such as رئة "lung" is treated as if it were spelled ريه and placed alphabetically between رين and ريو; similarly, مؤرخ "historian" is listed right before مورد "source." Baʕlabakki (1988), on the other hand, treats all forms of *hamzah* (أإآئؤء) and the *ʔalif maqṣuurah* as equivalent to bare *ʔalif*, and *taaʔ marbuuṭah* as a variant of *taaʔ maftuuħah* (ت). Under this scheme مؤرخ is listed alphabetically right before مارد "giant; genie."

Using a different set of conventions, the school dictionary *al-Qaamuus al-jadiid* (Ibn al-Ħaajj Yaħyaa et al. 1979) alphabetizes in first place words that begin with the *madda-ʔalif* combination, so *ʔaayah* (آية) "verse," for example, is listed before *ʔab* (أب) "father." This dictionary also sorts geminate letters after their nongeminate forms, so that between *sardiin* "sardine" and *sarata* "to swallow," for example, we find (among other words) *sirr*, *sarraaj*, *sarraba*, and *sarraa*.[9] Similarly, *qudduus* "very holy" and *qiddiis* "holy" are listed right before *qadara* "to be able."

24.2.5.3 *Variation in Practice among Alphabetically Arranged Dictionaries*

It is important to note that the leading Western lexicographers who have employed the alphabetical method, namely, Krotkoff (1976) and Kropfitsch (1996), as well as their precursor Wahrmund (1870–1877), do not list verbs alphabetically but rather employ the traditional arrangement of grouping these by root and then listing the root alphabetically (as in root-based dictionaries). In doing so they also follow the presentation format observed in Wehr (all editions) where derived verbs are designated via their conventional Roman numerals and are listed together in a single paragraph. This grouping of derived verbs appears to be the logical choice, given that the semantic and grammatical relationship among derived forms is often so clear and compelling that in many instances it is perfectly good lexicographic technique to define an entry in one derived form entirely through reference to another form, such as "passive of I" (فعل) for many form VII (انفعل) verbs or "passive of II" (فعّل) for many form V (تفعّل) verbs.

The alphabetically arranged Arabic–Hebrew dictionary by Sharoni (1991) is worth mentioning for the attention it gives to roots and root-based cross-referencing. The root

[9] *sirr* "secret," *sarraaj* "saddler," *sarraba* "to leak (water, news)," and *sarraa* "to dispel (worries)."

of each entry is provided in square brackets immediately after the headword, and each root is itself listed alphabetically in the dictionary in the form of a cross-reference that lists all headwords and broken plurals belonging to that root. For example, the entry for *miizaan* "scales" (840) lists its root (وزن), and the entry for this root (906) consists of a cross-reference to the headwords *ittizaan* "equilibrium," *ittazana* "to be balanced," *ʔawzaan* "weights, measures," *tawaazana* "to be balanced," and a handful more, listed in straight alphabetical order.

It is interesting to note that a similar form of cross-referencing headwords and roots was practiced earlier by Elias (1922), although within the root-based arrangement. His system consisted of filling in the alphabetical "gaps" between roots with headwords cross-referenced to their respective roots. For example, between the roots *m-d-y* and *m-đ-r*, he lists six headwords and provides their respective roots: *madiid* (*m-d-d*) "extended"; *mudiir* (*d-w-r*) "director"; *mudiin* (*d-y-n*) "creditor"; *madiinah* (*m-d-n*) "city"; *muđ* (*m-n-đ*) "since"; and *mađaaq* (*đ-w-q*) "taste."

24.2.5.4 *Lookup Difficulties in Alphabetically Arranged Dictionaries*

Alphabetically arranged dictionaries cannot claim to have solved all word lookup problems, especially those where some knowledge of inflectional morphology is still required. Kropfitsch (1996), especially, appears to have anticipated these difficulties with his generous use of cross-references for broken plurals. It is interesting to note, however, that for broken plurals it appears more difficult (for learners of Arabic, at least) to deduce the singular form of these plurals than it is to extract a plausible root. Take, for example, the following broken plural entries in Kropfitsch (1996: 34), listed alphabetically as follows: أدواء, أدوات, أدواح, أدوار, and أدوية.[10] In a root-based dictionary one could look up a hypothetical root for these broken plurals with a fair amount of success *without knowing their singular forms*. But in an alphabetically arranged dictionary, it is absolutely necessary to know the singular form to locate the entry—hence, the need for cross-references. In this case Kropfitsch provides the following:

أدواء ← داء, أدوات ← أداة, أدواح ← دوحة, أدوار ← دور, and أدوية ← دواء.

24.2.5.5 *The Phonetic Alphabetical Arrangement in Dictionaries of Dialect*

Dialect dictionaries that present the Arabic words in Latin script use the familiar A to Z Latin character sort sequence, with some conventions established for the alphabetical sorting of phonemes such as *hamzah* and ʕ*ayn*, and phonemes typically represented by Greek letters or Latin characters with diacritics. This arrangement is typically used in glossaries and compilations of limited size, but occasionally in dictionaries that aim at comprehensive coverage. The most notable works in this category are the Moroccan Arabic–English dictionary by Harrell (1966) and the more recent Palestinian Arabic–English *Olive Tree* by Elihay (2004). The Moroccan Arabic–Dutch dictionary by Otten

[10] أدوار "roles," أدواح "family trees," أدوات "tools," أدواء "diseases," أدوية "remedies."

and Hoogland (1983) is also worth citing for its phonetic level of detail and for alphabetizing conventions similar to those used by Harrell, where the user is instructed to ignore as many as four "extra short" vowels when looking up words. Both dictionaries require from the user some familiarity with these conventions as well as better-than-average listening skills (for distinguishing the "extra short" vowels).

And finally, the dictionary of Hassaniya Arabic by Heath (2004) is noteworthy in that it follows a hybrid phonetic arrangement. Although lexical entries are lemmatized by root, the roots themselves are presented in Latin alphabetical order, with a fairly intuitive treatment of non-Latin symbols: for example, a, b, d/ḍ, ð/ḍ̣, e, f, g, h/ħ.

24.2.6 Macrostructure Conclusion: Root versus Alphabetic Arrangement

In a fairly comprehensive discussion of the merits and demerits of both systems, Bobzin (1989: 127) concludes that for a practical general-purpose dictionary it would make sense to follow the alphabetical arrangement. Before stating this conclusion, Bobzin provides several examples of how word lookup in dictionaries arranged by roots is a two-step process that involves first extracting the root, then locating the headword among other entries based on the same root that have been arranged according to specific conventions that may differ from one dictionary to another. These criteria are usually outlined under the title "User Notes" in the front matter of each dictionary.

Bobzin (1989: 127) points out that the alphabetically arranged dictionary is a better choice as a practical tool for the general user for two reasons: (1) it involves the application of a single lookup strategy (rather than the two-step method in dictionaries arranged by root); and (2) it obviates the need to create duplicate entries and cross-references at different locations, because all entries, whether they are based on Arabic roots or are of foreign origin, are entered according to purely alphabetical criteria.

Without denying the facts as presented by Bobzin, we would note that it is still possible to make good use of root-based dictionaries without the benefit of a good understanding of the root-internal conventions of the author, provided one does not mind perusing several headwords on one's way to finding (eventually) the one sought. In fact, this perusal of root-related headwords is one of the (possibly unintended) pedagogical strengths of root-based dictionaries, although it is easy to see why this might be considered a nuisance for users who want immediate access to a specific headword and do not wish to scan a handful of root-related headwords while trying to find it.

In defense of root-based dictionaries it should also be pointed out that, when a word is not listed in this type of dictionary, the user can often still extract the root and hazard an educated guess based on words already entered under that root. This is often the case with many lexicalized nominal and adjectival forms based on active and passive participle patterns.

When this issue is reexamined in the context of online electronic dictionaries, the logical conclusion is that, when the dictionary user retrieves a given entry, it is still useful to display (or make available for display) other entries from the same root. In fact, this is already the default display method for many online dictionaries.

24.3 Microstructure of the Lexicon: The Structure and Content of Entries

24.3.1 Introduction

In this section we discuss issues concerning the structure and content of dictionary entries, including the orthography and phonology of headwords, the use of explicit versus implicit part of speech and grammatical tags, the use of sense discriminators and numbered senses, and the treatment of multiword expressions and collocations.

24.3.2 The Orthography and Phonology of Dictionary Entries

The goal of dictionary lookup in Arabic is often to ascertain not just the meaning of a word but also its vocalization or pronunciation. In dictionaries of SA it is assumed that fully diacritized script represents canonical pronunciation. This is for the most part correct, with the exception of a few words of unusual orthography (e.g., مائة *mi'a* "one hundred"), including words of exceptional phonology (e.g., *aḷḷaah* "Allah"), and loanwords with non-SA phonemes (e.g., ڤيتو *viito* "veto"). In these cases it is useful to represent pronunciation via phonetic script (although this does not preclude also citing the fully voweled canonical form; e.g., مُوتُور *motoor* "engine").

Dictionaries of Arabic dialects typically make use of IPA-based symbols that are generally familiar to Arabic linguists, with adjustments based on the author's preferences but also according to the availability of certain typographic symbols. Among the more noteworthy differences is the approach taken to represent secondary emphatic consonants. In Harrell (1966) and Woodhead and Beene (1967) these are marked via the familiar underdots widely used for the emphatics: /ṭ/, /ḍ/, /ṣ/, and /ð̣/. In the Georgetown Moroccan dictionary the underdot is added to /b/, /l/, /m/, /r/, and /z/ (/ḅ/, /ḷ/, /ṃ/, /ṛ/, /ẓ/), and the Georgetown Iraqi dictionary includes underdots for /n/ (/ṇ/) and /p/ as well. Hinds and Badawi (1986), however, mark only the [a]/[ɑ] front/back vowel contrast, as seen in the contrastive pair /gaari/ "current" and /gɑɑr-i/ "my neighbor." An analogous approach is taken in the SA dictionaries of Krotkoff (1976) and Kropfitsch (1996), where the [a]/[ɑ] distinction is marked in the pronunciation, which is provided in the International Phonetic Alphabet (IPA) for each entry.

A significant decision in the phonological description of headwords is whether to retain representation of long vowel signs in contexts where they are reduced. Ideally, both forms would be available: the original (in Arabic script) and the corresponding phonetic representation with long vowel reduction. This is the case in Hinds and Badawi (1986), although for headwords only, where the original long vowel is provided in Arabic (unvoweled) script, and the reduced form, when it occurs, is provided in the accompanying phonetic script. The Arabic script thus allows the reader to make note of the underlying form (i.e., phonetic value) of words such as *rafahiyyah* (*rafaahiyyah* رفاهية "comfort"). Broken plural forms, however, are available only in phonetic script, so when these contain reduced forms, the reader must have sufficient linguistic knowledge to reconstruct the original (unreduced) form: for example, to know that the underlying form of *ṣawariix* is *ṣawaariix* (صواريخ "missiles").

Typesetting considerations, including readability factors, can also influence the decision whether to use fully voweled script or a combination of unvoweled script and phonetic notation. Given that most naturally occurring text is unvoweled leads us to favor an approach that treats the undiacritized headword as the orthographic lemma or homograph with two or more vocalizations or phonetic script representations. We see this approach in Kropfitsch (1996) in numbered homograph entries such as دَفعة 1 *dafʕah* "push" and دُفعة 2 *dufʕah* "year (alumni)." The inability of some desktop publishing systems to produce a dagger *ʔalif* has resulted in incorrect forms in such dictionaries as Hoogland et al. (2003) and Badawi and Abdel Haleem (2008), where a *fatħah* is used instead to mark the long vowel /aa/.

24.3.3 Grammatical Information: Part of Speech Labels

Wehr (all editions) makes use of remarkably few explicit part of speech labels, as most categories are assumed to be evident either through the conventions of the presentation (e.g., verbs are grouped first) or can be deduced from the glosses themselves (e.g., noun and adjective, although these categories are not always clear). The opposite trend, toward explicit and systematic application of part of speech labels, can be seen in dialect dictionaries such as Hinds and Badawi (1986) and Holes (2001) and more recently in SA dictionaries, such as the Arabic–Dutch works of Van Mol (2001) and Hoogland et al. (2003) and the Arabic–Czech lexicon of Zemánek et al. (2006).

It needs to be admitted that what appear to be straightforward part of speech labels in the lexicon are in reality more elusive when one examines corpus evidence directly.

24.3.4 Sense Divisions: The Use of Sense Discriminators and Numbered Senses

In systems with no numbered senses, such as Wehr (all editions), a semicolon is used to separate different (i.e., nonsynonymous) senses. This is in contrast with predominant practice, which has been to number the different senses. The pedagogical Arabic–Dutch dictionary of Van Mol (2001) also orders senses by frequency and uses sense discriminators (in the form of Arabic glosses, synonyms, explanatory text, or labels) for differentiating senses. For example, the entry for *saaʕah* "hour" has five numbered senses, with the sense discriminator labels *waqt* "time, moment," *muddah* "time period," *ʔaalah* "clock," *fatrah* "phase," and *ʕaddaad* "counter, meter." Hoogland et al. (2003) also use numbered senses and add sense discriminators, in the form of Arabic text (usually synonyms) or Dutch domain labels, as appropriate.

Baʕlabakki's (1988) Arabic–English dictionary stands out for its extensive use of sense discriminators in the form of Arabic synonyms, antonyms, and even brief Arabic definitions in its entries. In fact, in many respects this could be regarded as an Arabic/Arabic–English dictionary. Rather than reflecting a particular presentation strategy or lexicographic approach, this presentation format perhaps reflects the Arabic–Arabic dictionary sources used to draft many of the entries, as well as the fact that this dictionary is strongly oriented toward native speakers of Arabic.

24.3.5 Phrasal Entries: Collocations

Although the focus on collocations in Arabic lexicography is relatively recent, it cannot be said that collocations have been totally neglected in Arabic dictionaries. Wehr, for example, provides especially detailed and comprehensive coverage of the grammatical collocations of verbs, and in terms of lexical collocations Wehr (1985) covers more than 17,500 multiword expressions. The Arabic–Dutch work by Hoogland et al. (2003) contains a phenomenal 42,700 phrases and example sentences, and the Arabic–Czech dictionary by Zemánek et al. (2006) covers 18,000 phrases and expressions, which is remarkable for a dictionary of "only" 21,000 entries. At the same time, we should note that among general-purpose dictionaries there has been no systematic effort to catalogue all collocations, although this is due to the fact that these dictionaries were designed primarily for decoding (mostly reading comprehension) rather than encoding or active production of Arabic, especially by nonnative speakers.

24.4 Current Issues and Future Trends

24.4.1 Electronic and Online Dictionaries

Since the 1990s the leading monolingual dictionaries of the Classical period—and a few from the modern period—have been digitized and made available as text files. A few websites have also indexed this data by root or by word form and provide access to entries via interactive search engines.

One of the more popular long-standing resources for online dictionaries is the Ajeeb website (http://lexicons.ajeeb.com), which provides simultaneous search in eight monolingual Arabic dictionaries, three of which are modern publications: *al-Muʕjam al-wasiiṭ* (Muṣṭafaa 1960–1961); *al-Muhiiṭ* (al-Lajmi and al-Razzaaz 1993); and *al-γani* (ʔAbu al-ʕAzm c. 1998). The search mode is not specified but appears to favor root-based retrieval, with some limited stemming (affix stripping) performed on searches involving complex word forms. The search results are displayed in table format, with links provided to the full text of entries. All entries for a root are displayed in the search results for *al-Muʕjam al-wasiiṭ*, but results for *al-Muhiiṭ* and *al-γani* are displayed for individual entries only.

Most of the classical monolingual lexicons are available for download online (http://almeshkat.net). Sawalha and Atwell (2010) process and restructure the machine-readable data of 23 of these dictionaries to make them amenable to search and retrieval of entries. A root-based dictionary lookup system for six of these classic lexicons can be accessed online (http://www.comp.leeds.ac.uk/sawalha/). Five dictionaries from the Classical and premodern period can also be searched simultaneously online (http://baheth.info). The Lane *Lexicon* (1863–1893) was digitized in the early 2000s at Harvard University, and a version with user interface became available in 2011 at the Perseus Digital Library of Tufts University (http://www.perseus.tufts.edu/hopper/).

Two modern Arabic–L2 dictionaries are currently available online: the Arabic–Hebrew work by Ayalon and Shinar (1972) (http://ayalosh.snunit.k12.i/) and the Arabic–Danish lexicon by Pétrod and Barzenji (1997; http://www.ordbogen.com). Both of these dictionaries allow for searching either by root or word form, including broken plurals, and both display all entries for a root when the search mode is root based. The Ayalon and Shinar dictionary goes a step further by displaying all root-related entries when the search is for a word form (i.e., headword or broken plural), which facilitates the examination of related entries, as in root-based print dictionaries.

The dictionaries of Iraqi, Syrian, and Moroccan dialects published by Georgetown University Press are being digitized and converted to lexical databases by the Linguistic Data Consortium to provide interactive computer access as well as updated versions of the print copies.

The most important electronic publication so far is undoubtedly the digital version of the Arabic–Dutch dictionary by Hoogland et al. (2009, 2d ed.), which is provided free of cost for research purposes by the Institute for Dutch Lexicology (http://www.inl.nl). The lexicon is in Extensible Markup Language (XML) format and follows the proposed lexical markup framework (LMF) standard, thereby setting an important precedent in Arabic lexicography. It is not unrealistic to assume that the structural framework and Arabic content of this dictionary could be used as a template or starting point for Arabic–English or Arabic–French versions, for example, and perhaps even the first fully corpus-based Arabic–Arabic dictionary.

24.4.2 Dictionary Compilation Methods and the Corpus-Based Approach

In a review of Wehr's first Arabic–German edition (1958, third printing) and *Supplement* (1959), R. B. Serjeant (1959: 583) rightly noted, "... There is no organized method of recording new words as they appear or as they become established ...." He reiterated this important argument in his subsequent review (Serjeant 1962: 342) of the first Arabic–English edition (1961): "there is still no proper means devised whereby the current of new words and expressions that appear daily in Contemporary Arabic can be recorded and added to the lexicons." Indeed, the principal method of updating dictionaries has often been one of ad hoc addenda, mostly by way of contributions from users who discover missing entries or missing new meanings or usages when consulting the dictionary, usually during a reading activity. In a particularly thorough review of Wehr (1961), M. M. Bravmann (1963) contributes a list of over 60 addenda based on his perusal of several works of fiction by Mahmud Taymur and Najib Mahfuz. Most of Bravmann's addenda were incorporated by Wehr (1966, 2d ed.).

The tradition of citing corpus evidence has been practiced in the lexicography of the dialects, most notably in the works of Barthélemy (1935–1954), Denizeau (1960), and Holes (2001). As Holes (1995) points out, dialect dictionaries tend to be more accurate and comprehensive because they are based on corpus data, the best example of this being Hinds and Badawi (1986). What is needed, says Holes, is dictionaries of SA compiled on "a representative database of usage-in-context."

The need for corpus-based methods in the lexicography of SA has been addressed to a great extent in the methodology and Arabic–Dutch compilations of Van Mol (2001) and Hoogland et al. (2003). The modern corpus-based approach that was used in compiling the pedagogical dictionary by Van Mol is discussed in Van Mol and Paulussen (2001). A fairly detailed description of the corpus and the process used in compiling the comprehensive Arabic-Dutch dictionary by Hoogland et al is available online (http://www.let.ru.nl/wba). It can be said that corpus-based lexicography is now the new norm, especially for Western lexicographers of Arabic. The most recent compilation, the Arabic–Czech dictionary by Zemánek et al. (2006), is based almost entirely on a balanced corpus of 50 million words dating from the years 1980–2000.

Arabic lexicography and corpus linguistics research in general have been stimulated by the availability of online corpora and search tools. Among the more popular and useful we find the following:

The arabiCorpus website at Brigham Young University (http://arabicorpus.byu.edu) provides a fairly effective search mechanism in which the user specifies whether the search term is a noun, adjective, adverb, or verb. The search term is then expanded morphologically according to its inflectional category, and all appropriate prefixes and suffixes are added. Results (hits) are displayed in concordance format, and statistics are provided on the search term's collocates and its distribution over various subcorpora.

Aralex is an online lexical database based on an automatically tagged SA corpus of 40 million words. It provides statistical information on orthographic forms, word stems, roots, and word patterns as well as on the bigram and trigram frequencies of orthographic forms, roots, and patterns (Boudelaa and Marslen-Wilson 2010: 484). Although Aralex was designed primarily as a tool to aid in the selection of stimuli for Arabic cognitive processing research, it has ready applications in pedagogy and natural language processing. It can be accessed online (http://www.mrc-cbu.cam.ac.uk:8081/aralex.online/login.jsp).

The Arabic Web Corpus at the University of Leeds (Sawalha and Atwell 2009) (http://corpus.leeds.ac.uk/internet.html) allows for queries on a lemmatized corpus of 100 million words, with concordance views of the results, including tables of collocations and frequency statistics. An alternative interface with access to additional Arabic corpora, such as the Arabic Wikipedia, can be found online (http://corpus.leeds.ac.uk/query-ar.html).

24.4.3 SA and the Dialects

Although Hoogland (2008: 26–27) states, "The inclusion of colloquial Arabic in Modern Standard Arabic dictionaries... is very rare and considered improper," he does concede that dictionaries covering more than one variety of Arabic, such as Hinds and Badawi (1986), which includes a considerable amount of appropriately labeled SA, "might become more widespread in future" given that the dialects are increasingly being used in written communication ([Holes, "Orality"]; [Bentahila et al., "Code Switching"]).

This trend of including what are judged to be SA lexical items in dialect dictionaries is not a recent development. Lexicons of dialects have been known to list many SA and even classical terms. For example, in his review of the fourth fascicle of Barthélemy (1935–1954), M. Fakhry (1953: 178) complains that "the reader is unable to tell, in perusing his dictionary, whether the author intends it as a purely colloquial dictionary, or as a mixed (i.e. classical-colloquial) one. The book is full of words of indisputable classical extraction... whose usage does not differ from the classical at all."

It is not unheard of for dictionaries of dialect to use SA dictionaries as a model and to adapt their content when describing usage and meaning in a specific dialect. The close relationship between Wehr (1961) and the dictionary of Iraqi by Woodhead and Beene (1967) is quite evident in many of the entries that cover more formal and SA-like usage among educated Iraqis. In many instances, Woodhead and Beene actually improve on Wehr in the organization of sense divisions within lemmas and in the level of detail provided. Compare, for example, the description and internal structure of the entry *saakin* "quiet; resident" in Wehr (1961: 419) with the same in Woodhead and Beene (1967: 221). The Iraqi dictionary marks six different senses clearly and assigns the appropriate inflectional properties (and one idiomatic usage) to the corresponding meanings.

In appreciating the clarity of presentation in this entry, it is easy to forget that this is primarily a dialect dictionary rather than a dictionary of SA.

The Hinds and Badawi (1986) dictionary of Egyptian Arabic is outstanding in its coverage of educated spoken Arabic ([Davies et al., "Code Switching"]; [Al-Wer, "Sociolinguistics"]). It is worth noting that some 1600 items have been labeled (with the upward arrow) as belonging to *ʕaammiyyat al-muθaqqafiin* in Badawi's well-known five-level sociolinguistic hierarchy, which is summarized in the front matter (viii–xi). Most of the entries carrying this tag would be regarded today as fairly established SA items, and many were already listed in Wehr (1979, 4th ed.).

One contemporary dictionary that stands out for its explicit side-by-side coverage of both SA and a dialect (Palestinian) is the trilingual literary Arabic–Hebrew–colloquial Arabic dictionary by Rosenhouse (2004). In this dictionary, the entry for *laysa* "not," for example, offers the example phrase *laysa bi-l-ʔimkaan* "it is not possible," which is glossed in Palestinian Arabic as *miš mumkin* (in Hebrew phonetic script).

24.4.4 Coverage of Arabic Names

Knowledge of Arabic names, including the cultural baggage associated with names, is an integral part of the linguistic competence of native speakers. Because of the peculiarities of Arabic orthography (i.e., the absence of capitalization), names are especially difficult for learners of Arabic. It is therefore surprising that Arabic dictionaries have given little attention to names beyond what is often already known, such as the names of countries and principal cities, and the occasional historical figure. Wehr (all editions), for example, focused primarily on the names of historical figures from Islamic, Judeo-Christian, and Western Classical history: for example, Abraham, Aristotle, Jeremiah, Ishmael, Isaiah, Plato, Plotinus, Euclid, Job, Peter, Ptolemy, and Hippocrates. Among the addenda in Kropfitch (2003) we find the names of old Arab tribes (e.g., *Banu Laxm*, *Kindah*, and *al-Xazraj*), several uses and meanings specific to the Quran (e.g., *Aħmad*), and the names of major Arab cities. It appears that these are names that university students typically encounter in their studies of Arab and Islamic history and that lexicographers simply neglected to include. Hoogland et al. (2003) provide coverage for some 134 given names, tagged as masculine or feminine and as Christian or dual Christian–Muslim (the default is Muslim). Among the addenda to Hoogland et al. (2009, 2d ed.) are the names of all 114 Quranic chapters.[11]

It is likely that future dictionaries will provide additional coverage of Arabic names, although as part of a larger effort to include encyclopedic information, in which case the scope would be expanded beyond personal names. We sense that this would be handled more effectively in online dictionaries, with links provided to the relevant entries in additional online resources, such as Arabic Wikipedia.

[11] We wish to acknowledge Jan Hoogland's kind assistance in providing us with an electronic copy of these addenda.

24.5 Conclusion

In this chapter we devoted considerable attention to reviewing the basic features of the root-based and alphabetical arrangement methods. The choice of which of these two systems to use is still a very basic and relevant decision for lexicographers of Arabic today. Even when compiling a dictionary that is to be used primarily as an online interactive reference, the lexicographer must decide whether other root-related entries should be included in the display and, if so, in what sort of arrangement scheme. As we have seen, even in the internal arrangement of entries for root-based dictionaries there is much room for creativity. Perhaps with electronic and online dictionaries each user will have the option to configure his or her own custom layout.

In discussing various issues in modern Arabic lexicography we have emphasized the impact that corpus-based methods have had on dictionary compilation. Van Mol (2008: 39) identifies two critical areas for corpus-based research: the development of accurate tagging software (i.e., software that can disambiguate words in context); and the selection of representative corpora. In our view, this last point is the key, for if one selects only SA corpora then the lexicography will perforce be limited to SA. Perhaps the greatest challenge ahead, especially for corpus-based lexicographers, is the need to come to terms with the growing corpus of nonstandard Arabic, which is in great evidence these days on social networking websites. Written Arabic now includes much more than the *Schriftsprache der Gegenwart*, the "contemporary written Arabic" that Wehr documented so well. Also, a vast corpus of spontaneous (unscripted) spoken communication, often with accompanying video, is being produced and widely disseminated daily in the Arabic-speaking world. Much of it is educated spoken Arabic with varying amounts of regional and dialectal features and is quite suitable for use as corpus data in any dictionary that aims at describing contemporary Arabic.

We would argue for a lexicographic description of Arabic in the broadest terms, where the simultaneous treatment of both SA and the more salient lexical items from the major dialects becomes possible through the systematic application of the appropriate register and regional labels. One of the first lexicographic steps in this direction was our *Frequency Dictionary of Arabic* (Buckwalter and Parkinson 2011), where the corpus-based approach required that all varieties of Arabic and levels of usage be accounted for.

References

ʕAbd al-Masiiħ, Jurj Mitri. 1993–. *Luγat al-ʕArab: muʕjam muṭawwal lil-luγah al-ʕArabiyyah wa-muṣṭalaħaatihaa al-ħadiiθah*. Beirut: Maktabat Lubnaan.

ʕAbd al-Nuur, Jabbuur. 1983. *Muʕjam ʕAbd al-Nuur al-mufaṣṣal: ʕarabi-faransi*. 2 vols. Beirut: Daar al-ʕIlm lil-Malaayiin.

ʔAbu al-ʕAzm, ʕAbd al-γani. c. 1998. *al-γani*. Available at http://lexicons.sakhr.com.

ʔAbu Ħaaqah, Aħmad. 2007. *Muʕjam al-nafaaʔis al-kabiir*. Beirut: Daar al-Nafaaʔis.

al-ʕAlaayili, ʕAbd Allaah. 1963–. *al-Marjiʕ: muʕjam wasiiṭ ʕilmi, luɣawi, fanni murattab wafqa al-mufrad bi-ħasab lafẓih*, vol. 1. Beirut: Daar al-Muʕjam al-ʕArabi.

Ayalon, David and Pessah Shinar. 1972. *Milon ʕaravi-ʕivri la-lashon ha-ʕaravit ha-hadashah* [Arabic–Hebrew dictionary of Modern Arabic]. Jerusalem: Magnes Press. Available at http://ayalosh.snunit.k12.i/.

Badawi, Elsaid M. and Muhammad Abdel Haleem. 2008. *Arabic-English dictionary of Qurʾanic usage*. Leiden: Brill.

Baʕlabakki, Ruuħi. 1988. *al-Mawrid:qaamuus ʕarabi-inkiliizi*. Beirut: Dar al-ʕIlm lil-Malaayiin.

Barthélemy, Adrien. 1935–1954. *Dictionnaire arabe-français. Dialectes de Syrie: Alep, Damas, Liban, Jérusalem*. Paris: Librairie orientaliste Paul Geuthner.

Bobzin, Hartmut. 1989. Zum Problem der Anordnung von Einträgen in zweisprachigen Lexika des modernen Arabisch. *ZDMG* 8: 118–127.

Boudelaa, Sami and William Marslen-Wilson. 2010. Aralex: A lexical database for Modern Standard Arabic. *Behavior Research Methods* 42: 481–487.

Bravmann, M. M. 1963. Review of Wehr (1961). *Journal of the American Oriental Society* 83: 367–373.

Buckwalter, Tim and Dilworth Parkinson. 2011. *A frequency dictionary of Arabic: Core vocabulary for learners*. New York: Routledge.

Corriente, Federico and Ignacio Ferrando. 2005. *Diccionario avanzado árabe*, 2d ed., vol. 1, árabe-español. Barcelona: Herder.

Cortés, Julio. 1996. *Diccionario de árabe culto moderno: árabe-español*. Madrid: Gredos.

Denizeau, Claude. 1960. *Dictionnaire des parlers arabes de Syrie, Liban et Palestine: Supplément au dictionnaire arabe-français de A. Barthélemy*. Paris: G.-P. Maisonneuve.

Elias, Elias A. 1922. *Elias' modern dictionary, Arabic-English*. Cairo: Elias. (7th ed., 1954; 10th ed., 1974; 14th ed., 1983)

Elihay, J. 2004. *The olive tree dictionary: A transliterated dictionary of conversational Eastern Arabic (Palestinian)*. Jerusalem: Minerva.

Fakhry, M. 1953. Review of Barthélemy (1935–1954). *BSOAS* 15: 178–179.

Ħajjaar, Juuzif. 2002. *al-Marjiʕ: qaamuus muʕaaṣir: ʕarabi-faransi*. Beirut: Maktabat Lubnaan Naaširuun.

Ħamaawi, Ṣubħi. 2000. *al-Munjid fi al-luɣah al-ʕarabiyyah al-muʕaaṣirah*. Beirut: Daar al-Mašriq.

Harrell, Richard S. (ed.). [1966] 2004[2]. *A dictionary of Moroccan Arabic: Moroccan–English*. Washington, DC: Georgetown University Press.

Hava, J. G. 1899. *Arabic-English dictionary for the use of students = al-Faraaʔid al-durriyyah fi al-luɣatayn al-ʕarabiyyah wa-al-ʔinkiliiziyyah*. Beirut: Catholic Press.

Haywood, John. 1991. Bilingual lexicography with Arabic. In *Wörterbücher: ein internationales Handbuch zur Lexikographie*, vol. 3, ed. Franz J. Hausmann et al., 3086–3096. Berlin: de Gruyter.

Heath, Jeffrey. 2004. *Hassaniya Arabic (Mali)-English-French dictionary*. Wiesbaden: Harrassowitz.

Hinds, Martin and El-Said Badawi. 1986. *A dictionary of Egyptian Arabic: Arabic–English*. Beirut: Librairie du Liban.

Holes, Clive. 1995. Review of Selim, George D. *Arabic-English and English-Arabic dictionaries in the Library of Congress*. *British Journal of Middle Eastern Studies* 22: 224–225.

——. 2001. *Dialect, culture, and society in Eastern Arabia*. vol. 1, *Glossary*. Leiden: Brill.

Hoogland, Jan. 2008. Lexicography: Bilingual dictionaries. In *Encyclopedia of Arabic Language and Linguistics*, vol. 3, ed. Kees Versteegh, Associate Editors: Mushira Eid, Alaa Elgibali, Manfred Woidich, Andrzej Zaborski, 21–30. Leiden: Brill.

Hoogland, Jan, Kees Versteegh, and Manfred Woidich. [2003] 2009². *Woordenboek Arabisch-Nederlands*. Amsterdam: Bulaaq.

Ibn al-Ħaajj Yaħyaa, al-Jiilaani, Bilħasan al-Baliiš, and ʕAlii Bin Haadiyah. 1979. *al-Qaamuus al-jadiid lil-ṭullaab: muʕjam ʕarabi madrasi ʔalifbaaʔi*. Tunis: al-Šarikah al-Tuunisiyyah lil-Tawziiʕ; Algiers: al-Šarikah al-Waṭaniyyah lil-Našr wa-al-Tawziiʕ. (5th ed., 1984)

al-Jurr, Xaliil. 1973. *Laaruus: al-Muʕjam al-ʕarabi al-ħadiiθ*. Paris: Larousse.

al-Karmi, Ħasan Saʕiid. 1999. *al-Muγni al-wasiiṭ: qaamuus ʕarabi-ʔinkiliizi*. Beirut: Librairie du Liban.

——. 2000. *al-Muγni al-fariid: qaamuus al-jayb al-ḍaxm, ʕarabi-ʔinkiliizi*. Beirut: Librairie du Liban.

Krahl, Günther and Gharieb Mohamed Gharieb. 1984. *Wörterbuch Arabisch-Deutsch*. Leipzig: VEB Verlag Enzyklopädie.

Kropfitsch, Lorenz. 1993. *Langenscheidt Taschenwörterbuch Arabisch. Teil I: Arabisch-Deutsch*. Berlin: Langenscheidt. (2d ed., 2010)

——. 1996. *Langenscheidt Handwörterbuch Arabisch-Deutsch*. Berlin: Langenscheidt. (2d ed., 2003)

Krotkoff, Georg. 1976. *Langenscheidts Taschenwörterbuch der arabischen und deutschen Sprache. Teil I: Arabisch-Deutsch*. Berlin: Langenscheidt.

al-Lajmi, ʔAdib and Nabiilah al-Razzaaz. 1993. *al-Muħiiṭ: muʕjam al-luγah al-ʕarabiyyah*. Paris: Al Mouhit.

Lane, Edward William. [1863–1893] 1984. *Arabic-English lexicon*. Cambridge, UK: Islamic Texts Society.

Madina, Maan Z. 1973. *Arabic-English dictionary of the modern literary language*. New York: Pocket Books.

Maʕluuf, Luwiis. 1908. *al-Munjid fi al-luγah*. Beirut: Daar al-Mašriq.

——. [1956] 2007. *al-Munjid fi al-luγah wa-al-aʕlaam*. Beirut: Daar al-Mašriq. (42nd printing, 2007)

Masʕuud, Jibraan. [1964] 1992. *al-Raaʔid: muʕjam luγawi ʕaṣri ruttibat mufradaatuhu wafqan li-ħuruufihaa al-ʔuulaa*. Beirut: Daar al-ʕIlm lil-Malaayiin.

——. 2003. *al-Raaʔid, muʕjam ʔalifbaaʔi fi al-luγah wa-al-ʔaʕlaam*. Beirut: Daar al-ʕIlm lil-Malaayiin.

Muṣṭafaa, ʔIbraahiim et al. 1960–1961. *al-Muʕjam al-wasiiṭ*. Cairo: Daar al-Maʕaarif. (2d ed., 1972–1973; 4th ed., 2004, Cairo: Maktabat al-Šuruuq al-Dawliyyah)

Otten, Roel and Jan Hoogland. 1983. *Basiswoordenboek van het Marokkaans Arabisch: Marokkaans/Nederlands, Nederlands/Marokkaans*. Muiderberg: Dick Coutinho.

Pétrod, Martine and Fuad Barzenji. 1997. *Arabisk-dansk ordbog = Qaamuus ʕarabi-daanimarki*. Copenhagen: Gad. Available at http://www.ordbogen.com.

Qafisheh, Hamdi. 1997. *NTC's Gulf Arabic-English dictionary*. Lincolnwood, IL: NTC Publishing Group.

Riḍaa, Yuusuf Muħammad. 2006. *Muʕjam al-ʕarabiyyah al-kilaasiikiyyah wa-al-muʕaaṣirah*. Beirut: Maktabat Lubnaan Naaširuun.

Rosenhouse, Judith. 2004 *Milon telat-leshone shimushi: ʕAravi-ʕIvri: le-ʕAravit śifrutit ule-ʕAravit meduberet*. [Practical trilingual dictionary: Literary Arabic-Hebrew-Colloquial Arabic]. Rosh Ha-ʕAyin: Prolog.

Sawalha, Majdi and Eric Atwell. 2009. Linguistically informed and corpus informed morphological analysis of Arabic. In *Proceedings of the 5th international corpus linguistics conference (CL 2009)*, July 20–23, Liverpool, UK. Available at http://ucrel.lancs.ac.uk/publications/cl2009/.

——. 2010. Constructing and using broad-coverage lexical resource for enhancing morphological analysis of Arabic. In *Proceedings of the language resource and evaluation conference (LREC 2010)*, 282–287. Malta: Valleta.

Schregle, Götz. 1981–1992. *Arabisch-Deutsches Wörterbuch. vol. 1: Hamzah to ḍaad; vol. 2: Ṭaaʔ to qusanṭiinah*. Wiesbaden: Steiner.

Serjeant, R. B. 1959. Review of Wehr (1952 and 1959). *BSOAS* 22: 582–583.

——. 1962. Review of Wehr (1961). *BSOAS* 25: 341–342.

Sharoni, Avraham. 1991. *Milon ʕarvi-ʕivri shimushi = al-Muʕjam al-muʕaaṣir ʕarabi-ʕibri*. Tel Aviv: Misrad ha-bitahon. (14th ed., 2006)

Shivtiel, Avihai. 1993. Root-dictionary or alphabetical dictionary: a methodological dilemma. In *Proceedings of the colloquium on Arabic lexicology and lexicography*, ed. Kinga Dévényi, Tamás Iványi, and Avihai Shivtiel, 13–25. Budapest: Eötvös Loránd University and Csoma de Kőrös Society.

Van Mol, Mark. 2001. *Leerwoordenboek Arabisch-Nederlands*. Amsterdam: Bulaaq.

——. 2008. Arabic and the computer: Possibilities and perspectives for scientific research and educational purposes. In *Linguistics in an age of globalization: Perspectives on Arabic language and teaching*, ed. Zeinab Ibrahim and Sanaa Makhlouf, 46–72. Cairo: American University in Cairo.

Van Mol, Mark and Hans Paulussen. 2001. AraLat: A relational database for the development of bilingual Arabic dictionaries. In *Proceedings of Asialex 2001, Asian bilingualism and the dictionary*, 206–211. Seoul, Korea: Yonsei University.

Wahrmund, Adolf. 1870–1877. *Handwörterbuch der arabischen und deutschen Sprache*. Giessen: J. Ricker.

Wehr, Hans. [1952] 1985. *Arabisches Wörterbuch für die Schriftsprache der Gegenwart*. Wiesbaden: Harrassowitz. (1st ed. printed in Leipzig; 5th ed. 1985)

——. 1958. *Supplement zum arabischen Wörterbuch für die Schriftsprache der Gegenwart*. Wiesbaden: Harrassowitz.

——. [1961] 1979[4]. *A dictionary of modern written Arabic*. Trans. J. Milton Cowan. Wiesbaden: Harrassowitz. (2nd ed., 1966; 3rd ed., 1971; 4th ed., 1979)

Woodhead, D. R. and Wayne Beene (eds.). [1967] 2003[2]. *A dictionary of Iraqi Arabic: Arabic-English*. Washington, DC: Georgetown University Press.

Zemánek, Petr, František Ondráš, Andrea Moustafa, and Naděžda Obadalová. 2006. *Arabsko-český slovník*. Praha: Set Out.

Index of Names

Note: for purposes of alphabetization, Arabic names transliterated with a definite article al- (small "a") followed by a hyphen (al-) are alphabetized according to the first letter of the stem.

Subject Index